THE OXFORD
ILLUSTRATED DICKENS

THE UNCOMMERCIAL TRAVELLER
AND
REPRINTED PIECES
ETC.

THE OXFORD ILLUSTRATED DICKENS

Charles John Huffham Dickens was born on 7 February 1812 at Landport near Portsmouth, where his father was a Navy pay clerk. His family moved to London in 1815 and in 1817 to Chatham, where Dickens spent the happiest time of his boyhood. This was followed by a period of misery during which his father was imprisoned for debt in the Marshalsea and Dickens was withdrawn from school and, at the age of 12, sent to work in a blacking warehouse. These experiences deeply affected him and his future work. He returned to school, and left at 15 to become a clerk, a shorthand reporter in the law courts, and a reporter of debates in the Commons. In 1833 he began contributing articles to periodicals, which were later reprinted as *Sketches by Boz* (1836–7); these led to an approach from publishers, resulting in the creation of Mr Pickwick and the publication in monthly numbers of *The Posthumous Papers of the Pickwick Club* (1836–7). In 1836 he married Catherine Hogarth; they had ten children over the next 16 years. Dickens began to publish *Oliver Twist* in 1837 in *Bentley's Miscellany*, a periodical of which he was the first editor. *Nicholas Nickleby* followed in 1838–9. *The Old Curiosity Shop* (1840–1) and *Barnaby Rudge* (1841) were intended for *Master Humphrey's Clock*, a weekly written by Dickens, but he eventually abandoned 'Master Humphrey'.

Dickens's visit to America in 1842 resulted in *American Notes* (1842) and an American section in *Martin Chuzzlewit* (1843–4). He lost readership with the latter but regained it with 'A Christmas Carol' (1843), the first of his five *Christmas Books*. In 1844 he visited Italy, and contributed 'Pictures from Italy' (1846) to the *Daily News*, a paper he founded. *Dombey and Son* appeared in 1846–8 and *David Copperfield* in 1849–50. In 1850 Dickens began the weekly journal *Household Words*, incorporated in 1859 into *All The Year Round*, which he edited until his death. In these appeared essays later issued as *Reprinted Pieces* (1858) and *The Uncommercial Traveller* (1861), and his *Christmas Stories*. *A Child's History of England* was published in 1851–3, *Bleak House* in 1852–3, *Hard Times* in 1854, *Little Dorrit* in 1855–7, *A Tale of Two Cities* in 1859, *Great Expectations* in 1860–1, and *Our Mutual Friend* in 1864–5. In 1856 Dickens bought a country house, Gad's Hill Place, near Rochester, and in 1858 he and his wife separated. He threw himself into public readings of his works, which were greatly successful but draining. His last work, *The Mystery of Edwin Drood*, was left unfinished when he died suddenly on 9 June 1870.

Time and his Wife

THE
UNCOMMERCIAL TRAVELLER
AND
REPRINTED PIECES
ETC.

By
CHARLES DICKENS

With Eleven Illustrations
by G. J. Pinwell
F. Walker, and 'W. M.'
and an Introduction by
LESLIE C. STAPLES

OXFORD   NEW YORK   TORONTO   MELBOURNE
OXFORD UNIVERSITY PRESS

Oxford University Press, Walton Street, Oxford OX2 6DP
Oxford New York Toronto
Delhi Bombay Calcutta Madras Karachi
Petaling Jaya Singapore Hong Kong Tokyo
Nairobi Dar es Salaam Cape Town
Melbourne Auckland
and associated companies in
Berlin Ibadan

Oxford is a trade mark of Oxford University Press

The Uncommercial Traveller was first published in 1860 and containe·
seventeen essays which had appeared that year in All the Year
Round. A further eleven essays from All the Year Round were addeu
to the first Cheap Edition, 1865, and eight more to the Illustrated
Library Edition, 1875. 'A Fly-leaf in a Life' was added to the Gad's
Hill Edition, 1890, completing the thirty-seven essays.

Reprinted Pieces, consisting of contributions to Household Words
between 1850 and 1856, was first added to the Collected Works
in a volume published in 1868 which also included American Notes.

Sunday under Three Heads was first issued in wrappers, 1836. The
Lamplighter, originally written as a farce for Macready at Covent
Garden but not acted, appeared in its present form in The Picnic
Papers, 1841. To be Read at Dusk was written for The Keepsake, 1852.

Hunted Down first appeared in the New York Ledger, 1859; Holiday
Romance in Our Young Folks, Boston, Mass., January, March, April,
and May, 1868; and George Silverman's Explanation in the Atlantic
Monthly, 1868.

The illustrations are taken from the Illustrated Library Edition,
1862–8.

In the Oxford Illustrated Dickens (known before 1966 as the
New Oxford Illustrated Dickens) this volume was first published
in 1958, and reprinted in 1964, 1968, 1973, 1978, 1981, 1987, 1989,
1989, 1991.

Published in the United States by Oxford University Press, USA

This volume: ISBN 0 19 254521 3
21-volume set: ISBN 0 19 254522 1

Printed in the United States of America

INTRODUCTION

by LESLIE C. STAPLES

(Honorary Editor of *The Dickensian*)

THE genius of Dickens needed space to attain its full stature. Twenty monthly 'parts' of thirty-two pages each were not too much for the telling of his tales. In the preface to the best known of his shorter works he complained of the difficulty of its construction within a 'narrow space'. He remarked that he 'never attempted great elaboration of detail in the working out of character within such limits, believing that it could not succeed'. And yet what memorable characters he did in fact create within the narrowest limits. In the novels one immediately recalls Trabb's boy and, within the narrowest limits imaginable, the nervous young man interposing in a conversation and getting no further than *Esker . . .?* and then stopping dead. In the short articles we are to consider in this volume, when space was indeed narrow, examples abound, perhaps less known but scarcely less remarkable.

It was as a journalist that Dickens first made his mark with the reading public, and a good case could be made out for the theory that if Dickens had never published a novel his collected journalistic pieces would have secured for him some small niche in the temple of fame. His earliest essays, collected under the title *Sketches by Boz*, make up a book which has been described as the Overture to the Opera of Dickens. Almost all the themes dealt with in the novels are foreshadowed here. They were the work of a high-spirited young man in his early twenties, and exhibit a gusto that is infectious and was to reach its fine flowering a year or two later in *Pickwick*.

The journalism presented in this volume is of a very different character, and is contemporary with his maturity, as is self-evident in much of *The Uncommercial Traveller*. There are no undisciplined high spirits here, but the polished prose of the established master. Yet for all their apparent

effortlessness a world of pains had gone into their composition. One of the most revealing things to be seen at the
Dickens House in London is a page of the manuscript of
Pickwick, a masterpiece written at the age of twenty-four,
which has no more than half a dozen words corrected,
lying side by side with that of one of his later journalistic
papers, which has hardly a line that was not scored out and
rewritten.

Dickens's weekly journal *All the Year Round* had been
running for two years, following its predecessor's eight,
when he commenced the series he called *The Uncommercial
Traveller*. Until then, all the contributions in these journals,
with the exception of his own serialized novels, had been
anonymous; but he was announced to be the author of
these articles, among which are to be found the finest of his
fugitive writings, and in which, as he explains in the pre-
fatory paper, *His General Line of Business*, he proposed to
travel, uncommercially, for the firm of Human Interest
Brothers. In addition to recounting current experiences, he
frequently drew upon his memories of the past, and not the
least interesting feature of the papers is the autobiographical
material that is to be found in many of them. Here is much
that he probably originally intended for the autobiography
that he never wrote, and much to supplement what we
gather about his early life in *David Copperfield*.

The city of Rochester, 'the birthplace of his fancy', as it
has been called, figures in many of his works, but in *Dullborough Town* we have his picture of it as the background
of his own childhood, and not as a setting for his characters.
His vivid memories of it should be read alongside the pictures painted of it in his first book, *Pickwick*, and again in
his last, *Edwin Drood*. In every case the old city inspires
him with the tenderest affection.

Of course the town had shrunk fearfully since I was a child
there. I had entertained the impression that the High Street
was at least as wide as Regent Street, London, or the Italian
Boulevard at Paris. I found it little better than a lane. There
was a public clock in it, which I had supposed to be the finest
clock in the world; whereas it now turned out to be as inexpressive, moon-faced, weak a clock as ever I saw. It belonged to a Town Hall . . . a mean little brick heap, like a
demented chapel, with a few yawning persons in leather gaiters,

in the last extremity for something to do, lounging at the door with their hands in their pockets, and calling themselves a Corn Exchange!

In *Travelling Abroad* there is the oft-quoted story of his being taken to Gad's Hill as 'a queer small boy' by his father, and shown the great house there. If he worked hard, he was told, he might one day come to live in a house like that. A parental prophecy that came true, for he did indeed come to live, and to die, there. More childhood memories are to be found in *Nurse's Stories*, in which Dickens makes yet another plea that a child's imagination should be treated with the most delicate care.

Memories of his early manhood are no less interesting. In *City of London Churches* we get a delightful glimpse of his first love affair. For Angelica, beside whom he writes of himself as sitting in an all but empty city church one Sunday morning, must surely have been Maria Beadnell, alias Dora Spenlow.

I mind when I, turned of eighteen, went with my Angelica to a city church on account of a shower (by this special coincidence that it was in Huggin Lane), and when I said to my Angelica, 'Let the blessed event, Angelica, occur at no altar but this!' and when my Angelica consented that it should occur at no other—which it certainly never did, for it never occurred anywhere, and oh Angelica, what has become of you, this present Sunday morning, when I can't attend to the sermon; and more difficult than that, what has become of Me, as I was when I sat by your side?

In *Recollections of Mortality* there is a humorous account of the purchase of his first horse, when he was living at Devonshire Terrace, and in the same paper the story of his serving on a coroner's jury empanelled to investigate the death of 'a very little mite of a child'. The story of his purchase of a performing goldfinch, and the little creature's refusal to perform without the personal attendance of its vendor, is to be found in *Shy Neighbourhoods*.

Later recollections include those of his eccentric sculptor friend, Angus Fletcher, whose portrait as Mr. Kindheart in *Medicine Men of Civilisation* is not unworthy to stand beside many more elaborate portraits in the novels; and of his visit to the little house in Shadwell that was the seed of a great children's hospital, in *A Small Star in the East*. And

how delightful it is to meet again the little wooden midshipman of *Dombey and Son* in *Wapping Workhouse*.

In addition to the autobiographical, the series has the
widest of range, and embraces most of the author's extremely varied interests and styles; maritime rescue work
in *The Shipwreck*, popular entertainment in *Two Views of a
Cheap Theatre*, a very familiar subject such as the description of *Titbull's Alms-houses*, and characteristic imaginative
writing such as *Arcadian London*, and *Chambers*, in which
latter paper Dickens once again inveighs against Gray's Inn.
Why, one wonders, did he so seldom miss an opportunity of
doing so? Was he unhappy there, as a lawyer's clerk?

I look upon Gray's Inn generally as one of the most depressing
institutions in bricks and mortar known to the children of men.
Can anything be more dreary than its arid Square, Sahara
Desert of the law . . .

Despite the passage of a century, not to speak of the falling of high explosives, a great deal of the old London
described in these chapters is still to be seen, and explora-
tions in the author's footsteps are among the most rewarding
experiences of the Dickensian in London. Many of the city
churches so vividly characterized are still to be identified.

An interesting example occurs here of Dickens making
amends for mistaken criticism. In *A Small Star in the East*
he had something to say about the conditions under which
people worked in East London lead mills. The passage
coming to the notice of the gentlemen who ran the mills with
which Dickens dealt, they got into touch with him and invited him to see how carefully they sought to protect their
workers. Dickens made honourable amends in *On an
Amateur Beat*, and his correspondence with the firm is now
in the Dickens House in London.

Some attention has been paid in recent years to *The
Ruffian*, but it is too controversial a matter to be usefully
discussed in the limited space available here. The paper is
long likely to remain fruitful material for assessing Dickens's
social conscience.

Turning to *Reprinted Pieces*, we have a somewhat earlier
collection, all the items of which appeared in *Household
Words* between 1850 and 1856, and all anonymously. This
selection of his contributions to that journal was made by

Dickens himself for the Library Edition of his works. In this edition a few of these papers have been transferred to *Christmas Stories*, a convenient and not uncommon practice.

Here again, the autobiographical element is of great interest. Again we are taken back to his earlier days. *Our School* gives a vivid picture of his brief schooldays at Wellington House Academy in Hampstead Road: that part of it which was not sliced away by the construction of the London and Birmingham Railway, as described in the paper, remains to this day. Clearly it was not a remarkable school, but Dickens was glad to be at any kind of school after the misery of the blacking factory. Some of his recollections of it went into the creation of Creakle's school in *David Copperfield*. And then we have a delightful picture of Broadstairs, to which he regularly returned, summer after summer, from 1836 to 1851, in *Our English Watering-Place*. Although considerably larger than in Dickens's day, the older part of the town has retained its character to a remarkable degree and the landmarks with which he deals are still to be seen. Readers of this chapter will also hail an old friend with a great deal of pleasure, Miss Julia Mills, from *David Copperfield*.

Miss Julia Mills has read the whole collection of these books [in the circulating library]. She has left marginal notes on the pages, as 'Is not this truly touching? J. M.' 'How thrilling! J. M.' 'Entranced here by the Magician's potent spell. J. M.' She has italicized her favourite traits in the description of the hero, as 'his hair, which was *dark* and *wavy*, clustered in *rich profusion* around a *marble brow*, whose lofty paleness bespoke the intellect within.' It reminds her of another hero. She adds, 'How like B. L. Can this be mere coincidence? J. M.

Our French Watering-Place is Boulogne, which almost replaced Broadstairs in Dickens's affection for a season or two. Apart from the autobiographical, the series deals with the widest range of subjects, from *A Child's Dream of a Star*, among the most sentimental of his writings, to *A Monument of French Folly*, a fierce attack on what Dickens regarded as a great public scandal.

After presenting three miscellaneous items written at different periods of Dickens's life—*The Lamplighter*, *To be Read at Dusk*, and *Sunday under Three Heads*—this volume concludes with three pieces commissioned for publication in America. The author received a thousand pounds for each of these; Forster comments on the unprecedented figure for writings of their length. Julius Slinkton in *Hunted Down* was founded upon Thomas Griffiths Wainewright, the poisoner and forger. Prominent in the contemporary world of letters, he was 'Janus Weathercock' of the *London Magazine*. We probably read more of him in Dickens's Jonas Chuzzlewit. *Holiday Romance* contains the favourite *Magic Fishbone*. To one of its companion pieces, *Captain Boldheart*, its author was especially partial. *George Silverman's Explanation* has mystified most of the critics. It is possibly the least characteristic of Dickens's shorter writings. The key to it, in all probability, is psychological, as at least one commentator has demonstrated.

To know Dickens one must be familiar with a dozen major novels, but the knowledge is incomplete without some familiarity with his journalistic work, much of the best of which is to be found in this volume.

CONTENTS

LIST OF ILLUSTRATIONS

CHARACTERS

JOHN ANDERSON, a tramp. *Tramps*

MRS. ANDERSON, wife of the preceding. *Ibid.*

ANTONIO, a young Spanish guitar-player. *Poor Mercantile Jack*

MR. BATTENS, an old pensioner. *Titbull's Alms-houses*

BULLFINCH, a friend of the Uncommercial Traveller's. *A Little Dinner in an Hour*

GIOVANNI CARLAVERO, keeper of a small wine-shop. *The Italian Prisoner*

CHIPS, a shipwright. *Nurse's Stories*

THE CLERGYMAN, a good Christian minister. *The Shipwreck*

MR. INDIGNATION COCKER, an irate diner. *A Little Dinner in an Hour*

SUSANNAH CLEVERLY, a Mormon emigrant. *Bound for the Great Salt Lake*

WILLIAM CLEVERLY, brother of the preceding. *Ibid.*

MR. SAMPSON DIBBLE, an aged Mormon emigrant. *Ibid.*

MRS. DOROTHY DIBBLE, wife of the preceding. *Ibid.*

MONSIEUR THE FACE-MAKER. *In the French-Flemish Country.*

SALLY FLANDERS, a former nurse of the Uncommercial Traveller. *Medicine Men of Civilisation*

MR. FLIPFIELD, a friend of the Uncommercial Traveller's. *Birthday Celebrations*

MISS FLIPFIELD, elder sister of the preceding. *Ibid.*

MR. TOM FLIPFIELD, brother of the preceding. *Ibid.*

MRS. FLIPFIELD, mother of the preceding. *Ibid.*

BULLY GLOBSON, a schoolmate of the Uncommercial Traveller's. *Ibid.*

MR. ALEXANDER GRAZINGLANDS, a country gentleman from the Midlands. *Refreshments for Travellers*

MRS. ARABELLA GRAZINGLANDS, wife of the preceding. *Ibid.*

DARK JACK, a negro sailor. *Poor Mercantile Jack*

MERCANTILE JACK, a merchant sailor. *Ibid.*

JESSIE JOBSON, a Mormon emigrant. *Bound for the Great Salt Lake*

MR. BANJO JONES, an Ethiopic minstrel. *Poor Mercantile Jack*

THE

UNCOMMERCIAL TRAVELLER

I

HIS GENERAL LINE OF BUSINESS

ALLOW me to introduce myself—first negatively.

No landlord is my friend and brother, no chambermaid loves me, no waiter worships me, no boots admires and envies me. No round of beef or tongue or ham is expressly cooked for me, no pigeon-pie is especially made for me, no hotel-advertisement is personally addressed to me, no hotel-room tapestried with great-coats and railway wrappers is set apart for me, no house of public entertainment in the United Kingdom greatly cares for my opinion of its brandy or sherry. When I go upon my journeys, I am not usually rated at a low figure in the bill; when I come home from my journeys, I never get any commission. I know nothing about prices, and should have no idea, if I were put to it, how to wheedle a man into ordering something he doesn't want. As a town traveller, I am never to be seen driving a vehicle externally like a young and volatile pianoforte van, and internally like an oven in which a number of flat boxes are baking in layers. As a country traveller, I am rarely to be found in a gig, and am never to be encountered by a pleasure train, waiting on the platform of a branch station, quite a Druid in the midst of a light Stonehenge of samples.

And yet—proceeding now, to introduce myself positively —I am both a town traveller and a country traveller, and am always on the road. Figuratively speaking, I travel for the great house of Human Interest Brothers, and have rather a large connection in the fancy goods way. Literally speaking, I am always wandering here and there from my rooms in Covent-garden, London—now about the city streets: now, about the country by-roads—seeing many little things, and some great things, which, because they interest me, I think may interest others.

These are my brief credentials as the Uncommercial Traveller.

THE SHIPWRECK

NEVER had I seen a year going out, or going on, under quieter circumstances. Eighteen hundred and fifty-nine had but another day to live, and truly its end was Peace on that sea-shore that morning.

So settled and orderly was everything seaward, in the bright light of the sun and under the transparent shadows of the clouds, that it was hard to imagine the bay otherwise, for years past or to come, than it was that very day. The Tug-steamer lying a little off the shore, the Lighter lying still nearer to the shore, the boat alongside the Lighter, the regularly-turning windlass aboard the Lighter, the methodical figures at work, all slowly and regularly heaving up and down with the breathing of the sea, all seemed as much a part of the nature of the place as the tide itself. The tide was on the flow, and had been for some two hours and a half; there was a slight obstruction in the sea within a few yards of my feet: as if the stump of a tree, with earth enough about it to keep it from lying horizontally on the water, had slipped a little from the land—and as I stood upon the beach and observed it dimpling the light swell that was coming in, I cast a stone over it.

So orderly, so quiet, so regular—the rising and falling of the Tug-steamer, the Lighter, and the boat—the turning of the windlass—the coming in of the tide—that I myself seemed, to my own thinking, anything but new to the spot. Yet, I had never seen it in my life, a minute before, and had traversed two hundred miles to get at it. That very morning I had come bowling down, and struggling up, hill-country roads; looking back at snowy summits; meeting courteous peasants well to do, driving fat pigs and cattle to market: noting the neat and thrifty dwellings, with their unusual quantity of clean white linen, drying on the bushes; having windy weather suggested by every cotter's little rick, with its thatch straw-ridged and extra straw-ridged into overlapping compartments like the back of a rhinoceros. Had I not given a lift of fourteen miles to the Coast-guardsman (kit and all), who was coming to his spell of duty there, and had we not just now parted company? So it was; but the journey seemed to glide down into the placid sea, with other chafe and trouble, and for the moment nothing was so calmly and monotonously real under the sunlight as the gentle rising and falling of the water with its freight, the regular turning of the windlass aboard the Lighter, and the slight obstruction so very near my feet.

O reader, haply turning this page by the fireside at Home, and hearing the night wind rumble in the chimney, that slight obstruction was the uppermost fragment of the Wreck of the Royal Charter, Australian trader and passenger ship, Homeward bound, that struck here on the terrible morning of the twenty-sixth of this October, broke into three parts, went down with her treasure of at least five hundred human lives, and has never stirred since!

From which point, or from which, she drove ashore, stern foremost; on which side, or on which, she passed the little Island in the bay, for ages henceforth to be aground certain yards outside her; these are rendered bootless questions by the darkness of that night and the darkness of death. Here she went down.

Even as I stood on the beach with the words "Here she went down!" in my ears, a diver in his grotesque dress, dipped heavily over the side of the boat alongside the Lighter, and dropped to the bottom. On the shore by the water's edge, was a rough tent, made of fragments of wreck, where other divers and workmen sheltered themselves, and where they had kept Christmas-day with rum and roast beef, to the destruction of their frail chimney. Cast up among the stones and boulders of the beach, were great spars of the lost vessel, and masses of iron twisted by the fury of the sea into the strangest forms. The timber was already bleached and iron rusted, and even these objects did no violence to the prevailing air the whole scene wore, of having been exactly the same for years and years.

Yet, only two short months had gone, since a man, living on the nearest hill-top overlooking the sea, being blown out of bed at about daybreak by the wind that had begun to strip his roof off, and getting upon a ladder with his nearest neighbour to construct some temporary device for keeping his house over his head, saw from the ladder's elevation as he looked down by chance towards the shore, some dark troubled object close in with the land. And he and the other, descending to the beach, and finding the sea mercilessly beating over a great broken ship, had clambered up the stony ways, like staircases without stairs, on which the wild village hangs in little clusters, as fruit hangs on boughs, and had given the alarm. And so, over the hill-slopes, and past the waterfall, and down the gullies where the land drains off into the ocean, the scattered quarrymen and fishermen inhabiting that part of Wales had come running to the dismal sight—their clergyman among them. And as they stood in the leaden morning, stricken with pity, leaning hard against the wind, their breath and vision often failing as the sleet and spray rushed at them from the ever forming and dissolving mountains of sea, and as the wool which was a part of the vessel's cargo blew in with the salt foam and remained upon the land when the foam melted, they saw the ship's life-boat put off from one of the heaps of wreck; and first, there were three men in her, and in a moment she capsized, and there were but two; and again, she was struck by a vast mass of water, and there was but one; and again, she was thrown bottom upward, and that one, with his arm struck through the broken planks and waving as if for the help that could never reach him, went down into the deep.

It was the clergyman himself from whom I heard this, while I stood on the shore, looking in his kind wholesome face as it turned to the spot where the boat had been. The divers were down then, and busy. They were "lifting" to-day the gold found yesterday—some five-and-twenty thousand pounds. Of three hundred and fifty thousand pounds' worth of gold, three hundred thousand pounds' worth, in round numbers, was at that time recovered. The great bulk of the remainder was surely and steadily coming up. Some loss of sovereigns there would be, of course; indeed, at first sovereigns had drifted in with the sand, and been scattered far and wide over the beach, like sea-shells; but most other golden treasure would be found. As it was brought up, it went aboard the Tug-steamer, where good account was taken of it. So tremendous had the force of the sea been when it broke the ship, that it had beaten one

great ingot of gold, deep into a strong and heavy piece of
her solid iron-work: in which, also, several loose sovereigns
that the ingot had swept in before it, had been found, as
firmly embedded as though the iron had been liquid when
they were forced there. It had been remarked of such
bodies come ashore, too, as had been seen by scientific men,
that they had been stunned to death, and not suffocated.
Observation, both of the internal change that had been
wrought in them, and of their external expression, showed
death to have been thus merciful and easy. The report was
brought, while I was holding such discourse on the beach,
that no more bodies had come ashore since last night. It
began to be very doubtful whether many more would be
thrown up, until the north-east winds of the early spring
set in. Moreover, a great number of the passengers, and
particularly the second-class women-passengers, were known
to have been in the middle of the ship when she parted, and
thus the collapsing wreck would have fallen upon them
after yawning open, and would keep them down. A diver
made known, even then, that he had come upon the body
of a man, and had sought to release it from a great super-
incumbent weight; but that, finding he could not do so
without mutilating the remains, he had left it where it was.

It was the kind and wholesome face I have made mention
of as being then beside me, that I had purposed to myself to
see, when I left home for Wales. I had heard of that
clergyman, as having buried many scores of the shipwrecked
people ; of his having opened his house and heart to their
agonised friends ; of his having used a most sweet and patient
diligence for weeks and weeks, in the performance of the
forlornest offices that Man can render to his kind ; of his
having most tenderly and thoroughly devoted himself to
the dead, and to those who were sorrowing for the dead.
I had said to myself, " In the Christmas season of the year,
I should like to see that man !" And he had swung the
gate of his little garden in coming out to meet me, not half
an hour ago.

So cheerful of spirit and guiltless of affectation, as true
practical Christianity ever is ! I read more of the New
Testament in the fresh frank face going up the village beside
me, in five minutes, than I have read in anathematising
discourses (albeit put to press with enormous flourishing of
trumpets), in all my life. I heard more of the Sacred Book

in the cordial voice that had nothing to say about its owner, than in all the would-be celestial pairs of bellows that have ever blown conceit at me.

We climbed towards the little church, at a cheery pace, among the loose stones, the deep mud, the wet coarse grass, the outlying water, and other obstructions from which frost and snow had lately thawed. It was a mistake (my friend was glad to tell me, on the way) to suppose that the peasantry had shown any superstitious avoidance of the drowned; on the whole, they had done very well, and had assisted readily. Ten shillings had been paid for the bringing of each body up to the church, but the way was steep, and a horse and cart (in which it was wrapped in a sheet) were necessary, and three or four men, and, all things considered, it was not a great price. The people were none the richer for the wreck, for it was the season of the herring-shoal—and who could cast nets for fish, and find dead men and women in the draught?

He had the church keys in his hand, and opened the churchyard gate, and opened the church door; and we went in.

It is a little church of great antiquity; there is reason to believe that some church has occupied the spot, these thousand years or more. The pulpit was gone, and other things usually belonging to the church were gone, owing to its living congregation having deserted it for the neighbouring schoolroom, and yielded it up to the dead. The very Commandments had been shouldered out of their places, in the bringing in of the dead; the black wooden tables on which they were painted, were askew, and on the stone pavement below them, and on the stone pavement all over the church, were the marks and stains where the drowned had been laid down. The eye, with little or no aid from the imagination, could yet see how the bodies had been turned, and where the head had been and where the feet. Some faded traces of the wreck of the Australian ship may be discernible on the stone pavement of this little church, hundreds of years hence, when the digging for gold in Australia shall have long and long ceased out of the land.

Forty-four shipwrecked men and women lay here at one time, awaiting burial. Here, with weeping and wailing in every room of his house, my companion worked alone for hours, solemnly surrounded by eyes that could not see him, and by lips that could not speak to him, patiently examining the tattered clothing, cutting off buttons, hair, marks from linen, anything that might lead to subsequent identification, studying faces, looking for a scar, a bent finger, a crooked toe, comparing letters sent to him with the ruin about him. "My dearest brother had bright grey eyes and a pleasant smile," one sister wrote. O poor sister! well for you to be far from here, and keep that as your last remembrance of him!

The ladies of the clergyman's family, his wife and two sisters-in-law, came in among the bodies often. It grew to be the business of their lives to do so. Any new arrival of a bereaved woman would stimulate their pity to compare the description brought, with the dread realities. Sometimes, they would go back able to say, "I have found him," or, "I think she lies there." Perhaps, the mourner, unable to bear the sight of all that lay in the church, would be led in blindfold. Conducted to the spot with many compassionate words, and encouraged to look, she would say, with a piercing cry, "This is my boy!" and drop insensible on the insensible figure.

He soon observed that in some cases of women, the identification of persons, though complete, was quite at variance with the marks upon the linen; this led him to notice that even the marks upon the linen were sometimes inconsistent with one another; and thus he came to understand that they had dressed in great haste and agitation, and that their clothes had become mixed together. The identification of men by their dress, was rendered extremely difficult, in consequence of a large proportion of them being dressed alike —in clothes of one kind, that is to say, supplied by slopsellers and outfitters, and not made by single garments but by hundreds. Many of the men were bringing over parrots, and had receipts upon them for the price of the birds; others had bills of exchange in their pockets, or in belts. Some of these documents, carefully unwrinkled and dried, were little less fresh in appearance that day, than the present page will be under ordinary circumstances, after having been opened three or four times.

In that lonely place, it had not been easy to obtain even such common commodities in towns, as ordinary disinfectants. Pitch had been burnt in the church, as the readiest thing at hand, and the frying-pan in which it had bubbled

over a brazier of coals was still there, with its ashes. Hard
by the Communion-Table, were some boots that had been
taken off the drowned and preserved—a gold-digger's boot,
cut down the leg for its removal—a trodden-down man's
ankle-boot with a buff cloth top—and others—soaked and
sandy, weedy and salt.

From the church, we passed out into the churchyard.
Here, there lay, at that time, one hundred and forty-five
bodies, that had come ashore from the wreck. He had
buried them, when not identified, in graves containing four
each. He had numbered each body in a register describing
it, and had placed a corresponding number on each coffin,
and over each grave. Identified bodies he had buried singly,
in private graves, in another part of the churchyard. Several
bodies had been exhumed from the graves of four, as relatives had come from a distance and seen his register; and,
when recognised, these have been reburied in private graves,
so that the mourners might erect separate headstones over
the remains. In all such cases he had performed the
funeral service a second time, and the ladies of his house
had attended. There had been no offence in the poor
ashes when they were brought again to the light of day;
the beneficent Earth had already absorbed it. The drowned
were buried in their clothes. To supply the great sudden
demand for coffins, he had got all the neighbouring people
handy at tools, to work the livelong day, and Sunday
likewise. The coffins were neatly formed;—I had seen
two, waiting for occupants, under the lee of the ruined
walls of a stone hut on the beach, within call of the tent
where the Christmas Feast was held. Similarly, one of
the graves for four was lying open and ready, here, in the
churchyard. So much of the scanty space was already
devoted to the wrecked people, that the villagers had begun
to express uneasy doubts whether they themselves could lie
in their own ground, with their forefathers and descendants,
by-and-by. The churchyard being but a step from the
clergyman's dwelling-house, we crossed to the latter; the
white surplice was hanging up near the door ready to
be put on at any time, for a funeral service.

The cheerful earnestness of this good Christian minister
was as consolatory, as the circumstances out of which it
shone were sad. I never have seen anything more delightfully genuine than the calm dismissal by himself and his

household of all they had undergone, as a simple duty that was quietly done and ended. In speaking of it, they spoke of it with great compassion for the bereaved; but laid no stress upon their own hard share in those weary weeks, except as it had attached many people to them as friends, and elicited many touching expressions of gratitude. This clergyman's brother—himself the clergyman of two adjoining parishes, who had buried thirty-four of the bodies in his own churchyard, and who had done to them all that his brother had done as to the larger number—must be understood as included in the family. He was there, with his neatly arranged papers, and made no more account of his trouble than anybody else did. Down to yesterday's post outward, my clergyman alone had written one thousand and seventy-five letters to relatives and friends of the lost people. In the absence of self-assertion, it was only through my now and then delicately putting a question as the occasion arose, that I became informed of these things. It was only when I had remarked again and again, in the church, on the awful nature of the scene of death he had been required so closely to familiarise himself with for the soothing of the living, that he had casually said, without the least abatement of his cheerfulness, "indeed, it had rendered him unable for a time to eat or drink more than a little coffee now and then, and a piece of bread."

In this noble modesty, in this beautiful simplicity, in this serene avoidance of the least attempt to "improve" an occasion which might be supposed to have sunk of its own weight into my heart, I seemed to have happily come, in a few steps, from the churchyard with its open grave, which was the type of Death, to the Christian dwelling side by side with it, which was the type of Resurrection. I never shall think of the former, without the latter. The two will always rest side by side in my memory. If I had lost any one dear to me in this unfortunate ship, if I had made a voyage from Australia to look at the grave in the churchyard, I should go away, thankful to God that that house was so close to it, and that its shadow by day and its domestic lights by night fell upon the earth in which its Master had so tenderly laid my dear one's head.

The references that naturally arose out of our conversation, to the descriptions sent down of shipwrecked persons, and to the gratitude of relations and friends, made me very anxious to see some of those letters. I was presently seated before a shipwreck of papers, all bordered with black, and from them I made the following few extracts.

A mother writes:

REVEREND SIR. Amongst the many who perished on your shore was numbered my beloved son. I was only just recovering from a severe illness, and this fearful affliction has caused a relapse, so that I am unable at present to go to identify the remains of the loved and lost. My darling son would have been sixteen on Christmas-day next. He was a most amiable and obedient child, early taught the way of salvation. We fondly hoped that as a British seaman he might be an ornament to his profession, but, "it is well;" I feel assured my dear boy is now with the redeemed. Oh, he did not wish to go this last voyage! On the fifteenth of October, I received a letter from him from Melbourne, date August twelfth; he wrote in high spirits, and in conclusion he says: "Pray for a fair breeze, dear mamma, and I'll not forget to whistle for it! and, God permitting, I shall see you and all my little pets again. Good-bye, dear mother—good-bye, dearest parents. Good-bye, dear brother." Oh, it was indeed an eternal farewell. I do not apologise for thus writing you, for oh, my heart is so very sorrowful.

A husband writes:

MY DEAR KIND SIR. Will you kindly inform me whether there are any initials upon the ring and guard you have in possession, found, as the Standard says, last Tuesday? Believe me, my dear sir, when I say that I cannot express my deep gratitude in words sufficiently for your kindness to me on that fearful and appalling day. Will you tell me what I can do for you, and will you write me a consoling letter to prevent my mind from going astray?

A widow writes:

Left in such a state as I am, my friends and I thought it best that my dear husband should be buried where he lies, and, much as I should have liked to have had it otherwise, I must submit. I feel, from all I have heard of you, that you will see it done decently and in order. Little does it signify to us, when the soul has departed, where this poor body lies, but we who are left behind would do all we can to show how we loved them. This is denied me, but it is God's hand that afflicts us, and I try to submit. Some day I may be able to visit the spot, and see where he lies, and erect a simple stone to his memory. Oh! it will be long, long before I forget that dreadful night! Is there such a thing in the vicinity, or any shop in Bangor, to which I could send for a small picture of Moelfra or Llanallgo church, a spot now sacred to me?

Another widow writes:

I have received your letter this morning, and do thank you most kindly for the interest you have taken about my dear husband, as well for the sentiments yours contains, evincing the spirit of a Christian who can sympathise with those who, like myself, are broken down with grief.

May God bless and sustain you, and all in connection with you, in this great trial. Time may roll on and bear all ·its sons away, but your name as a disinterested person will stand in history, and, as successive years pass, many a widow will think of your noble conduct, and the tears of gratitude flow down many a cheek, the tribute of a thankful heart, when other things are forgotten for ever.

A father writes:

I am at a loss to find words to sufficiently express my gratitude to you for your kindness to my son Richard upon the melancholy occasion of his visit to his dear brother's body, and also for your ready attention in pronouncing our beautiful burial service over my poor unfortunate son's remains. God grant that your prayers over him may reach the Mercy Seat, and that his soul may be received (through Christ's intercession) into heaven!

His dear mother begs me to convey to you her heartfelt thanks.

Those who were received at the clergyman's house, write thus, after leaving it:

DEAR AND NEVER-TO-BE-FORGOTTEN FRIENDS. I arrived here yesterday morning without accident, and am about to proceed to my home by railway.

I am overpowered when I think of you and your hospitable home. No words could speak language suited to my heart. I refrain. God reward you with the same measure you have meted with!

I enumerate no names, but embrace you all.

MY BELOVED FRIENDS. This is the first day that I have been able to leave my bedroom since I returned, which will explain the reason of my not writing sooner.

If I could only have had my last melancholy hope realised in recovering the body of my beloved and lamented son, I should have returned home somewhat comforted, and I think I could then have been comparatively resigned.

I fear now there is but little prospect, and I mourn as one without hope.

The only consolation to my distressed mind is in having been so feelingly allowed by you to leave the matter in your hands, by whom I well know that everything will be done that can be, according to arrangements made before I left the scene of the awful catastrophe, both as to the identification of my dear son, and also his interment.

I feel most anxious to hear whether anything fresh has transpired since I left you; will you add another to the many deep obligations I am under to you by writing to me? And should the body of my dear and unfortunate son be identified, let me hear from you immediately, and I will come again.

Words cannot express the gratitude I feel I owe to you all for your benevolent aid, your kindness, and your sympathy.

MY DEARLY BELOVED FRIENDS. I arrived in safety at my house yesterday, and a night's rest has restored and tranquillised me. I must again repeat, that language has no words by which I can express my sense of obligation to you. You are enshrined in my heart of hearts.

I have seen him! and can now realise my misfortune more than I have hitherto been able to do. Oh, the bitterness of the cup I drink! But I bow submissive. God *must* have done right. I do not want to feel less, but to acquiesce more simply.

There were some Jewish passengers on board the Royal Charter, and the gratitude of the Jewish people is feelingly

expressed in the following letter bearing date from   the
office of the Chief Rabbi:"

'REVEREND SIR. I cannot refrain from expressing to you
my heartfelt thanks on behalf of those of my flock whose
relatives have unfortunately been among those who perished
at the late wreck of the Royal Charter. You have, indeed,
like Boaz, "not left off your kindness to the living and the
dead."

You have not alone acted kindly towards the living by
receiving them hospitably at your house, and energetically
assisting them in their mournful duty, but also towards the
dead, by exerting yourself to have our co-religionists buried
in our ground, and according to our rites. May our heavenly
Father reward you for your acts of humanity and true
philanthropy !

The "Old Hebrew congregation of Liverpool" thus express themselves through their secretary:

REVEREND SIR. The wardens of this congregation have
learned with great pleasure that, in addition to those
indefatigable exertions, at the scene of the late disaster to
the Royal Charter, which have received universal recognition, you have very benevolently employed your valuable
efforts to assist such members of our faith as have sought
the bodies of lost friends to give them burial in our consecrated grounds, with the observances and rites prescribed
by the ordinances of our religion.

The wardens desire me to take the earliest available
opportunity to offer to you, on behalf of our community,
the expression of their warm acknowledgments and grateful
thanks, and their sincere wishes for your continued welfare
and prosperity.

A Jewish gentleman writes:

REVEREND AND DEAR SIR. I take the opportunity of
thanking you right earnestly for the promptness you displayed in answering my note with full particulars concerning
my much lamented brother, and I also herein beg to express
my sincere regard for the willingness you displayed and for
the facility you afforded for getting the remains of my poor
brother exhumed. It has been to us a most sorrowful and
painful event, but when we meet with such friends as your-

self, it in a measure, somehow or other, abates that mental anguish, and makes the suffering so much easier to be borne. Considering the circumstances connected with my poor brother's fate, it does, indeed, appear a hard one. He had been away in all seven years ; he returned four years ago to see his family. He was then engaged to a very amiable young lady. He had been very successful abroad, and was now returning to fulfil his sacred vow; he brought all his property with him in gold uninsured. We heard from him when the ship stopped at Queenstown, when he was in the highest of hope, and in a few short hours afterwards all was washed away.

Mournful in the deepest degree, but too sacred for quotation here, were the numerous references to those miniatures of women worn round the necks of rough men (and found there after death), those locks of hair, those scraps of letters, those many many slight memorials of hidden tenderness. One man cast up by the sea bore about him, printed on a perforated lace card, the following singular (and unavailing) charm

A BLESSING.

May the blessing of God await thee. May the sun of glory shine around thy bed ; and may the gates of plenty, honour, and happiness be ever open to thee. May no sorrow distress thy days ; may no grief disturb thy nights. May the pillow of peace kiss thy cheek, and the pleasures of imagination attend thy dreams ; and when length of years makes thee tired of earthly joys, and the curtain of death gently closes around thy last sleep of human existence, may the Angel of God attend thy bed, and take care that the expiring lamp of life shall not receive one rude blast to hasten on its extinction.

A sailor had these devices on his right arm. "Our Saviour on the Cross, the forehead of the Crucifix and the vesture stained red; on the lower part of the arm, a man and woman ; on one side of the Cross, the appearance of a half moon, with a face ; on the other side, the sun; on the top of the Cross, the letters I.H.S. ; on the left arm, a man and woman dancing, with an effort to delineate the female's dress ; under which, initials." Another seaman

" had, on the lower part of the right arm, the device of a sailor and a female ; the man holding the Union Jack with a streamer, the folds of which waved over her head, and the end of it was held in her hand. On the upper part of the arm, a device of Our Lord on the Cross, with stars surrounding the head of the Cross, and one large star on the side in Indian ink. On the left arm, a flag, a true lover's knot, a face, and initials." This tattooing was found still plain, below the discoloured outer surface of a mutilated arm, when such surface was carefully scraped away with a knife. It is not improbable that the perpetuation of this marking custom among seamen, may be referred back to their desire to be identified, if drowned and flung ashore.

It was some time before I could sever myself from the many interesting papers on the table, and then I broke bread and drank wine with the kind family before I left them. As I brought the Coast-guard down, so I took the Postman back, with his leathern wallet, walking-stick, bugle, and terrier dog. Many a heart-broken letter had he brought to the Rectory House within two months ; many a benignantly painstaking answer had he carried back.

As I rode along, I thought of the many people, inhabit-ants of this mother country, who would make pilgrimages to the little churchyard in the years to come ; I thought of the many people in Australia, who would have an interest in such a shipwreck, and would find their way here when they visit the Old World ; I thought of the writers of all the wreck of letters I had left upon the table ; and I resolved to place this little record where it stands. Convocations, Conferences, Diocesan Epistles, and the like, will do a great deal for Religion, I dare say, and Heaven send they may ! but I doubt if they will ever do their Master's service half so well, in all the time they last, as the Heavens have seen it done in this bleak spot upon the rugged coast of Wales.

Had I lost the friend of my life, in the wreck of the Royal Charter ; had I lost my betrothed, the more than friend of my life ; had I lost my maiden daughter, had I lost my hopeful boy, had I lost my little child ; I would kiss the hands that worked so busily and gently in the church, and say, " None better could have touched the form, though it had lain at home." I could be sure of it, I could be thankful for it : I could be content to leave the grave near the house the good family pass in and out of every day, undisturbed, in the little churchyard where so many are so strangely brought together.

Without the name of the clergyman to whom—I hope, not without carrying comfort to some heart at some time—I have referred, my reference would be as nothing. He is the Reverend Stephen Roose Hughes, of Llanallgo, near Moelfra, Anglesey. His brother is the Reverend Hugh Robert Hughes, of Penrhes, Alligwy.

WAPPING WORKHOUSE

My day's no-business beckoning me to the East-end of
London, I had turned my face to that point of the metropolitan compass on leaving Covent-garden, and had got past
the India House, thinking in my idle manner of Tippoo-Sahib
and Charles Lamb, and had got past my little wooden midshipman, after affectionately patting him on one leg of his
knee-shorts for old acquaintance' sake, and had got past
Aldgate Pump, and had got past the Saracen's Head (with
an ignominious rash of posting bills disfiguring his swarthy
countenance), and had strolled up the empty yard of his
ancient neighbour the Black or Blue Boar, or Bull, who
departed this life I don't know when, and whose coaches
are all gone I don't know where; and I had come out again
into the age of railways, and I had got past Whitechapel
Church, and was—rather inappropriately for an Uncommercial Traveller—in the Commercial Road.   Pleasantly wallowing in the abundant mud of that thoroughfare, and greatly
enjoying the huge piles of building belonging to the sugar
refiners, the little masts and vanes in small back gardens in
back streets, the neighbouring canals and docks, the India
vans lumbering along their stone tramway, and the pawn-
brokers' shops where hard-up Mates had pawned so many
sextants and quadrants, that I should have bought a few
cheap if I had the least notion how to use them, I at last
began to file off to the right, towards Wapping.

Not that I intended to take boat at Wapping Old Stairs,
or that I was going to look at the locality, because I believe
(for I don't) in the constancy of the young woman who told
her sea-going lover, to such a beautiful old tune, that she
had ever continued the same, since she gave him the 'baccer-
box marked with his name; I am afraid he usually got the
worst of those transactions, and was frightfully taken in.
No, I was going to Wapping, because an Eastern police

magistrate had said, through the morning papers, that there was no classification at the Wapping workhouse for women, and that it was a disgrace and a shame, and divers other hard names, and because I wished to see how the fact really stood. For, that Eastern police magistrates are not always the wisest men of the East, may be inferred from their course of procedure respecting the fancy-dressing and panto-mime-posturing at St. George's in that quarter : which is usually, to discuss the matter at issue, in a state of mind betokening the weakest perplexity, with all parties concerned and unconcerned, and, for a final expedient, to consult the complainant as to what he thinks ought to be done with the defendant, and take the defendant's opinion as to what he would recommend to be done with himself.

Long before I reached Wapping, I gave myself up as having lost my way, and, abandoning myself to the narrow streets in a Turkish frame of mind, relied on predestination to bring me somehow or other to the place I wanted if I were ever to get there. When I had ceased for an hour or so to take any trouble about the matter, I found myself on a swing-bridge looking down at some dark locks in some dirty water. Over against me, stood a creature remotely in the likeness of a young man, with a puffed sallow face, and a figure all dirty and shiny and slimy, who may have been the youngest son of his filthy old father, Thames, or the drowned man about whom there was a placard on the granite post like a large thimble, that stood between us.

I asked this apparition what it called the place? Unto which, it replied, with a ghastly grin and a sound like gurgling water in its throat :

"Mr. Baker's trap."

As it is a point of great sensitiveness with me on such occasions to be equal to the intellectual pressure of the conversation, I deeply considered the meaning of this speech, while I eyed the apparition—then engaged in hug-ging and sucking a horizontal iron bar at the top of the locks. Inspiration suggested to me that Mr. Baker was the acting coroner of that neighbourhood.

"A common place for suicide," said I, looking down at the locks.

"Sue ? " returned the ghost, with a stare. "Yes! And Poll. Likewise Emily. And Nancy. And Jane;" he sucked the iron between each name ; "and all the bileing.

Ketches off their bonnets or shorls, takes a run, and headers down here, they doos. Always a headerin' down here, they is. Like one o'clock."

"And at about that hour of the morning, I suppose?"

"Ah!" said the apparition. "*They* an't partickler. Two ull do for *them*. Three. All times o' night. On'y mind you!" Here the apparition rested his profile on the bar, and gurgled in a sarcastic manner. "There must be somebody comin'. They don't go a headerin' down here, wen there an't no Bobby nor gen'ral Cove, fur to hear the splash."

According to my interpretation of these words, I was myself a General Cove, or member of the miscellaneous public. In which modest character I remarked:

"They are often taken out, are they, and restored?"

"I dunno about restored," said the apparition, who, for some occult reason, very much objected to that word; "they're carried into the werkiss and put into a 'ot bath, and brought round. But I dunno about restored," said the apparition; "blow *that!*"—and vanished.

As it had shown a desire to become offensive, I was not sorry to find myself alone, especially as the "werkiss" it had indicated with a twist of its matted head, was close at hand. So I left Mr. Baker's terrible trap (baited with a scum that was like the soapy rinsing of sooty chimneys), and made bold to ring at the workhouse gate, where I was wholly unexpected and quite unknown.

A very bright and nimble little matron, with a bunch of keys in her hand, responded to my request to see the House. I began to doubt whether the police magistrate was quite right in his facts, when I noticed her quick active little figure and her intelligent eyes.

The Traveller (the matron intimated) should see the worst first. He was welcome to see everything. Such as it was, there it all was.

This was the only preparation for our entering "the Foul wards." They were in an old building squeezed away in a corner of a paved yard, quite detached from the more modern and spacious main body of the workhouse. They were in a building most monstrously behind the time—a mere series of garrets or lofts, with every inconvenient and objectionable circumstance in their construction, and only accessible by steep and narrow staircases, infamously ill-adapted for the passage up-stairs of the sick or down-stairs of the dead.

A-bed in these miserable rooms, here on bedsteads, there (for a change, as I understood it) on the floor, were women in every stage of distress and disease. None but those who have attentively observed such scenes, can conceive the extraordinary variety of expression still latent under the general monotony and uniformity of colour, attitude, and condition. The form a little coiled up and turned away, as though it had turned its back on this world for ever; the uninterested face at once lead-coloured and yellow, looking passively upward from the pillow; the haggard mouth a little dropped, the hand outside the coverlet, so dull and indifferent, so light, and yet so heavy; these were on every pallet; but when I stopped beside a bed, and said ever so slight a word to the figure lying there, the ghost of the old character came into the face, and made the Foul ward as various as the fair world. No one appeared to care to live, but no one complained; all who could speak, said that as much was done for them as could be done there, that the attendance was kind and patient, that their suffering was very heavy, but they had nothing to ask for. The wretched rooms were as clean and sweet as it is possible for such rooms to be; they would become a pest-house in a single week, if they were ill-kept.

I accompanied the brisk matron up another barbarous staircase, into a better kind of loft devoted to the idiotic and imbecile. There was at least Light in it, whereas the windows in the former wards had been like sides of school-boys' bird-cages. There was a strong grating over the fire here, and, holding a kind of state on either side of the hearth, separated by the breadth of this grating, were two old ladies in a condition of feeble dignity, which was surely the very last and lowest reduction of self-complacency, to be found in this wonderful humanity of ours. They were evidently jealous of each other, and passed their whole time (as some people do, whose fires are not grated) in mentally disparaging each other, and contemptuously watching their neighbours. One of these parodies on provincial gentle-women was extremely talkative, and expressed a strong desire to attend the service on Sundays, from which she represented herself to have derived the greatest interest and consolation when allowed that privilege. She gossiped so

well, and looked altogether so cheery and harmless, that
I began to think this a case for the Eastern magistrate,
until I found that on the last occasion of her attending
chapel she had secreted a small stick, and had caused some
confusion in the responses by suddenly producing it and
belabouring the congregation.

So, these two old ladies, separated by the breadth of the
grating—otherwise they would fly at one another's caps—
sat all day long, suspecting one another, and contemplating
a world of fits. For, everybody else in the room had fits,
except the wards-woman; an elderly, able-bodied pauperess,
with a large upper lip, and an air of repressing and saving
her strength, as she stood with her hands folded before her,
and her eyes slowly rolling, biding her time for catching or
holding somebody. This civil personage (in whom I re-
gretted to identify a reduced member of my honourable
friend Mrs. Gamp's family) said, "They has 'em continiwal,
sir. They drops without no more notice than if they was
coach-horses dropped from the moon, sir. And when one
drops, another drops, and sometimes there'll be as many as
four or five on 'em at once, dear me, a rolling and a tearin',
bless you!—this young woman, now, has 'em dreadful bad."

She turned up this young woman's face with her hand as
she said it. This young woman was seated on the floor,
pondering in the foreground of the afflicted. There was
nothing repellant either in her face or head. Many, apparently worse, varieties of epilepsy and hysteria were about
her, but she was said to be the worst here. When I had
spoken to her a little, she still sat with her face turned up,
pondering, and a gleam of the mid-day sun shone in upon
her.

—Whether this young woman, and the rest of these so
sorely troubled, as they sit or lie pondering in their confused
dull way, ever get mental glimpses among the motes in the
sunlight, of healthy people and healthy things? Whether
this young woman, brooding like this in the summer season,
ever thinks that somewhere there are trees and flowers, even
mountains and the great sea? Whether, not to go so far,
this young woman ever has any dim revelation of that young
woman—that young woman who is not here and never will
come here; who is courted, and caressed, and loved, and has
a husband, and bears children, and lives in a home, and who
never knows what it is to have this lashing and tearing

coming upon her? And whether this young woman, God help her, gives herself up then and drops like a coach-horse from the moon?

I hardly knew whether the voices of infant children, penetrating into so hopeless a place, made a sound that was pleasant or painful to me. It was something to be reminded that the weary world was not all aweary, and was ever renewing itself; but, this young woman was a child not long ago, and a child not long hence might be such as she. Howbeit, the active step and eye of the vigilant matron conducted me past the two provincial gentlewomen (whose dignity was ruffled by the children), and into the adjacent nursery.

There were many babies here, and more than one hand-some young mother. There were ugly young mothers also, and sullen young mothers, and callous young mothers. But, the babies had not appropriated to themselves any bad expression yet, and might have been, for anything that appeared to the contrary in their soft faces, Princes Imperial, and Princesses Royal. I had the pleasure of giving a poetical commission to the baker's man to make a cake with all despatch and toss it into the oven for one red-headed young pauper and myself, and felt much the better for it. Without that refreshment, I doubt if I should have been in a condition for "the Refractories," towards whom my quick little matron—for whose adaptation to her office I had by this time conceived a genuine respect—drew me next, and marshalled me the way that I was going.

The Refractories were picking oakum, in a small room giving on a yard. They sat in line on a form, with their backs to a window; before them, a table, and their work. The oldest Refractory was, say twenty; youngest Refractory, say sixteen. I have never yet ascertained in the course of my uncommercial travels, why a Refractory habit should affect the tonsils and uvula; but, I have always observed that Refractories of both sexes and every grade, between a Ragged School and the Old Bailey, have one voice, in which the tonsils and uvula gain a diseased ascendency.

"Five pound indeed! I hain't a going fur to pick five pound," said the Chief of the Refractories, keeping time to herself with her head and chin. "More than enough to pick what we picks now, in sich a place as this, and on wot we gets here!"

(This was in acknowledgment of a delicate intimation that the amount of work was likely to be increased. It certainly was not heavy then, for one Refractory had already done her day's task—it was barely two o'clock—and was sitting behind it, with a head exactly matching it.)

"A pretty Ouse this is, matron, ain't it?" said Refractory Two, "where a pleeseman's called in, if a gal says a word!"

"And wen you're sent to prison for nothink or less!" said the Chief, tugging at her oakum as if it were the matron's hair. "But any place is better than this; that's one thing, and be thankful!"

A laugh of Refractories led by Oakum Head with folded arms—who originated nothing, but who was in command of the skirmishers outside the conversation.

"If any place is better than this," said my brisk guide, in the calmest manner, "it is a pity you left a good place when you had one."

"Ho, no, I didn't, matron," returned the Chief, with another pull at her oakum, and a very expressive look at the enemy's forehead. "Don't say that, matron, cos it's lies!"

Oakum Head brought up the skirmishers again, skirmished, and retired.

"And *I* warn't a going," exclaimed Refractory Two, "though I was in one place for as long as four year— *I* warn't a going fur to stop in a place that warn't fit for me—there! And where the family warn't 'spectable characters—there! And where I fort'nately or hunfort'nately, found that the people warn't what they pretended to make theirselves out to be—there! And where it wasn't their faults, by chalks, if I warn't made bad and ruinated—Hah!"

During this speech, Oakum Head had again made a diversion with the skirmishers, and had again withdrawn.

The Uncommercial Traveller ventured to remark that he supposed Chief Refractory and Number One, to be the two young women who had been taken before the magistrate?

"Yes!" said the Chief, "we har! and the wonder is, that a pleeseman an't 'ad in now, and we took off agen. You can't open your lips here, without a pleeseman."

Number Two laughed (very uvularly), and the skirmishers followed suit.

"I'm sure I'd be thankful," protested the Chief, looking sideways at the Uncommercial, "if I could be got into a

place, or got abroad. I'm sick and tired of this precious
Ouse, I am, with reason."

So would be, and so was, Number Two. So would be,
and so was, Oakum Head. So would be, and so were,
Skirmishers.

The Uncommercial took the liberty of hinting that he
hardly thought it probable that any lady or gentleman in
want of a likely young domestic of retiring manners, would
be tempted into the engagement of either of the two leading
Refractories, on her own presentation of herself as per
sample.

"It ain't no good being nothink else here," said the
Chief.

The Uncommercial thought it might be worth trying.

"Oh no, it ain't," said the Chief.

"Not a bit of good," said Number Two.

"And I'm sure I'd be very thankful to be got into a place,
or got abroad," said the Chief.

"And so should I," said Number Two. "Truly thankful,
I should."

Oakum Head then rose, and announced as an entirely
new idea, the mention of which profound novelty might be
naturally expected to startle her unprepared hearers, that
she would be very thankful to be got into a place, or got
abroad. And, as if she had then said, "Chorus, ladies!" all
the Skirmishers struck up to the same purpose. We left
them, thereupon, and began a long walk among the women
who were simply old and infirm ; but whenever, in the course
of this same walk, I looked out of any high window that
commanded the yard, I saw Oakum Head and all the other
Refractories looking out at their low window for me, and
never failing to catch me, the moment I showed my head.

In ten minutes I had ceased to believe in such fables of
a golden time as youth, the prime of life, or a hale old age.
In ten minutes, all the lights of womankind seemed to have
been blown out, and nothing in that way to be left this vault
to brag of, but the flickering and expiring snuffs.

And what was very curious, was, that these dim old women
had one company notion which was the fashion of the place.
Every old woman who became aware of a visitor and was
not in bed hobbled over a form into her accustomed seat,
and became one of a line of dim old women confronting
another line of dim old women across a narrow table. There

was no obligation whatever upon them to range themselves
in this way; it was their manner of "receiving." As a rule,
they made no attempt to talk to one another, or to look at
the visitor, or to look at anything, but sat silently working
their mouths, like a sort of poor old Cows. In some of
these wards, it was good to see a few green plants; in
others, an isolated Refractory acting as nurse, who did well
enough in that capacity, when separated from her compeers;
every one of these wards, day room, night room, or both
combined, was scrupulously clean and fresh. I have seen
as many such places as most travellers in my line, and
I never saw one such, better kept.

Among the bedridden there was great patience, great
reliance on the books under the pillow, great faith in GOD.
All cared for sympathy, but none much cared to be encouraged
with hope of recovery; on the whole, I should say, it was
considered rather a distinction to have a complication of
disorders, and to be in a worse way than the rest. From
some of the windows, the river could be seen with all its
life and movement; the day was bright, but I came upon
no one who was looking out.

In one large ward, sitting by the fire in arm-chairs of
distinction, like the President and Vice of the good company,
were two old women, upwards of ninety years of age. The
younger of the two, just turned ninety, was deaf, but not
very, and could easily be made to hear. In her early time
she had nursed a child, who was now another old woman,
more infirm than herself, inhabiting the very same chamber.
She perfectly understood this when the matron told it, and,
with sundry nods and motions of her forefinger, pointed out
the woman in question. The elder of this pair, ninety-three,
seated before an illustrated newspaper (but not reading it),
was a bright-eyed old soul, really not deaf, wonderfully
preserved, and amazingly conversational. She had not long
lost her husband, and had been in that place little more
than a year. At Boston, in the State of Massachusetts,
this poor creature would have been individually addressed,
would have been tended in her own room, and would have
had her life gently assimilated to a comfortable life out of
doors. Would that be much to do in England for a woman
who has kept herself out of a workhouse more than ninety
rough long years? When Britain first, at Heaven's command,
arose, with a great deal of allegorical confusion, from out the

azure main, did her guardian angels positively forbid it in the Charter which has been so much besung?

The object of my journey was accomplished when the nimble matron had no more to show me. As I shook hands with her at the gate, I told her that I thought Justice had not used her very well, and that the wise men of the East were not infallible.

Now, I reasoned with myself, as I made my journey home again, concerning those Foul wards. They ought not to exist; no person of common decency and humanity can see them and doubt it. But what is this Union to do? The necessary alteration would cost several thousands of pounds; it has already to support three workhouses; its inhabitants work hard for their bare lives, and are already rated for the relief of the Poor to the utmost extent of reasonable endurance. One poor parish in this very Union is rated to the amount of FIVE AND SIXPENCE in the pound, at the very same time when the rich parish of Saint George's, Hanover-square, is rated at about SEVENPENCE in the pound, Paddington at about FOURPENCE, Saint James's, Westminster, at about TENPENCE! It is only through the equalisation of Poor Rates that what is left undone in this wise, can be done. Much more is left undone, or is ill-done, than I have space to suggest in these notes of a single uncommercial journey; but, the wise men of the East, before they can reasonably hold forth about it, must look to the North and South and West; let them also, any morning before taking the seat of Solomon, look into the shops and dwellings all around the Temple, and first ask themselves "how much more can these poor people—many of whom keep themselves with difficulty enough out of the workhouse—bear?"

I had yet other matter for reflection as I journeyed home, inasmuch as, before I altogether departed from the neighbourhood of Mr. Baker's trap, I had knocked at the gate of the workhouse of St. George's-in-the-East, and had found it to be an establishment highly creditable to those parts, and thoroughly well administered by a most intelligent master. I remarked in it, an instance of the collateral harm that obstinate vanity and folly can do. "This was the Hall where those old paupers, male and female, whom I had just seen, met for the Church service, was it?"—"Yes."—"Did they sing the Psalms to any instrument?"—"They would like to, very much; they would have an extraordinary

interest in doing so."—"And could none be got?"—"Well,
a piano could even have been got for nothing, but these
unfortunate dissensions——" Ah! better, far better, my
Christian friend in the beautiful garment, to have let the
singing boys alone, and left the multitude to sing for themselves! You should know better than I, but I think I have
read that they did so, once upon a time, and that "when
they had sung an hymn," Some one (not in a beautiful
garment) went up unto the Mount of Olives.

It made my heart ache to think of this miserable trifling,
in the streets of a city where every stone seemed to call to
me, as I walked along, "Turn this way, man, and see what
waits to be done!" So I decoyed myself into another train
of thought to ease my heart. But, I don't know that I did
it, for I was so full of paupers, that it was, after all, only
a change to a single pauper, who took possession of my
remembrance instead of a thousand.

"I beg your pardon, sir," he had said, in a confidential
manner, on another occasion, taking me aside; "but I have
seen better days."

"I am very sorry to hear it."

"Sir, I have a complaint to make against the master."

"I have no power here, I assure you. And if I had——"

"But, allow me, sir, to mention it, as between yourself and
a man who has seen better days, sir. The master and myself
are both masons, sir, and I make him the sign continually;
but, because I am in this unfortunate position, sir, he won't
give me the countersign!"

TWO VIEWS OF A CHEAP THEATRE

As I shut the door of my lodging behind me, and came out into the streets at six on a drizzling Saturday evening in the last past month of January, all that neighbourhood of Covent-garden looked very desolate. It is so essentially a neighbourhood which has seen better days, that bad weather affects it sooner than another place which has not come down in the world. In its present reduced condition it bears a thaw almost worse than any place I know. It gets so dreadfully low-spirited when damp breaks forth. Those wonderful houses about Drury-lane Theatre, which in the palmy days of theatres were prosperous and long-settled places of business, and which now change hands every week, but never change their character of being divided and subdivided on the ground floor into mouldy dens of shops where an orange and half-a-dozen nuts, or a pomatum-pot, one cake of fancy soap, and a cigar box, are offered for sale and never sold, were most ruefully contemplated that evening, by the statue of Shakespeare, with the rain-drops coursing one another down its innocent nose. Those inscrutable pigeon-hole offices, with nothing in them (not so much as an inkstand) but a model of a theatre before the curtain, where, in the Italian Opera season, tickets at reduced prices are kept on sale by nomadic gentlemen in smeary hats too tall for them, whom one occasionally seems to have seen on race-courses, not wholly unconnected with strips of cloth of various colours and a rolling ball—those Bedouin establishments, deserted by the tribe, and tenantless, except when sheltering in one corner an irregular row of ginger-beer bottles, which would have made one shudder on such a night, but for its being plain that they had nothing in them, shrunk from the shrill cries of the newsboys at their Exchange in the kennel of Catherine-street, like guilty things upon a fearful summons. At the pipe shop in Great Russell-street, the Death's-head pipes were like theatrical memento mori, admonishing beholders of the decline of the playhouse as an Institution. I walked up Bow-street, disposed to be angry with the shops there, that were letting out theatrical secrets by exhibiting to work-a-day humanity the stuff of which diadems and robes of kings are made. I noticed that some shops which had once been in the dramatic line, and had struggled out of it, were not getting on prosperously—like some actors I have known, who took to business and failed to make it answer. In a word, those streets looked so dull, and, considered as theatrical streets, so broken and bankrupt, that the FOUND DEAD on the black board at the police station might have announced the decease of the Drama, and the pools of water outside the fire-engine makers at the corner of Long-acre might have been occasioned by his having brought out the whole of his stock to play upon its last smouldering ashes.

And yet, on such a night in so degenerate a time, the object of my journey was theatrical. And yet within half an hour I was in an immense theatre, capable of holding nearly five thousand people.

What Theatre? Her Majesty's? Far better. Royal Italian Opera? Far better. Infinitely superior to the latter for hearing in; infinitely superior to both, for seeing in. To every part of this Theatre, spacious fire-proof ways of ingress and egress. For every part of it, convenient places of refreshment and retiring rooms. Everything to eat and d ink carefully supervised as to quality, and sold at an appointed price; respectable female attendants ready for the commonest women in the audience; a general air of consideration, decorum, and supervision, most commendable; an unquestionably humanising influence in all the social arrangements of the place.

Surely a dear Theatre, then? Because there were in London (not very long ago) Theatres with entrance-prices up to half-a-guinea a head, whose arrangements were not half so civilised. Surely, therefore, a dear Theatre? Not very dear. A gallery at threepence, another gallery at four-pence, a pit at sixpence, boxes and pit-stalls at a shilling, and a few private boxes at half-a-crown.

My uncommercial curiosity induced me to go into every nook of this great place, and among every class of the audience assembled in it—amounting that evening, as I cal-

culated, to about two thousand and odd hundreds. Magnifi
cently lighted by a firmament of sparkling chandeliers, the
building was ventilated to perfection. My sense of smell,
without being particularly delicate, has been so offended in
some of the commoner places of public resort, that I have
often been obliged to leave them when I have made an
uncommercial journey expressly to look on. The air of this
Theatre was fresh, cool, and wholesome. To help towards
this end, very sensible precautions had been used, ingeniously combining the experience of hospitals and railway
stations. Asphalt pavements substituted for wooden floors,
honest bare walls of glazed brick and tile—even at the back
of the boxes—for plaster and paper, no benches stuffed, and
no carpeting or baize used; a cool material with a light
glazed surface, being the covering of the seats.

These various contrivances are as well considered in the
place in question as if it were a Fever Hospital; the result
is, that it is sweet and healthful. It has been constructed
from the ground to the roof, with a careful reference to sight
and sound in every corner; the result is, that its form is
beautiful, and that the appearance of the audience, as seen
from the proscenium—with every face in it commanding the
stage, and the whole so admirably raked and turned to that
centre, that a hand can scarcely move in the great assemblage
without the movement being seen from thence—is highly
remarkable in its union of vastness with compactness. The
stage itself, and all its appurtenances of machinery, cellarage,
height and breadth, are on a scale more like the Scala at
Milan, or the San Carlo at Naples, or the Grand Opera at
Paris, than any notion a stranger would be likely to form of
the Britannia Theatre at Hoxton, a mile north of St. Luke's
Hospital in the Old-street-road, London. The Forty Thieves
might be played here, and every thief ride his real horse,
and the disguised captain bring in his oil jars on a train of
real camels, and nobody be put out of the way. This really
extraordinary place is the achievement of one man's enterprise, and was erected on the ruins of an inconvenient old
building in less than five months, at a round cost of five-
and-twenty thousand pounds. To dismiss this part of my
subject, and still to render to the proprietor the credit that
is strictly his due, I must add that his sense of the responsibility upon him to make the best of his audience, and to do
his best for them, is a highly agreeable sign of these times.

As the spectators at this theatre, for a reason I will presently show, were the object of my journey, I entered on the play of the night as one of the two thousand and odd hundreds, by looking about me at my neighbours. We were a motley assemblage of people, and we had a good many boys and young men among us; we had also many girls and young women. To represent, however, that we did not include a very great number, and a very fair proportion of family groups, would be to make a gross mis-statement. Such groups were to be seen in all parts of the house; in the boxes and stalls particularly, they were composed of persons of very decent appearance, who had many children with them. Among our dresses there were most kinds of shabby and greasy wear, and much fustian and corduroy that was neither sound nor fragrant. The caps of our young men were mostly of a limp character, and we who wore them, slouched, high-shouldered, into our places with our hands in our pockets, and occasionally twisted our cravats about our necks like eels, and occasionally tied them down our breasts like links of sausages, and occasionally had a screw in our hair over each cheek-bone with a slight Thief-flavour in it. Besides prowlers and idlers, we were mechanics, dock-labourers, costermongers, petty tradesmen, small clerks, milliners, stay-makers, shoe-binders, slop-workers, poor workers in a hundred highways and byways. Many of us—on the whole, the majority—were not at all clean, and not at all choice in our lives or conversation. But we had all come together in a place where our convenience was well consulted, and where we were well looked after, to enjoy an evening's entertainment in common. We were not going to lose any part of what we had paid for through anybody's caprice, and as a community we had a character to lose. So, we were closely attentive, and kept excellent order; and let the man or boy who did otherwise instantly get out from this place, or we would put him out with the greatest expedition.

We began at half-past six with a pantomime—with a pantomime so long, that before it was over I felt as if I had been travelling for six weeks—going to India, say, by the Overland Mail. The Spirit of Liberty was the principal personage in the Introduction, and the Four Quarters of the World came out of the globe, glittering, and discoursed with the Spirit, who sang charmingly. We were delighted to

A Cheap Theatre—Saturday Night

understand that there was no liberty anywhere but among ourselves, and we highly applauded the agreeable fact. In an allegorical way, which did as well as any other way, we and the Spirit of Liberty got into a kingdom of Needles and Pins, and found them at war with a potentate who called in to his aid their old arch enemy Rust, and who would have got the better of them if the Spirit of Liberty had not in the nick of time transformed the leaders into Clown, Pantaloon, Harlequin, Columbine, Harlequina, and a whole family of Sprites, consisting of a remarkably stout father and three spineless sons. We all knew what was coming when the Spirit of Liberty addressed the king with a big face, and His Majesty backed to the side-scenes and began untying himself behind, with his big face all on one side. Our excitement at that crisis was great, and our delight unbounded. After this era in our existence, we went through all the incidents of a pantomime ; it was not by any means a savage panto-mime, in the way of burning or boiling people, or throwing them out of window, or cutting them up ; was often very droll ; was always liberally got up, and cleverly presented. I noticed that the people who kept the shops, and who represented the passengers in the thoroughfares, and so forth, had no conventionality in them, but were unusually like the real thing—from which I infer that you may take that audience in (if you wish to) concerning Knights and Ladies, Fairies, Angels, or such like, but they are not to be done as to anything in the streets. I noticed, also, that when two young men, dressed in exact imitation of the eel-and-sausage-cravated portion of the audience, were chased by policemen, and, finding themselves in danger of being caught, dropped so suddenly as to oblige the policemen to tumble over them, there was great rejoicing among the caps —as though it were a delicate reference to something they had heard of before.

The Pantomime was succeeded by a Melo-Drama. Throughout the evening I was pleased to observe Virtue quite as triumphant as she usually is out of doors, and indeed I thought rather more so. We all agreed (for the time) that honesty was the best policy, and we were as hard as iron upon Vice, and we wouldn't hear of Villainy getting on in the world—no, not on any consideration whatever.

Between the pieces, we almost all of us went out and refreshed. Many of us went the length of drinking beer at the bar of the neighbouring public-house, some of us drank spirits, crowds of us had sandwiches and ginger-beer at the refreshment-bars established for us in the Theatre. The sandwich—as substantial as was consistent with portability, and as cheap as possible—we hailed as one of our greatest institutions. It forced its way among us at all stages of the entertainment, and we were always delighted to see it; its adaptability to the varying moods of our nature was surprising; we could never weep so comfortably as when our tears fell on our sandwich; we could never laugh so heartily as when we choked with sandwich; Virtue never looked so beautiful or Vice so deformed as when we paused, sandwich in hand, to consider what would come of that resolution of Wickedness in boots, to sever Innocence in flowered chintz from Honest Industry in striped stockings. When the curtain fell for the night, we still fell back upon sandwich, to help us through the rain and mire, and home to bed.

This, as I have mentioned, was Saturday night. Being Saturday night, I had accomplished but the half of my un-commercial journey; for, its object was to compare the play on Saturday evening with the preaching in the same Theatre on Sunday evening.

Therefore, at the same hour of half-past six on the similarly damp and muddy Sunday evening, I returned to this Theatre. I drove up to the entrance (fearful of being late, or I should have come on foot), and found myself in a large crowd of people who, I am happy to state, were put into excellent spirits by my arrival. Having nothing to look at but the mud and the closed doors, they looked at me, and highly enjoyed the comic spectacle. My modesty inducing me to draw off, some hundreds of yards, into a dark corner, they at once forgot me, and applied themselves to their former occupation of looking at the mud and looking in at the closed doors: which, being of grated ironwork, allowed the lighted passage within to be seen. They were chiefly people of respectable appearance, odd and impulsive as most crowds are, and making a joke of being there as most crowds do.

In the dark corner I might have sat a long while, but that a very obliging passer-by informed me that the Theatre was already full, and that the people whom I saw in the street were all shut out for want of room. After that, I lost no time in warming myself into the building, and creeping to a place in a Proscenium box that had been kept for me.

There must have been full four thousand people present. Carefully estimating the pit alone, I could bring it out as holding little less than fourteen hundred. Every part of the house was well filled, and I had not found it easy to make my way along the back of the boxes to where I sat. The chandeliers in the ceiling were lighted ; there was no light on the stage ; the orchestra was empty. The green curtain was down, and, packed pretty closely on chairs on the small space of stage before it, were some thirty gentlemen, and two or three ladies. In the centre of these, in a desk or pulpit covered with red baize, was the presiding minister. The kind of rostrum he occupied will be very well under-stood, if I liken it to a boarded-up fireplace turned towards the audience, with a gentleman in a black surtout standing in the stove and leaning forward over the mantelpiece.

A portion of Scripture was being read when I went in. It was followed by a discourse, to which the congregation listened with most exemplary attention and uninterrupted silence and decorum. My own attention comprehended both the auditory and the speaker, and shall turn to both in this recalling of the scene, exactly as it did at the time.

"A very difficult thing," I thought, when the discourse began, "to speak appropriately to so large an audience, and to speak with tact. Without it, better not to speak at all. Infinitely better, to read the New Testament well, and to let *that* speak. In this congregation there is indubitably one pulse ; but I doubt if any power short of genius can touch it as one, and make it answer as one."

I could not possibly say to myself as the discourse proceeded, that the minister was a good speaker. I could not possibly say to myself that he expressed an understanding of the general mind and character of his audience. There was a supposititious working-man introduced into the homily, to make supposititious objections to our Christian religion and be reasoned down, who was not only a very disagreeable person, but remarkably unlike life—very much more unlike it than anything I had seen in the pantomime. The native independence of character this artisan was supposed to pos-sess, was represented by a suggestion of a dialect that I certainly never heard in my uncommercial travels, and with a coarse swing of voice and manner anything but agreeable

to his feelings, I should conceive, considered in the light of
a portrait, and as far away from the fact as a Chinese Tartar.
There was a model pauper introduced in like manner, who
appeared to me to be the most intolerably arrogant pauper
ever relieved, and to show himself in absolute want and dire
necessity of a course of Stone Yard.   For, how did this
pauper testify to his having received the gospel of humility ?
A gentleman met him in the workhouse, and said (which
I myself really thought good-natured of him), " Ah, John !
I am sorry to see you here. I am sorry to see you so poor."
" Poor, sir ! " replied that man, drawing himself up, " I am
the son of a Prince !   *My* father is the King of Kings.   *My*
father is the Lord of Lords.   *My* father is the ruler of all
the Princes of the Earth ! " &c.   And this was what all the
preacher's fellow-sinners might come to, if they would embrace this blessed book—which I must say it did some
violence to my own feelings of reverence, to see held out at
arm's length at frequent intervals and soundingly slapped,
like a slow lot at a sale.   Now, could I help asking myself
the question, whether the mechanic before me, who must
detect the preacher as being wrong about the visible manner
of himself and the like of himself, and about such a noisy
lip-server as that pauper, might not, most unhappily for the
usefulness of the occasion, doubt that preacher's being right
about things not visible to human senses ?

Again.   Is it necessary or advisable to address such an
audience continually as " fellow-sinners " ?   Is it not enough
to be fellow-creatures, born yesterday, suffering and striving
to-day, dying to-morrow ?   By our common humanity, my
brothers and sisters, by our common capacities for pain and
pleasure, by our common laughter and our common tears,
by our common aspiration to reach something better than
ourselves, by our common tendency to believe in something
good, and to invest whatever we love or whatever we lose
with some qualities that are superior to our own failings and
weaknesses as we know them in our own poor hearts—by
these, Hear me !—Surely, it is enough to be fellow-creatures.
Surely, it includes the other designation, and some touching
meanings over and above.

Again.   There was a personage introduced into the discourse (not an absolute novelty, to the best of my remembrance of my reading), who had been personally known to
the preacher, and had been quite a Crichton in all the ways

of philosophy, but had been an infidel. Many a time had the preacher talked with him on that subject, and many a time had he failed to convince that intelligent man. But he fell ill, and died, and before he died he recorded his conversion—in words which the preacher had taken down, my fellow-sinners, and would read to you from this piece of paper. I must confess that to me, as one of an uninstructed audience, they did not appear particularly edifying. I thought their tone extremely selfish, and I thought they had a spiritual vanity in them which was of the before-mentioned refractory pauper's family.

All slangs and twangs are objectionable everywhere, but the slang and twang of the conventicle— as bad in its way as that of the House of Commons, and nothing worse can be said of it—should be studiously avoided under such circumstances as I describe. The avoidance was not complete on this occasion. Nor was it quite agreeable to see the preacher addressing his pet "points" to his backers on the stage, as if appealing to those disciples to show him up, and testify to the multitude that each of those points was a clincher.

But, in respect of the large Christianity of his general tone; of his renunciation of all priestly authority; of his earnest and reiterated assurance to the people that the commonest among them could work out their own salvation if they would, by simply, lovingly, and dutifully following Our Saviour, and that they needed the mediation of no erring man; in these particulars, this gentleman deserved all praise. Nothing could be better than the spirit, or the plain emphatic words of his discourse in these respects. And it was a most significant and encouraging circumstance that whenever he struck that chord, or whenever he described anything which Christ himself had done, the array of faces before him was very much more earnest, and very much more expressive of emotion, than at any other time.

And now, I am brought to the fact, that the lowest part of the audience of the previous night, *was not there*. There is no doubt about it. There was no such thing in that building, that Sunday evening. I have been told since, that the lowest part of the audience of the Victoria Theatre has been attracted to its Sunday services. I have been very glad to hear it, but on this occasion of which I write, the lowest part of the usual audience of the Britannia Theatre, decidedly and unquestionably stayed away. When I first took my seat and looked at the house, my surprise at the change in its occupants was as great as my disappointment. To the most respectable class of the previous evening, was added a great number of respectable strangers attracted by curiosity, and drafts from the regular congregations of various chapels. It was impossible to fail in identifying the character of these last, and they were very numerous. I came out in a strong, slow tide of them setting from the boxes. Indeed, while the discourse was in progress, the respectable character of the auditory was so manifest in their appearance, that when the minister addressed a supposititious "outcast," one really felt a little impatient of it, as a figure of speech not justified by anything the eye could discover.

The time appointed for the conclusion of the proceedings was eight o'clock. The address having lasted until full that time, and it being the custom to conclude with a hymn, the preacher intimated in a few sensible words that the clock had struck the hour, and that those who desired to go before the hymn was sung, could go now, without giving offence. No one stirred. The hymn was then sung, in good time and tune and unison, and its effect was very striking. A comprehensive benevolent prayer dismissed the throng, and in seven or eight minutes there was nothing left in the Theatre but a light cloud of dust.

That these Sunday meetings in Theatres are good things, I do not doubt. Nor do I doubt that they will work lower and lower down in the social scale, if those who preside over them will be very careful on two heads: firstly, not to disparage the places in which they speak, or the intelligence of their hearers; secondly, not to set themselves in antagonism to the natural inborn desire of the mass of mankind to recreate themselves and to be amused.

There is a third head, taking precedence of all others, to which my remarks on the discourse I heard, have tended. In the New Testament there is the most beautiful and affecting history conceivable by man, and there are the terse models for all prayer and for all preaching. As to the models, imitate them, Sunday preachers—else why are they there, consider? As to the history, tell it. Some people cannot read, some people will not read, many people (this especially holds among the young and ignorant) find it hard to pursue the verse-form in which the book is presented to them, and imagine that those breaks imply gaps and want of continuity. Help them over that first stumbling-block, by. setting forth the history in narrative, with no fear of exhausting it. You will never preach so well, you will never move them so profoundly, you will never send them away with half so much to think of. Which is the better interest : Christ's choice of twelve poor men to help in those merciful wonders among the poor and rejected ; or the pious bullying of a whole Union-full of paupers ? What is your changed philosopher to wretched me, peeping in at the door out of the mud of the streets and of my life, when you have the widow's son to tell me about, the ruler's daughter, the other figure at the door when the brother of the two sisters was dead, and one of the two ran to the mourner, crying, " The Master is come, and calleth for thee " ?—Let the preacher who will thoroughly forget himself and remember no individuality but one, and no eloquence but one, stand up before four thousand men and women at the Britannia Theatre any Sunday night, recounting that narrative to them as fellow creatures, and he shall see a sight !

V

POOR MERCANTILE JACK

Is the sweet little cherub who sits smiling aloft and keeps watch on the life of poor Jack, commissioned to take charge of Mercantile Jack, as well as Jack of the national navy? If not, who is? What is the cherub about, and what are we all about, when poor Mercantile Jack is having his brains slowly knocked out by pennyweights, aboard the brig Beelzebub, or the barque Bowie-knife—when he looks his last at that infernal craft, with the first officer's iron boot-heel in his remaining eye, or with his dying body towed overboard in the ship's wake, while the cruel wounds in it do "the multitudinous seas incarnadine"?

Is it unreasonable to entertain a belief that if, aboard the brig Beelzebub or the barque Bowie-knife, the first officer did half the damage to cotton that he does to men, there would presently arise from both sides of the Atlantic so vociferous an invocation of the sweet little cherub who sits calculating aloft, keeping watch on the markets that pay, that such vigilant cherub would, with a winged sword, have that gallant officer's organ of destructiveness out of his head in the space of a flash of lightning?

If it be unreasonable, then am I the most unreasonable of men, for I believe it with all my soul.

This was my thought as I walked the dock-quays at Liverpool, keeping watch on poor Mercantile Jack. Alas for me! I have long outgrown the state of sweet little cherub; but there I was, and there Mercantile Jack was, and very busy he was, and very cold he was: the snow yet lying in the frozen furrows of the land, and the north-east winds snipping off the tops of the little waves in the Mersey, and rolling them into hailstones to pelt him with. Mercantile Jack was hard at it, in the hard weather: as he mostly is in all weathers, poor Jack. He was girded to ships' masts and

funnels of steamers, like a forester to a great oak, scraping
and painting; he was lying out on yards, furling sails that
tried to beat him off; he was dimly discernible up in a world
of giant cobwebs, reefing and splicing; he was faintly
audible down in holds, stowing and unshipping cargo; he
was winding round and round at capstans melodious,
monotonous, and drunk; he was of a diabolical aspect, with
coaling for the Antipodes; he was washing decks barefoot,
with the breast of his red shirt open to the blast, though
it was sharper than the knife in his leathern girdle; he was
looking over bulwarks, all eyes and hair; he was standing
by at the shoot of the Cunard steamer, off to-morrow, as the
stocks in trade of several butchers, poulterers, and fish-
mongers, poured down into the icehouse; he was coming
aboard of other vessels, with his kit in a tarpaulin bag,
attended by plunderers to the very last moment of his
shore-going existence. As though his senses, when released
from the uproar of the elements, were under obligation to
be confused by other turmoil, there was a rattling of wheels,
a clattering of hoofs, a clashing of iron, a jolting of cotton
and hides and casks and timber, an incessant deafening disturbance on the quays, that was the very madness of sound.
And as, in the midst of it, he stood swaying about, with his
hair blown all manner of wild ways, rather crazedly taking
leave of his plunderers, all the rigging in the docks was
shrill in the wind, and every little steamer coming and
going across the Mersey was sharp in its blowing off, and
every buoy in the river bobbed spitefully up and down, as
if there were a general taunting chorus of "Come along,
Mercantile Jack! Ill-lodged, ill-fed, ill-used, hocussed, entrapped, anticipated, cleaned out. Come along, Poor Mercantile Jack, and be tempest-tossed till you are drowned!"

The uncommercial transaction which had brought me and
Jack together, was this:—I had entered the Liverpool police
force, that I might have a look at the various unlawful traps
which are every night set for Jack. As my term of service
in that distinguished corps was short, and as my personal
bias in the capacity of one of its members has ceased, no
suspicion will attach to my evidence that it is an admirable
force. Besides that it is composed, without favour, of the
best men that can be picked, it is directed by an unusual
intelligence. Its organisation against Fires, I take to be
much better than the metropolitan system, and in all

respects it tempers its remarkable vigilance with a still more remarkable discretion.

Jack had knocked off work in the docks some hours, and I had taken, for purposes of identification, a photograph-likeness of a thief, in the portrait-room at our head police office (on the whole, he seemed rather complimented by the proceeding), and I had been on police parade, and the small hand of the clock was moving on to ten, when I took up my lantern to follow Mr. Superintendent to the traps that were set for Jack. In Mr. Superintendent I saw, as anybody might, a tall well-looking well-set-up man of a soldierly bearing, with a cavalry air, a good chest, and a resolute but not by any means ungentle face. He carried in his hand a plain black walking-stick of hard wood; and whenever and wherever, at any after-time of the night, he struck it on the pavement with a ringing sound, it instantly produced a whistle out of the darkness, and a policeman. To this remarkable stick, I refer an air of mystery and magic which pervaded the whole of my perquisition among the traps that were set for Jack.

We began by diving into the obscurest streets and lanes of the port. Suddenly pausing in a flow of cheerful discourse, before a dead wall, apparently some ten miles long, Mr. Superintendent struck upon the ground, and the wall opened and shot out, with military salute of hand to temple, two policemen—not in the least surprised themselves, not in the least surprising Mr. Superintendent.

" All right, Sharpeye ? "

" All right, sir."

" All right, Trampfoot ? "

" All right, sir."

" Is Quickear there ? "

" Here am I, sir."

" Come with us."

" Yes, sir."

So, Sharpeye went before, and Mr. Superintendent and I went next, and Trampfoot and Quickear marched as rear-guard. Sharpeye, I soon had occasion to remark, had a skilful and quite professional way of opening doors—touched latches delicately, as if they were keys of musical instruments—opened every door he touched, as if he were perfectly confident that there was stolen property behind it —instantly insinuated himself, to prevent its being shut.

Sharpeye opened several doors of traps that were set for Jack, but Jack did not happen to be in any of them. They were all such miserable places that really, Jack, if I were you, I would give them a wider berth. In every trap, somebody was sitting over a fire, waiting for Jack. Now, it was a crouching old woman, like the picture of the Norwood Gipsy in the old sixpenny dream-books; now, it was a crimp of the male sex, in a checked shirt and without a coat; reading a newspaper; now, it was a man crimp and a woman crimp, who always introduced themselves as united in holy matrimony ; now, it was Jack's delight, his (un)lovely Nan ; but they were all waiting for Jack, and were all frightfully disappointed to see us.

"Who have you got up-stairs here?" says Sharpeye, generally. (In the Move-on tone.)

"Nobody, surr; sure not a blessed sowl!" (Irish feminine reply.)

"What do you mean by nobody? Didn't I hear a woman's step go up-stairs when my hand was on the latch?"

"Ah! sure thin you're right, surr, I forgot her! 'Tis on'y Betsy White, surr. Ah! you know Betsy, surr. Come down, Betsy darlin', and say the gintlemin."

Generally, Betsy looks over the banisters (the steep staircase is in the room) with a forcible expression in her protesting face, of an intention to compensate herself for the present trial by grinding Jack finer than usual when he does come. Generally, Sharpeye turns to Mr. Superintendent, and says, as if the subjects of his remarks were wax-work :

"One of the worst, sir, this house is. This woman has been indicted three times. This man's a regular bad one likewise. His real name is Pegg. Gives himself out as Waterhouse."

"Never had sitch a name as Pegg near me back, thin, since I was in this house, bee the good Lard!" says the woman.

Generally, the man says nothing at all, but becomes exceedingly round-shouldered, and pretends to read his paper with rapt attention. Generally, Sharpeye directs our observation with a look, to the prints and pictures that are invariably numerous on the walls. Always, Trampfoot and Quickear are taking notice on the doorstep. In default of Sharpeye being acquainted with the exact individuality of any gentleman encountered, one of these two is sure to proclaim from the outer air, like a gruff spectre, that Jack-

son is not Jackson, but knows himself to be Fogle; or that
Canlon is Walker's brother, against whom there was not
sufficient evidence; or that the man who says he never was
at sea since he was a boy, came ashore from a voyage last
Thursday, or sails to-morrow morning. "And that is a bad
class of man, you see," says Mr. Superintendent, when he
got out into the dark again, " and very difficult to deal with,
who, when he has made this place too hot to hold him,
enters himself for a voyage as steward or cook, and is out
of knowledge for months, and then turns up again worse
than ever."

When we had gone into many such houses, and had
come out (always leaving everybody relapsing into waiting
for Jack), we started off to a singing-house where Jack was
expected to muster strong.

The vocalisation was taking place in a long low room
up-stairs; at one end, an orchestra of two performers, and
a small platform; across the room, a series of open pews
for Jack, with an aisle down the middle; at the other end
a larger pew than the rest, entitled SNUG, and reserved for
mates and similar good company. About the room, some
amazing coffee-coloured pictures varnished an inch deep, and
some stuffed creatures in cases; dotted among the audience,
in Snug and out of Snug, the " Professionals ;" among them,
the celebrated comic favourite Mr. Banjo Bones, looking
very hideous with his blackened face and limp sugar-loaf
hat; beside him, sipping rum-and-water, Mrs. Banjo Bones,
in her natural colours—a little heightened.

It was a Friday night, and Friday night was considered
not a good night for Jack. At any rate, Jack did not show
in very great force even here, though the house was one to
which he much resorts, and where a good deal of money is
taken. There was British Jack, a little maudlin and sleepy,
lolling over his empty glass, as if he were trying to read his
fortune at the bottom; there was Loafing Jack of the Stars
and Stripes, rather an unpromising customer, with his long
nose, lank cheek, high cheek-bones, and nothing soft about
him but his cabbage-leaf hat; there was Spanish Jack, with
curls of black hair, rings in his ears, and a knife not far
from his hand, if you get into trouble with him; there
were Maltese Jack, and Jack of Sweden, and Jack the Finn,
looming through the smoke of their pipes, and turning faces
that looked as if they were carved out of dark wood, towards

tho young lady dancing the hornpipe: who found the platform so exceedingly small for it, that I had a nervous expectation of seeing her, in the backward steps, disappear through the window. Still, if all hands had been got together, they would not have more than half-filled the room. Observe, however, said Mr. Licensed Victualler, the host, that it was Friday night, and, besides, it was getting on for twelve, and Jack had gone aboard. A sharp and watchful man, Mr. Licensed Victualler, the host, with tight lips and a complete edition of Cocker's arithmetic in each eye. Attended to his business himself, he said. Always on the spot. When he heard of talent, trusted nobody's account of it, but went off by rail to see it. If true talent, engaged it. Pounds a week for talent—four pound—five pound. Banjo Bones was undoubted talent. Hear this instrument that was going to play—it was real talent! In truth it was very good; a kind of piano-accordion, played by a young girl of a delicate prettiness of face, figure, and dress, that made the audience look coarser. She sang to the instrument, too; first, a song about village bells, and how they chimed; then a song about how I went to sea; winding up with an imitation of the bagpipes, which Mercantile Jack seemed to understand much the best. A good girl, said Mr. Licensed Victualler. Kept herself select. Sat in Snug, not listening to the blandishments of Mates. Lived with mother. Father dead. Once a merchant well to do, but over-speculated himself. On delicate inquiry as to salary paid for item of talent under consideration, Mr. Victualler's pounds dropped suddenly to shillings—still it was a very comfortable thing for a young person like that, you know; she only went on six times a night, and was only required to be there from six at night to twelve. What was more conclusive was, Mr. Victualler's assurance that he "never allowed any language, and never suffered any disturbance." Sharpeye confirmed the statement, and the order that prevailed was the best proof of it that could have been cited. So, I came to the conclusion that poor Mercantile Jack might do (as I am afraid he does) much worse than trust himself to Mr. Victualler, and pass his evenings here.

But we had not yet looked, Mr. Superintendent—said Trampfoot, receiving us in the street again with military salute—for Dark Jack. True, Trampfoot. Ring the wonderful stick, rub the wonderful lantern, and cause the spirits of the stick and lantern to convey us to the Darkies.

There was no disappointment in the matter of Dark Jack; *he* was producible. The Genii set us down in the little first floor of a little public-house, and there, in a stiflingly close atmosphere, were Dark Jack, and Dark Jack's delight, his *white* unlovely Nan, sitting against the wall all round the -room. More than that: Dark Jack's delight was the least unlovely Nan, both morally and physically, that I saw that night.

As a fiddle and tambourine band were sitting among the company, Quickear suggested why not strike up? "Ah, la'ads!" said a negro sitting by the door, "gib the jebblem a darnse. Tak' yah pardlers, jebblem, for 'um QUAD-rill."

This was the landlord, in a Greek cap, and a dress half Greek and half English. As master of the ceremonies, he called all the figures, and occasionally addressed himself parenthetically—after this manner. When he was very loud, I use capitals.

"Now den! Hoy! ONE. Right and left. (Put a steam on, gib 'um powder.) LA-dies' chail. BAL-loon say. Lemonade! Two. AD-warnse and go back (gib 'ell a break-down, shake it out o' yerselbs, keep a movil). SWING-corners, BAL-loon say, and Lemonade! (Hoy!) THREE. GENT come for'ard with a lady and go back, hoppersite come for'ard and do what yer can. (Aeiohoy!) BAL-loon say, and leetle lemonade (Dat hair nigger by 'um fireplace 'hind a' time, shake it out o' yerselbs, gib 'ell a breakdown.) Now den! Hoy! FOUR! Lemonade. BAL-loon say, and swing. FOUR ladies meets in 'um middle, FOUR gents goes round 'um ladies, FOUR gents passes out under 'um ladies' arms, SWING—and Lemonade till 'a moosic can't play no more! (Hoy, Hoy!)"

The male dancers were all blacks, and one was an unusually powerful man of six feet three or four. The sound of their flat feet on the floor was as unlike the sound of white feet as their faces were unlike white faces. They toed and heeled, shuffled, double-shuffled, double-double-shuffled, covered the buckle, and beat the time out, rarely, dancing with a great show of teeth, and with a childish good-humoured enjoyment that was very prepossessing. They generally kept together, these poor fellows, said Mr. Superintendent, because they were at a disadvantage singly, and liable to slights in the neighbouring streets. But, if I were Light Jack, I should be very slow to interfere oppressively with Dark Jack, for, whenever I have had to do with him I have found him a simple and a gentle fellow. Bearing this in mind, I asked his friendly permission to leave him restoration of beer, in wishing him good night, and thus it fell out that the last words I heard him say as I blundered down the worn stairs, were, "Jebblem's elth! Ladies drinks fust!"

The night was now well on into the morning, but, for miles and hours we explored a strange world, where nobody ever goes to bed, but everybody is eternally sitting up, waiting for Jack. This exploration was among a labyrinth of dismal courts and blind alleys, called Entries, kept in wonderful order by the police, and in much better order than by the corporation : the want of gaslight in the most dangerous and infamous of these places being quite unworthy of so spirited a town. I need describe but two or three of the houses in which Jack was waited for as specimens of the rest. Many we attained by noisome passages so profoundly dark that we felt our way with our hands. Not one of the whole number we visited, was without its show of prints and ornamental crockery ; the quantity of the latter set forth on little shelves and in little cases, in otherwise wretched rooms, indicating that Mercantile Jack must have an extraordinary fondness for crockery, to necessitate so much of that bait in his traps.

Among such garniture, in one front parlour in the dead of the night, four women were sitting by a fire. One of them had a male child in her arms. On a stool among them was a swarthy youth with a guitar, who had evidently stopped playing when our footsteps were heard.

"Well! how do *you* do?" says Mr. Superintendent, looking about him.

"Pretty well, sir, and hope you gentlemen are going to treat us ladies, now you have come to see us."

"Order there!" says Sharpeye.

"None of that!" says Quickear.

Trampfoot, outside, is heard to confide to himself, "Meggisson's lot this is. And a bad 'un!"

"Well!" says Mr. Superintendent, laying his hand on the shoulder of the swarthy youth, "and who's this?"

"Antonio, sir."

"And what does *he* do here?"

"Come to give us a bit of music. No harm in that, I suppose?"

"A young foreign sailor?"

"Yes. He's a Spaniard. You're a Spaniard, ain't you, Antonio?"

"Me Spanish."

"And he don't know a word you say, not he; not if you was to talk to him till doomsday." (Triumphantly, as if it redounded to the credit of the house.)

"Will he play something?"

"Oh, yes, if you like. Play something, Antonio. *You* ain't ashamed to play something; are you?"

The cracked guitar raises the feeblest ghost of a tune, and three of the women keep time to it with their heads, and the fourth with the child. If Antonio has brought any money in with him, I am afraid he will never take it out, and it even strikes me that his jacket and guitar may be in a bad way. But, the look of the young man and the tinkling of the instrument so change the place in a moment to a leaf out of Don Quixote, that I wonder where his mule is stabled, until he leaves off.

I am bound to acknowledge (as it tends rather to my uncommercial confusion), that I occasioned a difficulty in this establishment, by having taken the child in my arms. For, on my offering to restore it to a ferocious joker not unstimulated by rum, who claimed to be its mother, that unnatural parent put her hands behind her, and declined to accept it; backing into the fireplace, and very shrilly declaring, regardless of remonstrance from her friends, that she knowed it to be Law, that whoever took a child from its mother of his own will, was bound to stick to it. The uncommercial sense of being in a rather ridiculous position with the poor little child beginning to be frightened, was relieved by my worthy friend and fellow-constable, Trampfoot; who, laying hands on the article as if it were a Bottle, passed it on to the nearest woman, and bade her "take hold of that." As we came out the Bottle was passed to the ferocious joker, and they all sat down as before, including Antonio and the guitar. It was clear that there was no such thing as a nightcap to this baby's head, and that even he never went to bed, but was always kept up—and would grow up, kept up—waiting for Jack.

Later still in the night, we came (by the court "where

the man was murdered," and by the other court across the
street, into which his body was dragged) to another parlour
in another Entry, where several people were sitting round
a fire in just the same way. It was a dirty and offensive
place, with some ragged clothes drying in it; but there was
a high shelf over the entrance-door (to te out of the reach of
marauding hands, possibly) with two large white loaves on
it, and a great piece of Cheshire cheese.

"Well!" says Mr. Superintendent, with a comprehensive
look all round. "How do *you* do?"

"Not much to boast of, sir." From the curtseying woman
of the house. "This is my good man, sir."

"You are not registered as a common Lodging House?"

"No, sir."

Sharpeye (in the Move-on tone) puts in the pertinent
inquiry, "Then why ain't you?"

"Ain't got no one here, Mr. Sharpeye," rejoin the woman
and my good man together, "but our own family."

"How many are you in family?"

The woman takes time to count, under pretence of coughing, and adds, as one scant of breath, "Seven, sir."

But she has missed one, so Sharpeye, who knows all
about it, says:

"Here's a young man here makes eight, who ain't of your
family?"

"No, Mr. Sharpeye, he's a weekly lodger."

"What does he do for a living?"

The young man here, takes the reply upon himself, and
shortly answers, "Ain't got nothing to do."

The young man here, is modestly brooding behind a damp
apron pendent from a clothes-line. As I glance at him
I become—but I don't know why—vaguely reminded of
Woolwich, Chatham, Portsmouth, and Dover. When we
get out, my respected fellow-constable Sharpeye, addressing
Mr. Superintendent, says:

"You noticed that young man, sir, at Darby's?"

"Yes. What is he?"

"Deserter, sir."

Mr. Sharpeye further intimates that when we have done
with his services, he will step back and take that young man.
Which in course of time he does: feeling at perfect ease
about finding him, and knowing for a moral certainty that
nobody in that region will be gone to bed.

Later still in the night, we came to another parlour up a step or two from the street, which was very cleanly, neatly, even tastefully, kept, and in which, set forth on a draped chest of drawers masking the staircase, was such a profusion of ornamental crockery, that it would have furnished forth a handsome sale-booth at a fair. It backed up a stout old lady—HOGARTH drew her exact likeness more than once —and a boy who was carefully writing a copy in a copybook.

" Well, ma'am, how do *you* do ? "

Sweetly, she can assure the dear gentlemen, sweetly. Charmingly, charmingly. And overjoyed to see us !

" Why, this is a strange time for this boy to be writing his copy. In the middle of the night ! "

" So it is, dear gentlemen, Heaven bless your welcome faces and send ye prosperous, but he has been to the Play with a young friend for his diversion, and he combinates his improvement with entertainment, by doing his school-writing afterwards, God be good to ye ! "

The copy admonished human nature to subjugate the fire of every fierce desire. One might have thought it recommended stirring the fire, the old lady so approved it. There she sat, rosily beaming at the copy-book and the boy, and invoking showers of blessings on our heads, when we left her in the middle of the night, waiting for Jack.

Later still in the night, we came to a nauseous room with an earth floor, into which the refuse scum of an alley trickled. The stench of this habitation was abominable ; the seeming poverty of it, diseased and dire. Yet, here again, was visitor or lodger—a man sitting before the fire, like the rest of them elsewhere, and apparently not distasteful to the mistress's niece, who was also before the fire. The mistress herself had the misfortune of being in jail.

Three weird old women of transcendent ghastliness, were at needlework at a table in this room. Says Trampfoot to First Witch, " What are you making ? " Says she, " Money-bags."

" *What* are you making ? " retorts Trampfoot, a little off his balance.

" Bags to hold your money," says the witch, shaking her head, and setting her teeth, " you as has got it."

She holds up a common cash-bag, and on the table is a heap of such bags. Witch Two laughs at us. Witch Three scowls at us. Witch sisterhood all, stitch, stitch. First Witch has a circle round each eye. I fancy it like the beginning of the development of a perverted diabolical halo, and that when it spreads all round her head, she will die in the odour of devilry.

Trampfoot wishes to be informed what First Witch has got behind the table, down by the side of her, there? Witches Two and Three croak angrily, "Show him the child!"

She drags out a skinny little arm from a brown dustheap on the ground. Adjured not to disturb the child, she lets it drop again. Thus we find at last that there is one child in the world of Entries who goes to bed—if this be bed. •

Mr. Superintendent asks how long are they going to work at those bags?

How long? First Witch repeats. Going to have supper presently. See the cups and saucers, and the plates.

"Late? Ay! But we has to 'arn our supper afore we eats it!" Both the other witches repeat this after First Witch, and take the Uncommercial measurement with their eyes, as for a charmed winding-sheet. Some grim discourse ensues, referring to the mistress of the cave, who will be released from jail to-morrow. Witches pronounce Trampfoot "right there," when he deems it a trying distance for the old lady to walk; she shall be fetched by niece in a spring-cart.

As I took a parting look at First Witch in turning away, the red marks round her eyes seemed to have already grown larger, and she hungrily and thirstily looked out beyond me into the dark doorway, to see if Jack was there. For, Jack came even here, and the mistress had got into jail through deluding Jack.

When I at last ended this night of travel and got to bed, I failed to keep my mind on comfortable thoughts of Seaman's Homes (not overdone with strictness), and improved dock regulations giving Jack greater benefit of fire and candle aboard ship, through my mind's wandering among the vermin I had seen. Afterwards the same vermin ran all over my sleep. Evermore, when on a breezy day I see Poor Mercantile Jack running into port with a fair wind under all sail, I shall think of the unsleeping host of devourers who never go to bed, and are always in their set traps waiting for him.

VI

REFRESHMENTS FOR TRAVELLERS

In the late high winds I was blown to a great many places
—and indeed, wind or no wind, I generally have. extensive
transactions on hand in the article of Air—but I have not
been blown to any English place lately, and I very seldom
have blown to any English place in my life, where I could
get anything good to eat and drink in five minutes, or where,
if I sought it, I was received with a welcome.

This is a curious thing to consider. But before (stimulated by my own experiences and the representations of
many fellow-travellers of every uncommercial and commercial degree) I consider it further, I must utter a passing
word of wonder concerning high winds.

I wonder why metropolitan gales always blow so hard at
Walworth. I cannot imagine what Walworth has done, to
bring such windy punishment upon itself, as I never fail to
find recorded in the newspapers when the wind has blown at
all hard. Brixton seems to have something on its conscience; Peckham suffers more than a virtuous Peckham
might be supposed to deserve; the howling neighbourhood
of Deptford figures largely in the accounts of the ingenious
gentlemen who are out in every wind that blows, and to
whom it is an ill high wind that blows no good; but, there
can hardly be any Walworth left by this time. It must
surely be blown away. I have read of more chimney-stacks
and house-copings coming down with terrific smashes at
Walworth, and of more sacred edifices being nearly (not
quite) blown out to sea from the same accursed locality,
than I have read of practised thieves with the appearance
and manners of gentlemen—a popular phenomenon which
never existed on earth out of fiction and a police report.
Again: I wonder why people are always blown into the
Surrey Canal, and into no other piece of water! Why do
people get up early and go out in groups, to be blown into

the Surrey Canal? Do they say to one another, "Welcome death, so that we get into the newspapers?" Even that would be an insufficient explanation, because even then they might sometimes put themselves in the way of being blown into the Regent's Canal, instead of always saddling Surrey for the field. Some nameless policeman, too, is constantly, on the slightest provocation, getting himself blown into this same Surrey Canal. Will SIR RICHARD MAYNE see to it, and restrain that weak-minded and feeble-bodied constable?

To resume the consideration of the curious question of Refreshment. I am a Briton, and, as such, I am aware that I never will be a slave—and yet I have latent suspicion that there must be some slavery of wrong custom in this matter.

I travel by railroad. I start from home at seven or eight in the morning, after breakfasting hurriedly. What with skimming over the open landscape, what with mining in the damp bowels of the earth, what with banging booming and shrieking the scores of miles away, I am hungry when I arrive at the "Refreshment" station where I am expected. Please to observe, expected. I have said, I am hungry; perhaps I might say, with greater point and force, that I am to some extent exhausted, and that I need—in the expressive French sense of the word—to be restored. What is provided for my restoration? The apartment that is to restore me is a wind-trap, cunningly set to inveigle all the draughts in that country-side, and to communicate a special intensity and velocity to them as they rotate in two hurricanes: one, about my wretched head: one, about my wretched legs. The training of the young ladies behind the counter who are to restore me, has been from their infancy directed to the assumption of a defiant dramatic show that I am *not* expected. It is in vain for me to represent to them by my humble and conciliatory manners, that I wish to be liberal. It is in vain for me to represent to myself, for the encouragement of my sinking soul, that the young ladies have a pecuniary interest in my arrival. Neither my reason nor my feelings can make head against the cold glazed glare of eye with which I am assured that I am not expected, and not wanted. The solitary man among the bottles would sometimes take pity on me, if he dared, but he is powerless against the rights and mights of Woman.

(Of the page I make no account, for, he is a boy, and there-fore the natural enemy of Creation.) Chilling fast, in the deadly tornadoes to which my upper and lower extremities are exposed, and subdued by the moral disadvantage at which I stand, I turn my disconsolate eyes on the refresh-ments that are to restore me. I find that I must either scald my throat by insanely ladling into it, against time and for no wager, brown hot water stiffened with flour ; or I must make myself flaky and sick with Banbury cake ; or, I must stuff into my delicate organisation, a currant pin-cushion which I know will swell into immeasurable dimen-sions when it has got there ; or, I must extort from an iron-bound quarry, with a fork, as if I were farming an inhospitable soil, some glutinous lumps of gristle and grease, called pork-pie. While thus forlornly occupied, I find that the depressing banquet on the table is, in every phase of its profoundly unsatisfactory character, so like the banquet at the meanest and shabbiest of evening parties, that I begin to think I must have "brought down" to supper, the old lady unknown, blue with cold, who is setting her teeth on edge with a cool orange at my elbow—that the pastrycook who has compounded for the company on the lowest terms per head, is a fraudulent bankrupt, redeeming his contract with the stale stock from his window—that, for some unex-plained reason, the family giving the party have become my mortal foes, and have given it on purpose to affront me. Or, I fancy that I am "breaking up" again, at the evening conversazione at school, charged two-and-sixpence in the half-year's bill ; or breaking down again at that celebrated evening party given at Mrs. Bogles's boarding-house when I was a boarder there, on which occasion Mrs. Bogles was taken in execution by a branch of the legal profession who got in as the harp, and was removed (with the keys and subscribed capital) to a place of durance, half an hour prior to the commencement of the festivities.

Take another case.

Mr. Grazinglands, of the Midland Counties, came to London by railroad one morning last week, accompanied by the amiable and fascinating Mrs. Grazinglands. Mr. G. is a gentleman of a comfortable property, and had a little business to transact at the Bank of England, which required the con-currence and signature of Mrs. G. Their business disposed of, Mr. and Mrs. Grazinglands viewed the Royal Exchange, and the exterior of St. Paul's Cathedral. The spirits of Mrs. Grazinglands then gradually beginning to flag, Mr. Grazinglands (who is the tenderest of husbands) remarked with sympathy, "Arabella, my dear, I fear you are faint." Mrs. Grazinglands replied, "Alexander, I am rather faint; but don't mind me, I shall be better presently." Touched by the feminine meekness of this answer, Mr. Grazinglands looked in at a pastry-cook's window, hesitating as to the expediency of lunching at that establishment. He beheld nothing to eat, but butter in various forms, slightly charged with jam, and languidly frizzling over tepid water. Two ancient turtle-shells, on which was inscribed the legend, "Soups," decorated a glass partition within, enclosing a stuffy alcove, from which a ghastly mockery of a marriage-breakfast spread on a rickety table, warned the terrified traveller. An oblong box of stale and broken pastry at reduced prices, mounted on a stool, ornamented the door-way; and two high chairs that looked as if they were performing on stilts, embellished the counter. Over the whole, a young lady presided, whose gloomy haughtiness as she surveyed the street, announced a deep-seated grievance against society, and an implacable determination to be avenged. From a beetle-haunted kitchen below this institution, fumes arose, suggestive of a class of soup which Mr. Grazinglands knew, from painful experience, enfeebles the mind, distends the stomach, forces itself into the complexion, and tries to ooze out at the eyes. As he decided against entering, and turned away, Mrs. Grazinglands becoming perceptibly weaker, repeated, "I am rather faint, Alexander, but don't mind me." Urged to new efforts by these words of resignation, Mr. Grazinglands looked in at a cold and floury baker's shop, where utilitarian buns unrelieved by a currant, consorted with hard biscuits, a stone filter of cold water, a hard pale clock, and a hard little old woman with flaxen hair, of an undeveloped-farinaceous aspect, as if she had been fed upon seeds. He might have entered even here, but for the timely remembrance coming upon him that Jairing's was but round the corner.

Now, Jairing's being an hotel for families and gentlemen, in high repute among the midland counties, Mr. Grazinglands plucked up a great spirit when he told Mrs. Grazinglands she should have a chop there. That lady likewise felt that she was going to see Life. Arriving on that gay

and festive scene, they found the second waiter, in a flabby
undress, cleaning the windows of the empty coffee-room;
and the first waiter, denuded of his white tie, making up
his cruets behind the Post-Office Directory. The latter
(who took them in hand) was greatly put out by their
patronage, and showed his mind to be troubled by a sense
of the pressing necessity of instantly smuggling Mrs. Grazinglands into the obscurest corner of the building. This slighted
lady (who is the pride of her division of the county) was
immediately conveyed, by several dark passages, and up and
down several steps, into a penitential apartment at the back
of the house, where five invalided old plate-warmers leaned
up against one another under a discarded old melancholy
sideboard, and where the wintry leaves of all the dining-
tables in the house lay thick. Also, a sofa, of incomprehensible form regarded from any sofane point of view,
murmured "Bed;" while an air of mingled fluffiness and
heeltaps, added, "Second Waiter's." Secreted in this dismal
hold, objects of a mysterious distrust and suspicion, Mr.
Grazinglands and his charming partner waited twenty
minutes for the smoke (for it never came to a fire), twenty-
five minutes for the sherry, half an hour for the tablecloth,
forty minutes for the knives and forks, three-quarters of an
hour for the chops, and an hour for the potatoes. On
settling the little bill—which was not much more than the
day's pay of a Lieutenant in the navy—Mr. Grazinglands
took heart to remonstrate against the general quality and
cost of his reception. To whom the waiter replied, sub-
stantially, that Jairing's made it a merit to have accepted
him on any terms: "for," added the waiter (unmistakably
coughing at Mrs. Grazinglands, the pride of her division of
the county), "when indiwiduals is not staying in the 'Ouse,
their favours is not as a rule looked upon as making it
worth Mr. Jairing's while; nor is it, indeed, a style of
business Mr. Jairing wishes." Finally, Mr. and Mrs.
Grazinglands passed out of Jairing's hotel for Families
and Gentlemen, in a state of the greatest depression, scorned
by the bar; and did not recover their self-respect for several
days.

Or take another case. Take your own case.

You are going off by railway, from any Terminus. You
have twenty minutes for dinner, before you go. You want
your dinner, and like Dr. Johnson, Sir, you like to dine,

You present to your mind, a picture of the refreshment-table at that terminus. The conventional shabby evening-party supper—accepted as the model for all termini and all refreshment stations, because it is the last repast known to this state of existence of which any human creature would partake, but in the direst extremity—sickens your contemplation, and your words are these : "I cannot dine on stale sponge-cakes that turn to sand in the mouth. I cannot dine on shining brown patties, composed of unknown animals within, and offering to my view the device of an indigestible star-fish in leaden pie-crust without. I cannot dine on a sandwich that has long been pining under an exhausted receiver. I cannot dine on barley-sugar. I cannot dine on Toffee." You repair to the nearest hotel, and arrive, agitated, in the coffee-room.

It is a most astonishing fact that the waiter is very cold to you. Account for it how you may, smooth it over how you will, you cannot deny that he is cold to you. He is not glad to see you, he does not want you, he would much rather you hadn't come. He opposes to your flushed condition, an immovable composure. As if this were not enough, another waiter, born, as it would seem, expressly to look at you in this passage of your life, stands at a little distance, with his napkin under his arm and his hands folded, looking at you with all his might. You impress on your waiter that you have ten minutes for dinner, and he proposes that you shall begin with a bit of fish which will be ready in twenty. That proposal declined, he suggests— as a neat originality—" a weal or mutton cutlet." You close with either cutlet, any cutlet, anything. He goes, leisurely, behind a door and calls down some unseen shaft. A ventriloquial dialogue ensues, tending finally to the effect that weal only, is available on the spur of the moment. You anxiously call out, "Veal, then ! " Your waiter having settled that point, returns to array your tablecloth, with a table napkin folded cocked-hat-wise (slowly, for something out of window engages his eye), a white wine-glass, a green wine-glass, a blue finger-glass, a tumbler, and a powerful field battery of fourteen casters with nothing in them ; or at all events—which is enough for your purpose—with nothing in them that will come out. All this time, the other waiter looks at you—with an air of mental comparison and curiosity, now, as if it had occurred to him that you are

rather like his brother.   Half your time gone, and nothing
come but the jug of ale and the bread, you implore your
waiter to "see after that cutlet, waiter; pray do!"   He
cannot go at once, for he is carrying in seventeen pounds
of American cheese for you to finish with, and a small
Landed Estate of celery and water-cresses.   The other waiter
changes his leg, and takes a new view of you, doubtfully,
now, as if he had rejected the resemblance to his brother,
and had begun to think you more like his aunt or his grandmother.   Again you beseech your waiter with pathetic
indignation, to "see after that cutlet!"   He steps out to
see after it, and by-and-by, when you are going away without it, comes back with it.   Even then, he will not take
the sham silver cover off, without a pause for a flourish, and
a look at the musty cutlet as if he were surprised to see
it—which cannot possibly be the case, he must have seen
it so often before.   A sort of fur has been produced upon
its surface by the cook's art, and in a sham silver vessel
staggering on two feet instead of three, is a cutaneous kind
of sauce, of brown pimples and pickled cucumber.   You
order the bill, but your waiter cannot bring your bill yet,
because he is bringing, instead, three flinty-hearted potatoes
and two grim head of broccoli, like the occasional ornaments
on area railings, badly boiled.   You know that you will
never come to this pass, any more than to the cheese and
celery, and you imperatively demand your bill; but, it takes
time to get, even when gone for, because your waiter has
to communicate with a lady who lives behind a sash-window
in a corner, and who appears to have to refer to several
Ledgers before she can make it out—as if you had been
staying there a year.   You become distracted to get away,
and the other waiter, once more changing his leg, still looks
at you—but suspiciously, now, as if you had begun to
remind him of the party who took the great-coats last
winter.   Your bill at last brought and paid, at the rate of
sixpence a mouthful, your waiter reproachfully reminds
you that "attendance is not charged for a single meal,"
and you have to search in all your pockets for sixpence
more.   He has a worse opinion of you than ever, when
you have given it to him, and lets you out into the street
with the air of one saying to himself, as you cannot doubt
he is, "I hope we shall never see *you* here again!"

Or, take any other of the numerous travelling instances

in which, with more time at your disposal, you are, have been, or may be, equally ill served. Take the old-established Bull's Head with its old-established knife-boxes on its old-established sideboards, its old-established flue under its old-established four-post bedsteads in its old-established airless rooms, its old-established frouziness up-stairs and down-stairs, its old-established cookery, and its old-established principles of plunder. Count up your injuries, in its side-dishes of ailing sweetbreads in white poultices, of apoth-caries' powders in rice for curry, of pale stewed bits of calf ineffectually relying for an adventitious interest on forcemeat balls. You have had experience of the old-established Bull's Head stringy fowls, with lower extremities like wooden legs, sticking up out of the dish; of its canni-balic boiled mutton, gushing horribly among its capers, when carved; of its little dishes of pastry—roofs of spermaceti ointment, erected over half an apple or four gooseberries. Well for you if you have yet forgotten the old-established Bull's Head fruity port: whose reputation was gained solely by the old-established price the Bull's Head put upon it, and by the old-established air with which the Bull's Head set the glasses and D'Oyleys on, and held that Liquid Gout to the three-and-sixpenny wax-candle, as if its old-established colour hadn't come from the dyer's.

Or lastly, take to finish with, two cases that we all know, every day.

We all know the new hotel near the station, where it is always gusty, going up the lane which is always muddy, where we are sure to arrive at night, and where we make the gas start awfully when we open the front door. We all know the flooring of the passages and staircases that is too new, and the walls that are too new, and the house that is haunted by the ghost of mortar. We all know the doors that have cracked, and the cracked shutters through which we get a glimpse of the disconsolate moon. We all know the new people, who have discome to keep the new hotel, and who wish they had never come, and who (inevitable result) wish *we* had never come. We all know how much too scant and smooth and bright the new furniture is, and how it has never settled down, and cannot fit itself into right places, and will get into wrong places. We all know how the gas, being lighted, shows maps of Damp upon the walls. We all know how the ghost of mortar passes into our sandwich, stirs our negus, goes up to bed with us, ascends the pale bedroom chimney, and prevents the smoke from following. We all know how a leg of our chair comes off at breakfast in the morning, and how the dejected waiter attributes the accident to a general greenness pervading the establishment, and informs us, in reply to a local inquiry, that he is thankful to say he is an entire stranger in that part of the country, and is going back to his own connexion on Saturday.

We all know, on the other hand, the great station hotel belonging to the company of proprietors, which has suddenly sprung up in the back outskirts of any place we like to name, and where we look out of our palatial windows, at little back yards and gardens, old summer-houses, fowl-houses, pigeon-traps, and pigsties. We all know this hotel in which we can get anything we want, after its kind, for money ; but where nobody is glad to see us, or sorry to see us, or minds (our bill paid) whether we come or go, or how, or when, or why, or cares about us. We all know this hotel, where we have no individuality, but put ourselves into the general post, as it were, and are sorted and disposed of according to our division. We all know that we can get on very well indeed at such a place, but still not perfectly well ; and this may be, because the place is largely wholesale, and there is a lingering personal retail interest within us that asks to be satisfied.

To sum up. My uncommercial travelling has not yet brought me to the conclusion that we are close to perfection in these matters. And just as I do not believe that the end of the world will ever be near at hand, so long as any of the very tiresome and arrogant people who constantly predict that catastrophe are left in it, so, I shall have small faith in the Hotel Millennium, while any of the uncomfortable superstitions I have glanced at remain in existence.

TRAVELLING ABROAD

I GOT into the travelling chariot—it was of German make, roomy, heavy, and unvarnished—I got into the travelling chariot, pulled up the steps after me, shut myself in with a smart bang of the door, and gave the word, "Go on!"

Immediately, all that W. and S.W. division of London began to slide away at a pace so lively, that I was over the river, and past the Old Kent Road, and out on Blackheath, and even ascending Shooter's Hill, before I had had time to look about me in the carriage, like a collected traveller.

I had two ample Imperials on the roof, other fitted storage for luggage in front, and other up behind; I had a net for books overhead, great pockets to all the windows, a leathern pouch or two hung up for odds and ends, and a reading lamp fixed in the back of the chariot, in case I should be benighted. I was amply provided in all respects, and had no idea where I was going (which was delightful), except that I was going abroad.

So smooth was the old high road, and so fresh were the horses, and so fast went I, that it was midway between Gravesend and Rochester, and the widening river was bearing the ships, white-sailed or black-smoked, out to sea, when I noticed by the wayside a very queer small boy.

"Holloa!" said I, to the very queer small boy, "where do you live?"

"At Chatham," says he.

"What do you do there?" says I.

"I go to school," says he.

I took him up in a moment, and we went on. Presently, the very queer small boy says, "This is Gads-hill we are coming to, where Falstaff went out to rob those travellers, and ran away."

"You know something about Falstaff, eh?" said I.

"All about him," said the very queer small boy. "I am old (I am nine), and I read all sorts of books. But *do* let us stop at the top of the hill, and look at the house there, if you please!"

"You admire that house?" said I.

"Bless you, sir," said the very queer small boy, "when I was not more than half as old as nine, it used to be a treat for me to be brought to look at it. And now, I am nine, I come by myself to look at it. And ever since I can recollect, my father, seeing me so fond of it, has often said to me, 'If you were to be very persevering and were to work hard, you might some day come to live in it.' Though that's impossible!" said the very queer small boy, drawing a low breath, and now staring at the house out of window with all his might.

I was rather amazed to be told this by the very queer small boy; for that house happens to be *my* house, and I have reason to believe that what he said was true.

Well! I made no halt there, and I soon dropped the very queer small boy and went on. Over the road where the old Romans used to march, over the road where the old Canterbury pilgrims used to go, over the road where the travelling trains of the old imperious priests and princes used to jingle on horseback between the continent and this Island through the mud and water, over the road where Shakespeare hummed to himself, "Blow, blow, thou winter wind," as he sat in the saddle at the gate of the inn yard noticing the carriers; all among the cherry orchards, apple orchards, corn-fields, and hop-gardens; so went I, by Canterbury to Dover. There, the sea was tumbling in, with deep sounds, after dark, and the revolving French light on Cape Grinez was seen regularly bursting out and becoming obscured, as if the head of a gigantic light-keeper in an anxious state of mind were interposed every half-minute, to look how it was burning.

Early in the morning I was on the deck of the steam-packet, and we were aiming at the bar in the usual intolerable manner, and the bar was aiming at us in the usual intolerable manner, and the bar got by far the best of it, and we got by far the worst—all in the usual intolerable manner.

But, when I was clear of the Custom House on the other side, and when I began to make the dust fly on the thirsty French roads, and when the twigsome trees by the wayside (which, I suppose, never will grow leafy, for they never did) guarded here and there a dusty soldier, or field labourer, baking on a heap of broken stones, sound asleep in a fiction of shade, I began to recover my travelling spirits. Coming upon the breaker of the broken stones, in a hard hot shining hat, on which the sun played at a distance as on a burning-glass, I felt that now, indeed, I was in the dear old France of my affections. I should have known it, without the well-remembered bottle of rough ordinary wine, the cold roast fowl, the loaf, and the pinch of salt, on which I lunched with unspeakable satisfaction, from one of the stuffed pockets of the chariot.

I must have fallen asleep after lunch, for when a bright face looked in at the window, I started, and said :

" Good God, Louis, I dreamed you were dead ! "

My cheerful servant laughed, and answered :

" Me ? Not at all, sir."

" How glad I am to wake ! What are we doing, Louis ? "

" We go to take relay of horses. Will you walk up the hill ? "

" Certainly."

Welcome the old French hill, with the old French lunatic (not in the most distant degree related to Sterne's Maria) living in a thatched dog-kennel half-way up, and flying out with his crutch and his big head and extended nightcap, to be beforehand with the old men and women exhibiting crippled children, and with the children exhibiting old men and women, ugly and blind, who always seemed by resurrectionary process to be recalled out of the elements for the sudden peopling of the solitude ! "

" It is well," said I, scattering among them what small coin I had ; " here comes Louis, and I am quite roused from my nap."

We journeyed on again, and I welcomed every new assurance that France stood where I had left it. There were the posting-houses, with their archways, dirty stable-yards, and clean postmasters' wives, bright women of business, looking on at the putting-to of the horses ; there were the postilions counting what money they got, into their hats, and never making enough of it ; there were the standard population of grey horses of Flanders descent, invariably biting one another when they got a chance ; there were the fleecy sheep-skins, looped on over their uniforms by the postilions, like bibbed aprons when it blew and rained ; there were their jack-

boots, and their cracking whips ; there were the cathedrals
that I got out to see, as under some cruel bondage, in no
wise desiring to see them ; there were the little towns that
appeared to have no reason for being towns, since most of
their houses were to let and nobody could be induced to look
at them, except the people who couldn't let them and had
nothing else to do but look at them all day. I lay a night
upon the road and enjoyed delectable cookery of potatoes,
and some other sensible things, adoption of which at home
would inevitably be shown to be fraught with ruin, somehow
or other, to that rickety national blessing, the British farmer ;
and at last I was rattled, like a single pill in a box, over
leagues of stones, until—madly cracking, plunging, and
flourishing two grey tails about—I made my triumphal entry
into Paris.

At Paris, I took an upper apartment for a few days in one
of the hotels of the Rue de Rivoli ; my front windows looking into the garden of the Tuileries (where the principal
difference between the nursemaids and the flowers seemed to
be that the former were locomotive and the latter not) : my
back windows looking at all the other back windows in the
hotel, and deep down into a paved yard, where my German
chariot had retired under a tight-fitting archway, to all appearance for life, and where bells rang all day without anybody's
minding them but certain chamberlains with feather brooms
and green baize caps, who here and there leaned out of some
high window placidly looking down, and where neat waiters
with trays on their left shoulders passed and repassed from
morning to night.

Whenever I am at Paris, I am dragged by invisible force
into the Morgue. I never want to go there, but am always
pulled there. One Christmas Day, when I would rather
have been anywhere else, I was attracted in, to see an old
grey man lying all alone on his cold bed, with a tap of water
turned on over his grey hair, and running, drip, drip, drip,
down his wretched face until it got to the corner of his
mouth, where it took a turn, and made him look sly. One
New Year's Morning (by the same token, the sun was shining
outside, and there was a mountebank balancing a feather on
his nose, within a yard of the gate), I was pulled in again to
look at a flaxen-haired boy of eighteen, with a heart hanging
on his breast—"from his mother," was engraven on it—who
had come into the net across the river, with a bullet wound

Leaving the Morgue

in his fair forehead and his hands cut with a knife, but whence or how was a blank mystery. This time, I was forced into the same dread place, to see a large dark man whose disfigurement by water was in a frightful manner comic, and whose expression was that of a prize-fighter who had closed his eyelids under a heavy blow, but was going immediately to open them, shake his head, and "come up smiling." Oh what this large dark man cost me in that bright city!

It was very hot weather, and he was none the better for that, and I was much the worse. Indeed, a very neat and pleasant little woman with the key of her lodging on her forefinger, who had been showing him to her little girl while she and the child ate sweetmeats, observed monsieur looking poorly as we came out together, and asked monsieur, with her wondering little eyebrows prettily raised, if there were anything the matter? Faintly replying in the negative, monsieur crossed the road to a wine-shop, got some brandy, and resolved to freshen himself with a dip in the great floating bath on the river.

The bath was crowded in the usual airy manner, by a male population in striped drawers of various gay colours, who walked up and down arm in arm, drank coffee, smoked cigars, sat at little tables, conversed politely with the damsels who dispensed the towels, and every now and then pitched themselves into the river head foremost, and came out again to repeat this social routine. I made haste to participate in the water part of the entertainments, and was in the full enjoyment of a delightful bath, when all in a moment I was seized with an unreasonable idea that the large dark body was floating straight at me.

I was out of the river, and dressing instantly. In the shock I had taken some water into my mouth, and it turned me sick, for I fancied that the contamination of the creature was in it. I had got back to my cool darkened room in the hotel, and was lying on a sofa there, before I began to reason with myself.

Of course, I knew perfectly well that the large dark creature was stone dead, and that I should no more come upon him out of the place where I had seen him dead, than I should come upon the cathedral of Notre-Dame in an entirely new situation. What troubled me was the picture of the creature; and that had so curiously and strongly painted itself upon my brain, that I could not get rid of it until it was worn out.

I noticed the peculiarities of this possession, while it was a real discomfort to me. That very day, at dinner, some morsel on my plate looked like a piece of him, and I was glad to get up and go out. Later in the evening, I was walking along the Rue St. Honore, when I saw a bill at a public room there, announcing small-sword exercise, broad-sword exercise, wrestling, and other such feats. I went in, and some of the sword-play being very skilful, remained. A specimen ·of our own national sport, The British Boaxe, was announced to be given at the close of the evening. In an evil hour, I determined to wait for this Boaxe, as became a Briton. It was a clumsy specimen (executed by two English grooms out of place), but one of the combatants, receiving a straight right-hander with the glove between his eyes, did exactly what the large dark creature in the Morgue had seemed going to do — and finished me for that night.

There was rather a sickly smell (not at all an unusual fragrance in Paris) in the little ante-room of my apartment at the hotel. The large dark creature in the Morgue was by no direct experience associated ‚with my sense of smell, because, when I came to the knowledge of him, he lay behind a wall of thick plate-glass as good as a wall of steel or marble for that matter. Yet the whiff of the room never failed to reproduce him. What was more curious, was the capriciousness with which his portrait seemed to light itself up in my mind, elsewhere. I might be walking in the Palais Royal, lazily enjoying the shop windows, and might be regaling myself with one of the ready-made clothes shops that are set out there. My eyes, wandering over impossible-waisted dressing-gowns and luminous waistcoats, would fall upon the master, or the shopman, or even the very dummy at the door, and would suggest to me, "Something like him!"—and instantly I was sickened again.

This would happen at the theatre, in the same manner. Often it would happen in the street, when I certainly was not looking for the likeness, and when probably there was no likeness there. It was not because the creature was dead that I was so haunted, because I know that I might have been (and I know it because I have been) equally attended by the image of a living aversion. This lasted about a week. The picture did not fade by degrees, in the sense that it became a whit less forcible and distinct, but in the sense that it obtruded itself less and less frequently. The experience may be worth considering by some who have the care of children. It would be difficult to overstate the intensity and accuracy of an intelligent child's observation At that impressible time of life, it must sometimes produce a fixed impression. If the fixed impression be of an object terrible to the child, it will be (for want of reasoning upon) inseparable from great fear. Force the child at such a time, be Spartan with it, send it into the dark against its will, leave it in a lonely bedroom against its will, and you had better murder it.

On a bright morning I rattled away from Paris, in the German chariot, and left the large dark creature behind me for good. I ought to confess, though, that I had been drawn back to the Morgue, after he was put underground, to look at his clothes, and that I found them frightfully like him—particularly his boots. However, I rattled away for Switzerland, looking forward and not backward, and so we parted company.

Welcome again, the long long spell of France. with the queer country inns, full of vases of flowers and clocks, in the dull little town, and with the little population not at all dull on the little Boulevard in the evening, under the little trees! Welcome Monsieur the Curé, walking alone in the early morning a short way out of the town, reading that eternal Breviary of yours, which surely might be almost read, without book, by this time! Welcome Monsieur the Curé, later in the day, jolting through the highway dust (as if you had already ascended to the cloudy region), in a very big-headed cabriolet, with the dried mud of a dozen winters on it. Welcome again Monsieur the Curé, as we exchange salutations; you, straightening your back to look at the German chariot, while picking in your little village garden a vegetable or two for the day's soup: I, looking out of the German chariot window in that delicious traveller's trance which knows no cares, no yesterdays, no to-morrows, nothing but the passing objects and the passing scents and sounds! And so I came, in due course of delight, to Strasbourg, where I passed a wet Sunday evening at a window, while an idle trifle of a vaudeville was played for me at the opposite house.

How such a large house came to have only three people living in it, was its own affair. There were at least a score

of windows in its high roof alone ; how many in its grotesque
front, I soon gave up counting. The owner was a shopkeeper,
by name Straudenheim ; by trade—I couldn't make out what
by trade, for he had forborne to write that up, and his shop
was shut.

At first, as I looked at Straudenheim's, through the steadily
falling rain, I set him up in business in the goose-liver line.
But, inspection of Straudenheim, who became visible at
a window on the second floor, convinced me that there was
something more precious than liver in the case.   He wore
a black velvet skull-cap, and looked usurious and rich.
A large-lipped, pear-nosed old man, with white hair, and
keen eyes, though near-sighted.   He was writing at a desk,
was Straudenheim, and ever and again left off writing, put
his pen in his mouth, and went through actions with his
right hand, like a man steadying piles of cash.   Five-franc
pieces, Straudenheim, or golden Napoleons ?   A jeweller,
Straudenheim, a dealer in money, a diamond merchant, or
what ?

Below Straudenheim, at a window on the first floor, sat
his housekeeper—far from young, but of a comely presence,
suggestive of a well-matured foot and ankle.   She was
cheerily dressed, had a fan in her hand, and wore large gold
earrings and a large gold cross.   She would have been out
holiday-making (as I settled it) but for the pestilent rain.
Strasbourg had given up holiday-making for that once, as
a bad job, because the rain was jerking in gushes out of the
old roof-spouts, and running in a brook down the middle of
the street.   The housekeeper, her arms folded on her bosom
and her fan tapping her chin, was bright and smiling at her
open window, but otherwise Straudenheim's house front was
very dreary.   The housekeeper's was the only open window in
it ; Straudenheim kept himself close, though it was a sultry
evening when air is pleasant, and though the rain had brought
into the town that vague refreshing smell of grass which
rain does bring in the summer-time.

The dim appearance of a man at Straudenheim's shoulder,
inspired me with a misgiving that somebody had come to
murder that flourishing merchant for the wealth with which
I had handsomely endowed him : the rather, as it was an
excited man, lean and long of figure, and evidently stealthy
of foot.   But, he conferred with Straudenheim instead of
doing him a mortal injury, and then they both softly opened

the other window of that room—which was immediately over
the housekeeper's—and tried to see her by looking down.
And my opinion of Straudenheim was much lowered when
I saw that eminent citizen spit out of window, clearly with
the hope of spitting on the housekeeper.

The unconscious housekeeper fanned herself, tossed her
head, and laughed. Though unconscious of Straudenheim,
she was conscious of somebody else—of me ?—there was
nobody else.

After leaning so far out of the window, that I confidently
expected to see their heels tilt up, Straudenheim and the
lean man drew their heads in and shut the window.   Presently, the house door secretly opened, and they slowly and
spitefully crept forth into the pouring rain. They were coming
over to me (I thought) to demand satisfaction for my looking
at the housekeeper, when they plunged into a recess in the
architecture under my window and dragged out the puniest
of little soldiers, begirt with the most innocent of little
swords. The tall glazed head-dress of this warrior, Straudenheim instantly knocked off, and out of it fell two sugar-
sticks, and three or four large lumps of sugar.

The warrior made no effort to recover his property or to
pick up his shako, but looked with an expression of attention
at Straudenheim when he kicked him five times, and also at
the lean man when *he* kicked him five times, and again at
Straudenheim when he tore the breast of his (the warrior's)
little coat open, and shook all his ten fingers in his face, as
if they were ten thousand.   When these outrages had been
committed, Straudenheim and his man went into the house
again and barred the door.   A wonderful circumstance was,
that the housekeeper who saw it all (and who could have
taken six such warriors to her buxom bosom at once), only
fanned herself and laughed as she had laughed before, and
seemed to have no opinion about it, one way or other.

But, the chief effect of the drama was the remarkable
vengeance taken by the little warrior.   Left alone in the
rain, he picked up his shako ; put it on, all wet and dirty
as it was ; retired into a court, of which Straudenheim's
house formed the corner ; wheeled about ; and bringing his
two forefingers close to the top of his nose, rubbed them
over one another, cross-wise, in derision, defiance, and contempt of Straudenheim.   Although Straudenheim could not
possibly be supposed to be conscious of this strange pro-

ceeding, it so inflated and comforted the little warrior's soul, that twice he went away, and twice came back into the court to repeat it, as though it must goad his enemy to madness. Not only that, but he afterwards came back with two other small warriors, and they all three did it together. Not only that—as I live to tell the tale!—but just as it was falling quite dark, the three came back, bringing with them a huge bearded Sapper, whom they moved, by recital of the original wrong, to go through the same performance, with the same complete absence of all possible knowledge of it on the part of Straudenheim. And then they all went away, arm in arm, singing.

I went away too, in the German chariot at sunrise, and rattled on, day after day, like one in a sweet dream ; with so many clear little bells on the harness of the horses, that the nursery rhyme about Banbury Cross and the venerable lady who rode in state there, was always in my ears. And now I came to the land of wooden houses, innocent cakes, thin butter soup, and spotless little inn bedrooms with a family likeness to Dairies. And now the Swiss marksmen were for ever rifle-shooting at marks across gorges, so exceedingly near my ear, that I felt like a new Gesler in a Canton of Tells, and went in highly-deserved danger of my tyrannical life. The prizes at these shootings, were watches, smart handkerchiefs, hats, spoons, and (above all) tea-trays ; and at these contests I came upon a more than usually accomplished and amiable countryman of my own, who had shot himself deaf in whole years of competition, and had won so many tea-trays that he went about the country with his carriage full of them, like a glorified Cheap-Jack.

In the mountain-country into which I had now travelled, a yoke of oxen were sometimes hooked on before the post-horses, and I went lumbering up, up, up, through mist and rain, with the roar of falling water for change of music. Of a sudden, mist and rain would clear away, and I would come down into picturesque little towns with gleaming spires and odd towers ; and would stroll afoot into market-places in steep winding streets, where a hundred women in bodices, sold eggs and honey, butter and fruit, and suckled their children as they sat by their clean baskets, and had such enormous goîtres (or glandular swellings in the throat) that it became a science to know where the nurse ended and the child began. About this time, I deserted my German chariot for the back of a mule (in colour and consistency so very like a dusty old hair trunk I once had at school, that I half expected to see my initials in brass-headed nails on his back-bone), and went up a thousand rugged ways, and looked down at a thousand woods of fir and pine, and would on the whole have preferred my mule's keeping a little nearer to the inside, and not usually travelling with a hoof or two over the precipice—though much consoled by explanation that this was to be attributed to his great sagacity, by reason of his carrying broad loads of wood at other times, and not being clear but that I myself belonged to that station of life, and required as much room as they. He brought me safely, in his own wise way, among the passes of the Alps, and here I enjoyed a dozen climates a day; being now (like Don Quixote on the back of the wooden horse) in the region of wind, now in the region of fire, now in the region of unmelting ice and snow. Here, I passed over trembling domes of ice, beneath which the cataract was roaring; and here was received under arches of icicles, of unspeakable beauty; and here the sweet air was so bracing and so light, that at halting-times I rolled in the snow when I saw my mule do it, thinking that he must know best. At this part of the journey we would come, at mid-day, into half an hour's thaw: when the rough mountain inn would be found on an island of deep mud in a sea of snow, while the baiting strings of mules, and the carts full of casks and bales, which had been in an Arctic condition a mile off, would steam again. By such ways and means, I would come to the cluster of châlets where I had to turn out of the track to see the water-fall; and then, uttering a howl like a young giant, on espying a traveller—in other words, something to eat—coming up the steep, the idiot lying on the wood-pile who sunned him-self and nursed his goître, would rouse the woman-guide within the hut, who would stream out hastily, throwing her child over one of her shoulders and her goître over the other, as she came along. I slept at religious houses, and bleak refuges of many kinds, on this journey, and by the stove at night heard stories of travellers who had perished within call, in wreaths and drifts of snow. One night the stove within, and the cold outside, awakened childish associations long forgotten, and I dreamed I was in Russia—the identical serf out of a picture-book I had, before I could read it for myself—and that I was going to be knouted by a noble personage in a fur cap, boots, and earrings, who, I think, must have come out of some melodrama.

Commend me to the beautiful waters among these mountains! Though I was not of their mind: they, being inveterately bent on getting down into the level country, and I ardently desiring to linger where I was. What desperate leaps they took, what dark abysses they plunged into, what rocks they wore away, what echoes they invoked! In one part where I went, they were pressed into the service of carrying wood down, to be burnt next winter, as costly fuel, in Italy. But, their fierce savage nature was not to be easily constrained, and they fought with every limb of the wood; whirling it round and round, stripping its bark away, dashing it against pointed corners, driving it out of the course, and roaring and flying at the peasants who steered it back again from the bank with long stout poles. Alas! concurrent streams of time and water carried *me* down fast, and I came, on an exquisitely clear day, to the Lausanne shore of the Lake of Geneva, where I stood looking at the bright blue water, the flushed white mountains opposite, and the boats at my feet with their furled Mediterranean sails, showing like enormous magnifications of this goose-quill pen that is now in my hand.

—The sky became overcast without any notice; a wind very like the March east wind of England, blew across me; and a voice said, "How do you like it? Will it do?"

I had merely shut myself, for half a minute, in a German travelling chariot that stood for sale in the Carriage Department of the London Pantechnicon. I had a commission to buy it, for a friend who was going abroad; and the look and manner of the chariot, as I tried the cushions and the springs, brought all these hints of travelling remembrance before me.

"It will do very well," said I, rather sorrowfully, as I got out at the other door, and shut the carriage up.

THE GREAT TASMANIA'S CARGO

I TRAVEL constantly, up and down a certain line of railway
that has a terminus in London. It is the railway for a
large military depôt, and for other large barracks. To the
best of my serious belief, I have never been on that railway
by daylight, without seeing some handcuffed deserters in
the train.

It is in the nature of things that such an institution as
our English army should have many bad and troublesome
characters in it. But, this is a reason for, and not against,
its being made as acceptable as possible to well-disposed
men of decent behaviour. Such men are assuredly not
tempted into the ranks, by the beastly inversion of natural
laws, and the compulsion to live in worse than swinish
foulness. Accordingly, when any such Circumlocutional
embellishments of the soldier's condition have of late been
brought to notice, we civilians, seated in outer darkness
cheerfully meditating on an Income Tax, have considered
the matter as being our business, and have shown a tendency
to declare that we would rather not have it misregulated,
if such declaration may, without violence to the Church
Catechism, be hinted to those who are put in authority
over us.

Any animated description of a modern battle, any private
soldier's letter published in the newspapers, any page of the
records of the Victoria Cross, will show that in the ranks of
the army, there exists under all disadvantages as fine a sense
of duty as is to be found in any station on earth. Who
doubts that if we all did our duty as faithfully as the soldier
does his, this world would be a better place? There may
be greater difficulties in our way than in the soldier's. Not
disputed. But, let us at least do our duty towards *him*.

I had got back again to that rich and beautiful port where
I had looked after Mercantile Jack, and I was walking up

a hill there, on a wild March morning. My conversation with my official friend Pangloss, by whom I was accidentally accompanied, took this direction as we took the up-hill direction, because the object of my uncommercial journey was to see some discharged soldiers who had recently come home from India. There were men of HAVELOCK's among them; there were men who had been in many of the great battles of the great Indian campaign, among them; and I was curious to note what our discharged soldiers looked like, when they were done with.

I was not the less interested (as I mentioned to my official friend Pangloss) because these men had claimed to be discharged, when their right to be discharged was not admitted. They had behaved with unblemished fidelity and bravery; but, a change of circumstances had arisen, which, as they considered, put an end to their compact and entitled them to enter on a new one. Their demand had been blunderingly resisted by the authorities in India; but, it is to be presumed that the men were not far wrong, inasmuch as the bungle had ended in their being sent home discharged, in pursuance of orders from home. (There was an immense waste of money, of course.)

Under these circumstances—thought I, as I walked up the hill, on which I accidentally encountered my official friend—under these circumstances of the men having successfully opposed themselves to the Pagoda Department of that great Circumlocution Office on which the sun never sets and the light of reason never rises, the Pagoda Department will have been particularly careful of the national honour. It will have shown these men, in the scrupulous good faith, not to say the generosity, of its dealing with them, that great national authorities can have no small retaliations and revenges. It will have made every provision for their health on the passage home, and will have landed them, restored from their campaigning fatigues by a sea-voyage, pure air, sound food, and good medicines. And I pleased myself with dwelling beforehand, on the great accounts of their personal treatment which these men would carry into their various towns and villages, and on the increasing popularity of the service that would insensibly follow. I almost began to hope that the hitherto-never-failing deserters on my railroad would by-and-by become a phenomenon.

In this agreeable frame of mind I entered the workhouse of Liverpool.—For, the cultivation of laurels in a sandy soil, had brought the soldiers in question to *that* abode of Glory.

Before going into their wards to visit them, I inquired how they had made their triumphant entry there? They had been brought through the rain in carts, it seemed, from the landing-place to the gate, and had then been carried upstairs on the backs of paupers. Their groans and pains during the performance of this glorious pageant, had been so distressing, as to bring tears into the eyes of spectators but too well accustomed to scenes of suffering. The men were so dreadfully cold, that those who could get near the fires were hard to be restrained from thrusting their feet in among the blazing coals. They were so horribly reduced, that they were awful to look upon. Racked with dysentery and blackened with scurvy, one hundred and forty wretched soldiers had been revived with brandy and laid in bed.

My official friend Pangloss is lineally descended from a learned doctor of that name, who was once tutor to Candide, an ingenious young gentleman of some celebrity. In his personal character, he is as humane and worthy a gentleman as any I know; in his official capacity, he unfortunately preaches the doctrines of his renowned ancestor, by demonstrating on all occasions that we live in the best of all possible official worlds.

"In the name of Humanity," said I, "how did the men fall into this deplorable state? Was the ship well found in stores?"

"I am not here to asseverate that I know the fact, of my own knowledge," answered Pangloss, "but I have grounds for asserting that the stores were the best of all possible stores."

A medical officer laid before us, a handful of rotten biscuit, and a handful of split peas. The biscuit was a honeycombed heap of maggots, and the excrement of maggots. The peas were even harder than this filth. A similar handful had been experimentally boiled six hours, and had shown no signs of softening. These were the stores on which the soldiers had been fed.

"The beef——" I began, when Pangloss cut me short.

"Was the best of all possible beef," said he.

But, behold, there was laid before us certain evidence

given at the Coroner's Inquest, holden on some of the men (who had obstinately died of their treatment), and from that evidence it appeared that the beef was the worst of possible beef!

"Then I lay my hand upon my heart, and take my stand," said Pangloss, " by the pork, which was the best of all possible pork."

"But look at this food before our eyes, if one may so misuse the word," said I.   "Would any Inspector who did his duty, pass such abomination ? "

" It ought not to have been passed," Pangloss admitted.

" Then the authorities out there——" I began, when Pangloss cut me short again.

"There would certainly seem to have been something wrong somewhere," said he ;   "but I am prepared to prove that the authorities out there, are the best of all possible authorities."

I never heard of any impeached public authority in my life, who was not the best public authority in existence.

" We are told of these unfortunate men being laid low by scurvy," said I.   "Since lime-juice has been regularly stored and served out in our navy, surely that disease, which used to devastate it, has almost disappeared ?   Was there lime-juice aboard this transport? "

My official friend was beginning "the best of all possible——"when an inconvenient medical forefinger pointed out another passage in the evidence, from which it appeared that the lime-juice had been bad too.   Not to mention that the vinegar had been bad too, the vegetables bad too, the cooking accommodation insufficient (if there had been anything worth mentioning to cook), the water supply exceedingly inadequate, and the beer sour.

" Then the men," said Pangloss, a little irritated, " were the worst of all possible men."

" In what respect ? " I asked.

" Oh !   Habitual drunkards," said Pangloss.

But, again the same incorrigible medical forefinger pointed out another passage in the evidence, showing that the dead men had been examined after death, and that they, at least, could not possibly have been habitual drunkards, because the organs within them which must have shown traces of that habit, were perfectly sound.

" And besides," said the three doctors present, one and

all, "habitual drunkards brought as low as these men have been, could not recover under care and food, as the great majority of these men are recovering. They would not have strength of constitution to do it."

"Reckless and improvident dogs, then," said Pangloss. "Always are—nine times out of ten."

I turned to the master of the workhouse, and asked him whether the men had any money?

"Money?" said he. "I have in my iron safe, nearly four hundred pounds of theirs; the agents have nearly a hundred pounds more; and many of them have left money in Indian banks besides."

"Hah!" said I to myself, as we went up-stairs, "this is not the best of all possible stories, I doubt!"

We went into a large ward, containing some twenty or five-and-twenty beds. We went into several such wards, one after another. I find it very difficult to indicate what a shocking sight I saw in them, without frightening the reader from the perusal of these lines, and defeating my object of making it known.

O the sunken eyes that turned to me as I walked between the rows of beds, or—worse still—that glazedly looked at the white ceiling, and saw nothing and cared for nothing! Here, lay the skeleton of a man, so lightly covered with a thin unwholesome skin, that not a bone in the anatomy was clothed, and I could clasp the arm above the elbow, in my finger and thumb. Here, lay a man with the black scurvy eating his legs away, his gums gone, and his teeth all gaunt and bare. This bed was empty, because gangrene had set in, and the patient had died but yesterday. That bed was a hopeless one, because its occupant was sinking fast, and could only be roused to turn the poor pinched mask of face upon the pillow, with a feeble moan. The awful thinness of the fallen cheeks, the awful brightness of the deep set eyes, the lips of lead, the hands of ivory, the recumbent human images lying in the shadow of death with a kind of solemn twilight on them, like the sixty who had died aboard the ship and were lying at the bottom of the sea, O Pangloss, GOD forgive you!

In one bed, lay a man whose life had been saved (as it was hoped) by deep incisions in the feet and legs. While I was speaking to him, a nurse came up to change the poultices which this operation had rendered necessary, and

D

I had an instinctive feeling that it was not well to turn
away, merely to spare myself. He was sorely wasted and
keenly susceptible, but the efforts he made to subdue any
expression of impatience or suffering, were quite heroic. It
was easy to see, in the shrinking of the figure, and the
drawing of the bed-clothes over the head, how acute the
endurance was, and it made me shrink too, as if *I* were in
pain ; but, when the new bandages were on, and the poor
feet were composed again, he made an apology for himself
(though he had not uttered a word), and said plaintively,
" I am so tender and weak, you see, sir ! " Neither from
him nor from any one sufferer of the whole ghastly number,
did I hear a complaint. Of thankfulness for present solicitude and care, I heard much ; of complaint, not a word.

I think I could have recognised in the dismalest skeleton
there, the ghost of a soldier. Something of the old air was
still latent in the palest shadow of life I talked to. One
emaciated creature, in the strictest literality worn to the
bone, lay stretched on his back, looking so like death that
I asked one of the doctors if he were not dying, or dead ?
A few kind words from the doctor, in his ear, and he opened
his eyes, and smiled—looked, in a moment, as if he would
have made a salute, if he could. " We shall pull him
through, please God," said the Doctor. " Plase God, surr,
and thankye," said the patient. " You are much better to-
day ; are you not ? " said the Doctor. " Plase God, surr ;
tis the slape I want, surr ; 'tis my breathin' makes the nights
so long." " He is a careful fellow this, you must know,"
said the Doctor, cheerfully ; " it was raining hard when
they put him in the open cart to bring him here, and he had
the presence of mind to ask to have a sovereign taken out of
his pocket that he had there, and a cab engaged. Probably
it saved his life." The patient rattled out the skeleton of
a laugh, and said, proud of the story, " 'Deed, surr, an open
cairt was a comical means o' bringin' a dyin' man here, and
a clever way to kill him." You might have sworn to him
for a soldier when he said it.

One thing had perplexed me very much in going from
bed to bed. A very significant and cruel thing. I could
find no young man but one. He had attracted my notice,
by having got up and dressed himself in his soldier's jacket
and trousers, with the intention of sitting by the fire ; but
he had found himself too weak, and had crept back to his

bed and laid himself down on the outside of it. I could have pronounced him, alone, to be a young man aged by famine and sickness. As we were standing by the Irish soldier's bed, I mentioned my perplexity to the Doctor. He took a board with an inscription on it from the head of the Irishman's bed, and asked me what age I supposed that man to be ? I had observed him with attention while talking to him, and answered, confidently, " Fifty." The Doctor, with a pitying glance at the patient, who had dropped into a stupor again, put the board back, and said, " Twenty-four."

All the arrangements of the wards were excellent. They could not have been more humane, sympathising, gentle, attentive, or wholesome. The owners of the ship, too, had done all they could, liberally. There were bright fires in every room, and the convalescent men were sitting round them, reading various papers and periodicals. I took the liberty of inviting my official friend Pangloss to look at those convalescent men, and to tell me whether their faces and bearing were or were not, generally, the faces and bearing of steady respectable soldiers ? The master of the work-house, overhearing me, said he had had a pretty large experience of troops, and that better conducted men than these he had never had to do with. They were always (he added) as we saw them. And of us visitors (I add) they knew nothing whatever, except that we were there.

It was audacious in me, but I took another liberty with Pangloss. Prefacing it with the observation that, of course, I knew beforehand that there was not the faintest desire, anywhere, to hush up any part of this dreadful business, and that the Inquest was the fairest of all possible Inquests. I besought four things of Pangloss. Firstly, to observe that the Inquest *was not held in that place*, but at some distance off. Secondly, to look round upon those helpless spectres in their beds. Thirdly, to remember that the witnesses produced from among them before that Inquest, could not have been selected because they were the men who had the most to tell it, but because they happened to be in a state admitting of their safe removal. Fourthly, to say whether the coroner and Jury could have come there, to those pillows, and taken a little evidence ? My official friend declined to commit himself to a reply.

There was a sergeant, reading, in one of the fireside groups. As he was a man of very intelligent countenance, and as I have a great respect for non-commissioned officers as a class, I sat down on the nearest bed, to have some talk with him. (It was the bed of one of the grisliest of the poor skeletons, and he died soon afterwards.)

"I was glad to see, in the evidence of an officer at the Inquest, sergeant, that he never saw men behave better on board ship than these men."

"They did behave very well, sir."

"I was glad to see, too, that every man had a hammock."

The sergeant gravely shook his head. "There must be some mistake, sir. The men of my own mess had no hammocks. There were not hammocks enough on board, and the men of the two next messes laid hold of hammocks for themselves as soon as they got on board, and squeezed my men out, as I may say."

"Had the squeezed-out men none then?"

"None, sir. As men died, their hammocks were used by other men, who wanted hammocks; but many men had none at all."

"Then you don't agree with the evidence on that point?"

"Certainly not, sir. A man can't, when he knows to the contrary."

"Did any of the men sell their bedding for drink?"

"There is some mistake on that point too, sir. Men were under the impression—I knew it for a fact at the time—that it was not allowed to take blankets or bedding on board, and so men who had things of that sort came to sell them purposely."

"Did any of the men sell their clothes for drink?"

"They did, sir." (I believe there never was a more truthful witness than the sergeant. He had no inclination to make out a case.)

"Many?"

"Some, sir" (considering the question). "Soldier-like. They had been long marching in the rainy season, by bad roads—no roads at all, in short—and when they got to Calcutta, men turned to and drank, before taking a last look at it. Soldier-like."

"Do you see any men in this ward, for example, who sold clothes for drink at that time?"

The sergeant's wan eye, happily just beginning to rekindle with health, travelled round the place and came back to me. "Certainly, sir."

"The marching to Calcutta in the rainy season must have been severe?"

"It was very severe, sir."

"Yet what with the rest and the sea air, I should have thought that the men (even the men who got drunk) would have soon begun to recover on board ship?"

"So they might; but the bad food told upon them, and when we got into a cold latitude, it began to tell more, and the men dropped."

"The sick had a general disinclination for food, I am told, sergeant?"

"Have you seen the food, sir?"

"Some of it."

"Have you seen the state of their mouths, sir?"

If the sergeant, who was a man of a few orderly words, had spoken the amount of this volume, he could not have settled that question better. I believe the sick could as soon have eaten the ship, as the ship's provisions.

I took the additional liberty with my friend Pangloss, when I had left the sergeant with good wishes, of asking Pangloss whether he had ever heard of biscuit getting drunk and bartering its nutritious qualities for putrefaction and vermin; of peas becoming hardened in liquor; of hammocks drinking themselves off the face of the earth; of lime-juice, vegetables, vinegar, cooking accommodation, water supply, and beer, all taking to drinking together and going to ruin? "If not (I asked him), what did he say in defence of the officers condemned by the Coroner's Jury, who, by signing the General Inspection report relative to the ship Great Tasmania, chartered for these troops, had deliberately asserted all that bad and poisonous dunghill refuse, to be good and wholesome food?" My official friend replied that it was a remarkable fact, that whereas some officers were only positively good, and other officers only comparatively better, those particular officers were superlatively the very best of all possible officers.

My hand and my heart fail me, in writing my record of this journey. The spectacle of the soldiers in the hospital-beds of that Liverpool workhouse (a very good workhouse, indeed, be it understood), was so shocking and so shameful, that as an Englishman I blush to remember it. It would have been simply unbearable at the time, but for the consideration and pity with which they were soothed in their sufferings.

No punishment that our inefficient laws provide, is worthy of the name when set against the guilt of this transaction. But, if the memory of it die out unavenged, and if it do not result in the inexorable dismissal and disgrace of those who are responsible for it, their escape will be infamous to the Government (no matter of what party) that so neglects its duty, and infamous to the nation that tamely suffers such intolerable wrong to be done in its name.

CITY OF LONDON CHURCHES

IF the confession that I have often travelled from this Covent Garden lodging of mine on Sundays, should give offence to those who never travel on Sundays, they will be satisfied (I hope) by my adding that the journeys in question were made to churches.

Not that I have any curiosity to hear powerful preachers. Time was, when I was dragged by the hair of my head, as one may say, to hear too many. On summer evenings, when every flower, and tree, and bird, might have better address d my soft young heart, I have in my day been caught in the palm of a female hand by the crown, have been violently scrubbed from the neck to the roots of the hair as a purification for the Temple, and have then been carried off highly charged with saponaceous electricity, to be steamed like a potato in the unventilated breath of the powerful Boanerges Boiler and his congregation, until what small mind I had, was quite steamed out of me. In which pitiable plight I have been haled out of the place of meeting, at the conclusion of the exercises, and catechised respecting Boanerges Boiler, his fifthly, his sixthly, and his seventhly, until I have regarded that reverend person in the light of a most dismal and oppressive Charade. Time was, when I was carried off to platform assemblages at which no human child, whether of wrath or grace, could possibly keep its eyes open, and when I felt the fatal sleep stealing, stealing over me, and when I gradually heard the orator in possession, spinning and humming like a great top, until he rolled, collapsed, and tumbled over, and I discovered to my burning shame and fear, that as to that last stage it was not he, but I. I have sat under Boanerges when he has specifically addressed himself to us—us, the infants—and at this present writing I hear his lumbering jocularity (which never amused us, though we basely pretended that it did), and I behold his big round face, and I look up the inside of his out-stretched coat-sleeve as if it were a telescope with the stopper on, and I hate him with an unwholesome hatred for two hours. Through such means did it come to pass that I knew the powerful preacher from beginning to end, all over and all through, while I was very young, and that I left him behind at an early period of life. Peace be with him! More peace than he brought to me!

Now, I have heard many preachers since that time—not powerful; merely Christian, unaffected, and reverential—and I have had many such preachers on my roll of friends. But, it was not to hear these, any more than the powerful class, that I made my Sunday journeys. They were journeys of curiosity to the numerous churches in the City of London. It came into my head one day, here had I been cultivating a familiarity with all the churches of Rome, and I knew nothing of the insides of the old churches of London! This befell on a Sunday morning. I began my expeditions that very same day, and they lasted me a year.

I never wanted to know the names of the churches to which I went, and to this hour I am profoundly ignorant in that particular of at least nine-tenths of them. Indeed, saving that I know the church of old GOWER's tomb (he lies in effigy with his head upon his books) to be the church of Saint Saviour's, Southwark; and the church of MILTON's tomb to be the church of Cripplegate; and the church on Cornhill with the great golden keys to be the church of Saint Peter; I doubt if I could pass a competitive examination in any of the names. No question did I ever ask of living creature concerning these churches, and no answer to any antiquarian question on the subject that I ever put to books, shall harass the reader's soul. A full half of my pleasure in them arose out of their mystery; mysterious I found them; mysterious they shall remain for me.

Where shall I begin my round of hidden and forgotten old churches in the City of London?

It is twenty minutes short of eleven on a Sunday morning, when I stroll down one of the many narrow hilly streets in the City that tend due south to the Thames. It is my first experiment, and I have come to the region of Whittington in an omnibus, and we have put down a fierce-eyed spare old woman, whose slate-coloured gown smells of herbs, and who walked up Aldersgate-street to some chapel where she comforts herself with brimstone doctrine, I warrant. We have also put down a stouter and sweeter old lady, with a pretty large prayer-book in an unfolded pocket-handkerchief, who got out at a corner of a court near Stationers' Hall, and who I think must go to church there, because she is the widow of some* deceased old Company's Beadle. The rest of our freight were mere chance pleasure-seekers and rural walkers, and went on to the Blackwall railway. So many bells are ringing, when I stand undecided at a street corner, that every sheep in the ecclesiastical fold might be a bell-wether. The discordance is fearful. My state of indecision is referable to, and about equally divisible among, four great churches, which are all within sight and sound, all within the space of a few square yards.

As I stand at the street corner, I don't see as many as four people at once going to church, though I see as many as four churches with their steeples clamouring for people. I choose my church, and go up the flight of steps to the great entrance in the tower. A mouldy tower within, and like a neglected washhouse. A rope comes through the beamed roof, and a man in the corner pulls it and clashes the bell— a whity-brown man, whose clothes were once black—a man with flue on him, and cobweb. He stares at me, wondering how I come there, and I stare at him, wondering how he comes there. Through a screen of wood and glass, I peep into the dim church. About twenty people are discernible, waiting to begin. Christening would seem to have faded out of this church long ago, for the font has the dust of desuetude thick upon it, and its wooden cover (shaped like an old-fashioned tureen-cover) looks as if it wouldn't come off, upon requirement. I perceive the altar to be rickety and the Commandments damp. Entering after this survey, I jostle the clergyman in his canonicals, who is entering too from a dark lane behind a pew of state with curtains, where nobody sits. The pew is ornamented with four blue wands, once carried by four somebodys, I suppose, before somebody else, but which there is nobody now to hold or receive honour from. I open the door of a family pew, and shut myself in ; if I could occupy twenty family pews at once I might have them. The clerk, a brisk young man (how does *he* come here ?), glances at me knowingly, as who should say, " You have done it now ; you must stop." Organ plays. Organ-loft is in a small gallery across the church ; gallery congregation, two girls. I wonder within myself what will happen when we are required to sing.

There is a pale heap of books in the corner of my pew, and while the organ, which is hoarse and sleepy, plays in such fashion that I can hear more of the rusty working of the stops than of any music, I look at the books, which are mostly bound in faded baize and stuff. They belonged in 1754, to the Dowgate family; and who were they? Jane Comport must have married Young Dowgate, and come into the family that way; Young Dowgate was courting Jane Comport when he gave her her prayer-book, and recorded the presentation in the fly-leaf; if Jane were fond of Young Dowgate, why did she d e and leave the book here? Perhaps at the rickety altar, and before the damp Commandments, she, Comport, had taken him, Dowgate, in a flush of youthful hope and joy, and perhaps it had not turned out in the long run as great a success as was expected?

The opening of the service recalls my wandering thoughts. I then find, to my astonishment, that I have been, and still am, taking a strong kind of invisible snuff, up my nose, into my eyes, and down my throat. I wink, sneeze, and cough. The clerk sneezes; the clergyman winks; the unseen organist sneezes and coughs (and probably winks); all our little party wink, sneeze, and cough. The snuff seems to be made of the decay of matting, wood, cloth, stone, iron, earth, and something else. Is the something else, the decay of dead citizens in the vaults below? As sure as Death it is! Not only in the cold damp February day, do we cough and sneeze dead citizens, all through the service, but dead citizens have got into the very bellows of the organ, and half choked the same. We stamp our feet to warm them, and dead citizens arise in heavy clouds. Dead citizens stick upon the walls, and lie pulverised on the sounding-board over the clergyman's head, and, when a gust of air comes, tumble down upon him.

In this first experience I was so nauseated by too much snuff, made of the Dowgate family, the Comport branch, and other families and branches, that I gave but little heed to our dull manner of ambling through the service; to the brisk clerk's manner of encouraging us to try a note or two at psalm time; to the gallery-congregation's manner of enjoying a shrill duet, without a notion of time or tune; to the whity-brown man's manner of shutting the minister into the pulpit, and being very particular with the lock of the door, as if he were a dangerous animal. But, I tried again next Sunday, and soon accustomed myself to the dead citizens when I found that I could not possibly get on without them among the City churches.

Another Sunday.

After being again rung for by conflicting bells, like a leg of mutton or a laced hat a hundred years ago, I make selection of a church oddly put away in a corner among a number of lanes—a smaller church than the last, and an ugly: of about the date of Queen Anne. As a congregation, we are fourteen strong: not counting an exhausted charity school in a gallery, which has dwindled away to four boys, and two girls. In the porch, is a benefaction of loaves of bread, which there would seem to be nobody left in the exhausted congregation to claim, and which I saw an exhausted beadle, long faded out of uniform, eating with his eyes for self and family when I passed in. There is also an exhausted clerk in a brown wig, and two or three exhausted doors and windows have been bricked up, and the service books are musty, and the pulpit cushions are threadbare, and the whole of the church furniture is in a very advanced stage of exhaustion. We are three old women (habitual), two young lovers (accidental), two tradesmen, one with a wife and one alone, an aunt and nephew, again two girls (these two girls dressed out for church with everything about them limp that should be stiff, and *vice versâ*, are an invariable experience,) and three sniggering boys. The clergyman is, perhaps, the chaplain of a civic company; he has the moist and vinous look, and eke the bulbous boots, of one acquainted with 'Twenty port, and comet vintages.

We are so quiet in our dulness that the three sniggering boys, who have got away into a corner by the altar-railing, give us a start, like crackers, whenever they laugh. And this reminds me of my own village church where, during sermon-time on bright Sundays when the birds are very musical indeed, farmers' boys patter out over the stone pavement, and the clerk steps out from his desk after them, and is distinctly heard in the summer repose to pursue and punch them in the churchyard, and is seen to return with a medi-tative countenance, making believe that nothing of the sort has happened. The aunt and nephew in this City church are much disturbed by the sniggering boys. The nephew is himself a boy, and the sniggerers tempt him to secular thoughts of marbles and string, by secretly offering such commodities to his distant contemplation. This young Saint Anthony for a while resists, but presently becomes a backslider, and in dumb show defies the sniggerers to " heave " a marble or two in his direction. Herein he is detected by the aunt (a rigorous reduced gentlewoman who has the charge of offices), and I perceive that worthy relative to poke him in the side, with the corrugated hooked handle of an ancient umbrella. The nephew revenges himself for this, by holding his breath and terrifying his kinswoman with the dread belief that he has made up his mind to burst. Regardless of whispers and shakes, he swells and becomes discoloured, and yet again swells and becomes discoloured, until the aunt can bear it no longer, but leads him out, with no visible neck, and with his eyes going before him like a prawn's. This causes the sniggerers to regard flight as an eligible move, and I know which of them will go out first, because of the over-devout attention that he suddenly concentrates on the clergyman. In a little while, this hypocrite, with an elaborate demonstration of hushing his footsteps, and with a face generally expressive of having until now forgotten a religious appointment elsewhere, is gone. Number two gets out in the same way, but rather quicker. Number three getting safely to the door, there turns reckless, and banging it open, flies forth with a Whoop! that vibrates to the top of the tower above us.

The clergyman, who is of a prandial presence and a muffled voice, may be scant of hearing as well as of breath, but he only glances up, as having an idea that somebody has said Amen in a wrong place, and continues his steady jog-trot, like a farmer's wife going to market. He does all he has to do, in the same easy way, and gives us a concise sermon, still like the jog-trot of the farmer's wife on a level road. Its drowsy cadence soon lulls the three old women asleep, and the unmarried tradesman sits looking out at window, and the married tradesman sits looking at his wife's bonnet, and the lovers sit looking at one another, so superlatively happy, that I mind when I, turned of eighteen, went with my Angelica to a City church on account of a shower (by this special coincidence that it was in Huggin-lane), and when I said to my Angelica, " Let the blessed event, Angelica, occur at no altar but

this!" and when my Angelica consented that it should
occur at no other—which it certainly never did, for it never
occurred anywhere. And O, Angelica, what has become
of you, this present Sunday morning when I can't attend
to the sermon; and, more difficult question than that, what
has become of Me as I was when I sat by your side?

But, we receive the signal to make that unanimous dive
which surely is a little conventional—like the strange
rustlings and settlings and clearings of throats and noses,
which are never dispensed with, at certain points of the
Church service, and are never held to be necessary under
any other circumstances. In a minute more it is all over,
and the organ expresses itself to be as glad of it as it can
be of anything in its rheumatic state, and in another minute
we are all of us out of the church, and Whity-brown has
locked it up. Another minute or little more, and, in the
neighbouring churchyard—not the yard of that church,
but of another—a churchyard like a great shabby old migno-
nette box, with two trees in it and one tomb—I meet
Whity-brown, in his private capacity, fetching a pint of
beer for his dinner from the public-house in the corner,
where the keys of the rotting fire-ladders are kept and were
never asked for, and where there is a ragged, white-seamed,
out-at-elbowed bagatelle board on the first floor.

In one of these City churches, and only in one, I found
an individual who might have been claimed as expressly
a City personage. I remember the church, by the feature
that the clergyman couldn't get to his own desk without going
through the clerk's, or couldn't get to the pulpit without
going through the reading-desk—I forget which, and it is
no matter—and by the presence of this personage among
the exceedingly sparse congregation. I doubt if we were
a dozen, and we had no exhausted charity school to help us
out. The personage was dressed in black of square cut,
and was stricken in years, and wore a black velvet cap, and
cloth shoes. He was of a staid, wealthy, and dissatisfied
aspect. In his hand, he conducted to church a mysterious
child: a child of the feminine gender. The child had a
beaver hat, with a stiff drab plume that surely never
belonged to any bird of the air. The child was further
attired in a nankeen frock and spencer, brown boxing-
gloves, and a veil. It had a blemish, in the nature of
currant jelly, on its chin; and was a thirsty child. Inso-

much that the personage carried in his pocket a green bottle, from which, when the first psalm was given out, the child was openly refreshed. At all other times throughout the service it was motionless, and stood on the seat of the large pew, closely fitted into the corner, like a rain-water pipe.

The personage never opened his book, and never looked at the clergyman. *He* never sat down either, but stood with his arms leaning on the top of the pew, and his forehead sometimes shaded with his right hand, always looking at the church door. It was a long church for a church of its size, and he was at the upper end, but he always looked at the door. That he was an old bookkeeper, or an old trader who had kept his own books, and that he might be seen at the Bank of England about Dividend times, no doubt. That he had lived in the City all his life and was disdainful of other localities, no doubt. Why he looked at the door, I never absolutely proved, but it is my belief that he lived in expectation of the time when the citizens would come back to live in the City, and its ancient glories would be renewed. He appeared to expect that this would occur on a Sunday, and that the wanderers would first appear, in the deserted churches, penitent and humbled. Hence, he looked at the door which they never darkened. Whose child the child was, whether the child of a disinherited daughter, or some parish orphan whom the personage had adopted, there was nothing to lead up to. It never played, or skipped, or smiled. Once, the idea occurred to me that it was an automaton, and that the personage had made it ; but following the strange couple out one Sunday, I heard the personage say to it, " Thirteen thousand pounds ; " to which it added in a weak human voice, " Seventeen and fourpence." Four Sundays I followed them out, and this is all I ever heard or saw them say. One Sunday, I followed them home. They lived behind a pump, and the personage opened their abode with an exceeding large key. The one solitary inscription on their house related to a fire-plug. The house was partly undermined by a deserted and closed gateway ; its windows were blind with dirt ; and it stood with its face disconsolately turned to a wall. Five great churches and two small ones rang their Sunday bells between this house and the church the couple frequented, so they must have had some special reason for going a quarter of a mile to it. The last time I saw them,

The City Personage

was on this wise. I had been to explore another church at a distance, and happened to pass the church they frequented, at about two of the afternoon when that edifice was closed. But, a little side-door, which I had never observed before, stood open, and disclosed certain cellarous steps. Methought "They are airing the vaults to-day," when the personage and the child silently arrived at the steps, and silently descended. Of course, I came to the conclusion that the personage had at last despaired of the looked-for return of the penitent citizens, and that he and the child went down to get themselves buried.

In the course of my pilgrimages I came upon one obscure church which had broken out in the melodramatic style, and was got up with various tawdry decorations, much after the manner of the extinct London may-poles. These attractions had induced several young priests or deacons in black bibs for waistcoats, and several young ladies interested in that holy order (the proportion being, as I estimated, seventeen young ladies to a deacon), to come into the City as a new and odd excitement. It was wonderful to see how these young people played out their little play in the heart of the City, all among themselves, without the deserted City's knowing anything about it. It was as if you should take an empty counting-house on a Sunday, and act one of the old Mysteries there. They had impressed a small school (from what neighbourhood I don't know) to assist in the performances, and it was pleasant to notice frantic garlands of inscription on the walls, especially addressing those poor innocents in characters impossible for them to decipher. There was a remarkably agreeable smell of pomatum in this congregation.

But, in other cases, rot and mildew and dead citizens formed the uppermost scent, while, infused into it in a dreamy way not at all displeasing, was the staple character of the neighbourhood. In the churches about Mark-lane, for example, there was a dry whiff of wheat; and I accidentally struck an airy sample of barley out of an aged hassock in one of them. From Rood-lane to Tower-street, and thereabouts, there was often a subtle flavour of wine: sometimes, of tea. One church near Mincing-lane smelt like a druggist's drawer. Behind the Monument the service had a flavour of damaged oranges, which, a little further down towards the river, tempered into herrings, and gradually toned into a cosmopolitan blast of fish. In one church, the exact counterpart of the church in the Rake's Progress where the hero is being married to the horrible old lady, there was no speciality of atmosphere, until the organ shook a perfume of hides all over us from some adjacent warehouse.

Be the scent what it would, however, there was no speciality in the people. There were never enough of them to represent any calling or neighbourhood. They had all gone elsewhere over-night, and the few stragglers in the many churches languished there inexpressively.

Among the Uncommercial travels in which I have engaged, this year of Sunday travel occupies its own place, apart from all the rest. Whether I think of the church where the sails of the oyster-boats in the river almost flapped against the windows, or of the church where the railroad made the bells hum as the train rushed by above the roof, I recall a curious experience. On summer Sundays, in the gentle rain or the bright sunshine—either, deepening the idleness of the idle City—I have sat, in that singular silence which belongs to resting-places usually astir, in scores of buildings at the heart of the world's metropolis, unknown to far greater numbers of people speaking the English tongue, than the ancient edifices of the Eternal City, or the Pyramids of Egypt. The dark vestries and registries into which I have peeped, and the little hemmed-in churchyards that have echoed to my feet, have left impressions on my memory as distinct and quaint as any it has in that way received. In all those dusty registers that the worms are eating, there is not a line but made some hearts leap, or some tears flow, in their day. Still and dry now, still and dry! and the old tree at the window with no room for its branches, has seen them all out. So with the tomb of the old Master of the old Company, on which it drips. His son restored it and died, his daughter restored it and died, and then he had been remembered long enough, and the tree took possession of him, and his name cracked out.

There are few more striking indications of the changes of manners and customs that two or three hundred years have brought about, than these deserted churches. Many of them are handsome and costly structures, several of them were designed by WREN, many of them arose from the ashes of the great fire, others of them outlived the plague and the fire too, to die a slow death in these later days. No one can be sure of the coming time; but it is not too much to say of it that it has no sign in its outsetting tides, of the reflux to these churches of their congregations and uses. They remain like the tombs of the old citizens who lie beneath them and around them, Monuments of another age. They are worth a Sunday-exploration, now and then, for they yet echo, not unharmoniously, to the time when the City of London really was London; when the 'Prentices and Trained Bands were of mark in the state; when even the Lord Mayor himself was a Reality—not a Fiction conventionally be-puffed on one day in the year by illustrious friends, who no less conventionally laugh at him on the remaining three hundred and sixty-four days.

X

SHY NEIGHBOURHOODS

So much of my travelling is done on foot, that if I cherished betting propensities, I should probably be found registered in sporting newspapers under some such title as the Elastic Novice, challenging all eleven stone mankind to competition in walking. My last special feat was turning out of bed at two, after a hard day, pedestrian and otherwise, and walking thirty miles into the country to breakfast. The road was so lonely in the night, that I fell asleep to the monotonous sound of my own feet, doing their regular four miles an hour. Mile after mile I walked, without the slightest sense of exertion, dozing heavily and dreaming constantly. It was only when I made a stumble like a drunken man, or struck out into the road to avoid a horseman close upon me on the path—who had no existence—that I came to myself and looked about. The day broke mistily (it was autumn time), and I could not disembarrass myself of the idea that I had to climb those heights and banks of cloud, and that there was an Alpine Convent somewhere behind the sun, where I was going to breakfast. This sleepy notion was so much stronger than such substantial objects as villages and haystacks, that, after the sun was up and bright, and when I was sufficiently awake to have a sense of pleasure in the prospect, I still occasionally caught myself looking about for wooden arms to point the right track up the mountain, and wondering there was no snow yet. It is a curiosity of broken sleep that I made immense quantities of verses on that pedestrian occasion (of course I never make any when I am in my right senses), and that I spoke a certain language once pretty familiar to me, but which I have nearly forgotten from disuse, with fluency. Of both these phenomena I have such frequent experience in the state between sleeping and waking, that I sometimes argue with myself that I know I cannot be awake, for, if I were, I should not be half so ready. The readiness is not imaginary, because I often recall long strings of the verses, and many turns of the fluent speech, after I am broad awake.

My walking is of two kinds: one, straight on end to a definite goal at a round pace; one, objectless, loitering, and purely vagabond. In the latter state, no gipsy on earth is a greater vagabond than myself; it is so natural to me, and strong with me, that I think I must be the descendant, at no great distance, of some irreclaimable tramp.

One of the pleasantest things I have lately met with, in a vagabond course of shy metropolitan neighbourhoods and small shops, is the fancy of a humble artist, as exemplified in two portraits representing Mr. Thomas Sayers, of Great Britain, and Mr. John Heenan, of the United States of America. These illustrious men are highly coloured in fighting trim, and fighting attitude. To suggest the pastoral and meditative nature of their peaceful calling, Mr. Heenan is represented on emerald sward, with primroses and other modest flowers springing up under the heels of his half-boots; while Mr. Sayers is impelled to the administration of his favourite blow, the Auctioneer, by the silent eloquence of a village church. The humble homes of England, with their domestic virtues and honeysuckle porches, urge both heroes to go in and win; and the lark and other singing birds are observable in the upper air, ecstatically carolling their thanks to Heaven for a fight. On the whole, the associations entwined with the pugilistic art by this artist are much in the manner of Izaak Walton.

But, it is with the lower animals of back streets and by-ways that my present purpose rests. For human notes we may return to such neighbourhoods when leisure and opportunity serve.

Nothing in shy neighbourhoods perplexes my mind more, than the bad company birds keep. Foreign birds often get into good society, but British birds are inseparable from low associates. There is a whole street of them in St. Giles's; and I always find them in poor and immoral neighbourhoods, convenient to the public-house and the pawnbroker's. They seem to lead people into drinking, and even the man who makes their cages usually gets into a chronic state of black eye. Why is this? Also, they will do things for people in short-skirted velveteen coats with bone buttons, or in sleeved waistcoats and fur caps, which they cannot be persuaded by the respectable orders of society to undertake. In a dirty court in Spitalfields, once, I found a goldfinch drawing his own water, and drawing as much of it as if he were in a consuming fever. That goldfinch lived at a bird-shop, and offered, in writing, to barter himself against old clothes, empty bottles, or even kitchen stuff. Surely a low thing and a depraved taste in any finch! I bought that goldfinch for money. He was sent home, and hung upon a nail over against my table. He lived outside a counterfeit dwelling-house, supposed (as I argued) to be a dyer's; otherwise it would have been impossible to account for his perch sticking out of the garret window. From the time of his appearance in my room, either he left off being thirsty—which was not in the bond—or he could not make up his mind to hear his little bucket drop back into his well when he let it go: a shock which in the best of times had made him tremble. He drew no water but by stealth and under the cloak of night. After an interval of futile and at length hopeless expectation, the merchant who had educated him was appealed to. The merchant was a bow-legged character, with a flat and cushiony nose, like the last new strawberry. He wore a fur cap, and shorts, and was of the velveteen race, velveteeny. He sent word that he would "look round." He looked round, appeared in the doorway of the room, and slightly cocked up his evil eye at the goldfinch. Instantly a raging thirst beset that bird; when it was appeased, he still drew several unnecessary buckets of water; and finally, leaped about his perch and sharpened his bill, as if he had been to the nearest wine vaults and got drunk.

Donkeys again. I know shy neighbourhoods where the Donkey goes in at the street door, and appears to live upstairs, for I have examined the back-yard from over the palings, and have been unable to make him out. Gentility, nobility, Royalty, would appeal to that donkey in vain to do what he does for a costermonger. Feed him with oats at the highest price, put an infant prince and princess in a pair of panniers on his back, adjust his delicate trappings to a nicety, take him to the softest slopes at Windsor, and try what pace you can get out of him. Then, starve him, harness him anyhow to a truck with a flat tray on it, and see him bowl from Whitechapel to Bayswater. There appears to be no particular private understanding between birds and donkeys, in a state of nature; but in the shy neighbourhood state, you shall see them always in the same hands and always developing their very best energies for the very worst company. I have known a donkey—by sight; we were not on speaking terms—who lived over on the Surrey side of London-bridge, among the fastnesses of Jacob's Island and Dockhead. It was the habit of that animal, when his services were not in immediate requisition, to go out alone, idling. I have met him a mile from his place of residence, loitering about the streets; and the expression of his countenance at such times was most degraded. He was attached to the establishment of an elderly lady who sold periwinkles, and he used to stand on Saturday nights with a cartful of those delicacies outside a gin-shop, pricking up his ears when a customer came to the cart, and too evidently deriving satisfaction from the knowledge that they got bad measure. His mistress was sometimes overtaken by inebriety. The last time I ever saw him (about five years ago) he was in circumstances of difficulty, caused by this failing. Having been left alone with the cart of periwinkles, and forgotten, he went off idling. He prowled among his usual low haunts for some time, gratifying his depraved tastes, until, not taking the cart into his calculations, he endeavoured to turn up a narrow alley, and became greatly involved. He was taken into custody by the police, and, the Green Yard of the district being near at hand, was backed into that place of durance. At that crisis, I encountered him; the stubborn sense he evinced of being—not to compromise the expression—a blackguard, I never saw exceeded in the human subject. A flaring candle in a paper shade, stuck in among his periwinkles, showed him, with his ragged harness broken and his cart extensively shattered, twitching his mouth and shaking his hanging head, a picture of disgrace and obduracy. I have seen boys being taken to station-houses, who were as like him as his own brother.

The dogs of shy neighbourhoods, I observe to avoid play, and to be conscious of poverty. They avoid work, too, if they can, of course; that is in the nature of all animals. I have the pleasure to know a dog in a back street in the neighbourhood of Walworth, who has greatly distinguished himself in the minor drama, and who takes his portrait with him when he makes an engagement, for the illustration of the play-bill. His portrait (which is not at all like him) represents him in the act of dragging to the earth a recreant Indian, who is supposed to have tomahawked, or essayed to tomahawk, a British officer. The design is pure poetry, for there is no such Indian in the piece, and no such incident. He is a dog of the Newfoundland breed, for whose honesty I would be bail to any amount; but whose intellectual qualities in association with dramatic fiction, I cannot rate high. Indeed, he is too honest for the profession he has entered. Being at a town in Yorkshire last summer, and seeing him posted in the bill of the night, I attended the performance. His first scene was eminently successful; but, as it occupied a second in its representation (and five lines in the bill), it scarcely afforded ground for a cool and deliberate judgment of his powers. He had merely to bark, run on, and jump through an inn window, after a comic fugitive. The next scene of importance to the fable was a little marred in its interest by his over-anxiety; forasmuch as while his master (a belated soldier in a den of robbers on a tempestuous night) was feelingly lamenting the absence of his faithful dog, and laying great stress on the fact that he was thirty leagues away, the faithful dog was barking furiously in the prompter's box, and clearly choking himself against his collar. But it was in his greatest scene of all, that his honesty got the better of him. He had to enter a dense and trackless forest, on the trail of the murderer, and there to fly at the murderer when he found him resting at the foot of a tree, with his victim bound ready for slaughter. It was a hot night, and he came into the forest from an altogether unexpected direction, in the sweetest temper, at a very deliberate trot, not in the least excited; trotted to the foot-lights with his tongue out; and there sat down, panting, and amiably surveying the audience, with his tail beating on the boards, like a Dutch clock. Meanwhile the murderer, impatient to receive his doom, was audibly calling to him "Co-o-ome here!" while the victim, struggling with his bonds, assailed him with the most injurious expressions. It happened through these means, that when he was in course of time persuaded to trot up and rend the murderer limb from limb, he made it (for dramatic purposes) a little too obvious that he worked out that awful retribution by licking butter off his blood-stained hands.

In a shy street, behind Long-acre, two honest dogs live,

who perform in Punch's shows. I may venture to say that I am on terms of intimacy with both, and that I never saw either guilty of the falsehood of failing to look down at the man inside the show, during the whole performance. The difficulty other dogs have in satisfying their minds about these dogs, appears to be never overcome by time. The same dogs must encounter them over and over again, as they trudge along in their off-minutes behind the legs of the show and beside the drum; but all dogs seem to suspect their frills and jackets, and to sniff at them as if they thought those articles of personal adornment, an eruption—a something in the nature of mange, perhaps. From this Covent-garden window of mine I noticed a country dog, only the other day, who had come up to Covent-garden Market under a cart, and had broken his cord, an end of which he still trailed along with him. He loitered about the corners of the four streets commanded by my window; and bad London dogs came up, and told him lies that he didn't believe; and worse London dogs came up, and made proposals to him to go and steal in the market, which his principles rejected; and the ways of the town confused him, and he crept aside and lay down in a doorway. He had scarcely got a wink of sleep, when up comes Punch with Toby. He was darting to Toby for consolation and advice, when he saw the frill, and stopped, in the middle of the street, appalled. The show was pitched, Toby retired behind the drapery, the audience formed, the drum and pipes struck up. My country dog remained immovable, intently staring at these strange appearances, until Toby opened the drama by appearing on his ledge, and to him entered Punch, who put a tobacco-pipe into Toby's mouth. At this spectacle, the country dog threw up his head, gave one terrible howl, and fled due west.

We talk of men keeping dogs, but we might often talk more expressively of dogs keeping men. I know a bull-dog in a shy corner of Hammersmith who keeps a man. He keeps him up a yard, and makes him go to public-houses and lay wagers on him, and obliges him to lean against posts and look at him, and forces him to neglect work for him, and keeps him under rigid coercion. I once knew a fancy terrier who kept a gentleman—a gentleman who had been brought up at Oxford, too. The dog kept the gentleman entirely for his glorification, and the gentleman never talked about anything but the terrier. This, however, was not in a shy neighbourhood, and is a digression consequently.

There are a great many dogs in shy neighbourhoods, who keep boys. I have my eye on a mongrel in Somerstown who keeps three boys. He feigns that he can bring down sparrows, and unburrow rats (he can do neither), and he takes the boys out on sporting pretences into all sorts of suburban fields. He has likewise made them believe that he possesses some mysterious knowledge of the art of fishing, and they consider themselves incompletely equipped for the Hampstead ponds, with a pickle-jar and wide-mouthed bottle, unless he is with them and barking tremendously. There is a dog residing in the Borough of Southwark who keeps a blind man. He may be seen, most days, in Oxford-street, haling the blind man away on expeditions wholly uncontemplated by, and unintelligible to, the man : wholly of the dog's conception and execution. Contrariwise, when the man has projects, the dog will sit down in a crowded thoroughfare and meditate. I saw him yesterday, wearing the money-tray like an easy collar, instead of offering it to the public, taking the man against his will, on the invitation of a disreputable cur, apparently to visit a dog at Harrow— he was so intent on that direction. The north wall of Burlington House Gardens, between the Arcade and the Albany, offers a shy spot for appointments among blind men at about two or three o'clock in the afternoon. They sit (very uncomfortably) on a sloping stone there, and compare notes. Their dogs may always be observed at the same time, openly disparaging the men they keep, to one another, and settling where they shall respectively take their men when they begin to move again. At a small butcher's, in a shy neighbourhood (there is no reason for suppressing the name ; it is by Notting-hill, and gives upon the district called the Potteries), I know a shaggy black and white dog who keeps a drover. He is a dog of an easy disposition, and too frequently allows this drover to get drunk. On these occasions, it is the dog's custom to sit outside the public-house, keeping his eye on a few sheep, and thinking. I have seen him with six sheep, plainly casting up in his mind how many he began with when he left the market, and at what places he has left the rest. I have seen him perplexed by not being able to account to himself for certain particular sheep. A light has gradually broken on him, he has remembered at what butcher's he left them, and in a burst of grave satisfaction has caught a fly off his nose, and shown himself much relieved. If I could at any time have doubted the fact that it was he who kept the drover, and not the drover who kept him, it would have been abundantly proved by his way of taking undivided charge of the six sheep, when the drover came out besmeared with red ochre and beer, and gave him wrong directions, which he calmly disregarded. He has taken the sheep entirely into his own hands, has merely remarked with respectful firmness, "That instruction would place them under an omnibus; you had better confine your attention to yourself—you will want it all;" and has driven his charge away, with an intelligence of ears and tail, and a knowledge of business, that has left his lout of a man very, very far behind.

As the dogs of shy neighbourhoods usually betray a slinking consciousness of being in poor circumstances—for the most part manifested in an aspect of anxiety, an awkwardness in their play, and a misgiving that somebody is going to harness them to something, to pick up a living—so the cats of shy neighbourhoods exhibit a strong tendency to relapse into barbarism. Not only are they made selfishly ferocious by ruminating on the surplus population around them, and on the densely crowded state of all the avenues to cat's meat; not only is there a moral and politico-economical haggardness in them, traceable to these reflections; but they evince a physical deterioration. Their linen is not clean, and is wretchedly got up; their black turns rusty, like old mourning; they wear very indifferent fur; and take to the shabbiest cotton velvet, instead of silk velvet. I am on terms of recognition with several small streets of cats, about the Obelisk in Saint George's Fields, and also in the vicinity of Clerkenwell-green, and also in the back settlements of Drury-lane. In appearance, they are very like the women among whom they live. They seem to turn out of their unwholesome beds into the street, without any preparation. They leave their young families to stagger about the gutters, unassisted, while they frouzily quarrel and swear and scratch and spit, at street corners. In particular, I remark that when they are about to increase their families (an event of frequent recurrence) the resemblance is strongly expressed in a certain dusty dowdiness, down-at-heel self-neglect, and general giving up of things.

I cannot honestly report that I have ever seen a feline matron of this class washing her face when in an interesting condition.

Not to prolong these notes of uncommercial travel among the lower animals of shy neighbourhoods, by dwelling at length upon the exasperated moodiness of the tom-cats, and their resemblance in many respects to a man and a brother, I will come to a close with a word on the fowls of the same localities.

That anything born of an egg and invested with wings, should have got to the pass that it hops contentedly down a ladder into a cellar, and calls *that* going home, is a circumstance so amazing as to leave one nothing more in this connexion to wonder at. Otherwise I might wonder at the completeness with which these fowls have become separated from all the birds of the air—have taken to grovelling in bricks and mortar and mud—have forgotten all about live trees, and make roosting-places of shop-boards, barrows, oyster-tubs, bulk-heads, and door-scrapers. I wonder at nothing concerning them, and take them as they are. I accept as products of Nature and things of course, a reduced Bantam family of my acquaintance in the Hackney-road, who are incessantly at the pawnbroker's. I cannot say that they enjoy themselves, for they are of a melancholy temperament; but what enjoyment they are capable of, they derive from crowding together in the pawnbroker's side-entry. Here, they are always to be found in a feeble flutter, as if they were newly come down in the world, and were afraid of being identified. I know a low fellow, originally of a good family from Dorking, who takes his whole establishment of wives, in single file, in at the door of the Jug Department of a disorderly tavern near the Haymarket, manœuvres them among the company's legs, emerges with them at the Bottle Entrance, and so passes his life: seldom, in the season, going to bed before two in the morning. Over Waterloo-bridge, there is a shabby old speckled couple (they belong to the wooden French-bedstead, washing-stand, and towel-horse-making trade), who are always trying to get in at the door of a chapel. Whether the old lady, under a delusion reminding one of Mrs. Southcott, has an idea of entrusting an egg to that particular denomination, or merely understands that she has no business in the building and is consequently frantic to enter it,

I cannot determine; but she is constantly endeavouring to undermine the principal door: while her partner, who is infirm upon his legs, walks up and down, encouraging her and defying the Universe. But, the family I have been best acquainted with, since the removal from this trying sphere of a Chinese circle at Brentford, reside in the densest part of Bethnal-green. Their abstraction from the objects among which they live, or rather their conviction that those objects have all come into existence in express sub-servience to fowls, has so enchanted me, that I have made them the subject of many journeys at divers hours. After careful observation of the two lords and the ten ladies of whom this family consists, I have come to the conclusion that their opinions are represented by the leading lord and leading lady: the latter, as I judge, an aged personage, afflicted with a paucity of feather and visibility of quill, that gives her the appearance of a bundle of office pens. When a railway goods van that would crush an elephant comes round the corner, tearing over these fowls, they emerge unharmed from under the horses, perfectly satisfied that the whole rush was a passing property in the air, which may have left something to eat behind it. They look upon old shoes, wrecks of kettles and saucepans, and fragments of bonnets, as a kind of meteoric discharge, for fowls to peck at. Peg-tops and hoops they account, I think, as a sort of hail; shuttlecocks, as rain, or dew. Gaslight comes quite as natural to them as any other light; and I have more than a suspicion that, in the minds of the two lords, the early public-house at the corner has superseded the sun. I have established it as a certain fact, that they always begin to crow when the public-house shutters begin to be taken down, and that they salute the potboy, the instant he appears to perform that duty, as if he were Phœbus in person.

XI

TRAMPS

THE chance use of the word "Tramp" in my last paper, brought that numerous fraternity so vividly before my mind's eye, that I had no sooner laid down my pen than a compulsion was upon me to take it up again, and make notes of the Tramps whom I perceived on all the summer roads in all directions.

Whenever a tramp sits down to rest by the wayside, he sits with his legs in a dry ditch; and whenever he goes to sleep (which is very often indeed), he goes to sleep on his back. Yonder, by the high road, glaring white in the bright sunshine, lies, on the dusty bit of turf under the bramble-bush that fences the coppice from the highway, the tramp of the order savage, fast asleep. He lies on the broad of his back, with his face turned up to the sky, and one of his ragged arms loosely thrown across his face. His bundle (what can be the contents of that mysterious bundle, to make it worth his while to carry it about?) is thrown down beside him, and the waking woman with him sits with her legs in the ditch, and her back to the road. She wears her bonnet rakishly perched on the front of her head, to shade her face from the sun in walking, and she ties her skirts round her in conventionally tight tramp-fashion with a sort of apron. You can seldom catch sight of her, resting thus, without seeing her in a despondently defiant manner doing something to her hair or her bonnet, and glancing at you between her fingers. She does not often go to sleep herself in the daytime, but will sit for any length of time beside the man. And his slumberous propensities would not seem to be referable to the fatigue of carrying the bundle, for she carries it much oftener and further than he. When they are afoot, you will mostly find him slouching on ahead, in a gruff temper, while she lags heavily behind with the burden. He is given to personally correcting her, too—

'*This is a Sweet Spot, Ain't It? A Lovelly Spot!*'

which phase of his character develops itself oftenest, on
benches outside alehouse doors—and she appears to become
strongly attached to him for these reasons ; it may usually
be noticed that when the poor creature has a bruised face,
she is the most affectionate. He has no occupation whatever,
this order of tramp, and has no object whatever in going
anywhere. He will sometimes call himself a brickmaker,
or a sawyer, but only when he takes an imaginative flight.
He generally represents himself, in a vague way, as looking
out for a job of work ; but he never did work, he never does,
and he never will. It is a favourite fiction with him, however (as if he were the most industrious character on earth),
that *you* never work ; and as he goes past your garden and
sees you looking at your flowers, you will overhear him
growl with a strong sense of contrast, " *You* are a lucky
hidle devil, *you* are ! "

The slinking tramp is of the same hopeless order, and has
the same injured conviction on him that you were born to
whatever you possess, and never did anything to get it : but
he is of a less audacious disposition. He will stop before
your gate, and say to his female companion with an air of
constitutional humility and propitiation—to edify any one
who may be within hearing behind a blind or a bush—" This
is a sweet spot, ain't it ? A lovelly spot ! And I wonder if
they'd give two poor footsore travellers like me and you,
a drop of fresh water out of such a pretty gen-teel crib ?
We'd take it wery koind on 'em, wouldn't us ? Wery koind,
upon my word, us would ? " He has a quick sense of a dog
in the vicinity, and will extend his modestly-injured propitiation to the dog chained up in your yard ; remarking, as
he slinks at the yard gate, " Ah ! You are a foine breed o'
dog, too, and *you* ain't kep for nothink ! I'd take it wery
koind o' your master if he'd elp a traveller and his woife as
envies no gentlefolk their good fortun, wi' a bit o' your
broken wittles. He'd never know the want of it, nor more
would you. Don't bark like that, at poor persons as never
done you no arm ; the poor is down-trodden and broke
enough without that ; O DON'T ! " He generally heaves
a prodigious sigh in moving away, and always looks up the
lane and down the lane, and up the road and down the road,
before going on.

Both of these orders of tramp are of a very robust habit ;
let the hard-working labourer at whose cottage-door they

prowl and beg, have the ague never so badly, these tramps are sure to be in good health.

There is another kind of tramp, whom you encounter this bright summer day—say, on a road with the sea-breeze making its dust lively, and sails of ships in the blue distance beyond the slope of Down. As you walk enjoyingly on, you descry in the perspective at the bottom of a steep hill up which your way lies, a figure that appears to be sitting airily on a gate, whistling in a cheerful and disengaged manner. As you approach nearer to it, you observe the figure to slide down from the gate, to desist from whistling, to uncock its hat, to become tender of foot, to depress its head and elevate its shoulders, and to present all the characteristics of profound despondency. Arriving at the bottom of the hill and coming close to the figure, you observe it to be the figure of a shabby young man. He is moving painfully forward, in the direction in which you are going, and his mind is so preoccupied with his misfortunes that he is not aware of your approach until you are close upon him at the hill-foot. When he is aware of you, you discover him to be a remarkably well-behaved young man, and a remarkably well-spoken young man. You know him to be well-behaved, by his respectful manner of touching his hat : you know him to be well-spoken, by his smooth manner of expressing himself. He says in a flowing confidential voice, and without punctuation, " I ask your pardon sir but if you would excuse the liberty of being so addressed upon the public Iway by one who is almost reduced to rags though it as not always been so and by no fault of his own but through ill elth in his family and many unmerited sufferings it would be a great obligation sir to know the time." You give the well-spoken young man the time. The well-spoken young man, keeping well up with you, resumes : " I am aware sir that it is a liberty to intrude a further question on a gentleman walking for his entertainment but might I make so bold as ask the favour of the way to Dover sir and about the distance ? " You inform the well-spoken young man that the way to Dover is straight on, and the distance some eighteen miles. The well-spoken young man becomes greatly agitated. " In the condition to which I am reduced," says he, " I could not ope to reach Dover before dark even if my shoes were in a state to take me there or my feet were in a state to old out over the flinty road and were not on the bare ground of which any gentleman has the means to satisfy himself by looking Sir may I take the liberty of speaking to you?" As the well-spoken young man keeps so well up with you that you can't prevent his taking the liberty of speaking to you, he goes on, with fluency : "Sir it is not begging that is my intention for I was brought up by the best of mothers and begging is not my trade I should not know sir how to follow it as a trade if such were my shameful wishes for the best of mothers long taught otherwise and in the best of omes though now reduced to take the present liberty on the Iway Sir my business was the law-stationering and I was favourably known to the Solicitor-General the Attorney-General the majority of the Judges and the ole of the legal profession but through ill elth in my family and the treachery of a friend for whom I became security and he no other than my own wife's brother the brother of my own wife I was cast forth with my tender partner and three young children not to beg for I will sooner die of deprivation but to make my way to the seaport town of Dover where I have a relative i in respect not only that will assist me but that would trust me with untold gold Sir in appier times and hare this calamity fell upon me I made for my amusement when I little thought that I should ever need it excepting for my air this "—here the well-spoken young man put his hand into his breast—" this comb ! Sir I implore you in the name of charity to purchase a tortoiseshell comb which is a genuine article at any price that your humanity may put upon it and may the blessings of a ouseless family awaiting with beating arts the return of a husband and a father from Dover upon the cold stone seats of London-bridge ever attend you Sir may I take the liberty of speaking to you I implore you to buy this comb ! " By this time, being a reasonably good walker, you will have been too much for the well-spoken young man, who will stop short and express his disgust and his want of breath, in a long expectoration, as you leave him behind.

Towards the end of the same walk, on the same bright summer day, at the corner of the next little town or village, you may find another kind of tramp, embodied in the persons of a most exemplary couple whose only improvidence appears to have been, that they spent the last of their little All on soap. They are a man and woman, spotless to behold—John Anderson, with the frost on his short smock-front instead of his "pow," attended by Mrs. Anderson. John is over-ostentatious of the frost upon his raiment, and wears a curious and, you would say, an almost unnecessary demonstration of girdle of white linen wound about his waist—a girdle, snowy as Mrs. Anderson's apron. This cleanliness was the expiring effort of the respectable couple, and nothing then remained to Mr. Anderson but to get chalked upon his spade in snow-white copy-book characters, HUNGRY! and to sit down here. Yes; one thing more remained to Mr. Anderson—his character; Monarchs could not deprive him of his hard-earned character. Accordingly, as you come up with this spectacle of virtue in distress, Mrs. Anderson rises, and with a decent curtsey presents for your consideration a certificate from a Doctor of Divinity, the reverend the Vicar of Upper Dodgington, who informs his Christian friends and all whom it may concern that the bearers, John Anderson and lawful wife, are persons to whom you cannot be too liberal. This benevolent pastor omitted no work of his hands to fit the good couple out, for with half an eye you can recognise his autograph on the spade.

Another class of tramp is a man, the most valuable part of whose stock-in-trade is a highly perplexed demeanour. He is got up like a countryman, and you will often come upon the poor fellow, while he is endeavouring to decipher the inscription on a milestone—quite a fruitless endeavour, for he cannot read. He asks your pardon, he truly does (he is very slow of speech, this tramp, and he looks in a bewildered way all round the prospect while he talks to you), but all of us shold do as we wold be done by, and he'll take it kind, if you'll put a power man in the right road fur to jine his eldest son as has broke his leg bad in the mason-ing, and is in this heere Orspit'l as is wrote down by Squire Pouncerby's own hand as wold not tell a lie fur no man. He then produces from under his dark frock (being always very slow and perplexed) a neat but worn old leathern purse, from which he takes a scrap of paper. On this scrap of paper is written, by Squire Pouncerby, of The Grove, "Please to direct the Bearer, a poor but very worthy man, to the Sussex County Hospital, near Brighton"—a matter of some difficulty at the moment, seeing that the request comes suddenly upon you in the depths of Hertfordshire. The more you endeavour to indicate where Brighton is—when you have with the greatest difficulty remembered—

the less the devoted father can be made to comprehend, and the more obtusely he stares at the prospect ; whereby, being reduced to extremity, you recommend the faithful parent to begin by going to St. Albans, and present him with half-a-crown. It does him good, no doubt, but scarcely helps him forward, since you find him lying drunk that same evening in the wheelwright's sawpit under the shed where the felled trees are, opposite the sign of the Three Jolly Hedgers.

But, the most vicious, by far, of all the idle tramps, is the tramp who pretends to have been a gentleman. "Educated," he writes, from the village beer-shop in pale ink of a ferruginous complexion ; "educated at Trin. Coll. Cam.—nursed in the lap of affluence—once in my small way the pattron of the Muses," &c. &c. &c.—surely a sympathetic mind will not withhold a trifle, to help him on to the market-town where he thinks of giving a Lecture to the *fruges consumere nati*, on things in general? This shameful creature lolling about hedge tap-rooms in his ragged clothes, now so far from being black that they look as if they never can have been black, is more selfish and insolent than even the savage tramp. He would sponge on the poorest boy for a farthing, and spurn him when he had got it ; he would interpose (if he could get anything by it) between the baby and the mother's breast. So much lower than the company he keeps, for his maudlin assumption of being higher, this pitiless rascal blights the summer road as he maunders on between the luxuriant hedges; where (to my thinking) even the wild convolvulus and rose and sweetbriar, are the worse for his going by, and need time to recover from the taint of him in the air.

The young fellows who trudge along barefoot, five or six together, their boots slung over their shoulders, their shabby bundles under their arms, their sticks newly cut from some roadside wood, are not eminently prepossessing, but are much less objectionable. There is a tramp-fellowship among them. They pick one another up at resting stations, and go on in companies. They always go at a fast swing—though they generally limp too—and there is invariably one of the company who has much ado to keep up with the rest. They generally talk about horses, and any other means of locomotion than walking: or, one of the company relates some recent experiences of the road—which are always disputes and difficulties. As for example. "So as I'm a standing at the pump in the market, blest if there don't come up a Beadle, and he ses,—'Mustn't stand here,' he ses. 'Why not?' I ses. 'No beggars allowed in this town,' he ses. 'Who's a beggar?' I ses. 'You are,' he ses. 'Who ever see *me* beg? Did *you*?' I ses. 'Then you're a tramp,' he ses. 'I'd rather be that than a Beadle,' I ses." (The company express great approval.) "'Would you?' he ses to me. 'Yes, I would,' I ses to him. 'Well,' he ses, 'anyhow, get out of this town.' 'Why, blow your little town!' I ses, 'who wants to be in it? Wot does your dirty little town mean by comin' and stickin' itself in the road to anywhere? Why don't you get a shovel and a barrer, and clear your town out o' people's way?'" (The company expressing the highest approval and laughing aloud, they all go down the hill.)

Then, there are the tramp handicraft men. Are they not all over England, in this Midsummer time? Where does the lark sing, the corn grow, the mill turn, the river run, and they are not among the lights and shadows, tinkering, chair-mending, umbrella-mending, clock-mending, knife-grinding? Surely, a pleasant thing, if we were in that condition of life, to grind our way through Kent, Sussex, and Surrey. For the worst six weeks or so, we should see the sparks we ground off, fiery bright against a background of green wheat and green leaves. A little later, and the ripe harvest would pale our sparks from red to yellow, until we got the dark newly-turned land for a background again, and they were red once more. By that time, we should have ground our way to the sea cliffs, and the whirr of our wheel would be lost in the breaking of the waves. Our next variety in sparks would be derived from contrast with the gorgeous medley of colours in the autumn woods, and, by the time we had ground our way round to the heathy lands between Reigate and Croydon, doing a prosperous stroke of business all along, we should show like a little firework in the light frosty air, and be the next best thing to the blacksmith's forge. Very agreeable, too, to go on a chair-mending tour. What judges we should be of rushes, and how knowingly (with a sheaf and a bottomless chair at our back) we should lounge on bridges, looking over at osier-beds! Among all the innumerable occupations that cannot possibly be transacted without the assistance of lookers-on, chair-mending may take a station in the first rank. When we sat down with our backs against the barn or the public-house, and began to mend, what a sense of popularity would grow upon us! When all the children came to look at us, and the tailor, and the general dealer, and the farmer who had been giving a small order at the little saddler's, and the groom from the great house, and the publican, and even the two skittle-players (and here note that, howsoever busy all the rest of village human-kind may be, there will always be two people with leisure to play at skittles, wherever village skittles are), what encouragement would be on us to plait and weave! No one looks at us while we plait and weave these words. Clock-mending again. Except for the slight inconvenience of carrying a clock under our arm, and the monotony of making the bell go, whenever we came to a human habitation, what a pleasant privilege to give a voice to the dumb cottage-clock, and set it talking to the cottage family again. Likewise we foresee great interest in going round by the park plantations, under the overhanging boughs (hares, rabbits, partridges, and pheasants, scudding like mad across and across the chequered ground before us), and so over the park ladder, and through the wood, until we came to the Keeper's lodge. Then, would the Keeper be discoverable at his door, in a deep nest of leaves, smoking his pipe. Then, on our accosting him in the way of our trade, would he call to Mrs. Keeper, respecting "t'ould clock" in the kitchen. Then, would Mrs. Keeper ask us into the lodge, and on due examination we should offer to make a good job of it for eighteenpence; which offer, being accepted, would set us tinkling and clinking among the chubby awe-struck little Keepers for an hour and more. So completely to the family's satisfaction would we achieve our work, that the Keeper would mention how that there was something wrong with the bell of the turret stable-clock up at the Hall, and that if we thought good of going up to the housekeeper on the chance of that job too, why he would take us. Then, should we go, among the branching oaks and the deep fern, by silent ways of mystery known to the Keeper, seeing the herd glancing here and there as we went along, until we came to the old Hall, solemn and grand. Under the Terrace Flower Garden, and round by the stables, would the Keeper take us in, and as we passed we should observe how

spacious and stately the stables, and how fine the painting
of the horses' names over their stalls, and how solitary all :
the family being in London. Then, should we find ourselves presented to the housekeeper, sitting, in hushed state,
at needlework, in a bay-window looking out upon a mighty
grim red-brick quadrangle, guarded by stone lions disrespect-
fully throwing somersaults over the escutcheons of the noble
family.   Then, our services accepted and we insinuated
with a candle into the stable-turret, we should find it to be
a mere question of pendulum, but one that would hold us
until dark. Then, should we fall to work, with a general
impression of Ghosts being about, and of pictures indoors
that of a certainty came out of their frames and "walked,"
if the family would only own it.   Then, should we work
and work, until the day gradually turned to dusk, and even
until the dusk gradually turned to dark.   Our task at
length accomplished, we should be taken into an enormous
servants' hall, and there regaled with beef and bread, and
powerful ale.   Then, paid freely, we should be at liberty to
go, and should be told by a pointing helper to keep round
over yinder by the blasted ash, and so straight through the
woods, till we should see the town-lights right afore us. Then,
feeling lonesome, should we desire upon the whole, that the
ash had not been blasted, or that the helper had had the
manners not to mention it.   However, we should keep on,
all right, till suddenly the stable bell would strike ten in
the dolefullest way, quite chilling our blood, though we had
so lately taught him how to acquit himself.   Then, as we
went on, should we recall old stories, and dimly consider
what it would be most advisable to do, in the event of a
tall figure, all in white, with saucer eyes, coming up and
saying, " I want you to come to a churchyard and mend a
church clock. Follow me !" Then, should we make a burst
to get clear of the trees, and should soon find ourselves in the
open, with the town-lights bright ahead of us. So should
we lie that night at the ancient sign of the Crispin and
Crispanus, and rise early next morning to be betimes on
tramp again.

Bricklayers often tramp, in twos and threes, lying by
night at their "lodges," which are scattered all over the
country.   Bricklaying is another of the occupations that
can by no means be transacted in rural parts, without the
assistance of spectators—of as many as can be convened. In

thinly-peopled spots, I have known bricklayers on tramp, coming up with bricklayers at work, to be so sensible of the indispensability of lookers-on, that they themselves have sat up in that capacity, and have been unable to subside into the acceptance of a proffered share in the job, for two or three days together. Sometimes the "navvy," on tramp, with an extra pair of half-boots over his shoulder, a bag, a bottle, and a can, will take a similar part in a job of excavation, and will look at it without engaging in it, until all his money is gone. The current of my uncommercial pursuits caused me only last summer to want a little body of workmen for a certain spell of work in a pleasant part of the country ; and I was at one time honoured with the attendance of as many as seven-and-twenty, who were looking at six.

Who can be familiar with any rustic highway in summer-time, without storing up knowledge of the many tramps who go from one oasis of town or village to another, to sell a stock in trade, apparently not worth a shilling when sold ? Shrimps are a favourite commodity for this kind of specula-tion, and so are cakes of a soft and spongy character, coupled with Spanish nuts and brandy balls. The stock is carried on the head in a basket, and, between the head and the basket, are the trestles on which the stock is displayed at trading times. Fleet of foot, but a careworn class of tramp this, mostly ; with a certain stiffness of neck, occasioned by much anxious balancing of baskets ; and also with a long Chinese sort of eye, which an overweighted forehead would seem to have squeezed into that form.

On the hot dusty roads near seaport towns and great rivers, behold the tramping Soldier. And if you should happen never to have asked yourself whether his uniform is suited to his work, perhaps the poor fellow's appearance as he comes distressfully towards you, with his absurdly tight jacket unbuttoned, his neck-gear in his hand, and his legs well chafed by his trousers of baize, may suggest the per-sonal inquiry, how you think *you* would like it. Much better the tramping Sailor, although his cloth is somewhat too thick for land service. But, why the tramping merchant-mate should put on a black velvet waistcoat, for a chalky country in the dog-days, is one of the great secrets of nature that will never be discovered.

I have my eye upon a piece of Kentish road, bordered on

either side by a wood, and having on one hand, between the road-dust and the trees, a skirting patch of grass. Wild flowers grow in abundance on this spot, and it lies high and airy, with a distant river stealing steadily away to the ocean, like a man's life. To gain the milestone here, which the moss, primroses, violets, blue-bells, and wild roses, would soon render illegible but for peering travellers pushing them aside with their sticks, you must come up a steep hill, come which way you may. So, all the tramps with carts or caravans—the Gipsy-tramp, the Show-tramp, the Cheap Jack—find it impossible to resist the temptations of the place, and all turn the horse loose when they come to it, and boil the pot. Bless the place, I love the ashes of the vagabond fires that have scorched its grass! What tramp children do I see here, attired in a handful of rags, making a gymnasium of the shafts of the cart, making a feather-bed of the flints and brambles, making a toy of the hobbled old horse who is not much more like a horse than any cheap toy would be! Here, do I encounter the cart of mats and brooms and baskets—with all thoughts of business given to the evening wind—with the stew made and being served out—with Cheap Jack and Dear Jill striking soft music out of the plates that are rattled like warlike cymbals when put up for auction at fairs and markets—their minds so influenced (no doubt) by the melody of the nightingales as they begin to sing in the woods behind them, that if I were to propose to deal, they would sell me anything at cost price. On this hallowed ground has it been my happy privilege (let me whisper it), to behold the White-haired Lady with the pink eyes, eating meat-pie with the Giant: while, by the hedge-side, on the box of blankets which I knew contained the snakes, were set forth the cups and saucers and the teapot. It was on an evening in August, that I chanced upon this ravishing spectacle, and I noticed that, whereas the Giant reclined half concealed beneath the overhanging boughs and seemed indifferent to Nature, the white hair of the gracious Lady streamed free in the breath of evening, and her pink eyes found pleasure in the landscape. I heard only a single sentence of her uttering, yet it bespoke a talent for modest repartee. The ill-mannered Giant—accursed be his evil race!—had interrupted the Lady in some remark, and, as I passed that enchanted corner of the wood, she gently reproved him, with the words, "Now, Cobby;"—

Cobby! so short a name!—" ain't one fool enough to talk at a time?"

Within appropriate distance of this magic ground, though not so near it as that the song trolled from tap or bench at door, can invade its woodland silence, is a little hostelry which no man possessed of a penny was ever known to pass in warm weather. Before its entrance are certain pleasant trimmed limes; likewise a cool well, with so musical a bucket-handle that its fall upon the bucket rim will make a horse prick up his ears and neigh, upon the droughty road half a mile off. This is a house of great resort for hay-making tramps and harvest tramps, insomuch that as they sit within, drinking their mugs of beer, their relinquished scythes and reaping-hooks glare out of the open windows, as if the whole establishment were a family war-coach of Ancient Britons. Later in the season, the whole country-side, for miles and miles, will swarm with hopping tramps. They come in families, men, women, and children, every family provided with a bundle of bedding, an iron pot, a number of babies, and too often with some poor sick creature quite unfit for the rough life, for whom they suppose the smell of the fresh hop to be a sovereign remedy. Many of these hoppers are Irish, but many come from London. They crowd all the roads, and camp under all the hedges and on all the scraps of common-land, and live among and upon the hops until they are all picked, and the hop-gardens, so beautiful through the summer, look as if they had been laid waste by an invading army. Then, there is a vast exodus of tramps out of the country; and if you ride or drive round any turn of any road, at more than a foot pace, you will be bewildered to find that you have charged into the bosom of fifty families, and that there are splashing up all around you, in the utmost prodigality of confusion, bundles of bedding, babies, iron pots, and a good-humoured multitude of both sexes and all ages, equally divided between perspiration and intoxication.

XII

DULLBOROUGH TOWN

It lately happened that I found myself rambling about the scenes among which my earliest days were passed; scenes from which I departed when I was a child, and which I did not revisit until I was a man. This is no uncommon chance, but one that befalls some of us any day; perhaps it may not be quite uninteresting to compare notes with the reader respecting an experience so familiar and a journey so uncommercial.

I call my boyhood's home (and I feel like a Tenor in an English Opera when I mention it) Dullborough. Most of us come from Dullborough who come from a country town.

As I left Dullborough in the days when there were no railroads in the land, I left it in a stage-coach. Through all the years that have since passed, have I ever lost the smell of the damp straw in which I was packed—like game—and forwarded, carriage paid, to the Cross Keys, Wood-street, Cheapside, London? There was no other inside passenger, and I consumed my sandwiches in solitude and dreariness, and it rained hard all the way, and I thought life sloppier than I had expected to find it.

With this tender remembrance upon me, I was cavalierly shunted back into Dullborough the other day, by train. My ticket had been previously collected, like my taxes, and my shining new portmanteau had had a great plaster stuck upon it, and I had been defied by Act of Parliament to offer an objection to anything that was done to it, or me, under a penalty of not less than forty shillings or more than five pounds, compoundable for a term of imprisonment. When I had sent my disfigured property on to the hotel, I began to look about me; and the first discovery I made, was, that the Station had swallowed up the playing-field.

It was gone. The two beautiful hawthorn-trees, the hedge, the turf, and all those buttercups and daisies, had given place to the stoniest of jolting roads: while, beyond the Station, an ugly dark monster of a tunnel kept its jaws open, as if it had swallowed them and were ravenous for more destruction. The coach that had carried me away, was melodiously called Timpson's Blue-Eyed Maid, and belonged to Timpson, at the coach-office up-street; the locomotive engine that had brought me back, was called severely No. 97, and belonged to S.E.R., and was spitting ashes and hot water over the blighted ground.

When I had been let out at the platform-door, like a prisoner whom his turnkey grudgingly released, I looked in again over the low wall, at the scene of departed glories. Here, in the haymaking time, had I been delivered from the dungeons of Seringapatam, an immense pile (of haycock), by my own countrymen, the victorious British (boy next door and his two cousins), and had been recognised with ecstasy by my affianced one (Miss Green), who had come all the way from England (second house in the terrace) to ransom me, and marry me. Here, had I first heard in confidence, from one whose father was greatly connected, being under Government, of the existence of a terrible banditti, called "The Radicals," whose principles were, that the Prince Regent wore stays, and that nobody had a right to any salary, and that the army and navy ought to be put down—horrors at which I trembled in my bed, after supplicating that the Radicals might be speedily taken and hanged. Here, too, had we, the small boys of Boles's, had that cricket match against the small boys of Coles's, when Boles and Coles had actually met upon the ground, and when, instead of instantly hitting out at one another with the utmost fury, as we had all hoped and expected, those sneaks had said respectively, "I hope Mrs. Boles is well," and "I hope Mrs. Coles and the baby are doing charmingly." Could it be that, after all this, and much more, the Playing-field was a Station, and No. 97 expectorated boiling water and redhot cinders on it, and the whole belonged by Act of Parliament to S.E.R. ?

As it could be, and was, I left the place with a heavy heart for a walk all over the town. And first of Timpson's up-street. When I departed from Dullborough in the strawy arms of Timpson's Blue-Eyed Maid, Timpson's was a moderate-sized coach-office (in fact, a little coach-office), with an oval transparency in the window, which looked beautiful by night, representing one of Timpson's coaches in the act

of passing a milestone on the London road with great velocity,
completely full inside and out, and all the passengers dressed
in the first style of fashion, and enjoying themselves tremendously. I found no such place as Timpson's now—no such
bricks and rafters, not to mention the name—no such edifice
on the teeming earth. Pickford had come and knocked
Timpson's down. Pickford had not only knocked Timpson's
down, but had knocked two or three houses down on each
side of Timpson's, and then had knocked the whole into one
great establishment with a pair of big gates, in and out of
which, his (Pickford's) waggons are, in these days, always
rattling, with their drivers sitting up so high, that they look
in at the second-floor windows of the old-fashioned houses in
the High-street as they shake the town. I have not the honour
of Pickford's acquaintance, but I felt that he had done me an
injury, not to say committed an act of boyslaughter, in running over my childhood in this rough manner ; and if ever
I meet Pickford driving one of his own monsters, and smoking a pipe the while (which is the custom of his men), he
shall know by the expression of my eye, if it catches his,
that there is something wrong between us.

Moreover, I felt that Pickford had no right to come rushing
into Dullborough and deprive the town of a public picture.
He is not Napoleon Bonaparte. When he took down the
transparent stage-coach, he ought to have given the town a
transparent van. With a gloomy conviction that Pickford
is wholly utilitarian and unimaginative, I proceeded on my
way.

It is a mercy I have not a red and green lamp and a night-
bell at my door, for in my very young days I was taken to
so many lyings-in that I wonder I escaped becoming a
professional martyr to them in after-life. I suppose I had
a very sympathetic nurse, with a large circle of married
acquaintance. However that was, as I continued my walk
through Dullborough, I found many houses to be solely
associated in my mind with this particular interest. At one
little greengrocer's shop, down certain steps from the street,
I remember to have waited on a lady who had had four
children (I am afraid to write five, though I fully believe it
was five) at a birth. This meritorious woman held quite
a reception in her room on the morning when I was introduced there, and the sight of the house brought vividly to
my mind how the four (five) deceased young people lay, side

by side, on a clean cloth on a chest of drawers; reminding me by a homely association, which I suspect their complexion to have assisted, of pigs' feet as they are usually displayed at a neat tripe-shop. Hot caudle was handed round on the occasion, and I further remembered as I stood contemplating the greengrocer's, that a subscription was entered into among the company, which became extremely alarming to my consciousness of having pocket-money on my person. This fact being known to my conductress, whoever she was, I was earnestly exhorted to contribute, but resolutely declined : therein disgusting the company, who gave me to understand that I must dismiss all expectations of going to Heaven.

How does it happen that when all else is change wherever one goes, there yet seem, in every place, to be some few people who never alter? As the sight of the greengrocer's house recalled these trivial incidents of long ago, the identical greengrocer appeared on the steps, with his hands in his pockets, and leaning his shoulder against the door-post, as my childish eyes had seen him many a time ; indeed, there was his old mark on the door-post yet, as if his shadow had become a fixture there. It was he himself ; he might formerly have been an old-looking young man, or he might now be a young-looking old man, but there he was. In walking along the street, I had as yet looked in vain for a familiar face, or even a transmitted face ; here was the very greengrocer who had been weighing and handling baskets on the morning of the reception. As he brought with him a dawning remembrance that he had had no proprietary interest in those babies, I crossed the road, and accosted him on the subject. He was not in the least excited or gratified, or in any way roused, by the accuracy of my recollection, but said, Yes, summut out of the common—he didn't remember how many it was (as if half-a-dozen babes either way made no difference) —had happened to a Mrs. What's-her-name, as once lodged there—but he didn't call it to mind, particular. Nettled by this phlegmatic conduct, I informed him that I had left the town when I was a child. He slowly returned, quite unsoftened, and not without a sarcastic kind of complacency, *Had* I? Ah! And did I find it had got on tolerably well without me? Such is the difference (I thought, when I had left him a few hundred yards behind, and was by so much in a better temper) between going away from a place and remaining in it. I had no right, I reflected, to be angry with the greengrocer for his want of interest, I was nothing to him : whereas he was the town, the cathedral, the bridge, the river, my childhood, and a large slice of my life, to me.

Of course the town had shrunk fearfully, since I was a child there. I had entertained the impression that the High-street was at least as wide as Regent-street, London, or the Italian Boulevard at Paris. I found it little better than a lane. There was a public clock in it, which I had supposed to be the finest clock in the world : whereas it now turned out to be as inexpressive, moon-faced, and weak a clock as ever I saw. It belonged to a Town Hall, where I had seen an Indian (who I now suppose wasn't an Indian) swallow a sword (which I now suppose he didn't). The edifice had appeared to me in those days so glorious a structure, that I had set it up in my mind as the model on which the Genie of the Lamp built the palace for Aladdin. A mean little brick heap, like a demented chapel, with a few yawning persons in leather gaiters, and in the last extremity for some-thing to do, lounging at the door with their hands in their pockets, and calling themselves a Corn Exchange !

The Theatre was in existence, I found, on asking the fish-monger, who had a compact show of stock in his window, consisting of a sole and a quart of shrimps—and I resolved to comfort my mind by going to look at it. Richard the Third, in a very uncomfortable cloak, had first appeared to me there, and had made my heart leap with terror by back-ing up against the stage-box in which I was posted, while struggling for life against the virtuous Richmond. It was within those walls that I had learnt as from a page of English history, how that wicked King slept in war-time on a sofa much too short for him, and how fearfully his conscience troubled his boots. There, too, had I first seen the funny countryman, but countryman of noble principles, in a flowered waistcoat, crunch up his little hat and throw it on the ground, and pull off his coat, saying, "Dom thee, squire, coom on with thy fistes then !" At which the lovely young woman who kept company with him (and who went out gleaning, in a narrow white muslin apron with five beautiful bars of five different-coloured ribbons across it) was so frightened for his sake, that she fainted away. Many wondrous secrets of Nature had I come to the know-ledge of in that sanctuary : of which not the least terrific were, that the witches in Macbeth bore an awful resemblance to the Thanes and other proper inhabitants of Scotland; and that the good King Duncan couldn't rest in his grave, but was constantly coming out of it and calling himself somebody else. To the Theatre, therefore, I repaired for consolation. But I found very little, for it was in a bad and declining way. A dealer in wine and bottled beer had already squeezed his trade into the box-office, and the theatrical money was taken—when it came—in a kind of meat-safe in the passage. The dealer in wine and bottled beer must have insinuated himself under the stage too; for he announced that he had various descriptions of alcoholic drinks "in the wood," and there was no possible stowage for the wood anywhere else. Evidently, he was by degrees eating the establishment away to the core, and would soon have sole possession of it. It was To Let, and hopelessly so, for its old purposes; and there had been no entertainment within its walls for a long time except a Panorama; and even that had been announced as "pleasingly instructive," and I know too well the fatal meaning and the leaden import of those terrible expressions. No, there was no comfort in the Theatre. It was mysteriously gone, like my own youth. Unlike my own youth, it might be coming back some day; but there was little promise of it.

As the town was placarded with references to the Dullborough Mechanics' Institution, I thought I would go and look at that establishment next. There had been no such thing in the town, in my young day, and it occurred to me that its extreme prosperity might have brought adversity upon the Drama. I found the Institution with some difficulty, and should scarcely have known that I had found it if I had judged from its external appearance only; but this was attributable to its never having been finished, and having no front: consequently, it led a modest and retired existence up a stable-yard. It was (as I learnt, on inquiry) a most flourishing Institution, and of the highest benefit to the town: two triumphs which I was glad to understand were not at all impaired by the seeming drawbacks that no mechanics belonged to it, and that it was steeped in debt to the chimney-pots. It had a large room, which was approached by an infirm step-ladder: the builder having declined to construct the intended staircase, without a present payment in cash, which Dullborough (though profoundly appreciative

of the Institution) seemed unaccountably bashful about sub-
scribing. The large room had cost—or would, when paid
for—five hundred pounds; and it had more mortar in it
and more echoes than one might have expected to get for
the money. It was fitted up with a platform, and the usual
lecturing tools, including a large black board of a menacing
appearance. On referring to lists of the courses of lectures
that had been given in this thriving Hall, I fancied I detected a shyness in admitting that human nature when at
leisure has any desire whatever to be relieved and diverted ;
and a furtive sliding in of any poor make-weight piece of
amusement, shamefacedly and edgewise. Thus, I observed
that it was necessary for the members to be knocked on the
head with Gas, Air, Water, Food, the Solar System, the
Geological periods, Criticism on Milton, the Steam-engine,
John Bunyan, and Arrow-Headed Inscriptions, before they
might be tickled by those unaccountable choristers, the
negro singers in the court costume of the reign of George
the Second. Likewise, that they must be stunned by a
weighty inquiry whether there was internal evidence in
Shakespeare's works, to prove that his uncle by the mother's
side lived for some years at Stoke Newington, before they
were brought-to by a Miscellaneous Concert. But, indeed,
the masking of entertainment, and pretending it was something else—as people mask bedsteads when they are obliged
to have them in sitting-rooms, and make believe that they
are book-cases, sofas, chests of drawers, anything rather
than bedsteads—was manifest even in the pretence of dreariness that the unfortunate entertainers themselves felt obliged
in decency to put forth when they came here. One very
agreeable professional singer, who travelled with two professional ladies, knew better than to introduce either of those
ladies to sing the ballad " Comin' through the Rye " without
prefacing it himself, with some general remarks on wheat
and clover ; and even then, he dared not for his life call the
song, a song, but disguised it in the bill as an " Illustration."
In the library, also—fitted with shelves for three thousand
books, and containing upwards of one hundred and seventy
(presented copies mostly), seething their edges in damp
plaster—there was such a painfully apologetic return of 62
offenders who had read Travels, Popular Biography, and
mere Fiction descriptive of the aspirations of the hearts and
souls of mere human creatures like themselves ; and such

an elaborate parade of 2 bright examples who had had down
Euclid after the day's occupation and confinement; and 3
who had had down Metaphysics after ditto; and 1 who had
had down Theology after ditto; and 4 who had worried
Grammar, Political Economy, Botany, and Logarithms all
at once after ditto; that I suspected the boasted class to be
one man, who had been hired to do it.

Emerging from the Mechanics' Institution and continuing
my walk about the town, I still noticed everywhere the
prevalence, to an extraordinary degree, of this custom of
putting the natural demand for amusement out of sight, as
some untidy housekeepers put dust, and pretending that
it was swept away.   And yet it was ministered to, in a dull
and abortive manner, by all who made this feint.   Looking
in at what is called in Dullborough "the serious book-
seller's," where, in my childhood, I had studied the faces
of numbers of gentlemen depicted in rostrums with a gaslight on each side of them, and casting my eyes over the
open pages of certain printed discourses there, I found a vast
deal of aiming at jocosity and dramatic effect, even in them
—yes, verily, even on the part of one very wrathful expounder who bitterly anathematised a poor little Circus.
Similarly, in the reading provided for the young people
enrolled in the Lasso of Love, and other excellent unions,
I found the writers generally under a distressing sense that
they must start (at all events) like story-tellers, and delude
the young persons into the belief that they were going to
be interesting.   As I looked in at this window for twenty
minutes by the clock, I am in a position to offer a friendly
remonstrance—not bearing on this particular point—to the
designers and engravers of the pictures in those publications.
Have they considered the awful consequences likely to flow
from their representations of Virtue?   Have they asked
themselves the question, whether the terrific prospect of
acquiring that fearful chubbiness of head, unwieldiness
of arm, feeble dislocation of leg, crispiness of hair, and
enormity of shirt-collar, which they represent as inseparable
from Goodness, may not tend to confirm sensitive waverers,
in Evil?   A most impressive example (if I had believed it)
of what a Dustman and a Sailor may come to, when they
mend their ways, was presented to me in this same shop-
window.   When they were leaning (they were intimate
friends) against a post, drunk and reckless, with surpass-

ingly bad hats on, and their hair over their foreheads, they were rather picturesque, and looked as if they might be agreeable men, if they would not be beasts. But, when they had got over their bad propensities, and when, as a consequence, their heads had swelled alarmingly, their hair had got so curly that it lifted their blown-out cheeks up, their coat-cuffs were so long that they never could do any work, and their eyes were so wide open that they never could do any sleep, they presented a spectacle calculated to plunge a timid nature into the depths of Infamy.

But, the clock that had so degenerated since I saw it last, admonished me that I had stayed here long enough ; and I resumed my walk.

I had not gone fifty paces along the street when I was suddenly brought up by the sight of a man who got out of a little phaeton at the doctor's door, and went into the doctor's house. Immediately, the air was filled with the scent of trodden grass, and the perspective of years opened, and at the end of it was a little likeness of this man keeping a wicket, and I said, "God bless my soul ! Joe Specks ! "

Through many changes and much work, I had preserved a tenderness for the memory of Joe, forasmuch as we had made the acquaintance of Roderick Random together, and had believed him to be no ruffian, but an ingenuous and engaging hero. Scorning to ask the boy left in the phaeton whether it was really Joe, and scorning even to read the brass plate on the door—so sure was I—I rang the bell and informed the servant maid that a stranger sought audience of Mr. Specks. Into a room, half surgery, half study, I was shown to await his coming, and I found it, by a series of elaborate accidents, bestrewn with testimonies to Joe. Portrait of Mr. Specks, bust of Mr. Specks, silver cup from grateful patient to Mr. Specks, presentation sermon from local clergyman, dedication poem from local poet, dinner-card from local nobleman, tract on balance of power from local refugee, inscribed *Hommage de l'auteur à Specks.*

When my old schoolfellow came in, and I informed him with a smile that I was not a patient, he seemed rather at a loss to perceive any reason for smiling in connexion with that fact, and inquired to what was he to attribute the honour ? I asked him, with another smile, could he remember me at all ? He had not (he said) that pleasure. I was beginning to have but a poor opinion of Mr. Specks, when he said reflectively, "And yet there's a something too." Upon that, I saw a boyish light in his eyes that looked well, and I asked him if he could inform me, as a stranger who desired to know and had not the means of reference at hand, what the name of the young lady was, who married Mr. Random? Upon that, he said "Narcissa," and, after staring for a moment, called me by my name, shook me by the hand, and melted into a roar of laughter. "Why, of course, you'll remember Lucy Green," he said, after we had talked a little. "Of course," said I. "Whom do you think she married?" said he. "You?" I hazarded. "Me," said Specks, "and you shall see her." So I saw her, and she was fat, and if all the hay in the world had been heaped upon her, it could scarcely have altered her face more than Time had altered it from my remembrance of the face that had once looked down upon me into the fragrant dungeons of Seringapatam. But when her youngest child came in after dinner (for I dined with them, and we had no other company than Specks, Junior, Barrister-at-law, who went away as soon as the cloth was removed, to look after the young lady to whom he was going to be married next week), I saw again, in that little daughter, the little face of the hayfield, unchanged, and it quite touched my foolish heart. We talked immensely, Specks and Mrs. Specks, and I, and we spoke of our old selves as though our old selves were dead and gone, and indeed indeed they were—dead and gone as the playing-field that had become a wilderness of rusty iron, and the property of S.E.R.

Specks, however, illuminated Dullborough with the rays of interest that I wanted and should otherwise have missed in it, and linked its present to its past, with a highly agreeable chain. And in Specks's society I had new occasion to observe what I had before noticed in similar communications among other men. All the schoolfellows and others of old, whom I inquired about, had either done superlatively well or super-latively ill—had either become uncertificated bankrupts, or been felonious and got themselves transported; or had made great hits in life, and done wonders. And this is so commonly the case, that I never can imagine what becomes of all the mediocre people of people's youth—especially considering that we find no lack of the species in our maturity. But, I did not propound this difficulty to Specks, for no pause in the conversation gave me an occasion. Nor, could I discover one single flaw in the good doctor—when he reads this, he will receive in a friendly spirit the pleasantly meant record—except that he had forgotten his Roderick Random, and that he confounded Strap with Lieutenant Hatchway ; who never knew Random, howsoever intimate with Pickle.

When I went alone to the Railway to catch my train at night (Specks had meant to go with me, but was inopportunely called out), I was in a more charitable mood with Dullborough than I had been all day ; and yet in my heart I had loved it all day too. Ah! who was I that I should quarrel with the town for being changed to me, when I myself had come back, so changed, to it ! All my early readings and early imaginations dated from this place, and I took them away so full of innocent construction and guileless belief, and I brought them back so worn and torn, so much the wiser and so much the worse !

XIII

SOME years ago, a temporary inability to sleep, referable to a distressing impression, caused me to walk about the streets all night, for a series of several nights. The disorder might have taken a long time to conquer, if it had been faintly experimented on in bed; but, it was soon defeated by the brisk treatment of getting up directly after lying down, and going out, and coming home tired at sunrise.

In the course of those nights, I finished my education in a fair amateur experience of houselessness. My principal object being to get through the night, the pursuit of it brought me into sympathetic relations with people who have no other object every night in the year.

The month was March, and the weather damp, cloudy, and cold. The sun not rising before half-past five, the night perspective looked sufficiently long at half-past twelve: which was about my time for confronting it.

The restlessness of a great city, and the way in which it tumbles and tosses before it can get to sleep, formed one of the first entertainments offered to the contemplation of us houseless people. It lasted about two hours. We lost a great deal of companionship when the late public-houses turned their lamps out, and when the potmen thrust the last brawling drunkards into the street; but stray vehicles and stray people were left us, after that. If we were very lucky, a policeman's rattle sprang and a fray turned up; but, in general, surprisingly little of this diversion was provided. Except in the Haymarket, which is the worst kept part of London, and about Kent-street in the Borough, and along a portion of the line of the Old Kent-road, the peace was seldom violently broken. But, it was always the case that London, as if in imitation of individual citizens belonging to it, had expiring fits and starts of restlessness.

After all seemed quiet, if one cab rattled by, half-a-dozen would surely follow; and Houselessness even observed that intoxicated people appeared to be magnetically attracted towards each other: so that we knew when we saw one drunken object staggering against the shutters of a shop, that another drunken object would stagger up before five minutes were out, to fraternise or fight with it. When we made a divergence from the regular species of drunkard, the thin-armed, puff-faced, leaden-lipped gin-drinker, and encountered a rarer specimen of a more decent appearance, fifty to one but that specimen was dressed in soiled mourning. As the street experience in the night, so the street experience in the day; the common folk who come unexpectedly into a little property, come unexpectedly into a deal of liquor.

At length these flickering sparks would die away, worn out—the last veritable sparks of waking life trailed from some late pieman or hot-potato man—and London would sink to rest. And then the yearning of the houseless mind would be for any sign of company, any lighted place, any movement, anything suggestive of any one being up—nay, even so much as awake, for the houseless eye looked out for lights in windows.

Walking the streets under the pattering rain, Houselessness would walk and walk and walk, seeing nothing but the interminable tangle of streets, save at a corner, here and there, two policemen in conversation, or the sergeant or inspector looking after his men. Now and then in the night—but rarely—Houselessness would become aware of a furtive head peering out of a doorway a few yards before him, and, coming up with the head, would find a man standing bolt upright to keep within the doorway's shadow, and evidently intent upon no particular service to society. Under a kind of fascination, and in a ghostly silence suitable to the time, Houselessness and this gentleman would eye one another from head to foot, and so, without exchange of speech, part, mutually suspicious. Drip, drip, drip, from ledge and coping, splash from pipes and water-spouts, and by-and-by the houseless shadow would fall upon the stones that pave the way to Waterloo-bridge; it being in the houseless mind to have a halfpenny worth of excuse for saying " Good night " to the toll-keeper, and catching a glimpse of his fire. A good fire and a good great-coat and a good woollen neck-shawl, were comfortable things to see in conjunction with the toll-keeper; also his brisk wakefulness was excellent company when he rattled the change of halfpence down upon that metal table of his, like a man who defied the night, with all its sorrowful thoughts, and didn't care for the coming of dawn.   There was need of encouragement on the threshold of the bridge, for the bridge was dreary.   The chopped-up murdered man, had not been lowered with a rope over the parapet when those nights were; he was alive, and slept then quietly enough most likely, and undisturbed by any dream of where he was to come.   But the river had an awful look, the buildings on the banks were muffled in black shrouds, and the reflected lights seemed to originate deep in the water, as if the spectres of suicides were holding them to show where they went down.   The wild moon and clouds were as restless as an evil conscience in a tumbled bed, and the very shadow of the immensity of London seemed to lie oppressively upon the river.

Between the bridge and the two great theatres, there was but the distance of a few hundred paces, so the theatres came next.   Grim and black within, at night, those great dry Wells, and lonesome to imagine, with the rows of faces faded out, the lights extinguished, and the seats all empty. One would think that nothing in them knew itself at such a time but Yorick's skull.   In one of my night walks, as the church steeples were shaking the March winds and rain with strokes of Four, I passed the outer boundary of one of these great deserts, and entered it.   With a dim lantern in my hand, I groped my well-known way to the stage and looked over the orchestra—which was like a great grave dug for a time of pestilence—into the void beyond.   A dismal cavern of an immense aspect, with the chandelier gone dead like everything else, and nothing visible through mist and fog and space, but tiers of winding-sheets.   The ground at my feet where, when last there, I had seen the peasantry of Naples dancing among the vines, reckless of the burning mountain which threatened to overwhelm them, was now in possession of a strong serpent of engine-hose, watchfully lying in wait for the serpent Fire, and ready to fly at it if it showed its forked tongue.   A ghost of a watchman, carrying a faint corpse candle, haunted the distant upper gallery and flitted away.   Retiring within the proscenium, and holding my light above my head towards the rolled-up curtain—green no more, but black as ebony—my sight lost itself in a gloomy vault, showing faint indications in it of a shipwreck of canvas and cordage. Methought I felt much as a diver might, at the bottom of the sea.

In those small hours when there was no movement in the streets, it afforded matter for reflection to take Newgate in the way, and, touching its rough stone, to think of the prisoners in their sleep, and then to glance in at the lodge over the spiked wicket, and see the fire and light of the watching turnkeys, on the white wall. Not an inappropriate time either, to linger by that wicked little Debtors' Door—shutting tighter than any other door one ever saw—which has been Death's Door to so many. In the days of the uttering of forged one-pound notes by people tempted up from the country, how many hundreds of wretched creatures of both sexes—many quite innocent—swung out of a pitiless and inconsistent world, with the tower of yonder Christian church of Saint Sepulchre monstrously before their eyes! Is there any haunting of the Bank Parlour, by the remorseful souls of old directors, in the nights of these later days, I wonder, or is it as quiet as this degenerate Aceldama of an Old Bailey?

To walk on to the Bank, lamenting the good old times and bemoaning the present evil period, would be an easy next step, so I would take it, and would make my houseless circuit of the Bank, and give a thought to the treasure within; likewise to the guard of soldiers passing the night there, and nodding over the fire. Next, I went to Billingsgate, in some hope of market-people, but it proving as yet too early, crossed London-bridge and got down by the waterside on the Surrey shore among the buildings of the great brewery. There was plenty going on at the brewery; and the reek, and the smell of grains, and the rattling of the plump dray horses at their mangers, were capital company. Quite refreshed by having mingled with this good society, I made a new start with a new heart, setting the old King's Bench prison before me for my next object, and resolving, when I should come to the wall, to think of poor Horace Kinch, and the Dry Rot in men.

A very curious disease the Dry Rot in men, and difficult to detect the beginning of. It had carried Horace Kinch inside the wall of the old King's Bench prison, and it had

carried him out with his feet foremost. He was a likely
man to look at, in the prime of life, well to do, as clever as
he needed to be, and popular among many friends. He was
suitably married, and had healthy and pretty children.
But, like some fair-looking houses or fair-looking ships, he
took the Dry Rot. The first strong external revelation of
the Dry Rot in men, is a tendency to lurk and lounge; to
be at street-corners without intelligible reason; to be going
anywhere when met; to be about many places rather than
at any; to do nothing tangible, but to have an intention of
performing a variety of intangible duties to-morrow or the
day after. When this manifestation of the disease is
observed, the observer will usually connect it with a vague
impression once formed or received, that the patient was
living a little too hard. He will scarcely have had leisure
to turn it over in his mind and form the terrible suspicion
"Dry Rot," when he will notice a change for the worse in
the patient's appearance: a certain slovenliness and deterioration, which is not poverty, nor dirt, nor intoxication,
nor ill-health, but simply Dry Rot. To this, succeeds a smell
as of strong waters, in the morning; to that, a looseness
respecting money; to that, a stronger smell as of strong
waters, at all times; to that, a looseness respecting everything; to that, a trembling of the limbs, somnolency,
misery, and crumbling to pieces. As it is in wood, so it is
in men. Dry Rot advances at a compound usury quite incalculable. A plank is found infected with it, and the
whole structure is devoted. Thus it had been with the
unhappy Horace Kinch, lately buried by a small subscription. Those who knew him had not nigh done saying,
"So well off, so comfortably established, with such hope
before him—and yet, it is feared, with a slight touch of Dry
Rot!" when lo! the man was all Dry Rot and dust.

From the dead wall associated on those houseless nights
with this too common story, I chose next to wander by
Bethlehem Hospital; partly, because it lay on my road
round to Westminster; partly, because I had a night fancy
in my head which could be best pursued within sight of
its walls and dome. And the fancy was this: Are not the
sane and the insane equal at night as the sane lie a dreaming? Are not all of us outside this hospital, who dream,
more or less in the condition of those inside it, every night
of our lives? Are we not nightly persuaded, as they daily

are, that we associate preposterously with kings and queens, emperors and empresses, and notabilities of all sorts? Do we not nightly jumble events and personages and times and places, as these do daily? Are we not sometimes troubled by our own sleeping inconsistencies; and do we not vexedly try to account for them or excuse them, just as these do sometimes in respect of their waking delusions? Said an afflicted man to me, when I was last in a hospital like this, " Sir, I can frequently fly." I was half ashamed to reflect that so could I—by night. Said a woman to me on the same occasion, " Queen Victoria frequently comes to dine with me, and her Majesty and I dine off peaches and maccaroni in our night-gowns, and his Royal Highness the Prince Consort does us the honour to make a third on horseback in a Field-Marshal's uniform." Could I refrain from reddening with consciousness when I remembered the amazing royal parties I myself had given (at night), the unaccountable viands I had put on table, and my extraordinary manner of conducting myself on those distinguished occasions? I wonder that the great master who knew everything, when he called Sleep the death of each day's life, did not call Dreams the insanity of each day's sanity.

By this time I had left the Hospital behind me, and was again setting towards the river; and in a short breathing space I was on Westminster-bridge, regaling my houseless eyes with the external walls of the British Parliament—the perfection of a stupendous institution, I know, and the admiration of all surrounding nations and succeeding ages, I do not doubt, but perhaps a little the better now and then for being pricked up to its work. Turning off into Old Palace-yard, the Courts of Law kept me company for a quarter of an hour; hinting in low whispers what numbers of people they were keeping awake, and how intensely wretched and horrible they were rendering the small hours to unfortunate suitors. Westminster Abbey was fine gloomy society for another quarter of an hour; suggesting a wonderful procession of its dead among the dark arches and pillars, each century more amazed by the century following it than by all the centuries going before. And indeed in those houseless night walks—which even included cemeteries where watchmen went round among the graves at stated times, and moved the tell-tale handle of an index which recorded that they had touched it at such an hour—it was a solemn consideration what enormous hosts of dead belong to one old great city, and how, if they were raised while the living slept, there would not be the space of a pin's point in all the streets and ways for the living to come out into. Not only that, but the vast armies of dead would overflow the hills and valleys beyond the city, and would stretch away all round it, God knows how far.

When a church clock strikes, on houseless ears in the dead of the night, it may be at first mistaken for company and hailed as such. But, as the spreading circles of vibration, which you may perceive at such a time with great clearness, go opening out, for ever and ever afterwards widening perhaps (as the philosopher has suggested) in eternal space, the mistake is rectified and the sense of loneliness is profounder. Once—it was after leaving the Abbey and turning my face north—I came to the great steps of St. Martin's church as the clock was striking Three. Suddenly, a thing that in a moment more I should have trodden upon without seeing, rose up at my feet with a cry of loneliness and houselessness, struck out of it by the bell, the like of which I never heard. We then stood face to face looking at one another, frightened by one another. The creature was like a beetle-browed hair-lipped youth of twenty, and it had a loose bundle of rags on, which it held together with one of its hands. It shivered from head to foot, and its teeth chattered, and as it stared at me—persecutor, devil, ghost, whatever it thought me—it made with its whining mouth as if it were snapping at me, like a worried dog. Intending to give this ugly object money, I put out my hand to stay it—for it recoiled as it whined and snapped—and laid my hand upon its shoulder. Instantly, it twisted out of its garment, like the young man in the New Testament, and left me standing alone with its rags in my hands.

Covent-garden Market, when it was market morning, was wonderful company. The great waggons of cabbages, with growers' men and boys lying asleep under them, and with sharp dogs from market-garden neighbourhoods looking after the whole, were as good as a party. But one of the worst night sights I know in London, is to be found in the children who prowl about this place; who sleep in the baskets, fight for the offal, dart at any object they think they can lay their thieving hands on, dive under the carts and barrows, dodge the constables, and are perpetually making a blunt pattering on the pavement of the Piazza with the rain of their naked feet. A painful and unnatural result comes of the comparison one is forced to institute between the growth of corruption as displayed in the so much improved and cared for fruits of the earth, and the growth of corruption as displayed in these all uncared for (except inasmuch as ever-hunted) savages.

There was early coffee to be got about Covent-garden Market, and that was more company—warm company, too, which was better. Toast of a very substantial quality, was likewise procurable: though the towzled-headed man who made it, in an inner chamber within the coffee-room, hadn't got his coat on yet, and was so heavy with sleep that in every interval of toast and coffee he went off anew behind the partition into complicated cross-roads of choke and snore, and lost his way directly. Into one of these establishments (among the earliest) near Bow-street, there came one morning as I sat over my houseless cup, pondering where to go next, a man in a high and long snuff-coloured coat, and shoes, and, to the best of my belief, nothing else but a hat, who took out of his hat a large cold meat pudding; a meat pudding so large that it was a very tight fit, and brought the lining of the hat out with it. This mysterious man was known by his pudding, for on his entering, the man of sleep brought him a pint of hot tea, a small loaf, and a large knife and fork and plate. Left to himself in his box, he stood the pudding on the bare table, and, instead of cutting it, stabbed it, overhand, with the knife, like a mortal enemy; then took the knife out, wiped it on his sleeve, tore the pudding asunder with his fingers, and ate it all up. The remembrance of this man with the pudding remains with me as the remembrance of the most spectral person my houselessness encountered. Twice only was I in that establishment, and twice I saw him stalk in (as I should say, just out of bed, and presently going back to bed), take out his pudding, stab his pudding, wipe the dagger, and eat his pudding all up. He was a man whose figure promised cadaverousness, but who had an excessively red face, though shaped like a horse's. On the second occasion of my seeing him, he said huskily to the man of sleep, "Am I red to-night?" "You are," he uncompromisingly answered. "My mother," said the spectre, "was a red-faced woman that liked drink, and I looked at her

hard when she laid in her coffin, and I took the complexion."
Somehow, the pudding seemed an unwholesome pudding
after that, and I put myself in its way no more.

When there was no market, or when I wanted variety,
a railway terminus with the morning mails coming in, was
remunerative company. But like most of the company to
be had in this world, it lasted only a very short time. The
station lamps would burst out ablaze, the porters would
emerge from places of concealment, the cabs and trucks
would rattle to their places (the post-office carts were already
in theirs), and, finally, the bell would strike up, and the train
would come banging in. But there were few passengers and
little luggage, and everything scuttled away with the greatest
expedition. The locomotive post-offices, with their great
nets—as if they had been dragging the country for bodies—
would fly open as to their doors, and would disgorge a smell
of lamp, an exhausted clerk, a guard in a red coat, and their
bags of letters; the engine would blow and heave and
perspire, like an engine wiping its forehead and saying
what a run it had had; and within ten minutes the lamps
were out, and I was houseless and alone again.

But now, there were driven cattle on the high road near,
wanting (as cattle always do) to turn into the midst of stone
walls, and squeeze themselves through six inches' width of
iron railing, and getting their heads down (also as cattle
always do) for tossing-purchase at quite imaginary dogs, and
giving themselves and every devoted creature associated with
them a most extraordinary amount of unnecessary trouble.
Now, too, the conscious gas began to grow pale with the
knowledge that daylight was coming, and straggling workpeople were already in the streets, and, as waking life had
become extinguished with the last pieman's sparks, so it
began to be rekindled with the fires of the first street-corner
breakfast-sellers. And so by faster and faster degrees, until
the last degrees were very fast, the day came, and I was tired
and could sleep. And it is not, as I used to think, going
home at such times, the least wonderful thing in London,
that in the real desert region of the night, the houseless
wanderer is alone there. I knew well enough where to
find Vice and Misfortune of all kinds, if I had chosen ; but
they were put out of sight, and my houselessness had many
miles upon miles of streets in which it could, and did, have
its own solitary way.

XIV

CHAMBERS

HAVING occasion to transact some business with a solicitor who occupies a highly suicidal set of chambers in Gray's Inn, I afterwards took a turn in the large square of that stronghold of Melancholy, reviewing, with congenial surroundings, my experiences of Chambers.

I began, as was natural, with the Chambers I had just left. They were an upper set on a rotten staircase, with a mysterious bunk or bulkhead on the landing outside them, of a rather nautical and Screw Collier-like appearance than otherwise, and painted an intense black. Many dusty years have passed since the appropriation of this Davy Jones's locker to any purpose, and during the whole period within the memory of living man, it has been hasped and padlocked. I cannot quite satisfy my mind whether it was originally meant for the reception of coals, or bodies, or as a place of temporary security for the plunder "looted" by laundresses ; but I incline to the last opinion. It is about breast high, and usually serves as a bulk for defendants in reduced circumstances to lean against and ponder at, when they come on the hopeful errand of trying to make an arrangement without money—under which auspicious circumstances it mostly happens that the legal gentleman they want to see, is much engaged, and they pervade the staircase for a considerable period. Against this opposing bulk, in the absurdest manner, the tomb-like outer door of the solicitor's chambers (which is also of an intense black) stands in dark ambush, half open, and half shut, all day. The solicitor's apartments are three in number ; consisting of a slice, a cell, and a wedge. The slice is assigned to the two clerks, the cell is occupied by the principal, and the wedge is devoted to stray papers, old game baskets from the country, a washing-stand, and a model of a patent Ship's Caboose which was exhibited in Chancery at the commencement of the present century on an application for an injunction to restrain infringement. At about half-past nine on every week-day morning, the younger of the two clerks (who, I have reason to believe, leads the fashion at Pentonville in the articles of pipes and shirts) may be found knocking the dust out of his official door-key on the bunk or locker before mentioned; and so exceedingly subject to dust is his key, and so very retentive of that superfluity, that in exceptional summer weather when a ray of sunlight has fallen on the locker in my presence, I have noticed its inexpressive countenance to be deeply marked by a kind of Bramah erysipelas or small-pox.

This set of chambers (as I have gradually discovered, when I have had restless occasion to make inquiries or leave messages, after office hours) is under the charge of a lady named Sweeney, in figure extremely like an old family-umbrella: whose dwelling confronts a dead wall in a court off Gray's Inn-lane, and who is usually fetched into the passage of that bower, when wanted, from some neighbouring home of industry, which has the curious property of imparting an inflammatory appearance to her visage. Mrs. Sweeney is one of the race of professed laundresses, and is the compiler of a remarkable manuscript volume entitled "Mrs. Sweeney's Book," from which much curious statistical information may be gathered respecting the high prices and small uses of soda, soap, sand, firewood, and other such articles. I have created a legend in my mind —and consequently I believe it with the utmost pertinacity —that the late Mr. Sweeney was a ticket-porter under the Honourable Society of Gray's Inn, and that, in considera-tion of his long and valuable services, Mrs. Sweeney was appointed to her present post. For, though devoid of personal charms, I have observed this lady to exercise a fascination over the elderly ticket-porter mind (particularly under the gateway, and in corners and entries), which I can only refer to her being one of the fraternity, yet not com-peting with it. All that need be said concerning this set of chambers, is said, when I have added that it is in a large double house in Gray's Inn-square, very much out of repair, and that the outer portal is ornamented in a hideous manner with certain stone remains, which have the appearance of the dismembered bust, torso, and limbs of a petrified bencher.

Indeed, I look upon Gray's Inn generally as one of the most depressing institutions in brick and mortar, known to

the children of men. Can anything be more dreary than its
arid Square, Sahara Desert of the law, with the ugly old
tiled-topped tenements, the dirty windows, the bills To Let,
To Let, the door-posts inscribed like gravestones, the crazy
gateway giving upon the filthy Lane, the scowling iron-
barred prison-like passage into Verulam-buildings, the
mouldy red-nosed ticket-porters with little coffin plates,
and why with aprons, the dry hard atomy-like appearance
of the whole dust-heap? When my uncommercial travels
tend to this dismal spot, my comfort is its rickety state.
Imagination gloats over the fulness of time when the
staircases shall have quite tumbled down—they are daily
wearing into an ill-savoured powder, but have not quite
tumbled down yet—when the last old prolix bencher all
of the olden time, shall have been got out of an upper
window by means of a Fire Ladder, and carried off to the
Holborn Union ; when the last clerk shall have engrossed
the last parchment behind the last splash on the last of the
mud-stained windows, which, all through the miry year,
are pilloried out of recognition in Gray's Inn-lane. Then,
shall a squalid little trench, with rank grass and a pump
in it, lying between the coffee-house and South-square, be
wholly given up to cats and rats, and not, as now, have its
empire divided between those animals and a few briefless
bipeds—surely called to the Bar by voices of deceiving
spirits, seeing that they are wanted there by no mortal—
who glance down, with eyes better glazed than their case-
ments, from their dreary and lack-lustre rooms. Then shall
the way Nor' Westward, now lying under a short grim
colonnade where in summer-time pounce flies from law-
stationering windows into the eyes of laymen, be choked
with rubbish and happily become impassable. Then shall
the gardens where turf, trees, and gravel wear a legal livery
of black, run rank, and pilgrims go to Gorhambury to see
Bacon's effigy as he sat, and not come here (which in truth
they seldom do) to see where he walked. Then, in a word,
shall the old-established vendor of periodicals sit alone in
his little crib of a shop behind the Holborn Gate, like that
lumbering Marius among the ruins of Carthage, who has sat
heavy on a thousand million of similes.

At one period of my uncommercial career I much
frequented another set of chambers in Gray's Inn-square.
They were what is familiarly called "a top set," and all

Laundresses

the eatables and drinkables introduced into them acquired a flavour of Cockloft. I have known an unopened Strasbourg pâté fresh from Fortnum and Mason's, to draw in this cockloft tone through its crockery dish, and become penetrated with cockloft to the core of its inmost truffle in three-quarters of an hour. This, however, was not the most curious feature of those chambers; that, consisted in the profound conviction entertained by my esteemed friend Parkle (their tenant) that they were clean. Whether it was an inborn hallucination, or whether it was imparted to him by Mrs. Miggot the laundress, I never could ascertain. But, I believe he would have gone to the stake upon the question. Now, they were so dirty that I could take off the distinctest impression of my figure on any article of furniture by merely lounging upon it for a few moments; and it used to be a private amusement of mine to print myself off—if I may use the expression—all over the rooms. It was the first large circulation I had. At other times I have accidentally shaken a window curtain while in animated conversation with Parkle, and struggling insects which were certainly red, and were certainly not ladybirds, have dropped on the back of my hand. Yet Parkle lived in that top set years, bound body and soul to the superstition that they were clean. He used to say, when congratulated upon them, "Well, they are not like chambers in one respect, you know; they are clean." Concurrently, he had an idea which he could never explain, that Mrs. Miggot was in some way connected with the Church. When he was in particularly good spirits, he used to believe that a deceased uncle of hers had been a Dean; when he was poorly and low, he believed that her brother had been a Curate. I and Mrs. Miggot (she was a genteel woman) were on confidential terms, but I never knew her to commit herself to any distinct assertion on the subject; she merely claimed a proprietorship in the Church, by looking when it was mentioned, as if the reference awakened the slumbering Past, and were personal. It may have been his amiable confidence in Mrs. Miggot's better days that inspired my friend with his delusion respecting the chambers, but he never wavered in his fidelity to it for a moment, though he wallowed in dirt seven years.

Two of the windows of these chambers looked down into the garden; and we have sat up there together many a

summer evening. saying how pleasant it was, and talking of
many things. To my intimacy with that top set, I am
indebted for three of my liveliest personal impressions of
the loneliness of life in chambers. They shall follow here,
in order; first, second, and third.

First. My Gray's Inn friend, on a time, hurt one of his
legs, and it became seriously inflamed. Not knowing of his
indisposition, I was on my way to visit him as usual, one
summer evening, when I was much surprised by meeting
a lively leech in Field-court, Gray's Inn, seemingly on his
way to the West End of London. As the leech was alone,
and was of course unable to explain his position, even if he
had been inclined to do so (which he had not the appearance
of being), I passed him and went on. Turning the corner of
Gray's Inn-square, I was beyond expression amazed by meeting another leech—also entirely alone, and also proceeding
in a westerly direction, though with less decision of purpose.
Ruminating on this extraordinary circumstance, and endeavouring to remember whether I had ever read, in the
Philosophical Transactions or any work on Natural History,
of a migration of Leeches, I ascended to the top set, past the
dreary series of closed outer doors of offices and an empty set
or two, which intervened between that lofty region and the
surface. Entering my friend's rooms, I found him stretched
upon his back, like Prometheus Bound, with a perfectly
demented ticket-porter in attendance on him instead of the
Vulture: which helpless individual, who was feeble and
frightened, and had (my friend explained to me, in great
choler) been endeavouring for some hours to apply leeches to
his leg, and as yet had only got on two out of twenty. To
this Unfortunate's distraction between a damp cloth on
which he had placed the leeches to freshen them, and the
wrathful adjurations of my friend to "Stick 'em on, sir!"
I referred the phenomenon I had encountered: the rather
as two fine specimens were at that moment going out at the
door, while a general insurrection of the rest was in progress
on the table. After a while our united efforts prevailed, and,
when the leeches came off and had recovered their spirits,
we carefully tied them up in a decanter. But I never heard
more of them than that they were all gone next morning,
and that the Out-of-door young man of Bickle Bush and
Bodger, on the ground floor, had been bitten and blooded
by some creature not identified. They never "took" on

Mrs. Miggot, the laundress; but, I have always preserved fresh, the belief that she unconsciously carried several about her, until they gradually found openings in life.

Second. On the same staircase with my friend Parkle, and on the same floor, there lived a man of law who pursued his business elsewhere, and used those chambers as his place of residence. For three or four years, Parkle rather knew of him than knew him, but after that—for Englishmen—short pause of consideration, they began to speak. Parkle exchanged words with him in his private character only, and knew nothing of his business ways, or means. He was a man a good deal about town, but always alone. We used to remark to one another, that although we often encountered him in theatres, concert-rooms, and similar public places, he was always alone. Yet he was not a gloomy man, and was of a decidedly conversational turn; insomuch that he would sometimes of an evening lounge with a cigar in his mouth, half in and half out of Parkle's rooms, and discuss the topics of the day by the hour. He used to hint on these occasions that he had four faults to find with life; firstly, that it obliged a man to be always winding up his watch; secondly, that London was too small; thirdly, that it therefore wanted variety; fourthly, that there was too much dust in it. There was so much dust in his own faded chambers, certainly, that they reminded me of a sepulchre, furnished in prophetic anticipation of the present time, which had newly been brought to light, after having remained buried a few thousand years. One dry hot autumn evening at twilight, this man, being then five years turned of fifty, looked in upon Parkle in his usual lounging way, with his cigar in his mouth as usual, and said, "I am going out of town." As he never went out of town, Parkle said, "Oh indeed! At last?" "Yes," says he, "at last. For what is a man to do? London is so small! If you go West, you come to Hounslow. If you go East, you come to Bow. If you go South, there's Brixton or Norwood. If you go North, you can't get rid of Barnet. Then, the monotony of all the streets, streets, streets—and of all the roads, roads, roads—and the dust, dust, dust!" When he had said this, he wished Parkle a good evening, but came back again and said, with his watch in his hand, "Oh, I really cannot go on winding up this watch over and over again; I wish you would take care

of it." So, Parkle laughed and consented, and the man went
out of town. The man remained out of town so long, that
his letter-box became choked, and no more letters could be
got into it, and they began to be left at the lodge and to
accumulate there. At last the head-porter decided, on conference with the steward, to use his master-key and look into
the chambers, and give them the benefit of a whiff of air.
Then, it was found that he had hanged himself to his bedstead, and had left this written memorandum: "I should
prefer to be cut down by my neighbour and friend (if he
will allow me to call him so), H. Parkle, Esq." This was
an end of Parkle's occupancy of chambers. He went into
lodgings immediately.

Third. While Parkle lived in Gray's Inn, and I myself
was uncommercially preparing for the Bar—which is done,
as everybody knows, by having a frayed old gown put on
in a pantry by an old woman in a chronic state of Saint
Anthony's fire and dropsy, and, so decorated, bolting a bad
dinner in a party of four, whereof each individual mistrusts
the other three—I say, while these things were, there was
a certain elderly gentleman who lived in a court of the
Temple, and was a great judge and lover of port wine.
Every day he dined at his club and drank his bottle or two
of port wine, and every night came home to the Temple and
went to bed in his lonely chambers. This had gone on
many years without variation, when one night he had a fit
on coming home, and fell and cut his head deep, but partly
recovered and groped about in the dark to find the door.
When he was afterwards discovered, dead, it was clearly
established by the marks of his hands about the room that he
must have done so. Now, this chanced on the night of
Christmas Eve, and over him lived a young fellow who had
sisters and young country friends, and who gave them a
little party that night, in the course of which they played
at Blindman's Buff. They played that game, for their
greater sport, by the light of the fire only; and once, when
they were all quietly rustling and stealing about, and the
blindman was trying to pick out the prettiest sister (for
which I am far from blaming him), somebody cried, Hark!
The man below must be playing Blindman's Buff by himself
to-night! They listened, and they heard sounds of some
one falling about and stumbling against furniture, and they
all laughed at the conceit, and went on with their play,

more light-hearted and merry than ever. Thus, those two so different games of life and death were played out together, blindfolded, in the two sets of chambers.

Such are the occurrences, which, coming to my knowledge, imbued me long ago with a strong sense of the loneliness of chambers. There was a fantastic illustration to much the same purpose implicitly believed by a strange sort of man now dead, whom I knew when I had not quite arrived at legal years of discretion, though I was already in the un-commercial line.

This was a man who, though not more than thirty, had seen the world in divers irreconcilable capacities—had been an officer in a South American regiment among other odd things—but had not achieved much in any way of life, and was in debt, and in hiding. He occupied chambers of the dreariest nature in Lyons Inn; his name, however, was not up on the door, or door-post, but in lieu of it stood the name of a friend who died in the chambers, and had given him the furniture. The story arose out of the furniture, and was to this effect :—Let the former holder of the chambers, whose name was still upon the door and door-post, be Mr. Testator.

Mr. Testator took a set of chambers in Lyons Inn when he had but very scanty furniture for his bedroom, and none for his sitting-room. He had lived some wintry months in this condition, and had found it very bare and cold. One night, past midnight, when he sat writing and still had writing to do that must be done before he went to bed, he found himself out of coals. He had coals down-stairs, but had never been to his cellar; however the cellar-key was on his mantelshelf, and if he went down and opened the cellar it fitted, he might fairly assume the coals in that cellar to be his. As to his laundress, she lived among the coal-waggons and Thames watermen—for there were Thames watermen at that time—in some unknown rat-hole by the river, down lanes and alleys on the other side of the Strand. As to any other person to meet him or obstruct him, Lyons Inn was dreaming, drunk, maudlin, moody, betting, brooding over bill-discounting or renewing—asleep or awake, minding its own affairs. Mr. Testator took his coal-scuttle in one hand, his candle and key in the other, and descended to the dismallest underground dens of Lyons Inn, where the late vehicles in the streets became thunderous, and all the water-pipes in the neighbourhood seemed to have Macbeth's Amen sticking in their throats, and to be trying to get it out. After groping here and there among low doors to no purpose, Mr. Testator at length came to a door with a rusty padlock which his key fitted. Getting the door open with much trouble, and looking in, he found, no coals, but a confused pile of furniture. Alarmed by this intrusion on another man's property, he locked the door again, found his own cellar, filled his scuttle, and returned up-stairs.

But the furniture he had seen, ran on castors across and across Mr. Testator's mind incessantly, when, in the chill hour of five in the morning, he got to bed. He particularly wanted a table to write at, and a table expressly made to be written at, had been the piece of furniture in the foreground of the heap. When his laundress emerged from her burrow in the morning to make his kettle boil, he artfully led up to the subject of cellars and furniture; but the two ideas had evidently no connexion in her mind. When she left him, and he sat at his breakfast, thinking about the furniture, he recalled the rusty state of the padlock, and inferred that the furniture must have been stored in the cellars for a long time —was perhaps forgotten—owner dead, perhaps? After thinking it over, a few days, in the course of which he could pump nothing out of Lyons Inn about the furniture, he became desperate, and resolved to borrow that table. He did so, that night. He had not had the table long, when he determined to borrow an easy-chair; he had not had that long, when he made up his mind to borrow a bookcase; then, a couch; then, a carpet and rug. By that time, he felt he was "in furniture stepped in so far," as that it could be no worse to borrow it all. Consequently, he borrowed it all, and locked up the cellar for good. He had always locked it, after every visit. He had carried up every separate article' in the dead of the night, and, at the best, had felt as wicked as a Resurrection Man. Every article was blue and furry when brought into his rooms, and he had had, in a murder-ous and guilty sort of way, to polish it up while London slept.

Mr. Testator lived in his furnished chambers two or three years, or more, and gradually lulled himself into the opinion that the furniture was his own. This was his convenient state of mind when, late one night, a step came up the stairs, and a hand passed over his door feeling for his knocker, and then one deep and solemn rap was rapped that might have been a spring in Mr. Testator's easy-chair to shoot him out of it; so promptly was it attended with that effect.

With a candle in his hand, Mr. Testator went to the door, and found there a very pale and very tall man; a man who stooped; a man with very high shoulders, a very narrow chest, and a very red nose; a shabby-genteel man. He was wrapped in a long threadbare black coat, fastened up the front with more pins than buttons, and under his arm he squeezed an umbrella without a handle, as if he were playing bagpipes. He said, "I ask your pardon, but can you tell me—" and stopped; his eyes resting on some object within the chambers.

"Can I tell you what?" asked Mr. Testator, noting his stoppage with quick alarm.

"I ask your pardon," said the stranger, "but—this is not the inquiry I was going to make—*do* I see in there, any small article of property belonging to *me*?"

Mr. Testator was beginning to stammer that he was not aware—when the visitor slipped past him into the chambers. There, in a goblin way which froze Mr. Testator to the marrow, he examined, first, the writing-table, and said, "Mine;" then, the easy-chair, and said, "Mine;" then, the bookcase, and said, "Mine;" then, turned up a corner of the carpet, and said, "Mine!"—in a word, inspected every item of furniture from the cellar, in succession, and said, "Mine!" Towards the end of this investigation, Mr. Testator perceived that he was sodden with liquor, and that the liquor was gin. He was not unsteady with gin, either in his speech or carriage; but he was stiff with gin in both particulars.

Mr. Testator was in a dreadful state, for (according to his making out of the story) the possible consequences of what he had done in recklessness and hardihood, flashed upon him in their fulness for the first time. When they had stood gazing at one another for a little while, he tremulously began:

"Sir, I am conscious that the fullest explanation, compensation, and restitution, are your due. They shall be yours. Allow me to entreat that, without temper, without even natural irritation on your part, we may have a little—"

"Drop of something to drink," interposed the stranger. "I am agreeable."

Mr. Testator had intended to say, "a little quiet conversation," but with great relief of mind adopted the amendment. He produced a decanter of gin, and was bustling about for hot water and sugar, when he found that his visitor had already drunk half of the decanter's contents. With hot water and sugar the visitor drank the remainder before he had been an hour in the chambers by the chimes of the church of St. Mary in the Strand; and during the process he frequently whispered to himself, "Mine!"

The gin gone, and Mr. Testator wondering what was to follow it, the visitor rose and said, with increased stiffness, "At what hour of the morning, sir, will it be convenient?" Mr. Testator hazarded, "At ten?" "Sir," said the visitor, "at ten, to the moment, I shall be here." He then contemplated Mr. Testator somewhat at leisure, and said, "God bless you! How is your wife?" Mr. Testator (who never had a wife) replied with much feeling, "Deeply anxious, poor soul, but otherwise well." The visitor thereupon turned and went away, and fell twice in going down-stairs. From that hour he was never heard of. Whether he was a ghost, or a spectral illusion of conscience, or a drunken man who had no business there, or the drunken rightful owner of the furniture, with a transitory gleam of memory; whether he got safe home, or had no home to get to; whether he died of liquor on the way, or lived in liquor ever afterwards; he n·ver was heard of more. This was the story, received with the furniture and held to be as substantial, by its second possessor in an upper set of chambers in grim Lyons Inn.

It is to be remarked of chambers in general, that they must have been built for chambers, to have the right kind of loneliness. You may make a great dwelling-house very lonely, by isolating suites of rooms and calling them chambers, but you cannot make the true kind of loneliness. In dwelling-houses, there have been family festivals; children have grown in them, girls have bloomed into women in them, courtships and marriages have taken place in them. True chambers never were young, childish, maidenly; never had dolls in them, or rocking-horses, or christenings, or betrothals, or little coffins. Let Gray's Inn identify the child who first touched hands and hearts with Robinson Crusoe, in any one of its many "sets," and that child's little statue, in white marble with a golden inscription, shall be at its service, at my cost and charge, as a drinking fountain for

the spirit, to freshen its thirsty square. Let Lincoln's produce from all its houses, a twentieth of the procession
derivable from any dwelling-house one-twentieth of its age,
of fair young brides who married for love and hope, not
settlements, and all the Vice-Chancellors shall thence-for-
ward be kept in nosegays for nothing, on application to the
writer hereof. It is not denied that on the terrace of the
Adelphi, or in any of the streets of that subterranean-stable-
haunted spot, or about Bedford-row, or James-street of that
ilk (a grewsome place), or anywhere among the neighbourhoods that have done flowering and have run to seed, you
may find Chambers replete with the accommodations of
Solitude, Closeness, and Darkness, where you may be as
low-spirited as in the genuine article, and might be as easily
murdered, with the placid reputation of having merely gone
down to the sea-side. But, the many waters of life did run
musical in those dry channels once ;—among the Inns, never.
The only popular legend known in relation to any one of
the dull family of Inns, is a dark Old Bailey whisper concerning Clement's, and importing how the black creature
who holds the sun-dial there, was a negro who slew his
master and built the dismal pile out of the contents of his
strong box—for which architectural offence alone he ought
to have been condemned to live in it. But, what populace
would waste fancy upon such a place, or on New Inn, Staple
Inn, Barnard's Inn, or any of the shabby crew ?

The genuine laundress, too, is an institution not to be
had in its entirety out of and away from the genuine
Chambers. Again, it is not denied that you may be robbed
elsewhere. Elsewhere you may have—for money—dishonesty, drunkenness, dirt, laziness, and profound in-
capacity. But the veritable shining-red-faced shameless
laundress ; the true Mrs. Sweeney—in figure, colour,
texture, and smell, like the old damp family umbrella ; the
tip-top complicated abomination of stockings, spirits, bonnet,
limpness, looseness, and larceny ; is only to be drawn at
the fountain-head. Mrs. Sweeney is beyond the reach of
individual art. It requires the united efforts of several
men to ensure that great result, and it is only developed in
perfection under an Honourable Society and in an Inn of
Court.

XV

THERE are not many places that I find it more agreeable to revisit when I am in an idle mood, than some places to which I have never been. For, my acquaintance with those spots is of such long standing, and has ripened into an intimacy of so· affectionate a nature, that I take a particular interest in assuring myself that they are unchanged.

I never was in Robinson Crusoe's Island, yet I frequently return there. The colony he established on it soon faded away, and it is uninhabited by any descendants of the grave and courteous Spaniards, or of Will Atkins and the other mutineers, and has relapsed into its original condition. Not a twig of its wicker houses remains, its goats have long run wild again, its screaming parrots would darken the sun with a cloud of many flaming colours if a gun were fired there, no face is ever reflected in the waters of the little creek which Friday swam across when pursued by his two brother cannibals with sharpened stomachs. After comparing notes with other travellers who have similarly revisited the Island and conscientiously inspected it, I have satisfied myself that it contains no vestige of Mr. Atkins's domesticity or theology, though his track on the memorable evening of his landing to set his captain ashore, when he was decoyed about and round about until it was dark, and his boat was stove, and his strength and spirits failed him, is yet plainly to be traced. So is the hill-top on which Robinson was struck dumb with joy when the reinstated captain pointed to the ship, riding within half a mile of the shore, that was to bear him away, in the nine-and-twentieth year of his seclusion in that lonely place. So is the sandy beach on which the memorable footstep was impressed, and where the savages hauled up their canoes when they came ashore for those dreadful public dinners, which led to a dancing worse than speech-making. So is the cave where the flaring eyes of the old goat made such a goblin appearance in the dark. So is the site of the hut where Robinson lived with the dog and the parrot and the cat, and where he endured those first agonies of solitude, which —strange to say—never involved any ghostly fancies; a circumstance so very remarkable, that perhaps he left out something in writing his record? Round hundreds of such objects, hidden in the dense tropical foliage, the tropical sea breaks evermore; and over them the tropical sky, saving in the short rainy season, shines bright and cloudless.

Neither was I ever belated among wolves, on the borders of France and Spain; nor did I ever, when night was closing in and the ground was covered with snow, draw up my little company among some felled trees which served as a breast-work, and there fire a train of gunpowder so dexterously that suddenly we had three or four score blazing wolves illuminating the darkness around us. Nevertheless, I occasionally go back to that dismal region and perform the feat again; when indeed to smell the singeing and the frying of the wolves afire, and to see them setting one another alight as they rush and tumble, and to behold them rolling in the snow vainly attempting to put themselves out, and to hear their howlings taken up by all the echoes as well as by all the unseen wolves within the woods, makes me tremble.

I was never in the robbers' cave, where Gil Blas lived, but I often go back there and find the trap-door just as heavy to raise as it used to be, while that wicked old disabled Black lies everlastingly cursing in bed. I was never in Don Quixote's study, where he read his books of chivalry until he rose and hacked at imaginary giants, and then refreshed himself with great draughts of water, yet you couldn't move a book in it without my knowledge, or with my consent. I was never (thank Heaven) in company with the little old woman who hobbled out of the chest and told the merchant Abudah to go in search of the Talisman of Oromanes, yet I make it my business to know that she is well preserved and as intolerable as ever. I was never at the school where the boy Horatio Nelson got out of bed to steal the pears: not because he wanted any, but because every other boy was afraid: yet I have several times been back to this Academy, to see him let down out of window with a sheet. So with Damascus, and Bagdad, and Brobingnag (which has the curious fate of being usually misspelt when written), and Lilliput, and Laputa, and the Nile, and Abyssinia, and the Ganges, and the North Pole, and many hundreds' of places—I was never at them, yet it is an affair of my life to keep them intact, and I am always going back to them.

But, when I was at Dullborough one day, revisiting the associations of my childhood as recorded in previous pages of these notes, my experience in this wise was made quite inconsiderable and of no account, by the quantity of places and people—utterly impossible places and people, but none the less alarmingly real—that I found I had been introduced to by my nurse before I was six years old, and used to be forced to go back to at night without at all wanting to go. If we all knew our own minds (in a more enlarged sense than the popular acceptation of that phrase), I suspect we should find our nurses responsible for most of the dark corners we are forced to go back to, against our wills.

The first diabolical character who intruded himself on my peaceful youth (as I called to mind that day at Dullborough), was a certain Captain Murderer. This wretch must have been an offshoot of the Blue Beard family, but I had no suspicion of the consanguinity in those times. His warning name would seem to have awakened no general prejudice against him, for he was admitted into the best society and possessed immense wealth. Captain Murderer's mission was matrimony, and the gratification of a cannibal appetite with tender brides. On his marriage morning, he always caused both sides of the way to church to be planted with curious flowers; and when his bride said, "Dear Captain Murderer, I never saw flowers like these before: what are they called?" he answered, "They are called Garnish for house-lamb," and laughed at his ferocious practical joke in a horrid manner, disquieting the minds of the noble bridal company, with a very sharp show of teeth, then displayed for the first time. He made love in a coach and six, and married in a coach and twelve, and all his horses were milk-white horses with one red spot on the back which he caused to be hidden by the harness. For, the spot *would* come there, though every horse was milk-white when Captain Murderer bought him. And the spot was young bride's blood,

(To this terrific point I am indebted for my first personal experience of a shudder and cold beads on the forehead.) When Captain Murderer had made an end of feasting and revelry, and had dismissed the noble guests, and was alone with his wife on the day month after their marriage, it was his whimsical custom to produce a golden rolling-pin and a silver pie-board. Now, there was this special feature in the Captain's courtships, that he always asked if the young lady could make pie-crust; and if she couldn't by nature or education, she was taught. Well. When the bride saw Captain Murderer produce the golden rolling-pin and silver pie-board, she remembered this, and turned up her laced-silk sleeves to make a pie. The Captain brought out a silver pie-dish of immense capacity, and the Captain brought out flour and butter and eggs and all things needful, except the inside of the pie; of materials for the staple of the pie itself, the Captain brought out none. Then said the lovely bride, " Dear Captain Murderer, what pie is this to be ? " He replied, " A meat pie." Then said the lovely bride, " Dear Captain Murderer, I see no meat." The Captain humorously retorted, " Look in the glass." She looked in the glass, but still she saw no meat, and then the Captain roared with laughter, and suddenly frowning and drawing his sword, bade her roll out the crust. So she rolled out the crust, dropping large tears upon it all the time because he was so cross, and when she had lined the dish with crust and had cut the crust all ready to fit the top, the Captain called out, " *I* see the meat in the glass ! " And the bride looked up at the glass, just in time to see the Captain cutting her head off; and he chopped her in pieces, and peppered her, and salted her, and put her in the pie, and sent it to the baker's, and ate it all, and picked the bones.

Captain Murderer went on in this way, prospering exceedingly, until he came to choose a bride from two twin sisters, and at first didn't know which to choose. For, though one was fair and the other dark, they were both equally beautiful. But the fair twin loved him, and the dark twin hated him, so he chose the fair one. The dark twin would have prevented the marriage if she could, but she couldn't; however, on the night before it, much suspecting Captain Murderer, she stole out and climbed his garden wall, and looked in at his window through a chink in the shutter, and saw him having his teeth filed sharp. Next day she listened all day, and heard him make his joke about the house-lamb. And that day month, he had the paste rolled out, and cut the fair twin's head off, and chopped her in pieces, and peppered her, and salted her, and put her in the pie, and sent it to the baker's, and ate it all. and picked the bones.

Now, the dark twin had had her suspicions much in-creased by the filing of the Captain's teeth, and again by the house-lamb joke. Putting all things together when he gave out that her sister was dead, she divined the truth, and determined to be revenged. So, she went up to Captain Murderer's house, and knocked at the knocker and pulled at the bell, and when the Captain came to the door, said : " Dear Captain Murderer, marry me next, for I always loved you and was jealous of my sister." The Captain took it as a compliment, and made a polite answer, and the marriage was quickly arranged. On the night before it, the bride again climbed to his window, and again saw him having his teeth filed sharp. At this sight she laughed such a terrible laugh at the chink in the shutter, that the Captain's blood curdled, and he said : " I hope nothing has disagreed with me ! " At that, she laughed again, a still more terrible laugh, and the shutter was opened and search made, but she was nimbly gone, and there was no one. Next day they went to church in a coach and twelve, and were married. And that day month, she rolled the pie-crust out, and Captain Murderer cut her head off, and chopped her in pieces, and peppered her, and salted her, and put her in the pie, and sent it to the baker's, and ate it all, and picked the bones.

But before she began to roll out the paste she had taken a deadly poison of a most awful character, distilled from toads' eyes and spiders' knees ; and Captain Murderer had hardly picked her last bone, when he began to swell, and to turn blue, and to be all over spots, and to scream. And he went on swelling and turning bluer, and being more all over spots and screaming, until he reached from floor to ceiling and from wall to wall; and then, at one o'clock in the morning, he blew up with a loud explosion. At the sound of it, all the milk-white horses in the stables broke their halters and went mad, and then they galloped over every-body in Captain Murderer's house (beginning with the family blacksmith who had filed his teeth) until the whole were dead, and then they galloped away.

Hundreds of times did I hear this legend of Captain Murderer, in my early youth, and added hundreds of times was there a mental compulsion upon me in bed, to peep in at his window as the dark twin peeped, and to revisit his horrible house, and look at him in his blue and spotty and screaming stage, as he reached from floor to ceiling and from wall to wall. The young woman who brought me acquainted with Captain Murderer had a fiendish enjoyment of my terrors, and used to begin, I remember—as a sort of introductory overture—by clawing the air with both hands, and uttering a long low hollow groan. So acutely did I suffer from this ceremony in combination with this infernal Captain, that I sometimes used to plead I thought I was hardly strong enough and old enough to hear the story again just yet. But, she never spared me one word of it, and indeed commended the awful chalice to my lips as the only preservative known to science against "The Black Cat"—a weird and glaring-eyed supernatural Tom, who was reputed to prowl about the world by night, sucking the breath of infancy, and who was endowed with a special thirst (as I was given to understand) for mine.

This female bard—may she have been repaid my debt of obligation to her in the matter of nightmares and perspirations!—reappears in my memory as the daughter of a shipwright. Her name was Mercy, though she had none on me. There was something of a shipbuilding flavour in the following story. As it always recurs to me in a vague association with calomel pills, I believe it to have been reserved for dull nights when I was low with medicine.

There was once a shipwright, and he wrought in a Government Yard, and his name was Chips. And his father's name before him was Chips, and *his* father's name before *him* was Chips, and they were all Chipses. And Chips the father had sold himself to the Devil for an iron pot and a bushel of tenpenny nails and half a ton of copper and a rat that could speak ; and Chips the grandfather had sold himself to the Devil for an iron pot and a bushel of tenpenny nails and half a ton of copper and a rat that could speak ; and Chips the great-grandfather had disposed of himself in the same direction on the same terms ; and the bargain had run in the family for a long long time. So, one day, when young

Chips was at work in the Dock Slip all alone, down in the
dark hold of an old Seventy-four that was haled up for
repairs, the Devil presented himself, and remarked:

"A Lemon has pips,
And a Yard has ships,
And *I*'ll have Chips!"

(I don't know why, but this fact of the Devil's expressing
himself in rhyme was peculiarly trying to me.) Chips looked
up when he heard the words, and there he saw the Devil with
saucer eyes that squinted on a terrible great scale, and that
struck out sparks of blue fire continually. And whenever
he winked his eyes, showers of blue sparks came out, and
his eyelashes made a clattering like flints and steels striking
lights. And hanging over one of his arms by the handle was
an iron pot, and under that arm was a bushel of tenpenny
nails, and under his other arm was half a ton of copper, and
sitting on one of his shoulders was a rat that could speak.
So, the Devil said again:

"A Lemon has pips,
And a Yard has ships,
And *I*'ll have Chips!"

(The invariable effect of this alarming tautology on the part
of the Evil Spirit was to deprive me of my senses for some
moments.) So, Chips answered never a word, but went on
with his work. "What are you doing, Chips?" said the rat
that could speak. "I am putting in new planks where you
and your gang have eaten old away," said Chips. "But
we'll eat them too," said the rat that could speak; "and
we'll let in the water and drown the crew, and we'll eat them
too." Chips, being only a shipwright, and not a Man-of-war's
man, said, "You are welcome to it." But he couldn't keep
his eyes off the half a ton of copper or the bushel of tenpenny
nails; for nails and copper are a shipwright's sweethearts,
and shipwrights will run away with them whenever they
can. So, the Devil said, "I see what you are looking at,
Chips. You had better strike the bargain. You know the
terms. Your father before you was well acquainted with
them, and so were your grandfather and great-grandfather
before him." Says Chips, "I like the copper, and I like the
nails, and I don't mind the pot, but I don't like the rat."
Says the Devil, fiercely, "You can't have the metal without
him—and *he's* a curiosity. I'm going." Chips, afraid of

losing the half a ton of copper and the bushel of nails, then said, "Give us hold!" So, he got the copper and the nails and the pot and the rat that could speak, and the Devil vanished. Chips sold the copper, and he sold the nails, and he would have sold the pot; but whenever he offered it for sale, the rat was in it, and the dealers dropped it, and would have nothing to say to the bargain. So, Chips resolved to kill the rat, and, being at work in the Yard one day with a great kettle of hot pitch on one side of him and the iron pot with the rat in it on the other, he turned the scalding pitch into the pot, and filled it full. Then, he kept his eye upon it till it cooled and hardened, and then he let it stand for twenty days, and then he heated the pitch again and turned it back into the kettle, and then he sank the pot in water for twenty days more, and then he got the smelters to put it in the furnace for twenty days more, and then they gave it him out, red hot, and looking like red-hot glass instead of iron—yet there was the rat in it, just the same as ever! And the moment it caught his eye, it said with a jeer:

> "A Lemon has pips,
> And a Yard has ships,
> And I'll have Chips!"

(For this Refrain I had waited since its last appearance, with inexpressible horror, which now culminated.) Chips now felt certain in his own mind that the rat would stick to him; the rat, answering his thought, said, "I will—like pitch!"

Now, as the rat leaped out of the pot when it had spoken, and made off, Chips began to hope that it wouldn't keep its word. But, a terrible thing happened next day. For, when dinner-time came, and the Dock-bell rang to strike work, he put his rule into the long pocket at the side of his trousers, and there he found a rat—not that rat, but another rat. And in his hat, he found another; and in his pocket-handkerchief, another; and in the sleeves of his coat, when he pulled it on to go to dinner, two more. And from that time he found himself so frightfully intimate with all the rats in the Yard, that they climbed up his legs when he was at work, and sat on his tools while he used them. And they could all speak to one another, and he understood what they said. And they got into his lodging, and into his bed, and into his teapot, and into his beer, and into his boots. And he was going to be married to a corn-chandler's daughter; and when he gave her a workbox he had himself made for her, a rat jumped out of it; and when he put his arm round her waist, a rat clung about her; so the marriage was broken off, though the banns were already twice put up—which the parish clerk well remembers, for, as he handed the book to the clergyman for the second time of asking, a large fat rat ran over the leaf. (By this time a special cascade of rats was rolling down my back, and the whole of my small listening person was overrun with them. At intervals ever since, I have been morbidly afraid of my own pocket, lest my exploring hand should find a specimen or two of those vermin in it.)

You may believe that all this was very terrible to Chips; but even all this was not the worst. He knew besides, what the rats were doing, wherever they were. So, sometimes he would cry aloud, when he was at his club at night, "Oh! Keep the rats out of the convicts' burying-ground! Don't let them do that!" Or, "There's one of them at the cheese down-stairs!" Or, "There's two of them smelling at the baby in the garret!" Or, other things of that sort. At last, he was voted mad, and lost his work in the Yard, and could get no other work. But King George wanted men, so before very long he got pressed for a sailor. And so he was taken off in a boat one evening to his ship, lying at Spithead, ready to sail. And so the first thing he made out in her as he got near her, was the figure-head of the old Seventy-four, where he had seen the Devil. She was called the Argonaut, and they rowed right under the bowsprit where the figure-head of the Argonaut, with a sheepskin in his hand and a blue gown on, was looking out to sea; and sitting staring on his forehead was the rat who could speak, and his exact words were these: "Chips ahoy! Old boy! We've pretty well eat them too, and we'll drown the crew, and will eat them too!" (Here I always became exceedingly faint, and would have asked for water, but that I was speechless.)

The ship was bound for the Indies; and if you don't know where that is, you ought to it, and angels will never love you. (Here I felt myself an outcast from a future state.) The ship set sail that very night, and she sailed, and sailed, and sailed. Chips's feelings were dreadful. Nothing ever equalled his terrors. No wonder. At last, one day he asked

leave to speak to the Admiral. The Admiral giv' leave.
Chips went down on his knees in the Great State Cabin.
"Your Honour, unless your Honour, without a moment's
loss of time, makes sail for the nearest shore, this is a
doomed ship, and her name is the Coffin!" "Young man,
your words are a madman's words." "Your Honour, no;
they are nibbling us away." "They?" "Your Honour,
them dreadful rats. Dust and hollowness where solid oak
ought to be! Rats nibbling a grave for every man on board!
Oh! Does your Honour love your Lady and your pretty
children?" "Yes, my man, to be sure." "Then, for God's
sake, make for the nearest shore, for at this present moment
the rats are all stopping in their work, and are all looking
straight towards you with bare teeth, and are all saying to
one another that you shall never, never, never, never, see
your Lady and your children more." "My poor fellow,
you are a case for the doctor. Sentry, take care of this
man!"

So, he was bled and he was blistered, and he was this and
that, for six whole days and nights. So, then he again asked
leave to speak to the Admiral. The Admiral giv' leave. He
went down on his knees in the Great State Cabin. "Now,
Admiral, you must die! You took no warning; you must
die! The rats are never wrong in their calculations, and
they make out that they'll be through, at twelve to-night.
So, you must die!—With me and all the rest!" And so at
twelve o'clock there was a great leak reported in the ship,
and a torrent of water rushed in and nothing could stop it,
and they all went down, every living soul. And what the
rats—being water-rats—left of Chips, at last floated to shore,
and sitting on him was an immense overgrown rat, laughing,
that dived when the corpse touched the beach and never
came up. And there was a deal of seaweed on the remains.
And if you get thirteen bits of seaweed, and dry them and
burn them in the fire, they will go off like in these thirteen
words as plain as plain can be:

> "A Lemon has pips,
> And a Yard has ships,
> And I've got Chips!"

The same female bard—descended, possibly, from those
terrible old Scalds who seem to have existed for the express
purpose of addling the brains of mankind when they begin

to investigate languages—made a standing pretence which
greatly assisted in forcing me back to a number of hideous
places that I would by all means have avoided. This pretence was, that all her ghost stories had occurred to her own
relations. Politeness towards a meritorious family, therefore, forbade my doubting them, and they acquired an air of
authentication that impaired my digestive powers for life.
There was a narrative concerning an unearthly animal fore-
boding death, which appeared in the open street to a parlour-
maid who "went to fetch the beer" for supper; first (as
I now recall it) assuming the likeness of a black dog, and
gradually rising on its hind-legs and swelling into the
semblance of some quadruped greatly surpassing a hippopotamus: which apparition—not because I deemed it in the
least improbable, but because I felt it to be really too large
to bear—I feebly endeavoured to explain away. But, on
Mercy's retorting with wounded dignity that the parlour-
maid was her own sister-in-law, I perceived there was no
hope, and resigned myself to this zoological phenomenon as
one of my many pursuers. There was another narrative
describing the apparition of a young woman who came out
of a glass-case and haunted another young woman until
the other young woman questioned it and elicited that its
bones (Lord ! To think of its being so particular about its
bones !) were buried under the glass-case, whereas she
required them to be interred, with every Undertaking
solemnity up to twenty-four pound ten, in another particular place. This narrative I considered I had a personal
interest in disproving, because we had glass-cases at home,
and how, otherwise, was I to be guaranteed from the
intrusion of young women requiring *me* to bury them up to
twenty-four pound ten, when I had only twopence a week?
But my remorseless nurse cut the ground from under my
tender feet, by informing me that She was the other young
woman ; and I couldn't say "I don't believe you ; " it was
not possible.

Such are a few of the uncommercial journeys that I was
forced to make, against my will, when I was very young
and unreasoning. And really, as to the latter part of them,
it is not so very long ago—now I come to think of it—that
I was asked to undertake them once again, with a steady
countenance.

XVI

ARCADIAN LONDON

BEING in a humour for complete solitude and uninterrupted meditation this autumn, I have taken a lodging for six weeks in the most unfrequented part of England—in a word, in London.

The retreat into which I have withdrawn myself, is Bond-street. From this lonely spot I make pilgrimages into the surrounding wilderness, and traverse extensive tracts of the Great Desert. The first solemn feeling of isolation overcome, the first oppressive consciousness of profound retirement conquered, I enjoy that sense of freedom, and feel reviving within me that latent wildness of the original savage, which has been (upon the whole somewhat frequently) noticed by Travellers.

My lodgings are at a hatter's—my own hatter's. After exhibiting no articles in his window for some weeks, but seaside wide-awakes, shooting-caps, and a choice of rough water-proof head-gear for the moors and mountains, he has put upon the heads of his family as much of this stock as they could carry, and has taken them off to the Isle of Thanet. His young man alone remains—and remains alone—in the shop. The young man has let out the fire at which the irons are heated, and, saving his strong sense of duty, I see no reason why he should take the shutters down.

Happily for himself and for his country, the young man is a Volunteer; most happily for himself, or I think he would become the prey of a settled melancholy. For, to live surrounded by human hats, and alienated from human heads to fit them on, is surely a great endurance. But, the young man, sustained by practising his exercise, and by constantly furbishing up his regulation plume (it is unnecessary to observe that, as a hatter, he is in a cock's-feather corps), is resigned and uncomplaining. On a Saturday, when he closes early and gets his Knickerbockers on, he is even cheerful. I am gratefully particular in this reference to him, because he is my companion through many peaceful hours. My hatter has a desk up certain steps behind his counter, enclosed like the clerk's desk at Church. I shut myself into this place of seclusion, after breakfast, and meditate. At such times, I observe the young man loading an imaginary rifle with the greatest precision, and maintaining a most galling and destructive fire upon the national enemy. I thank him publicly for his companionship and his patriotism.

The simple character of my life, and the calm nature of the scenes by which I am surrounded, occasion me to rise early. I go forth in my slippers, and promenade the pavement. It is pastoral to feel the freshness of the air in the uninhabited town, and to appreciate the shepherdess character of the few milkwomen who purvey so little milk that it would be worth nobody's while to adulterate it, if anybody were left to undertake the task. On the crowded sea-shore, the great demand for milk, combined with the strong local temptation of chalk, would betray itself in the lowered quality of the article. In Arcadian London I derive it from the cow.

The Arcadian simplicity of the metropolis altogether, and the primitive ways into which it has fallen in this autumnal Golden Age, make it entirely new to me. Within a few hundred yards of my retreat, is the house of a friend who maintains a most sumptuous butler. I never, until yesterday, saw that butler out of superfine black broadcloth. Until yesterday, I never saw him off duty, never saw him (he is the best of butlers) with the appearance of having any mind for anything but the glory of his master and his master's friends. Yesterday morning, walking in my slippers near the house of which he is the prop and ornament—a house now a waste of shutters—I encountered that butler, also in his slippers, and in a shooting suit of one colour, and in a low-crowned straw-hat, smoking an early cigar. He felt that we had formerly met in another state of existence, and that we were translated into a new sphere. Wisely and well, he passed me without recognition. Under his arm he carried the morning paper, and shortly afterwards I saw him sitting on a rail in the pleasant open landscape of Regent-street, perusing it at his ease under the ripening sun.

My landlord having taken his whole establishment to be salted down, I am waited on by an elderly woman labouring under a chronic sniff,. who, at the shadowy hour of half-past nine o'clock of every evening, gives admittance at the street door to a meagre and mouldy old man whom I have never yet seen detached from a flat pint of beer in a pewter pot. The meagre and mouldy old man is her husband, and the pair have a dejected consciousness that they are not justified in appearing on the surface of the earth. They come out of some hole when London empties itself, and go in again when it fills. I saw them arrive on the evening when I myself took possession, and they arrived with the flat pint of beer, and their bed in a bundle. The old man is a weak old man, and appeared to me to get the bed down the kitchen stairs by tumbling down with and upon it. They make their bed in the lowest and remotest corner of the basement, and they smell of bed, and have no possession but bed : unless it be (which I rather infer from an under-current of flavour in them) cheese. I know their name, through the chance of having called the wife's attention, at half-past nine on the second evening of our acquaintance, to the circumstance of there being some one at the house door ; when she apologetically explained, "It's only Mr. Klem." What becomes of Mr. Klem all day, or when he goes out, or why, is a mystery I cannot penetrate ; but at half-past nine he never fails to turn up on the door-step with the flat pint of beer. And the pint of beer, flat as it is, is so much more important than himself, that it always seems to my fancy as if it had found him drivelling in the street and had humanely brought him home. In making his way below, Mr. Klem never goes down the middle of the passage, like another Christian, but shuffles against the wall as if entreating me to take notice that he is occupying as little space as possible in the house ; and whenever I come upon him face to face, he backs from me in fascinated confusion. The most extraordinary circumstance I have traced in connexion with this aged couple, is, that there is a Miss Klem, their daughter, apparently ten years older than either of them, who has also a bed and smells of it, and carries it about the earth at dusk and hides it in deserted houses. I came into this piece of knowledge through Mrs. Klem's beseeching me to sanction the sheltering of Miss Klem under that roof for a single night, "between her takin' care of the upper part in Pall Mall which the family of his back, and a 'ouse in Serjameses-street, which the family of leaves towng ter-morrer." I gave my gracious consent (having nothing that I know of to do with it), and in the shadowy hours Miss Klem became perceptible on the door-step, wrestling with a bed in a bundle. Where she made it up for the night I cannot positively state, but, I think, in a sink. I know that with the instinct of a reptile or an insect, she stowed it and herself away in deep obscurity. In the Klem family, I have noticed another remarkable gift of nature, and that is a power they possess of converting everything into flue. Such broken victuals as they take by stealth, appear (whatever the nature of the viands) invariably to generate flue; and even the nightly pint of beer, instead of assimilating naturally, strikes me as breaking out in that form, equally on the shabby gown of Mrs. Klem, and the threadbare coat of her husband.

Mrs. Klem has no idea of my name—as to Mr. Klem he has no idea of anything—and only knows me as her good gentleman. Thus, if doubtful whether I am in my room or no, Mrs. Klem taps at the door and says, "Is my good gentleman here?" Or, if a messenger desiring to see me were consistent with my solitude, she would show him in with "Here is my good gentleman." I find this to be a generic custom. For, I meant to have observed before now, that in its Arcadian time all my part of London is indistinctly pervaded by the Klem species. They creep about with beds, and go to bed in miles of deserted houses. They hold no companionship except that sometimes, after dark, two of them will emerge from opposite houses, and meet in the middle of the road as on neutral ground, or will peep from adjoining houses over an interposing barrier of area railings, and compare a few reserved mistrustful notes respecting their good ladies or good gentlemen. This I have discovered in the course of various solitary rambles I have taken Northward from my retirement, along the awful perspectives of Wimpole-street, Harley-street, and similar frowning regions. Their effect would be scarcely distinguishable from that of the primeval forests, but for the Klem stragglers; these may be dimly observed, when the heavy shadows fall, flitting to and fro, putting up the door-chain, taking in the pint of beer, lowering like phantoms at the dark parlour windows, or secretly consorting underground with the dust-bin and the water-cistern.

In the Burlington Arcade, I observe, with peculiar pleasure, a primitive state of manners to have superseded the baneful influences of ultra civilisation. Nothing can surpass the innocence of the ladies' shoe-shops, the artificial-flower repositories, and the head-dress depôts. They are in strange hands at this time of year—hands of unaccustomed persons, who are imperfectly acquainted with the prices of the goods, and contemplate them with unsophisticated delight and wonder. The children of these virtuous people exchange familiarities in the Arcade, and temper the asperity of the two tall beadles. Their youthful prattle blends in an unwonted manner with the harmonious shade of the scene, and the general effect is, as of the voices of birds in a grove. In this happy restoration of the golden time, it has been my privilege even to see the bigger beadle's wife. She brought him his dinner in a basin, and he ate it in his arm-chair, and afterwards fell asleep like a satiated child. At Mr. Truefitt's, the excellent hair-dresser's, they are learning French to beguile the time ; and even the few solitaries left on guard at Mr. Atkinson's, the perfumer's round the corner (generally the most inexorable gentleman in London, and the most scornful of three-and-sixpence), condescend a little, as they drowsily bide or recall their turn for chasing the ebbing Neptune on the ribbed sea-sand. From Messrs. Hunt and Roskell's, the jewellers, all things are absent but the precious stones, and the gold and silver, and the soldierly pensioner at the door with his decorated breast. I might stand night and day for a month to come, in Saville-row, with my tongue cut, yet not find a doctor to look at it for love or money. The dentists' instruments are rusting in their drawers, and their horrible cool parlours, where people pretend to read the Every-Day Book and not to be afraid, are doing penance for their grimness in white sheets. The light-weight of shrewd appearance, with one eye always shut up, as if he were eating a sharp gooseberry in all seasons, who usually stands at the gateway of the livery-stables on very little legs under a very large waistcoat, has gone to Doncaster. Of such undesigning aspect is his guileless yard now, with its gravel and scarlet beans, and the yellow Break housed under a glass roof in a corner, that I almost believe I could not be taken in there, if I tried. In the places of business of the great tailors, the cheval-glasses are dim and dusty for lack of being looked into. Ranges of brown paper coat and waistcoat bodies look as funereal as if they were the hatch-ments of the customers with whose names they are inscribed ; the measuring tapes hang idle on the wall ; the order-taker, left on the hopeless chance of some one looking in, yawns in the last extremity over the book of patterns, as if he were trying to read that entertaining library. The hotels in Brook-street have no one in them, and the staffs of servants stare disconsolately for next season out of all the windows. The very man who goes about like an erect Turtle, between two boards recommendatory of the Sixteen Shilling Trousers, is aware of himself as a hollow mockery, and eats filberts while he leans his hinder shell against a wall.

Among these tranquillising objects, it is my delight to walk and meditate. Soothed by the repose around me, I wander insensibly to considerable distances, and guide myself back by the stars. Thus, I enjoy the contrast of a few still partially inhabited and busy spots where all the lights are not fled, where all the garlands are not dead, whence all but I have not departed. Then, does it appear to me that in this age three things are clamorously required of Man in the miscellaneous thoroughfares of the metropolis. Firstly, that he have his boots cleaned. Secondly, that he eat a penny ice. Thirdly, that he get himself photographed. Then do I speculate, What have those seam-worn artists been who stand at the photograph doors in Greek caps, sample in hand, and mysteriously salute the public—the female public with a pressing tenderness—to come in and be "took"? What did they do with their greasy blandish-ments, before the era of cheap photography? Of what class were their previous victims, and how victimised? And how did they get, and how did they pay for, that large collection of likenesses, all purporting to have been taken inside, with the taking of none of which had that establish-ment any more to do than with the taking of Delhi?

But, these are small oases, and I am soon back again in metropolitan Arcadia. It is my impression that much of its serene and peaceful character is attributable to the absence of customary Talk. How do I know but there may be

subtle influences in Talk, to vex the souls of men who don't
hear it? How do I know but that Talk, five, ten, twenty
miles off, may get into the air and disagree with me? If
I rise from my bed, vaguely troubled and wearied and sick
of my life, in the session of Parliament, who shall say that
my noble friend, my right reverend friend, my right honourable friend, my honourable friend, my honourable and
learned friend, or my honourable and gallant friend, may
not be responsible for that effect upon my nervous system?
Too much Ozone in the air, I am informed and fully believe
(though I have no idea what it is), would affect me in a
marvellously disagreeable way; why may not too much
Talk? I don't see or hear the Ozone; I don't see or hear
the Talk. And there is so much Talk; so much too much;
such loud cry, and such scant supply of wool; such a deal
of fleecing, and so little fleece! Hence, in the Arcadian
season, I find it a delicious triumph to walk down to
deserted Westminster, and see the Courts shut up; to walk
a little further and see the Two Houses shut up; to stand
in the Abbey Yard, like the New Zealander of the grand
English History (concerning which unfortunate man, a whole
rookery of mares' nests is generally being discovered), and
gloat upon the ruins of Talk. Returning to my primitive
solitude and lying down to sleep, my grateful heart expands
with the consciousness that there is no adjourned Debate,
no ministerial explanation, nobody to give notice of intention
to ask the noble Lord at the head of her Majesty's Government five-and-twenty bootless questions in one, no term time
with legal argument, no Nisi Prius with eloquent appeal to
British Jury; that the air will to-morrow, and to-morrow,
and to-morrow, remain untroubled by this superabundant
generating of Talk. In a minor degree it is a delicious
triumph to me to go into the club, and see the carpets up,
and the Bores and the other dust dispersed to the four
winds. Again New Zealander-like, I stand on the cold
hearth, and say in the solitude, "Here I watched Bore
A 1, with voice always mysteriously low and head always
mysteriously drooped, whispering political secrets into the
ears of Adam's confiding children. Accursed be his memory
for ever and a day!"

But, I have all this time been coming to the point, that
the happy nature of my retirement is most sweetly expressed
in its being the abode of Love. It is, as it were, an in-

expensive Agapemone: nobody's speculation: everybody's profit. The one great result of the resumption of primitive habits, and (convertible terms) the not having much to do, is, the abounding of Love.

The Klem species are incapable of the softer emotions; probably, in that low nomadic race, the softer emotions have all degenerated into flue. But, with this exception, all the sharers of my retreat make love.

I have mentioned Saville-row. We all know the Doctor's servant. We all know what a respectable man he is, what a hard dry man, what a firm man, what a confidential man: how he lets us into the waiting-room, like a man who knows minutely what is the matter with us, but from whom the rack should not wring the secret. In the prosaic "season," he has distinctly the appearance of a man conscious of money in the savings bank, and taking his stand on his respectability with both feet. At that time it is as impossible to associate him with relaxation, or any human weakness, as it is to meet his eye without feeling guilty of indisposition. In the blest Arcadian time, how changed! I have seen him, in a pepper-and-salt jacket—jacket—and drab trousers, with his arm round the waist of a bootmaker's housemaid, smiling in open day. I have seen him at the pump by the Albany, unsolicitedly pumping for two fair young creatures, whose figures as they bent over their cans, were—if I may be allowed an original expression—a model for the sculptor. I have seen him trying the piano in the Doctor's drawing-room with his forefinger, and have heard him humming tunes in praise of lovely woman. I have seen him seated on a fire-engine, and going (obviously in search of excitement) to a fire. I saw him, one moonlight evening when the peace and purity of our Arcadian west were at their height, polk with the lovely daughter of a cleaner of gloves, from the door-steps of his own residence, across Saville-row, round by Clifford-street and Old Burlington-street, back to Burlington-gardens. Is this the Golden Age revived, or Iron London?

The Dentist's servant. Is that man no mystery to us, no type of invisible power? The tremendous individual knows (who else does?) what is done with the extracted teeth; he knows what goes on in the little room where something is always being washed or filed; he knows what warm spicy infusion is put into the comfortable tumbler from which we rinse our wounded mouth, with a gap in it that feels a foot wide ; he knows whether the thing we spit into is a fixture communicating with the Thames, or could be cleared away for a dance ; he sees the horrible parlour when there are no patients in it, and he could reveal, if he would, what becomes of the Every-Day Book then. The conviction of my coward conscience when I see that man in a professional light, is, that he knows all the statistics of my teeth and gums, my double teeth, my single teeth, my stopped teeth, and my sound. In this Arcadian rest, I am fearless of him as of a harmless, powerless creature in a Scotch cap, who adores a young lady in a voluminous crinoline, at a neighbouring billiard-room, and whose passion would be uninfluenced if every one of her teeth were false. They may be. He takes them all on trust.

In secluded corners of the place of my seclusion, there are little shops withdrawn from public curiosity, and never two together, where servants' perquisites are bought. The cook may dispose of grease at these modest and convenient marts ; the butler, of bottles ; the valet and lady's maid, of clothes ; most servants, indeed, of most things they may happen to lay hold of. I have been told that in sterner times loving correspondence, otherwise interdicted, may be maintained by letter through the agency of some of these useful establishments. In the Arcadian autumn, no such device is necessary. Everybody loves, and openly and blamelessly loves. My landlord's young man loves the whole of one side of the way of Old Bond-street, and is beloved several doors up New Bond-street besides. I never look out of window but I see kissing of hands going on all around me. It is the morning custom to glide from shop to shop and exchange tender sentiments ; it is the evening custom for couples to stand hand in hand at house doors, or roam, linked in that flowery manner, through the unpeopled streets. There is nothing else to do but love ; and what there is to do, is done.

In unison with this pursuit, a chaste simplicity obtains in the domestic habits of Arcadia. Its few scattered people dine early, live moderately, sup socially, and sleep soundly. It is rumoured that the Beadles of the Arcade, from being the mortal enemies of boys, have signed with tears an address to Lord Shaftesbury, and subscribed to a ragged school. No wonder! For, they might turn their heavy maces into crooks and tend sheep in the Arcade, to the purling of the water-carts as they give the thirsty streets much more to drink than they can carry.

A happy Golden Age, and a serene tranquillity. Charming picture, but it will fade. The iron age will return, London will come back to town, if I show my tongue then in Saville-row for half a minute I shall be prescribed for, the Doctor's man and the Dentist's man will then pretend that these days of unprofessional innocence never existed. Where Mr. and Mrs. Klem and their bed will be at that time, passes human knowledge; but my hatter hermitage will then know them no more, nor will it then know me. The desk at which I have written these meditations will retributively assist at the making out of my account, and the wheels of gorgeous carriages and the hoofs of high-stepping horses will crush the silence out of Bond-street— will grind Arcadia away, and give it to the elements in granite powder.

XVII

THE ITALIAN PRISONER

THE rising of the Italian people from under their unutterable wrongs, and the tardy burst of day upon them after the long long night of oppression that has darkened their beautiful country, have naturally caused my mind to dwell often of late on my own small wanderings in Italy. Connected with them, is a curious little drama, in which the character I myself sustained was so very subordinate that I may relate its story without any fear of being suspected of self-display. It is strictly a true story.

I am newly arrived one summer evening, in a certain small town on the Mediterranean. I have had my dinner at the inn, and I and the mosquitoes are coming out into the streets together. It is far from Naples; but a bright brown plump little woman-servant at the inn, is a Neapolitan, and is so vivaciously expert in pantomimic action, that in the single moment of answering my request to have a pair of shoes cleaned which I have left up-stairs, she plies imaginary brushes, and goes completely through the motions of polishing the shoes up, and laying them at my feet. I smile at the brisk little woman in perfect satisfaction with her briskness; and the brisk little woman, amiably pleased with me because I am pleased with her, claps her hands and laughs delightfully. We are in the inn yard. As the little woman's bright eyes sparkle on the cigarette I am smoking, I make bold to offer her one; she accepts it none the less merrily, because I touch a most charming little dimple in her fat cheek, with its light paper end. Glancing up at the many green lattices to assure herself that the mistress is not looking on, the little woman then puts her two little dimple arms a-kimbo, and stands on tiptoe to light her cigarette at mine. "And now, dear little sir," says she, puffing out smoke in a most innocent and cherubic manner, "keep quite straight on, take the first to the right, and probably you will see him standing at his door."

I have a commission to "him," and I have been inquiring about him. I have carried the commission about Italy several months. Before I left England, there came to me one night a certain generous and gentle English nobleman (he is dead in these days when I relate the story, and exiles have lost their best British friend), with this request: "Whenever you come to such a town, will you seek out one Giovanni Carlavero, who keeps a little wine-shop there, mention my name to him suddenly, and observe how it affects him?" I accepted the trust, and am on my way to discharge it.

The sirocco has been blowing all day, and it is a hot unwholesome evening with no cool sea-breeze. Mosquitoes and fire-flies are lively enough, but most other creatures are faint. The coquettish airs of pretty young women in the tiniest and wickedest of dolls' straw hats, who lean out at opened lattice blinds, are almost the only airs stirring. Very ugly and haggard old women with distaffs, and with a grey tow upon them that looks as if they were spinning out their own hair (I suppose they were once pretty, too, but it is very difficult to believe so), sit on the footway leaning against house walls. Everybody who has come for water to the fountain, stays there, and seems incapable of any such energetic idea as going home. Vespers are over, though not so long but that I can smell the heavy resinous incense as I pass the church. No man seems to be at work, save the coppersmith. In an Italian town he is always at work, and always thumping in the deadliest manner.

I keep straight on, and come in due time to the first on the right: a narrow dull street, where I see a well-favoured man of good stature and military bearing, in a great cloak, standing at a door. Drawing nearer to this threshold, I see it is the threshold of a small wine-shop; and I can just make out, in the dim light, the inscription that it is kept by Giovanni Carlavero.

I touch my hat to the figure in the cloak, and pass in, and draw a stool to a little table. The lamp (just such another as they dig out of Pompeii) is lighted, but the place is empty. The figure in the cloak has followed me in, and stands before me.

"The master?"

"At your service, sir."

"Please to give me a glass of the wine of the country."

He turns to a little counter, to get it. As his striking face is pale, and his action is evidently that of an enfeebled man, I remark that I fear he has been ill. It is not much, he courteously and gravely answers, though bad while it lasts: the fever.

As he sets the wine on the little table, to his manifest surprise I lay my hand on the back of his, look him in the face, and say in a low voice: "I am an Englishman, and you are acquainted with a friend of mine. Do you recollect ——?" and I mentioned the name of my generous countryman.

Instantly, he utters a loud cry, bursts into tears, and falls on his knees at my feet, clasping my legs in both his arms and bowing his head to the ground.

Some years ago, this man at my feet, whose over-fraught heart is heaving as if it would burst from his breast, and whose tears are wet upon the dress I wear, was a galley-slave in the North of Italy. He was a political offender, having been concerned in the then last rising, and was sentenced to imprisonment for life. That he would have died in his chains, is certain, but for the circumstance that the Englishman happened to visit his prison.

It was one of the vile old prisons of Italy, and a part of it was below the waters of the harbour. The place of his confinement was an arched under-ground and under-water gallery, with a grill-gate at the entrance, through which it received such light and air as it got. Its condition was insufferably foul, and a stranger could hardly breathe in it, or see in it with the aid of a torch. At the upper end of this dungeon, and consequently in the worst position, as being the furthest removed from light and air, the Englishman first beheld him, sitting on an iron bedstead to which he was chained by a heavy chain. His countenance impressed the Englishman as having nothing in common with the faces of the malefactors with whom he was associated, and he talked with him, and learnt how he came to be there.

When the Englishman emerged from the dreadful den into the light of day, he asked his conductor, the governor of the jail, why Giovanni Carlavero was put into the worst place?

"Because he is particularly recommended," was the strin-gent answer.

"Recommended, that is to say, for death?"

"Excuse me; particularly recommended," was again the answer.

"He has a bad tumour in his neck, no doubt occasioned by the hardship of his miserable life. If he continues to be neglected, and he remains where he is, it will kill him."

"Excuse me, I can do nothing. He is particularly recommended."

The Englishman was staying in that town, and he went to his home there; but the figure of this man chained to the bedstead made it no home, and destroyed his rest and peace. He was an Englishman of an extraordinarily tender heart, and he could not bear the picture. He went back to the prison grate; went back again and again, and talked to the man and cheered him. He used the utmost influence to get the man unchained from the bedstead, were it only for ever so short a time in the day, and permitted to come to the grate. It took a long time, but the Englishman's station, personal character, and steadiness of purpose, wore out opposition so far, and that grace was at last accorded. Through the bars, when he could thus get light upon the tumour, the Englishman lanced it, and it did well, and healed. His strong interest in the prisoner had greatly increased by this time, and he formed the desperate resolu-tion that he would exert his utmost self-devotion and use his utmost efforts, to get Carlavero pardoned.

If the prisoner had been a brigand and a murderer, if he had committed every non-political crime in the Newgate Calendar and out of it, nothing would have been easier than for a man of any court or priestly influence to obtain his release. As it was, nothing could have been more difficult. Italian authorities, and English authorities who had interest with them, alike assured the Englishman that his object was hopeless. He met with nothing but evasion, refusal, and ridicule. His political prisoner became a joke in the place. It was especially observable that English Circum-locution, and English Society on its travels, were as humorous on the subject as Circumlocution and Society may be on any subject without loss of caste. But, the Englishman possessed (and proved it well in his life) a cour-age very uncommon among us: he had not the least fear

of being considered a bore, in a good humane cause. So he
went on persistently trying, and trying, and trying, to get
Giovanni Carlavero out. That prisoner had been rigorously
re-chained, after the tumour operation, and it was not likely
that his miserable life could last very long.

One day, when all the town knew about the Englishman
and his political prisoner, there came to the Englishman,
a certain sprightly Italian Advocate of whom he had some
knowledge ; and he made this strange proposal. " Give me
a hundred pounds to obtain Carlavero's release. I think
I can get him a pardon, with that money. But I cannot
tell you what I am going to do with the money, nor must
you ever ask me the question if I succeed, nor must you
ever ask me for an account of the money if I fail." The
Englishman decided to hazard the hundred pounds. He
did so, and heard not another word of the matter. For
half a year and more, the Advocate made no sign, and never
once " took on " in any way, to have the subject on his
mind. The Englishman was then obliged to change his
residence to another and more famous town in the North
of Italy. He parted from the poor prisoner with a sorrowful heart, as from a doomed man for whom there was no
release but Death.

The Englishman lived in his new place of abode another
half-year and more, and had no tidings of the wretched
prisoner. At length, one day, he received from the Advocate
a cool concise mysterious note, to this effect. " If you still
wish to bestow that benefit upon the man in whom you were
once interested, send me fifty pounds more, and I think it
can be ensured." Now, the Englishman had long settled in
his mind that the Advocate was a heartless sharper, who
had preyed upon his credulity and his interest in an unfortunate sufferer. So, he sat down and wrote a dry answer,
giving the Advocate to understand that he was wiser now
than he had been formerly, and that no more money was
extractable from his pocket.

He lived outside the city gates, some mile or two from
the post-office, and was accustomed to walk into the city
with his letters and post them himself. On a lovely spring
day, when the sky was exquisitely blue, and the sea Divinely
beautiful, he took his usual walk, carrying this letter to the
Advocate in his pocket. As he went along, his gentle heart
was much moved by the loveliness of the prospect, and by

the thought of the slowly dying prisoner chained to the bedstead, for whom the universe had no delights. As he drew nearer and nearer to the city where he was to post the letter, he became very uneasy in his mind. He debated with himself, was it remotely possible, after all, that this sum of fifty pounds could restore the fellow-creature whom he pitied so much, and for whom he had striven so hard, to liberty? He was not a conventionally rich Englishman— very far from that—but, he had a spare fifty pounds at the banker's. He resolved to risk it. Without doubt, GOD has recompensed him for the resolution.

He went to the banker's, and got a bill for the amount, and enclosed it in a letter to the Advocate that I wish I could have seen. He simply told the Advocate that he was quite a poor man, and that he was sensible it might be a great weakness in him to part with so much money on the faith of so vague a communication ; but, that there it was, and that he prayed the Advocate to make a good use of it. If he did otherwise no good could ever come of it, and it would lie heavy on his soul one day.

Within a week, the Englishman was sitting at his break-fast, when he heard some suppressed sounds of agitation on the staircase, and Giovanni Carlavero leaped into the room and fell upon his breast, a free man !

Conscious of having wronged the Advocate in his own thoughts, the Englishman wrote him an earnest and grateful letter, avowing the fact, and entreating him to confide by what means and through what agency he had succeeded so well. The Advocate returned for answer through the post, " There are many things, as you know, in this Italy of ours, that are safest and best not even spoken of—far less written of. We may meet some day, and then I may tell you what you want to know; not here, and now." But, the two never did meet again. The Advocate was dead when the Englishman gave me my trust; and how the man had been set free, remained as great a mystery to the Englishman, and to the man himself, as it was to me.

But, I knew this:—here was the man, this sultry night, on his knees at my feet, because I was the Englishman's friend ; here were his tears upon my dress ; here were his sobs choking his utterance; here were his kisses on my hands, because they had touched the hands that had worked out his release. He had no need to tell me it would be happiness to him to die for his benefactor; I doubt if I ever saw real, sterling, fervent gratitude of soul, before or since.

He was much watched and suspected, he said, and had had enough to do to keep himself out of trouble. This, and his not having prospered in his worldly affairs, had led to his having failed in his usual communications to the Englishman for—as I now remember the period—some two or three years. But, his prospects were brighter, and his wife who had been very ill had recovered, and his fever had left him, and he had bought a little vineyard, and would I carry to his benefactor the first of its wine? Ay, that I would (I told him with enthusiasm), and not a drop of it should be spilled or lost!

He had cautiously closed the door before speaking of himself, and had talked with such excess of emotion, and in a provincial Italian so difficult to understand, that I had more than once been obliged to stop him, and beg him to have compassion on me and be slower and calmer. By degrees he became so, and tranquilly walked back with me to the hotel. There, I sat down before I went to bed and wrote a faithful account of him to the Englishman: which I concluded by saying that I would bring the wine home, against any difficulties, every drop.

Early next morning, when I came out at the hotel door to pursue my journey, I found my friend waiting with one of those immense bottles in which the Italian peasants store their wine—a bottle holding some half-dozen gallons—bound round with basket-work for greater safety on the journey. I see him now, in the bright sunlight, tears of gratitude in his eyes, proudly inviting my attention to this corpulent bottle. (At the street-corner hard by, two high-flavoured able-bodied monks—pretending to talk together, but keeping their four evil eyes upon us.)

How the bottle had been got there, did not appear; but the difficulty of getting it into the ramshackle vetturino carriage in which I was departing, was so great, and it took up so much room when it was got in, that I elected to sit outside. The last I saw of Giovanni Carlavero was his running through the town by the side of the jingling wheels, clasping my hand as I stretched it down from the box, charging me with a thousand last loving and dutiful messages to his dear patron, and finally looking in at the bottle as it reposed inside, with an admiration of its honourable way of travelling that was beyond measure delightful.

And now, what disquiet of mind this dearly-beloved and highly-treasured Bottle began to cost me, no man knows. It was my precious charge through a long tour, and, for hundreds of miles, I never had it off my mind by day or by night. Over bad roads—and they were many—I clung to it with affectionate desperation. Up mountains, I looked in at it and saw it helplessly tilting over on its back, with terror. At innumerable inn doors when the weather was bad, I was obliged to be put into my vehicle before the Bottle could be got in, and was obliged to have the Bottle lifted out before human aid could come near me. The Imp of the same name, except that his associations were all evil and these associations were all good, would have been a less troublesome travelling companion. I might have served Mr. Cruikshank as a subject for a new illustration of the miseries of the Bottle. The National Temperance Society might have made a powerful Tract of me.

The suspicions that attached to this innocent Bottle, greatly aggravated my difficulties. It was like the apple-pie in the child's book. Parma pouted at it, Modena mocked it, Tuscany tackled it, Naples nibbled it, Rome refused it, Austria accused it, Soldiers suspected it, Jesuits jobbed it. I composed a neat Oration, developing my inoffensive intentions in connexion with this Bottle, and delivered it in an infinity of guard-houses, at a multitude of town gates, and on every drawbridge, angle, and rampart, of a complete system of fortifications. Fifty times a day, I got down to harangue an infuriated soldiery about the Bottle. Through the filthy degradation of the abject and vile Roman States, I had as much difficulty in working my way with the Bottle, as if it had bottled up a complete system of heretical theology. In the Neapolitan country, where everybody was a spy, a soldier, a priest, or a lazzarone, the shameless beggars of all four denominations incessantly pounced on the Bottle and made it a pretext for extorting money from me. Quires—quires do I say? Reams—of forms illegibly printed on whity-brown paper were filled up about the Bottle, and it was the subject of more stamping and sanding than I had ever seen before. In consequence of which haze of sand, perhaps, it was always irregular, and always latent with dismal penalties of going back or not going forward,

which were only to be abated by the silver crossing of
a base hand, poked shirtless out of a ragged uniform sleeve.
Under all discouragements, however, I stuck to my Bottle,
and held firm to my resolution that every drop of its
contents should reach the Bottle's destination.

The latter refinement cost me a separate heap of troubles
on its own separate account.   What corkscrews did I see
the military power bring out against that Bottle ; what
gimlets, spikes, divining rods, gauges, and unknown tests
and instruments !   At some places, they persisted in declaring that the wine must not be passed, without being opened
and tasted ; I, pleading to the contrary, used then to argue
the question seated on the Bottle lest they should open it in
spite of me.   In the southern parts of Italy more violent
shrieking, face-making, and gesticulating, greater vehemence
of speech and countenance and action, went on about that
Bottle, than would attend fifty murders in a northern
latitude.   It raised important functionaries out of their
beds, in the dead of night.   I have known half-a-dozen
military lanterns to disperse themselves at all points of
a great sleeping Piazza, each lantern summoning some
official creature to get up, put on his cocked-hat instantly,
and come and stop the Bottle.   It was characteristic that
while this innocent Bottle had such immense difficulty in
getting from little town to town, Signor Mazzini and the
fiery cross were traversing Italy from end to end.

Still, I stuck to my Bottle, like any fine old English
gentleman all of the olden time.   The more the Bottle was
interfered with, the stauncher I became (if possible) in my
first determination that my countryman should have it
delivered to him intact, as the man whom he had so nobly
restored to life and liberty had delivered it to me.   If ever
I had been obstinate in my days—and I may have been,
say, once or twice—I was obstinate about the Bottle.   But,
I made it a rule always to keep a pocket full of small coin
at its service, and never to be out of temper in its cause.
Thus, I and the Bottle made our way.   Once we had
a break-down ; rather a bad break-down, on a steep high
place with the sea below us, on a tempestuous evening
when it blew great guns.   We were driving four wild
horses abreast, Southern fashion, and there was some little
difficulty in stopping them.   I was outside, and not thrown
off ; but no words can describe my feelings when I saw the

Bottle—travelling inside, as usual—burst the door open, and roll obesely out into the road. A blessed Bottle with a charmed existence, he took no hurt, and we repaired damage, and went on triumphant.

A thousand representations were made to me that the Bottle must be left at this place, or that, and called for again. I never yielded to one of them, and never parted from the Bottle, on any pretence, consideration, threat, or entreaty. I had no faith in any official receipt for the Bottle, and nothing would induce me to accept one. These unmanageable politics at last brought me and the Bottle, still triumphant, to Genoa. There, I took a tender and reluctant leave of him for a few weeks, and consigned him to a trusty English captain, to be conveyed to the Port of London by sea.

While the Bottle was on his voyage to England, I read the Shipping Intelligence as anxiously as if I had been an underwriter. There was some stormy weather after I myself had got to England by way of Switzerland and France, and my mind greatly misgave me that the Bottle might be wrecked. At last to my great joy, I received notice of his safe arrival, and immediately went down to Saint Katharine's Docks, and found him in a state of honourable captivity in the Custom House.

The wine was mere vinegar when I set it down before the generous Englishman—probably it had been something like vinegar when I took it up from Giovanni Carlavero—but not a drop of it was spilled or gone. And the Englishman told me, with much emotion in his face and voice, that he had never tasted wine that seemed to him so sweet and sound. And long afterwards, the Bottle graced his table. And the last time I saw him in this world that misses him, he took me aside in a crowd, to say, with his amiable smile: "We were talking of you only to-day at dinner, and I wished you had been there, for I had some Claret up in Carlavero's Bottle."

XVIII

It is an unsettled question with me whether I shall leave Calais something handsome in my will, or whether I shall leave it my malediction. I hate it so much, and yet I am always so very glad to see it, that I am in a state of constant indecision on this subject. When I first made acquaintance with Calais, it was as a maundering young wretch in a clammy perspiration and dripping saline particles, who was conscious of no extremities but the one great extremity, sea-sickness—who was a mere bilious torso, with a mislaid headache somewhere in its stomach—who had been put into a horrible swing in Dover Harbour, and had tumbled giddily out of it on the French coast, or the Isle of Man, or anywhere. Times have changed, and now I enter Calais self-reliant and rational. I know where it is beforehand, I keep a look out for it, I recognise its landmarks when I see any of them, I am acquainted with its ways, and I know—and I can bear—its worst behaviour.

Malignant Calais! Low-lying alligator, evading the eyesight and discouraging hope! Dodging flat streak, now on this bow, now on that, now anywhere, now everywhere, now nowhere! In vain Cape Grinez, coming frankly forth into the sea, exhorts the failing to be stout of heart and stomach : sneaking Calais, prone behind its bar, invites emetically to despair. Even when it can no longer quite conceal itself in its muddy dock, it has an evil way of falling off, has Calais, which is more hopeless than its invisibility. The pier is all but on the bowsprit, and you think you are there—roll, roar, wash !—Calais has retired miles inland, and Dover has burst out to look for it. It has a last dip and slide in its character, has Calais, to be especially commended to the infernal gods. Thrice accursed be that garrison-town, when it dives under the boat's keel, and comes up a league or two to the right, with the packet shivering and spluttering and staring about for it !

Not but what I have my animosities towards -Dover. I particularly detest Dover for the self-complacency with which it goes to bed. It always goes to bed (when I am going to Calais) with a more brilliant display of lamp and candle than any other town. Mr. and Mrs. Birmingham, host and hostess of the Lord Warden Hotel, are my much esteemed friends, but they are too conceited about the comforts of that establishment when the Night Mail is starting. I know it is a good house to stay at, and I don't want the fact insisted upon in all its warm bright windows at such an hour. I know the Warden is a stationary edifice that never rolls or pitches, and I object to its big outline seeming to insist upon that circumstance, and, as it were, to come over me with it, when I am reeling on the deck of the boat. Beshrew the Warden likewise for obstructing that corner, and making the wind so angry as it rushes round. Shall I not know that it blows quite soon enough, without the officious Warden's interference ?

As I wait here on board the night packet, for the South-Eastern Train to come down with the Mail, Dover appears to me to be illuminated for some intensely aggravating festivity in my personal dishonour. All its noises smack of taunting praises of the land, and dispraises of the gloomy sea, and of me for going on it. The drums upon the heights have gone to bed, or I know they would rattle taunts against me for having my unsteady footing on this slippery deck. The many gas eyes of the Marine Parade twinkle in an offensive manner, as if with derision. The distant dogs of Dover bark at me in my mis-shapen wrappers, as if I were Richard the Third.

A screech, a bell, and two red eyes come gliding down the Admiralty Pier with a smoothness of motion rendered more smooth by the heaving of the boat. The sea makes noises against the pier, as if several hippopotami were lapping at it, and were prevented by circumstances over which they had no control from drinking peaceably. We, the boat, become violently agitated—rumble, hum, scream, roar, and establish an immense family washing-day at each paddle-box. Bright patches break out in the train as the doors of the post-office vans are opened, and instantly stooping figures with sacks upon their backs begin to be beheld among the piles, descending as it would seem in ghostly procession to Davy Jones's Locker. The passengers come on board ; a few shadowy Frenchmen, with hatboxes shaped like the stoppers of gigantic case-bottles ; a few shadowy Germans in immense fur coats and boots ; a few shadowy Englishmen prepared for the worst and pretending not to expect it. I cannot disguise from my uncommercial mind the miserable fact that we are a body of outcasts ; that the attendants on us are as scant in number as may serve to get rid of us with the least possible delay ; that there are no night-loungers interested in us; that the unwilling lamps shiver and shudder at us ; that the sole object is to commit us to the deep and abandon us. Lo. the two red eyes glaring in increasing distance, and then the very train itself has gone to bed before we are off !

What is the moral support derived by some sea-going amateurs from an umbrella? Why do certain voyagers across the Channel always put up that article, and hold it up with a grim and fierce tenacity ? A fellow-creature near me—whom I only know to *be* a fellow-creature, because of his umbrella : without which he might be a dark bit of cliff, pier, or bulkhead—clutches that instrument with a desperate grasp, that will not relax until he lands at Calais. Is there any analogy, in certain constitutions, between keeping an umbrella up, and keeping the spirits up ? A hawser thrown on board with a flop replies " Stand by ! " " Stand by, below ! " " Half a turn a head ! " " Half a turn a head ! " " Half speed ! " " Half speed ! " " Port ! " " Port ! " " Steady ! " " Steady ! " " Go on ! " " Go on ! "

A stout wooden wedge driven in at my right temple and out at my left, a floating deposit of lukewarm oil in my throat, and a compression of the bridge of my nose in a blunt pair of pincers,—these are the personal sensations by which I know we are off, and by which I shall continue to know it until I am on the soil of France. My symptoms have scarcely established themselves comfortably, when two or three skating shadows that have been trying to walk or stand, get flung together, and other two or three shadows in tarpaulin slide with them into corners and cover them up. Then the South Foreland lights begin to hiccup at us in a way that bodes no good.

It is at about this period that my detestation of Calais knows no bounds. Inwardly I resolve afresh that I never

will forgive that hated town. I have done so before, many
times, but that is past. Let me register a vow. Implacable animosity to Calais everm——that was an awkward sea, and the funnel seems of my opinion, for it gives
a complaining roar.

The wind blows stiffly from the Nor'-East, the sea runs
high, we ship a deal of water, the night is dark and cold,
and the shapeless passengers lie about in melancholy
bundles, as if they were sorted out for the laundress; but
for my own uncommercial part I cannot pretend that I am
much inconvenienced by any of these things. A general
howling whistling flopping gurgling and scooping, I am
aware of, and a general knocking about of Nature; but the
impressions I receive are very vague. In a sweet faint
temper, something like the smell of damaged oranges,
I think I should feel languidly benevolent if I had time.
I have not time, because I am under a curious compulsion
to occupy myself with the Irish melodies. "Rich and rare
were the gems she wore," is the particular melody to which
I find myself devoted. I sing it to myself in the most
charming manner and with the greatest expression. Now
and then, I raise my head (I am sitting on the hardest of
wet seats, in the most uncomfortable of wet attitudes, but
I don't mind it,) and notice that I am a whirling shuttlecock between a fiery battledore of a lighthouse on the
French coast and a fiery battledore of a lighthouse on
the English coast; but I don't notice it particularly, except
to feel envenomed in my hatred of Calais. Then I go on
again, " Rich and rare were the ge-ems she-e-e-e wore, And
a bright gold ring on her wa-and she bo-ore, But O her
beauty was fa-a-a-a-r beyond "—I am particularly proud of
my execution here, when I become aware of another awkward shock from the sea, and another protest from the
funnel, and a fellow-creature at the paddle-box more audibly
indisposed than I think he need be—" Her sparkling gems,
or snow-white wand, But O her beauty was fa-a-a-a-r beyond "—another awkward one here, and the fellow-creature
with the umbrella down and picked up—" Her spa-a-rkling
ge-ems, or her Port ! port ! steady ! steady ! snow-white
fellow-creature at the paddle-box very selfishly audible, bump
roar wash white wand."

As my execution of the Irish melodies partakes of my
imperfect perceptions of what is going on around me, so

what is going on around me becomes something else than what it is. The stokers open the furnace doors below, to feed the fires, and I am again on the box of the old Exeter Telegraph fast coach, and that is the light of the for ever extinguished coach-lamps, and the gleam on the hatches and paddle-boxes is *their* gleam on cottages and haystacks, and the monotonous noise of the engines is the steady jingle of the splendid team. Anon, the intermittent funnel roar of protest at every violent roll, becomes the regular blast of a high pressure engine, and I recognise the exceedingly explosive steamer in which I ascended the Mississippi when the American civil war was not, and when only its causes were. A fragment of mast on which the light of a lantern falls, an end of rope, and a jerking block or so, become suggestive of Franconi's Circus at Paris where I shall be this very night mayhap (for it must be morning now), and they dance to the self-same time and tune as the trained steed, Black Raven. What may be the speciality of these waves as they come rushing on, I cannot desert the pressing demands made upon me by the gems she wore, to inquire, but they are charged with something about Robinson Crusoe, and I think it was in Yarmouth Roads that he first went a seafaring and was near foundering (what a terrific sound that word had for me when I was a boy!) in his first gale of wind. Still, through all this, I must ask her (who *was* she, I wonder!) for the fiftieth time, and without ever stopping, Does she not fear to stray, So lone and lovely through this bleak way, And are Erin's sons so good or so cold, As not to be tempted by more fellow-creatures at the paddle-box or gold? Sir Knight I feel not the least alarm, No son of Erin will offer me harm, For though they love fellow-creature with umbrella down again and golden store, Sir Knight they what a tremendous one love honour and virtue more: For though they love Stewards with a bull's eye bright, they'll trouble you for your ticket, sir—rough passage to-night!

I freely admit it to be a miserable piece of human weakness and inconsistency, but I no sooner become conscious of those last words from the steward than I begin to soften towards Calais. Whereas I have been vindictively wishing that those Calais burghers who came out of their town by a short cut into the History of England, with those fatal ropes round their necks by which they have since been towed into so many cartoons, had all been hanged on the spot, I now begin to regard them as highly respectable and virtuous tradesmen. Looking about me, I see the light of Cape Grinez well astern of the boat on the davits to leeward, and the light of Calais Harbour undeniably at its old tricks, but still ahead and shining. Sentiments of forgiveness of Calais, not to say of attachment to Calais, begin to expand my bosom. I have weak notions that I will stay there a day or two on my way back. A faded and recumbent stranger pausing in a profound reverie over the rim of a basin, asked me what kind of place Calais is? I tell him (Heaven forgive me!) a very agreeable place indeed—rather hilly than otherwise.

So strangely goes the time, and on the whole so quickly — though still I seem to have been on board a week—that I am bumped rolled gurgled washed and pitched into Calais Harbour before her maiden smile has finally lighted her through the Green Isle, When blest for ever is she who relied, On entering Calais at the top of the tide. For we have not to land to-night down among those slimy timbers— covered with green hair as if it were the mermaids' favourite combing-place—where one crawls to the surface of the jetty, like a stranded shrimp, but we go steaming up the harbour to the Railway Station Quay. And as we go, the sea washes in and out among piles and planks, with dead heavy beats and in quite a furious manner (whereof we are proud), and the lamps shake in the wind, and the bells of Calais striking One seem to send their vibrations struggling against troubled air, as we have come struggling against troubled water. And now, in the sudden relief and wiping of faces, everybody on board seems to have had a prodigious double-tooth out, and to be this very instant free of the Dentist's hands. And now we all know for the first time how wet and cold we are, and how salt we are; and now I love Calais with my heart of hearts!

"Hôtel Dessin!" (but in this one case it is not a vocal cry; it is but a bright lustre in the eyes of the cheery representative of that best of inns). "Hôtel Meurice!" "Hôtel de France!" "Hôtel de Calais!" "The Royal Hôtel, Sir, Angaishe ouse!" "You going to Parry, Sir?" "Your baggage, registair froo, Sir?" Bless ye, my Touters, bless ye, my commissionaires, bless ye, my hungry-eyed mysteries in caps of a military form, who are always here, day or night, fair weather or foul, seeking inscrutable jobs

which I never see you get! Bless ye, my Custom House
officers in green and grey; permit me to grasp the welcome
hands that descend into my travelling-bag, one on each side,
and meet at the bottom to give my change of linen a peculiar
shake up, as if it were a measure of chaff or grain! I have
nothing to declare, Monsieur le Douanier, except that when
I cease to breathe, Calais will be found written on my heart.
No article liable to local duty have I with me, Monsieur
l'Officier de l'Octroi, unless the overflowing of a breast
devoted to your charming town should be in that wise
chargeable. Ah! see at the gangway by the twinkling
lantern, my dearest brother and friend, he once of the
Passport Office, he who collects the names! May he be
for ever changeless in his buttoned black surtout, with
his note-book in his hand, and his tall black hat surmounting his round smiling patient face! Let us embrace, my
dearest brother. I am yours à tout jamais—for the whole
of ever.

Calais up and doing at the railway station, and Calais
down and dreaming in its bed; Calais with something of
"an ancient and fish-like smell" about it, and Calais blown
and sea-washed pure; Calais represented at the Buffet by
savoury roast fowls, hot coffee, cognac, and Bordeaux; and
Calais represented everywhere by flitting persons with
a monomania for changing money—though I never shall
be able to understand in my present state of existence
how they live by it, but I suppose I should, if I understood
the currency question—Calais *en gros*, and Calais *en détail*,
forgive one who has deeply wronged you.—I was not fully
aware of it on the other side, but I meant Dover.

Ding, ding! To the carriages, gentlemen the travellers.
Ascend then, gentlemen the travellers, for Hazebroucke,
Lille, Douai, Bruxelles, Arras, Amiens, and Paris! I, humble
representative of the uncommercial interest, ascend with the
rest. The train is light to-night, and I share my compart-
ment with but two fellow-travellers; one, a compatriot in
an obsolete cravat, who thinks it a quite unaccountable
thing that they don't keep "London time" on a French
railway, and who is made angry by my modestly suggesting
the possibility of Paris time being more in their way; the
other, a young priest, with a very small bird in a very small
cage, who feeds the small bird with a quill, and then puts
him up in the network above his head, where he advances

twittering, to his front wires, and seems to address me in an electioneering manner. The compatriot (who crossed in the boat, and whom I judge to be some person of distinction, as he was shut up, like a stately species of rabbit, in a private hutch on deck) and the young priest (who joined us at Calais) are soon asleep, and then the bird and I have it all to ourselves.

A stormy night still; a night that sweeps the wires of the electric telegraph with a wild and fitful hand; a night so very stormy, with the added storm of the train-progress through it, that when the Guard comes clambering round to mark the tickets while we are at full speed (a really horrible performance in an express train, though he holds on to the open window by his elbows in the most deliberate manner), he stands in such a whirlwind that I grip him fast by the collar, and feel it next to manslaughter to let him go. Still, when he is gone, the small small bird remains at his front wires feebly twittering to me—twittering and twittering, until, leaning back in my place and looking at him in drowsy fascination, I find that he seems to jog my memory as we rush along.

Uncommercial travels (thus the small small bird) have lain in their idle thriftless way through all this range of swamp and dyke, as through many other odd places; and about here, as you very well know, are the queer old stone farm-houses, approached by drawbridges, and the windmills that you get at by boats. Here, are the lands where the women hoe and dig, paddling canoe-wise from field to field, and here are the cabarets and other peasant-houses where the stone dove-cotes in the littered yards are as strong as warders' towers in old castles. Here, are the long monotonous miles of canal, with the great Dutch-built barges garishly painted, and the towing girls, sometimes harnessed by the forehead, sometimes by the girdle and the shoulders, not a pleasant sight to see. Scattered through this country are mighty works of VAUBAN, whom you know about, and regiments of such corporals as you heard of once upon a time, and many a blue-eyed Bebelle. Through these flat districts, in the shining summer days, walk those long grotesque files of young novices in enormous shovel-hats, whom you remember blackening the ground checkered by the avenues of leafy trees. And now that Hazebroucke slumbers certain kilo-metres ahead, recall the summer evening when your dusty

feet strolling up from the station tended hap-hazard to
a Fair there, where the oldest inhabitants were circling
round and round a barrel-organ on hobby-horses, with the
greatest gravity, and where the principal show in the Fair
was a Religious Richardson's—literally, on its own announcement in great letters, THEATRE RELIGIEUX. In
which improving Temple, the dramatic representation was
of "all the interesting events in the life of our Lord, from
the Manger to the Tomb;" the principal female character,
without any reservation or exception, being at the moment
of your arrival, engaged in trimming the external Moderators
(as it was growing dusk), while the next principal female
character took the money, and the Young Saint John disported himself upside down on the platform.

Looking up at this point to confirm the small small bird
in every particular he has mentioned, I find he has ceased
to twitter, and has put his head under his wing.   Therefore,
in my different way I follow the good example.

XIX

SOME RECOLLECTIONS OF MORTALITY

I HAD parted from the small bird at somewhere about four o'clock in the morning, when he had got out at Arras, and had been received by two shovel-hats in waiting at the station, who presented an appropriately ornithological and crow-like appearance. My compatriot and I had gone on to Paris; my compatriot enlightening me occasionally with a long list of the enormous grievances of French railway travelling: every one of which, as I am a sinner, was perfectly new to me, though I have as much experience of French railways as most uncommercials. I had left him at the terminus (through his conviction, against all explanation and remonstrance, that his baggage-ticket was his passenger-ticket), insisting in a very high temper to the functionary on duty, that in his own personal identity he was four packages weighing so many kilogrammes—as if he had been Cassim Baba! I had bathed and breakfasted, and was strolling on the bright quays. The subject of my meditations was the question whether it is positively in the essence and nature of things, as a certain school of Britons would seem to think it, that a Capital must be ensnared and enslaved before it can be made beautiful: when I lifted up my eyes and found that my feet, straying like my mind, had brought me to Notre-Dame.

That is to say, Notre-Dame was before me, but there was a large open space between us. A very little while gone, I had left that space covered with buildings densely crowded; and now it was cleared for some new wonder in the way of public Street, Place, Garden, Fountain, or all four. Only the obscene little Morgue, slinking on the brink of the river and soon to come down, was left there, looking mortally ashamed of itself, and supremely wicked. I had but glanced at this old acquaintance, when I beheld an airy procession coming round in front of Notre-Dame, past the great hospital. It had something of a Masaniello look, with fluttering striped curtains in the midst of it, and it came dancing round the cathedral in the liveliest manner.

I was speculating on a marriage in Blouse-life, or a Christening, or some other domestic festivity which I would see out, when I found, from the talk of a quick rush of Blouses past me, that it was a Body coming to the Morgue. Having never before chanced upon this initiation, I constituted myself a Blouse likewise, and ran into the Morgue with the rest. It was a very muddy day, and we took in a quantity of mire with us, and the procession coming in upon our heels brought a quantity more. The procession was in the highest spirits, and consisted of idlers who had come with the curtained litter from its starting-place, and of all the reinforcements it had picked up by the way. It set the litter down in the midst of the Morgue, and then two Custodians proclaimed aloud that we were all "invited" to go out. This invitation was rendered the more pressing, if not the more flattering, by our being shoved out, and the folding-gates being barred upon us.

Those who have never seen the Morgue, may see it perfectly, by presenting to themselves an indifferently paved coach-house accessible from the street by a pair of folding-gates; on the left of the coach-house, occupying its width, any large London tailor's or linendraper's plate-glass window reaching to the ground; within the window, on two rows of inclined plane, what the coach-house has to show; hanging above, like irregular stalactites from the roof of a cave, a quantity of clothes—the clothes of the dead and buried shows of the coach-house.

We had been excited in the highest degree by seeing the Custodians pull off their coats and tuck up their shirt-sleeves, as the procession came along. It looked so interestingly like business. Shut out in the muddy street, we now became quite ravenous to know all about it. Was it river, pistol, knife, love, gambling, robbery, hatred, how many stabs, how many bullets, fresh or decomposed, suicide or murder? All wedged together, and all staring at one another with our heads thrust forward, we propounded these inquiries and a hundred more such. Imperceptibly, it came to be known that Monsieur the tall and sallow mason yonder, was acquainted with the facts. Would Monsieur the tall and sallow mason, surged at by a new wave of us, have the goodness to impart? It was but a poor old man, passing along the street under one of the new buildings, on whom a stone had fallen, and who had tumbled dead. His age? Another wave surged up against the tall and sallow mason, and our wave swept on and broke, and he was any age from sixty-five to ninety.

An old man was not much : moreover, we could have wished he had been killed by human agency—his own, or somebody else's : the latter, preferable—but our comfort was, that he had nothing about him to lead to his identification, and that his people must seek him here. Perhaps they were waiting dinner for him even now? We liked that. Such of us as had pocket-handkerchiefs took a slow intense protracted wipe at our noses, and then crammed our handkerchiefs into the breast of our blouses. Others of us who had no handker- chiefs administered a similar relief to our overwrought minds, by means of prolonged smears or wipes of our mouths on our sleeves. One man with a gloomy malformation of brow— a homicidal worker in white-lead, to judge from his blue tone of colour, and a certain flavour of paralysis pervading him—got his coat-collar between his teeth, and bit at it with an appetite. Several decent women arrived upon the out- skirts of the crowd, and prepared to launch themselves into the dismal coach-house when opportunity should come, among them, a pretty young mother, pretending to bite the forefinger of her baby-boy, kept it between her rosy lips that it might be handy for guiding to point at the show. Mean- time, all faces were turned towards the building, and we men waited with a fixed and stern resolution :—for the most part with folded arms. Surely, it was the only public French sight these uncommercial eyes had seen, at which the expectant people did not form *en queue*. But there was no such order of arrangement here ; nothing but a general determination to make a rush for it, and a disposition to object to some boys who had mounted on the two stone posts by the hinges of the gates, with the design of swoop- ing in when the hinges should turn.

Now, they turned, and we rushed ! Great pressure, and a scream or two from the front. Then a laugh or two, some expressions of disappointment, and a slackening of the pressure and subsidence of the struggle.—Old man not there.

"But what would you have?" the Custodian reasonably

argues, as he looks out at his little door. "Patience, patience! We make his toilette, gentlemen. He will be exposed presently. It is necessary to proceed according to rule. His toilette is not made all at a blow. He will be exposed in good time, gentlemen, in good time." And so retires, smoking, with a wave of his sleeveless arm towards the window, importing, "Entertain yourselves in the meanwhile with the other curiosities. Fortunately the Museum is not empty to-day."

Who would have thought of public fickleness even at the Morgue? But there it was, on that occasion. Three lately popular articles that had been attracting greatly when the litter was first descried coming dancing round the corner by the great cathedral, were so completely deposed now, that nobody save two little girls (one showing them to a doll) would look at them. Yet the chief of the three, the article in the front row, had received jagged injury of the left temple; and the other two in the back row, the drowned two lying side by side with their heads very slightly turned towards each other, seemed to be comparing notes about it. Indeed, those two of the back row were so furtive of appearance, and so (in their puffed way) assassinatingly knowing as to the one of the front, that it was hard to think the three had never come together in their lives, and were only chance companions after death. Whether or no this was the general, as it was the uncommercial, fancy, it is not to be disputed that the group had drawn exceedingly within ten minutes. Yet now, the inconstant public turned its back upon them, and even leaned its elbows carelessly against the bar outside the window and shook off the mud from its shoes, and also lent and borrowed fire for pipes.

Custodian re-enters from his door. "Again once, gentlemen, you are invited—— " No further invitation necessary. Ready dash into the street. Toilette finished. Old man coming out.

This time, the interest was grown too hot to admit of toleration of the boys on the stone posts. The homicidal white-lead worker made a pounce upon one boy who was hoisting himself up, and brought him to earth amidst general commendation. Closely stowed as we were, we yet formed into groups—groups of conversation, without separation from the mass—to discuss the old man. Rivals of the tall and sallow mason sprang into being, and here again was

popular inconstancy. These rivals attracted audiences, and
were greedily listened to ; and whereas they had derived
their information solely from the tall and sallow one, officious
members of the crowd now sought to enlighten *him* on their
authority. Changed by this social experience into an iron-
visaged and inveterate misanthrope, the mason glared at
mankind, and evidently cherished in his breast the wish that
the whole of the present company could change places with
the deceased old man. And now listeners became inattentive,
and people made a start forward at a slight sound, and an
unholy fire kindled in the public eye, and those next the
gates beat at them impatiently, as if they were of the
cannibal species and hungry.

Again the hinges creaked, and we rushed. Disorderly
pressure for some time ensued before the uncommercial unit
got figured into the front row of the sum. It was strange
to see so much heat and uproar seething about one poor
spare white-haired old man, quiet for evermore. He was
calm of feature and undisfigured, as he lay on his back—
having been struck upon the hinder part of the head, and
thrown forward—and something like a tear or two had
started from the closed eyes, and lay wet upon the face.
The uncommercial interest, sated at a glance, directed itself
upon the striving crowd on either side and behind : wondering whether one might have guessed, from the expression of
those faces merely, what kind of sight they were looking at.
The differences of expression were not many. There was
a little pity, but not much, and that mostly with a selfish
touch in it—as who would say, "Shall I, poor I, look like
that, when the time comes !" There was more of a secretly
brooding contemplation and curiosity, as "That man I don't
like, and have the grudge against ; would such be his appearance, if some one—not to mention names—by any chance
gave him an ugly knock ? " There was a wolfish stare at
the object, in which the homicidal white-lead worker shone
conspicuous. And there was a much more general, purpose-
less, vacant staring at it—like looking at waxwork, without
a catalogue, and not knowing what to make of it. But all
these expressions concurred in possessing the one under-
lying expression of *looking at something that could not return
a look.* The uncommercial notice had established this as
very remarkable, when a new pressure all at once coming
up from the street pinioned him ignominiously, and hurried

him into the arms (now sleeved again) of the Custodian smoking at his door, and answering questions, between puffs, with a certain placid meritorious air of not being proud, though high in office. And mentioning pride, it may be observed, by the way, that one could not well help investing the original sole occupant of the front row with an air depreciatory of the legitimate attraction of the poor old man: while the two in the second row seemed to exult at this superseded popularity.

Pacing presently round the garden of the Tower of St. Jacques de la Boucherie, and presently again in front of the Hôtel de Ville, I called to mind a certain desolate open-air Morgue that I happened to light upon in London, one day in the hard winter of 1861, and which seemed as strange to me, at the time of seeing it, as if I had found it in China. Towards that hour of a winter's afternoon when the lamp-lighters are beginning to light the lamps in the streets a little before they are wanted, because the darkness thickens fast and soon, I was walking in from the country on the northern side of the Regent's Park—hard frozen and deserted —when I saw an empty Hansom cab drive up to the lodge at Gloucester-gate, and the driver with great agitation call to the man there : who quickly reached a long pole from a tree, and, deftly collared by the driver, jumped to the step of his little seat, and so the Hansom rattled out at the gate, galloping over the iron-bound road. I followed running, though not so fast but that when I came to the right-hand Canal Bridge, near the cross-path to Chalk Farm, the Hansom was stationary, the horse was smoking hot, the long pole was idle on the ground, and the driver and the park-keeper were looking over the bridge parapet. Looking over too, I saw, lying on the towing-path with her face turned up towards us, a woman, dead a day or two, and under thirty, as I guessed, poorly dressed in black. The feet were lightly crossed at the ankles, and the dark hair, all pushed back from the face, as though that had been the last action of her desperate hands, streamed over the ground. Dabbled all about her, was the water and the broken ice that had dropped from her dress, and had splashed as she was got out. The policeman who had just got her out, and the passing costermonger who had helped him, were standing near the body ; the latter with that stare at it which I have likened to being at a waxwork exhibition without a catalogue ; the former, looking over his stock, with professional stiffness and coolness, in the direction in which the bearers he had sent for were expected. So dreadfully forlorn, so dreadfully sad, so dreadfully mysterious, this spectacle of our dear sister here departed! A barge came up, breaking the floating ice and the silence, and a woman steered it. The man with the horse that towed it, cared so little for the body, that the stumbling hoofs had been among the hair, and the tow-rope had caught and turned the head, before our cry of horror took him to the bridle. At which sound the steering woman looked up at us on the bridge, with contempt unutterable, and then looking down at the body with a similar expression—as if it were made in another likeness from herself, had been informed with other passions, had been lost by other chances, had had another nature dragged down to perdition—steered a spurning streak of mud at it, and passed on.

A better experience, but also of the Morgue kind, in which chance happily made me useful in a slight degree, arose to my remembrance as I took my way by the Boulevard de Sébastopol to the brighter scenes of Paris.

The thing happened, say five-and-twenty years ago. I was a modest young uncommercial then, and timid and inexperienced. Many suns and winds have browned me in the line, but those were my pale days. Having newly taken the lease of a house in a certain distinguished metropolitan parish —a house which then appeared to me to be a frightfully first-class Family Mansion, involving awful responsibilities— I became the prey of a Beadle. I think the Beadle must have seen me going in or coming out, and must have observed that I tottered under the weight of my grandeur. Or he may have been in hiding under straw when I bought my first horse (in the desirable stable-yard attached to the first-class Family Mansion), and when the vendor remarked to me, in an original manner, on bringing him for approval, taking his cloth off and smacking him, "There, Sir! *There's* a Orse!" And when I said gallantly, "How much do you want for him?" and when the vendor said, "No more than sixty guineas, from you," and when I said smartly, "Why not more than sixty from *me?*" And when he said crushingly, "Because upon my soul and body he'd be considered cheap at seventy, by one who understood the subject—but you don't."—I say, the Beadle may have been in hiding under straw, when this disgrace befell me, or he may have

noted that I was too raw and young an Atlas to carry the
first-class Family Mansion in a knowing manner. Be this
as it may, the Beadle did what Melancholy did to the youth
in Gray's Elegy—he marked me for his own. And the way
in which the Beadle did it, was this: he summoned me as
a Juryman on his Coroner's Inquests.

In my first feverish alarm I repaired "for safety and for
succour"—like those sagacious Northern shepherds who,
having had no previous reason whatever to believe in young
Norval, very prudently did not originate the hazardous idea
of believing in him—to a deep householder. This profound
man informed me that the Beadle counted on my buying
him off; on my bribing him not to summon me; and that
if I would attend an Inquest with a cheerful countenance,
and profess alacrity in that branch of my country's service,
the Beadle would be disheartened, and would give up the
game.

I roused my energies, and the next time the wily Beadle
summoned me, I went. The Beadle was the blankest Beadle
I have ever looked on when I answered to my name; and
his discomfiture gave me courage to go through with it.

We were impanelled to inquire concerning the death of a
very little mite of a child. It was the old miserable story.
Whether the mother had committed the minor offence of
concealing the birth, or whether she had committed the
major offence of killing the child, was the question on which
we were wanted. We must commit her on one of the two
issues.

The Inquest came off in the parish workhouse, and I have
yet a lively impression that I was unanimously received by
my brother Jurymen as a brother of the utmost conceivable
insignificance. Also, that before we began, a broker who had
lately cheated me fearfully in the matter of a pair of card-
tables, was for the utmost rigour of the law. I remember
that we sat in a sort of board-room, on such very large square
horse-hair chairs that I wondered what race of Patagonians
they were made for; and further, that an undertaker gave
me his card when we were in the full moral freshness of
having just been sworn, as "an inhabitant that was newly
come into the parish, and was likely to have a young family."
The case was then stated to us by the Coroner, and then we
went down-stairs—led by the plotting Beadle—to view the
body. From that day to this, the poor little figure, on which

that sounding legal appellation was bestowed, has lain in the same place and with the same surroundings, to my thinking. In a kind of crypt devoted to the warehousing of the parochial coffins, and in the midst of a perfect Panorama of coffins of all sizes, it was stretched on a box; the mother had put it in her box—this box—almost as soon as it was born, and it had been presently found there. It had been opened, and neatly sewn up, and regarded from that point of view, it looked like a stuffed creature. It rested on a clean white cloth, with a surgical instrument or so at hand, and regarded from that point of view, it looked as if the cloth were "laid," and the Giant were coming to dinner. There was nothing repellant about the poor piece of innocence, and it demanded a mere form of looking at. So, we looked at an old pauper who was going about among the coffins with a foot rule, as if he were a case of Self-Measurement; and we looked at one another; and we said the place was well whitewashed anyhow; and then our conversational powers as a British Jury flagged, and the foreman said, "All right, gentlemen? Back again, Mr. Beadle!"

The miserable young creature who had given birth to this child within a very few days, and who had cleaned the cold wet door-steps immediately afterwards, was brought before us when we resumed our horse-hair chairs, and was present during the proceedings. She had a horse-hair chair herself, being very weak and ill; and I remember how she turned to the unsympathetic nurse who attended her, and who might have been the figure-head of a pauper-ship, and how she hid her face and sobs and tears upon that wooden shoulder. I remember, too, how hard her mistress was upon her (she was a servant-of-all-work), and with what a cruel pertinacity that piece of Virtue spun her thread of evidence double, by intertwisting it with the sternest thread of construction. Smitten hard by the terrible low wail from the utterly friendless orphan girl, which never ceased during the whole inquiry, I took heart to ask this witness a question or two, which hopefully admitted of an answer that might give a favourable turn to the case. She made the turn as little favourable as it could be, but it did some good, and the Coroner, who was nobly patient and humane (he was the late Mr. Wakley), cast a look of strong encouragement in my direction. Then, we had the doctor who had made the examination, and the usual tests as to whether the child was

born alive; but he was a timid muddle-headed doctor, and
got confused and contradictory, and wouldn't say this, and
couldn't answer for that, and the immaculate broker was
too much for him, and our side slid back again. However,
I tried again, and the Coroner backed me again, for which
I ever afterwards felt grateful to him as I do now to his
memory; and we got another favourable turn, out of some
other witness, some member of the family with a strong
prepossession against the sinner; and I think we had the
doctor back again; and I know that the Coroner summed
up for our side, and that I and my British brothers turned
round to discuss our verdict, and get ourselves into great
difficulties with our large chairs and the broker. At that
stage of the case I tried hard again, being convinced that
I had cause for it; and at last we found for the minor
offence of only concealing the birth; and the poor desolate
creature, who had been taken out during our deliberation,
being brought in again to be told of the verdict, then
dropped upon her knees before us, with protestations that
we were right—protestations among the most affecting that
I have ever heard in my life—and was carried away insensible.

(In private conversation after this was all over, the Coroner
showed me his reasons as a trained surgeon, for perceiving
it to be impossible that the child could, under the most
favourable circumstances, have drawn many breaths, in the
very doubtful case of its having ever breathed at all; this,
owing to the discovery of some foreign matter in the wind-
pipe, quite irreconcilable with many moments of life.)

When the agonised girl had made those final protestations,
I had seen her face, and it was in unison with her distracted
heartbroken voice, and it was very moving. It certainly did
not impress me by any beauty that it had, and if I ever see
it again in another world I shall only know it by the help
of some new sense or intelligence. But it came to me in my
sleep that night, and I selfishly dismissed it in the most
efficient way I could think of. I caused some extra care to
be taken of her in the prison, and counsel to be retained for
her defence when she was tried at the Old Bailey; and her
sentence was lenient, and her history and conduct proved
that it was right. In doing the little I did for her, I
remember to have had the kind help of some gentle-hearted
functionary to whom I addressed myself—but what func-

tionary I have long forgotten—who I suppose was officially present at the Inquest.

I regard this as a very notable uncommercial experience, because this good came of a Beadle. And to the best of my knowledge, information, and belief, it is the only good that ever did come of a Beadle since the first Beadle put on his cocked-hat.

XX

IT came into my mind that I would recall in these notes a few of the many hostelries I have rested at in the course of my journeys ; and, indeed, I had taken up my pen for the purpose, when I was baffled by an accidental circumstance. It was the having to leave off, to wish the owner of a certain bright face that looked in at my door, "many happy returns of the day." Thereupon a new thought came into my mind, driving its predecessor out, and I began to recall—instead of Inns—the birthdays that I have put up at, on my way to this present sheet of paper.

I can very well remember being taken out to visit some peach-faced creature in a blue sash, and shoes to correspond, whose life I supposed to consist entirely of birthdays. Upon seed-cake, sweet wine, and shining presents, that glorified young person seemed to me to be exclusively reared. At so early a stage of my travels did I assist at the anniversary of her nativity (and become enamoured of her), that I had not yet acquired the recondite knowledge that a birthday is the common property of all who are born, but supposed it to be a special gift bestowed by the favouring Heavens on that one distinguished infant. There was no other company, and we sat in a shady bower—under a table, as my better (or worse) knowledge leads me to believe—and were regaled with saccharine substances and liquids, until it was time to part. A bitter powder was administered to me next morning, and I was wretched. On the whole, a pretty accurate fore-shadowing of my more mature experiences in such wise !

Then came the time when, inseparable from one's own birthday, was a certain sense of merit, a consciousness of well-earned distinction. When I regarded my birthday as a graceful achievement of my own, a monument of my perseverance, independence, and good sense, redounding greatly to my honour. This was at about the period when

H

Olympia Squires became involved in the anniversary. Olympia was most beautiful (of course), and I loved her to that degree, that I used to be obliged to get out of my little bed in the night, expressly to exclaim to Solitude, "O, Olympia Squires!" Visions of Olympia, clothed entirely in sage-green, from which I infer a defectively educated taste on the part of her respected parents, who were necessarily unacquainted with the South Kensington Museum, still arise before me. Truth is sacred, and the visions are crowned by a shining white beaver bonnet, impossibly suggestive of a little feminine postboy. My memory presents a birthday when Olympia and I were taken by an unfeeling relative—some cruel uncle, or the like—to a slow torture called an Orrery. The terrible instrument was set up at the local Theatre, and I had expressed a profane wish in the morning that it was a Play: for which a serious aunt had probed my conscience deep, and my pocket deeper, by reclaiming a bestowed half-crown. It was a venerable and a shabby Orrery, at least one thousand stars and twenty-five comets behind the age. Nevertheless, it was awful. When the low-spirited gentleman with a wand said, "Ladies and gentlemen" (meaning particularly Olympia and me), "the lights are about to be put out, but there is not the slightest cause for alarm," it was very alarming. Then the planets and stars began. Sometimes they wouldn't come on, sometimes they wouldn't go off, sometimes they had holes in them, and mostly they didn't seem to be good likenesses. All this time the gentleman with the wand was going on in the dark (tapping away at the heavenly bodies between whiles, like a wearisome woodpecker), about a sphere revolving on its own axis eight hundred and ninety-seven thousand millions of times —or miles—in two hundred and sixty-three thousand five hundred and twenty-four millions of something elses, until I thought if this was a birthday it were better never to have been born. Olympia, also, became much depressed, and we both slumbered and woke cross, and still the gentleman was going on in the dark—whether up in the stars, or down on the stage, it would have been hard to make out, if it had been worth trying—cyphering away about planes of orbits, to such an infamous extent that Olympia, stung to madness, actually kicked me. A pretty birthday spectacle, when the lights were turned up again, and all

the schools in the town (including the National, who had
come in for nothing, and serve them right, for they were
always throwing stones) were discovered with exhausted
countenances, screwing their knuckles into their eyes, or
clutching their heads of hair. A pretty birthday speech
when Dr. Sleek of the City-Free bobbed up his powdered
head in the stage-box, and said that before this assembly
dispersed he really must beg to express his entire approval
of a lecture as improving, as informing, as devoid of anything that could call a blush into the cheek of youth, as
any it had ever been his lot to hear delivered. A pretty
birthday altogether, when Astronomy couldn't leave poor
Small Olympia Squires and me alone, but must put an end
to our loves! For, we never got over it; the threadbare
Orrery outwore our mutual tenderness; the man with the
wand was too much for the boy with the bow.

When shall I disconnect the combined smells of oranges,
brown paper, and straw, from those other birthdays at school,
when the coming hamper casts its shadow before, and
when a week of social harmony—shall I add of admiring
and affectionate popularity—led up to that Institution?
What noble sentiments were expressed to me in the days
before the hamper, what vows of friendship were sworn
to me, what exceedingly old knives were given me, what
generous avowals of having been in the wrong emanated
from else obstinate spirits once enrolled among my enemies!
The birthday of the potted game and guava jelly, is still
made special to me by the noble conduct of Bully Globson.
Letters from home had mysteriously inquired whether
I should be much surprised and disappointed if among
the treasures in the coming hamper I discovered potted
game, and guava jelly from the Western Indies. I had
mentioned those hints in confidence to a few friends, and
had promised to give away, as I now see reason to believe,
a handsome covey of partridges potted, and about a hundred-
weight of guava jelly. It was now that Globson, Bully no
more, sought me out in the playground. He was a big
fat boy, with a big fat head and a big fat fist, and at the
beginning of that Half had raised such a bump on my forehead that I couldn't get my hat of state on, to go to church.
He said that after an interval of cool reflection (four months)
he now felt this blow to have been an error of judgment,
and that he wished to apologise for the same. Not only that,

but holding down his big head between his two big hands in order that I might reach it conveniently, he requested me, as an act of justice which would appease his awakened conscience, to raise a retributive bump upon it, in the presence of witnesses. This handsome proposal I modestly declined, and he then embraced me, and we walked away conversing. We conversed respecting the West India Islands, and, in the pursuit of knowledge he asked me with much interest whether in the course of my reading I had met with any reliable description of the mode of manufacturing guava jelly ; or whether I had ever happened to taste that conserve, which he had been given to under-stand was of rare excellence.

Seventeen, eighteen, nineteen, twenty ; and then with the waning months came an ever augmenting sense of the dignity of twenty-one. Heaven knows I had nothing to "come into," save the bare birthday, and yet I esteemed it as a great possession. I now and then paved the way to my state of dignity, by beginning a proposition with the casual words, "say that a man of twenty-one," or by the incidental assumption of a fact that could not sanely be disputed, as, "for when a fellow comes to be a man of twenty-one." I gave a party on the occasion. She was there. It is unnecessary to name Her more particularly ; She was older than I, and had pervaded every chink and crevice of my mind for three or four years. I had held volumes of Imaginary Conversations with her mother on the subject of our union, and I had written letters more in number than Horace Walpole's, to that discreet woman, soliciting her daughter's hand in marriage. I had never had the remotest intention of sending any of those letters ; but to write them, and after a few days tear them up, had been a sublime occupation. Sometimes, I had begun "Honoured Madam. I think that a lady gifted with those powers of observation which I know you to possess, and endowed with those womanly sympathies with the young and ardent which it were more than heresy to doubt, can scarcely have failed to discover that I love your ador-able daughter, deeply, devotedly." In less buoyant states of mind I had begun, "Bear with me, Dear Madam, bear with a daring wretch who is about to make a surprising confession to you, wholly unanticipated by yourself, and which he beseeches you to commit to the flames as soon as you have become aware to what a towering height his mad ambition soars." At other times—periods of profound mental depression, when She had gone out to balls where I was not—the draft took the affecting form of a paper to be left on my table after my departure to the confines of the globe. As thus : " For Mrs. Onowenever, these lines when the hand that traces them shall be far away. I could not bear the daily torture of hopelessly loving the dear one whom I will not name. Broiling on the coast of Africa, or congealing on the shores of Greenland, I am far far better there than here." (In this sentiment my cooler judgment perceives that the family of the beloved object would have most completely concurred.) " If I ever emerge from obscurity, and my name is ever heralded by Fame, it will be for her dear sake. If I ever amass Gold, it will be to pour it at her feet. Should I on the other hand become the prey of Ravens—— " I doubt if I ever quite made up my mind what was to be done in that affecting case ; I tried " then it is better so ; " but not feeling convinced that it would be better so, I vacillated between leaving all else blank, which looked expressive and bleak, or winding up with " Farewell ! "

This fictitious correspondence of mine is to blame for the foregoing digression. I was about to pursue the statement that on my twenty-first birthday I gave a party, and She was there. It was a beautiful party. There was not a single animate or inanimate object connected with it (except the company and myself) that I had ever seen before. Everything was hired, and the mercenaries in attendance were profound strangers to me. Behind a door, in the crumby part of the night when wine-glasses were to be found in unexpected spots, I spoke to Her—spoke out to Her. What passed, I cannot as a man of honour reveal. She was all angelical gentleness, but a word was mentioned —a short and dreadful word of three letters, beginning with a B—which, as I remarked at the moment, "scorched my brain." She went away soon afterwards, and when the hollow throng (though to be sure it was no fault of theirs) dispersed, I issued forth, with a dissipated scorner, and, as I mentioned expressly to him, "sought oblivion." It was found, with a dreadful headache in it, but it didn't last ; for, in the shaming light of next day's noon, I raised my heavy head in bed, looking back to the birthdays behind me, and tracking the circle by which I had got round, after all, to the bitter powder and the wretchedness again.

This reactionary powder (taken so largely by the human race, I am inclined to regard it as the Universal Medicine once sought for in Laboratories) is capable of being made up in another form for birthday use. Anybody's long-lost brother will do ill to turn up on a birthday. If I had a long-lost brother I should know beforehand that he would prove a tremendous fraternal failure if he appointed to rush into my arms on my birthday. The first Magic Lantern I ever saw, was secretly and elaborately planned to be the great effect of a very juvenile birthday; but it wouldn't act, and its images were dim. My experience of adult birthday Magic Lanterns may possibly have been unfortunate, but has certainly been similar. I have an illustrative birthday in my eye: a birthday of my friend Flipfield, whose birthdays had long been remarkable as social successes. There had been nothing set or formal about them; Flipfield having been accustomed merely to say, two or three days before, " Don't forget to come and dine, old boy, according to custom;"—I don't know what he said to the ladies he invited, but I may safely assume to have been "old girl." Those were delightful gatherings, and were enjoyed by all participators. In an evil hour, a long-lost brother of Flipfield's came to light in foreign parts. Where he had been hidden, or what he had been doing, I don't know, for Flipfield vaguely informed me that he had turned up " on the banks of the Ganges "—speaking of him as if he had been washed ashore. The Long-lost was coming home, and Flipfield made an unfortunate calculation, based on the well-known regularity of the P. and O. Steamers, that matters might be so contrived as that the Long-lost should appear in the nick of time on his (Flipfield's) birthday. Delicacy commanded that I should repress the gloomy anticipations with which my soul became fraught when I heard of this plan. The fatal day arrived, and we assembled in force. Mrs. Flipfield senior formed an interesting feature in the group, with a blue-veined miniature of the late Mr. Flipfield round her neck, in an oval, resembling a tart from the pastrycook's: his hair powdered, and the bright buttons on his coat, evidently very like. She was accompanied by Miss Flipfield, the eldest of her numerous family, who held her pocket-handkerchief to her bosom in a majestic manner, and spoke to all of us (none of us had ever seen her before), in pious and condoning tones, of all the quarrels that had taken place in the family, from her infancy—which must have been a long time ago—down to that hour. The Long-lost did not appear. Dinner, half an hour later than usual, was announced, and still no Long-lost. We sat down to table. The knife and fork of the Long-lost made a vacuum in Nature, and when the champagne came round for the first time, Flipfield gave him up for the day, and had them removed. It was then that the Long-lost gained the height of his popularity with the company ; for my own part, I felt convinced that I loved him dearly. Flipfield's dinners are perfect, and he is the easiest and best of entertainers. Dinner went on brilliantly, and the more the Long-lost didn't come, the more comfortable we grew, and the more highly we thought of him. Flipfield's own man (who has a regard for me) was in the act of struggling with an ignorant stipendiary, to wrest from him the wooden leg of a Guinea-fowl which he was pressing on my acceptance, and to substitute a slice of the breast, when a ringing at the door-bell suspended the strife. I looked round me, and perceived the sudden pallor which I knew my own visage revealed, reflected in the faces of the company. Flipfield hurriedly excused himself, went out, was absent for about a minute or two, and then re-entered with the Long lost.

I beg to say distinctly that if the stranger had brought Mont Blanc with him, or had come attended by a retinue of eternal snows, he could not have chilled the circle to the marrow in a more efficient manner. Embodied Failure sat enthroned upon the Long-lost's brow, and pervaded him to his Long-lost boots. In vain Mrs. Flipfield senior, opening her arms, exclaimed, "My Tom!" and pressed his nose against the counterfeit presentment of his other parent. In vain Miss Flipfield, in the first transports of this re-union, showed him a dint upon her maidenly cheek, and asked him if he remembered when he did that with the bellows ? We, the bystanders, were overcome, but overcome by the palpable, undisguisable, utter, and total breakdown of the Long-lost. Nothing he could have done would have set him right with us but his instant return to the Ganges. In the very same moments it became established that the feeling was reciprocal, and that the Long-lost detested us. When a friend of the family (not myself, upon my honour), wishing to set things going again, asked him, while he partook of soup—asked him with an amiability of intention beyond all praise, but with a weakness of execution open to defeat—what kind of river he considered the Ganges, the Long-lost, scowling at the friend of the family over his spoon, as one of an abhorrent race, replied, "Why a river of water, I suppose," and spooned his soup into himself with a malignancy of hand and eye that blighted the amiable questioner. Not an opinion could be elicited from the Long-lost, in unison with the sentiments of any individual present. He contradicted Flipfield dead, before he had eaten his salmon. He had no idea—or affected to have no idea—that it was his brother's birthday, and on the communication of that interesting fact to him, merely wanted to make him out four years older than he was. He was an antipathetical being, with a peculiar power and gift of treading on everybody's tenderest place. They talk in America of a man's "Platform." I should describe the Platform of the Long-lost as a Platform composed of other people's corns, on which he had stumped his way, with all his might and main, to his present position. It is needless to add that Flipfield's great birthday went by the board, and that he was a wreck when I pretended at parting to wish him many happy returns of it.

There is another class of birthdays at which I have so frequently assisted, that I may assume such birthdays to be pretty well known to the human race. My friend Mayday's birthday is an example. The guests have no knowledge of one another except on that one day in the year, and are annually terrified for a week by the prospect of meeting one another again. There is a fiction among us that we have uncommon reasons for being particularly lively and spirited on the occasion, whereas deep despondency is no phrase for the expression of our feelings. But the wonderful feature of the case is, that we are in tacit accordance to avoid the subject—to keep it as far off as possible, as long as possible —and to talk about anything else, rather than the joyful event. I may even go so far as to assert that there is a dumb compact among us that we will pretend that it is NOT Mayday's birthday. A mysterious and gloomy Being, who is said to have gone to school with Mayday, and who is

so lank and lean that he seriously impugns the Dietary of
the establishment at which they were jointly educated,
always leads us, as I may say, to the block, by laying his
grisly hand on a decanter and begging us to fill our glasses.
The devices and pretences that I have seen put in practice
to defer the fatal moment, and to interpose between this
man and his purpose, are innumerable. I have known
desperate guests, when they saw the grisly hand approaching
the decanter, wildly to begin, without any antecedent whatsoever, "That reminds me——" and to plunge into long
stories. When at last the hand and the decanter come
together, a shudder, a palpable perceptible shudder, goes
round the table. We receive the reminder that it is Mayday's birthday, as if it were the anniversary of some profound disgrace he had undergone, and we sought to comfort
him. And when we have drunk Mayday's health, and
wished him many happy returns, we are seized for some
moments with a ghastly blitheness, an unnatural levity, as
if we were in the first flushed reaction of having undergone
a surgical operation.

Birthdays of this species have a public as well as a private
phase. My "boyhood's home," Dullborough, presents a case
in point. An Immortal Somebody was wanted in Dullborough, to dimple for a day the stagnant face of the waters ;
he was rather wanted by Dullborough generally, and much
wanted by the principal hotel-keeper. The County history
was looked up for a locally Immortal Somebody, but the
registered Dullborough worthies were all Nobodies. In
this state of things, it is hardly necessary to record that
Dullborough did what every man does when he wants to
write a book or deliver a lecture, and is provided with all
the materials except a subject. It fell back upon Shakespeare.

No sooner was it resolved to celebrate Shakespeare's birthday in Dullborough, than the popularity of the immortal
bard became surprising. You might have supposed the
first edition of his works to have been published last week,
and enthusiastic Dullborough to have got half through them.
(I doubt, by the way, whether it had ever done half that,
but this is a private opinion.) A young gentleman with
a sonnet, the retention of which for two years had enfeebled
his mind and undermined his knees, got the sonnet into the
Dullborough Warden, and gained flesh. Portraits of Shake-

speare broke out in the bookshop windows, and our principal artist painted a large original portrait in oils for the decoration of the dining-room. It was not in the least like any of the other portraits, and was exceedingly admired, the head being much swollen. At the Institution, the Debating Society discussed the new question, Was there sufficient ground for supposing that the Immortal Shakespeare ever stole deer? This was indignantly decided by an over-whelming majority in the negative ; indeed, there was but one vote on the Poaching side, and that was the vote of the orator who had undertaken to advocate it, and who became quite an obnoxious character—particularly to the Dull-borough "roughs," who were about as well informed on the matter as most other people. Distinguished speakers were invited down, and very nearly came (but not quite). Sub-scriptions were opened, and committees sat, and it would have been far from a popular measure in the height of the excitement, to have told Dullborough that it wasn't Stratford-upon-Avon. Yet, after all these preparations, when the great festivity took place, and the portrait, elevated aloft, surveyed the company as if it were in danger of springing a mine of intellect and blowing itself up, it did undoubtedly happen, according to the inscrutable mysteries of things, that nobody could be induced, not to say to touch upon Shakespeare, but to come within a mile of him, until the crack speaker of Dullborough rose to propose the immortal memory. Which he did with the perplexing and astonishing result that before he had repeated the great name half-a-dozen times, or had been upon his legs as many minutes, he was assailed with a general shout of "Question."

XXI

THE SHORT-TIMERS

"Within so many yards of this Covent-garden lodging of mine, as within so many yards of Westminster Abbey, Saint Paul's Cathedral, the Houses of Parliament, the Prisons, the Courts of Justice, all the Institutions that govern the land, I can find—*must* find, whether I will or no—in the open streets, shameful instances of neglect of children, intolerable toleration of the engenderment of paupers, idlers, thieves, races of wretched and destructive cripples both in body and mind, a misery to themselves, a misery to the community, a disgrace to civilisation, and an outrage on Christianity. I know it to be a fact as easy of demonstration as any sum in any of the elementary rules of arithmetic, that if the State would begin its work and duty at the beginning, and would with the strong hand take those children out of the streets, while they are yet children, and wisely train them, it would make them a part of England's glory, not its shame—of England's strength, not its weakness—would raise good soldiers and sailors, and good citizens, and many great men, out of the seeds of its criminal population. Yet I go on bearing with the enormity as if it were nothing, and I go on reading the Parliamentary Debates as if they were something, and I concern myself far more about one railway-bridge across a public thoroughfare, than about a dozen generations of scrofula, ignorance, wickedness, prostitution, poverty, and felony. I can slip out at my door, in the small hours after any midnight, and, in one circuit of the purlieus of Covent-garden Market, can behold a state of infancy and youth, as vile as if a Bourbon sat upon the English throne; a great police force looking on with authority to do no more than worry and hunt the dreadful vermin into corners, and there leave them. Within the length of a few streets I can find a workhouse, mismanaged with that dull short sighted obstinacy that its greatest opportunities as to the children it receives are lost, and yet not a farthing saved to any one. But the wheel goes round, and round, and round; and because it goes round—so I am told by the politest authorities—it goes well."

Thus I reflected, one day in the Whitsun week last past, as I floated down the Thames among the bridges, looking—not inappropriately—at the drags that were hanging up at certain dirty stairs to hook the drowned out, and at the numerous conveniences provided to facilitate their tumbling in. My object in that uncommercial journey called up another train of thought, and it ran as follows:

"When I was at school, one of seventy boys, I wonder by what secret understanding our attention began to wander when we had pored over our books for some hours. I wonder by what ingenuity we brought on that confused state of mind when sense became nonsense, when figures wouldn't work, when dead languages wouldn't construe, when live languages wouldn't be spoken, when memory wouldn't come, when dulness and vacancy wouldn't go. I cannot remember that we ever conspired to be sleepy after dinner, or that we ever particularly wanted to be stupid, and to have flushed faces and hot beating heads, or to find blank hopelessness and obscurity this afternoon in what would become perfectly clear and bright in the freshness of to-morrow morning. We suffered for these things, and they made us miserable enough. Neither do I remember that we ever bound ourselves by any secret oath or other solemn obligation, to find the seats getting too hard to be sat upon after a certain time; or to have intolerable twitches in our legs, rendering us aggressive and malicious with those members; or to be troubled with a similar uneasiness in our elbows, attended with fistic consequences to our neighbours; or to carry two pounds of lead in the chest, four pounds in the head, and several active blue-bottles in each ear. Yet, for certain, we suffered under those distresses, and were always charged at for labouring under them, as if we had brought them on, of our own deliberate act and deed. As to the mental portion of them being my own fault in my own case—I should like to ask any well-trained and experienced teacher, not to say psychologist. And as to the physical portion—I should like to ask Professor Owen."

It happened that I had a small bundle of papers with

me, on what is called "The Half-Time System" in schools.
Referring to one of those papers I found that the indefatigable MR. CHADWICK had been beforehand with me, and
had already asked Professor Owen: who had handsomely
replied that I was not to blame, but that, being troubled
with a skeleton, and having been constituted according to
certain natural laws, I and my skeleton were unfortunately
bound by those laws—even in school—and had comported
ourselves accordingly.   Much comforted by the good Professor's being on my side, I read on to discover whether the
indefatigable Mr. Chadwick had taken up the mental part of
my afflictions.   I found that he had, and that he had gained
on my behalf, SIR BENJAMIN BRODIE, SIR DAVID WILKIE,
SIR WALTER SCOTT, and the common sense of mankind.   For
which I beg Mr. Chadwick, if this should meet his eye, to
accept my warm acknowledgments.

Up to that time I had retained a misgiving that the
seventy unfortunates of whom I was one, must have been,
without knowing it, leagued together by the spirit of evil in
a sort of perpetual Guy Fawkes Plot, to grope about in vaults
with dark lanterns after a certain period of continuous study.
But now the misgiving vanished, and I floated on with a
quieted mind to see the Half-Time System in action.   For
that was the purpose of my journey, both by steamboat on
the Thames, and by very dirty railway on the shore.   To
which last institution, I beg to recommend the legal use of
coke as engine-fuel, rather than the illegal use of coal; the
recommendation is quite disinterested, for I was most liberally
supplied with small coal on the journey, for which no charge
was made.   I had not only my eyes, nose, and ears filled,
but my hat, and all my pockets, and my pocket-book, and
my watch.

The V.D.S.C.R.C. (or Very Dirty and Small Coal Railway
Company) delivered me close to my destination, and I soon
found the Half-Time System established in spacious premises,
and freely placed at my convenience and disposal.

What would I see first of the Half-Time System?   I chose
Military Drill.   "Atten—tion!"   Instantly a hundred boys
stood forth in the paved yard as one boy; bright, quick,
eager, steady, watchful for the look of command, instant and
ready for the word.   Not only was there complete precision
—complete accord to the eye and to the ear—but an alert-
ness in the doing of the thing which deprived it, curiously,

of its monotonous or mechanical character. There was
perfect uniformity, and yet an individual spirit and emulation.
No spectator could doubt that the boys liked it. With non-
commissioned officers varying from a yard to a yard and
a half high, the result could not possibly have been attained
otherwise. They marched, and counter-marched, and formed
in line and square, and company, and single file and double
file, and performed a variety of evolutions; all most admirably. In respect of an air of enjoyable understanding of
what they were about, which seems to be forbidden to
English soldiers, the boys might have been small French
troops. When they were dismissed and the broadsword
exercise, limited to a much smaller number, succeeded, the
boys who had no part in that new drill, either looked on
attentively, or disported themselves in a gymnasium hard
by. The steadiness of the broadsword boys on their short
legs, and the firmness with which they sustained the different
positions, was truly remarkable.

The broadsword exercise over, suddenly there was great
excitement and a rush. Naval Drill!

In the corner of the ground stood a decked mimic ship,
with real masts, yards, and sails—mainmast seventy feet
high. At the word of command from the Skipper of this
ship—a mahogany-faced Old Salt, with the indispensable
quid in his cheek, the true nautical roll, and all wonderfully
complete—the rigging was covered with a swarm of boys: one,
the first to spring into the shrouds, outstripping all the others,
and resting on the truck of the main-topmast in no time.

And now we stood out to sea, in a most amazing manner;
the Skipper himself, the whole crew, the Uncommercial, and
all hands present, implicitly believing that there was not
a moment to lose, that the wind had that instant chopped
round and sprung up fair, and that we were away on a
voyage round the world. Get all sail upon her! With
a will, my lads! Lay out upon the main-yard there! Look
alive at the weather earring! Cheery, my boys! Let go the
sheet, now! Stand by at the braces, you! With a will,
aloft there! Belay, starboard watch! Fifer! Come aft, fifer,
and give 'em a tune! Forthwith, springs up fifer, fife in
hand—smallest boy ever seen—big lump on temple, having
lately fallen down on a paving-stone—gives 'em a tune with
all his might and main. Hooroar, fifer! With a will, my
lads! Tip 'em a livelier one, fifer! Fifer tips 'em a livelier

one, and excitement increases. Shake 'em out, my lads!
Well done! There you have her! Pretty, pretty! Every
rag upon her she can carry, wind right astarn, and ship
cutting through the water fifteen knots an hour!

At this favourable moment of her voyage, I gave the alarm
"A man overboard!" (on the gravel), but he was immediately recovered, none the worse. Presently, I observed the
Skipper overboard, but forbore to mention it, as he seemed
in no wise disconcerted by the accident. Indeed, I soon
came to regard the Skipper as an amphibious creature, for
he was so perpetually plunging overboard to look up at the
hands aloft, that he was oftener in the bosom of the ocean
than on deck. His pride in his crew on those occasions
was delightful, and the conventional unintelligibility of his
orders in the ears of uncommercial land-lubbers and loblolly
boys, though they were always intelligible to the crew, was
hardly less pleasant. But we couldn't expect to go on in
this way for ever; dirty weather came on, and then worse
weather, and when we least expected it we got into tremendous difficulties. Screw loose in the chart perhaps—
something certainly wrong somewhere—but here we were
with breakers ahead, my lads, driving head on, slap on a lee
shore! The Skipper broached this terrific announcement in
such great agitation, that the small fifer, not fifeing now,
but standing looking on near the wheel with his fife under
his arm, seemed for the moment quite unboyed, though he
speedily recovered his presence of mind. In the trying circumstances that ensued, the Skipper and the crew proved
worthy of one another. The Skipper got dreadfully hoarse,
but otherwise was master of the situation. The man at the
wheel did wonders; all hands (except the fifer) were turned
up to wear ship; and I observed the fifer, when we were at
our greatest extremity, to refer to some document in his
waistcoat-pocket, which I conceived to be his will. I think
she struck. I was not myself conscious of any collision,
but I saw the Skipper so very often washed overboard and
back again, that I could only impute it to the beating of
the ship. I am not enough of a seaman to describe the
manœuvres by which we were saved, but they made the
Skipper very hot (French polishing his mahogany face) and
the crew very nimble, and succeeded to a marvel; for, within
a few minutes of the-first alarm, we had wore ship and got
her off, and were all a-tauto—which I felt very grateful for:

not that I knew what it was, but that I perceived that we had not been all a-tauto lately. Land now appeared on our weather-bow, and we shaped our course for it, having the wind abeam, and frequently changing the man at the helm, in order that every man might have his spell. We worked into harbour under prosperous circumstances, and furled our sails, and squared our yards, and made all ship-shape and handsome, and so our voyage ended. When I complimented the Skipper at parting on his exertions and those of his gallant crew, he informed me that the latter were provided for the worst, all hands being taught to swim and dive ; and he added that the able seaman at the main-topmast truck especially, could dive as deep as he could go high.

The next adventure that befell me in my visit to the Short-Timers, was the sudden apparition of a military band. I had been inspecting the hammocks of the crew of the good ship, when I saw with astonishment that several musical instruments, brazen and of great size, appeared to have suddenly developed two legs each, and to be trotting about a yard. And my astonishment was heightened when I observed a large drum, that had previously been leaning helpless against a wall, taking up a stout position on four legs. Approaching this drum and looking over it, I found two boys behind it (it was too much for one), and then I found that each of the brazen instruments had brought out a boy, and was going to discourse sweet sounds. The boys —not omitting the fifer, now playing a new instrument— were dressed in neat uniform, and stood up in a circle at their music-stands, like any other Military Band. They played a march or two, and then we had Cheer boys, Cheer, and then we had Yankee Doodle, and we finished, as in loyal duty bound, with God Save the Queen. The band's proficiency was perfectly wonderful, and it was not at all wonderful that the whole body corporate of Short-Timers listened with faces of the liveliest interest and pleasure.

What happened next among the Short-Timers ? As if the band had blown me into a great class-room out of their brazen tubes, *in* a great class-room I found myself now, with the whole choral force of Short-Timers singing the praises of a summer's day to the harmonium, and my small but highly respected friend the fifer blazing away vocally, as if he had been saving up his wind for the last twelvemonth ; also the whole crew of the good ship Nameless swarming up and down the scale as if they had never swarmed up and down the rigging. This done, we threw our whole power into God bless the Prince of Wales, and blessed his Royal Highness to such an extent that, for my own Uncommercial part, I gasped again when it was over. The moment this was done, we formed, with surpassing freshness, into hollow squares, and fell to work at oral lessons, as if we never did, and had never thought of doing, anything else.

Let a veil be drawn over the self-committals into which the Uncommercial Traveller would have been betrayed but for a discreet reticence, coupled with an air of absolute wisdom on the part of that artful personage. Take the square of five, multiply it by fifteen, divide it by three, deduct eight from it, add four dozen to it, give me the result in pence, and tell me how many eggs I could get for it at three farthings apiece. The problem is hardly stated, when a dozen small boys pour out answers. Some wide, some very nearly right, some worked as far as they go with such accuracy, as at once to show what link of the chain has been dropped in the hurry. For the moment, none are quite right; but behold a labouring spirit beating the buttons on its corporeal waistcoat, in a process of internal calculation, and knitting an accidental bump on its corporeal forehead in a concentration of mental arithmetic! It is my honourable friend (if he will allow me to call him so) the fifer. With right arm eagerly extended in token of being inspired with an answer, and with right leg foremost, the fifer solves the mystery: then recalls both arm and leg, and with bump in ambush awaits the next poser. Take the square of three, multiply it by seven, divide it by four, add fifty to it, take thirteen from it, multiply it by two, double it, give me the result in pence, and say how many halfpence. ˙ Wise as the serpent is the four feet of performer on the nearest approach to that instrument, whose right arm instantly appears, and quenches this arithmetical fire. Tell me something about Great Britain, tell me something about its principal productions, tell me something about its ports, tell me something about its seas and rivers, tell me something about coal, iron, cotton, timber, tin, and turpentine. The hollow square bristles with extended right arms; but ever faithful to fact is the fifer, ever wise as the serpent is the performer on that instrument, ever prominently buoyant and brilliant are all members of the band. I observe the player of the cymbals to dash at a sounding answer now and then rather than not cut in at all ; but I take that to be in the way of his instru-ment. All these questions, and many such, are put on the spur of the moment, and by one who has never examined these boys. The Uncommercial, invited to add another, falteringly demands how many birthdays a man born on the twenty-ninth of February will have had on completing his fiftieth year? A general perception of trap and pitfall instantly arises, and the fifer is seen to retire behind the corduroys of his next neighbours, as perceiving special necessity for collecting himself and communing with his mind. Meanwhile, the wisdom of the serpent suggests that the man will have had only one birthday in all that time, for how can any man have more than one, seeing that he is born once and dies once? The blushing Uncommercial stands corrected, and amends the formula. Pondering ensues, two or three wrong answers are offered, and Cymbals strikes up "Six!" but doesn't know why. Then modestly emerging from his Academic Grove of corduroys appears the fifer, right arm extended, right leg foremost, bump irradiated. "Twelve, and two over!"

The feminine Short-Timers passed a similar examination, and very creditably too. Would have done better perhaps, with a little more geniality on the part of their pupil-teacher ; for a cold eye, my young friend, and a hard abrupt manner, are not by any means the powerful engines that your innocence supposes them to be. Both girls and boys wrote excellently, from copy and dictation ; both could cook ; both could mend their own clothes ; both could clean up everything about them in an orderly and skilful way, the girls having womanly household knowledge superadded. Order and method began in the songs of the Infant School which I visited likewise, and they were even in their dwarf degree to be found in the Nursery, where the Uncommercial walking-stick was carried off with acclamations, and where "the Doctor"—a medical gentleman of two, who took his degree on the night when he was found at an apothecary's door—did the honours of the establishment with great urbanity and gaiety.

These have long been excellent schools ; long before the days of the Short-Time. I first saw them, twelve or fifteen years ago. But since the introduction of the Short-Time system it has been proved here that eighteen hours a week of book-learning are more profitable than thirty-six, and that the pupils are far quicker and brighter than of yore. The good influences of music on the whole body of children have likewise been surprisingly proved. Obviously another of the immense advantages of the Short-Time system to the cause of good education is the great diminution of its cost, and of the period of time over which it extends. The last is a most important consideration, as poor parents are always impatient to profit by their children's labour.

It will be objected: Firstly, that this is all very well, but special local advantages and special selection of children must be necessary to such success. Secondly, that this is all very well, but must be very expensive. Thirdly, that this is all very well, but we have no proof of the results, sir, no proof.

On the first head of local advantages and special selection. Would Limehouse Hole be picked out for the site of a Children's Paradise? Or would the legitimate and illegitimate pauper children of the long-shore population of such a river-side district, be regarded as unusually favourable specimens to work with? Yet these schools are at Limehouse, and are the Pauper Schools of the Stepney Pauper Union.

On the second head of expense. Would sixpence a week be considered a very large cost for the education of each pupil, including all salaries of teachers and rations of teachers? But supposing the cost were not sixpence a week, not fivepence? It is FOURPENCE-HALFPENNY.

On the third head of no proof, sir, no proof. Is there any proof in the fact that Pupil Teachers more in number, and more highly qualified, have been produced here under the Short-Time system than under the Long-Time system? That the Short-Timers, in a writing competition, beat the Long-Timers of a first-class National School? That the sailor-boys are in such demand for merchant ships, that whereas, before they were trained, 10*l.* premium used to be given with each boy—too often to some greedy brute of a drunken skipper, who disappeared before the term of apprenticeship was out, if the ill-used boy didn't—captains of the best character now take these boys more than willingly, with no premium at all? That they are also much esteemed in the Royal Navy, which they prefer, "because everything is so neat and clean and orderly"? Or, is there any proof in Naval captains writing, "Your little fellows are all that

I can desire "? Or, is there any proof in such testimony as this: "The owner of a vessel called at the school, and said that as his ship was going down Channel on her last voyage, with one of the boys from the school on board, the pilot said, 'It would be as well if the royal were lowered ; I wish it were down.' Without waiting for any orders, and unobserved by the pilot, the lad, whom they had taken on board from the school, instantly mounted the mast and lowered the royal, and at the next glance of the pilot to the masthead, he perceived that the sail had been let down. He exclaimed, 'Who's done that job?' The owner, who was on board, said, 'That was the little fellow whom I put on board two days ago.' The pilot immediately said, 'Why, where could he have been brought up?' That boy had never seen the sea or been on a real ship before"? Or, is there any proof in these boys being in greater demand for Regimental Bands than the Union can meet? Or, in ninety-eight of them having gone into Regimental Bands in three years? Or, in twelve of them being in the band of one regiment? Or, in the colonel of that regiment writing, "We want six more boys; they are excellent lads"? Or, in one of the boys having risen to be band-corporal in the same regiment? Or, in employers of all kinds chorusing, "Give us drilled boys, for they are prompt, obedient, and punctual"? Other proofs I have myself beheld with these Uncommercial eyes, though I do not regard myself as having a right to relate in what social positions they have seen respected men and women who were once pauper children of the Stepney Union.

Into what admirable soldiers others of these boys have the capabilities for being turned, I need not point out. Many of them are always ambitious of military service; and once upon a time when an old boy came back to see the old place, a cavalry soldier all complete, *with his spurs on*, such a yearning broke out to get into cavalry regiments and wear those sublime appendages, that it was one of the greatest excitements ever known in the school. The girls make excellent domestic servants, and at certain periods come back, a score or two at a time, to see the old building, and to take tea with the old teachers, and to hear the old band, and to see the old ship with her masts towering up above the neighbouring roofs and chimneys. As to the physical health of these schools, it is so exceptionally remarkable (simply because the sanitary regulations are as good as the other educational arrangements), that when Mr. TUFNELL, the Inspector, first stated it in a report, he was supposed, in spite of his high character, to have been betrayed into some extraordinary mistake or exaggeration. In the moral health of these schools—where corporal punishment is unknown—Truthfulness stands high. When the ship was first erected, the boys were forbidden to go aloft, until the nets, which are now always there, were stretched as a precaution against accidents. Certain boys, in their eagerness, disobeyed the injunction, got out of window in the early daylight, and climbed to the masthead. One boy unfortunately fell, and was killed. There was no clue to the others; but all the boys were assembled, and the chairman of the Board addressed them. "I promise nothing; you see what a dreadful thing has happened; you know what a grave offence it is that has led to such a consequence; I cannot say what will be done with the offenders; but, boys, you have been trained here, above all things, to respect the truth. I want the truth. Who are the delinquents?" Instantly, the whole number of boys concerned, separated from the rest, and stood out.

Now, the head and heart of that gentleman (it is needless to say, a good head and a good heart) have been deeply interested in these schools for many years, and are so still; and the establishment is very fortunate in a most admirable master, and moreover the schools of the Stepney Union cannot have got to be what they are, without the Stepney Board of Guardians having been earnest and humane men strongly imbued with a sense of their responsibility. But what one set of men can do in this wise, another set of men can do; and this is a noble example to all other Bodies and Unions, and a noble example to the State. Followed, and enlarged upon by its enforcement on bad parents, it would clear London streets of the most terrible objects they smite the sight with—myriads of little children who awfully reverse Our Saviour's words, and are not of the Kingdom of Heaven, but of the Kingdom of Hell.

Clear the public streets of such shame, and the public conscience of such reproach? Ah! Almost prophetic, surely, the child's jingle:

> "When will that be,
> Say the bells of Step-ney!"

XXII

BOUND FOR THE GREAT SALT LAKE

BEHOLD me on my way to an Emigrant Ship, on a hot morning early in June. My road lies through that part of London generally known to the initiated as "Down by the Docks." Down by the Docks, is home to a good many people —to too many, if I may judge from the overflow of local population in the streets—but my nose insinuates that the number to whom it is Sweet Home might be easily counted. Down by the Docks, is a region I would choose as my point of embarkation aboard ship if I were an emigrant. It would present my intention to me in such a sensible light; it would show me so many things to be run away from.

Down by the Docks, they eat the largest oysters and scatter the roughest oyster-shells, known to the descendants of Saint George and the Dragon. Down by the Docks, they consume the slimiest of shell-fish, which seem to have been scraped off the copper bottoms of ships. Down by the Docks, the vegetables at greengrocers' doors acquire a saline and a scaly look, as if they had been crossed with fish and seaweed. Down by the Docks, they "board seamen" at the eating-houses, the public-houses, the slop-shops, the coffee-shops, the tally-shops, all kinds of shops mentionable and unmentionable—board them, as it were, in the piratical sense, making them bleed terribly, and giving no quarter. Down by the Docks, the seamen roam in mid-street and mid-day, their pockets inside out, and their heads no better. Down by the Docks, the daughters of wave-ruling Britannia also rove, clad in silken attire, with uncovered tresses streaming in the breeze, bandanna kerchiefs floating from their shoulders, and crinoline not wanting. Down by the Docks, you may hear the Incomparable Joe Jackson sing the Standard of England, with a hornpipe, any night; or any day may see at the waxwork, for a penny and no waiting, him as killed the policeman at Acton and suffered for it. Down by the Docks, you may buy polonies, saveloys, and sausage preparations various, if you are not particular what they are made of besides seasoning. Down by the Docks, the children of Israel creep into any gloomy cribs and entries they can hire, and hang slops there—pewter watches, sou'-wester hats, waterproof overalls—"firtht rate articleth, Thjack." Down by the Docks, such dealers exhibiting on a frame a complete nautical suit without the refinement of a waxen visage in the hat, present the imaginary wearer as drooping at the yard-arm, with his seafaring and earthfaring troubles over. Down by the Docks, the placards in the shops apostrophise the customer, knowing him familiarly beforehand, as, "Look here, Jack!" "Here's your sort, my lad!" "Try our sea-going mixed, at two and nine!" "The right kit for the British tar!" "Ship ahoy!" "Splice the main-brace, brother!" "Come, cheer up, my lads. We've the best liquors here, And you'll find something new In our wonderful Beer!" Down by the Docks, the pawnbroker lends money on Union-Jack pocket-handkerchiefs, on watches with little ships pitching fore and aft on the dial, on tele-scopes, nautical instruments in cases, and such-like. Down by the Docks, the apothecary sets up in business on the wretchedest scale—chiefly on lint and plaster for the strap-ping of wounds—and with no bright bottles, and with no little drawers. Down by the Docks, the shabby undertaker's shop will bury you for next to nothing, after the Malay or Chinaman has stabbed you for nothing at all: so you can hardly hope to make a cheaper end. Down by the Docks, anybody drunk will quarrel with anybody drunk or sober, and everybody else will have a hand in it, and on the shortest notice you may revolve in a whirlpool of red shirts, shaggy beards, wild heads of hair, bare tattooed arms, Britannia's daughters, malice, mud, maundering, and mad-ness. Down by the Docks, scraping fiddles go in the public-houses all day long, and, shrill above their din and all the din, rises the screeching of innumerable parrots brought from foreign parts, who appear to be very much astonished by what they find on these native shores of ours. Possibly the parrots don't know, possibly they do, that Down by the Docks is the road to the Pacific Ocean, with its lovely islands, where the savage girls plait flowers, and the savage boys carve cocoa-nut shells, and the grim blind idols muse in their shady groves to exactly the same purpose as the priests and chiefs. And possibly the parrots don't know, possibly they do, that the noble savage is a wearisome impostor wherever he is, and has five hundred thousand volumes of indifferent rhyme, and no reason, to answer for.

Shadwell church! Pleasant whispers of there being a fresher air down the river than down by the Docks, go pursuing one another, playfully, in and out of the openings in its spire. Gigantic in the basin just beyond the church, looms my Emigrant Ship: her name, the Amazon. Her figure-head is not *dis*figured as those beauteous founders of the race of strong-minded women are fabled to have been, for the convenience of drawing the bow; but I sympathise with the carver:

> "A flattering carver who made it his care
> To carve busts as they ought to be—not as they were."

My Emigrant Ship lies broadside-on to the wharf. Two great gangways made of spars and planks connect her with the wharf; and up and down these gangways, perpetually crowding to and fro and in and out, like ants, are the Emigrants who are going to sail in my Emigrant Ship. Some with cabbages, some with loaves of bread, some with cheese and butter, some with milk and beer, some with boxes, beds, and bundles, some with babies—nearly all with children—nearly all with bran-new tin cans for their daily allowance of water, uncomfortably suggestive of a tin flavour in the drink. To and fro, up and down, aboard and ashore, swarming here and there and everywhere, my Emigrants. And still as the Dock-Gate swings upon its hinges, cabs appear, and carts appear, and vans appear, bringing more of my Emigrants, with more cabbages, more loaves, more cheese and butter, more milk and beer, more boxes, beds, and bundles, more tin cans, and on those shipping investments accumulated compound interest of children.

I go aboard my Emigrant Ship. I go first to the great cabin, and find it in the usual condition of a Cabin at that pass. Perspiring landsmen, with loose papers, and with pens and inkstands, pervade it; and the general appearance of things is as if the late Mr. Amazon's funeral had just come home from the cemetery, and the disconsolate Mrs. Amazon's trustees found the affairs in great disorder, and were looking high and low for the will. I go out on the poop-deck, for air, and surveying the emigrants on the deck below (indeed they are crowded all about me, up there too), find more pens and inkstands in action, and more papers, and interminable complication respecting accounts with individuals for tin cans and what not. But nobody is in an ill-temper, nobody is the worse for drink, nobody swears an oath or uses a coarse word, nobody appears depressed, nobody is weeping, and down upon the deck in every corner where it is possible to find a few square feet to kneel, crouch, or lie in, people, in every unsuitable attitude for writing, are writing letters.

Now, I have seen emigrant ships before this day in June. And these people are so strikingly different from all other people in like circumstances whom I have ever seen, that I wonder aloud, "What *would* a stranger suppose these emigrants to be!"

The vigilant bright face of the weather-browned captain of the Amazon is at my shoulder, and he says, "What, indeed! The most of these came aboard yesterday evening. They came from various parts of England in small parties that had never seen one another before. Yet they had not been a couple of hours on board, when they established their own police, made their own regulations, and set their own watches at all the hatchways. Before nine o'clock, the ship was as orderly and as quiet as a man-of-war."

I looked about me again, and saw the letter-writing going on with the most curious composure. Perfectly abstracted in the midst of the crowd; while great casks were swinging aloft, and being lowered into the hold; while hot agents were hurrying up and down, adjusting the interminable accounts; while two hundred strangers were searching everywhere for two hundred other strangers, and were asking questions about them of two hundred more; while the children played up and down all the steps, and in and out among all the people's legs, and were beheld, to the general dismay, toppling over all the dangerous places; the letter-writers wrote on calmly. On the starboard side of the ship, a grizzled man dictated a long letter to another grizzled man in an immense fur cap: which letter was of so profound a quality, that it became necessary for the amanuensis at intervals to take off his fur cap in both his hands, for the ventilation of his brain, and stare at him who dictated, as a man of many mysteries who was worth looking at. On the larboard side, a woman had covered a belaying-pin with a white cloth to make a neat desk of it, and was sitting on a little box, writing with the delibera· tion of a bookkeeper. Down upon her breast on the planks of the deck at this woman's feet, with her head diving in under a beam of the bulwarks on that side, as an eligible place of refuge for her sheet of paper, a neat and pretty girl wrote for a good hour (she fainted at last), only rising to the surface occasionally for a dip of ink. Alongside the boat, close to me on the poop-deck, another girl, a fresh well-grown country girl, was writing another letter on the bare deck. Later in the day, when this self-same boat was filled with a choir who sang glees and catches for a long time, one of the singers, a girl, sang her part mechanically all the while, and wrote a letter in the bottom of the boat while doing so.

"A stranger would be puzzled to guess the right name for these people, Mr. Uncommercial," says the captain.

"Indeed he would."

"If you hadn't known, could you ever have supposed——?"

"How could I! I should have said they were in their degree, the pick and flower of England."

"So should I," says the captain.

"How many are they?"

"Eight hundred in round numbers."

I went between-decks, where the families with children swarmed in the dark, where unavoidable confusion had been caused by the last arrivals, and where the confusion was increased by the little preparations for dinner that were going on in each group. A few women here and there, had got lost, and were laughing at it, and asking their way to their own people, or out on deck again. A few of the poor children were crying; but otherwise the universal cheerfulness was amazing. "We shall shake down by to-morrow." "We shall come all right in a day or so." "We shall have more light at sea." Such phrases I heard everywhere, as I groped my way among chests and barrels and beams and unstowed cargo and ring-bolts and Emigrants, down to the lower-deck, and thence up to the light of day again, and to my former station.

Surely, an extraordinary people in their power of self· abstraction! All the former letter-writers were still writing

calmly, and many more letter-writers had broken out in my
absence. A boy with a bag of books in his hand and a slate
under his arm, emerged from below, concentrated himself
in my neighbourhood (espying a convenient skylight for his
purpose), and went to work at a sum as if he were stone
deaf. A father and mother and several young children,
on the main deck below me, had formed a family circle
close to the foot of the crowded restless gangway, where
the children made a nest for themselves in a coil of rope,
and the father and mother, she suckling the youngest,
discussed family affairs as peaceably as if they were in
perfect retirement. I think the most noticeable characteristic in the eight hundred as a mass, was their exemption
from hurry.

Eight hundred what? "Geese, villain?" EIGHT HUNDRED
MORMONS. I, Uncommercial Traveller for the firm of Human
Interest Brothers, had come aboard this Emigrant Ship
to see what Eight hundred Latter-day Saints were like,
and I found them (to the rout and overthrow of all my
expectations) like what I now describe with scrupulous
exactness.

The Mormon Agent who had been active in getting them
together, and in making the contract with my friends the
owners of the ship to take them as far as New York on
their way to the Great Salt Lake, was pointed out to me.
A compactly-made handsome man in black, rather short,
with rich-brown hair and beard, and clear bright eyes.
From his speech, I should set him down as American.
Probably, a man who had "knocked about the world"
pretty much. A man with a frank open manner, and
unshrinking look; withal a man of great quickness. I believe he was wholly ignorant of my Uncommercial individuality, and consequently of my immense Uncommercial
importance.

UNCOMMERCIAL. These are a very fine set of people you
have brought together here.

MORMON AGENT. Yes, sir, they are a *very* fine set of
people.

UNCOMMERCIAL (looking about). Indeed, I think it would
be difficult to find Eight hundred people together anywhere
else, and find so much beauty and so much strength and
capacity for work among them.

MORMON AGENT (not looking about. but looking steadily

at Uncommercial). I think so.—We sent out about a thousand more, yes'day, from Liverpool.

UNCOMMERCIAL. You are not going with these emigrants?

MORMON AGENT. No, sir. I remain.

UNCOMMERCIAL. But you have been in the Mormon
Territory?

MORMON AGENT. Yes; I left Utah about three years ago.

UNCOMMERCIAL. It is surprising to me that these people
are all so cheery, and make so little of the immense distance
before them.

MORMON AGENT. Well, you see; many of 'em have friends
out at Utah, and many of 'em look forward to meeting
friends on the way.

UNCOMMERCIAL. On the way?

MORMON AGENT. This way 'tis. This ship lands 'em in
New York City. Then they go on by rail right away beyond
St. Louis, to that part of the Banks of the Missouri where
they strike the Plains. There, waggons from the settlement
meet 'em to bear 'em company on their journey 'cross—
twelve hundred miles about. Industrious people who come
out to the settlement soon get waggons of their own, and so
the friends of some of these will come down in their own
waggons to meet 'em. They look forward to that, greatly.

UNCOMMERCIAL. On their long journey across the Desert,
do you arm them?

MORMON AGENT. Mostly you would find they have arms
of some kind or another already with them. Such as had
not arms we should arm across the Plains, for the general
protection and defence.

UNCOMMERCIAL. Will these waggons bring down any
produce to the Missouri?

MORMON AGENT. Well, since the war broke out, we've
taken to growing cotton, and they'll likely bring down
cotton to be exchanged for machinery. We want machinery.
Also we have taken to growing indigo, which is a fine
commodity for profit. It has been found that the climate
on the further side of the Great Salt Lake suits well for
raising indigo.

UNCOMMERCIAL. I am told that these people now on
board are principally from the South of England?

MORMON AGENT. And from Wales. That's true.

UNCOMMERCIAL. Do you get many Scotch?

MORMON AGENT. Not many.

UNCOMMERCIAL. Highlanders, for instance?

MORMON AGENT. No, not Highlanders. They ain't interested enough in universal brotherhood and peace and good will.

UNCOMMERCIAL. The old fighting blood is strong in them?

MORMON AGENT. Well, yes. And besides; they've no faith.

UNCOMMERCIAL (who has been burning to get at the Prophet Joe Smith, and seems to discover an opening). Faith in——!

MORMON AGENT (far too many for Uncommercial). Well. —In anything!

Similarly on this same head, the Uncommercial underwent discomfiture from a Wiltshire labourer: a simple fresh-coloured farm-labourer, of eight-and-thirty, who at one time stood beside him looking on at new arrivals, and with whom he held this dialogue:

UNCOMMERCIAL. Would you mind my asking you what part of the country you come from?

WILTSHIRE. Not a bit. Theer! (exultingly) I've worked all my life o' Salisbury Plain, right under the shadder o' Stonehenge. You mightn't think it, but I haive.

UNCOMMERCIAL. And a pleasant country too.

WILTSHIRE. Ah! 'Tis a pleasant country.

UNCOMMERCIAL. Have you any family on board?

WILTSHIRE. Two children, boy and gal. I am a widderer, *I* am, and I'm going out alonger my boy and gal. That's my gal, and she's a fine gal o' sixteen (pointing out the girl who is writing by the boat). I'll go and fetch my boy. I'd like to show you my boy. (Here Wiltshire disappears, and presently comes back with a big shy boy of twelve, in a superabundance of boots, who is not at all glad to be presented.) He is a fine boy too, and a boy fur to work! (Boy having undutifully bolted, Wiltshire drops him.)

UNCOMMERCIAL. It must cost you a great deal of money to go so far, three strong.

WILTSHIRE. A power of money. Theer! Eight shillen a week, eight shillen a week, eight shillen a week, put by out of the week's wages for ever so long.

UNCOMMERCIAL. I wonder how you did it.

WILTSHIRE (recognising in this a kindred spirit). See theer now! *I* wonder how I done it! But what with a bit o' subscription heer, and what with a bit o' help theer, it were done at last, though I don't hardly know how. Then it were unfort'net for us, you see, as we got kep' in Bristol so long—nigh a fortnight, it were—on accounts of a mistake wi' Brother Halliday. Swaller'd up money, 'it did, when we might have come straight on.

UNCOMMERCIAL (delicately approaching Joe Smith). You are of the Mormon religion, of course?

WILTSHIRE (confidently). O yes, I'm a Mormon. (Then reflectively). I'm a Mormon. (Then, looking round the ship, feigns to descry a particular friend in an empty spot, and evades the Uncommercial for evermore.)

After a noontide pause for dinner, during which my Emigrants were nearly all between-decks, and the Amazon looked deserted, a general muster took place. The muster was for the ceremony of passing the Government Inspector and the Doctor. Those authorities held their temporary state amidships, by a cask or two; and, knowing that the whole Eight hundred emigrants must come face to face with them, I took my station behind the two. They knew nothing whatever of me, I believe, and my testimony to the unpretending gentleness and good nature with which they discharged their duty, may be of the greater worth. There was not the slightest flavour of the Circumlocution Office about their proceedings.

The emigrants were now all on deck. They were densely crowded aft, and swarmed upon the poop-deck like bees. Two or three Mormon agents stood ready to hand them on to the Inspector, and to hand them forward when they had passed. By what successful means, a special aptitude for organisation had been infused into these people, I am, of course, unable to report. But I know that, even now, there was no disorder, hurry, or difficulty.

All being ready, the first group are handed on. That member of the party who is entrusted with the passenger-ticket for the whole, has been warned by one of the agents to have it ready, and here it is in his hand. In every instance through the whole eight hundred, without an exception, this paper is always ready.

INSPECTOR (reading the ticket). Jessie Jobson, Sophronia Jobson, Jessie Jobson again, Matilda Jobson, William Jobson, Jane Jobson, Matilda Jobson again, Brigham Jobson, Leonardo Jobson, and Orson Jobson. Are you all here? (glancing at the party, over his spectacles).

JESSIE JOBSON NUMBER TWO. All here, sir.

This group is composed of an old grandfather and grandmother, their married son and his wife, and *their* family of children. Orson Jobson is a little child asleep in his mother's arms. The Doctor, with a kind word or so, lifts up the corner of the mother's shawl, looks at the child's face, and touches the little clenched hand. If we were all as well as Orson Jobson, doctoring would be a poor profession.

INSPECTOR. Quite right, Jessie Jobson. Take your ticket, Jessie, and pass on.

And away they go. Mormon agent, skilful and quiet, hands them on. Mormon agent, skilful and quiet, hands next party up.

INSPECTOR (reading ticket again). Susannah Cleverly and William Cleverly. Brother and sister, eh ?

SISTER (young woman of business, hustling slow brother). Yes, sir.

INSPECTOR. Very good, Susannah Cleverly. Take your ticket, Susannah, and take care of it.

And away they go.

INSPECTOR (taking ticket again). Sampson Dibble and Dorothy Dibble (surveying a very old couple over his spectacles, with some surprise). Your husband quite blind, Mrs. Dibble ?

MRS. DIBBLE. Yes, sir, he be stone-blind.

MR. DIBBLE (addressing the mast). Yes, sir, I be stone-blind.

INSPECTOR. That's a bad job. Take your ticket, Mrs. Dibble, and don't lose it, and pass on.

Doctor taps Mr. Dibble on the eyebrow with his forefinger, and away they go.

INSPECTOR (taking ticket again). Anastatia Weedle.

ANASTATIA (a pretty girl, in a bright Garibaldi, this morning elected by universal suffrage the Beauty of the Ship). That is me, sir.

INSPECTOR. Going alone, Anastatia ?

ANASTATIA (shaking her curls). I am with Mrs. Jobson, sir, but I've got separated for the moment.

INSPECTOR. Oh ! You are with the Jobsons ? Quite right. That'll do, Miss Weedle. Don't lose your ticket.

Away she goes, and joins the Jobsons who are waiting for her, and stoops and kisses Brigham Jobson—who appears to be considered too young for the purpose, by several Mormons rising twenty, who are looking on. Before her extensive skirts have departed from the casks, a decent widow stands there with four children, and so the roll goes.

The faces of some of the Welsh people, among whom there were many old persons, were certainly the least intelligent. Some of these emigrants would have bungled sorely, but for the directing hand that was always ready. The intelligence here was unquestionably of a low order, and the heads were of a poor type. Generally the case was the reverse. There were many worn faces bearing traces of patient poverty and hard work, and there was great steadiness of purpose and much undemonstrative self-respect among this class. A few young men were going singly. Several girls were going, two or three together. These latter I found it very difficult to refer back, in my mind, to their relinquished homes and pursuits. Perhaps they were more like country milliners, and pupil teachers rather tawdrily dressed, than any other classes of young women. I noticed, among many little ornaments worn, more than one photograph-brooch of the Princess of Wales, and also of the late Prince Consort. Some single women of from thirty to forty, whom one might suppose to be embroiderers, or straw-bonnet-makers, were obviously going out in quest of husbands, as finer ladies go to India. That they had any distinct notions of a plurality of husbands or wives, I do not believe. To suppose the family groups of whom the majority of emigrants were composed, polygamically possessed, would be to suppose an absurdity, manifest to any one who saw the fathers and mothers.

I should say (I had no means of ascertaining the fact) that most familiar kinds of handicraft trades were represented here. Farm-labourers, shepherds, and the like, had their full share of representation, but I doubt if they preponderated. It was interesting to see how the leading spirit in the family circle never failed to show itself, even in the simple process of answering to the names as they were called, and checking off the owners of the names. Sometimes it was the father, much oftener the mother, sometimes a quick little girl second or third in order of seniority. It seemed to occur for the first time to some heavy fathers, what large families they had ; and their eyes rolled about, during the calling of the list, as if they half misdoubted some other family to have been smuggled into their own. Among all the fine handsome children, I observed but two with marks upon their necks that were probably scrofulous. Out of the whole number of emigrants, but one old woman was temporarily set aside by the doctor, on suspicion of fever; but even she afterwards obtained a clean bill of health.

When all had "passed," and the afternoon began to wear on, a black box became visible on deck, which box was in charge of certain personages also in black, of whom only one had the conventional air of an itinerant preacher. This box contained a supply of hymn-books, neatly printed and got up, published at Liverpool, and also in London at the "Latter-Day Saints' Book Depôt, 30, Florence-street." Some copies were handsomely bound; the plainer were the more in request, and many were bought. The title ran: "Sacred Hymns and Spiritual Songs for the Church of Jesus Christ of Latter-Day Saints." The Preface, dated Manchester, 1840, ran thus:—"The Saints in this country have been very desirous for a Hymn Book adapted to their faith and worship, that they might sing the truth with an understanding heart, and express their praise joy and gratitude in songs adapted to the New and Everlasting Covenant. In accordance with their wishes, we have selected the following volume, which we hope will prove acceptable until a greater variety can be added. With sentiments of high consideration and esteem, we subscribe ourselves your brethren in the New and Everlasting Covenant, BRIGHAM YOUNG, PARLEY P. PRATT, JOHN TAYLOR." From this book—by no means explanatory to myself of the New and Everlasting Covenant, and not at all making my heart an understanding one on the subject of that mystery—a hymn was sung, which did not attract any great amount of attention, and was supported by a rather select circle. But the choir in the boat was very popular and pleasant; and there was to have been a Band, only the Cornet was late in coming on board. In the course of the afternoon, a mother appeared from shore, in search of her daughter, "who had run away with the Mormons." She received every assistance from the Inspector, but her daughter was not found to be on board. The saints did not seem to me, particularly interested in finding her.

Towards five o'clock, the galley became full of tea-kettles, and an agreeable fragrance of tea pervaded the ship. There was no scrambling or jostling for the hot water, no ill humour, no quarrelling. As the Amazon was to sail with the next tide, and as it would not be high water before two o'clock in the morning, I left her with her tea in full action, and her idle Steam Tug lying by, deputing steam and smoke for the time being to the Tea-kettles.

I afterwards learned that a Despatch was sent home by the captain before he struck out into the wide Atlantic, highly extolling the behaviour of these Emigrants, and the perfect order and propriety of all their social arrangements. What is in store for the poor people on the shores of the Great Salt Lake, what happy delusions they are labouring under now, on what miserable blindness their eyes may be opened then, I do not pretend to say. But I went on board their ship to bear testimony against them if they deserved it, as I fully believed they would; to my great astonishment they did not deserve it; and my predispositions and tendencies must not affect me as an honest witness. I went over the Amazon's side, feeling it impossible to deny that, so far, some remarkable influence had produced a remarkable result, which better known influences have often missed.[1]

[1] After this Uncommercial Journey was printed, I happened to mention the experience it describes to Lord Houghton. That gentleman then showed me an article of his writing, in *The Edinburgh Review* for January, 1862, which is highly remarkable for its philosophical and literary research concerning these Latter-Day Saints. I find in it the following sentences :—"The Select Committee of the House of Commons on emigrant ships for 1854 summoned the Mormon agent and passenger-broker before it, and came to the conclusion that no ships under the provisions of the 'Passengers Act' could be depended upon for comfort and security in the same degree as those under his administration. The Mormon ship is a Family under strong and accepted discipline, with every provision for comfort, decorum, and internal peace."

XXIII

WHEN I think I deserve particularly well of myself, and have earned the right to enjoy a little treat, I stroll from Covent-garden into the City of London, after business-hours there, on a Saturday, or—better yet—on a Sunday, and roam about its deserted nooks and corners. It is necessary to the full enjoyment of these journeys that they should be made in summer-time, for then the retired spots that I love to haunt, are at their idlest and dullest. A gentle fall of rain is not objectionable, and a warm mist sets off my favourite retreats to decided advantage.

Among these, City Churchyards hold a high place. Such strange churchyards hide in the City of London ; churchyards sometimes so entirely detached from churches, always so pressed upon by houses ; so small, so rank, so silent, so forgotten, except by the few people who ever look down into them from their smoky windows. As I stand peeping in through the iron gates and rails, I can peel the rusty metal off, like bark from an old tree. The illegible tombstones are all lop-sided, the grave-mounds lost their shape in the rains of a hundred years ago, the Lombardy Poplar or Plane-Tree that was once a drysalter's daughter and several common-councilmen, has withered like those worthies, and its departed leaves are dust beneath it. Contagion of slow ruin overhangs the place. The discoloured tiled roofs of the, environing buildings stand so awry, that they can hardly be proof against any stress of weather. Old crazy stacks of chimneys seem to look down as they overhang, dubiously calculating how far they will have to fall. In an angle of the walls, what was once the tool-house of the grave-digger rots away, encrusted with toadstools. Pipes and spouts for carrying off the rain from the encompassing gables, broken or feloniously cut for old lead long ago, now let the rain drip and splash as it list, upon the weedy earth. Sometimes there

is a rusty pump somewhere near, and, as I look in at the
rails and meditate, I hear it working under an unknown
hand with a creaking protest: as though the departed in the
churchyard urged, "Let us lie here in peace; don't suck us
up and drink us!"

One of my best beloved churchyards, I call the churchyard
of Saint Ghastly Grim; touching what men in general call
it, I have no information. It lies at the heart of the City,
and the Blackwall Railway shrieks at it daily. It is a small
small churchyard, with a ferocious strong spiked iron gate,
like a jail. This gate is ornamented with skulls and cross-
bones, larger than the life, wrought in stone; but it likewise
came into the mind of Saint Ghastly Grim, that to stick iron
spikes a-top of the stone skulls, as though they were impaled,
would be a pleasant device. Therefore the skulls grin aloft
horribly, thrust through and through with iron spears.
Hence, there is attraction of repulsion for me in Saint Ghastly
Grim, and, having often contemplated it in the daylight and
the dark, I once felt drawn towards it in a thunderstorm at
midnight. "Why not?" I said, in self-excuse. "I have been
to see the Colosseum by the light of the moon; is it worse to
go to see Saint Ghastly Grim by the light of the lightning?"
I repaired to the Saint in a hackney cab, and found the
skulls most effective, having the air of a public execution,
and seeming, as the lightning flashed, to wink and grin with
the pain of the spikes. Having no other person to whom to
impart my satisfaction, I communicated it to the driver. So
far from being responsive, he surveyed me—he was naturally
a bottle-nosed, red-faced man—with a blanched countenance.
And as he drove me back, he ever and again glanced in over
his shoulder through the little front window of his carriage,
as mistrusting that I was a fare originally from a grave in
the churchyard of Saint Ghastly Grim, who might have flitted
home again without paying.

Sometimes, the queer Hall of some queer Company gives
upon a churchyard such as this, and, when the Livery dine,
you may hear them (if you are looking in through the iron
rails, which you never are when I am) toasting their own
Worshipful prosperity. Sometimes, a wholesale house of
business, requiring much room for stowage, will occupy one
or two or even all three sides of the enclosing space, and the
backs of bales of goods will lumber up the windows, as if
they were holding some crowded trade-meeting of them-

selves within. Sometimes, the commanding windows are
all blank, and show no more sign of life than the graves
below—not so much, for *they* tell of what once upon a time
was life undoubtedly. Such was the surrounding of one
City churchyard that I saw last summer, on a Volunteering
Saturday evening towards eight of the clock, when with
astonishment I beheld an old old man and an old old woman
in it, making hay. Yes, of all occupations in this world,
making hay! It was a very confined patch of churchyard
lying between Gracechurch-street and the Tower, capable of
yielding, say an apronful of hay. By what means the old
old man and woman had got into it, with an almost toothless hay-making rake, I could not fathom. No open window
was within view; no window at all was within view, sufficiently near the ground to have enabled their old legs to
descend from it; the rusty churchyard-gate was locked, the
mouldy church was locked. Gravely among the graves,
they made hay, all alone by themselves. They looked like
Time and his wife. There was but the one rake between
them, and they both had hold of it in a pastorally-loving
manner, and there was hay on the old woman's black
bonnet, as if the old man had recently been playful. The
old man was quite an obsolete old man, in knee-breeches and
coarse grey stockings, and the old woman wore mittens like
unto his stockings in texture and in colour. They took no
heed of me as I looked on, unable to account for them. The
old woman was much too bright for a pew-opener, the old
man much too meek for a beadle. On an old tombstone in
the foreground between me and them, were two cherubim;
but for those celestial embellishments being represented as
having no possible use for knee-breeches, stockings, or mittens, I should have compared them with the hay-makers,
and sought a likeness. I coughed and awoke the echoes,
but the hay-makers never looked at me. They used the rake
with a measured action, drawing the scanty crop towards
them; and so I was fain to leave them under three yards
and a half of darkening sky, gravely making hay among the
graves, all alone by themselves. Perhaps they were Spectres,
and I wanted a Medium.

In another City churchyard of similar cramped dimen-
sions, I saw, that selfsame summer, two comfortable charity
children. They were making love—tremendous proof of
the vigour of that immortal article, for they were in the

graceful uniform under which English Charity delights to
hide herself—and they were overgrown, and their legs (his
legs at least, for I am modestly incompetent to speak of
hers) were as much in the wrong as mere passive weakness
of character can render legs. O it was a leaden churchyard,
but no doubt a golden ground to those young persons! I
first saw them on a Saturday evening, and, perceiving from
their occupation that Saturday evening was their trysting-
time, I returned that evening se'nnight, and renewed the
contemplation of them. They came there to shake the bits
of matting which were spread in the church aisles, and they
afterwards rolled them up, he rolling his end, she rolling
hers, until they met, and over the two once divided now
united rolls—sweet emblem!—gave and received a chaste
salute. It was so refreshing to find one of my faded churchyards blooming into flower thus, that I returned a second
time, and a third, and ultimately this befell:—They had
left the church door open, in their dusting and arranging.
Walking in to look at the church, I became aware, by the
dim light, of him in the pulpit, of her in the reading-
desk, of him looking down, of her looking up, exchanging
tender discourse. Immediately both dived, and became as
it were non-existent on this sphere. With an assumption of
innocence I turned to leave the sacred edifice, when an obese
form stood in the portal, puffily demanding Joseph, or in
default of Joseph, Celia. Taking this monster by the
sleeve, and luring him forth on pretence of showing him
whom he sought, I gave time for the emergence of Joseph
and Celia, who presently came towards us in the churchyard, bending under dusty matting, a picture of thriving
and unconscious industry. It would be superfluous to hint
that I have ever since deemed this the proudest passage in
my life.

But such instances, or any tokens of vitality, are rare
indeed in my City churchyards. A few sparrows occasionally try to raise a lively chirrup in their solitary tree—
perhaps, as taking a different view of worms from that
entertained by humanity—but they are flat and hoarse of
voice, like the clerk, the organ, the bell, the clergyman, and
all the rest of the Church-works when they are wound up
for Sunday. Caged larks, thrushes, or blackbirds, hanging
in neighbouring courts, pour forth their strains passionately,
as scenting the tree, trying to break out, and see leaves again

before they die, but their song is Willow, Willow—of a churchyard cast. So little light lives inside the churches of my churchyards, when the two are co-existent, that it is often only by an accident and after long acquaintance that I discover their having stained glass in some odd window. The westering sun slants into the churchyard by some unwonted entry, a few prismatic tears drop on an old tomb-stone, and a window that I thought was only dirty, is for the moment all bejewelled. Then the light passes and the colours die. Though even then, if there be room enough for me to fall back so far as that I can gaze up to the top of the Church Tower, I see the rusty vane new burnished, and seeming to look out with a joyful flash over the sea of smoke at the distant shore of country.

Blinking old men who are let out of workhouses by the hour, have a tendency to sit on bits of coping stone in these churchyards, leaning with both hands on their sticks and asthmatically gasping. The more depressed class of beggars too, bring hither broken meats, and munch. I am on nodding terms with a meditative turncock who lingers in one of them, and whom I suspect of a turn for poetry; the rather, as he looks out of temper when he gives the fire-plug a disparaging wrench with that large tuning-fork of his which would wear out the shoulder of his coat, but for a precautionary piece of inlaid leather. Fire-ladders, which I am satisfied nobody knows anything about, and the keys of which were lost in ancient times, moulder away in the larger churchyards, under eaves like wooden eyebrows; and so removed are those corners from the haunts of men and boys, that once on a fifth of November I found a "Guy" trusted to take care of himself there, while his pro-prietors had gone to dinner. Of the expression of his face I cannot report, because it was turned to the wall; but his shrugged shoulders and his ten extended fingers, appeared to denote that he had moralised in his little straw chair on the mystery of mortality until he gave it up as a bad job.

You do not come upon these churchyards violently; there are shades of transition in the neighbourhood. An anti-quated news shop, or barber's shop, apparently bereft of customers in the earlier days of George the Third, would warn me to look out for one, if any discoveries in this respect were left for me to make. A very quiet court, in combina-tion with an unaccountable dyer's and scourer's, would prepare me for a churchyard. An exceedingly retiring public-house, with a bagatelle-board shadily visible in a sawdusty parlour shaped like an omnibus, and with a shelf of punch-bowls in the bar, would apprise me that I stood near consecrated ground. A " Dairy," exhibiting in its modest window one very little milk-can and three eggs, would suggest to me the certainty of finding the poultry hard by, pecking at my forefathers. I first inferred the vicinity of Saint Ghastly Grim, from a certain air of extra repose and gloom pervading a vast stack of warehouses.

From the hush of these places, it is congenial to pass into the hushed resorts of business. Down the lanes I like to see the carts and waggons huddled together in repose, the cranes idle, and the warehouses shut. Pausing in the alleys behind the closed Banks of mighty Lombard-street, it gives one as good as a rich feeling to think of the broad counters with a rim along the edge, made for telling money out on, the scales for weighing precious metals, the ponderous ledgers, and, above all, the bright copper shovels for shovelling gold. When I draw money, it never seems so much money as when it is shovelled at me out of a bright copper shovel. I like to say, " In gold," and to see seven pounds musically pouring out of the shovel, like seventy ; the Bank appearing to remark to me—I italicise *appearing*—" if you want more of this yellow earth, we keep it in barrows at your service." To think of the banker's clerk with his deft finger turning the crisp edges of the Hundred-Pound Notes he has taken in a fat roll out of a drawer, is again to hear the rustling of that delicious south-cash wind. " How will you have it ? " I once heard this usual question asked at a Bank Counter of an elderly female, habited in mourning and steeped in simplicity, who answered, open-eyed, crook-fingered, laughing with expectation, " Anyhow ! " Calling these things to mind as I stroll among the Banks, I wonder whether the other solitary Sunday man I pass, has designs upon the Banks. For the interest and mystery of the matter, I almost hope he may have, and that his confederate may be at this moment taking impressions of the keys of the iron closets in wax, and that a delightful robbery may be in course of transaction. About College-hill, Mark-lane, and so on towards the Tower, and Dockward, the deserted wine-merchants' cellars are fine subjects for consideration ; but the deserted money-cellars of the Bankers, and their plate-cellars, and their jewel-cellars, what subterranean regions of the Wonderful Lamp are these! And again: possibly some shoeless boy in rags passed through this street yesterday, for whom it is reserved to be a Banker in the fulness of time, and to be surpassing rich. Such reverses have been, since the days of Whittington ; and were, long before. I want to know whether the boy has any foreglittering of that glittering fortune now, when he treads these stones, hungry. Much as I also want to know whether the next man to be hanged at Newgate yonder, had any suspicion upon him that he was moving steadily towards that fate, when he talked so much about the last man who paid the same great debt at the same small Debtors' Door.

Where are all the people who on busy working-days pervade these scenes ? The locomotive banker's clerk, who carries a black portfolio chained to him by a chain of steel, where is he ? Does he go to bed with his chain on—to church with his chain on—or does he lay it by ? And if he lays it by, what becomes of his portfolio when he is unchained for a holiday ? The wastepaper baskets of these closed counting-houses would let me into many hints of business matters if I had the exploration of them ; and what secrets of the heart should I discover on the "pads" of the young clerks—the sheets of cartridge-paper and blotting-paper interposed between their writing and their desks ! Pads are taken into confidence on the tenderest occasions, and oftentimes when I have made a business visit, and have sent in my name from the outer office, have I had it forced on my discursive notice that the officiating young gentleman has over and over again inscribed AMELIA, in ink of various dates, on corners of his pad. Indeed, the pad may be regarded as the legitimate modern successor of the old forest-tree : whereon these young knights (having no attainable forest nearer than Epping) engrave the names of their mistresses. After all, it is a more satisfactory process than carving, and can be oftener repeated. So these courts in their Sunday rest are courts of Love Omnipotent (I rejoice to bethink myself), dry as they look. And here is Garraway's, bolted and shuttered hard and fast ! It is possible to imagine the man who cuts the sandwiches, on his back in a hayfield ; it is possible to imagine his desk, like the desk of a clerk at church, without him ; but imagination is unable to pursue the men who wait at Garraway's all the week for the men who never come. When they are forcibly put out of Garraway's on Saturday night—which they must be, for they never would go out of their own accord—where do they vanish until Monday morning? On the first Sunday that I ever strayed here, I expected to find them hovering about these lanes, like restless ghosts, and trying to peep into Garraway's through chinks in the shutters, if not endeavouring to turn the lock of the door with false keys, picks, and screw-drivers. But the wonder is, that they go clean away! And now I think of it, the wonder is, that every working-day pervader of these scenes goes clean away. The man who sells the dogs' collars and the little toy coal-scuttles, feels under as great an obligation to go afar off, as Glyn and Co., or Smith, Payne, and Smith. There is an old monastery-crypt under Garraway's (I have been in it among the port wine), and perhaps Garraway's, taking pity on the mouldy men who wait in its public-room all their lives, gives them cool house-room down there over Sundays ; but the catacombs of Paris would not be large enough to hold the rest of the missing. This characteristic of London City greatly helps its being the quaint place it is in the weekly pause of business, and greatly helps my Sunday sen-sation in it of being the Last Man. In my solitude, the ticket-porters being all gone with the rest, I venture to breathe to the quiet bricks and stones my confidential won-derment why a ticket-porter, who never does any work with his hands, is bound to wear a white apron, and why a great Ecclesiastical Dignitary, who never does any work with his hands either, is equally bound to wear a black one.

XXIV

AN OLD STAGE-COACHING HOUSE

BEFORE the waitress had shut the door, I had forgotten how many stage-coaches she said used to change horses in the town every day. But it was of little moment; any high number would do as well as another. It had been a great stage-coaching town in the great stage-coaching times, and the ruthless railways had killed and buried it.

The sign of the house was the Dolphin's Head. Why only head, I don't know ; for the Dolphin's effigy at full length, and upside down—as a Dolphin is always bound to be when artistically treated, though I suppose he is sometimes right side upward in his natural condition—graced the sign-board. The sign-board chafed its rusty hooks outside the bow-window of my room, and was a shabby work. No visitor could have denied that the Dolphin was dying by inches, but he showed no bright colours. He had once served another master ; there was a newer streak of paint below him, displaying with inconsistent freshness the legend, By J. MELLOWS.

My door opened again, and J. Mellows's representative came back. I had asked her what I could have for dinner, and she now returned with the counter question, what would I like ? As the Dolphin stood possessed of nothing that I do like, I was fain to yield to the suggestion of a duck, which I don't like. J. Mellows's representative was a mournful young woman, with one eye susceptible of guidance, and one uncontrollable eye ; which latter, seeming to wander in quest of stage-coaches, deepened the melancholy in which the Dolphin was steeped.

This young woman had but shut the door on retiring again when I bethought me of adding to my order, the words, "with nice vegetables." Looking out at the door to give them emphatic utterance, I found her already in a state of pensive catalepsy in the deserted gallery, picking her teeth with a pin.

At the Railway Station seven miles off, I had been the subject of wonder when I ordered a fly in which to come here. And when I gave the direction "To the Dolphin's Head," I had observed an ominous stare on the countenance of the strong young man in velveteen, who was the platform servant of the Company. He had also called to my driver at parting, "All ri-ight ! Don't hang yourself when you get there, Geo-o-rge ! " in a sarcastic tone, for which I had entertained some transitory thoughts of reporting him to the General Manager.

I had no business in the town—I never have any business in any town—but I had been caught by the fancy that I would come and look at it in its degeneracy. My purpose was fitly inaugurated by the Dolphin's Head, which everywhere expressed past coachfulness and present coachlessness. Coloured prints of coaches, starting, arriving, changing horses, coaches in the sunshine, coaches in the snow, coaches in the wind, coaches in the mist and rain, coaches on the King's birthday, coaches in all circumstances compatible with their triumph and victory, but never in the act of breaking down or overturning, pervaded the house. Of these works of art, some, framed and not glazed, had holes in them ; the varnish of others had become so brown and cracked, that they looked like overdone pie-crust ; the designs of others were almost obliterated by the flies of many summers. Broken glasses, damaged frames, lop-sided hanging, and consignment of incurable cripples to places of refuge in dark corners, attested the desolation of the rest. The old room on the ground floor where the passengers of the Highflyer used to dine, had nothing in it but a wretched show of twigs and flower-pots in the broad window to hide the nakedness of the land, and in a corner little Mellows's perambulator, with even its parasol-head turned despondently to the wall. The other room, where post-horse company used to wait while relays were getting ready down the yard, still held its ground, but was as airless as I conceive a hearse to be : insomuch that Mr. Pitt, hanging high against the partition (with spots on him like port wine, though it is mysterious how port wine ever got squirted up there), had good reason for perking his nose and sniffing. The stopperless cruets on the spindle-shanked sideboard were in a miserably dejected state : the anchovy sauce having turned blue some years ago, and the cayenne pepper (with a scoop in it like a small model of a wooden leg) having turned solid. The old fraudulent candles which were always being paid for and never used, were burnt out at last; but their tall stilts of candlesticks still lingered, and still outraged the human intellect by pretending to be silver. The mouldy old unreformed Borough Member, with his right hand buttoned up in the breast of his coat, and his back characteristically turned on bales of petitions from his constituents, was there too; and the poker which never had been among the fire-irons, lest post-horse company should overstir the fire, was *not* there, as of old.

Pursuing my researches in the Dolphin's Head, I found it sorely shrunken. When J. Mellows came into possession, he had walled off half the bar, which was now a tobacco-shop with its own entrance in the yard—the once glorious yard where the postboys, whip in hand and always buttoning their waistcoats at the last moment, used to come running forth to mount and away. A " Scientific Shoeing-Smith and Veterinary Surgeon," had further encroached upon the yard ; and a grimly satirical Jobber, who announced himself as having to Let " A neat one-horse fly, and a one-horse cart," had established his business, himself, and his family, in a part of the extensive stables. Another part was lopped clean off from the Dolphin's Head, and now comprised a chapel, a wheelwright's, and a Young Men's Mutual Improvement and Discussion Society (in a loft) : the whole forming a back lane. No audacious hand had plucked down the vane from the central cupola of the stables, but it had grown rusty and stuck at N—Nil : while the score or two of pigeons that remained true to their ancestral traditions and the place, had collected in a row on the roof-ridge of the only out-house retained by the Dolphin, where all the inside pigeons tried to push the outside pigeon off. This I accepted as emblematical of the struggle for post and place in railway times.

Sauntering forth into the town, by way of the covered and pillared entrance to the Dolphin's Yard, once redolent of soup and stable-litter, now redolent of musty disuse, I paced the street. It was a hot day, and the little sun-blinds of the shops were all drawn down, and the more enterprising trades-men had caused their 'Prentices to trickle water on the pavement appertaining to their frontage. It looked as if they had been shedding tears for the stage-coaches, and drying

their ineffectual pocket-handkerchiefs. Such weakness would
have been excusable ; for business was—as one dejected pork-
man who kept a shop which refused to reciprocate the compliment by keeping him, informed me—"bitter bad." Most
of the harness-makers and corn-dealers were gone the way of
the coaches, but it was a pleasant recognition of the eternal
procession of Children down that old original steep Incline,
the Valley of the Shadow, that those tradesmen were mostly
succeeded by vendors of sweetmeats and cheap toys. The
opposition house to the Dolphin, once famous as the New
White Hart, had long collapsed. In a fit of abject depression,
it had cast whitewash on its windows, and boarded up its
front door, and reduced itself to a side entrance ; but even
that had proved a world too wide for the Literary Institution which had been its last phase ; for the Institution had
collapsed too, and of the ambitious letters of its inscription
on the White Hart's front, all had fallen off but these:

L   Y INS   T

—suggestive of Lamentably Insolvent. As to the neighbouring market-place, it seemed to have wholly relinquished
marketing to the dealer in crockery whose pots and pans
straggled half across it, and to the Cheap Jack who sat with
folded arms on the shafts of his cart, superciliously gazing
around ; his velveteen waistcoat, evidently harbouring grave
doubts whether it was worth his while to stay a night in
such a place.

The church bells began to ring as I left this spot, but
they by no means improved the case, for they said, in a
petulant way, and speaking with some difficulty in their irritation, WHAT's-be-come-of-the-coach-es !" Nor would they
(I found on listening) ever vary their emphasis, save in
respect of growing more sharp and vexed, but invariably
went on, "WHAT's-be-come-of-the-coach-es !"—always beginning the inquiry with an unpolite abruptness. Perhaps
from their elevation they saw the railway, and it aggravated
them.

Coming upon a coachmaker's workshop, I began to look
about me with a revived spirit, thinking that perchance I
might behold there some remains of the old times of the
town's greatness. There was only one man at work—a dry
man, grizzled, and far advanced in years, but tall and upright,
who, becoming aware of me looking on, straightened his

back, pushed up his spectacles against his brown-paper cap, and appeared inclined to defy me. To whom I pacifically said:

"Good day, sir!"

"What?" said he.

"Good day, sir."

He seemed to consider about that, and not to agree with me.—"Was you a looking for anything?" he then asked, in a pointed manner.

"I was wondering whether there happened to be any fragment of an old stage-coach here."

"Is that all?"

"That's all."

"No, there ain't."

It was now my turn to say "Oh!" and I said it. Not another word did the dry and grizzled man say, but bent to his work again. In the coach-making days, the coach-painters had tried their brushes on a post beside him; and quite a Calendar of departed glories was to be read upon it, in blue and yellow and red and green, some inches thick. Presently he looked up again.

"You seem to have a deal of time on your hands," was his querulous remark.

I admitted the fact.

"I think it's a pity you was not brought up to something," said he.

I said I thought so too.

Appearing to be informed with an idea, he laid down his plane (for it was a plane he was at work with), pushed up his spectacles again, and came to the door.

"Would a po-shay do for you?" he asked.

"I am not sure that I understand what you mean."

"Would a po-shay," said the coachmaker, standing close before me, and folding his arms in the manner of a cross-examining counsel—"would a po-shay meet the views you have expressed? Yes, or no?"

"Yes."

"Then you keep straight along down there till you see one. *You'll* see one if you go fur enough."

With that, he turned me by the shoulder in the direction I was to take, and went in and resumed his work against a background of leaves and grapes. For, although he was a soured man and a discontented, his workshop was that agreeable mixture of town and country, street and garden, which is often to be seen in a small English town.

I went the way he had turned me, and I came to the Beer-shop with the sign of The First and Last, and was out of the town on the old London road. I came to the Turnpike, and I found it, in its silent way, eloquent respecting the change that had fallen on the road. The Turnpike-house was all overgrown with ivy; and the Turnpike-keeper, unable to get a living out of the tolls, plied the trade of a cobbler. Not only that, but his wife sold ginger-beer, and, in the very window of espial through which the Toll-takers of old times used with awe to behold the grand London coaches coming on at a gallop, exhibited for sale little barber's-poles of sweetstuff in a sticky lantern.

The political economy of the master of the turnpike thus expressed itself.

"How goes turnpike business, master?" said I to him, as he sat in his little porch, repairing a shoe.

"It don't go at all, master," said he to me. "It's stopped."

"That's bad," said I.

"Bad?" he repeated. And he pointed to one of his sun-burnt dusty children who was climbing the turnpike-gate, and said, extending his open right hand in remonstrance with Universal Nature. "Five on 'em!"

"But how to improve Turnpike business?" said I.

"There's a way, master," said he, with the air of one who had thought deeply on the subject.

"I should like to know it."

"Lay a toll on everything as comes through; lay a toll on walkers. Lay another toll on everything as don't come through; lay a toll on them as stops at home."

"Would the last remedy be fair?"

"Fair? Them as stops at home, could come through if they liked; couldn't they?"

"Say they could."

"Toll 'em. If they don't come through, it's *their* look out. Anyways,—Toll 'em!"

Finding it was as impossible to argue with this financial genius as if he had been Chancellor of the Exchequer and consequently the right man in the right place, I passed on meekly.

My mind now began to misgive me that the disappointed coachmaker had sent me on a wild-goose errand, and that there was no post-chaise in those parts. But coming within view of certain allotment-gardens by the roadside, I retracted the suspicion, and confessed that I had done him an injustice. For, there I saw, surely, the poorest superannuated post-chaise left on earth.

It was a post-chaise taken off its axletree and wheels, and plumped down on the clayey soil among a ragged growth of vegetables. It was a post-chaise not even set straight upon the ground, but tilted over, as if it had fallen out of a balloon. It was a post-chaise that had been a long time in those decayed circumstances, and against which scarlet beans were trained. It was a post-chaise patched and mended with old tea-trays, or with scraps of iron that looked like them, and boarded up as to the windows, but having A KNOCKER on the off-side door. Whether it was a post-chaise used as tool-house, summer-house, or dwelling-house, I could not discover, for there was nobody at home at the post-chaise when I knocked; but it was certainly used for something, and locked up. In the wonder of this discovery, I walked round and round the post-chaise many times, and sat down by the post-chaise, waiting for further elucidation. None came. At last, I made my way back to the old London road by the further end of the allotment-gardens, and consequently at a point beyond that from which I had diverged. I had to scramble through a hedge and down a steep bank, and I nearly came down a-top of a little spare man who sat breaking stones by the roadside.

He stayed his hammer, and said, regarding me mysteriously through his dark goggles of wire:

"Are you aware, sir, that you've been trespassing?"

"I turned out of the way," said I, in explanation, "to look at that odd post-chaise. Do you happen to know anything about it?"

"I know it was many a year upon the road," said he.

"So I supposed. Do you know to whom it belongs?"

The stone-breaker bent his brows and goggles over his heap of stones, as if he were considering whether he should answer the question or not. Then, raising his barred eyes to my features as before, he said:

"To me."

Being quite unprepared for the reply, I received it with a sufficiently awkward "Indeed! Dear me!" Presently I added, "Do you——" I was going to say "live there," but it seemed so absurd a question, that I substituted "live near here ?"

The stone-breaker, who had not broken a fragment since we began to converse, then did as follows. He raised himself by poising his finger on his hammer, and took his coat, on which he had been seated, over his arm. He then backed to an easier part of the bank than that by which I had come down, keeping his dark goggles silently upon me all the time, and then shouldered his hammer, suddenly turned, ascended, and was gone. His face was so small, and his goggles were so large, that he left me wholly uninformed as to his countenance; but he left me a profound impression that the curved legs I had seen from behind as he vanished, were the legs of an old postboy. It was not until then that I noticed he had been working by a grass-grown milestone, which looked like a tombstone erected over the grave of the London road.

My dinner-hour being close at hand, I had no leisure to pursue the goggles or the subject then, but made my way back to the Dolphin's Head. In the gateway I found J. Mellows, looking at nothing, and apparently experiencing that it failed to raise his spirits.

"*I* don't care for the town," said J. Mellows, when I complimented him on the sanitary advantages it may or may not possess; "I wish I had never seen the town!"

"You don't belong to it, Mr. Mellows?"

"Belong to it!" repeated Mellows. "If I didn't belong to a better style of town than this, I'd take and drown myself in a pail." It then occurred to me that Mellows, having so little to do, was habitually thrown back on his internal resources—by which I mean the Dolphin's cellar.

"What we want," said Mellows, pulling off his hat, and making as if he emptied it of the last load of Disgust that had exuded from his brain, before he put it on again for another load; "what we want, is a Branch. The Petition for the Branch Bill is in the coffee-room. Would you put your name to it? Every little helps."

I found the document in question stretched out flat on the coffee-room table by the aid of certain weights from the kitchen, and I gave it the additional weight of my uncommercial signature. To the best of my belief, I bound myself to the modest statement that universal traffic, happiness, prosperity, and civilisation, together with unbounded national triumph in competition with the foreigner, would infallibly flow from the Branch.

Having achieved this constitutional feat, I asked Mr. Mellows if he could grace my dinner with a pint of good wine? Mr. Mellows thus replied:

"If I couldn't give you a pint of good wine, I'd-- there! —I'd take and drown myself in a pail. But I was deceived when I bought this business, and the stock was higgledy-piggledy, and I haven't yet tasted my way quite through it with a view to sorting it. Therefore, if you order one kind and get another, change till it comes right. For what," said Mellows, unloading his hat as before, "what would you or any gentleman do, if you ordered one kind of wine and was required to drink another? Why, you'd (and naturally and properly, having the feelings of a gentleman), you'd take and drown yourself in a pail!"

XXV

THE shabbiness of our English capital, as compared with Paris, Bordeaux, Frankfort, Milan, Geneva—almost any important town on the continent of Europe—I find very striking after an absence of any duration in foreign parts. London is shabby in contrast with Edinburgh, with Aberdeen, with Exeter, with Liverpool, with a bright little town like Bury St. Edmunds. London is shabby in contrast with New York, with Boston, with Philadelphia. In detail, one would say it can rarely fail to be a disappointing piece of shabbiness to a stranger from any of those places. There is nothing shabbier than Drury-lane, in Rome itself. The meanness of Regent-street, set against the great line of Boulevards in Paris, is as striking as the abortive ugliness of Trafalgar-square, set against the gallant beauty of the Place de la Concorde. London is shabby by daylight, and shabbier by gaslight. No Englishman knows what gaslight is, until he sees the Rue de Rivoli and the Palais Royal after dark.

The mass of London people are shabby. The absence of distinctive dress has, no doubt, something to do with it. The porters of the Vintners' Company, the draymen, and the butchers, are about the only people who wear distinctive dresses ; and even these do not wear them on holidays. We have nothing which for cheapness, cleanliness, convenience, or picturesqueness, can compare with the belted blouse. As to our women ;—next Easter or Whitsuntide, look at the bonnets at the British Museum or the National Gallery, and think of the pretty white French cap, the Spanish mantilla, or the Genoese mezzero.

Probably there are not more second-hand clothes sold in London than in Paris, and yet the mass of the London population have a second-hand look which is not to be detected on the mass of the Parisian population. I think this is mainly because a Parisian workman does not in the least trouble himself about what is worn by a Parisian idler, but dresses in the way of his own class, and for his own comfort. In London, on the contrary, the fashions descend; and you never fully know how inconvenient or ridiculous a fashion is, until you see it in its last descent. It was but the other day, on a race-course, that I observed four people in a barouche deriving great entertainment from the contemplation of four people on foot. The four people on foot were two young men and two young women; the four people in the barouche were two young men and two young women. The four young women were dressed in exactly the same style; the four young men were dressed in exactly the same style. Yet the two couples on wheels were as much amused by the two couples on foot, as if they were quite unconscious of having themselves set those fashions, or of being at that very moment engaged in the display of them.

Is it only in the matter of clothes that fashion descends here in London—and consequently in England—and thence shabbiness arises? Let us think a little, and be just. The " Black Country " round about Birmingham, is a very black country; but is it quite as black as it has been lately painted? An appalling accident happened at the People's Park near Birmingham, this last July, when it was crowded with people from the Black Country—an appalling accident consequent on a shamefully dangerous exhibition. Did the shamefully dangerous exhibition originate in the moral blackness of the Black Country, and in the Black People's peculiar love of the excitement attendant on great personal hazard, which they looked on at, but in which they did not participate? Light is much wanted in the Black Country. O we are all agreed on that. But, we must not quite forget the crowds of gentlefolks who set the shamefully dangerous fashion, either. We must not quite forget the enterprising Directors of an Institution vaunting mighty educational pretences, who made the low sensation as strong as they possibly could make it, by hanging the Blondin rope as high as they possibly could hang it. All this must not be eclipsed in the Blackness of the Black Country. The reserved seats high up by the rope, the cleared space below it, so that no one should be smashed but the performer, the

pretence of slipping and falling off, the baskets for the feet
and the sack for the head, the photographs everywhere,
and the virtuous indignation nowhere—all this must not
be wholly swallowed up in the blackness of the jet-black
country.

Whatsoever fashion is set in England, is certain to descend.
This is a text for a perpetual sermon on care in setting
fashions. When you find a fashion low down, look back for
the time (it will never be far off) when it was the fashion
high up. This is the text for a perpetual sermon on social
justice. From imitations of Ethiopian Serenaders, to imitations of Prince's coats and waistcoats, you will find the
original model in St. James's Parish. When the Serenaders
become tiresome, trace them beyond the Black Country;
when the coats and waistcoats become insupportable, refer
them to their source in the Upper Toady Regions.

Gentlemen's clubs were once maintained for purposes of
savage party warfare ; working men's clubs of the same day
assumed the same character. Gentlemen's clubs became
places of quiet inoffensive recreation ; working men's clubs
began to follow suit. If working men have seemed rather
slow to appreciate advantages of combination which have
saved the pockets of gentlemen, and enhanced their comforts, it is because working men could scarcely, for want of
capital, originate such combinations without help ; and
because help has not been separable from that great impertinence, Patronage. The instinctive revolt of his spirit
against patronage, is a quality much to be respected in the
English working man. It is the base of the base of his best
qualities. Nor is it surprising that he should be unduly
suspicious of patronage, and sometimes resentful of it even
where it is not, seeing what a flood of washy talk has been
let loose on his devoted head, or with what complacent
condescension the same devoted head has been smoothed
and patted. It is a proof to me of his self-control that he
never strikes out pugilistically, right and left, when addressed
as one of " My friends," or " My assembled friends ; " that
he does not become inappeasable, and run amuck like a
Malay, whenever he sees a biped in broadcloth getting on
a platform to talk to him ; that any pretence of improving
his mind, does not instantly drive him out of his mind,
and cause him to toss his obliging patron like a mad bull.

For, how often have I heard the unfortunate working

man lectured, as if he were a little charity-child, humid as to his nasal development, strictly literal as to his Catechism, and called by Providence to walk all his days in a station in life represented on festive occasions by a mug of warm milk-and-water and a bun ! What popguns of jokes have these ears tingled to hear let off at him, what asinine sentiments, what impotent conclusions, what spelling-book moralities, what adaptations of the orator's insufferable tediousness to the assumed level of his understanding ! If his sledge-hammers, his spades and pick-axes, his saws and chisels, his paint-pots and brushes, his forges, furnaces, and engines, the horses that he drove at his work, and the machines that drove him at his work, were all toys in one little paper box, and he the baby who played with them, he could not have been discoursed to, more impertinently and absurdly than I have heard him discoursed to times innumerable. Consequently, not being a fool or a fawner, he has come to acknowledge his patronage by virtually saying : " Let me alone. If you understand me no better than *that*, sir and madam, let me alone. You mean very well, I dare say, but I don't like it, and I won't come here again to have any more of it."

Whatever is done for the comfort and advancement of the working man must be so far done by himself as that it is maintained by himself. And there must be in it no touch of condescension, no shadow of patronage. In the great working districts, this truth is studied and understood. When the American civil war rendered it necessary, first in Glasgow, and afterwards in Manchester, that the working people should be shown how to avail themselves of the advantages derivable from system, and from the combination of numbers, in the purchase and the cooking of their food, this truth was above all things borne in mind. The quick consequence was, that suspicion and reluctance were vanquished, and that the effort resulted in an astonishing and a complete success.

Such thoughts passed through my mind on a July morning of this summer, as I walked towards Commercial Street (not Uncommercial Street), Whitechapel. The Glasgow and Manchester system had been lately set a-going there, by certain gentlemen who felt an interest in its diffusion, and I had been attracted by the following hand-bill printed on rose-coloured paper :

SELF-SUPPORTING

C O O K I N G   D E P Ô T

FOR THE WORKING CLASSES

Commercial-street, Whitechapel,

Where Accommodation is provided for Dining comfortably
300 Persons at a time.

Open from 7 A.M. till 7 P.M.

PRICES.

All Articles of the BEST QUALITY.

Cup of Tea or Coffee. . . .	One Penny
Bread and Butter	One Penny
Bread and Cheese	One Penny
Slice of bread . One half-penny or	One Penny
Boiled Egg	One Penny
Ginger Beer	One Penny

The above Articles always ready.

Besides the above may be had, from 12 to 3 o'clock,

Bowl of Scotch Broth . . .	One Penny
Bowl of Soup	One Penny
Plate of Potatoes	One Penny
Plate of Minced Beef . . .	Twopence
Plate of Cold Beef	Twopence
Plate of Cold Ham	Twopence
Plate of Plum Pudding or Rice .	One Penny

As the Economy of Cooking depends greatly upon the
simplicity of the arrangements with which a great number
of persons can be served at one time, the Upper Room of
this Establishment will be especially set apart for a

PUBLIC DINNER EVERY DAY

From 12 till 3 o'clock,

Consisting of the following Dishes:

Bowl of Broth, or Soup,
Plate of Cold Beef or Ham,
Plate of Potatoes,
Plum Pudding, or Rice.

FIXED CHARGE 4½d.

THE DAILY PAPERS PROVIDED.

N.B.—This Establishment is conducted on the strictest business principles, with the full intention of making it self-supporting, so that every one may frequent it with a feeling of perfect independence.

The assistance of all frequenting the Depôt is confidently expected in checking anything interfering with the comfort, quiet, and regularity of the establishment.

Please do not destroy this Hand Bill, but hand it to some other person whom it may interest.

The Self-Supporting Cooking Depôt (not a very good name, and one would rather give it an English one) had hired a newly-built warehouse that it found to let; therefore it was not established in premises specially designed for the purpose. But, at a small cost they were exceedingly well adapted to the purpose: being light, well ventilated, clean, and cheerful. They consisted of three large rooms. That on the basement story was the kitchen; that on the ground floor was the general dining-room; that on the floor above was the Upper Room referred to in the hand-bill, where the Public Dinner at fourpence-halfpenny a head was provided every day. The cooking was done, with much economy of space and fuel, by American cooking-stoves, and by young women not previously brought up as cooks; the walls and pillars of the two dining-rooms were agreeably brightened with ornamental colours; the tables were capable of accommodating six or eight persons each; the attendants were all young women, becomingly and neatly dressed, and dressed alike. I think the whole staff was female, with the exception of the steward or manager.

My first inquiries were directed to the wages of this staff; because, if any establishment claiming to be self-supporting, live upon the spoliation of anybody or anything, or eke out a feeble existence by poor mouths and beggarly resources (as too many so-called Mechanics' Institutions do), I make bold to express my Uncommercial opinion that it has no business to live, and had better die. It was made clear to me by the account books, that every person employed was properly paid. My next inquiries were directed to the quality of the provisions purchased, and to the terms on which they were bought. It was made equally clear to me that the quality was the very best, and that all bills were paid weekly. My next inquiries were directed to the balance-sheet for the last two weeks—only the third and fourth of the establishment's career. It was made equally clear to me, that after everything bought was paid for, and after each week was charged with its full share of wages, rent and taxes, depreciation of plant in use, and interest on capital at the rate of four per cent. per annum, the last week had yielded a profit of (in round numbers) one pound ten; and the previous week a profit of six pounds ten. By this time I felt that I had a healthy appetite for the dinners.

It had just struck twelve, and a quick succession of faces had already begun to appear at a little window in the wall of the partitioned space where I sat looking over the books. Within this little window, like a pay-box at a theatre, a neat and brisk young woman presided to take money and issue tickets. Every one coming in must take a ticket. Either the fourpence-halfpenny ticket for the upper room (the most popular ticket, I think), or a penny ticket for a bowl of soup, or as many penny tickets as he or she choose to buy. For three penny tickets one had quite a wide range of choice. A plate of cold boiled beef and potatoes; or a plate of cold ham and potatoes; or a plate of hot minced beef and potatoes; or a bowl of soup, bread and cheese, and a plate of plum-pudding. Touching what they should have, some customers on taking their seats fell into a reverie—became mildly distracted—postponed decision, and said in bewilderment, they would think of it. One old man I noticed when I sat among the tables in the lower room, who was startled by the bill of fare, and sat contemplating it as if it were something of a ghostly nature. The decision of the boys was as rapid as their execution, and always included pudding.

There were several women among the diners, and several clerks and shopmen. There were carpenters and painters from the neighbouring buildings under repair, and there were nautical men, and there were, as one diner observed to me, "some of most sorts." Some were solitary, some came two together, some dined in parties of three or four, or six. The latter talked together, but assuredly no one was louder than at my club in Pall-Mall. One young fellow whistled in rather a shrill manner while he waited for his dinner, but I was gratified to observe that he did so in evident defiance of my Uncommercial individuality. Quite agreeing with him, on consideration, that I had no business to be there, unless I dined like the rest, I "went in," as the phrase is, for fourpence-halfpenny.

The room of the fourpence-halfpenny banquet had, like the lower room, a counter in it, on which were ranged a great number of cold portions ready for distribution. Behind this counter, the fragrant soup was steaming in deep cans, and the best-cooked of potatoes were fished out of similar receptacles. Nothing to eat was touched with the hand. Every waitress had her own tables to attend to. As soon as she saw a new customer seat himself at one of her tables, she took from the counter all his dinner—his soup, potatoes, meat, and pudding—piled it up dexterously in her two hands, set it before him, and took his ticket. This serving of the whole dinner at once, had been found greatly to simplify the business of attendance, and was also popular with the customers: who were thus enabled to vary the meal by varying the routine of dishes: beginning with soup to-day, putting soup in the middle to-morrow, putting soup at the end the day after to-morrow, and ringing similar changes on meat and pudding. The rapidity with which every new-comer got served, was remarkable ; and the dexterity with which the waitresses (quite new to the art a month before) discharged their duty, was as agreeable to see, as the neat smartness with which they wore their dress and had dressed their hair.

If I seldom saw better waiting, so I certainly never ate better meat, potatoes, or pudding. And the soup was an honest and stout soup, with rice and barley in it, and "little matters for the teeth to touch," as had been observed to me by my friend below stairs already quoted. The dinner-service, too, was neither conspicuously hideous for High Art nor for Low Art, but was of a pleasant and pure appearance. Concerning the viands and their cookery, one last remark. I dined at my club in Pall-Mall aforesaid, a few days afterwards, for exactly twelve times the money, and not half as well.

The company thickened after one o'clock struck, and changed pretty quickly. Although experience of the place had been so recently attainable, and although there was still considerable curiosity out in the street and about the entrance, the general tone was as good as could be, and the customers fell easily into the ways of the place. It was clear to me, however, that they were there to have what

they paid for, and to be on an independent footing. To the
best of my judgment, they might be patronised out of the
building in a month. With judicious visiting, and by dint
of being questioned, read to, and talked at, they might even
be got rid of (for the next quarter of a century) in half the
time.

This disinterested and wise movement is fraught with
so many wholesome changes in the lives of the working
people, and with so much good in the way of overcoming
that suspicion which our own unconscious impertinence has
engendered, that it is scarcely gracious to criticise details as
yet ; the rather, because it is indisputable that the managers
of the Whitechapel establishment most thoroughly feel that
they are upon their honour with the customers, as to the
minutest points of administration. But, although the
American stoves cannot roast, they can surely boil one kind
of meat as well as another, and need not always circumscribe
their boiling talents within the limits of ham and beef.
The most enthusiastic admirer of those substantials, would
probably not object to occasional inconstancy in respect of
pork and mutton : or, especially in cold weather, to a little
innocent trifling with Irish stews, meat pies, and toads in
holes. Another drawback on the Whitechapel establishment, is the absence of beer. Regarded merely as a question
of policy, it is very impolitic, as having a tendency to send
the working men to the public-house, where gin is reported
to be sold. But, there is a much higher ground on which
this absence of beer is objectionable. It expresses distrust
of the working man. It is a fragment of that old mantle of
patronage in which so many estimable Thugs, so darkly
wandering up and down the moral world, are sworn to
muffle him. Good beer is a good thing for him, he says,
and he likes it ; the Depôt could give it him good, and he
now gets it bad. Why does the Depôt not give it him good ?
Because he would get drunk. Why does the Depôt not let
him have a pint with his dinner, which would not make
him drunk ? Because he might have had another pint, or
another two pints, before he came. Now, this distrust is
an affront, is exceedingly inconsistent with the confidence
the managers express in their hand-bills, and is a timid
stopping-short upon the straight highway. It is unjust and
unreasonable, also. It is unjust, because it punishes the
sober man for the vice of the drunken man. It is un-

reasonable, because any one at all experienced in such things knows that the drunken workman does not get drunk where he goes to eat and drink, but where he goes to drink—expressly to drink. To suppose that the working man cannot state this question to himself quite as plainly as I state it here, is to suppose that he is a baby, and is again to tell him in the old wearisome condescending patronising way that he must be goody-poody, and do as he is toldy-poldy, and not be a manny-panny or a voter-poter, but fold his handy-pandys, and be a childy-pildy.

I found from the accounts of the Whitechapel Self-Supporting Cooking Depôt, that every article sold in it, even at the prices I have quoted, yields a certain small profit! Individual speculators are of course already in the field, and are of course already appropriating the name. The classes for whose benefit the real depôts are designed, will distinguish between the two kinds of enterprise.

XXVI

THERE are some small out-of-the-way landing-places on the Thames and the Medway, where I do much of my summer idling. Running water is favourable to day-dreams, and a strong tidal river is the best of running water for mine. I like to watch the great ships standing out to sea or coming home richly laden, the active little steam-tugs confidently puffing with them to and from the sea-horizon, the fleet of barges that seem to have plucked their brown and russet sails from the ripe trees in the landscape, the heavy old colliers, light in ballast, floundering down before the tide, the light screw barks and schooners imperiously holding a straight course while the others patiently tack and go about, the yachts with their tiny hulls and great white sheets of canvas, the little sailing-boats bobbing to and fro on their errands of pleasure or business, and—as it is the nature of little people to do—making a prodigious fuss about their small affairs. Watching these objects, I still am under no obligation to think about them, or even so much as to see them, unless it perfectly suits my humour. As little am I obliged to hear the plash and flop of the tide, the ripple at my feet, the clinking windlass afar off, or the humming steam-ship paddles further away yet. These, with the creaking little jetty on which I sit, and the gaunt high-water marks and low-water marks in the mud, and the broken causeway, and the broken bank, and the broken stakes and piles leaning forward as if they were vain of their personal appearance and looking for their reflection in the water, will melt into any train of fancy. Equally adaptable to any purpose or to none, are the pasturing sheep and kine upon the marshes, the gulls that wheel and dip around me, the crows (well out of gunshot) going home from the rich harvest-fields, the heron that has been out a-fishing and looks as melancholy, up there in the sky, as if it hadn't agreed with him. Everything within the range of the senses will, by the aid of the running water, lend itself to everything beyond that range, and work into a drowsy whole, not unlike a kind of tune, but for which there is no exact definition.

One of these landing-places is near an old fort (I can see the Nore Light from it with my pocket-glass), from which fort mysteriously emerges a boy, to whom I am much indebted for additions to my scanty stock of knowledge. He is a young boy, with an intelligent face burnt to a dust colour by the summer sun, and with crisp hair of the same hue. He is a boy in whom I have perceived nothing incompatible with habits of studious inquiry and meditation, unless an evanescent black eye (I was delicate of inquiring how occasioned) should be so considered. To him am I indebted for ability to identify a Custom-house boat at any distance, and for acquaintance with all the forms and ceremonies observed by a homeward-bound Indiaman coming up the river, when the Custom-house officers go aboard her. But for him, I might never have heard of "the dumb-ague," respecting which malady I am now learned. Had I never sat at his feet, I might have finished my mortal career and never known that when I see a white horse on a barge's sail, that barge is a lime barge. For precious secrets in reference to beer, am I likewise beholden to him, involving warning against the beer of a certain establishment, by reason of its having turned sour through failure in point of demand : though my young sage is not of opinion that similar deterioration has befallen the ale. He has also enlightened me touching the mushrooms of the marshes, and has gently reproved my ignorance in having supposed them to be impregnated with salt. His manner of imparting information, is thoughtful, and appropriate to the scene. As he reclines beside me, he pitches into the river, a little stone or piece of grit, and then delivers himself oracularly, as though he spoke out of the centre of the spreading circle that it makes in the water. He never improves my mind without observing this formula.

With the wise boy—whom I know by no other name than the Spirit of the Fort—I recently consorted on a breezy day when the river leaped about us and was full of life. I had seen the sheaved corn carrying in the golden fields as I came down to the river; and the rosy farmer, watching his labouring-men in the saddle on his cob, had told me how he had reaped his two hundred and sixty acres of long-strawed corn last week, and how a better week's work he had never done in all his days. Peace and abundance were on the country-side in beautiful forms and beautiful colours, and the harvest seemed even to be sailing out to grace the never-reaped sea in the yellow-laden barges that mellowed the distance.

It was on this occasion that the Spirit of the Fort, directing his remarks to a certain floating iron battery lately lying in that reach of the river, enriched my mind with his opinions on naval architecture, and informed me that he would like to be an engineer. I found him up to everything that is done in the contracting line by Messrs. Peto and Brassey—cunning in the article of concrete—mellow in the matter of iron— great on the subject of gunnery. When he spoke of pile- driving and sluice-making, he left me not a leg to stand on, and I can never sufficiently acknowledge his forbearance with me in my disabled state. While he thus discoursed, he several times directed his eyes to one distant quarter of the landscape, and spoke with vague mysterious awe of "the Yard." Pondering his lessons after we had parted, I be- thought me that the Yard was one of our large public Dockyards, and that it lay hidden among the crops down in the dip behind the windmills, as if it modestly kept itself out of view in peaceful times, and sought to trouble no man. Taken with this modesty on the part of the Yard, I resolved to improve the Yard's acquaintance.

My good opinion of the Yard's retiring character was not dashed by nearer approach. It resounded with the noise of hammers beating upon iron; and the great sheds or slips under which the mighty men-of-war are built, loomed business-like when contemplated from the opposite side of the river. For all that, however, the Yard made no display, but kept itself snug under hill-sides of corn-fields, hop- gardens, and orchards; its great chimneys smoking with a quiet—almost a lazy—air, like giants smoking tobacco; and the great Shears moored off it, looking meekly and inoffen- sively out of proportion, like the Giraffe of the machinery creation. The store of cannon on the neighbouring gun- wharf, had an innocent toy-like appearance, and the one red-coated sentry on duty over them was a mere toy figure, with a clock-work movement. As the hot sunlight sparkled on him he might have passed for the identical little man who had the little gun, and whose bullets they were made of lead, lead, lead.

Crossing the river and landing at the Stairs, where a drift of chips and weed had been trying to land before me and had not succeeded, but had got into a corner instead, I found the very street posts to be cannon, and the architectural ornaments to be shells. And so I came to the Yard, which was shut up tight and strong with great folded gates, like an enormous patent safe. These gates devouring me, I became digested into the Yard; and it had, at first, a clean-swept holiday air, as if it had given over work until next war-time. Though indeed a quantity of hemp for rope was tumbling out of store-houses, even there, which would hardly be lying like so much hay on the white stones if the Yard were as placid as it pretended.

Ding, Clash, Dong, BANG, Boom, Rattle, Clash, BANG, Clink, BANG, Dong, BANG, Clatter, BANG BANG BANG! What on earth is this! This is, or soon will be, the Achilles, iron armour-plated ship. Twelve hundred men are working at her now; twelve hundred men working on stages over her sides, over her bows, over her stern, under her keel, between her decks, down in her hold, within her and without, crawling and creeping into the finest curves of her lines wherever it is possible for men to twist. Twelve hundred hammerers, measurers, caulkers, armourers, forgers, smiths, shipwrights; twelve hundred dingers, clashers, dongers, rattlers, clinkers, bangers bangers bangers! Yet all this stupendous uproar around the rising Achilles is as nothing to the reverberations with which the perfected Achilles shall resound upon the dreadful day when the full work is in hand for which this is but note of preparation—the day when the scuppers that are now fitting like great dry thirsty conduit-pipes, shall run red. All these busy figures between decks, dimly seen bending at their work in smoke and fire, are as nothing to the figures that shall do work here of another kind in smoke and fire, that day. These steam-worked engines alongside, helping the ship by travelling to and fro, and wafting tons of iron plates about, as though they were so many leaves of trees, would be rent limb from limb if they stood by her for a minute then. To think that this Achilles, monstrous compound of iron tank and oaken chest, can ever swim or roll! To think that any force of wind and wave could ever break her! To think that wherever I see a glowing red-hot iron point thrust out of her side from within—as I do now, there,, and there, and there!—and two watching men on a stage without, with bared arms and sledge-hammers, strike at it fiercely, and repeat their blows until it is black and flat, I see a rivet being driven home, of which there are many in every iron plate, and thousands upon thousands in the ship! To think that the difficulty I experience in appreciating the ship's size when I am on board, arises from her being a series of iron tanks and oaken chests, so that internally she is ever finishing and ever beginning, and half of her might be smashed, and yet the remaining half suffice and be sound. Then, to go over the side again and down among the ooze and wet to the bottom of the dock, in the depths of the sub-terranean forest of dog-shores and stays that hold her up, and to see the immense mass bulging out against the upper light, and tapering down towards me, is, with great pains and much clambering, to arrive at an impossibility of realising that this is a ship at all, and to become possessed by the fancy that it is an enormous immovable edifice set up in an ancient amphitheatre (say, that at Verona), and almost filling it! Yet what would even these things be, without the tributary workshops and the mechanical powers for piercing the iron plates—four inches and a half thick—for rivets, shaping them under hydraulic pressure to the finest tapering turns of the ship's lines, and paring them away, with knives shaped like the beaks of strong and cruel birds, to the nicest requirements of the design! These machines of tremendous force, so easily directed by one attentive face and presiding hand, seem to me to have in them something of the retiring character of the Yard. "Obedient monster, please to bite this mass of iron through and through, at equal distances, where these regular chalk-marks are, all round." Monster looks at its work, and lifting its ponderous head, replies, "I don't par-ticularly want to do it; but if it must be done——!" The solid metal wriggles out, hot from the monster's crunching tooth, and it *is* done. "Dutiful monster, observe this other mass of iron. It is required to be pared away, according to this delicately lessening and arbitrary line, which please to look at." Monster (who has been in a reverie) brings down its blunt head, and, much in the manner of Doctor Johnson, closely looks along the line—very closely, being somewhat near-sighted. "I don't particularly want to do it; but if it must be done——!" Monster takes another near-sighted look, takes aim, and the tortured piece writhes off, and falls, a hot tight-twisted snake, among the ashes. The making of the rivets is merely a pretty round game, played by a man and a boy, who put red-hot barley sugar in a Pope Joan board, and immediately rivets fall out of window ; but the tone of the great machines is the tone of the great Yard and the great country : "We don't particularly want to do it ; but if it must be done——!"

How such a prodigious mass as the Achilles can ever be held by such comparatively little anchors as those intended for her and lying near her here, is a mystery of seamanship which I will refer to the wise boy. For my own part, I should as soon have thought of tethering an elephant to a tent-peg, or the larger hippopotamus in the Zoological Gardens to my shirt-pin. Yonder in the river, alongside a hulk, lie two of this ship's hollow iron masts. *They* are large enough for the eye, I find, and so are all her other appliances. I wonder why only her anchors look small.

I have no present time to think about it, for I am going to see the workshops where they make all the oars used in the British Navy. A pretty large pile of building, I opine, and a pretty long job ! As to the building, I am soon disappointed, because the work is all done in one loft. And as to a long job—what is this ? Two rather large mangles with a swarm of butterflies hovering over them ? What can there be in the mangles that attracts butterflies ?

Drawing nearer, I discern that these are not mangles, but intricate machines, set with knives and saws and planes, which cut smooth and straight here, and slantwise there, and now cut such a depth, and now miss cutting altogether, according to the predestined requirements of the pieces of wood that are pushed on below them : each of which pieces is to be an oar, and is roughly adapted to that purpose before it takes its final leave of far-off forests, and sails for England. Likewise I discern that the butterflies are not true butterflies, but wooden shavings, which, being spirted up from the wood by the violence of the machinery, and kept in rapid and not equal movement by the impulse of its rotation on the air, flutter and play, and rise and fall, and conduct themselves as like butterflies as heart could wish. Suddenly the noise and motion cease, and the butterflies drop dead. An oar has been made since I came in, wanting the shaped handle. As quickly as I can follow it with my eye and thought, the

same oar is carried to a turning lathe. A whirl and a Nick!
Handle made. Oar finished.

The exquisite beauty and efficiency of this machinery need
no illustration, but happen to have a pointed illustration to-
day. A pair of oars of unusual size chance to be wanted for
a special purpose, and they have to be made by hand. Side
by side with the subtle and facile machine, and side by side
with the fast-growing pile of oars on the floor, a man shapes
out these special oars with an axe. Attended by no butterflies, and chipping and dinting, by comparison as leisurely
as if he were a labouring Pagan getting them ready against
his decease at threescore and ten, to take with him as a
present to Charon for his boat, the man (aged about thirty)
plies his task. The machine would make a regulation oar
while the man wipes his forehead. The man might be
buried in a mound made of the strips of thin broad wooden
ribbon torn from the wood whirled into oars as the minutes
fall from the clock, before he had done a forenoon's work
with his axe.

Passing from this wonderful sight to the Ships again—for
my heart, as to the Yard, is where the ships are—I notice
certain unfinished wooden walls left seasoning on the stocks,
pending the solution of the merits of the wood and iron
question, and having an air of biding their time with surly
confidence. The names of these worthies are set up beside
them, together with their capacity in guns—a custom highly
conducive to ease and satisfaction in social intercourse, if it
could be adapted to mankind. By a plank more gracefully
pendulous than substantial, I make bold to go aboard a transport ship (iron screw) just sent in from the contractor's yard
to be inspected and passed. She is a very gratifying
experience, in the simplicity and humanity of her arrangements for troops, in her provision for light and air and cleanliness, and in her care for women and children. It occurs
to me, as I explore her, that I would require a handsome sum
of money to go aboard her, at midnight by the Dockyard
bell, and stay aboard alone till morning; for surely she must
be haunted by a crowd of ghosts of obstinate old martinets,
mournfully flapping their cherubic epaulettes over the changed
times. Though still we may learn from the astounding ways
and means in our Yards now, more highly than ever to respect
the forefathers who got to sea, and fought the sea, and held
the sea, without them. This remembrance putting me in the

best of tempers with an old hulk, very green as to her copper, and generally dim and patched, I pull off my hat to her. Which salutation a callow and downy-faced young officer of Engineers, going by at the moment, perceiving, appropriates — and to which he is most heartily welcome, I am sure.

Having been torn to pieces (in imagination) by the steam circular saws, perpendicular saws, horizontal saws, and saws of eccentric action, I come to the sauntering part of my expedition, and consequently to the core of my Uncommercial pursuits.

Everywhere, as I saunter up and down the Yard, I meet with tokens of its quiet and retiring character. There is a gravity upon its red brick offices and houses, a staid pretence of having nothing worth mentioning to do, an avoidance of display, which I never saw out of England. The white stones of the pavement present no other trace of Achilles and his twelve hundred banging men (not one of whom strikes an attitude) than a few occasional echoes. But for a whisper in the air suggestive of sawdust and shavings, the oar-making and the saws of many movements might be miles away. Down below here, is the great reservoir of water where timber is steeped in various temperatures, as a part of its seasoning process. Above it, on a tramroad supported by pillars, is a Chinese Enchanter's Car, which fishes the logs up, when sufficiently steeped, and rolls smoothly away with them to stack them. When I was a child (the Yard being then familiar to me) I used to think that I should like to play at Chinese Enchanter, and to have that apparatus placed at my disposal for the purpose by a beneficent country. I still think that I should rather like to try the effect of writing a book in it. Its retirement is complete, and to go gliding to and fro among the stacks of timber would be a convenient kind of travelling in foreign countries—among the forests of North America, the sodden Honduras swamps, the dark pine woods, the Norwegian frosts, and the tropical heats, rainy seasons, and thunder-storms. The costly store of timber is stacked and stowed away in sequestered places, with the pervading avoidance of flourish or effect. It makes as little of itself as possible, and calls to no one " Come and look at me ! " And yet it is picked out from the trees of the world ; picked out for length, picked out for breadth, picked out for straightness, picked out for crookedness, chosen with an eye to every need

of ship and boat.   Strangely twisted pieces lie about, precious
in the sight of shipwrights.   Sauntering through these
groves, I come upon an open glade where workmen are
examining some timber recently delivered.   Quite a pastoral
scene, with a background of river and windmill! and no
more like War than the American States are at present like
an Union.

Sauntering among the ropemaking, I am spun into a state
of blissful indolence, wherein my rope of life seems to be so
untwisted by the process as that I can see back to very early
days indeed, when my bad dreams—they were frightful,
though my more mature understanding has never made out
why—were of an interminable sort of ropemaking, with long
minute filaments for strands, which, when they were spun
home together close to my eyes, occasioned screaming.   Next,
I walk among the quiet lofts of stores—of sails, spars, rigging,
ships' boats—determined to believe that somebody in
authority wears a girdle and bends beneath the weight of
a massive bunch of keys, and that, when such a thing is
wanted, he comes telling his keys like Blue Beard, and opens
such a door.   Impassive as the long lofts look, let the electric
battery send down the word, and the shutters and doors shall
fly open, and such a fleet of armed ships, under steam and
under sail, shall burst forth as will charge the old Medway—
where the merry Stuart let the Dutch come, while his not so
merry sailors starved in the streets—with something worth
looking at to carry to the sea.   Thus I idle round to the
Medway again, where it is now flood tide; and I find the
river evincing a strong solicitude to force a way into the dry
dock where Achilles is waited on by the twelve hundred
bangers, with intent to bear the whole away before they are
ready.

To the last, the Yard puts a quiet face upon it; for I make
my way to the gates through a little quiet grove of trees,
shading the quaintest of Dutch landing-places, where the
leaf-speckled shadow of a shipwright just passing away at
the further end might be the shadow of Russian Peter himself.   So, the doors of the great patent safe at last close upon
me, and I take boat again: somehow, thinking as the oars
dip, of braggart Pistol and his brood, and of the quiet
monsters of the Yard, with their "We don't particularly
want to do it; but if it must be done——!"   Scrunch.

XXVII

"It is neither a bold nor a diversified country," said I to myself, "this country which is three-quarters Flemish, and a quarter French; yet it has its attractions too. Though great lines of railway traverse it, the trains leave it behind, and go puffing off to Paris and the South, to Belgium and Germany, to the Northern Sea-Coast of France, and to England, and merely smoke it a little in passing. Then I don't know it, and that is a good reason for being here; and I can't pronounce half the long queer names I see inscribed over the shops, and that is another good reason for being here, since I surely ought to learn how." In short, I was "here," and I wanted an excuse for not going away from here, and I made it to my satisfaction, and stayed here.

What part in my decision was borne by Monsieur P. Salcy, is of no moment, though I own to encountering that gentleman's name on a red bill on the wall, before I made up my mind. Monsieur P. Salcy, "par permission de M. le Maire," had established his theatre in the whitewashed Hôtel de Ville, on the steps of which illustrious edifice I stood. And Monsieur P. Salcy, privileged director of such theatre, situate in "the first theatrical arrondissement of the department of the North," invited French-Flemish mankind to come and partake of the intellectual banquet provided by his family of dramatic artists, fifteen subjects in number. "La Famille P. Salcy, composée d'artistes dramatiques, au nombre de 15 sujets."

Neither a bold nor a diversified country, I say again, and withal an untidy country, but pleasant enough to ride in, when the paved roads over the flats and through the hollows, are not too deep in black mud. A country so sparely inhabited, that I wonder where the peasants who till and sow and reap the ground, can possibly dwell, and also by what invisible balloons they are conveyed from their distant homes into the fields at sunrise and back again at sunset. The occasional few poor cottages and farms in this region, surely cannot afford shelter to the numbers necessary to the cultivation, albeit the work is done so very deliberately, that on one long harvest day I have seen, in twelve miles, about twice as many men and women (all told) reaping and binding. Yet have I seen more cattle, more sheep, more pigs, and all in better case, than where there is purer French spoken, and also better ricks —round swelling peg-top ricks, well thatched: not a shapeless brown heap, like the toast of a Giant's toast-and-water, pinned to the earth with one of the skewers out of his kitchen. A good custom they have about here, likewise, of prolonging the sloping tiled roof of farm or cottage, so that it overhangs three or four feet, carrying off the wet, and making a good drying-place wherein to hang up herbs, or implements, or what not. A better custom than the popular one of keeping the refuse-heap and puddle close before the house door : which, although I paint my dwelling never so brightly blue (and it cannot be too blue for me, hereabouts), will bring fever inside my door. Wonderful poultry of the French-Flemish country, why take the trouble to *be* poultry ? Why not stop short at eggs in the rising generation, and die out and have done with it ? Parents of chickens have I seen this day, followed by their wretched young families, scratching nothing out of the mud with an air—tottering about on legs so scraggy and weak, that the valiant word drumsticks becomes a mockery when applied to them, and the crow of the lord and master has been a mere dejected case of croup. Carts have I seen, and other agricultural instruments, unwieldy, dislocated, monstrous. Poplar-trees by the thousand fringe the fields and fringe the end of the flat landscape, so that I feel, looking straight on before me, as if, when I pass the extremest fringe on the low horizon, I shall tumble over into space. Little whitewashed black holes of chapels, with barred doors and Flemish inscriptions, abound at roadside corners, and often they are garnished with a sheaf of wooden crosses, like children's swords ; or, in their default, some hollow old tree with a saint roosting in it, is similarly decorated, or a pole with a very diminutive saint enshrined aloft in a sort of sacred pigeon-house. Not that we are deficient in such decoration in the town here, for, over at the church yonder, outside the building, is a scenic representation of the Crucifixion, built up with old bricks and stones, and made out with painted canvas and wooden figures:

the whole surmounting the dusty skull of some holy personage (perhaps), shut up behind a little ashy iron grate, as if it
were originally put there to be cooked, and the fire had long
gone out. A windmilly country this, though the windmills
are so damp and rickety, that they nearly knock themselves
off their legs at every turn of their sails, and creak in loud
complaint. A weaving country, too, for in the wayside
cottages the loom goes wearily—rattle and click, rattle and
click—and, looking in, I see the poor weaving peasant, man
or woman, bending at the work, while the child, working
too, turns a little handwheel put upon the ground to suit its
height. An unconscionable monster, the loom in a small
dwelling, asserting himself ungenerously as the bread-winner,
straddling over the children's straw beds, cramping the
family in space and air, and making himself generally objectionable and tyrannical. He is tributary, too, to ugly mills
and factories and bleaching-grounds, rising out of the sluiced
fields in an abrupt bare way, disdaining, like himself, to be
ornamental or accommodating. Surrounded by these things,
here I stood on the steps of the Hôtel de Ville, persuaded to
remain by the P. Salcy family, fifteen dramatic subjects
strong.

There was a Fair besides. The double persuasion being
irresistible, and my sponge being left behind at the last
Hotel, I made the tour of the little town to buy another.
In the small sunny shops—mercers, opticians, and druggist-
grocers, with here and there an emporium of religious images
—the gravest of old spectacled Flemish husbands and wives
sat contemplating one another across bare counters, while
the wasps, who seemed to have taken military possession of
the town, and to have placed it under wasp-martial law,
executed warlike manœuvres in the windows. Other shops
the wasps had entirely to themselves, and nobody cared
and nobody came when I beat with a five-franc piece upon the
board of custom. What I sought was no more to be found
than if I had sought a nugget of Californian gold : so I went,
spongeless, to pass the evening with the Family P. Salcy.

The members of the Family P. Salcy were so fat and so
like one another—fathers, mothers, sisters, brothers, uncles,
and aunts—that I think the local audience were much confused about the plot of the piece under representation, and
to the last expected that everybody must turn out to be
the long-lost relative of everybody else. The Theatre was

established on the top story of the Hôtel de Ville, and was
approached by a long bare staircase, whereon, in an airy
situation, one of the P. Salcy Family—a stout gentleman
imperfectly repressed by a belt—took the money. This
occasioned the greatest excitement of the evening; for, no
sooner did the curtain rise on the introductory Vaudeville,
and reveal in the person of the young lover (singing a very
short song with his eyebrows) apparently the very same
identical stout gentleman imperfectly repressed by a belt,
than everybody rushed out to the paying-place, to ascertain
whether he could possibly have put on that dress-coat, that
clear complexion, and those arched black vocal eyebrows, in
so short a space of time. It then became manifest that this
was another stout gentleman imperfectly repressed by a belt:
to whom, before the spectators had recovered their presence
of mind, entered a third stout gentleman imperfectly repressed by a belt, exactly like him. These two "subjects,"
making with the money-taker three of the announced fifteen,
fell into conversation touching a charming young widow:
who, presently appearing, proved to be a stout lady altogether irrepressible by any means—quite a parallel case
to the American Negro—fourth of the fifteen subjects, and
sister of the fifth who presided over the check-department.
In good time the whole of the fifteen subjects were dramatic-
ally presented, and we had the inevitable Ma Mère, Ma
Mère! and also the inevitable malédiction d'un père, and
likewise the inevitable Marquis, and also the inevitable provincial young man, weak-minded but faithful, who followed
Julie to Paris, and cried and laughed and choked all at once.
The story was wrought out with the help of a virtuous
spinning-wheel in the beginning, a vicious set of diamonds
in the middle, and a rheumatic blessing (which arrived by
post) from Ma Mère towards the end ; the whole resulting
in a small sword in the body of one of the stout gentlemen
imperfectly repressed by a belt, fifty thousand francs per
annum and a decoration to the other stout gentleman imperfectly repressed by a belt, and an assurance from everybody to the provincial young man that if he were not
supremely happy—which he seemed to have no reason
whatever for being—he ought to be. This afforded him a
final opportunity of crying and laughing and choking all at
once, and sent the audience home sentimentally delighted.
Audience more attentive or better behaved there could not

possibly be, though the places of second rank in the Theatre of the Family P. Salcy were sixpence each in English money, and the places of first rank a shilling. How the fifteen subjects ever got so fat upon it, the kind Heavens know.

What gorgeous china figures of knights and ladies, gilded till they gleamed again, I might have bought at the Fair for the garniture of my home, if I had been a French-Flemish peasant, and had had the money! What shining coffee-cups and saucers I might have won at the turntables, if I had had the luck! Ravishing perfumery also, and sweet-meats, I might have speculated in, or I might have fired for prizes at a multitude of little dolls in niches, and might have hit the doll of dolls, and won francs and fame. Or, being a French-Flemish youth, I might have been drawn in a handcart by my compeers, to tilt for municipal re-wards at the water-quintain; which, unless I sent my lance clean through the ring, emptied a full bucket over me; to fend off which, the competitors wore grotesque old scare-crow hats. Or, being French-Flemish man or woman, boy or girl, I might have circled all night on my hobby-horse in a stately cavalcade of hobby-horses four abreast, interspersed with triumphal cars, going round and round and round and round, we the goodly company singing a ceaseless chorus to the music of the barrel-organ, drum, and cymbals. On the whole, not more monotonous than the Ring in Hyde Park, London, and much merrier; for when do the circling com-pany sing chorus, there, to the barrel-organ, when do the ladies embrace their horses round the neck with both arms, when do the gentlemen fan the ladies with the tails of their gallant steeds? On all these revolving delights, and on their own especial lamps and Chinese lanterns revolving with them, the thoughtful weaver-face brightens, and the Hôtel de Ville sheds an illuminated line of gaslight: while above it, the Eagle of France, gas-outlined and apparently afflicted with the prevailing infirmities that have lighted on the poultry, is in a very undecided state of policy, and as a bird moulting. Flags flutter all around. Such is the prevailing gaiety that the keeper of the prison sits on the stone steps outside the prison-door, to have a look at the world that is not locked up; while that agreeable retreat, the wine-shop opposite to the prison in the prison-alley (its sign La Tranquillité, because of its charming situation), resounds with the voices of the shepherds and shepherdesses who resort there this festive night. And it reminds me that only this afternoon, I saw a shepherd in trouble, tending this way, over the jagged stones of a neighbouring street. A magnificent sight it was, to behold him in his blouse, a feeble little jog-trot rustic, swept along by the wind of two immense gendarmes, in cocked-hats for which the street was hardly wide enough, each carrying a bundle of stolen property that would not have held his shoulder-knot, and clanking a sabre that dwarfed the prisoner.

"Messieurs et Mesdames, I present to you at this Fair, as a mark of my confidence in the people of this so-renowned town, and as an act of homage to their good sense and fine taste, the Ventriloquist, the Ventriloquist! Further, Messieurs et Mesdames, I present to you the Face-Maker, the Physiognomist, the great Changer of Countenances, who transforms the features that Heaven has bestowed upon him into an endless succession of surprising and extraordinary visages, comprehending, Messieurs et Mesdames, all the contortions, energetic and expressive, of which the human face is capable, and all the passions of the human heart, as Love, Jealousy, Revenge, Hatred, Avarice, Despair! Hi hi, Ho ho, Lu lu, Come in!" To this effect, with an occasional smite upon a sonorous kind of tambourine—bestowed with a will, as if it represented the people who won't come in—holds forth a man of lofty and severe demeanour; a man in stately uniform, gloomy with the knowledge he possesses of the inner secrets of the booth. "Come in, come in! Your opportunity presents itself to-night; to-morrow it will be gone for ever. To-morrow morning by the Express Train the railroad will reclaim the Ventriloquist and the Face-Maker! Algeria will reclaim the Ventriloquist and the Face-Maker! Yes! For the honour of their country they have accepted propositions of a magnitude incredible, to appear in Algeria. See them for the last time before their departure! We go to commence on the instant. Hi hi! Ho ho! Lu lu! Come in! Take the money that now ascends, Madame; but after that, no more, for we commence! Come in!"

Nevertheless, the eyes both of the gloomy Speaker and of Madame receiving sous in a muslin bower, survey the crowd pretty sharply after the ascending money has ascended, to detect any lingering sous at the turning-point. "Come in, come in ! Is there any more money, Madame, on the point of ascending? If so, we wait for it. If not, we commence!" The orator looks back over his shoulder to say it, lashing the spectators with the conviction that he beholds through the folds of the drapery into which he is about to plunge, the Ventriloquist and the Face-Maker. Several sous burst out of pockets, and ascend. "Come up, then, Messieurs!" exclaims Madame in a shrill voice, and beckoning with a bejewelled finger. "Come up! This presses. Monsieur has commanded that they commence!" Monsieur dives into his Interior, and the last half-dozen of us follow. His Interior is comparatively severe ; his Exterior also. A true Temple of Art needs nothing but seats, drapery, a small table with two moderator lamps hanging over it, and an ornamental looking-glass let into the wall. Monsieur in uniform gets behind the table and surveys us with disdain, his forehead becoming diabolically intellectual under the moderators. "Messieurs et Mesdames, I present to you the Ventriloquist. He will commence with the celebrated Experience of the bee in the window. The bee, apparently the veritable bee of Nature, will hover in the window, and about the room. He will be with difficulty caught in the hand of Monsieur the Ventriloquist—he will escape—he will again hover—at length he will be recaptured by Monsieur the Ventriloquist, and will be with difficulty put into a bottle. Achieve then, Monsieur!" Here the proprietor is replaced behind the table by the Ventriloquist, who is thin and sallow, and of a weakly aspect. While the bee is in progress, Monsieur the Proprietor sits apart on a stool, immersed in dark and remote thought. The moment the bee is bottled, he stalks forward, eyes us gloomily as we applaud, and then announces, sternly waving his hand: "The magnificent Experience of the child with the whooping-cough!" The child disposed of, he starts up as before. "The superb and extraordinary Experience of the dialogue between Monsieur Tatambour in his dining-room, and his domestic, Jerome, in the cellar ; concluding with the songsters of the grove, and the Concert of domestic Farm-yard animals." All this done, and well done, Monsieur the Ventriloquist withdraws, and Monsieur the Face-Maker bursts in, as if his retiring-room were a mile long instead of a yard. A corpulent little man in a large white waistcoat, with a comic countenance, and with a wig in his hand. Irreverent disposition to laugh, instantly checked by the tremendous gravity of the Face-Maker, who intimates in his bow that if we expect that sort of thing we are mistaken. A very little shaving-glass with a leg behind it is handed in, and placed on the table before the Face-Maker. "Messieurs et Mesdames, with no other assistance than this mirror and this wig, I shall have the honour of showing you a thousand characters." As a preparation, the Face-Maker with both hands gouges himself, and turns his mouth inside out. He then becomes frightfully grave again, and says to the Proprietor, "I am ready!" Proprietor stalks forth from baleful reverie, and announces "The Young Conscript!" Face-Maker claps his wig on, hind side before, looks in the glass, and appears above it as a conscript so very imbecile, and squinting so extremely hard, that I should think the State would never get any good of him. Thunders of applause. Face-Maker dips behind the looking-glass, brings his own hair forward, is himself again, is awfully grave. "A distinguished inhabitant of the Faubourg St. Germain." Face-Maker dips, rises, is supposed to be aged, blear-eyed, toothless, slightly palsied, supernaturally polite, evidently of noble birth. "The oldest member of the Corps of Invalides on the fête-day of his master." Face-Maker dips, rises, wears the wig on one side, has become the feeblest military bore in existence, and (it is clear) would lie frightfully about his past achievements, if he were not confined to pantomime. "The Miser!" Face-Maker dips, rises, clutches a bag, and every hair of the wig is on end to express that he lives in continual dread of thieves. "The Genius of France!" Face-Maker dips, rises, wig pushed back and smoothed flat, little cocked hat (artfully concealed till now) put a-top of it, Face-Maker's white waistcoat much advanced, Face-Maker's left hand in bosom of white waistcoat, Face-Maker's right hand behind his back. Thunders. This is the first of three positions of the Genius of France. In the second position, the Face-Maker takes snuff; in the third, rolls up his right hand, and surveys illimitable armies through that pocket-glass. The Face-Maker then, by putting out his tongue, and wearing the wig nohow in particular, becomes the Village Idiot. The most remarkable feature in the whole of his ingenious performance, is, that whatever he does to disguise himself, has the effect of rendering him rather more like himself than he was at first.

There were peep-shows in this Fair, and I had the pleasure of recognising several fields of glory with which I became well acquainted a year or two ago as Crimean battles, now doing duty as Mexican victories. The change was neatly effected by some extra smoking of the Russians, and by permitting the camp followers free range in the foreground to despoil the enemy of their uniforms. As no British troops had ever happened to be within sight when the artist took his original sketches, it followed fortunately that none were in the way now.

The Fair wound up with a ball. Respecting the particular night of the week on which the ball took place, I decline to commit myself; merely mentioning that it was held in a stable-yard so very close to the railway, that it is a mercy the locomotive did not set fire to it. (In Scotland, I suppose it would have done so.) There, in a tent prettily decorated with looking-glasses and a myriad of toy-flags, the people danced all night. It was not an expensive recreation, the price of a double ticket for a cavalier and lady being one and threepence in English money, and even of that small sum fivepence was reclaimable for "consommation:" which word I venture to translate into refreshments of no greater strength, at the strongest, than ordinary wine made hot, with sugar and lemon in it. It was a ball of great good humour and of great enjoyment, though very many of the dancers must have been as poor as the fifteen subjects of the P. Salcy Family.

In short, not having taken my own pet national pint pot with me to this Fair, I was very well satisfied with the measure of simple enjoyment that it poured into the dull French-Flemish country life. How dull that is, I had an opportunity of considering when the Fair was over—when the tri-coloured flags were withdrawn from the windows of the houses on the Place where the Fair was held—when the windows were close shut, apparently until next Fair-time—when the Hôtel de Ville had cut off its gas and put away its eagle—when the two paviours, whom I take to form the entire paving population of the town, were ramming down the stones which had been pulled up for the erection of decorative poles—when the jailer had slammed his gate, and sulkily locked himself in with his charges. But then, as I paced the ring which marked the track of the departed hobby-horses on the market-place, pondering in my mind how long some hobby-horses do leave their tracks in public ways, and how difficult they are to erase, my eyes were greeted with a goodly sight. I beheld four male personages thoughtfully pacing the Place together, in the sunlight, evidently not belonging to the town, and having upon them a certain loose cosmopolitan air of not belonging to any town. One was clad in a suit of white canvas, another in a cap and blouse, the third in an old military frock, the fourth in a shapeless dress that looked as if it had been made out of old umbrellas. All wore dust-coloured shoes. My heart beat high; for, in those four male personages, although complexionless and eyebrowless, I beheld four subjects of the Family P. Salcy. Blue-bearded though they were, and bereft of the youthful smoothness of cheek which is imparted by what is termed in Albion a "Whitechapel shave" (and which is, in fact, whitening, judiciously applied to the jaws with the palm of the hand), I recognised them. As I stood admiring, there emerged from the yard of a lowly Cabaret, the excellent Ma Mère, Ma Mère, with the words, "The soup is served;" words which so elated the subject in the canvas suit, that when they all ran in to partake, he went last, dancing with his hands stuck angularly into the pockets of his canvas trousers, after the Pierrot manner. Glancing down the Yard, the last I saw of him was, that he looked in through a window (at the soup, no doubt) on one leg.

Full of this pleasure, I shortly afterwards departed from the town, little dreaming of an addition to my good fortune. But more was in reserve. I went by a train which was heavy with third-class carriages, full of young fellows (well guarded) who had drawn unlucky numbers in the last conscription, and were on their way to a famous French garrison town where much of the raw military material is worked up into soldiery. At the station they had been sitting about, in their threadbare homespun blue garments, with their poor little bundles under their arms, covered with dust and clay, and the various soils of France; sad enough at heart, most of them, but putting a good face upon it, and slapping their breasts and singing choruses on the smallest provocation; the gayer spirits shouldering half loaves of black bread speared upon their walking-sticks. As we went along, they were audible at every station, chorusing wildly out of tune, and feigning the highest hilarity. After a while, however, they began to leave off singing, and to laugh naturally, while at intervals there mingled with their laughter the barking of a dog. Now, I had to alight short of their destination, and, as that stoppage of the train was attended with a quantity of horn blowing, bell ringing, and proclamation of what Messieurs les Voyageurs were to do, and were not to do, in order to reach their respective destinations, I had ample leisure to go forward on the platform to take a parting look at my recruits, whose heads were all out at window, and who were laughing like delighted children. Then I perceived that a large poodle with a pink nose, who had been their travelling companion and the cause of their mirth, stood on his hind-legs presenting arms on the extreme verge of the platform, ready to salute them as the train went off. This poodle wore a military shako (it is unnecessary to add, very much on one side over one eye), a little military coat, and the regulation white gaiters. He was armed with a little musket and a little sword-bayonet, and he stood presenting arms in perfect attitude, with his unobscured eye on his master or superior officer, who stood by him. So admirable was his discipline, that, when the train moved, and he was greeted with the parting cheers of the recruits, and also with a shower of centimes, several of which struck his shako, and had a tendency to discompose him, he remained staunch on his post, until the train was gone. He then resigned his arms to his officer, took off his shako by rubbing his paw over it, dropped on four legs, bringing his uniform coat into the absurdest relations with the overarching skies, and ran about the platform in his white gaiters, wagging his tail to an exceeding great extent. It struck me that there was more waggery than this in the poodle, and that he knew that the recruits would neither get through their exercises, nor get rid of their uniforms, as easily as he; revolving which in my thoughts, and seeking in my pockets some small money to bestow upon him, I casually directed my eyes to the face of his superior officer, and in him beheld the Face-Maker! Though it was not the way to Algeria, but quite the reverse, the military poodle's Colonel was the Face-Maker in a dark blouse, with a small bundle dangling over his shoulder at the end of an umbrella, and taking a pipe from his breast to smoke as he and the poodle went their mysterious way.

XXVIII

MEDICINE MEN OF CIVILISATION

My voyages (in paper boats) among savages often yield me
matter for reflection at home. It is curious to trace the
savage in the civilised man, and to detect the hold of some
savage customs on conditions of society rather boastful of
being high above them.

I wonder, is the Medicine Man of the North American
Indians never to be got rid of, out of the North American
country? He comes into my Wigwam on all manner of
occasions, and with the absurdest "Medicine." I always find
it extremely difficult, and I often find it simply impossible,
to keep him out of my Wigwam. For his legal "Medicine"
he sticks upon his head the hair of quadrupeds, and plasters
the same with fat, and dirty white powder, and talks a
gibberish quite unknown to the men and squaws of his tribe.
For his religious "Medicine" he puts on puffy white sleeves,
little black aprons, large black waistcoats of a peculiar cut,
collarless coats with Medicine button-holes, Medicine stockings and gaiters and shoes, and tops the whole with a
highly grotesque Medicinal hat. In one respect, to be sure,
I am quite free from him. On occasions when the Medicine
Men in general, together with a large number of the miscellaneous inhabitants of his village, both male and female, are
presented to the principal Chief, his native "Medicine" is
a comical mixture of old odds and ends (hired of traders)
and new things in antiquated shapes, and pieces of red cloth
(of which he is particularly fond), and white and red and
blue paint for the face. The irrationality of this particular
Medicine culminates in a mock battle-rush, from which many
of the squaws are borne out, much dilapidated. I need not
observe how unlike this is to a Drawing Room at St. James's
Palace.

The African magician I find it very difficult to exclude

from my Wigwam too. This creature takes cases of death and mourning under his supervision, and will frequently impoverish a whole family by his preposterous enchantments. He is a great eater and drinker, and always conceals a rejoicing stomach under a grieving exterior. His charms consist of an infinite quantity of worthless scraps, for which he charges very high. He impresses on the poor bereaved natives, that the more of his followers they pay to exhibit such scraps on their persons for an hour or two (though they never saw the deceased in their lives, and are put in high spirits by his decease), the more honourably and piously they grieve for the dead. The poor people submitting themselves to this conjurer, an expensive procession is formed, in which bits of stick, feathers of birds, and a quantity of other unmeaning objects besmeared with black paint, are carried in a certain ghastly order of which no one understands the meaning, if it ever had any, to the brink of the grave, and are then brought back again.

In the Tonga Islands everything is supposed to have a soul, so that when a hatchet is irreparably broken, they say, "His immortal part has departed; he is gone to the happy hunting-plains." This belief leads to the logical sequence that when a man is buried, some of his eating and drinking vessels, and some of his warlike implements, must be broken and buried with him. Superstitious and wrong, but surely a more respectable superstition than the hire of antic scraps for a show that has no meaning based on any sincere belief.

Let me halt on my Uncommercial road, to throw a passing glance on some funeral solemnities that I have seen where North American Indians, African Magicians, and Tonga Islanders, are supposed not to be.

Once, I dwelt in an Italian city, where there dwelt with me for a while, an Englishman of an amiable nature, great enthusiasm, and no discretion. This friend discovered a desolate stranger, mourning over the unexpected death of one very dear to him, in a solitary cottage among the vineyards of an outlying village. The circumstances of the bereavement were unusually distressing; and the survivor, new to the peasants and the country, sorely needed help, being alone with the remains. With some difficulty, but with the strong influence of a purpose at once gentle, dis-

interested, and determined, my friend—Mr. Kindheart—
obtained access to the mourner, and undertook to arrange
the burial.

There was a small Protestant cemetery near the city walls,
and as Mr. Kindheart came back to me, he turned into it
and chose the spot. He was always highly flushed when
rendering a service unaided, and I knew that to make him
happy I must keep aloof from his ministration. But when
at dinner he warmed with the good action of the day, and
conceived the brilliant idea of comforting the mourner with
"an English funeral," I ventured to intimate that I thought
that institution, which was not absolutely sublime at home,
might prove a failure in Italian hands. However, Mr. Kindheart was so enraptured with his conception, that he presently wrote down into the town requesting the attendance
with to-morrow's earliest light of a certain little upholsterer.
This upholsterer was famous for speaking the unintelligible
local dialect (his own) in a far more unintelligible manner
than any other man alive.

When from my bath next morning I overheard Mr. Kindheart and the upholsterer in conference on the top of an
echoing staircase; and when I overheard Mr. Kindheart
rendering English Undertaking phrases into very choice
Italian, and the upholsterer replying in the unknown
Tongues ; and when I furthermore remembered that the
local funerals had no resemblance to English funerals ;
I became in my secret bosom apprehensive. But Mr. Kindheart informed me at breakfast that measures had been taken.
to ensure a signal success.

As the funeral was to take place at sunset, and as I knew
to which of the city gates it must tend, I went out at
that gate as the sun descended, and walked along the dusty,
dusty road. I had not walked far, when I encountered this
procession :

1. Mr. Kindheart, much abashed, on an immense grey
horse.

2. A bright yellow coach and pair, driven by a coachman
in bright red velvet knee-breeches and waistcoat. (This was
the established local idea of State.) Both coach doors kept
open by the coffin, which was on its side within, and sticking
out at each.

3. Behind the coach, the mourner, for whom the coach
was intended, walking in the dust.

4. Concealed behind a roadside well for the irrigation of a garden, the unintelligible Upholsterer, admiring.

It matters little now. Coaches of all colours are alike to poor Kindheart, and he rests far North of the little cemetery with the cypress-trees, by the city walls where the Mediterranean is so beautiful.

My first funeral, a fair representative funeral after its kind, was that of the husband of a married servant, once my nurse. She married for money. Sally Flanders, after a year or two of matrimony, became the relict of Flanders, a small master builder; and either she or Flanders had done me the honour to express a desire that I should "follow." I may have been seven or eight years old;—young enough, certainly, to feel rather alarmed by the expression, as not knowing where the invitation was held to terminate, and how far I was expected to follow the deceased Flanders. Consent being given by the heads of houses, I was jobbed up into what was pronounced at home decent mourning (comprehending somebody else's shirt, unless my memory deceives me), and was admonished that if, when the funeral was in action, I put my hands in my pockets, or took my eyes out of my pocket-handkerchief, I was personally lost, and my family disgraced. On the eventful day, having tried to get myself into a disastrous frame of mind, and having formed a very poor opinion of myself because I couldn't cry, I repaired to Sally's. Sally was an excellent creature, and had been a good wife to old Flanders, but the moment I saw her I knew that she was not in her own real natural state. She formed a sort of Coat of Arms, grouped with a smelling-bottle, a handkerchief, an orange, a bottle of vinegar, Flanders's sister, her own sister, Flanders's brother's wife, and two neighbouring gossips—all in mourning, and all ready to hold her whenever she fainted. At sight of poor little me she became much agitated (agitating me much more), and having exclaimed, "O here's dear Master Uncommercial!" became hysterical, and swooned as if I had been the death of her. An affecting scene followed, during which I was handed about and poked at her by various people, as if I were the bottle of salts. Reviving a little, she embraced me, said, "You knew him well, dear Master Uncommercial, and he knew you!" and fainted again: which, as the rest of the Coat of Arms soothingly said, "done her credit." Now, I knew that she needn't have fainted unless she liked, and that she wouldn't have fainted unless it had been expected of her, quite as well as I know it at this day. It made me feel uncomfortable and hypocritical besides. I was not sure but that it might be manners in *me* to faint next, and I resolved to keep my eye on Flanders's uncle, and if I saw any signs of his going in that direction, to go too, politely. But Flanders's uncle (who was a weak little old retail grocer) had only one idea, which was that we all wanted tea; and he handed us cups of tea all round, incessantly, 'whether we refused or not. There was a young nephew of Flanders's present, to whom Flanders, it was rumoured, had left nineteen guineas. He drank all the tea that was offered him, this nephew— amounting, I should say, to several quarts—and ate as much plum-cake as he could possibly come by; but he felt it to be decent mourning that he should now and then stop in the midst of a lump of cake, and appear to forget that his mouth was full, in the contemplation of his uncle's memory. I felt all this to be the fault of the undertaker, who was handing us gloves on a tea-tray as if they were muffins, and tying us into cloaks (mine had to be pinned up all round, it was so long for me), because I knew that he was making game. So, when we got out into the streets, and I constantly disarranged the procession by tumbling on the people before me because my handkerchief blinded my eyes, and tripping up the people behind me because my cloak was so long, I felt that we were all making game. I was truly sorry for Flanders, but I knew that it was no reason why we should be trying (the women with their heads in hoods like coal-scuttles with the black side outward) to keep step with a man in a scarf, carrying a thing like a mourning spy-glass, which he was going to open presently and sweep the horizon with. I knew that we should not all have been speaking in one particular key-note struck by the undertaker, if we had not been making game. Even in our faces we were every one of us as like the undertaker as if we had been his own family, and I perceived that this could not have happened unless we had been making game. When we returned to Sally's, it was all of a piece. The continued impossibility of getting on without plum-cake; the ceremonious apparition of a pair of decanters containing port and sherry and cork; Sally's sister at the tea-table, clinking the best crockery and shaking her head mournfully every time she looked down into the teapot, as if it were the tomb; the

Coat of Arms again, and Sally as before; lastly, the words
of consolation administered to Sally when it was considered
right that she should "come round nicely:" which were,
that the deceased had had "as com-for-ta-ble a fu-ne-ral as
comfortable could be!"

Other funerals have I seen with grown-up eyes, since that
day, of which the burden has been the same childish burden.
Making game. Real affliction, real grief and solemnity, have
been outraged, and the funeral has been "performed." The
waste for which the funeral customs of many tribes of savages
are conspicuous, has attended these civilised obsequies; and
once, and twice, have I wished in my soul that if the waste
must be, they would let the undertaker bury the money, and
let me bury the friend.

In France, upon the whole, these ceremonies are more
sensibly regulated, because they are upon the whole less
expensively regulated. I cannot say that I have ever been
much edified by the custom of tying a bib and apron on the
front of the house of mourning, or that I would myself particularly care to be driven to my grave in a nodding and
bobbing car, like an infirm four-post bedstead, by an inky
fellow-creature in a cocked-hat. But it may be that I am
constitutionally insensible to the virtues of a cocked-hat. In
provincial France, the solemnities are sufficiently hideous,
but are few and cheap. The friends and townsmen of the
departed, in their own dresses and not masquerading under
the auspices of the African Conjurer, surround the hand-bier,
and often carry it. It is not considered indispensable to stifle
the bearers, or even to elevate the burden on their shoulders;
consequently it is easily taken up, and easily set down, and
is carried through the streets without the distressing floundering and shuffling that we see at home. A dirty priest or
two, and a dirtier acolyte or two, do not lend any especial
grace to the proceedings; and I regard with personal
animosity the bassoon, which is blown at intervals by the
big-legged priest (it is always a big-legged priest who blows
the bassoon), when his fellows combine in a lugubrious
stalwart drawl. But there is far less of the Conjurer and the
Medicine Man in the business than under like circumstances
here. The grim coaches that we reserve expressly for such
shows, are non-existent; if the cemetery be far out of the
town, the coaches that are hired for other purposes of life are
hired for this purpose; and although the honest vehicles

make no pretence of being overcome, I have never noticed that the people in them were the worse for it. In Italy, the hooded Members of Confraternities who attend on funerals, are dismal and ugly to look upon ; but the services they render are at least voluntarily rendered, and impoverish no one, and cost nothing. Why should high civilisation and low savagery ever come together on the point of making them a wantonly wasteful and contemptible set of forms?

Once I lost a friend by death, who had been troubled in his time by the Medicine Man and the Conjurer, and upon whose limited resources there were abundant claims. The Conjurer assured me that I must positively "follow," and both he and the Medicine Man entertained no doubt that I must go in a black carriage, and must wear "fittings." I objected to fittings as having nothing to do with my friendship, and I objected to the black carriage as being in more senses than one a job. So, it came into my mind to try what would happen if I quietly walked, in my own way, from my own house to my friend's burial-place, and stood beside his open grave in my own dress and person, reverently listening to the best of Services. It satisfied my mind, I found, quite as well as if I had been disguised in a hired hatband and scarf both trailing to my very heels, and as if I had cost the orphan children, in their greatest need, ten guineas.

Can any one who ever beheld the stupendous absurdities attendant on "A message from the Lords" in the House of Commons, turn upon the Medicine Man of the poor Indians? Has he any "Medicine" in that dried skin pouch of his, so supremely ludicrous as the two Masters in Chancery holding up their black petticoats and butting their ridiculous wigs at Mr. Speaker? Yet there are authorities innumerable to tell me—as there are authorities innumerable among the Indians to tell them—that the nonsense is indispensable, and that its abrogation would involve most awful consequences. What would any rational creature who had never heard of judicial and forensic "fittings," think of the Court of Common Pleas on the first day of Term? Or with what an awakened sense of humour would LIVINGSTONE's account of a similar scene be perused, if the fur and red cloth and goats' hair and horse hair and powdered chalk and black patches on the top of the head, were all at Tala Mungongo instead of Westminster? That model missionary and good brave man found at least one tribe of blacks with a very strong sense of the ridiculous, insomuch that although an amiable and docile people, they never could see the Missionaries dispose of their legs in the attitude of kneeling, or hear them begin a hymn in chorus, without bursting into roars of irrepressible laughter. It is much to be hoped that no member of this facetious tribe may ever find his way to England and get committed for contempt of Court.

In the Tonga Island already mentioned, there are a set of personages called Mataboos—or some such name—who are the masters of all the public ceremonies, and who know the exact place in which every chief must sit down when a solemn public meeting takes place : a meeting which bears a family resemblance to our own Public Dinner, in respect of its being a main part of the proceedings that every gentleman present is required to drink something nasty. These Mataboos are a privileged order, so important is their avocation, and they make the most of their high functions. A long way out of the Tonga Islands, indeed, rather near the British Islands, was there no calling in of the Mataboos the other day to settle an earth-convulsing question of precedence ; and was there no weighty opinion delivered on the part of the Mataboos which, being interpreted to that unlucky tribe of blacks with the sense of the ridiculous, would infallibly set the whole population screaming with laughter ?

My sense of justice demands the admission, however, that this is not quite a one-sided question. If we submit ourselves meekly to the Medicine Man and the Conjurer, and are not exalted by it, the savages may retort upon us that we act more unwisely than they in other matters wherein we fail to imitate them. It is a widely diffused custom among savage tribes, when they meet to discuss any affair of public importance, to sit up all night making a horrible noise, dancing, blowing shells, and (in cases where they are familiar with fire-arms) flying out into open spaces and letting off guns. It is questionable whether our legislative assemblies might not take a hint from this. A shell is not a melodious wind-instrument, and it is monotonous ; but it is as musical as, and not more monotonous than, my Honourable friend's own trumpet, or the trumpet that he blows so hard for the Minister. The uselessness of arguing with any supporter of a Government or of an Opposition, is well known. Try dancing. It is a better exercise, and has the unspeakable recommendation that it couldn't be reported. The honourable and savage member who has a loaded gun, and has grown impatient of debate, plunges out of doors, fires in the air, and returns calm and silent to the Palaver. Let the honourable and civilised member similarly charged with a speech, dart into the cloisters of Westminster Abbey in the silence of night, let his speech off, and come back harmless. It is not at first sight a very rational custom to paint a broad blue stripe across one's nose and both cheeks, and a broad red stripe from the forehead to the chin, to attach a few pounds of wood to one's under lip, to stick fish-bones in one's ears and a brass curtain-ring in one's nose, and to rub one's body all over with rancid oil, as a preliminary to entering on business. But this is a question of taste and ceremony, and so is the Windsor Uniform. The manner of entering on the business itself is another question. A council of six hundred savage gentlemen entirely independent of tailors, sitting on their hams in a ring, smoking, and occasionally grunting, seem to me, according to the experience I have gathered in my voyages and travels, somehow to do what they come together for; whereas that is not at all the general experience of a council of six hundred civilised gentlemen very dependent on tailors and sitting on mechanical contrivances. It is better that an Assembly should do its utmost to envelop itself in smoke, than that it should direct its endeavours to enveloping the public in smoke; and I would rather it buried half a hundred hatchets than buried one subject demanding attention.

XXIX

TITBULL'S ALMS-HOUSES

By the side of most railways out of London, one may see
Alms-Houses and Retreats (generally with a Wing or a
Centre wanting, and ambitious of being much bigger than
they are), some of which are newly-founded Institutions,
and some old establishments transplanted.   There is a
tendency in these pieces of architecture to shoot upward
unexpectedly, like Jack's bean-stalk, and to be ornate in
spires of Chapels and lanterns of Halls, which might lead
to the embellishment of the air with many castles of
questionable beauty but for the restraining consideration
of expense.   However, the managers, being always of a
sanguine temperament, comfort themselves with plans and
elevations of Loomings in the future, and are influenced
in the present by philanthropy towards the railway passengers.   For, the question how prosperous and promising
the buildings can be made to look in their eyes, usually
supersedes the lesser question how they can be turned to
the best account for the inmates.

Why none of the people who reside in these places ever
look out of window, or take an airing in the piece of ground
which is going to be a garden by-and-by, is one of the
wonders I have added to my always-lengthening list of the
wonders of the world.   I have got it into my mind that
they live in a state of chronic injury and resentment, and
on that account refuse to decorate the building with a human
interest.   As I have known legatees deeply injured by a
bequest of five hundred pounds because it was not five
thousand, and as I was once acquainted with a pensioner
on the Public to the extent of two hundred a year, who
perpetually anathematised his Country because he was not
in the receipt of four, having no claim whatever to sixpence :
so perhaps it usually happens, within certain limits, that
to get a little help is to get a notion of being defrauded of

more. "How do they pass their lives in this beautiful and peaceful place?" was the subject of my speculation with a visitor who once accompanied me to a charming rustic retreat for old men and women : a quaint ancient foundation in a pleasant English county, behind a picturesque church and among rich old convent gardens. There were but some dozen or so of houses, and we agreed that we would talk with the inhabitants, as they sat in their groined rooms between the light of their fires and the light shining in at their latticed windows, and would find out. They passed their lives in considering themselves mulcted of certain ounces of tea by a deaf old steward who lived among them in the quadrangle. There was no reason to suppose that any such ounces of tea had ever been in existence, or that the old steward so much as knew what was the matter ; —he passed *his* life in considering himself periodically defrauded of a birch-broom by the beadle.

But it is neither to old Alms-Houses in the country, nor to new Alms-Houses by the railroad, that these present Uncommercial notes relate. They refer back to journeys made among those common-place smoky-fronted London Alms-Houses, with a little paved court-yard in front enclosed by iron railings, which have got snowed up, as it were, by bricks and mortar ; which were once in a suburb, but are now in the densely populated town ; gaps in the busy life around them, parentheses in the close and blotted texts of the streets.

Sometimes, these Alms-Houses belong to a Company or Society. Sometimes, they were established by individuals, and are maintained out of private funds bequeathed in perpetuity long ago. My favourite among them is Titbull's, which establishment is a picture of many. Of Titbull I know no more than that he deceased in 1723, that his Christian name was Sampson, and his social designation Esquire, and that he founded these Alms-Houses as Dwellings for Nine Poor Women and Six Poor Men by his Will and Testament. I should not know even this much, but for its being inscribed on a grim stone very difficult to read, let into the front of the centre house of Titbull's Alms-Houses, and which stone is ornamented a-top with a piece of sculptured drapery resembling the effigy of Titbull's bath-towel.

Titbull's Alms-Houses are in the east of London, in a great highway, in a poor busy and thronged neighbourhood.

Old iron and fried fish, cough drops and artificial flowers, boiled pigs'-feet and household furniture that looks as if it were polished up with lip-salve, umbrellas full of vocal literature and saucers full of shell-fish in a green juice which I hope is natural to them when their health is good, garnish the paved sideways as you go to Titbull's. I take the ground to have risen in those parts since Titbull's time, and you drop into his domain by three stone steps. So did I first drop into it, very nearly striking my brows against Titbull's pump, which stands with its back to the thorough-fare just inside the gate, and has a conceited air of reviewing Titbull's pensioners.

"And a worse one," said a virulent old man with a pitcher, "there isn't nowhere. A harder one to work, nor a grudginer one to yield, there isn't nowhere!" This old man wore a long coat, such as we see Hogarth s Chairmen represented with, and it was of that peculiar green-pea hue without the green, which seems to come of poverty. It had also that peculiar smell of cupboard which seems to come of poverty.

"The pump is rusty, perhaps," said I.

"Not *it*," said the old man, regarding it with undiluted virulence in his watery eye. "It never were fit to be termed a pump. That's what's the matter with *it*."

"Whose fault is that?" said I.

The old man, who had a working mouth which seemed to be trying to masticate his anger and to find that it was too hard and there was too much of it, replied, "Them gentlemen."

"What gentlemen?"

"Maybe you're one of 'em?" said the old man, suspi-ciously.

"The trustees?"

"I wouldn't trust 'em myself," said the virulent old man.

"If you mean the gentlemen who administer this place, no, I am not one of them; nor have I ever so much as heard of them."

"I wish *I* never heard of them," gasped the old man: "at my time of life—with the rheumatics—drawing water —from that thing!" Not to be deluded into calling it a Pump, the old man gave it another virulent look, took up his pitcher, and carried it into a corner dwelling-house, shutting the door after him.

Looking around and seeing that each little house was a house of two little rooms; and seeing that the little oblong court-yard in front was like a graveyard for the inhabitants, saving that no word was engraven on its flat dry stones; and seeing that the currents of life and noise ran to and fro outside, having no more to do with the place than if it were a soft of low-water mark on a lively beach; I say, seeing this and nothing else, I was going out at the gate when one of the doors opened.

"Was you looking for anything, sir?" asked a tidy well-favoured woman.

Really, no; I couldn't say I was.

"Not wanting any one, sir?"

"No—at least I—pray what is the name of the elderly gentleman who lives in the corner there?"

The tidy woman stepped out to be sure of the door I indicated, and she and the pump and I stood all three in a row with our backs to the thoroughfare.

"Oh! *His* name is Mr. Battens," said the tidy woman, dropping her voice.

"I have just been talking with him."

"Indeed?" said the tidy woman. "Ho! I wonder Mr. Battens talked!"

"Is he usually so silent?"

"Well, Mr. Battens is the oldest here—that is to say, the oldest of the old gentlemen—in point of residence."

She had a way of passing her hands over and under one another as she spoke, that was not only tidy but propitiatory; so I asked her if I might look at her little sitting-room? She willingly replied Yes, and we went into it together: she leaving the door open, with an eye as I understood to the social proprieties. The door opening at once into the room without any intervening entry, even scandal must have been silenced by the precaution.

It was a gloomy little chamber, but clean, and with a mug of wallflower in the window. On the chimney-piece were two peacock's feathers, a carved ship, a few shells, and a black profile with one eyelash; whether this portrait purported to be male or female passed my comprehension, until my hostess informed me that it was her only son, and "quite a speaking one."

"He is alive, I hope?"

"No, sir," said the widow, "he were cast away in China."

This was said with a modest sense of its reflecting a certain geographical distinction on his mother.

"If the old gentlemen here are not given to talking," said I, "I hope the old ladies are?—not that you are one."

She shook her head. "You see they get so cross."

"How is that?"

"Well, whether the gentlemen really do deprive us of any little matters which ought to be ours by rights, I cannot say for certain; but the opinion of the old ones is they do. And Mr. Battens he do even go so far as to doubt whether credit is due to the Founder. For Mr. Battens he do say, anyhow he got his name up by it and he done it cheap."

"I am afraid the pump has soured Mr. Battens."

"It may be so," returned the tidy widow, "but the handle does go very hard. Still, what I say to myself is, the gentlemen *may* not pocket the difference between a good pump and a bad one, and I would wish to think well of them. And the dwellings," said my hostess, glancing round her room; "perhaps they were convenient dwellings in the Founder's time, considered *as* his time, and therefore he should not be blamed. But Mrs. Saggers is very hard upon them."

"Mrs. Saggers is the oldest here?"

"The oldest but one. Mrs. Quinch being the oldest, and have totally lost her head."

"And you?"

"I am the youngest in residence, and consequently am not looked up to. But when Mrs. Quinch makes a happy release, there will be one below me. Nor is it to be expected that Mrs. Saggers will prove herself immortal."

"True. Nor Mr. Battens."

"Regarding the old gentlemen," said my widow slightingly, "they count among themselves. They do not count among us. Mr. Battens is that exceptional that he have written to the gentlemen many times and have worked the case against them. Therefore he have took a higher ground. But we do not, as a rule, greatly reckon the old gentlemen."

Pursuing the subject, I found it to be traditionally settled among the poor ladies that the poor gentlemen, whatever their ages, were all very old indeed, and in a state of dotage. I also discovered that the juniors and newcomers preserved, for a time, a waning disposition to believe in Titbull and his trustees, but that as they gained social standing they lost this faith, and disparaged Titbull and all his works.

Improving my acquaintance subsequently with this respected lady, whose name was Mrs. Mitts, and occasionally dropping in upon her with a little offering of sound Family Hyson in my pocket, I gradually became familiar with the inner politics and ways of Titbull's Alms-Houses. But I never could find out who the trustees were, or where they were : it being one of the fixed ideas of the place that those authorities must be vaguely and mysteriously mentioned as " the gentlemen " only. The secretary of " the gentlemen " was once pointed out to me, evidently engaged in championing the obnoxious pump against the attacks of the discontented Mr. Battens ; but I am not in a condition to report further of him than that he had the sprightly bearing of a lawyer's clerk. I had it from Mrs. Mitts's lips in a very confidential moment, that Mr. Battens was once "had up before the gentlemen " to stand or fall by his accusations, and that an old shoe was thrown after him on his departure from the building on this dread errand;—not ineffectually, for, the interview resulting in a plumber, was considered to have encircled the temples of Mr. Battens with the wreath of victory.

In Titbull's Alms-Houses, the local society is not regarded as good society. A gentleman or lady receiving visitors from without, or going out to tea, counts, as it were, accordingly ; but visitings or tea-drinkings interchanged among Titbullians do not score. Such interchanges, however, are rare, in consequence of internal dissensions occasioned by Mrs. Saggers's pail : which household article has split Titbull's into almost as many parties as there are dwellings in that precinct. The extremely complicated nature of the conflicting articles of belief on the subject prevents my stating them here with my usual perspicuity, but I think they have all branched off from the root-and-trunk question, Has Mrs. Saggers any right to stand her pail outside her dwelling? The question has been much refined upon, but roughly stated may be stated in those terms.

There are two old men in Titbull's Alms-Houses who, I have been given to understand, knew each other in the world beyond its pump and iron railings, when they were both " in trade." They make the best of their reverses, and are looked upon with great contempt. They are little stooping blear-eyed old men of cheerful countenance, and they hobble up and down the court-yard wagging their chins and talking together quite gaily. This has given offence, and has, moreover, raised the question whether they are justified in passing any other windows than their own. Mr. Battens, however, permitting them to pass *his* windows, on the disdainful ground that their imbecility almost amounts to irresponsibility, they are allowed to take their walk in peace. They live next door to one another, and take it by turns to read the newspaper aloud (that is to say, the newest newspaper they can get), and they play cribbage at night. On warm and sunny days they have been known to go so far as to bring out two chairs and sit by the iron railings, looking forth ; but this low conduct, being much remarked upon throughout Titbull's, they were deterred by an outraged public opinion from repeating it. There is a rumour—but it may be malicious—that they hold the memory of Titbull in some weak sort of veneration, and that they once set off together on a pilgrimage to the parish churchyard to find his tomb. To this, perhaps, might be traced a general suspicion that they are spies of " the gentlemen : " to which they were supposed to have given colour in my own presence on the occasion of the weak attempt at justification of the pump by the gentlemen's clerk ; when they emerged bare-headed from the doors of their dwellings, as if their dwellings and themselves constituted an old-fashioned weather-glass of double action with two figures of old ladies inside, and deferentially bowed to him at intervals until he took his departure. They are understood to be perfectly friendless and relationless. Unquestionably the two poor fellows make the very best of their lives in Titbull's Alms-Houses, and unquestionably they are (as before mentioned) the subjects of unmitigated contempt there.

On Saturday nights, when there is a greater stir than usual outside, and when itinerant vendors of miscellaneous wares even take their stations and light up their smoky lamps before the iron railings, Titbull's becomes flurried. Mrs. Saggers has her celebrated palpitations of the heart, for the most part, on Saturday nights. But Titbull's is unfit to strive with the uproar of the streets in any of its phases. It is religiously believed at Titbull's that people push more

than they used, and likewise that the foremost object of the
population of England and Wales is to get you down and
trample on you. Even of railroads they know, at Titbull's,
little more than the shriek (which Mrs. Saggers says goes
through her, and ought to be taken up by Government);
and the penny postage may even yet be unknown there,
for I have never seen a letter delivered to any inhabitant.
But there is a tall straight sallow lady resident in Number
Seven, Titbull's, who never speaks to anybody, who is surrounded by a superstitious halo of lost wealth, who does her
household work in housemaid's gloves, and who is secretly
much deferred to, though openly cavilled at; and it has
obscurely leaked out that this old lady has a son, grandson,
nephew, or other relative, who is "a Contractor," and who
would think it nothing of a job to knock down Titbull's,
pack it off into Cornwall, and knock it together again. An
immense sensation was made by a gipsy-party calling in
a spring-van, to take this old lady up to go for a day's
pleasure into Epping Forest, and notes were compared as
to which of the company was the son, grandson, nephew,
or other relative, the Contractor. A thick-set personage
with a white hat and a cigar in his mouth, was the favourite :
though as Titbull's had no other reason to believe that the
Contractor was there at all, than that this man was supposed
to eye the chimney stacks as if he would like to knock them
down and cart them off, the general mind was much unsettled in arriving at a conclusion. As a way out of this
difficulty, it concentrated itself on the acknowledged Beauty
of the party, every stitch in whose dress was verbally un-
ripped by the old ladies then and there, and whose "goings
on " with another and a thinner personage in a white hat
might have suffused the pump (where they were principally
discussed) with blushes, for months afterwards. Herein
Titbull's was to Titbull's true, for it has a constitutional
dislike of all strangers. As concerning innovations and
improvements, it is always of opinion that what it doesn't
want itself, nobody ought to want. But I think I have met
with this opinion outside Titbull's.

Of the humble treasures of furniture brought into Titbull's by the inmates when they establish themselves in
that place of contemplation for the rest of their days, by far
the greater and more valuable part belongs to the ladies.
I may claim the honour of having either crossed the

threshold, or looked in at the door, of every one of the nine ladies, and I have noticed that they are all particular in the article of bedsteads, and maintain favourite and long-established bedsteads and bedding as a regular part of their rest. Generally an antiquated chest of drawers is among their cherished possessions ; a tea-tray always is. I know of at least two rooms in which a little tea-kettle of genuine burnished copper, vies with the cat in winking at the fire; and one old lady has a tea-urn set forth in state on the top of her chest of drawers, which urn is used as her library, and contains four duodecimo volumes, and a black-bordered newspaper giving an account of the funeral of Her Royal Highness the Princess Charlotte. Among the poor old gentlemen there are no such niceties. Their furniture has the air of being contributed, like some obsolete Literary Miscellany, "by several hands;" their few chairs never match; old patchwork coverlets linger among them; and they have an untidy habit of keeping their wardrobes in hat-boxes. When I recall one old gentleman who is rather choice in his shoe-brushes and blacking-bottle, I have summed up the domestic elegances of that side of the building.

On the occurrence of a death in Titbull's, it is invariably agreed among the survivors—and it is the only subject on which they do agree—that the departed did something "to bring it on." Judging by Titbull's, I should say the human race need never die, if they took care. But they don't take care, and they do die, and when they die in Titbull's they are buried at the cost of the Foundation. Some provision has been made for the purpose, in virtue of which (I record this on the strength of having seen the funeral of Mrs. Quinch) a lively neighbouring undertaker dresses up four of the old men, and four of the old women, hustles them into a procession of four couples, and leads off with a large black bow at the back of his hat, looking over his shoulder at them airily from time to time to see that no member of the party has got lost, or has tumbled down ; as if they were a company of dim old dolls.

Resignation of a dwelling is of very rare occurrence in Titbull's. A story does obtain there, how an old lady's son once drew a prize of Thirty Thousand Pounds in the Lottery, and presently drove to the gate in his own carriage, with French Horns playing up behind, and whisked his mother away, and left ten guineas for a Feast. But I have been unable to substantiate it by any evidence, and regard it as an Alms-House Fairy Tale. It is curious that the only proved case of resignation happened within my knowledge.

It happened on this wise. There is a sharp competition among the ladies respecting the gentility of their visitors, and I have so often observed visitors to be dressed as for a holiday occasion, that I suppose the ladies to have besought them to make all possible display when they come. In these circumstances much excitement was one day occasioned by Mrs. Mitts receiving a visit from a Greenwich Pensioner. He was a Pensioner of a bluff and warlike appearance, with an empty coat-sleeve, and he was got up with unusual care; his coat-buttons were extremely bright, he wore his empty coat-sleeve in a graceful festoon, and he had a walking-stick in his hand that must have cost money. When, with the head of his walking-stick, he knocked at Mrs. Mitts's door—there are no knockers in Titbull's—Mrs. Mitts was overheard by a next-door neighbour to utter a cry of surprise expressing much agitation; and the same neighbour did afterwards solemnly affirm that when he was admitted into Mrs. Mitts's room, she heard a smack. Heard a smack which was not a blow.

There was an air about this Greenwich Pensioner when he took his departure, which imbued all Titbull's with the conviction that he was coming again. He was eagerly looked for, and Mrs. Mitts was closely watched. In the meantime, if anything could have placed the unfortunate six old gentlemen at a greater disadvantage than that at which they chronically stood, it would have been the apparition of this Greenwich Pensioner. They were well shrunken already, but they shrunk to nothing in comparison with the Pensioner. Even the poor old gentlemen themselves seemed conscious of their inferiority, and to know submissively that they could never hope to hold their own against the Pensioner with his warlike and maritime experience in the past, and his tobacco money in the present: his chequered career of blue water, black gunpowder, and red bloodshed for England, home, and beauty.

Before three weeks were out, the Pensioner reappeared. Again he knocked at Mrs. Mitts's door with the handle of his stick, and again was he admitted. But not again did

A Phenomenon at Titbull's

he depart alone; for Mrs. Mitts, in a bonnet identified as
having been re-embellished, went out walking with him,
and stayed out till the ten o'clock beer, Greenwich time.

There was now a truce, even as to the troubled waters of
Mrs. Saggers's pail; nothing was spoken of among the
ladies but the conduct of Mrs. Mitts and its blighting influence on the reputation of Titbull's. It was agreed that
Mr. Battens "ought to take it up," and Mr. Battens was
communicated with on the subject. That unsatisfactory
individual replied "that he didn't see his way yet," and it
was unanimously voted by the ladies that aggravation was
in his nature.

How it came to pass, with some appearance of inconsistency, that Mrs. Mitts was cut by all the ladies and the
Pensioner admired by all the ladies, matters not. Before
another week was out, Titbull's was startled by another
phenomenon. At ten o'clock in the forenoon appeared a
cab, containing not only the Greenwich Pensioner with one
arm, but, to boot, a Chelsea Pensioner with one leg. Both
dismounting to assist Mrs. Mitts into the cab, the Greenwich Pensioner bore her company inside, and the Chelsea
Pensioner mounted the box by the driver: his wooden
leg sticking out after the manner of a bowsprit, as if in
jocular homage to his friend's sea-going career. Thus
the equipage drove away. No Mrs. Mitts returned that
night.

What Mr. Battens might have done in the matter of
taking it up, goaded by the infuriated state of public feeling
next morning, was anticipated by another phenomenon. A
Truck, propelled by the Greenwich Pensioner and the
Chelsea Pensioner, each placidly smoking a pipe, and pushing his warrior breast against the handle.

The display on the part of the Greenwich Pensioner of
his "marriage-lines," and his announcement that himself
and friend had looked in for the furniture of Mrs. G. Pensioner, late Mitts, by no means reconciled the ladies to the
conduct of their sister; on the contrary, it is said that they
appeared more than ever exasperated. Nevertheless, my
stray visits to Titbull's since the date of this occurrence,
have confirmed me in an impression that it was a wholesome
fillip. The nine ladies are smarter, both in mind and dress,
than they used to be, though it must be admitted that they
despise the six gentlemen to the last extent. They have

a much greater interest in the external thoroughfare too, than they had when I first knew Titbull's. And whenever I chance to be leaning my back against the pump or the iron railings, and to be talking to one of the junior ladies, and to see that a flush has passed over her face, I immediately know without looking round that a Greenwich Pensioner has gone past.

XXX

THE RUFFIAN

I ENTERTAIN so strong an objection to the euphonious softening of Ruffian into Rough, which has lately become popular, that I restore the right word to the heading of this paper; the rather, as my object is to dwell upon the fact that the Ruffian is tolerated among us to an extent that goes beyond all unruffianly endurance. I take the liberty to believe that if the Ruffian besets my life, a professional Ruffian at large in the open streets of a great city, notoriously having no other calling than that of Ruffian, and of disquieting and despoiling me as I go peacefully about my lawful business, interfering with no one, then the Government under which I have the great constitutional privilege, supreme honour and happiness, and all the rest of it, to exist, breaks down in the discharge of any Government's most simple elementary duty.

What did I read in the London daily papers, in the early days of this last September? That the Police had "AT LENGTH SUCCEEDED IN CAPTURING TWO OF THE NOTORIOUS GANG THAT HAVE SO LONG INFESTED THE WATERLOO ROAD." Is it possible? What a wonderful Police! Here is a straight, broad, public thoroughfare of immense resort; half a mile long; gas-lighted by night; with a great gas-lighted railway station in it, extra the street lamps; full of shops; traversed by two popular cross thoroughfares of considerable traffic; itself the main road to the South of London; and the admirable Police have, after long infestment of this dark and lonely spot by a gang of Ruffians, actually got hold of two of them. Why, can it be doubted that any man of fair London knowledge and common resolution, armed with the powers of the Law, could have captured the whole confederacy in a week?

It is to the saving up of the Ruffian class by the Magistracy and Police—to the conventional preserving of them, as if they were Partridges—that their number and audacity must be in great part referred. Why is a notorious Thief and Ruffian ever left at large? He never turns his liberty to any account but violence and plunder, he never did a day's work out of gaol, he never will do a day's work out of gaol. As a proved notorious Thief he is always consignable to prison for three months. When he comes out, he is surely as notorious a Thief as he was when he went in. Then send him back again. "Just Heaven!" cries the Society for the protection of remonstrant Ruffians. "This is equivalent to a sentence of perpetual imprisonment!" Precisely for that reason it has my advocacy. I demand to have the Ruffian kept out of my way, and out of the way of all decent people. I demand to have the Ruffian employed, perforce, in hewing wood and drawing water somewhere for the general service, instead of hewing at her Majesty's subjects and drawing their watches out of their pockets. If this be termed an unreasonable demand, then the tax-gatherer's demand on me must be far more unreasonable, and cannot be otherwise than extortionate and unjust.

It will be seen that I treat of the Thief and Ruffian as one. I do so, because I know the two characters to be one, in the vast majority of cases, just as well as the Police know it. (As to the Magistracy, with a few exceptions, they know nothing about it but what the Police choose to tell them.) There are disorderly classes of men who are not thieves; as railway-navigators, brickmakers, wood-sawyers, coster-mongers. These classes are often disorderly and trouble-some; but it is mostly among themselves, and at any rate they have their industrious avocations, they work early and late, and work hard. The generic Ruffian—honourable member for what is tenderly called the Rough Element—is either a Thief, or the companion of Thieves. When he infamously molests women coming out of chapel on Sunday evenings (for which I would have his back scarified often and deep) it is not only for the gratification of his pleasant instincts, but that there may be a confusion raised by which either he or his friends may profit, in the commission of highway robberies or in picking pockets. When he gets a police-constable down and kicks him helpless for life, it is because that constable once did his duty in bringing him to justice. When he rushes into the bar of a public-house and scoops an eye out of one of the company there, or bites his ear off, it is because the man he maims gave evidence against him. When he and a line of comrades extending across the footway—say of that solitary mountain-spur of the Abruzzi, the Waterloo Road—advance towards me "skylarking" among themselves, my purse or shirt-pin is in predestined peril from his playfulness. Always a Ruffian, always a Thief. Always a Thief, always a Ruffian.

Now, when I, who am not paid to know these things, know them daily on the evidence of my senses and experience; when I know that the Ruffian never jostles a lady in the streets, or knocks a hat off, but in order that the Thief may profit, is it surprising that I should require from those who *are* paid to know these things, prevention of them?

Look at this group at a street corner. Number one is a shirking fellow of five-and-twenty, in an ill-favoured and ill-savoured suit, his trousers of corduroy, his coat of some indiscernible groundwork for the deposition of grease, his neckerchief like an eel, his complexion like dirty dough, his mangy fur cap pulled low upon his beetle brows to hide the prison cut of his hair. His hands are in his pockets. He puts them there when they are idle, as naturally as in other people's pockets when they are busy, for he knows that they are not roughened by work, and that they tell a tale. Hence, whenever he takes one out to draw a sleeve across his nose—which is often, for he has weak eyes and a constitutional cold in his head—he restores it to its pocket immediately afterwards. Number two is a burly brute of five-and-thirty, in a tall stiff hat; is a composite as to his clothes of betting-man and fighting-man; is whiskered; has a staring pin in his breast, along with his right hand; has insolent and cruel eyes; large shoulders; strong legs, booted and tipped for kicking. Number three is forty years of age; is short, thick-set, strong, and bow-legged; wears knee cords and white stockings, a very long-sleeved waist-coat, a very large neckerchief doubled or trebled round his throat, and a crumpled white hat crowns his ghastly parch-ment face. This fellow looks like an executed postboy of other days, cut down from the gallows too soon, and restored and preserved by express diabolical agency. Numbers five, six, and seven, are hulking, idle, slouching young men, patched and shabby, too short in the sleeves and too tight in the legs, slimily clothed, foul-spoken, repulsive wretches inside and out. In all the party there obtains a certain twitching character of mouth and furtiveness of eye, that hint how the coward is lurking under the bully. The hint is quite correct, for they are a slinking sneaking set, far more prone to lie down on their backs and kick out, when in difficulty, than to make a stand for it. (This may account for the street mud on the backs of Numbers five, six, and seven, being much fresher than the stale splashes on their legs.)

These engaging gentry a Police-constable stands contemplating. His Station, with a Reserve of assistance, is very near at hand. They cannot pretend to any trade, not even to be porters or messengers. It would be idle if they did, for he knows them, and they know that he knows them, to be nothing but professed Thieves and Ruffians. He knows where they resort, knows by what slang names they call one another, knows how often they have been in prison, and how long, and for what. All this is known at his Station, too, and is (or ought to be) known at Scotland Yard, too. But does he know, or does his Station know, or does Scotland Yard know, or does anybody know, why these fellows should be here at liberty, when, as reputed Thieves to whom a whole Division of Police could swear, they might all be under lock and key at hard labour? Not he; truly he would be a wise man if he did! He only knows that these are members of the "notorious gang," which, according to the newspaper Police-office reports of this last past September, "have so long infested" the awful solitudes of the Waterloo Road, and out of which almost impregnable fastnesses the Police have at length dragged Two, to the unspeakable admiration of all good civilians.

The consequences of this contemplative habit on the part of the Executive—a habit to be looked for in a hermit, but not in a Police System—are familiar to us all. The Ruffian becomes one of the established orders of the body politic. Under the playful name of Rough (as if he were merely a practical joker) his movements and successes are recorded on public occasions. Whether he mustered in large numbers, or small; whether he was in good spirits, or depressed; whether he turned his generous exertions to very prosperous account, or Fortune was against him; whether he was in a sanguinary mood, or robbed with amiable horse-play and a gracious consideration for life and limb; all this is chronicled as if he were an Institution. Is there any city in Europe, out of England, in which these terms are held with the pests of Society? Or in which, at this day, such violent robberies from the person are constantly committed as in London?

The Preparatory Schools of Ruffianism are similarly borne with. The young Ruffians of London—not Thieves yet, but training for scholarships and fellowships in the Criminal Court Universities—molest quiet people and their property, to an extent that is hardly credible. The throwing of stones in the streets has become a dangerous and destructive offence, which surely could have got to no greater height though we had had no Police but our own riding-whips and walking-sticks—the Police to which I myself appeal on these occasions. The throwing of stones at the windows of railway carriages in motion—an act of wanton wickedness with the very Arch-Fiend's hand in it—had become a crying evil, when the railway companies forced it on Police notice. Constabular contemplation had until then been the order of the day.

Within these twelve months, there arose among the young gentlemen of London aspiring to Ruffianism, and cultivating that much-encouraged social art, a facetious cry of "I'll have this!" accompanied with a clutch at some article of a passing lady's dress. I have known a lady's veil to be thus humorously torn from her face and carried off in the open streets at noon; and I have had the honour of myself giving chase, on Westminster Bridge, to another young Ruffian, who, in full daylight early on a summer evening, had nearly thrown a modest young woman into a swoon of indignation and confusion, by his shameful manner of attacking her with this cry as she harmlessly passed along before me. Mr. CARLYLE, some time since, awakened a little pleasantry by writing of his own experience of the Ruffian of the streets. I have seen the Ruffian act in exact accordance with Mr. Carlyle's description, innumerable times, and I never saw him checked.

The blaring use of the very worst language possible, in our public thoroughfares—especially in those set apart for recreation—is another disgrace to us, and another result of constabular contemplation, the like of which I have never heard in any other country to which my uncommercial travels have extended. Years ago, when I had a near interest in certain children who were sent with their nurses,

for air and exercise, into the Regent's Park, I found this evil
to be so abhorrent and horrible there, that I called public
attention to it, and also to its contemplative reception by
the Police. Looking afterwards into the newest Police
Act, and finding that the offence was punishable under it,
I resolved, when striking occasion should arise, to try my
hand as prosecutor. The occasion arose soon enough, and
I ran the following gauntlet.

The utterer of the base coin in question was a girl of
seventeen or eighteen, who, with a suitable attendance of
blackguards, youths, and boys, was flaunting along the streets,
returning from an Irish funeral, in a Progress interspersed
with singing and dancing. She had turned round to me and
expressed herself in the most audible manner, to the great
delight of that select circle. I attended the party, on the
opposite side of the way, for a mile further, and then encountered a Police-constable. The party had made themselves
merry at my expense until now, but seeing me speak to the
constable, its male members instantly took to their heels,
leaving the girl alone. I asked the constable did he know
my name? Yes, he did. "Take that girl into custody, on
my charge, for using bad language in the streets." He had
never heard of such a charge. I had. Would he take my
word that he should get into no trouble? Yes, sir, he would
do that. So he took the girl, and I went home for my
Police Act.

With this potent instrument in my pocket, I literally as
well as figuratively "returned to the charge," and presented
myself at the Police Station of the district. There, I found
on duty a very intelligent Inspector (they are all intelligent
men), who, likewise, had never heard of such a charge.
I showed him my clause, and we went over it together
twice or thrice. It was plain, and I engaged to wait
upon the suburban Magistrate to-morrow morning at ten
o'clock.

In the morning I put my Police Act in my pocket again,
and waited on the suburban Magistrate. I was not quite so
courteously received by him as I should have been by The
Lord Chancellor or The Lord Chief Justice, but that was
a question of good breeding on the suburban Magistrate's
part, and I had my clause ready with its leaf turned down.
Which was enough for *me*.

Conference took place between the Magistrate and clerk

respecting the charge. During conference I was evidently regarded as a much more objectionable person than the prisoner;—one giving trouble by coming there voluntarily, which the prisoner could not be accused of doing. The prisoner had been got up, since I last had the pleasure of seeing her, with a great effect of white apron and straw bonnet. She reminded me of an elder sister of Red Riding Hood, and I seemed to remind the sympathising Chimney Sweep by whom she was attended, of the Wolf.

The Magistrate was doubtful, Mr. Uncommercial Traveller, whether this charge could be entertained. It was not known. Mr. Uncommercial Traveller replied that he wished it were better known, and that, if he could afford the leisure, he would use his endeavours to make it so. There was no question about it, however, he contended. Here was the clause.

The clause was handed in, and more conference resulted. After which I was asked the extraordinary question: "Mr. Uncommercial, do you really wish this girl to be sent to prison?" To which I grimly answered, staring: "If I didn't, why should I take the trouble to come here?" Finally, I was sworn, and gave my agreeable evidence in detail, and White Riding Hood was fined ten shillings, under the clause, or sent to prison for so many days. "Why, Lord bless you, sir," said the Police-officer, who showed me out, with a great enjoyment of the jest of her having been got up so effectively, and caused so much hesitation: "if she goes to prison, that will be nothing new to *her*. She comes from Charles Street, Drury Lane!"

The Police, all things considered, are an excellent force, and I have borne my small testimony to their merits. Constabular contemplation is the result of a bad system; a system which is administered, not invented, by the man in constable's uniform, employed at twenty shillings a week. He has his orders, and would be marked for discouragement if he overstepped them. That the system is bad, there needs no lengthened argument to prove, because the fact is self-evident. If it were anything else, the results that have attended it could not possibly have come to pass. Who will say that under a good system, our streets could have got into their present state?

The objection to the whole Police system, as concerning the Ruffian, may be stated, and its failure exemplified, as follows. It is well known that on all great occasions, when they come together in numbers, the mass of the English people are their own trustworthy Police. It is well known that wheresoever there is collected together any fair general representation of the people, a respect for law and order, and a determination to discountenance lawlessness and disorder, may be relied upon. As to one another, the people are a very good Police, and yet are quite willing in their good-nature that the stipendiary Police should have the credit of the people's moderation. But we are all of us powerless against the Ruffian, because we submit to the law, and it is his only trade, by superior force and by violence, to defy it. Moreover, we are constantly admonished from high places (like so many Sunday-school children out for a holiday of buns and milk-and-water) that we are not to take the law into our own hands, but are to hand our defence over to it. It is clear that the common enemy to be punished and ex-terminated first of all is the Ruffian. It is clear that he is, of all others, *the* offender for whose repressal we maintain a costly system of Police. Him, therefore, we expressly present to the Police to deal with, conscious that, on the whole, we can, and do, deal reasonably well with one another. Him the Police deal with so inefficiently and absurdly that he flourishes, and multiplies, and, with all his evil deeds upon his head as notoriously as his hat is, pervades the streets with no more let or hindrance than ourselves.

XXXI

ABOARD SHIP

My journeys as Uncommercial Traveller for the firm of Human Interest Brothers have not slackened since I last reported of them, but have kept me continually on the move. I remain in the same idle employment. I never solicit an order, I never get any commission, I am the rolling stone that gathers no moss,—unless any should by chance be found among these samples.

Some half a year ago, I found myself in my idlest, dreamiest, and least accountable condition altogether, on board ship, in the harbour of the city of New York, in the United States of America. Of all the good ships afloat, mine was the good steamship "Russia," Capt. Cook, Cunard Line, bound for Liverpool. What more could I wish for?

I had nothing to wish for but a prosperous passage. My salad-days, when I was green of visage and sea-sick, being gone with better things (and no worse), no coming event cast its shadow before.

I might but a few moments previously have imitated Sterne, and said, " 'And yet, methinks, Eugenius,'—laying my forefinger wistfully on his coat-sleeve, thus, — 'and yet, methinks, Eugenius, 'tis but sorry work to part with thee, for what fresh fields, . . . my dear Eugenius, . . . can be fresher than thou art, and in what pastures new shall I find Eliza, or call her, Eugenius, if thou wilt, Annie ? ' "— I say I might have done this ; but Eugenius was gone, and I hadn't done it.

I was resting on a skylight on the hurricane - deck, watching the working of the ship very slowly about, that she might head for England. It was high noon on a most brilliant day in April, and the beautiful bay was glorious and glowing. Full many a time, on shore there, had I seen the snow come down, down, down (itself like down), until it lay deep in all the ways of men, and particularly,

as it seemed, in my way, for I had not gone dry-shod many
hours for months. Within two or three days last past
had I watched the feathery fall setting in with the ardour
of a new idea, instead of dragging at the skirts of a worn-
out winter, and permitting glimpses of a fresh young spring.
But a bright sun and a clear sky had melted the snow
in the great crucible of nature; and it had been poured
out again that morning over sea and land, transformed into
myriads of gold and silver sparkles.

The ship was fragrant with flowers. Something of the
old Mexican passion for flowers may have gradually passed
into North America, where flowers are luxuriously grown,
and tastefully combined in the richest profusion; but,
be that as it may, such gorgeous farewells in flowers had
come on board, that the small officer's cabin on deck, which
I tenanted, bloomed over into the adjacent scuppers, and
banks of other flowers that it couldn't hold made a garden
of the unoccupied tables in the passengers' saloon. These
delicious scents of the shore, mingling with the fresh airs
of the sea, made the atmosphere a dreamy, an enchanting
one. And so, with the watch aloft setting all the sails, and
with the screw below revolving at a mighty rate, and
occasionally giving the ship an angry shake for resisting,
I fell into my idlest ways, and lost myself.

As, for instance, whether it was I lying there, or some
other entity even more mysterious, was a matter I was far
too lazy to look into. What did it signify to me if it were
I? or to the more mysterious entity, if it were he? Equally
as to the remembrances that drowsily floated by me, or by
him, why ask when or where the things happened? Was it
not enough that they befell at some time, somewhere?

There was that assisting at the church service on board
another steamship, one Sunday, in a stiff breeze. Perhaps
on the passage out. No matter. Pleasant to hear the ship's
bells go as like church-bells as they could; pleasant to see
the watch off duty mustered and come in : best hats, best
Guernseys, washed hands and faces, smoothed heads. But
then arose a set of circumstances so rampantly comical, that
no check which the gravest intentions could put upon them
would hold them in hand. Thus the scene. Some seventy
passengers assembled at the saloon tables. Prayer-books on
tables. Ship rolling heavily. Pause. No minister. Rumour
has related that a modest young clergyman on board has

responded to the captain's request that he will officiate.
Pause again, and very heavy rolling.

Closed double doors suddenly burst open, and two strong
stewards skate in, supporting minister between them.
General appearance as of somebody picked up drunk and
incapable, and under conveyance to station-house. Stoppage,
pause, and particularly heavy rolling. Stewards watch their
opportunity, and balance themselves, but cannot balance
minister; who, struggling with a drooping head and a backward tendency, seems determined to return below, while they
are as determined that he shall be got to the reading-desk in
mid-saloon. Desk portable, sliding away down a long table,
and aiming itself at the breasts of various members of the
congregation. Here the double doors, which have been carefully closed by other stewards, fly open again, and worldly
passenger tumbles in, seemingly with pale-ale designs: who,
seeking friend, says "Joe!" Perceiving incongruity, says,
"Hullo! Beg yer pardon!" and tumbles out again. All
this time the congregation have been breaking up into sects,
—as the manner of congregations often is,—each sect sliding
away by itself, and all pounding the weakest sect which slid
first into the corner. Utmost point of dissent soon attained
in every corner, and violent rolling. Stewards at length
make a dash; conduct minister to the mast in the centre
of the saloon, which he embraces with both arms; skate
out; and leave him in that condition to arrange affairs
with flock.

There was another Sunday, when an officer of the ship
read the service. It was quiet and impressive, until we fell
upon the dangerous and perfectly unnecessary experiment
of striking up a hymn. After it was given out, we all rose,
but everybody left it to somebody else to begin. Silence
resulting, the officer (no singer himself) rather reproachfully
gave us the first line again, upon which a rosy pippin of an
old gentleman, remarkable throughout the passage for his
cheerful politeness, gave a little stamp with his boot (as if
he were leading off a country dance), and blithely warbled
us into a show of joining. At the end of the first verse we
became, through these tactics, so much refreshed and encouraged, that none of us, howsoever unmelodious, would
submit to be left out of the second verse; while as to the
third we lifted up our voices in a sacred howl that left it
doubtful whether we were the more boastful of the senti-

ments we united in professing, or of professing them with a most discordant defiance of time and tune.

"Lord bless us!" thought I, when the fresh remembrance of these things made me laugh heartily alone in the dead water-gurgling waste of the night, what time I was wedged into my berth by a wooden bar, or I must have rolled out of it, "what errand was I then upon, and to what Abyssinian point had public events then marched? No matter as to me. And as to them, if the wonderful popular rage for a play-thing (utterly confounding in its inscrutable unreason) had not then lighted on a poor young savage boy, and a poor old screw of a horse, and hauled the first off by the hair of his princely head to 'inspect' British volunteers, and hauled the second off by the hair of his equine tail to the Crystal Palace, why so much the better for all of us outside Bedlam!"

So, sticking to the ship, I was at the trouble of asking myself would I like to show the grog distribution in "the fiddle" at noon to the Grand United Amalgamated Total Abstinence Society? Yes, I think I should. I think it would do them good to smell the rum, under the circum-stances. Over the grog, mixed in a bucket, presides the boatswain's mate, small tin can in hand. Enter the crew, the guilty consumers, the grown-up brood of Giant Despair, in contradistinction to the band of youthful angel Hope. Some in boots, some in leggings, some in tarpaulin overalls, some in frocks, some in pea-coats, a very few in jackets, most with sou'wester hats, all with something rough and rugged round the throat; all dripping salt water where they stand; all pelted by weather, besmeared with grease, and blackened by the sooty rigging.

Each man's knife in its sheath in his girdle, loosened for dinner. As the first man, with a knowingly kindled eye, watches the filling of the poisoned chalice (truly but a very small tin mug, to be prosaic), and, tossing back his head, tosses the contents into himself, and passes the empty chalice and passes on, so the second man with an antici-patory wipe of his mouth on sleeve or handkerchief, bides his turn, and drinks and hands and passes on, in whom, and in each as his turn approaches, beams a knowingly kindled eye, a brighter temper, and a suddenly awakened tendency to be jocose with some shipmate. Nor do I even observe that the man in charge of the ship's lamps, who in right of his office has a double allowance of poisoned chalices, seems thereby vastly degraded, even though he empties the chalices into himself, one after the other, much as if he were delivering their contents at some absorbent establishment in which he had no personal interest. But vastly comforted, I note them all to be, on deck presently, even to the circulation of redder blood in their cold blue knuckles; and when I look up at them lying out on the yards, and holding on for life among the beating sails, I cannot for *my* life see the justice of visiting on them—or on me—the drunken crimes of any number of criminals arraigned at the heaviest of assizes.

Abetting myself in my idle humour, I closed my eyes, and recalled life on board of one of those mail-packets, as I lay, part of that day, in the Bay of New York, O! The regular life began—mine always did, for I never got to sleep afterwards—with the rigging of the pump while it was yet dark, and washing down of decks. Any enormous giant at a prodigious hydropathic establishment, conscientiously undergoing the water-cure in all its departments, and extremely particular about cleaning his teeth, would make those noises. Swash, splash, scrub, rub, toothbrush, bubble; swash, splash, bubble, toothbrush, splash, splash, bubble, rub. Then the day would break, and, descending from my berth by a graceful ladder composed of half-opened drawers beneath it, I would reopen my outer dead-light and my inner sliding window (closed by a watchman during the water-cure), and would look out at the long-rolling, lead-coloured, white-topped waves over which the dawn, on a cold winter morning, cast a level, lonely glance, and through which the ship fought her melancholy way at a terrific rate. And now, lying down again, awaiting the season for broiled ham and tea, I would be compelled to listen to the voice of conscience,—the screw.

It might be, in some cases, no more than the voice of stomach; but I called it in my fancy by the higher name. Because it seemed to me that we were all of us, all day long, endeavouring to stifle the voice. Because it was under everybody's pillow, everybody's plate, everybody's camp-stool, everybody's book, everybody's occupation. Because we pretended not to hear it, especially at meal-times, evening whist, and morning conversation on deck; but it was always among us in an under monotone, not to be drowned in pea-soup, not to be shuffled with cards, not to be diverted by books, not to be knitted into any pattern, not to be walked away from. It was smoked in the weediest cigar, and drunk in the strongest cocktail; it was conveyed on deck at noon with limp ladies, who lay there in their wrappers until the stars shone; it waited at table with the stewards; nobody could put it out with the lights. It was considered (as on shore) ill-bred to acknowledge the voice of conscience. It was not polite to mention it. One squally day an amiable gentleman in love gave much offence to a surrounding circle, including the object of his attachment, by saying of it, after it had goaded him over two easy-chairs and a skylight, "Screw!"

Sometimes it would appear subdued. In fleeting moments, when bubbles of champagne pervaded the nose, or when there was "hot pot" in the bill of fare, or when an old dish we had had regularly every day was described in that official document by a new name,—under such excitements, one would almost believe it hushed. The ceremony of washing plates on deck, performed after every meal by a circle as of ringers of crockery triple-bob majors for a prize, would keep it down. Hauling the reel, taking the sun at noon, posting the twenty-four hours' run, altering the ship's time by the meridian, casting the waste food overboard, and attracting the eager gulls that followed in our wake,—these events would suppress it for a while. But the instant any break or pause took place in any such diversion, the voice would be at it again, importuning us to the last extent. A newly married young pair, who walked the deck affectionately some twenty miles per day, would, in the full flush of their exercise, suddenly become stricken by it, and stand trembling, but otherwise immovable, under its reproaches.

When this terrible monitor was most severe with us was when the time approached for our retiring to our dens for the night; when the lighted candles in the saloon grew fewer and fewer; when the deserted glasses with spoons in them grew more and more numerous; when waifs of toasted cheese and strays of sardines fried in batter slid languidly to and fro in the table-racks; when the man who always read had shut up his book, and blown out his candle; when the man who always talked had ceased from troubling; when the man who was always medically reported as going to have delirium tremens had put it off till to-morrow; when

the man who every night devoted himself to a midnight
smoke on deck two hours in length, and who every night
was in bed within ten minutes afterwards, was buttoning
himself up in his third coat for his hardy vigil: for then, as
we fell off one by one, and, entering our several hutches,
came into a peculiar atmosphere of bilge-water and Windsor
soap, the voice would shake us to the centre. Woe to us
when we sat down on our sofa, watching the swinging
candle for ever trying and retrying to stand upon his head!
or our coat upon its peg, imitating us as we appeared in our
gymnastic days by sustaining itself horizontally from the
wall, in emulation of the lighter and more facile towels!
Then would the voice especially claim us for its prey, and
rend us all to pieces.

Lights out, we in our berths, and the wind rising, the
voice grows angrier and deeper. Under the mattress and
under the pillow, under the sofa and under the washing-
stand, under the ship and under the sea, seeming to rise
from the foundations under the earth with every scoop of
the great Atlantic (and oh ! why scoop so ?), always the
voice. Vain to deny its existence in the night season ;
impossible to be hard of hearing; screw, screw, screw !
Sometimes it lifts out of the water, and revolves with
a whirr, like a ferocious 'firework,—except that it never
expends itself, but is always ready to go off again ; sometimes it seems to be in anguish, and shivers ; sometimes it
seems to be terrified by its last plunge, and has a fit which
causes it to struggle, quiver, and for an instant stop. And
now the ship sets in rolling, as only ships so fiercely screwed
through time and space, day and night, fair weather and
foul, *can* roll.

Did she ever take a roll before like that last? Did she
ever take a roll before like this worse one that is coming
now ? Here is the partition at my ear down in the deep on
the lee side. Are we ever coming up again together? I
think not ; the partition and I are so long about it that
I really do believe we have overdone it this time. Heavens,
what a scoop! What a deep scoop, what a hollow scoop,
what a long scoop! Will it ever end, and can we bear the
heavy mass of water we have taken on board, and which has
let loose all the table furniture in the officers' mess, and has
beaten open the door of the little passage between the purser
and me, and is swashing about, even there and even here ?

The purser snores reassuringly, and the ship's bells striking, I hear the cheerful "All's well!" of the watch musically given back the length of the deck, as the lately diving partition, now high in air, tries (unsoftened by what we have gone through together) to force me out of bed and berth.

"All's well!" Comforting to know, though surely all might be better. Put aside the rolling and the rush of water, and think of darting through such darkness with such velocity. Think of any other similar object coming in the opposite direction !

Whether there may be an attraction in two such moving bodies out at sea, which may help accident to bring them into collision ? Thoughts, too, arise (the voice never silent all the while, but marvellously suggestive) of the gulf below ; of the strange unfruitful mountain ranges and deep valleys over which we are passing ; of monstrous fish midway ; of the ship's suddenly altering her course on her own account, and with a wild plunge settling down, and making *that* voyage with a crew of dead discoverers. Now, too, one recalls an almost universal tendency on the part of passengers to stumble, at some time or other in the day, on the topic of a certain large steamer making this same run, which was lost at sea, and never heard of more. Everybody has seemed under a spell, compelling approach to the threshold of the grim subject, stoppage, discomfiture, and pretence of never having been near it. The boatswain's whistle sounds ! A change in the wind, hoarse orders issuing, and the watch very busy. Sails come crashing home overhead, ropes (that seem all knot) ditto ; every man engaged appears to have twenty feet, with twenty times the average amount of stamping power in each. Gradually the noise slackens, the hoarse cries die away, the boatswain's whistle softens into the soothing and contented notes, which rather reluctantly admit that the job is done for the time, and the voice sets in again.

Thus come unintelligible dreams of up hill and down, and swinging and swaying, until consciousness revives of atmospherical Windsor soap and bilge-water, and the voice announces that the giant has come for the water-cure again.

Such were my fanciful reminiscences as I lay, part of that day, in the Bay of New York, O ! Also as we passed clear of the Narrows, and got out to sea ; also in many an idle hour at sea in sunny weather ! At length the observations and

computations showed that we should make the coast of
Ireland to-night. So I stood watch on deck all night to-
night, to see how we made the coast of Ireland.

Very dark, and the sea most brilliantly phosphorescent.
Great way on the ship, and double look-out kept. Vigilant
captain on the bridge, vigilant first officer looking over the
port side, vigilant second officer standing by the quarter-
master at the compass, vigilant third officer posted at the
stern rail with a lantern. No passengers on the quiet decks,
but expectation everywhere nevertheless. The two men at
the wheel very steady, very serious, and very prompt to
answer orders. An order issued sharply now and then, and
echoed back ; otherwise the night drags slowly, silently, with
no change.

All of a sudden, at the blank hour of two in the morning,
a vague movement of relief from a long strain expresses itself
in all hands ; the third officer's lantern tinkles, and he fires a
rocket, and another rocket. A sullen solitary light is pointed
out to me in the black sky yonder. A change is expected
in the light, but none takes place. " Give them two more
rockets, Mr. Vigilant." Two more, and a blue-light burnt.
All eyes watch the light again. At last a little toy sky-
rocket is flashed up from it ; and, even as that small streak
in the darkness dies away, we are telegraphed to Queenstown, Liverpool, and London, and back again under the
ocean to America.

Then up come the half-dozen passengers who are going
ashore at Queenstown, and up comes the mail-agent in charge
of the bags, and up come the men who are to carry the bags
into the mail-tender that will come off for them out of the
harbour. Lamps and lanterns gleam here and there about
the decks, and impeding bulks are knocked away with hand-
spikes ; and the port-side bulwark, barren but a moment
ago, bursts into a crop of heads of seamen, stewards, and
engineers.

The light begins to be gained upon, begins to be alongside,
begins to be left astern. More rockets, and, between us and
the land, steams beautifully the Inman steamship City of
Paris, for New York, outward bound. We observe with
complacency that the wind is dead against her (it being *with*
us), and that she rolls and pitches. (The sickest passenger
on board is the most delighted by this circumstance.) Time
rushes by as we rush on ; and now we see the light in

Queenstown Harbour, and now the lights of the mail-tender coming out to us. What vagaries the mail-tender performs on the way, in every point of the compass, especially in those where she has no business, and why she performs them, Heaven only knows! At length she is seen plunging within a cable's length of our port broadside, and is being roared at through our speaking-trumpets to do this thing, and not to do that, and to stand by the other, as if she were a very demented tender indeed. Then, we slackening amidst a deafening roar of steam, this much-abused tender is made fast to us by hawsers, and the men in readiness carry the bags aboard, and return for more, bending under their burdens, and looking just like the pasteboard figures of the miller and his men in the theatre of our boyhood, and comporting themselves almost as unsteadily. All the while the unfortunate tender plunges high and low, and is roared at. Then the Queenstown passengers are put on board of her, with infinite plunging and roaring, and the tender gets heaved up on the sea to that surprising extent that she looks within an ace of washing aboard of us, high and dry. Roared at with contumely to the last, this wretched tender is at length let go, with a final plunge of great ignominy, and falls spinning into our wake.

The voice of conscience resumed its dominion as the day climbed up the sky, and kept by all of us passengers into port ; kept by us as we passed other lighthouses, and dangerous islands off the coast, where some of the officers, with whom I stood my watch, had gone ashore in sailing-ships in fogs (and of which by that token they seemed to have quite an affectionate remembrance), and past the Welsh coast, and past the Cheshire coast, and past every-thing and everywhere lying between our ship and her own special dock in the Mersey. Off which, at last, at nine of the clock, on a fair evening early in May, we stopped, and the voice ceased. A very curious sensation, not unlike having my own ears stopped, ensued upon that silence ; and it was with a no less curious sensation that I went over the side of the good Cunard ship " Russia " (whom prosperity attend through all her voyages !) and surveyed the outer hull of the gracious monster that the voice had inhabited. So, perhaps, shall we all, in the spirit, one day survey the frame that held the busier voice from which my vagrant fancy derived this similitude.

XXXII

A SMALL STAR IN THE EAST

I HAD been looking, yesternight, through the famous "Dance of Death," and to-day the grim old woodcuts arose in my mind with the new significance of a ghastly monotony not to be found in the original. The weird skeleton rattled along the streets before me, and struck fiercely; but it was never at the pains of assuming a disguise. It played on no dulcimer here, was crowned with no flowers, waved no plume, minced in no flowing robe or train, lifted no wine-cup, sat at no feast, cast no dice, counted no gold. It was simply a bare, gaunt, famished skeleton, slaying his way along.

The borders of Ratcliff and Stepney, eastward of London, and giving on the impure river, were the scene of this uncompromising dance of death, upon a drizzling November day. A squalid maze of streets, courts, and alleys of miser-able houses let out in single rooms. A wilderness of dirt, rags, and hunger. A mud-desert, chiefly inhabited by a tribe from whom employment has departed, or to whom it comes but fitfully and rarely. They are not skilled mechanics in any wise. They are but labourers,—dock-labourers, water-side labourers, coal-porters, ballast-heavers, such-like hewers of wood and drawers of water. But they have come into existence, and they propagate their wretched race.

One grisly joke alone, methought, the skeleton seemed to play off here. It had stuck election-bills on the walls, which the wind and rain had deteriorated into suitable rags. It had even summed up the state of the poll, in chalk, on the shutters of one ruined house. It adjured the free and independent starvers to vote for Thisman and vote for Thatman; not to plump, as they valued the state of parties and the national prosperity (both of great importance to them, I think); but, by returning Thisman and Thatman, each naught without the other, to compound a glorious and immortal whole.. Surely the skeleton is nowhere more cruelly ironical in the original monkisk idea!

Pondering in my mind the far-seeing schemes of Thisman and Thatman, and of the public blessing called Party, for staying the degeneracy, physical and moral, of many thousands (who shall say how many ?) of the English race ; for devising employment useful to the community for those who want but to work and live ; for equalising rates, cultivating waste lands, facilitating emigration, and, above all things, saving and utilising the oncoming generations, and thereby changing ever-growing national weakness into strength : pondering in my mind, I say, these hopeful exertions, I turned down a narrow street to look into a house or two.

It was a dark street with a dead wall on one side. Nearly all the outer doors of the houses stood open. I took the first entry, and knocked at a parlour-door. Might I come in ? I might, if I plased, sur.

The woman of the room (Irish) had picked up some long strips of wood, about some wharf or barge ; and they had just now been thrust into the otherwise empty grate to make two iron pots boil. There was some fish in one, and there were some potatoes in the other. The flare of the burning wood enabled me to see a table, and a broken chair or so, and some old cheap crockery ornaments about the chimney-piece. It was not until I had spoken with the woman a few minutes, that I saw a horrible brown heap on the floor in the corner, which, but for previous experience in this dismal wise, I might not have suspected to be "the bed." There was something thrown upon it ; and I asked what. that was.

"'Tis the poor craythur that stays here, sur; and 'tis very bad she is, and 'tis very bad she's been this long time, and 'tis better she'll never be, and 'tis slape she does all day, and 'tis wake she does all night, and 'tis the lead, sur."

"The what ? "

"The lead, sur.   Sure 'tis the lead-mills, where the women gets took on at eighteen-pence a day, sur, when they makes application early enough, and is lucky and wanted ; and 'tis lead-pisoned she is, sur, and some of them gets lead-pisoned soon, and some of them gets lead-pisoned later, and some, but not many, niver; and 'tis all according to the constitooshun, sur, and some constitooshuns is strong, and some

is weak , and her constitooshun is lead-pisoned, bad as can
be, sur ; and her brain is coming out at her ear, and it hurts
her dreadful ; and that's what it is, and niver no more, and
niver no less, sur."

The sick young woman moaning here, the speaker bent
over her, took a bandage from her head, and threw open
a back door to let in the daylight upon it, from the smallest
and most miserable back-yard I ever saw.

" That's what cooms from her, sur, being lead-pisoned ;
and it cooms from her night and day, the poor, sick craythur ; and the pain of it is dreadful ; and God he knows
that my husband has walked the sthreets these four days,
being a labourer, and is walking them now, and is ready to
work, and no work for him, and no fire and no food but the
bit in the pot, and no more than ten shillings in a fortnight ;
God be good to us ! and it is poor we are, and dark it is and
could it is indeed."

Knowing that I could compensate myself thereafter for
my self-denial, if I saw fit, I had resolved that I would give
nothing in the course of these visits. I did this to try the
people. I may state at once that my closest observation
could not detect any indication whatever of an expectation
that I would give money : they were grateful to be talked
to about their miserable affairs, and sympathy was plainly
a comfort to them ; but they neither asked for money in
any case, nor showed the least trace of surprise or disappointment or resentment at my giving none.

The woman's married daughter had by this time come
down from her room on the floor above, to join in the
conversation. She herself had been to the lead-mills
very early that morning to be "took on," but had not
succeeded. She had four children ; and her husband, also
a water-side labourer, and then out seeking work, seemed
in no better case as to finding it than her father. She was
English, and by nature of a buxom figure and cheerful.
Both in her poor dress and in her mother's there was an
effort to keep up some appearance of neatness. She knew
all about the sufferings of the unfortunate invalid, and all
about the lead-poisoning, and how the symptoms came on,
and how they grew,—having often seen them. The very
smell when you stood inside the door of the works was
enough to knock you down, she said : yet she was going
back again to get "took on:" What could she do ? Better

be ulcerated and paralyzed for eighteen-pence a day, while it lasted, than see the children starve.

A dark and squalid cupboard in this room, touching the back door and all manner of offence, had been for some time the sleeping-place of the sick young woman. But the nights being now wintry, and the blankets and coverlets "gone to the leaving shop," she lay all night where she lay all day, and was lying then. The woman of the room, her husband, this most miserable patient, and two others, lay on the one brown heap together for warmth.

"God bless you, sir, and thank you!" were the parting words from these people,—gratefully spoken too,—with which I left this place.

Some streets away, I tapped at another parlour-door on another ground-floor. Looking in, I found a man, his wife, and four children, sitting at a washing-stool by way of table, at their dinner of bread and infused tea-leaves. There was a very scanty cinderous fire in the grate by which they sat; and there was a tent bedstead in the room with a bed upon it and a coverlet. The man did not rise when I went in, nor during my stay, but civilly inclined his head on my pulling off my hat, and, in answer to my inquiry whether I might ask him a question or two, said, "Certainly." There being a window at each end of this room, back and front, it might have been ventilated; but it was shut up tight, to keep the cold out, and was very sickening.

The wife, an intelligent, quick woman, rose and stood at her husband's elbow; and he glanced up at her as if for help. It soon appeared that he was rather deaf. He was a slow, simple fellow of about thirty.

"What was he by trade?"

"Gentleman asks what are you by trade, John?"

"I am a boilermaker;" looking about him with an exceedingly perplexed air, as if for a boiler that had unaccountably vanished.

"He ain't a mechanic, you understand, sir," the wife put in: "he's only a labourer."

"Are you in work?"

He looked up at his wife again. "Gentleman says are you in work, John?"

"In work!" cried this forlorn boilermaker, staring aghast at his wife, and then working his vision's way very slowly round to me: "Lord no!"

"Ah, he ain't indeed!" said the poor woman, shaking her head, as she looked at the four children in succession, and then at him.

"Work!" said the boilermaker, still seeking that evaporated boiler, first in my countenance, then in the air, and then in the features of his second son at his knee: "I wish I *was* in work! I haven't had more than a day's work to do this three weeks."

"How have you lived?"

A faint gleam of admiration lighted up the face of the would-be boilermaker, as he stretched out the short sleeve of his threadbare canvas jacket, and replied, pointing her out, "On the work of the wife."

I forget where boilermaking had gone to, or where he supposed it had gone to; but he added some resigned information on that head, coupled with an expression of his belief that it was never coming back.

The cheery helpfulness of the wife was very remarkable. She did slop-work; made pea-jackets. She produced the pea-jacket then in hand, and spread it out upon the bed,— the only piece of furniture in the room on which to spread it. She showed how much of it she made, and how much was afterwards finished off by the machine. According to her calculation at the moment, deducting what her trimming cost her, she got for making a pea-jacket tenpence half-penny, and she could make one in something less than two days.

But, you see, it come to her through two hands, and of course it didn't come through the second hand for nothing. Why did it come through the second hand at all? Why, this way. The second hand took the risk of the given-out work, you see. If she had money enough to pay the security deposit,—call it two pound,—she could get the work from the first hand, and so the second would not have to be deducted for. But, having no money at all, the second hand come in and took its profit, and so the whole worked down to tenpence half-penny. Having explained all this with great intelligence, even with some little pride, and without a whine or murmur, she folded her work again, sat down by her husband's side at the washing-stool, and resumed her dinner of dry bread. Mean as the meal was, on the bare board, with its old gallipots for cups, and what not other sordid makeshifts: shabby as

the woman was in dress, and toning down towards the
Bosjesman colour, with want of nutriment and washing,—
there was positively a dignity in her, as the family anchor
just holding the poor shipwrecked boilermaker's bark.
When I left the room, the boilermaker's eyes were slowly
turned towards her, as if his last hope of ever again seeing
that vanished boiler lay in her direction.

These people had never applied for parish relief but once;
and that was when the husband met with a disabling accident
at his work.

Not many doors from here, I went into a room on the first
floor. The woman apologised for its being in "an untidy
mess." The day was Saturday, and she was boiling the
children's clothes in a saucepan on the hearth. There was
nothing else into which she could have put them. There
was no crockery, or tinware, or tub, or bucket. There was
an old gallipot or two, and there was a broken bottle or so,
and there were some broken boxes for seats. The last small
scraping of coals left was raked together in a corner of the
floor. There were some rags in an open cupboard, also on
the floor. In a corner of the room was a crazy old French
bedstead, with a man lying on his back upon it in a ragged
pilot jacket, and rough oil-skin fantail hat. The room was
perfectly black. It was difficult to believe, at first, that it was
not purposely coloured black, the walls were so begrimed.

As I stood opposite the woman boiling the children's
clothes,—she had not even a piece of soap to wash them
with,—and apologising for her occupation, I could take in
all these things without appearing to notice them, and could
even correct my inventory. I had missed, at the first
glance, some half a pound of bread in the otherwise empty
safe, an old red ragged crinoline hanging on the handle
of the door by which I had entered, and certain fragments
of rusty iron scattered on the floor, which looked like broken
tools and a piece of stove-pipe. A child stood looking on.
On the box nearest to the fire sat two younger children;
one a delicate and pretty little creature, whom the other
sometimes kissed.

This woman, like the last, was wofully shabby, and was
degenerating to the Bosjesman complexion. But her figure,
and the ghost of a certain vivacity about her, and the
spectre of a dimple in her cheek, carried my memory
strangely back to the old days of the Adelphi Theatre,

London, when Mrs. Fitzwilliam was the friend of Victorine.

"May I ask you what your husband is?"

"He's a coal-porter, sir,"—with a glance and a sigh towards the bed.

"Is he out of work?"

"Oh, yes, sir! and work's at all times very, very scanty with him; and now he's laid up."

"It's my legs," said the man upon the bed. "I'll unroll 'em." And immediately began.

"Have you any older children?"

"I have a daughter that does the needle-work, and I have a son that does what he can. She's at her work now, and he's trying for work."

"Do they live here?"

"They sleep here. They can't afford to pay more rent, and so they come here at night. The rent is very hard upon us. It's rose upon us too, now,—sixpence a week,—on account of these new changes in the law, about the rates. We are a week behind; the landlord's been shaking and rattling at that door frightfully; he says he'll turn us out. I don't know what's to come of it."

The man upon the bed ruefully interposed, "Here's my legs. The skin's broke, besides the swelling. I have had a many kicks, working, one way and another."

He looked at his legs (which were much discoloured and misshapen) for a while, and then appearing to remember that they were not popular with his family, rolled them up again, as if they were something in the nature of maps or plans that were not wanted to be referred to, lay hopelessly down on his back once more with his fantail hat over his face, and stirred not.

"Do your eldest son and daughter sleep in that cupboard?"

"Yes," replied the woman.

"With the children?"

"Yes. We have to get together for warmth. We have little to cover us."

"Have you nothing by you to eat but the piece of bread I see there?"

"Nothing. And we had the rest of the loaf for our breakfast, with water. I don't know what's to come of it."

"Have you no prospect of improvement?"

"If my eldest son earns anything to-day, he'll bring it

M

home. Then we shall have something to eat to-night, and may be able to do something towards the rent. If not, I don't know what's to come of it."

"This is a sad state of things."

"Yes, sir; it's a hard, hard life. Take care of the stairs as you go, sir,—they're broken,—and good day, sir!"

These people had a mortal dread of entering the work-house, and received no out-of-door relief.

In another room, in still another tenement, I found a very decent woman with five children,—the last a baby, and she herself a patient of the parish doctor,—to whom, her husband being in the hospital, the Union allowed for the support of herself and family, four shillings a week and five loaves. I suppose when Thisman, M.P., and Thatman, M.P., and the Public-blessing Party, lay their heads together in course of time, and come to an equalization of rating, she may go down to the dance of death to the tune of six-pence more.

I could enter no other houses for that one while, for I could not bear the contemplation of the children. Such heart as I had summoned to sustain me against the miseries of the adults failed me when I looked at the children. I saw how young they were, how hungry, how serious and still. I thought of them, sick and dying in those lairs. I think of them dead without anguish; but to think of them so suffering and so dying quite unmanned me.

Down by the river's bank in Ratcliff, I was turning upward by a side street, therefore, to regain the railway, when my eyes rested on the inscription across the road, "East London Children's Hospital." I could scarcely have seen an inscription better suited to my frame of mind; and I went across and went straight in.

I found the children's hospital established in an old sail-loft or storehouse, of the roughest nature, and on the simplest means. There were trap-doors in the floors, where goods had been hoisted up and down; heavy feet and heavy weights had started every knot in the well-trodden plank-ing: inconvenient bulks and beams and awkward staircases perplexed my passage through the wards. But I found it airy, sweet, and clean. In its seven and thirty beds I saw but little beauty; for starvation in the second or third generation takes a pinched look: but I saw the sufferings both of infancy and childhood tenderly assuaged; I heard the little patients answering to pet playful names, the light touch of a delicate lady laid bare the wasted sticks of arms for me to pity; and the claw-like little hands, as she did so, twined themselves lovingly around her wedding-ring.

One baby mite there was as pretty as any of Raphael's angels. The tiny head was bandaged for water on the brain; and it was suffering with acute bronchitis too, and made from time to time a plaintive, though not impatient or complaining, little sound. The smooth curve of the cheeks and of the chin was faultless in its condensation of infantine beauty, and the large bright eyes were most lovely. It happened as I stopped at the foot of the bed, that these eyes rested upon mine with that wistful expression of wondering thoughtfulness which we all know sometimes in very little children. They remained fixed on mine, and never turned from me while I stood there. When the utterance of that plaintive sound shook the little form, the gaze still remained unchanged. I felt as though the child implored me to tell the story of the little hospital in which it was sheltered to any gentle heart I could address. Laying my world-worn hand upon the little unmarked clasped hand at the chin, I gave it a silent promise that I would do so.

A gentleman and lady, a young husband and wife, have bought and fitted up this building for its present noble use, and have quietly settled themselves in it as its medical officers and directors. Both have had considerable practical experience of medicine and surgery; he as house-surgeon of a great London hospital; she as a very earnest student, tested by severe examination, and also as a nurse of the sick poor during the prevalence of cholera.

With every qualification to lure them away, with youth and accomplishments and tastes and habits that can have no response in any breast near them, close begirt by every repulsive circumstance inseparable from such a neighbour-hood, there they dwell. They live in the hospital itself, and their rooms are on its first floor. Sitting at their dinner-table, they could hear the cry of one of the children in pain. The lady's piano, drawing-materials, books, and other such evidences of refinement are as much a part of the rough place as the iron bedsteads of the little patients. They are put to shifts for room, like passengers on board ship. The dispenser of medicines (attracted to them not by self-interest, but by their own magnetism and that of their cause) sleeps in a recess in the dining-room, and has his washing apparatus in the sideboard.

Their contented manner of making the best of the things around them, I found so pleasantly inseparable from their usefulness! Their pride in this partition that we put up ourselves, or in that partition that we took down, or in that other partition that we moved, or in the stove that was given us for the waiting-room, or in our nightly conversion of the little consulting-room into a smoking-room! Their admiration of the situation, if we could only get rid of its one objectionable incident, the coal-yard at the back! "Our hospital carriage, presented by a friend, and very useful." That was my presentation to a perambulator, for which a coach-house had been discovered in a corner down-stairs, just large enough to hold it. Coloured prints, in all stages of preparation for being added to those already decorating the wards, were plentiful; a charming wooden phenomenon of a bird, with an impossible top-knot, who ducked his head when you set a counter weight going, had been inaugurated as a public statue that very morning; and trotting about among the beds, on familiar terms with all the patients, was a comical mongrel dog, called Poodles. This comical dog (quite a tonic in himself) was found characteristically starving at the door of the institution, and was taken in and fed, and has lived here ever since. An admirer of his mental endowments has presented him with a collar bearing the legend, "Judge not Poodles by external appearances." He was merrily wagging his tail on a boy's pillow when he made this modest appeal to me.

When this hospital was first opened, in January of the present year, the people could not possibly conceive but that somebody paid for the services rendered there; and were disposed to claim them as a right, and to find fault if out of temper. They soon came to understand the case better, and have much increased in gratitude. The mothers of the patients avail themselves very freely of the visiting rules; the fathers often on Sundays. There is an unreasonable (but still, I think, touching and intelligible) tendency in the parents to take a child away to its wretched home, if on the point of death. One boy who had been thus carried off on a rainy night, when in a violent state of inflammation, and who had been afterwards brought back, had been recovered with exceeding difficulty; but he was a jolly boy, with a specially strong interest in his dinner, when I saw him.

Insufficient food and unwholesome living are the main causes of disease among these small patients. So nourishment, cleanliness, and ventilation are the main remedies. Discharged patients are looked after, and invited to come and dine now and then; so are certain famishing creatures who were never patients. Both the lady and the gentleman are well acquainted, not only with the histories of the patients and their families, but with the characters and circumstances of great numbers of their neighbours: of these they keep a register. It is their common experience, that people, sinking down by inches into deeper and deeper poverty, will conceal it, even from them, if possible, unto the very last extremity.

The nurses of this hospital are all young,—ranging, say, from nineteen to four and twenty. They have even within these narrow limits, what many well-endowed hospitals would not give them, a comfortable room of their own in which to take their meals. It is a beautiful truth, that interest in the children and sympathy with their sorrows bind these young women to their places far more strongly than any other consideration could. The best skilled of the nurses came originally from a kindred neighbourhood, almost as poor; and she knew how much the work was needed. She is a fair dressmaker. The hospital cannot pay her as many pounds in the year as there are months in it; and one day the lady regarded it as a duty to speak to her about her improving her prospects and following her trade. "No," she said: she could never be so useful or so happy elsewhere any more; she must stay among the children. And she stays. One of the nurses, as I passed her, was washing a baby-boy. Liking her pleasant face, I stopped to speak to her charge,—a common, bullet-headed, frowning charge enough, laying hold of his own nose with a slippery grasp, and staring very solemnly out of a blanket. The melting of the pleasant face into delighted smiles, as this young gentleman gave an unexpected kick, and laughed at me, was almost worth my previous pain.

An affecting play was acted in Paris years ago, called "The Children's Doctor." As I parted from my children's doctor, now in question, I saw in his easy black necktie, in his loose buttoned black frock-coat, in his pensive face, in the flow of his dark hair, in his eyelashes, in the very turn of his moustache, the exact realisation of the Paris artist's ideal as it was presented on the stage. But no romancer that I know of has had the boldness to prefigure the life and home of this young husband and young wife in the Children's Hospital in the east of London.

I came away from Ratcliff by the Stepney railway station to the terminus at Fenchurch Street. Any one who will reverse that route may retrace my steps.

XXXIII

A LITTLE DINNER IN AN HOUR

It fell out on a day in this last autumn, that I had to go down from London to a place of seaside resort, on an hour's business, accompanied by my esteemed friend Bullfinch. Let the place of seaside resort be, for the nonce, called Namelesston.

I had been loitering about Paris in very hot weather, pleasantly breakfasting in the open air in the garden of the Palais Royal or the Tuileries, pleasantly dining in the open air in the Elysian Fields, pleasantly taking my cigar and lemonade in the open air on the Italian Boulevard towards the small hours after midnight. Bullfinch—an excellent man of business—had summoned me back across the Channel, to transact this said hour's business at Namelesston; and thus it fell out that Bullfinch and I were in a railway carriage together on our way to Namelesston, each with his return-ticket in his waistcoat-pocket.

Says Bullfinch, "I have a proposal to make. Let us dine at the Temeraire."

I asked Bullfinch, did he recommend the Temeraire? inasmuch as I had not been rated on the books of the Temeraire for many years.

Bullfinch declined to accept the responsibility of recommending the Temeraire, but on the whole was rather sanguine about it. He "seemed to remember," Bullfinch said, that he had dined well there. A plain dinner, but good. Certainly not like a Parisian dinner (here Bullfinch obviously became the prey of want of confidence), but of its kind very fair.

I appeal to Bullfinch's intimate knowledge of my wants and ways to decide whether I was usually ready to be pleased with any dinner, or—for the matter of that—with anything that was fair of its kind and really what it claimed to be. Bullfinch doing me the honour to respond in the affirmative, I agreed to ship myself as an able trencherman on board the Temeraire.

"Now, our plan shall be this," says Bullfinch, with his forefinger at his nose. "As soon as we get to Namelesston, we'll drive straight to the Temeraire, and order a little dinner in an hour. And as we shall not have more than enough time in which to dispose of it comfortably, what do you say to giving the house the best opportunities of serving it hot and quickly by dining in the coffee-room ?"

What I had to say was, Certainly. Bullfinch (who is by nature of a hopeful constitution) then began to babble of green geese. But I checked him in that Falstaffian vein, urging considerations of time and cookery.

In due sequence of events we drove up to the Temeraire, and alighted. A youth in livery received us on the doorstep. "Looks well," said Bullfinch confidentially. And then aloud, "Coffee-room ! "

The youth in livery (now perceived to be mouldy) conducted us to the desired haven, and was enjoined by Bullfinch to send the waiter at once, as we wished to order a little dinner in an hour. Then Bullfinch and I waited for the waiter, until, the waiter continuing to wait in some unknown and invisible sphere of action, we rang for the waiter ; which ring produced the waiter, who announced himself as not the waiter who ought to wait upon us, and who didn't wait a moment longer.

So Bullfinch approached the coffee-room door, and melodiously pitching his voice into a bar where two young ladies were keeping the books of the Temeraire, apologetically explained that we wished to order a little dinner in an hour, and that we were debarred from the execution of our inoffensive purpose by consignment to solitude.

Hereupon one of the young ladies rang a bell, which reproduced—at the bar this time—the waiter who was not the waiter who ought to wait upon us ; that extraordinary man, whose life seemed consumed in waiting upon people to say that he wouldn't wait upon them, repeated his former protest with great indignation, and retired.

Bullfinch, with a fallen countenance, was about to say to me, "This won't do," when the waiter who ought to wait upon us left off keeping us waiting at last. "Waiter," said Bullfinch piteously, "we have been a long time waiting."

The waiter who ought to wait upon us laid the blame upon the waiter who ought not to wait upon us, and said it was all that waiter's fault.

"We wish," said Bullfinch, much depressed, "to order a little dinner in an hour. What can we have?"

"What would you like to have, gentlemen?"

Bullfinch, with extreme mournfulness of speech and action, and with a forlorn old fly-blown bill of fare in his hand which the waiter had given him, and which was a sort of general manuscript index to any cookery-book you please, moved the previous question.

We could have mock-turtle soup, a sole, curry, and roast duck. Agreed. At this table by this window. Punctually in an hour.

I had been feigning to look out of this window; but I had been taking note of the crumbs on all the tables, the dirty table-cloths, the stuffy, soupy, airless atmosphere, the stale leavings everywhere about, the deep gloom of the waiter who ought to wait upon us, and the stomach-ache with which a lonely traveller at a distant table in a corner was too evidently afflicted. I now pointed out to Bullfinch the alarming circumstance that this traveller had *dined.* We hurriedly debated whether, without infringement of good breeding, we could ask him to disclose if he had partaken of mock-turtle, sole, curry, or roast duck? We decided that the thing could not be politely done, and we had set our own stomachs on a cast, and they must stand the hazard of the die.

I hold phrenology, within certain limits, to be true; I am much of the same mind as to the subtler expressions of the hand; I hold physiognomy to be infallible; though all these sciences demand rare qualities in the student. But I also hold that there is no more certain index to personal character than the condition of a set of casters is to the character of any hotel. Knowing, and having often tested this theory of mine, Bullfinch resigned himself to the worst, when, laying aside any remaining veil of disguise, I held up before him in succession the cloudy oil and furry vinegar, the clogged cayenne, the dirty salt, the obscene dregs of soy, and the anchovy sauce in a flannel waistcoat of decomposition.

We went out to transact our business. So inspiriting was the relief of passing into the clean and windy streets

of Namelesston from the heavy and vapid closeness of the
coffee-room of the Temeraire, that hope began to revive
within us. We began to consider that perhaps the lonely
traveller had taken physic, or done something injudicious
to bring his complaint on. Bullfinch remarked that he
thought the waiter who ought to wait upon us had brightened a little when suggesting curry; and although I knew
him to have been at that moment the express image of
despair, I allowed myself to become elevated in spirits. As
we walked by the softly-lapping sea, all the notabilities of
Namelesston, who are for ever going up and down with the
changelessness of the tides, passed to and fro in procession.
Pretty girls on horseback, and with detested riding-masters;
pretty girls on foot; mature ladies in hats,—spectacled,
strong-minded, and glaring at the opposite or weaker sex.
The Stock Exchange was strongly represented, Jerusalem
was strongly represented, the bores of the prosier London
clubs were strongly represented. Fortune-hunters of all
denominations were there, from hirsute insolvency, in a
curricule, to closely-buttoned swindlery in doubtful boots,
on the sharp look-out for any likely young gentleman disposed to play a game at billiards round the corner. Masters
of languages, their lessons finished for the day, were going
to their homes out of sight of the sea; mistresses of accomplishments, carrying small portfolios, likewise tripped homeward; pairs of scholastic pupils, two and two, went
languidly along the beach, surveying the face of the waters
as if waiting for some Ark to come and take them off.
Spectres of the George the Fourth days flitted unsteadily
among the crowd, bearing the outward semblance of ancient
dandies, of every one of whom it might be said, not that he
had one leg in the grave, or both legs, but that he was
steeped in grave to the summit of his high shirt-collar, and
had nothing real about him but his bones. Alone stationary
in the midst of all the movements, the Namelesston boatmen leaned against the railings and yawned, and looked out
to sea, or looked at the moored fishing-boats and at nothing.
Such is the unchanging manner of life with this nursery of
our hardy seamen; and very dry nurses they are, and
always wanting something to drink. The only two nautical
personages detached from the railing were the two fortunate
possessors of the celebrated monstrous unknown barking-
fish, just caught (frequently just caught off Namelesston),

who carried him about in a hamper, and pressed the scientific to look in at the lid.

The sands of the hour had all run out when we got back
to the Temeraire. Says Bullfinch, then, to the youth in
livery, with boldness, "Lavatory!"

When we arrived at the family vault with a skylight,
which the youth in livery presented as the institution
sought, we had already whisked off our cravats and coats;
but finding ourselves in the presence of an evil smell, and
no linen but two crumpled towels newly damp from the
countenances of two somebody elses, we put on our cravats
and coats again, and fled unwashed to the coffee-room.

There the waiter who ought to wait upon us had set
forth our knives and forks and glasses, on the cloth whose
dirty acquaintance we had already had the pleasure of
making, and which we were pleased to recognise by the
familiar expression of its stains. And now there occurred
the truly surprising phenomenon, that the waiter who ought
not to wait upon us swooped down upon us, clutched our
loaf of bread, and vanished with the same.

Bullfinch, with distracted eyes, was following this unaccountable figure "out at the portal," like the ghost in
Hamlet, when the waiter who ought to wait upon us jostled
against it, carrying a tureen.

"Waiter!" said a severe diner, lately finished, perusing
his bill fiercely through his eye-glass.

The waiter put down our tureen on a remote side-table,
and went to see what was amiss in this new direction.

"This is not right, you know, waiter. Look here!
here's yesterday's sherry, one and eightpence, and here we
are again, two shillings. And what does sixpence mean?"

So far from knowing what sixpence meant, the waiter
protested that he didn't know what anything meant. He
wiped the perspiration from his clammy brow, and said it
was impossible to do it,—not particularising what,—and the
kitchen was so far off.

"Take the bill to the bar, and get it altered," said Mr.
Indignation Cocker, so to call him.

The waiter took it, looked intensely at it, didn't seem
to like the idea of taking it to the bar, and submitted, as
a new light upon the case, that perhaps sixpence meant
sixpence.

"I tell you again," said Mr. Indignation Cocker, "here's

yesterday's sherry—can't you see it?—one and eightpence,
and here we are again, two shillings.   What do you make
of one and eightpence and two shillings?"

Totally unable to make anything of one and eightpence
and two shillings, the waiter went out to try if anybody
else could; merely casting a helpless backward glance at
Bullfinch, in acknowledgment of his pathetic entreaties
for our soup-tureen.   After a pause, during which Mr. Indignation Cocker read a newspaper and coughed defiant
coughs, Bullfinch arose to get the tureen, when the waiter
reappeared and brought it,—dropping Mr. Indignation
Cocker's altered bill on Mr. Indignation Cocker's table as
he came along.

"It's quite impossible to do it, gentlemen," murmured the
waiter ; " and the kitchen is so far off."

"Well, you don't keep the house ; it's not your fault, we
suppose.   Bring some sherry."

"Waiter!" from Mr. Indignation Cocker, with a new and
burning sense of injury upon him.

The waiter, arrested on his way to our sherry, stopped
short, and came back to see what was wrong now.

"Will you look here?   This is worse than before.   *Do*
you understand?   Here's yesterday's sherry, one and eightpence, and here we are again two shillings.   And what the
devil does ninepence mean?"

This new portent utterly confounded the waiter.   He
wrung his napkin, and mutely appealed to the ceiling.

"Waiter, fetch that sherry," says Bullfinch, in open
wrath and revolt.

"I want to know," persisted Mr. Indignation Cocker,
"the meaning of ninepence.   I want to know the meaning
of sherry one and eightpence yesterday, and of here we are
again two shillings.   Send somebody."

The distracted waiter got out of the room on pretext of
sending somebody, and by that means got our wine.   But
the instant he appeared with our decanter, Mr. Indignation
Cocker descended on him again.

"Waiter!"

"You will now have the goodness to attend to our dinner,
waiter," said Bullfinch, sternly.

"I am very sorry, but it's quite impossible to do it,
gentlemen," pleaded the waiter ; "and the kitchen—— "

"Waiter!" said Mr. Indignation Cocker.

"—Is," resumed the waiter, "so far off, that—— "

"Waiter!" persisted Mr. Indignation Cocker, "send somebody."

We were not without our fears that the waiter rushed out to hang himself; and we were much relieved by his fetching somebody,—in graceful, flowing skirts and with a waist,—who very soon settled Mr. Indignation Cocker's business.

"Oh!" said Mr. Cocker, with his fire surprisingly quenched by this apparition; "I wished to ask about this bill of mine, because it appears to me that there's a little mistake here. Let me show you. Here's yesterday's sherry one and eightpence, and here we are again two shillings. And how do you explain ninepence?"

However, it was explained, in tones too soft to be overheard. Mr. Cocker was heard to say nothing more than "Ah-h-h! Indeed; thank you! Yes," and shortly afterwards went out, a milder man.

The lonely traveller with the stomach-ache had all this time suffered severely, drawing up a leg now and then, and sipping hot brandy-and-water with grated ginger in it. When we tasted our (very) mock-turtle soup, and were instantly seized with symptoms of some disorder simulating apoplexy, and occasioned by the surcharge of nose and brain with lukewarm dish-water holding in solution sour flour, poisonous condiments, and (say) seventy-five per cent. of miscellaneous kitchen stuff rolled into balls, we were inclined to trace his disorder to that source. On the other hand, there was a silent anguish upon him too strongly resembling the results established within ourselves by the sherry, to be discarded from alarmed consideration. Again, we observed him, with terror, to be much overcome by our sole's being aired in a temporary retreat close to him, while the waiter went out (as we conceived) to see his friends. And when the curry made its appearance he suddenly retired in great disorder.

In fine, for the uneatable part of this little dinner (as contradistinguished from the undrinkable) we paid only seven shillings and sixpence each. And Bullfinch and I agreed unanimously, that no such ill-served, ill-appointed, ill-cooked, nasty little dinner could be got for the money anywhere else under the sun. With that comfort to our backs, we turned them on the dear old Temeraire, the charging Temeraire, and resolved (in the Scotch dialect) to gang nae mair to the flabby Temeraire.

XXXIV

MR. BARLOW

A GREAT reader of good fiction at an unusually early age, it seems to me as though I had been born under the superintendence of the estimable but terrific gentleman whose name stands at the head of my present reflections. The instructive monomaniac, Mr. Barlow, will be remembered as the tutor of Master Harry Sandford and Master Tommy Merton. He knew everything, and didactically improved all sorts of occasions, from the consumption of a plate of cherries to the contemplation of a starlight night. What youth came to without Mr. Barlow was displayed in the history of Sandford and Merton, by the example of a certain awful Master Mash. This young wretch wore buckles and powder, conducted himself with insupportable levity at the theatre, had no idea of facing a mad bull single-handed (in which I think him less reprehensible, as remotely reflecting my own character), and was a frightful instance of the enervating effects of luxury upon the human race.

Strange destiny on the part of Mr. Barlow, to go down to posterity as childhood's experience of a bore! Immortal Mr. Barlow, boring his way through the verdant freshness of ages!

My personal indictment against Mr. Barlow is one of many counts. I will proceed to set forth a few of the injuries he has done me.

In the first place, he never made or took a joke. This insensibility on Mr. Barlow's part not only cast its own gloom over my boyhood, but blighted even the sixpenny jest-books of the time; for, groaning under a moral spell constraining me to refer all things to Mr. Barlow, I could not choose but ask myself in a whisper when tickled by a printed jest, "What would *he* think of it? What would *he* see in it?" The point of the jest immediately became

a sting, and stung my conscience. For my mind's eye
saw him stolid, frigid, perchance taking from its shelf some
dreary Greek book, and translating at full length what some
dismal sage said (and touched up afterwards, perhaps, for
publication), when he banished some unlucky joker from
Athens.

The incompatibility of Mr. Barlow with all other portions
of my young life but himself, the adamantine inadaptability
of the man to my favourite fancies and amusements, is the
thing for which I hate him most. What right had he to
bore his way into my Arabian Nights? Yet he did. He
was always hinting doubts of the veracity of Sindbad the
Sailor. If he could have got hold of the Wonderful Lamp,
I knew he would have trimmed it and lighted it, and
delivered a lecture over it on the qualities of sperm-oil, with
a glance at the whale fisheries. He would so soon have
found out—on mechanical principles—the peg in the neck
of the Enchanted Horse, and would have turned it the right
way in so workmanlike a manner, that the horse could
never have got any height into the air, and the story
couldn't have been. He would have proved, by map and
compass, that there was no such kingdom as the delightful
kingdom of Casgar, on the frontiers of Tartary. He would
have caused that hypocritical young prig Harry to make an
experiment,—with the aid of a temporary building in the
garden and a dummy,—demonstrating that you couldn't let
a choked hunchback down an Eastern chimney with a cord,
and leave him upright on the hearth to terrify the sultan's
purveyor.

The golden sounds of the overture to the first metropolitan
pantomime, I remember, were alloyed by Mr. Barlow. Click
click, ting ting, bang bang, weedle weedle weedle, bang!
I recall the chilling air that ran across my frame and cooled
my hot delight, as the thought occurred to me, "This would
never do for Mr. Barlow!" After the curtain drew up,
dreadful doubts of Mr. Barlow's considering the costumes of
the Nymphs of the Nebula as being sufficiently opaque,
obtruded themselves on my enjoyment. In the clown I
perceived two persons; one a fascinating unaccountable
creature of a hectic complexion, joyous in spirits though
feeble in intellect, with flashes of brilliancy; the other
a pupil for Mr. Barlow. I thought how Mr. Barlow would
secretly rise early in the morning, and butter the pavement

for *him*, and, when he had brought him down, would look severely out of his study window and ask *him* how he enjoyed the fun.

I thought how Mr. Barlow would heat all the pokers in the house, and singe him with the whole collection, to bring him better acquainted with the properties of incandescent iron, on which he (Barlow) would fully expatiate. I pictured Mr. Barlow's instituting a comparison between the clown's conduct at his studies,—drinking up the ink, licking his copy-book, and using his head for blotting-paper,—and that of the already mentioned young prig of prigs, Harry, sitting at the Barlovian feet, sneakingly pretending to be in a rapture of youthful knowledge. I thought how soon Mr. Barlow would smooth the clown's hair down, instead of letting it stand erect in three tall tufts ; and how, after a couple of years or so with Mr. Barlow, he would keep his legs close together when he walked, and would take his hands out of his big loose pockets, and wouldn't have a jump left in him.

That I am particularly ignorant what most things in the universe are made of, and how they are made, is another of my charges against Mr. Barlow. With the dread upon me of developing into a Harry, and with a further dread upon me of being Barlowed if I made inquiries, by bringing down upon myself a cold shower-bath of explanations and experiments, I forbore enlightenment in my youth, and became, as they say in melodramas, "the wreck you now behold." That I consorted with idlers and dunces is another of the melancholy facts for which I hold Mr. Barlow responsible. That pragmatical prig, Harry, became so detestable in my sight, that, he being reported studious in the South, I would have fled idle to the extremest North. Better to learn misconduct from a Master Mash than science and statistics from a Sandford ! So I took the path, which, but for Mr. Barlow, I might never have trodden. Thought I, with a shudder, "Mr. Barlow is a bore, with an immense constructive power of making bores. His prize specimen is a bore. He seeks to make a bore of me. That knowledge is power I am not prepared to gainsay; but, with Mr. Barlow, knowledge is power to bore." Therefore I took refuge in the caves of ignorance, wherein I have resided ever since, and which are still my private address.

But the weightiest charge of all my charges against Mr.

Barlow is, that he still walks the earth in various disguises, seeking to make a Tommy of me, even in my maturity. Irrepressible, instructive monomaniac, Mr. Barlow fills my life with pitfalls, and lies hiding at the bottom to burst out upon me when I least expect him.

A few of these dismal experiences of mine shall suffice.

Knowing Mr. Barlow to have invested largely in the moving panorama trade, and having on various occasions identified him in the dark with a long wand in his hand, holding forth in his old way (made more appalling in this connection by his sometimes cracking a piece of Mr. Carlyle's own Dead-Sea fruit in mistake for a joke), I systematically shun pictorial entertainment on rollers. Similarly, I should demand responsible bail and guaranty against the appearance of Mr. Barlow, before committing myself to attendance at any assemblage of my fellow-creatures where a bottle of water and a note-book were conspicuous objects; for in either of those associations, I should expressly expect him. But such is the designing nature of the man, that he steals in where no reasoning precaution or prevision could expect him. As in the following case:—

Adjoining the Caves of Ignorance is a country town. In this country town the Mississippi Momuses, nine in number, were announced to appear in the town-hall, for the general delectation, this last Christmas week. Knowing Mr. Barlow to be unconnected with the Mississippi, though holding republican opinions, and deeming myself secure, I took a stall. My object was to hear and see the Mississippi Momuses in what the bills described as their "National ballads, plantation break-downs, nigger part-songs, choice conundrums, sparkling repartees, &c." I found the nine dressed alike, in the black coat and trousers, white waistcoat, very large shirt-front, very large shirt-collar, and very large white tie and wristbands, which constitute the dress of the mass of the African race, and which has been observed by travellers to prevail over a vast number of degrees of latitude. All the nine rolled their eyes exceedingly, and had very red lips. At the extremities of the curve they formed, seated in their chairs, were the performers on the tambourine and bones. The centre Momus, a black of melancholy aspect (who inspired me with a vague uneasiness for which I could not then account), performed on a Mississippi instrument closely resembling what was once called in this island a hurdy-

gurdy. The Momuses on either side of him had each another
instrument peculiar to the Father of Waters, which may be
likened to a stringed weather-glass held upside down. There
were likewise a little flute and a violin. All went well for
awhile, and we had had several sparkling repartees exchanged
between the performers on the tambourine and bones, when
the black of melancholy aspect, turning .to the latter, and
addressing him in a deep and improving voice as "Bones,
sir," delivered certain grave remarks to him concerning
the juveniles present, and the season of the year; whereon
I perceived that I was in the presence of Mr. Barlow—
corked !

Another night—and this was in.London—I attended the
representation of a little comedy. As the characters were
life-like (and consequently not improving), and as they went
upon their several ways and designs without personally
addressing themselves to me, I felt rather confident of coming
through it without being regarded as Tommy, the more so,
as we were clearly getting close to the end. But I deceived
myself. All of a sudden, àpropos of nothing, everybody
concerned came to a check and halt, advanced to the foot-
lights in a general rally to take dead aim at me, and brought
me down with a moral homily, in which I detected the
dread hand of Barlow.

Nay, so intricate and subtle are the toils of this hunter,
that on the very next night after that, I was again entrapped, where no vestige of a spring could have been
apprehended by the timidest. It was a burlesque that I saw
performed ; an uncompromising burlesque, where everybody
concerned, but especially the ladies, carried on at a very
considerable rate indeed. Most prominent and active among
the corps of performers was what I took to be (and she really
gave me very fair opportunities of coming to a right conclusion) a young lady of a pretty figure. She was dressed as
a picturesque young gentleman, whose pantaloons had been
cut off in their infancy ; and she had very neat knees and
very neat satin boots. Immediately after singing a slang
song and dancing a slang dance, this engaging figure approached the fatal lamps, and, bending over them, delivered
in a thrilling voice a random eulogium on, and exhortation
to pursue, the virtues. "Great Heaven !" was my exclamation ; "Barlow !"

There is still another aspect in which Mr. Barlow per-

petually insists on my sustaining the character of Tommy,
which is more unendurable yet, on account of its extreme
aggressiveness. For the purposes of a review or newspaper,
he will get up an abstruse subject with infinite pains, will
Barlow, utterly regardless of the price of midnight oil, and
indeed of everything else, save cramming himself to the
eyes.

But mark. When Mr., Barlow blows his information off,
he is not contented with having rammed it home, and discharged it upon me, Tommy, his target, but he pretends
that he was always in possession of it, and made nothing of
it,—that he imbibed it with mother's milk,—and that I, the
wretched Tommy, am most abjectly behindhand in not
having done the same. I ask, why is Tommy to be always
the foil of Mr. Barlow to this extent ? What Mr. Barlow
had not the slightest notion of himself, a week ago, it surely
cannot be any very heavy backsliding in me not to have
at my fingers' ends to-day ! And yet Mr. Barlow systematically carries it over me with a high hand, and will
tauntingly ask me, in his articles, whether it is possible that
I am not aware that every school-boy knows that the
fourteenth turning on the left in the steppes of Russia will
conduct to such and such a wandering tribe? with other
disparaging questions of like nature. So, when Mr. Barlow
addresses a letter to any journal as a volunteer correspondent
(which I frequently find him doing), he will previously have
gotten somebody to tell him some tremendous technicality,
and will write in the coolest manner, " Now, sir, I may
assume that every reader of your columns, possessing average
information and intelligence, knows as well as I do that "—
say that the draught from the touch-hole of a cannon of
such a calibre bears such a proportion in the nicest fractions
to the draught from the muzzle ; or some equally familiar
little fact. But whatever it is, be certain that it always
tends to the exaltation of Mr. Barlow, and the depression of
his enforced and enslaved pupil.

Mr. Barlow's knowledge of my own pursuits I find to be
so profound, that my own knowledge of them becomes as
nothing. Mr. Barlow (disguised and bearing a feigned name,
but detected by me) has occasionally taught me, in a sonorous
voice, from end to end of a long dinner-table, trifles that
I took the liberty of teaching him five-and-twenty years ago.
My closing article of impeachment against Mr. Barlow is,

that he goes out to breakfast, goes out to dinner, goes out everywhere, high and low, and that he WILL preach to me, and that I CAN'T get rid of him. He makes of me a Promethean Tommy, bound ; and he is the vulture that gorges itself upon the liver of my uninstructed mind.

XXXV

ON AN AMATEUR BEAT

It is one of my fancies, that even my idlest walk must always have its appointed destination. I set myself a task before I leave my lodging in Covent-garden on a street expedition, and should no more think of altering my route by the way, or turning back and leaving a part of it un-achieved, than I should think of fraudulently violating an agreement entered into with somebody else. The other day, finding myself under this kind of obligation to proceed to Limehouse, I started punctually at noon, in compliance with the terms of the contract with myself to which my good faith was pledged.

On such an occasion, it is my habit to regard my walk as my beat, and myself as a higher sort of police-constable doing duty on the same. There is many a ruffian in the streets whom I mentally collar and clear out of them, who would see mighty little of London, I can tell him, if I could deal with him physically.

Issuing forth upon this very beat, and following with my eyes three hulking garrotters on their way home,—which home I could confidently swear to be within so many yards of Drury-lane, in such a narrow and restricted direction (though they live in their lodging quite as undisturbed as I in mine),—I went on duty with a consideration which I respectfully offer to the new Chief Commissioner,—in whom I thoroughly confide as a tried and efficient public servant. How often (thought I) have I been forced to swallow, in police-reports, the intolerable stereotyped pill of nonsense, how that the police-constable informed the worthy magistrate how that the associates of the prisoner did, at that present speaking, dwell in a street or court which no man dared go down, and how that the worthy magistrate had heard of the dark reputation of such street or court, and how that our readers would doubtless remember that it was always the same street or court which was thus edifyingly discoursed about, say once a fortnight.

Now, suppose that a Chief Commissioner sent round a circular to every division of police employed in London, requiring instantly the names in all districts of all such much-puffed streets or courts which no man durst go down; and suppose that in such circular he gave plain warning, "If those places really exist, they are a proof of police inefficiency which I mean to punish; and if they do not exist, but are a conventional fiction, then they are a proof of lazy tacit police connivance with professional crime, which I also mean to punish"—what then? Fictions or realities, could they survive the touchstone of this atom of common sense? To tell us in open court, until it has become as trite a feature of news as the great gooseberry, that a costly police-system such as was never before heard of, has left in London, in the days of steam and gas and photographs of thieves and electric telegraphs, the sanctuaries and stews of the Stuarts! Why, a parity of practice, in all departments, would bring back the Plague in two summers, and the Druids in a century!

Walking faster under my share of this public injury, I overturned a wretched little creature, who, clutching at the rags of a pair of trousers with one of its claws, and at its ragged hair with the other, pattered with bare feet over the muddy stones. I stopped to raise and succour this poor weeping wretch, and fifty like it, but of both sexes, were about me in a moment, begging, tumbling, fighting, clamouring, yelling, shivering in their nakedness and hunger. The piece of money I had put into the claw of the child I had overturned was clawed out of it, and was again clawed out of that wolfish gripe, and again out of that, and soon I had no notion in what part of the obscene scuffle in the mud, of rags and legs and arms and dirt, the money might be. In raising the child, I had drawn it aside out of the main thoroughfare, and this took place among some wooden hoardings and barriers and ruins of demolished buildings, hard by Temple Bar.

Unexpectedly, from among them emerged a genuine police constable, before whom the dreadful brood dispersed in various directions, he making feints and darts in this direction and in that, and catching nothing. When all were frightened away, he took off his hat, pulled out a handkerchief from it, wiped his heated brow, and restored the handkerchief and hat to their places, with the air of a man who had dis-charged a great moral duty,—as indeed he had, in doing what was set down for him. I looked at him, and I looked about at the disorderly traces in the mud, and I thought of the drops of rain and the footprints of an extinct creature, hoary ages upon ages old, that geologists have identified on the face of a clift; and this speculation came over me: If this mud could petrify at this moment, and could lie con-cealed here for ten thousand years, I wonder whether the race of men then to be our successors on the earth could, from these or any marks, by the utmost force of the human intellect, unassisted by tradition, deduce such an astounding inference as the existence of a polished state of society that bore with the public savagery of neglected children in the streets of its capital city, and was proud of its power by sea and land, and never used its power to seize and save them!

After this, when I came to the Old Bailey and glanced up it towards Newgate, I found that the prison had an inconsistent look. There seemed to be some unlucky in-consistency in the atmosphere that day; for though the proportions of St. Paul's Cathedral are very beautiful, it had an air of being somewhat out of drawing, in my eyes. I felt as though the cross were too high up, and perched upon the intervening golden ball too far away.

Facing eastward, I left behind me Smithfield and Old Bailey,—fire and faggot, condemned hold, public hanging, whipping through the city at the cart-tail, pillory, branding-iron, and other beautiful ancestral landmarks, which rude hands have rooted up, without bringing the stars quite down upon us as yet,—and went my way upon my beat, noting how oddly characteristic neighbourhoods are divided from one another, hereabout, as though by an invisible line across the way. Here shall cease the bankers and the money-changers; here shall begin the shipping interest and the nautical-instrument shops; here shall follow a scarcely perceptible flavouring of groceries and drugs; here shall come a strong infusion of butchers; now, small hosiers shall be in the ascendant; henceforth, everything exposed for sale shall have its ticketed price attached. All this as if specially ordered and appointed.

A single stride at Houndsditch Church, no wider than

sufficed to cross the kennel at the bottom of the Canon-gate, which the debtors in Holyrood sanctuary were wont to relieve their minds by skipping over, as Scott relates, and standing in delightful daring of catchpoles on the free side,—a single stride, and everything is entirely changed in grain and character. West of the stride, a table, or a chest of drawers on sale, shall be of mahogany and French-polished; east of the stride, it shall be of deal, smeared with a cheap counterfeit resembling lip-salve. West of the stride, a penny loaf or bun shall be compact and self-contained; east of the stride, it shall be of a sprawling and splay-footed character, as seeking to make more of itself for the money. My beat lying round by Whitechapel Church, and the adjacent sugar-refineries,—great buildings, tier upon tier, that have the appearance of being nearly related to the dock-warehouses at Liverpool,—I turned off to my right, and, passing round the awkward corner on my left, came suddenly on an apparition familiar to London streets afar off.

What London peripatetic of these times has not seen the woman who has fallen forward, double, through some affection of the spine, and whose head has of late taken a turn to one side, so that it now droops over the back of one of her arms at about the wrist? Who does not know her staff, and her shawl, and her basket, as she gropes her way along, capable of seeing nothing but the pavement, never begging, never stopping, for ever going somewhere on no business? How does she live, whence does she come, whither does she go, and why? I mind the time when her yellow arms were naught but bone and parchment. Slight changes steal over her: for there is a shadowy suggestion of human skin on them now. The Strand may be taken as the central point about which she revolves in a half-mile orbit. How comes she so far east as this? And coming back too! Having been how much farther? She is a rare spectacle in this neighbourhood. I receive intelligent information to this effect from a dog—a lop-sided mongrel with a foolish tail, plodding along with his tail up, and his ears pricked, and displaying an amiable interest in the ways of his fellow-men,—if I may be allowed the expression. After pausing at a pork-shop, he is jogging eastward like myself, with a benevolent countenance and a watery mouth, as though musing on the many excellences of pork, when he beholds this doubled-up bundle approaching.

Poodles Going the Round

He is not so much astonished at the bundle (though amazed by that), as the circumstance that it has within itself the means of locomotion. He stops, pricks his ears higher, makes a slight point, stares, utters a short, low growl, and glistens at the nose,—as I conceive with terror. The bundle continuing to approach, he barks, turns tail, and is about to fly, when, arguing with himself that flight is not becoming in a dog, he turns, and once more faces the advancing heap of clothes. After much hesitation, it occurs to him that there may be a face in it somewhere. Desperately resolving to undertake the adventure, and pursue the inquiry, he goes slowly up to the bundle, goes slowly round it, and coming at length upon the human countenance down there where never human countenance should be, gives a yelp of horror, and flies for the East India Docks.

Being now in the Commercial Road district of my beat, and bethinking myself that Stepney Station is near, I quicken my pace that I may turn out of the road at that point, and see how my small eastern star is shining.

The Children's Hospital, to which I gave that name, is in full force. All its beds are occupied. There is a new face on the bed where my pretty baby lay, and that sweet little child is now at rest for ever. Much kind sympathy has been here since my former visit, and it is good to see the walls profusely garnished with dolls. I wonder what Poodles may think of them, as they stretch out their arms above the beds, and stare, and display their splendid dresses. Poodles has a greater interest in the patients. I find him making the round of the beds, like a house-surgeon, attended by another dog,—a friend,—who appears to trot about with him in the character of his pupil dresser. Poodles is anxious to make me known to a pretty little girl looking wonderfully healthy, who had had a leg taken off for cancer of the knee. A difficult operation, Poodles intimates, wagging his tail on the counterpane, but perfectly successful, as you see, dear sir! The patient, patting Poodles, adds with a smile, "The leg was so much trouble to me, that I am glad it's gone." I never saw anything in doggery finer than the deportment of Poodles, when another little girl opens her mouth to show a peculiar enlargement of the tongue. Poodles (at that time on a table, to be on a level with the occasion) looks at the tongue (with his own sympathetically out) so very gravely and knowingly, that I feel inclined to put my hand in my waistcoat-pocket, and give him a guinea, wrapped in paper.

On my beat again, and close to Limehouse Church, its termination, I found myself near to certain "Lead-Mills." Struck by the name, which was fresh in my memory, and finding, on inquiry, that these same lead-mills were identified with those same lead-mills of which I made mention when I first visited the East London Children's Hospital and its neighbourhood as Uncommercial Traveller, I resolved to have a look at them.

Received by two very intelligent gentlemen, brothers, and partners with their father in the concern, and who testified every desire to show their works to me freely, I went over the lead-mills. The purport of such works is the conversion of pig-lead into white-lead. This conversion is brought about by the slow and gradual effecting of certain successive chemical changes in the lead itself. The processes are picturesque and interesting,—the most so, being the burying of the lead, at a certain stage of preparation, in pots, each pot containing a certain quantity of acid besides, and all the pots being buried in vast numbers, in layers, under tan, for some ten weeks.

Hopping up ladders, and across planks, and on elevated perches, until I was uncertain whether to liken myself to a bird or a bricklayer, I became conscious of standing on nothing particular, looking down into one of a series of large cocklofts, with the outer day peeping in through the chinks in the tiled roof above. A number of women were ascending to, and descending from, this cockloft, each carrying on the upward journey a pot of prepared lead and acid, for deposition under the smoking tan. When one layer of pots was completely filled, it was carefully covered in with planks, and those were carefully covered with tan again, and then another layer of pots was begun above; sufficient means of ventilation being preserved through wooden tubes. Going down into the cockloft then filling, I found the heat of the tan to be surprisingly great, and also the odour of the lead and acid to be not absolutely exquisite, though I believe not noxious at that stage. In other cocklofts, where the pots were being exhumed, the heat of the steaming tan was much greater, and the smell was penetrating and peculiar. There were cocklofts in all stages ; full and empty, half filled and half emptied ; strong, active women were clambering about them busily ; and the whole thing had rather the air of the upper part of the house of some immensely rich old Turk, whose faithful seraglio were hiding his money because the sultan or the pasha was coming.

As is the case with most pulps or pigments, so in the instance of this white-lead, processes of stirring, separating, washing, grinding, rolling, and pressing succeed. Some of these are unquestionably inimical to health, the danger arising from inhalation of particles of lead, or from contact between the lead and the touch, or both. Against these dangers, I found good respirators provided (simply made of flannel and muslin, so as to be inexpensively renewed, and in some instances washed with scented soap), and gauntlet gloves, and loose gowns. Everywhere, there was as much fresh air as windows, well placed and opened, could possibly admit. And it was explained that the precaution of frequently changing the women employed in the worst parts of the work (a precaution originating in their own experience or apprehension of its ill effects) was found salutary. They had a mysterious and singular appearance, with the mouth and nose covered, and the loose gown on, and yet bore out the simile of the old Turk and the seraglio all the better for the disguise.

At last this vexed white-lead, having been buried and resuscitated, and heated and cooled and stirred, and separated and washed and ground, and rolled and pressed, is subjected to the action of intense fiery heat. A row of women, dressed as above described, stood, let us say, in a large stone bake-house, passing on the baking-dishes as they were given out by the cooks, from hand to hand, into the ovens. The oven, or stove, cold as yet, looked as high as an ordinary house, and was full of men and women on temporary foot-holds, briskly passing up and stowing away the dishes. The door of another oven, or stove, about to be cooled and emptied, was opened from above, for the uncommercial countenance to peer down into. The uncommercial countenance withdrew itself, with expedition and a sense of suffocation, from the dull-glowing heat and the overpowering smell. On the whole, perhaps the going into these stoves to work, when they are freshly opened, may be the worst part of the occupation.

But I made it out to be indubitable that the owners of

these lead-mills honestly and sedulously try to reduce the dangers of the occupation to the lowest point.

A washing-place is provided for the women (I thought there might have been more towels), and a room in which they hang their clothes, and take their meals, and where they have a good fire-range and fire, and a female attendant to help them, and to watch that they do not neglect the cleansing of their hands before touching their food. An experienced medical attendant is provided for them, and any premonitory symptoms of lead-poisoning are carefully treated. Their teapots and such things were set out on tables ready for their afternoon meal, when I saw their room; and it had a homely look. It is found that they bear the work much better than men: some few of them have been at it for years, and the great majority of those I observed were strong and active. On the other hand, it should be remembered that most of them are very capricious and irregular in their attendance.

American inventiveness would seem to indicate that before very long white-lead may be made entirely by machinery. The sooner, the better. In the meantime, I parted from my two frank conductors over the mills, by telling them that they had nothing there to be concealed, and nothing to be blamed for. As to the rest, the philosophy of the matter of lead-poisoning and workpeople seems to me to have been pretty fairly summed up by the Irishwoman whom I quoted in my former paper: "Some of them gets lead-pisoned soon, and some of them gets lead-pisoned later, and some, but not many, niver; and 'tis all according to the constitooshun, sur; and some constitooshuns is strong and some is weak."

Retracing my footsteps over my beat, I went off duty.

XXXVI

A FLY-LEAF IN A LIFE

ONCE upon a time (no matter when), I was engaged in a pursuit (no matter what), which could be transacted by myself alone; in which I could have no help; which imposed a constant strain on the attention, memory, observation, and physical powers; and which involved an almost fabulous amount of change of place and rapid railway travelling. I had followed this pursuit through an exceptionally trying winter in an always trying climate, and had resumed it in England after but a brief repose. Thus it came to be prolonged until, at length—and, as it seemed, all of a sudden—it so wore me out that I could not rely, with my usual cheerful confidence, upon myself to achieve the constantly recurring task, and began to feel (for the first time in my life) giddy, jarred, shaken, faint, uncertain of voice and sight and tread and touch, and dull of spirit. The medical advice I sought within a few hours, was given in two words: "instant rest." Being accustomed to observe myself as curiously as if I were another man, and knowing the advice to meet my only need, I instantly halted in the pursuit of which I speak, and rested.

My intention was, to interpose, as it were, a fly-leaf in the book of my life, in which nothing should be written from without for a brief season of a few weeks. But some very singular experiences recorded themselves on this same fly-leaf, and I am going to relate them literally. I repeat the word: literally.

My first odd experience was of the remarkable coincidence between my case, in the general mind, and one Mr. Merdle's as I find it recorded in a work of fiction called LITTLE DORRIT. To be sure, Mr. Merdle was a swindler, forger, and thief, and my calling had been of a less harmful (and less remunerative) nature; but it was all one for that.

Here is Mr. Merdle's case :

" At first, he was dead of all the diseases that ever were known, and of several bran-new maladies invented with the speed of Light to meet the demand of the occasion. He had concealed a dropsy from infancy, he had inherited a large estate of water on the chest from his grandfather, he had had an operation performed upon him every morning of his life for eighteen years, he had been subject to the explosion of important veins in his body after the manner of fireworks, he had had something the matter with his lungs, he had had something the matter with his heart, he had had something the matter with his brain. Five hundred people who sat down to breakfast entirely uninformed on the whole subject, believed before they had done breakfast, that they privately and personally knew Physician to have said to Mr. Merdle, 'You must expect to go out, some day, like the snuff of a candle ; ' and that they knew Mr. Merdle to have said to Physician, 'A man can die but once.' By about eleven o'clock in the forenoon, something the matter with the brain, became the favourite theory against the field ; and by twelve the something had been distinctly ascertained to be 'Pressure.'

" Pressure was so entirely satisfactory to the public mind, and seemed to make every one so comfortable, that it might have lasted all day but for Bar's having taken the real state of·the case into Court at half-past nine. Pressure, however, so far from being overthrown by the discovery, became a greater favourite than ever. There was a general moralising upon Pressure, in every street. All the people who had tried to make money and had not been able to do it, said, There you were ! You no sooner began to devote yourself to the pursuit of wealth, than you got Pressure. The idle people improved the occasion in a similar manner. See, said they, what you brought yourself to by work, work, work ! You persisted in working, you overdid it, Pressure came on, and you were done for ! This consideration was very potent in many quarters, but nowhere more so than among the young clerks and partners who had never been in the slightest danger of overdoing it. These, one and all declared, quite piously, that they hoped they would never forget the warning as long as they lived, and that their conduct might be so regulated as to keep off Pressure, and preserve them, a comfort to their friends, for many years."

Just my case—if I had only known it—when I was quietly basking in the sunshine in my Kentish meadow !

But while I so rested, thankfully recovering every hour, I had experiences more odd than this. I had experiences of spiritual conceit, for which, as giving me a new warning against that curse of mankind, I shall always feel grateful to the supposition that I was too far gone to protest against playing sick lion to any stray donkey with an itching hoof. All sorts of people seemed to become vicariously religious at my expense. I received the most uncompromising warning that I was a Heathen : on the conclusive authority of a field preacher, who, like the most of his ignorant and vain and daring class, could not construct a tolerable sentence in his native tongue or pen a fair letter. This inspired individual called me to order roundly, and knew in the freest and easiest way where I was going to, and what would become of me if I failed to fashion myself on his bright example, and was on terms of blasphemous confidence with the Heavenly Host. He was in the secrets of my heart, and in the lowest soundings of my soul—he !—and could read the depths of my nature better than his A B C, and could turn me inside out, like his own clammy glove. But what is far more extraordinary than this—for such dirty water as this could alone be drawn from such a shallow and muddy source— I found from the information of a beneficed clergyman, of whom I never heard and whom I never saw, that I had not, as I rather supposed I had, lived a life of some reading, contemplation, and inquiry ; that I had not studied, as I rather supposed I had, to inculcate some Christian lessons in books ; that I had never tried, as I rather supposed I had, to turn a child or two tenderly towards the knowledge and love of our Saviour ; that I had never had, as I rather supposed I had had, departed friends, or stood beside open graves ; but that I had lived a life of "uninterrupted prosperity," and that I needed this " check, overmuch," and that the way to turn it to account was to read these sermons and these poems, enclosed, and written and issued by my correspondent ! I beg it may be understood that I relate facts of my own uncommercial experience, and no vain imaginings. The documents in proof lie near my hand.

Another odd entry on the fly-leaf, of a more entertaining character, was the wonderful persistency with which kind sympathisers assumed that I had injuriously coupled with the so suddenly relinquished pursuit, those personal habits of mine most obviously incompatible with it, and most plainly impossible of being maintained along with it. As, all that exercise, all that cold bathing, all that wind and weather, all that uphill training—all that everything else, say, which is usually carried about by express trains in a portmanteau and hat-box, and partaken of under a flaming row of gas-lights in the company of two thousand people. This assuming of a whole case against all fact and likeli-hood, struck me as particularly droll, and was an oddity of which I certainly had had no adequate experience in life until I turned that curious fly-leaf.

My old acquaintances the begging-letter writers came out on the fly-leaf, very piously indeed. They were glad, at such a serious crisis, to afford me another opportunity of sending that Post-office order. I needn't make it a pound, as previously insisted on ; ten shillings might ease my mind. And Heaven forbid that they should refuse, at such an insignificant figure, to take a weight off the memory of an erring fellow-creature ! One gentleman, of an artistic turn (and copiously illustrating the books of the Mendicity Society), thought it might soothe my conscience, in the tender respect of gifts misused, if I would immediately cash up in aid of his lowly talent for original design— as a specimen of which he enclosed me a work of art which I recognised as a tracing from a woodcut originally published in the late Mrs. Trollope's book on America, forty or fifty years ago. The number of people who were prepared to live long years after me, untiring benefactors to their species, for fifty pounds apiece down, was astonishing. Also, of those who wanted bank-notes for stiff penitential amounts, to give away :—not to keep, on any account.

Divers wonderful medicines and machines insinuated recommendations of themselves into the fly-leaf that was to have been so blank. It was specially observable that every prescriber, whether in a moral or physical direction, knew me thoroughly—knew me from head to heel, in and out, through and through, upside down. I was a glass piece of general property, and everybody was on the most surprisingly intimate terms with me. A few public insti-tutions had complimentary perceptions of corners in my mind, of which, after considerable self-examination, I have not discovered any indication. Neat little printed forms were addressed to those corners, beginning with the words: "I give and bequeath."

Will it seem exaggerative to state my belief that the most honest, the most modest, and the least vain-glorious of all the records upon this strange fly-leaf, was a letter from the self-deceived discoverer of the recondite secret "how to live four or five hundred years"? . Doubtless it will seem so, yet the statement is not exaggerative by any means, but is made in my serious and sincere conviction. With this, and with a laugh at the rest that shall not be cynical, I turn the Fly-leaf, and go on again.

XXXVII

A PLEA FOR TOTAL ABSTINENCE

ONE day this last Whitsuntide, at precisely eleven o'clock in the forenoon, there suddenly rode into the field of view commanded by the windows of my lodging an equestrian phenomenon. It was a fellow-creature on horseback, dressed in the absurdest manner. The fellow-creature wore high boots; some other (and much larger) fellow-creature's breeches, of a slack-baked doughy colour and a baggy form; a blue shirt, whereof the skirt, or tail, was puffily tucked into the waist-band of the said breeches; no coat; a red shoulder-belt; and a demi-semi-military scarlet hat, with a feathered ornament in front, which, to the uninstructed human vision, had the appearance of a moulting shuttlecock. I laid down the newspaper with which I had been occupied, and surveyed the fellow-man in question with astonishment. Whether he had been sitting to any painter as a frontispiece for a new edition of "Sartor Resartus;" whether "the husk or shell of him," as the esteemed Herr Teufelsdroch might put it, were founded on a jockey, on a circus, on General Garibaldi, on cheap porcelain, on a toy shop, on Guy Fawkes, on waxwork, on gold-digging, on Bedlam, or on all,—were doubts that greatly exercised my mind. Meanwhile, my fellow-man stumbled and slided, excessively against his will, on the slippery stones of my Covent-garden street, and elicited shrieks from several sympathetic females, by convulsively restraining himself from pitching over his horse's head. In the very crisis of these evolutions, and indeed at the trying moment when his charger's tail was in a tobacconist's shop, and his head anywhere about town, this cavalier was joined by two similar portents, who, likewise stumbling and sliding, caused him to stumble and slide the more distressingly. At length this Gilpinian triumvirate effected a halt, and, looking northward, waved their three right hands as commanding unseen troops, to "Up, guards! and at 'em." Hereupon a brazen band burst forth, which caused them to be instantly bolted with to some remote spot of earth in the direction of the Surrey Hills.

Judging from these appearances that a procession was under way, I threw up my window, and, craning out, had the satisfaction of beholding it advancing along the streets. It was a Teetotal procession, as I learnt from its banners, and was long enough to consume twenty minutes in passing. There were a great number of children in it, some of them so very young in their mothers' arms as to be in the act of practically exemplifying their abstinence from fermented liquors, and attachment to an unintoxicating drink, while the procession defiled. The display was, on the whole, pleasant to see, as any good-humoured holiday assemblage of clean, cheerful, and well-conducted people should be. It was bright with ribbons, tinsel, and shoulder-belts, and abounded in flowers, as if those latter trophies had come up in profusion under much watering. The day being breezy, the insubordination of the large banners was very reprehensible. Each of these being borne aloft on two poles and stayed with some half-dozen lines, was carried, as polite books in the last century used to be written, by "various hands," and the anxiety expressed in the upturned faces of those officers,— something between the anxiety attendant on the balancing art, and that inseparable from the pastime of kite-flying, with a touch of the angler's quality in landing his scaly prey,— much impressed me. Suddenly, too, a banner would shiver in the wind, and go about in the most inconvenient manner. This always happened oftenest with such gorgeous standards as those representing a gentleman in black, corpulent with tea and water, in the laudable act of summarily reforming a family, feeble and pinched with beer. The gentleman in black distended by wind would then conduct himself with the most unbecoming levity, while the beery family, growing beerier, would frantically try to tear themselves away from his ministration. Some of the inscriptions accompanying the banners were of a highly determined character, as "We never, never will give up the temperance cause," with similar sound resolutions rather suggestive to the profane mind of Mrs. Micawber's "I never will desert Mr. Micawber," and of Mr. Micawber's retort, "Really, my dear, I am not aware that you were ever required by any human being to do anything of the sort."

At intervals, a gloom would fall on the passing members of the procession, for which I was at first unable to account. But this I discovered, after a little observation, to be occasioned by the coming on of the executioners,—the terrible official beings who were to make the speeches by-and-by,— who were distributed in open carriages at various points of the cavalcade. A dark cloud and a sensation of dampness, as from many wet blankets, invariably preceded the rolling on of the dreadful cars containing these headsmen; and I noticed that the wretched people who closely followed them, and who were in a manner forced to contemplate their folded arms, complacent countenances, and threatening lips, were more overshadowed by the cloud and damp than those in front. Indeed, I perceived in some of these so moody an implacability towards the magnates of the scaffold, and so plain a desire to tear them limb from limb, that I would respectfully suggest to the managers the expediency of conveying the executioners to the scene of their dismal labours by unfrequented ways, and in closely-tilted carts, next Whitsuntide.

The procession was composed of a series of smaller processions, which had come together, each from its own metropolitan district. An infusion of allegory became perceptible when patriotic Peckham advanced. So I judged, from the circumstance of Peckham's unfurling a silken banner that fanned heaven and earth with the words, "The Peckham Lifeboat." No boat being in attendance, though life, in the likeness of "a gallant, gallant crew," in nautical uniform, followed the flag, I was led to meditate on the fact that Peckham is described by geographers as an inland settlement, with no larger or nearer shore-line than the towing-path of the Surrey Canal, on which stormy station I had been given to understand no lifeboat exists. Thus I deduced an allegorical meaning, and came to the conclusion, that if patriotic Peckham picked a peck of pickled poetry, this *was* the peck of pickled poetry which patriotic Peckham picked.

I have observed that the aggregate procession was on the whole pleasant to see. I made use of that qualified expression with a direct meaning, which I will now explain. It involves the title of this paper, and a little fair trying of teetotalism by its own tests. There were many people on foot, and many people in vehicles of various kinds. The former were pleasant to see, and the latter were not pleasant

to see; for the reason that I never, on any occasion or under
any circumstances, have beheld heavier overloading of horses
than in this public show.   Unless the imposition of a great
van laden with from ten to twenty people on a single horse
be a moderate tasking of the poor creature, then the
temperate use of horses was immoderate and cruel.   From
the smallest and lightest horse to the largest and heaviest,
there were many instances in which the beast of burden was
so shamefully overladen, that the Society for the Prevention
of Cruelty to Animals have frequently interposed in less
gross cases.

Now, I have always held that there may be, and that
there unquestionably is, such a thing as use without abuse,
and that therefore the total abolitionists are irrational and
wrong-headed.   But the procession completely converted me.
For so large a number of the people using draught-horses in
it were so clearly unable to use them without abusing them,
that I perceived total abstinence from horseflesh to be the
only remedy of which the case admitted.   As it is all one
to teetotalers whether you take half a pint of beer or half
a gallon, so it was all one here whether the beast of burden
were a pony or a cart-horse.   Indeed, my case had the
special strength that the half-pint quadruped underwent as
much suffering as the half-gallon quadruped.   Moral: total
abstinence from horseflesh through the whole length and
breadth of the scale.   This pledge will be in course of
administration to all teetotal processionists, not pedestrians,
at the publishing office of "All the Year Round," on the
1st day of April, 1870.

Observe a point for consideration.   This procession comprised many persons in their gigs, broughams, tax-carts,
barouches, chaises, and what not, who were merciful to the
dumb beasts that drew them, and did not overcharge their
strength.   What is to be done with those unoffending
persons?   I will not run amuck and vilify and defame
them, as teetotal tracts and platforms would most assuredly
do, if the question were one of drinking instead of driving:
I merely ask what is to be done with them!   The reply
admits of no dispute whatever.   Manifestly, in strict accordance with teetotal doctrines, THEY must come in too, and
take the total abstinence from horseflesh pledge.   It is not
pretended that those members of the procession misused
certain auxiliaries which in most countries and all ages have

been bestowed upon man for his use, but it is undeniable that other members of the procession did. Teetotal mathematics demonstrate that the less includes the greater; that the guilty include the innocent, the blind the seeing, the deaf the hearing, the dumb the speaking, the drunken the sober. If any of the moderate users of draught-cattle in question should deem that there is any gentle violence done to their reason by these elements of logic, they are invited to come out of the procession next Whitsuntide, and look at it from my window.

REPRINTED PIECES

with

THE LAMPLIGHTER

TO BE READ AT DUSK

SUNDAY UNDER THREE HEADS

HUNTED DOWN

HOLIDAY ROMANCE

and

GEORGE SILVERMAN'S
EXPLANATION

CONTENTS

REPRINTED PIECES

LIST OF ILLUSTRATIONS

By F. WALKER

CHARACTERS

THE LONG VOYAGE

CAPTAIN BLIGH, master of the *Bounty*
MR. BRIMER, fifth mate of the *Halsewell*
FLETCHER CHRISTIAN, an officer of the *Bounty*; a mutineer
MR. MACMANUS, a midshipman on the *Halsewell*
MISS MANSEL, a passenger in the *Halsewell*
MR. HENRY MERITON, second mate of the *Halsewell*
CAPTAIN PIERCE, master of the *Halsewell*
MR. ROGERS, third mate of the *Halsewell*

'BIRTHS. MRS. MEEK, OF A SON'

MRS. BIGBY, mother of Mrs. Meek
AUGUSTUS GEORGE MEEK, infant son of Mr. George Meek
MR. GEORGE MEEK, a quiet man, of small stature and weak voice
MRS. MEEK, his wife
MRS. PRODGIT, nurse to Mrs. Meek

A POOR MAN'S TALE OF A PATENT

WILLIAM BUTCHER, a Chartist
JOHN, a working smith, who endeavours to patent an invention
THOMAS JOY, a carpenter with whom John lodges

A FLIGHT

THE COMPACT ENCHANTRESS, a French actress
DON DIEGO, inventor of the last new flying-machine
LAMIEL, a tall, grave, melancholy Frenchman

THE DETECTIVE POLICE; AND THREE 'DETECTIVE' ANECDOTES

MR. CLARKSON, counsel for Shepherdson and other thieves
SERGEANT DORNTON, a detective police-officer
DR. DUNDEY, a man who robs an Irish bank
SERGEANT FENDALL, a detective police-officer
FIKEY, a man accused of forgery

ELIZA GRIMWOOD, a handsome young woman, called 'The Countess'
AARON MESHECK, a fraudulent Jewish bill-broker
SERGEANT MITH, a detective police-officer
MR. PHIBBS, a haberdasher
THOMAS PIGEON (*alias* TALLY-HO THOMPSON), a famous horse-stealer
SHEPHERDSON, a thief
INSPECTOR STALKER }
SERGEANT STRAW } detective police-officers
MR. TATT, an amateur detective
MR. TRINKLE, a young man suspected of murder
INSPECTOR WIELD }
SERGEANT WITCHEM } detective police-officers

ON DUTY WITH INSPECTOR FIELD

BULLY BARK, a lodging-house keeper and receiver of stolen goods
BLACKEY, a beggar with a painted skin to represent disease
MR. CLICK, a rogue
INSPECTOR FIELD, a detective officer
BOB MILES, a rogue and jail-bird
THE EARL OF WARWICK, a thief, so styled

PRINCE BULL. A FAIRY TALE

PRINCE BEAR [Russia], an enemy of Prince Bull
PRINCE BULL [the English Government], a powerful but corpulent
    and rather sleepy Prince
TAPE, a tyrannical old godmother to Prince Bull

OUR SCHOOL

MR. BLINKINS, the Latin master
MASTER DUMBLEDON, a goggle-eyed parlour-boarder
MISS FROST, a schoolgirl
MASTER MAWLS, a schoolboy of uncouth manners
MASTER MAXBY, a schoolboy, favoured by the usher
PHIL, a serving-man

OUR VESTRY

CAPTAIN BANGER, a vestryman, and opponent of Mr. Tiddypot
MR. CHIB, the Father of the Vestry
MR. DOGGINSON, a vestryman regarded as 'a regular John Bull'
MR. MAGG, one of the first orators of the Vestry
MR. TIDDYPOT, a vestryman, opposed to Captain Banger
MR. WIGSBY, a debater of great eminence

REPRINTED PIECES

THE LONG VOYAGE

WHEN the wind is blowing and the sleet or rain is driving against the dark windows, I love to sit by the fire, thinking of what I have read in books of voyage and travel. Such books have had a strong fascination for my mind from my earliest childhood; and I wonder it should have come to pass that I never have been round the world, never have been shipwrecked, ice-environed, tomahawked, or eaten.

Sitting on my ruddy hearth in the twilight of New Year's Eve, I find incidents of travel rise around me from all the latitudes and longitudes of the globe. They observe no order or sequence, but appear and vanish as they will— "come like shadows, so depart." Columbus, alone upon the sea with his disaffected crew, looks over the waste of waters from his high station on the poop of his ship, and sees the first uncertain glimmer of the light, "rising and falling with the waves, like a torch in the bark of some fisherman," which is the shining star of a new world. Bruce is caged in Abyssinia, surrounded by the gory horrors which shall often startle him out of his sleep at home when years have passed away. Franklin, come to the end of his unhappy overland journey—would that it had been his last!—lies perishing of hunger with his brave companions: each emaciated figure stretched upon its miserable bed without the power to rise: all, dividing the weary days between their prayers, their remembrances of the dear ones at home, and conversation on the pleasures of eating; the last-named topic being ever present to them, likewise, in their dreams. All the African travellers, wayworn, solitary and sad, submit themselves again to drunken, murderous, man-selling despots, of the lowest order of humanity ; and Mungo Park, fainting under a tree and succoured by a woman, gratefully remembers how his Good Samaritan has always come to him in woman's shape, the wide world over.

A shadow on the wall, in which my mind's eye can discern some traces of a rocky sea-coast, recalls to me a fearful story of travel derived from that unpromising narrator of such stories, a parliamentary blue-book. A convict is its chief figure, and this man escapes with other prisoners from a penal settlement. It is an island, and they seize a boat, and get to the main land. Their way is by a rugged and precipitous sea-shore, and they have no earthly hope of ultimate escape, for the party of soldiers despatched by an easier course to cut them off, must inevitably arrive at their distant bourne long before them, and retake them if by any hazard they survive the horrors of the way. Famine, as they all must have foreseen, besets them early in their course. Some of the party die and are eaten ; some are murdered by the rest and eaten. This one awful creature eats his fill, and sustains his strength, and lives on to be recaptured and taken back. The unrelateable experiences through which he has passed have been so tremendous, that he is not hanged as he might be, but goes back to his old chained-gang work. A little time, and he tempts one other prisoner away, seizes another boat, and flies once more— necessarily in the old hopeless direction, for he can take no other. He is soon cut off, and met by the pursuing party face to face, upon the beach. He is alone. In his former journey he acquired an inappeasable relish for his dreadful food. He urged the new man away, expressly to kill him and eat him. In the pockets on one side of his coarse convict-dress, are portions of the man's body, on which he is regaling ; in the pockets on the other side is an untouched store of salted pork (stolen before he left the island) for which he has no appetite. He is taken back, and he is hanged. But I shall never see that sea-beach on the wall or in the fire, without him, solitary monster, eating as he prowls along, while the sea rages and rises at him.

Captain Bligh (a worse man to be entrusted with arbitrary power there could scarcely be) is handed over the side of the Bounty, and turned adrift on the wide ocean in an open boat, by order of Fletcher Christian, one of his officers, at this very minute. Another flash of my fire, and "Thursday

October Christian," five-and-twenty years of age, son of the dead and gone Fletcher by a savage mother, leaps aboard His Majesty's ship Briton, hove-to off Pitcairn's Island; says his simple grace before eating, in good English; and knows that a pretty little animal on board is called a dog, because in his childhood he had heard of such strange creatures from his father and the other mutineers, grown grey under the shade of the bread-fruit trees, speaking of their lost country far away.

See the Halsewell, East Indiaman outward bound, driving madly on a January night towards the rocks near Seacombe, on the island of Purbeck! The captain's two dear daughters are aboard, and five other ladies. The ship has been driving many hours, has seven feet of water in her hold, and her mainmast has been cut away. The description of her loss, familiar to me from my early boyhood, seems to be read aloud as she rushes to her destiny.

" About two in the morning of Friday the sixth of January, the ship still driving, and approaching very fast to the shore, Mr. Henry Meriton, the second mate, went again into the cuddy, where the captain then was. Another conversation taking place, Captain Pierce expressed extreme anxiety for the preservation of his beloved daughters, and earnestly asked the officer if he could devise any method of saving them. On his answering with great concern, that he feared it would be impossible, but that their only chance would be to wait for morning, the captain lifted up his hands in silent and distressful ejaculation.

" At this dreadful moment the ship struck, with such violence as to dash the heads of those standing in the cuddy against the deck above them, and the shock was accompanied by a shriek of horror that burst at one instant from every quarter of the ship.

" Many of the seamen, who had been remarkably inattentive and remiss in their duty during great part of the storm, now poured upon deck, where no exertions of the officers could keep them, while their assistance might have been useful. They had actually skulked in their hammocks, leaving the working of the pumps and other necessary labours to the officers of the ship and the soldiers, who had made uncommon exertions. Roused by a sense of their danger, the same seamen, at this moment, in frantic exclamations, demanded of heaven and their fellow-sufferers that succour which their own efforts, timely made, might possibly have procured.

" The ship continued to beat on the rocks ; and soon bilging, fell with her broadside towards the shore. When she struck, a number of the men climbed up the ensign-staff, under an apprehension of her immediately going to pieces.

" Mr. Meriton, at this crisis, offered to these unhappy beings the best advice which could be given ; he recommended that all should come to the side of the ship lying lowest on the rocks, and singly to take the opportunities which might then offer, of escaping to the shore.

" Having thus provided, to the utmost of his power, for the safety of the desponding crew, he returned to the round-house, where, by this time, all the passengers and most of the officers had assembled. The latter were employed in offering consolation to the unfortunate ladies ; and, with unparalleled magnanimity, suffering their compassion for the fair and amiable companions of their misfortunes to prevail over the sense of their own danger.

" In this charitable work of comfort Mr. Meriton now joined, by assurances of his opinion, that the ship would hold together till the morning, when all would be safe. Captain Pierce, observing one of the young gentlemen loud in his exclamations of terror, and frequently cry that the ship was parting, cheerfully bid him be quiet, remarking that though the ship should go to pieces, he would not, but would be safe enough.

" It is difficult to convey a correct idea of the scene of this deplorable catastrophe, without describing the place where it happened. The Halsewell struck on the rocks at a part of the shore where the cliff is of vast height, and rises almost perpendicular from its base. But at this particular spot, the foot of the cliff is excavated into a cavern of ten or twelve yards in depth, and of breadth equal to the length of a large ship. The sides of the cavern are so nearly upright, as to be of extremely difficult access ; and the bottom is strewed with sharp and uneven rocks, which seem, by some convulsion of the earth, to have been de-tached from its roof.

" The ship lay with her broadside opposite to the mouth of this cavern, with her whole length stretched almost from side to side of it. But when she struck, it was too dark for the unfortunate persons on board to discover the real magnitude of the danger, and the extreme horror of such a situation.

"In addition to the company already in the round-house, they had admitted three black women and two soldiers' wives; who, with the husband of one of them, had been allowed to come in, though the seamen, who had tumultuously demanded entrance to get the lights, had been opposed and kept out by Mr. Rogers and Mr. Brimer, the third and fifth mates. The numbers there were, therefore, now increased to near fifty. Captain Pierce sat on a chair, a cot, or some other moveable, with a daughter on each side, whom he alternately pressed to his affectionate breast. The rest of the melancholy assembly were seated on the deck, which was strewed with musical instruments, and the wreck of furniture and other articles.

"Here also Mr. Meriton, after having cut several wax-candles in pieces, and stuck them up in various parts of the round-house, and lighted up all the glass lanthorns he could find, took his seat, intending to wait the approach of dawn, and then assist the partners of his dangers to escape. But, observing that the poor ladies appeared parched and exhausted, he brought a basket of oranges and prevailed on some of them to refresh themselves by sucking a little of the juice. At this time they were all tolerably composed, except Miss Mansel, who was in hysteric fits on the floor of the deck of the round-house.

"But on Mr. Meriton's return to the company, he perceived a considerable alteration in the appearance of the ship; the sides were visibly giving way; the deck seemed to be lifting, and he discovered other strong indications that she could not hold much longer together. On this account, he attempted to go forward to look out, but immediately saw that the ship had separated in the middle, and that the forepart having changed its position, lay rather further out towards the sea. In such an emergency, when the next moment might plunge him into eternity, he determined to seize the present opportunity, and follow the example of the crew and the soldiers, who were now quitting the ship in numbers, and making their way to the shore, though quite ignorant of its nature and description.

"Among other expedients, the ensign-staff had been unshipped, and attempted to be laid between the ship's side and some of the rocks, but without success, for it snapped asunder before it reached them. However, by the light of a lanthorn, which a seaman handed through the skylight of the round-house to the deck, Mr. Meriton discovered a spar which appeared to be laid from the ship's side to the rocks, and on this spar he resolved to attempt his escape.

"Accordingly, lying down upon it, he thrust himself forward ; however, he soon found that it had no communication with the rock ; he reached the end of it, and then slipped off, receiving a very violent bruise in his fall, and before he could recover his legs, he was washed off by the surge. He now supported himself by swimming, until a returning wave dashed him against the back part of the cavern. Here he laid hold of a small projection in the rock, but was so much benumbed that he was on the point of quitting it, when a seaman, who had already gained a footing, extended his hand, and assisted him until he could secure himself a little on the rock ; from which he clambered on a shelf still higher, and out of the reach of the surf.

"Mr. Rogers, the third mate, remained with the captain and the unfortunate ladies and their companions nearly twenty minutes after Mr. Meriton had quitted the ship. Soon after the latter left the round-house, the captain asked what was become of him, to which Mr. Rogers replied, that he was gone on deck to see what could be done. After this, a heavy sea breaking over the ship, the ladies exclaimed, 'Oh poor Meriton ! he is drowned ; had he stayed with us he would have been safe !' and they all, particularly Miss Mary Pierce, expressed great concern at the apprehension of his loss.

"The sea was now breaking in at the fore part of the ship, and reached as far as the mainmast. Captain Pierce gave Mr. Rogers a nod, and they took a lamp and went together into the stern-gallery, where, after viewing the rocks for some time, Captain Pierce asked Mr. Rogers if he thought there was any possibility of saving the girls ; to which he replied, he feared there was none ; for they could only discover the black face of the perpendicular rock, and not the cavern which afforded shelter to those who escaped. They then returned to the round-house, where Mr. Rogers hung up the lamp, and Captain Pierce sat down between his two daughters.

"The sea continuing to break in very fast, Mr. Macmanus, a midshipman, and Mr. Schutz, a passenger, asked Mr. Rogers what they could do to escape. ' Follow me,' he replied, and they all went into the stern-gallery, and from thence to the upper-quarter-gallery on the poop. While there, a very heavy sea fell on board, and the round-house gave way; Mr. Rogers heard the ladies shriek at intervals, as if the water reached them; the noise of the sea at other times drowning their voices.

"Mr. Brimer had followed him to the poop, where they remained together about five minutes, when on the breaking of this heavy sea, they jointly seized a hen-coop. The same wave which proved fatal to some of those below, carried him and his companion to the rock, on which they were violently dashed and miserably bruised.

"Here on the rock were twenty-seven men; but it now being low water, and as they were convinced that on the flowing of the tide all must be washed off, many attempted to get to the back or the sides of the cavern, beyond the reach of the returning sea. Scarcely more than six, besides Mr. Rogers and Mr. Brimer, succeeded.

"Mr. Rogers, on gaining this station, was so nearly exhausted, that had his exertions been protracted only a few minutes longer, he must have sunk under them. He was now prevented from joining Mr. Meriton, by at least twenty men between them, none of whom could move, without the imminent peril of his life.

"They found that a very considerable number of the crew, seamen and soldiers, and some petty officers, were in the same situation as themselves, though many who had reached the rocks below perished in attempting to ascend. They could yet discern some part of the ship, and in their dreary station solaced themselves with the hopes of its remaining entire until day-break; for, in the midst of their own distress, the sufferings of the females on board affected them with the most poignant anguish; and every sea that broke inspired them with terror for their safety.

"But, alas, their apprehensions were too soon realised! Within a very few minutes of the time that Mr. Rogers gained the rock, an universal shriek, which long vibrated in their ears, in which the voice of female distress was lamentably distinguished, announced the dreadful catastrophe. In a few moments all was hushed, except the roaring of the winds and the dashing of the waves; the wreck was buried in the deep, and not an atom of it was ever afterwards seen."

The most beautiful and affecting incident I know, associated with a shipwreck, succeeds this dismal story for a winter night. The Grosvenor, East Indiaman, homeward bound, goes ashore on the coast of Caffraria. It is resolved that the officers, passengers, and crew, in number one hundred and thirty-five souls, shall endeavour to penetrate on foot, across trackless deserts, infested by wild beasts and cruel savages, to the Dutch settlements at the Cape of Good Hope. With this forlorn object before them, they finally separate into two parties—never more to meet on earth.

There is a solitary child among the passengers—a little boy of seven years old who has no relation there; and when the first party is moving away he cries after some member of it who has been kind to him. The crying of a child might be supposed to be a little thing to men in such great extremity; but it touches them, and he is immediately taken into that detachment.

From which time forth, this child is sublimely made a sacred charge. He is pushed, on a little raft, across broad rivers by the swimming sailors; they carry him by turns through the deep sand and long grass (he patiently walking at all other times); they share with him such putrid fish as they find to eat; they lie down and wait for him when the rough carpenter, who becomes his especial friend, lags behind. Beset by lions and tigers, by savages, by thirst, by hunger, by death in a crowd of ghastly shapes, they never— O Father of all mankind, thy name be blessed for it !—forget this child. The captain stops exhausted, and his faithful coxswain goes back and is seen to sit down by his side, and neither of the two shall be any more beheld until the great last day; but, as the rest go on for their lives, they take the child with them. The carpenter dies of poisonous berries eaten in starvation; and the steward, succeeding to the command of the party, succeeds to the sacred guardianship of the child.

God knows all he does for the poor baby; how he cheerfully carries him in his arms when he himself is weak and ill; how he feeds him when he himself is griped with want; how he folds his ragged jacket round him, lays his little

The Long Voyage

worn face with a woman's tenderness upon his sunburnt breast, soothes him in his sufferings, sings to him as he limps along, unmindful of his own parched and bleeding feet. Divided for a few days from the rest, they dig a grave in the sand and bury their good friend the cooper—these two companions alone in the wilderness—and then the time comes when they both are ill, and beg their wretched partners in despair, reduced and few in number now, to wait by them one day. They wait by them one day, they wait by them two days. On the morning of the third, they move very softly about, in making their preparations for the resumption of their journey; for the child is sleeping by the fire, and it is agreed with one consent that he shall not be disturbed until the last moment. The moment comes, the fire is dying—and the child is dead.

His faithful friend, the steward, lingers but a little while behind him. His grief is great, he staggers on for a few days, lies down in the desert, and dies. But he shall be re-united in his immortal spirit—who can doubt it!—with the child, where he and the poor carpenter shall be raised up with the words, "Inasmuch as ye have done it unto the least of these, ye have done it unto Me."

As I recall the dispersal and disappearance of nearly all the participators in this once famous shipwreck (a mere handful being recovered at last), and the legends that were long afterwards revived from time to time among the English officers at the Cape, of a white woman with an infant, said to have been seen weeping outside a savage hut far in the interior, who was whisperingly associated with the remembrance of the missing ladies saved from the wrecked vessel, and who was often sought but never found, thoughts of another kind of travel came into my mind.

Thoughts of a voyager unexpectedly summoned from home, who travelled a vast distance, and could never return. Thoughts of this unhappy wayfarer in the depths of his sorrow, in the bitterness of his anguish, in the helplessness of his self-reproach, in the desperation of his desire to set right what he had left wrong, and do what he had left undone.

For there were many many things he had neglected. Little matters while he was at home and surrounded by them, but things of mighty moment when he was at an immeasurable distance. There were many many blessings that he had inadequately felt, there were many trivial injuries that he had not forgiven, there was love that he had but poorly returned, there was friendship that he had too lightly prized : there were a million kind words that he might have spoken, a million kind looks that he might have given, uncountable slight easy deeds in which he might have been most truly great and good. O for a day (he would exclaim), for but one day to make amends ! But the sun never shone upon that happy day, and out of his remote captivity he never came.

Why does this traveller's fate obscure, on New Year's Eve, the other histories of travellers with which my mind was filled but now, and cast a solemn shadow over me ! Must I one day make his journey? Even so. Who shall say, that I may not then be tortured by such late regrets : that I may not then look from my exile on my empty place and undone work? I stand upon a sea-shore, where the waves are years. They break and fall, and I may little heed them ; but with every wave the sea is rising, and I know that it will float me on this traveller's voyage at last.

THE BEGGING-LETTER WRITER

THE amount of money he annually diverts from wholesome and useful purposes in the United Kingdom, would be a set-off against the Window Tax. He is one of the most shameless frauds and impositions of this time. In his idleness, his mendacity, and the immeasurable harm he does to the deserving,—dirtying the stream of true benevolence, and muddling the brains of foolish justices, with inability to distinguish between the base coin of distress, and the true currency we have always among us,—he is more worthy of Norfolk Island than three-fourths of the worst characters who are sent there. Under any rational system, he would have been sent there long ago.

I, the writer of this paper, have been, for some time, a chosen receiver of Begging Letters. For fourteen years, my house has been made as regular a Receiving House for such communications as any one of the great branch Post-Offices is for general correspondence. I ought to know something of the Begging-Letter Writer. He has besieged my door at all hours of the day and night; he has fought my servant; he has lain in ambush for me, going out and coming in; he has followed me out of town into the country; he has appeared at provincial hotels, where I have been staying for only a few hours; he has written to me from immense distances, when I have been out of England. He has fallen sick; he has died and been buried; he has come to life again, and again departed from this transitory scene: he has been his own son, his own mother, his own baby, his idiot brother, his uncle, his aunt, his aged grandfather. He has wanted a greatcoat, to go to India in; a pound to set him up in life for ever; a pair of boots to take him to the coast of China; a hat to get him into a permanent situation under Government. He has frequently been exactly seven-and-sixpence short of independence. He has had such openings at Liverpool—posts of great trust and confidence in merchants' houses, which nothing but seven-and-sixpence was wanting to him to secure—that I wonder he is not Mayor of that flourishing town at the present moment.

The natural phenomena of which he has been the victim, are of a most astounding nature. He has had two children who have never grown up ; who have never had anything to cover them at night ; who have been continually driving him mad, by asking in vain for food ; who have never come out of fevers and measles (which, I suppose, has accounted for his fuming his letters with tobacco smoke, as a disinfectant) ; who have never changed in the least degree through fourteen long revolving years. As to his wife, what that suffering woman has undergone, nobody knows. She has always been in an interesting situation through the same long period, and has never been confined yet. His devotion to her has been unceasing. He has never cared for himself ; *he* could have perished—he would rather, in short—but was it not his Christian duty as a man, a husband, and a father, to write begging letters when he looked at her ? (He has usually remarked that he would call in the evening for an answer to this question.)

He has been the sport of the strangest misfortunes. What his brother has done to him would have broken anybody else's heart. His brother went into business with him, and ran away with the money ; his brother got him to be security for an immense sum and left him to pay it ; his brother would have given him employment to the tune of hundreds a-year, if he would have consented to write letters on a Sunday ; his brother enunciated principles incompatible with his religious views, and he could not (in consequence) permit his brother to provide for him.. His landlord has never shown a spark of human feeling. When he put in that execution I don't know, but he has never taken it out. The broker's man has grown grey in possession. They will have to bury him some day.

He has been attached to every conceivable pursuit. He has been in the army, in the navy, in the church, in the law ; connected with the press, the fine arts, public institutions, every description and grade of business. He has been brought up as a gentleman ; he has been at every college in Oxford and Cambridge ; he can quote Latin in his letters (but generally mis-spells some minor English word) ; he can tell you what Shakespeare says about begging, better than you know it. It is to be observed, that in the midst of his afflictions he always reads the newspapers; and rounds off his appeal with some allusion, that may be supposed to be in my way, to the popular subject of the hour.

His life presents a series of inconsistencies. Sometimes he has never written such a letter before. He blushes with shame. That is the first time; that shall be the last. Don't answer it, and let it be understood that, then, he will kill himself quietly. Sometimes (and more frequently) he *has* written a few such letters. Then he encloses the answers, with an intimation that they are of inestimable value to him, and a request that they may be carefully returned. He is fond of enclosing something—verses, letters, pawn-brokers' duplicates, anything to necessitate an answer. He is very severe upon "the pampered minion of fortune," who refused him the half-sovereign referred to in the enclosure number two—but he knows me better.

He writes in a variety of styles; sometimes in low spirits; sometimes quite jocosely. When he is in low spirits he writes down-hill and repeats words—these little indications being expressive of the perturbation of his mind. When he is more vivacious, he is frank with me; he is quite the agreeable rattle. I know what human nature is,—who better? Well! He had a little money once, and he ran through it—as many men have done before him. He finds his old friends turn away from him now—many men have done that before him too! Shall he tell me why he writes to me? Because he has no kind of claim upon me. He puts it on that ground plainly; and begs to ask for the loan (as I know human nature) of two sovereigns, to be repaid next Tuesday six weeks, before twelve at noon.

Sometimes, when he is sure that I have found him out, and that there is no chance of money, he writes to inform me that I have got rid of him at last. He has enlisted into the Company's service, and is off directly—but he wants a cheese. He is informed by the serjeant that it is essential to his prospects in the regiment that he should take out a single Gloucester cheese, weighing from twelve to fifteen pounds. Eight or nine shillings would buy it. He does not ask for money, after what has passed; but if he calls at nine to-morrow morning may he hope to find a cheese? And is there anything he can do to show his gratitude in Bengal?

Once he wrote me rather a special letter, proposing relief in kind. He had got into a little trouble by leaving parcels of mud done up in brown paper, at people's houses, on pretence of being a Railway-Porter, in which character he received carriage money. This sportive fancy he expiated in the House of Correction. Not long after his release, and on a Sunday morning, he called with a letter (having first dusted himself all over), in which he gave me to understand that, being resolvod to earn an honest livelihood, he had been travelling about the country with a cart of crockery. That he had been doing pretty well until the day before, when his horse had dropped down dead near Chatham, in Kent. That this had reduced him to the unpleasant necessity of getting into the shafts himself, and drawing the cart of crockery to London—a somewhat exhausting pull of thirty miles. That he did not venture to ask again for money; but that if I would have the goodness *to leave him out a donkey,* he would call for the animal before breakfast!

At another time my friend (I am describing actual experiences) introduced himself as a literary gentleman in the last extremity of distress. He had had a play accepted at a certain Theatre—which was really open; its representation was delayed by the indisposition of a leading actor—who was really ill; and he and his were in a state of absolute starvation. If he made his necessities known to the Manager of the Theatre, he put it to me to say what kind of treatment he might expect? Well! we got over that difficulty to our mutual satisfaction. A little while afterwards he was in some other strait. I think Mrs. Southcote, his wife, was in extremity—and we adjusted that point too. A little while afterwards he had taken a new house, and was going headlong to ruin for want of a water-butt. I had my misgivings about the water-butt, and did not reply to that epistle. But a little while afterwards, I had reason to feel penitent for my neglect. He wrote me a few broken-hearted lines, informing me that the dear partner of his sorrows died in his arms last night at nine o'clock!

I despatched a trusty messenger to comfort the bereaved mourner and his poor children; but the messenger went so soon, that the play was not ready to be played out; my friend was not at home, and his wife was in a most delightful state of health. He was taken up by the Mendicity Society (informally it afterwards appeared), and I presented myself at a London Police-Office with my testimony against him. The Magistrate was wonderfully struck by his educational acquirements, deeply impressed by the excellence of his letters, exceedingly sorry to see a man of his attainments there, complimented him highly on his powers of composition, and was quite charmed to have the agreeable duty of discharging him. A collection was made for the "poor fellow," as he was called in the reports, and I left the court with a comfortable sense of being universally regarded as a sort of monster. Next day comes to me a friend of mine, the governor of a large prison. "Why did you ever go to the Police-Office against that man," says he, " without coming to me first? I know all about him and his frauds. He lodged in the house of one of my warders, at the very time when he first wrote to you; and then he was eating spring-lamb at eighteen-pence a pound, and early asparagus at I don't know how much a bundle!" On that very same day, and in that very same hour, my injured gentleman wrote a solemn address to me, demanding to know what compensation I proposed to make him for his having passed the night in a "loathsome dungeon." And next morning an Irish gentleman, a member of the same fraternity, who had read the case, and was very well persuaded I should be chary of going to that Police-Office again, positively refused to leave my door for less than a sovereign, and resolved to besiege me into compliance, literally "sat down" before it for ten mortal hours. The garrison being well provisioned, I remained within the walls; and he raised the siege at midnight with a prodigious alarum on the bell.

The Begging-Letter Writer often has an extensive circle of acquaintance. Whole pages of the "Court Guide" are ready to be references for him. Noblemen and gentlemen write to say there never was such a man for probity and virtue. They have known him time out of mind, and there is nothing they wouldn't do for him. Somehow, they don't give him that one pound ten he stands in need of; but perhaps it is not enough—they want to do more, and his modesty will not allow it. It is to be remarked of his trade that it is a very fascinating one. He never leaves it; and those who are near to him become smitten with a love of it, too, and sooner or later set up for themselves. He employs a messenger—man, woman, or child. That messenger is certain ultimately to become an independent Begging-Letter

Writer. His sons and daughters succeed to his calling, and write begging-letters when he is no more. He throws off the infection of begging-letter writing, like the contagion of disease. What Sydney Smith so happily called "the dangerous luxury of dishonesty" is more tempting, and more catching, it would seem, in this instance than in any other.

He always belongs to a Corresponding-Society of Begging-Letter Writers. Any one who will, may ascertain this fact. Give money to-day in recognition of a begging-letter, —no matter how unlike a common begging-letter,—and for the next fortnight you will have a rush of such communications. Steadily refuse to give; and the begging-letters become Angels' visits, until the Society is from some cause or other in a dull way of business, and may as well try you as anybody else. It is of little use inquiring into the Begging-Letter Writer's circumstances. He may be sometimes accidentally found out, as in the case already mentioned (though that was not the first inquiry made); but apparent misery is always a part of his trade, and real misery very often is, in the intervals of spring-lamb and early asparagus. It is naturally an incident of his dissipated and dishonest life.

That the calling is a successful one, and that large sums of money are gained by it, must be evident to anybody who reads the Police Reports of such cases. But prosecutions are of rare occurrence, relatively to the extent to which the trade is carried on. The cause of this is to be found (as no one knows better than the Begging-Letter Writer, for it is a part of his speculation) in the aversion people feel to exhibit themselves as having been imposed upon, or as having weakly gratified their consciences with a lazy, flimsy substitute for the noblest of all virtues. There is a man at large, at the moment when this paper is preparing for the press (on the 29th of April, 1850), and never once taken up yet, who, within these twelve months, has been probably the most audacious and the most successful swindler that even this trade has ever known. There has been something singularly base in this fellow's proceedings; it has been his business to write to all sorts and conditions of people, in the names of persons of high reputation and unblemished honour, professing to be in distress—the general admiration and respect for whom has ensured a ready and generous reply.

Now, in the hope that the results of the real experience of a real person may do something more to induce reflection on this subject than any abstract treatise—and with a personal knowledge of the extent to which the Begging-Letter Trade has been carried on for some time, and has been for some time constantly increasing—the writer of this paper entreats the attention of his readers to a few concluding words. His experience is a type of the experience of many ; some on a smaller, some on an infinitely larger scale. All may judge of the soundness or unsoundness of his conclusions from it.

Long doubtful of the efficacy of such assistance in any case whatever, and able to recall but .one, within his whole individual knowledge, in which he had the least after-reason to suppose that any good was done by it, he was led, last autumn, into some serious considerations. The begging-letters flying about by every post made it perfectly manifest that a set of lazy vagabonds were interposed between the general desire to do something to relieve the sickness and misery under which the poor were suffering, and the suffering poor themselves. That many who sought to do some little to repair the social wrongs, inflicted in the way of preventible sickness and death upon the poor, were strengthening those wrongs, however innocently, by wasting money on pestilent knaves cumbering society. That imagination,—soberly following one of these knaves into his life of punishment in jail, and comparing it with the life of one of these poor in a cholera-stricken alley, or one of the children of one of these poor, soothed in its dying hour by the late lamented Mr. Drouet,—contemplated a grim farce, impossible to be 'presented very much longer before God or man. That the crowning miracle of all the miracles summed up in the New Testament, after the miracle of the blind seeing, and the lame walking, and the restoration of the dead to life, was the miracle that the poor had the Gospel preached to them. That while the poor were unnaturally and unnecessarily cut off by the thousand, in the prematurity of their age, or in the rottenness of their youth—for of flower or blossom such youth has none—the Gospel was NOT preached to them, saving in hollow and unmeaning voices. That of all wrongs, this was the first mighty wrong the Pestilence warned us to set right. And that no Post-Office Order to any amount, given to a Begging-Letter Writer for the quieting of an uneasy breast, would be presentable on the Last Great Day as anything towards it.

The poor never write these letters. Nothing could be more unlike their habits. The writers are public robbers; and we who support them are parties to their depredations. They trade upon every circumstance within their knowledge that affects us, public or private, joyful or sorrowful; they pervert the lessons of our lives; they change what ought to be our strength and virtue into weakness and encouragement of vice. There is a plain remedy, and it is in our own hands. We must resolve, at any sacrifice of feeling, to be deaf to such appeals, and crush the trade.

There are degrees in murder. Life must be held sacred among us in more ways than one—sacred, not merely from the murderous weapon, or the subtle poison, or the cruel blow, but sacred from preventible diseases, distortions, and pains. That is the first great end we have to set against this miserable imposition. Physical life respected, moral life comes next. What will not content a Begging-Letter Writer for a week, would educate a score of children for a year. Let us give all we can; let us give more than ever. Let us do all we can; let us do more than ever. But let us give, and do, with a high purpose; not to endow the scum of the earth, to its own greater corruption, with the offals of our duty.

A CHILD'S DREAM OF A STAR

THERE was once a child, and he strolled about a good deal, and thought of a number of things. He had a sister, who was a child too, and his constant companion. These two used to wonder all day long. They wondered at the beauty of the flowers; they wondered at the height and blueness of the sky; they wondered at the depth of the bright water; they wondered at the goodness and the power of GOD who made the lovely world.

They used to say to one another, sometimes, Supposing all the children upon earth were to die, would the flowers, and the water, and the sky be sorry? They believed they would be sorry. For, said they, the buds are the children of the flowers, and the little playful streams that gambol down the hill-sides are the children of the water; and the smallest bright specks playing at hide and seek in the sky all night, must surely be the children of the stars; and they would all be grieved to see their playmates, the children of men, no more.

There was one clear shining star that used to come out in the sky before the rest, near the church spire, above the graves. It was larger and beautiful, they thought, than all the others, and every night they watched for it, standing hand in hand at a window. Whoever saw it first cried out, "I see the star!" And often they cried out both together, knowing so well when it would rise, and where. So they grew to be such friends with it, that, before lying down in their beds, they always looked out once again, to bid it good night; and when they were turning round to sleep, they used to say, " God bless the star! "

But while she was still very young, oh very very young, the sister drooped, and came to be so weak that she could no longer stand in the window at night; and then the child looked sadly out by himself, and when he saw the star turned round and said to the patient pale face on the bed,

" I see the star ! " and then a smile would come upon the
face, and a little weak voice used to say, " God bless my
brother and the star ! "

And so the time came all too soon ! when the child
looked out alone, and when there was no face on the bed ;
and when there was a little grave among the graves, not
there before ; and when the star made long rays down
towards him, as he saw it through his tears.

Now, these rays were so bright, and they seemed to make
such a shining way from earth to Heaven, that when the
child went to his solitary bed, he dreamed about the star ;
and dreamed that, lying where he was, he saw a train of
people taken up that sparkling road by angels. And the
star, opening, showed him a great world of light, where
many more such angels waited to receive them.

All these angels, who were waiting, turned their beaming
eyes upon the people who were carried up into the star ; and
some came out from the long rows in which they stood, and
fell upon the people's necks, and kissed them tenderly, and
went away with them down avenues of light, and were so
happy in their company, that lying in his bed he wept for
joy.

But there were many angels who did not go with them,
and among them one he knew. The patient face that once
had lain upon the bed was glorified and radiant, but his
heart found out his sister among all the host.

His sister's angel lingered near the entrance of the star,
and said to the leader among those who had brought the
people thither :

" Is my brother come ? "

And he said " No."

She was turning hopefully away, when the child stretched
out his arms, and cried, " O, sister, I am here ! Take me ! "
and then she turned her beaming eyes upon him, and it was
night ; and the star was shining into the room, making
long rays down towards him as he saw it through his
tears.

From that hour forth, the child looked out upon the star
as on the home he was to go to, when his time should
come ; and he thought that he did not belong to the earth
alone, but to the star too, because of his sister's angel gone
before.

There was a baby born to be a brother to the child ;

and while he was so little that he never yet had spoken word, he stretched his tiny form out on his bed, and died.

Again the child dreamed of the open star, and of the company of angels, and the train of people, and the rows of angels with their beaming eyes all turned upon those people's faces.

Said his sister's angel to the leader:

"Is my brother come?"

And he said, "Not that one, but another."

As the child beheld his brother's angel in her arms, he cried, "O, sister, I am here! Take me!" And she turned and smiled upon him, and the star was shining.

He grew to be a young man, and was busy at his books when an old servant came to him and said:

"Thy mother is no more. I bring her blessing on her darling son!"

Again at night he saw the star, and all that former company. Said his sister's angel to the leader:

"Is my brother come?"

And he said, "Thy mother!"

A mighty cry of joy went forth through all the star, because the mother was re-united to her two children. And he stretched out his arms and cried, "O, mother, sister, and brother, I am here! Take me!" And they answered him, "Not yet," and the star was shining.

He grew to be a man, whose hair was turning grey, and he was sitting in his chair by the fireside, heavy with grief, and with his face bedewed with tears, when the star opened once again.

Said his sister's angel to the leader: "Is my brother come?"

And he said, "Nay, but his maiden daughter."

And the man who had been the child saw his daughter, newly lost to him, a celestial creature among those three, and he said, "My daughter's head is on my sister's bosom, and her arm is around my mother's neck, and at her feet there is the baby of old time, and I can bear the parting from her, God be praised!"

And the star was shining.

Thus the child came to be an old man, and his once smooth face was wrinkled, and his steps were slow and feeble, and his back was bent. And one night as he lay upon his bed, his children standing round, he cried, as he had cried so long ago :

"I see the star!"

They whispered one another, "He is dying."

And he said, "I am. My age is falling from me like a garment, and I move towards the star as a child. And O, my Father, now I thank thee that it has so often opened, to receive those dear ones who await me!"

And the star was shining ; and it shines upon his grave.

OUR ENGLISH WATERING-PLACE

In the Autumn-time of the year, when the great metropolis is so much hotter, so much noisier, so much more dusty or so much more water-carted, so much more crowded, so much more disturbing and distracting in all respects, than it usually is, a quiet sea-beach becomes indeed a blessed spot. Half awake and half asleep, this idle morning in our sunny window on the edge of a chalk-cliff in the old-fashioned watering-place to which we are a faithful resorter, we feel a lazy inclination to sketch its picture.

The place seems to respond. Sky, sea, beach, and village, lie as still before us as if they were sitting for the picture. It is dead low-water. A ripple plays among the ripening corn upon the cliff, as if it were faintly trying from recollection to imitate the sea; and the world of butterflies hovering over the crop of radish-seed are as restless in their little way as the gulls are in their larger manner when the wind blows. But the ocean lies winking in the sunlight like a drowsy lion—its glassy waters scarcely curve upon the shore—the fishing-boats in the tiny harbour are all stranded in the mud —our two colliers (our watering-place has a maritime trade employing that amount of shipping) have not an inch of water within a quarter of a mile of them, and turn, exhausted, on their sides, like faint fish of an antediluvian species. Rusty cables and chains, ropes and rings, undermost parts of posts and piles and confused timber-defences against the waves, lie strewn about, in a brown litter of tangled sea-weed and fallen cliff which looks as if a family of giants had been making tea here for ages, and had observed an untidy custom of throwing their tea-leaves on the shore.

In truth, our watering-place itself has been left somewhat high and dry by the tide of years. Concerned as we are for its honour, we must reluctantly admit that the time when this pretty little semi-circular sweep of houses tapering off at the end of the wooden pier into a point in the sea, was a gay place, and when the lighthouse overlooking it shone at daybreak on company dispersing from public balls, is but dimly traditional now. There is a bleak chamber in our watering-place which is yet called the Assembly " Rooms," and understood to be available on hire for balls or concerts ; and, some few seasons since, an ancient little gentleman came down and stayed at the hotel, who said that he had danced there, in bygone ages, with the Honourable Miss Peepy, well known to have been the Beauty of her day and the cruel occasion of innumerable duels. But he was so old and shrivelled, and so very rheumatic in the legs, that it demanded more imagination than our watering-place can usually muster, to believe him ; therefore, except the Master of the " Rooms " (who to this hour wears knee-breeches, and who confirmed the statement with tears in his eyes), nobody did believe in the little lame old gentleman, or even in the Honourable Miss Peepy, long deceased.

As to subscription balls in the Assembly Rooms of our watering-place now red-hot cannon balls are less improbable. Sometimes, a misguided wanderer of a Ventriloquist, or an Infant Phenomenon, or a Juggler, or somebody with an Orrery that is several stars behind the time, takes the place for a night, and issues bills with the name of his last town lined out, and the name of ours ignominiously written in, but you may be sure this never happens twice to the same unfortunate person. On such occasions the discoloured old Billiard Table that is seldom played at (unless the ghost of the Honourable Miss Peepy plays at pool with other ghosts) is pushed into a corner, and benches are solemnly constituted into front seats, back seats, and reserved seats—which are much the same after you have paid—and a few dull candles are lighted—wind permitting—and the performer and the scanty audience play out a short match which shall make the other most low-spirited—which is usually a drawn game. After that the performer instantly departs with maledictory expressions, and is never heard of more.

But the most wonderful feature of our Assembly Rooms, is, that an annual sale of " Fancy and other China," is announced here with mysterious constancy and perseverance. Where the china comes from, where it goes to, why it is annually put up to auction when nobody ever thinks of bidding for it, how it comes to pass that it is always the same china, whether it would not have been cheaper, with the sea at hand, to have thrown it away, say in eighteen hundred and thirty, are standing enigmas. Every year the bills come out, every year the Master of the Rooms gets into a little pulpit on a table, and offers it for sale, every year nobody buys it, every year it is put away somewhere till next year, when it appears again as if the whole thing were a new idea. We have a faint remembrance of an unearthly collection of clocks, purporting to be the work of Parisian and Genevese artists—chiefly bilious-faced clocks, supported on sickly white crutches, with their pendulums dangling like lame legs—to which a similar course of events occurred for several years, until they seemed to lapse away, of mere imbecility.

Attached to our Assembly Rooms is a library. There is a wheel of fortune in it, but it is rusty and dusty, and never turns. A large doll, with moveable eyes, was put up to be raffled for, by five-and-twenty members at two shillings, seven years ago this autumn, and the list is not full yet. We are rather sanguine, now, that the raffle will come off next year. We think so, because we only want nine members, and should only want eight, but for number two having grown up since her name was entered, and withdrawn it when she was married. Down the street, there is a toy-ship of considerable burden, in the same condition. Two of the boys who were entered for that raffle have gone to India in real ships, since; and one was shot, and died in the arms of his sister's lover, by whom he sent his last words home.

This is the library for the Minerva Press. If you want that kind of reading, come to our watering-place. The leaves of the romances, reduced to a condition very like curl-paper, are thickly studded with notes in pencil: sometimes complimentary, sometimes jocose. Some of these commentators, like commentators in a more extensive way, quarrel with one another. One young gentleman who sarcastically writes " Oh ! ! ! " after every sentimental passage, is pursued through his literary career by another, who writes " Insulting Beast!" Miss Julia Mills has read the whole collection of these books. She has left marginal notes on the pages, as " Is not this truly touching ? J. M." " How thrilling ! J. M." " Entranced here by the Magician's potent spell. J. M." She has also italicised her favourite traits in the description of the hero, as " his hair, which was *dark* and *wavy*, clustered in *rich profusion* around a *marble brow*, whose lofty paleness bespoke the intellect within." It reminds her of another

hero. She adds, "How like B. L. Can this be mere coincidence? J. M."

You would hardly guess which is the main street of our
watering-place, but you may know it by its being always
stopped up with donkey-chaises. Whenever you come here,
and see harnessed donkeys eating clover out of barrows
drawn completely across a narrow thoroughfare, you may
be quite sure you are in our High Street. Our Police you
may know by his uniform, likewise by his never on any
account interfering with anybody—especially the tramps
and vagabonds. In our fancy shops we have a capital
collection of damaged goods, among which the flies of countless summers "have been roaming." We are great in
obsolete seals, and in faded pin-cushions, and in rickety
camp-stools, and in exploded cutlery, and in miniature
vessels, and in stunted little telescopes, and in objects made
of shells that pretend not to be shells. Diminutive spades,
barrows, and baskets, are our principal articles of commerce ;
but even they don't look quite new somehow. They always
seem to have been offered and refused somewhere else, before
they came down to our watering-place.

Yet it must not be supposed that our watering-place is
an empty place, deserted by all visitors except a few staunch
persons of approved fidelity. On the contrary, the chances
are that if you came down here in August or September,
you wouldn't find a house to lay your head in. As to
finding either house or lodging of which you could reduce
the terms, you could scarcely engage in a more hopeless
pursuit. For all this, you are to observe that every season
is the worst season ever known, and that the householding
population of our watering-place are ruined regularly every
autumn. They are like the farmers, in regard that it is
surprising how much ruin they will bear. We have an
excellent hotel—capital baths, warm, cold, and shower—
firstrate bathing-machines—and as good butchers, bakers,
and grocers, as heart could desire. They all do business,
it is to be presumed, from motives of philanthropy—but it is
quite certain that they are all being ruined. Their interest
in strangers, and their politeness under ruin, bespeak their
amiable nature. You would say so, if you only saw the
baker helping a new comer to find suitable apartments.

So far from being at a discount as to company, we are in
fact what would be popularly called rather a nobby place.

Some tip-top " Nobbs " come down occasionally—even Dukes
and Duchesses. We have known such carriages to blaze
among the donkey-chaises, as made beholders wink. Attendant on these equipages come resplendent creatures in plush
and powder, who are sure to be stricken disgusted with the
indifferent accommodation of our watering-place, and who,
of an evening (particularly when it rains), may be seen very
much out of drawing, in rooms far too small for their fine
figures, looking discontentedly out of little back windows
into bye-streets. The lords and ladies get on well enough
and quite good-humouredly : but if you want to see the
gorgeous phenomena who wait upon them at a perfect non-
plus, you should come and look at the resplendent creatures
with little back parlours for servants' halls, and turn-up
bedsteads to sleep in, at our watering-place. You have no
idea how they take it to heart.

We have a pier—a queer old wooden pier, fortunately
without the slightest pretensions to architecture, and very
picturesque in consequence. Boats are hauled up upon it,
ropes are coiled all over it ; lobster-pots, nets, masts, oars,
spars, sails, ballast, and rickety capstans, make a perfect
labyrinth of it. For ever hovering about this pier, with
their hands in their pockets, or leaning over the rough
bulwark it opposes to the sea, gazing through telescopes
which they carry about in the same profound receptacles,
are the Boatmen of our watering-place. Looking at them,
you would say that surely these must be the laziest boatmen
in the world. They lounge about, in obstinate and inflexible
pantaloons that are apparently made of wood, the whole
season through. Whether talking together about the shipping in the Channel, or gruffly unbending over mugs of beer
at the public-house, you would consider them the slowest
of men. The chances are a thousand to one that you might
stay here for ten seasons, and never see a boatman in a
hurry. A certain expression about his loose hands, when
they are not in his pockets, as if he were carrying a considerable lump of iron in each, without any inconvenience, suggests strength, but he never seems to use it. He has the
appearance of perpetually strolling—running is too inappropriate a word to be thought of—to seed. The only
subject on which he seems to feel any approach to enthusiasm, is pitch. He pitches everything he can lay hold of,—
the pier, the palings, his boat, his house,—when there is

nothing else left he turns to and even pitches his hat, or his rough-weather clothing. Do not judge him by deceitful appearances. These are among the bravest and most skilful mariners that exist. Let a gale arise and swell into a storm, let a sea run that might appal the stoutest heart that ever beat, let the Light-boat on these dangerous sands throw up a rocket in the night, or let them hear through the angry roar the signal-guns of a ship in distress, and these men spring up into activity so dauntless, so valiant, and heroic, that the world cannot surpass it. Cavillers may object that they chiefly live upon the salvage of valuable cargoes. So they do, and God knows it is no great living that they get out of the deadly risks they run. But put that hope of gain aside. Let these rough fellows be asked, in any storm, who volunteers for the life-boat to save some perishing souls, as poor and empty-handed as themselves, whose lives the perfection of human reason does not rate at the value of a farthing each; and that boat will be manned, as surely and as cheerfully, as if a thousand pounds were told down on the weather-beaten pier. For this, and for the recollection of their comrades whom we have known, whom the raging sea has engulfed before their children's eyes in such brave efforts, whom the secret sand has buried, we hold the boatmen of our watering-place in our love and honour, and are tender of the fame they well deserve.

So many children are brought down to our watering-place that, when they are not out of doors, as they usually are in fine weather, it is wonderful where they are put: the whole village seeming much too small to hold them under cover. In the afternoons, you see no end of salt and sandy little boots drying on upper window-sills. At bathing-time in the morning, the little bay re-echoes with every shrill variety of shriek and splash—after which, if the weather be at all fresh, the sands teem with small blue mottled legs. The sands are the children's great resort. They cluster there, like ants: so busy burying their particular friends, and making castles with infinite labour which the next tide overthrows, that it is curious to consider how their play, to the music of the sea, foreshadows the realities of their after lives.

It is curious, too, to observe a natural ease of approach that there seems to be between the children and the boatmen. They mutually make acquaintance, and take indi-

vidual likings, without any help. You will come upon one
of those slow heavy fellows sitting down patiently mending
a little ship for a mite of a boy, whom he could crush to
death by throwing his lightest pair of trousers on him. You
will be sensible of the oddest contrast between the smooth
little creature, and the rough man who seems to be carved
out of hard-grained wood—between the delicate hand ex-
pectantly held out, and the immense thumb and finger that
can hardly feel the rigging of thread they mend—between
the small voice and the gruff growl—and yet there is a
natural propriety in the companionship : always to be noted
in confidence between a child and a person who has any
merit of reality and genuineness : which is admirably
pleasant.

We have a preventive station at our watering-place, and
much the same thing may be observed—in a lesser degree,
because of their official character—of the coast blockade ;
a steady, trusty, well-conditioned, well-conducted set of men,
with no misgiving about looking you full in the face, and
with a quiet thorough-going way of passing along to their
duty at night, carrying huge sou'-wester clothing in reserve,
that is fraught with all good prepossession. They are handy
fellows—neat about their houses—industrious at gardening
—would get on with their wives, one thinks, in a desert
island—and people it, too, soon.

As to the naval officer of the station, with his hearty
fresh face, and his blue eye that has pierced all kinds of
weather, it warms our hearts when he comes into church
on a Sunday, with that bright mixture of blue coat, buff
waistcoat, black neckerchief, and gold epaulette, that is
associated in the minds of all Englishmen with brave, unpretending, cordial, national service. We like to look at
him in his Sunday state ; and if we were First Lord (really
possessing the indispensable qualification for the office of
knowing nothing whatever about the sea), we would give
him a ship to-morrow.

We have a church, by-the-by, of course—a hideous temple
of flint, like a great petrified haystack. Our chief clerical
dignitary, who, to his honour, has done much for education
both in time and money, and has established excellent
schools, is a sound, shrewd, healthy gentleman, who has
got into little occasional difficulties with the neighbouring
farmers, but has had a pestilent trick of being right. Under

a new regulation, he has yielded the church of our watering-place to another clergyman. Upon the whole we get on in church well. We are a little bilious sometimes, about these days of fraternisation, and about nations arriving at a new and more unprejudiced knowledge of each other (which our Christianity don't quite approve), but it soon goes off, and then we get on very well.

There are two dissenting chapels, besides, in our small watering-place; being in about the proportion of a hundred and twenty guns to a yacht. But the dissension that has torn us lately, has not been a religious one. It has arisen on the novel question of Gas. Our watering-place has been convulsed by the agitation, Gas or No Gas. It was never reasoned why No Gas, but there was a great No Gas party. Broadsides were printed and stuck about—a startling circumstance in our watering-place. The No Gas party rested content with chalking ".No Gas!" and "Down with Gas!" and other such angry war-whoops, on the few back gates and scraps of wall which the limits of our watering-place afford; but the Gas party printed and posted bills, wherein they took the high ground of proclaiming against the No Gas party, that it was said Let there be light and there was light; and that not to have light (that is gas-light) in our watering-place, was to contravene the great decree. Whether by these thunderbolts or not, the No Gas party were defeated; and in this present season we have had our handful of shops illuminated for the first time. Such of the No Gas party, however, as have got shops, remain in opposition and burn tallow—exhibiting in their windows the very picture of the sulkiness that punishes itself, and a new illustration of the old adage about cutting off your nose to be revenged on your face, in cutting off their gas to be revenged on their business.

Other population than we have indicated, our watering-place has none. There are a few old used-up boatmen who creep about in the sunlight with the help of sticks, and there is a poor imbecile shoemaker who wanders his lonely life away among the rocks, as if he were looking for his reason—which he will never find. Sojourners in neighbouring watering-places come occasionally in flys to stare at us, and drive away again as if they thought us very dull; Italian boys come, Punch comes, the Fantoccini come, the Tumblers come, the Ethiopians come; Glee-singers come at night, and hum and vibrate (not always melodiously) under our windows. But they all go soon, and leave us to ourselves again. We once had a travelling Circus and Wombwell's Menagerie at the same time. They both know better than ever to try it again; and the Menagerie had nearly razed us from the face of the earth in getting the elephant away—his caravan was so large, and the watering-place so small. We have a fine sea, wholesome for all people; profitable for the body, profitable for the mind. The poet's words are sometimes on its awful lips:

> And the stately ships go on
> To their haven under the hill;
> But O for the touch of a vanish'd hand,
> And the sound of a voice that is still!
>
> Break, break, break,
> At the foot of thy crags, O sea!
> But the tender grace of a day that is dead
> Will never come back to me.

Yet it is not always so, for the speech of the sea is various, and wants not abundant resource of cheerfulness, hope, and lusty encouragement. And since I have been idling at the window here, the tide has risen. The boats are dancing on the bubbling water; the colliers are afloat again; the white bordered waves rush in; the children

> Do chase the ebbing Neptune, and do fly him
> When he comes back;

the radiant sails are gliding past the shore, and shining on the far horizon; all the sea is sparkling, heaving, swelling up with life and beauty, this bright morning.

OUR FRENCH WATERING-PLACE

HAVING earned by many years of fidelity, the right to be sometimes inconstant to our English watering-place, we have dallied for two or three seasons with a French watering-place : once solely known to us as a town with a very long street, beginning with an abattoir and ending with a steam-boat, which it seemed our fate to behold only at daybreak on winter mornings, when (in the days before continental railroads), just sufficiently awake to know that we were most uncomfortably asleep, it was our destiny always to clatter through it, in the coupé of the diligence from Paris, with a sea of mud behind us, and a sea of tumbling waves before. In relation to which latter monster, our mind's eye now recalls a worthy Frenchman in a seal-skin cap with a braided hood over it, once our travelling companion in the coupé aforesaid, who, waking up with a pale and crumpled visage, and looking ruefully out at the grim row of breakers enjoying themselves fanatically on an instrument of torture called "the Bar," inquired of us whether we were ever sick at sea? Both to prepare his mind for the abject creature we were presently to become, and also to afford him consolation, we replied, "Sir, your servant is always sick when it is possible to be so." He returned, altogether uncheered by the bright example, "Ah, Heaven, but I am always sick, even when it is *im*possible to be so."

The means of communication between the French capital and our French watering-place are wholly changed since those days ; but the Channel remains unbridged as yet, and the old floundering and knocking about go on there. It must be confessed that saving in reasonable (and therefore rare) sea-weather, the act of arrival at our French watering-place from England is difficult to be achieved with dignity. Several little circumstances combine to render the visitor an object of humiliation. In the first place, the steamer no sooner touches the port, than all the passengers fall into captivity : being boarded by an overpowering force of Custom-house officers, and marched into a gloomy dungeon.

In the second place, the road to this dungeon is fenced off with ropes breast-high, and outside those ropes all the English in the place who have lately been sea-sick and are now well, assemble in their best clothes to enjoy the degradation of their dilapidated fellow-creatures. " Oh, my gracious ! how ill this one has been ! " " Here's a damp one coming next ! " " *Here's* a pale one ! " " Oh ! Ain't he green in the face, this next one ! " Even we ourself (not deficient in natural dignity) have a lively remembrance of staggering up this detested lane one September day in a gale of wind, when we were received like an irresistible comic actor, with a burst of laughter and applause, occasioned by the extreme imbecility of our legs.

We were coming to the third place. In the third place, the captives, being shut up in the gloomy dungeon, are strained, two or three at a time, into an inner cell, to be examined as to passports ; and across the doorway of communication, stands a military creature making a bar of his arm. Two ideas are generally present to the British mind during these ceremonies ; first, that it is necessary to make for the cell with violent struggles, as if it were a life-boat and the dungeon a ship going down ; secondly, that the military creature's arm is a national affront, which the government at home ought instantly to " take up." The British mind and body becoming heated by these fantasies, delirious answers are made to inquiries, and extravagant actions performed. Thus, Johnson persists in giving Johnson as his baptismal name, and substituting for his ancestral designation the national " Dam ! " Neither can he by any means be brought to recognise the distinction between a portmanteau-key and a passport, but will obstinately persevere in tendering the one when asked for the other. This brings him to the fourth place, in a state of mere idiotcy ; and when he is, in the fourth place, cast out at a little door into a howling wilderness of touters, he becomes a lunatic with wild eyes and floating hair until rescued and soothed. If friendless and unrescued, he is generally put into a railway omnibus and taken to Paris.

But our French watering-place, when it is once got into, is a very enjoyable place. It has a varied and beautiful country around it, and many characteristic and agreeable things within it. To be sure, it might have fewer bad smells and less decaying refuse, and it might be better drained, and

much cleaner in many parts, and therefore infinitely more
healthy.   Still, it is a bright, airy, pleasant, cheerful town;
and if you were to walk down either of its three well-paved
main streets, towards five o'clock in the afternoon, when
delicate odours of cookery fill the air, and its hotel windows
(it is full of hotels) give glimpses of long tables set out for
dinner, and made to look sumptuous by the aid of napkins
folded fan-wise, you would rightly judge it to be an uncommonly good town to eat and drink in.

We have an old walled town, rich in cool public wells of
water, on the top of a hill within and above the present
business-town; and if it were some hundreds of miles further
from England, instead of being, on a clear day, within sight
of the grass growing in the crevices of the chalk-cliffs of
Dover, you would long ago have been bored to death about
that town.   It is more picturesque and quaint than half the
innocent places which tourists, following their leader like
sheep, have made impostors of.   To say nothing of its houses
with grave courtyards, its queer by-corners, and its many-
windowed streets white and quiet in the sunlight, there is an
ancient belfry in it that would have been in all the Annuals
and Albums, going and gone, these hundred years, if it had
but been more expensive to get at.   Happily it has escaped
so well, being only in our French watering-place, that you
may like it of your own accord in a natural manner, without
being required to go into convulsions about it.   We regard
it as one of the later blessings of our life, that BILKINS, the
only authority on Taste, never took any notice that we can
find out, of our French watering-place.   Bilkins never wrote
about it, never pointed out anything to be seen in it, never
measured anything in it, always left it alone.   For which
relief, Heaven bless the town and the memory of the immortal Bilkins likewise !

There is a charming walk, arched and shaded by trees, on
the old walls that form the four sides of this High Town,
whence you get glimpses of the streets below, and changing
views of the other town and of the river, and of the hills and
of the sea.   It is made more agreeable and peculiar by some
of the solemn houses that are rooted in the deep streets
below, bursting into a fresher existence a-top, and having
doors and windows, and even gardens, on these ramparts.   A
child going in at the courtyard gate of one of these houses,
climbing up the many stairs, and coming out at the fourth-

floor window, might conceive himself another Jack, alighting on enchanted ground from another bean-stalk. It is a place wonderfully populous in children ; English children, with governesses reading novels as they walk down the shady lanes of trees, or nursemaids interchanging gossip on the seats ; French children with their smiling bonnes in snow-white caps, and themselves—if little boys—in straw head-gear like beehives, work-baskets and church hassocks. Three years ago, there were three weazen old men, one bearing a frayed red ribbon in his threadbare button-hole, always to be found walking together among these children, before dinner-time. If they walked for an appetite, they doubtless lived en pension—were contracted for—otherwise their poverty would have made it a rash action. They were stooping, blear-eyed, dull old men, slip-shod and shabby, in long-skirted short-waisted coats and meagre trousers, and yet with a ghost of gentility hovering in their company. They spoke little to each other, and looked as if they might have been politically discontented if they had had vitality enough. Once, we overheard red-ribbon feebly complain to the other two that somebody, or something, was "a Robber;" and then they all three set their mouths so that they would have ground their teeth if they had had any. The ensuing winter gathered red-ribbon unto the great company of faded ribbons, and next year the remaining two were there—getting themselves entangled with hoops and dolls—familiar mysteries to the children—probably in the eyes of most of them, harmless creatures who had never been like children, and whom children could never be like. Another winter came, and another old man went, and so, this present year, the last of the triumvirate left off walking —it was no good, now—and sat by himself on a little solitary bench, with the hoops and the dolls as lively as ever all about him.

In the Place d'Armes of this town, a little decayed market is held, which seems to slip through the old gateway, like water, and go rippling down the hill, to mingle with the murmuring market in the lower town, and get lost in its movement and bustle. It is very agreeable on an idle summer morning to pursue this market-stream from the hill-top. It begins, dozingly and dully, with a few sacks of corn ; starts into a surprising collection of boots and shoes ; goes brawling down the hill in a diversified channel of old

cordage, old iron, old crockery, old clothes, civil and military, old rags, new cotton goods, flaming prints of saints,
little looking-glasses, and incalculable lengths of tape;
dives into a backway, keeping out of sight for a little while,
as streams will, or only sparkling for a moment in the
shape of a market drinking-shop; and suddenly reappears
behind the great church, shooting itself into a bright confusion of white-capped women and blue-bloused men,
poultry, vegetables, fruits, flowers, pots, pans, praying-
chairs, soldiers, country butter, umbrellas and other sun-
shades, girl-porters waiting to be hired with baskets at their
backs, and one weazen little old man in a cocked hat, wearing a cuirass of drinking-glasses and carrying on his
shoulder a crimson temple fluttering with flags, like a glorified pavior's rammer without the handle, who rings a little
bell in all parts of the scene, and cries his cooling drink
Hola, Hola, Ho-o-o! in a shrill cracked voice that somehow
makes itself heard, above all the chaffering and vending
hum. Early in the afternoon, the whole course of the
stream is dry. The praying-chairs are put back in the
church, the umbrellas are folded up, the unsold goods are
carried away, the stalls and stands disappear, the square is
swept, the hackney coaches lounge there to be hired, and on
all the country roads (if you walk about, as much as we do)
you will see the peasant women, always neatly and comfortably dressed, riding home, with the pleasantest saddle-furni-
ture of clean milk-pails, bright butter-kegs, and the like, on
the jolliest little donkeys in the world.

We have another market in our French watering-place —
that is to say, a few wooden hutches in the open street,
down by the Port—devoted to fish. Our fishing-boats are
famous everywhere; and our fishing people, though they
love lively colours and taste is neutral (see Bilkins), are
among the most picturesque people we ever encountered.
They have not only a quarter of their own in the town
itself, but they occupy whole villages of their own on the
neighbouring cliffs. Their churches and chapels are their
own; they consort with one another, they intermarry
among themselves, their customs are their own, and their
costume is their own and never changes. As soon as one of
their boys can walk, he is provided with a long bright red
nightcap; and one of their men would as soon think of
going afloat without his head, as without that indispensable

appendage to it. Then, they wear the noblest boots, with the hugest tops—flapping and bulging over anyhow; above which, they encase themselves in such wonderful overalls and petticoat trousers, made to all appearance of tarry old sails, so additionally stiffened with pitch and salt, that the wearers have a walk of their own, and go straddling and swinging about among the boats and barrels and nets and rigging, a sight to see. Then, their younger women, by dint of going down to the sea barefoot, to fling their baskets into the boats as they come in with the tide, and bespeak the first fruits of the haul with propitiatory promises to love and marry that dear fisherman who shall fill that basket like an Angel, have the finest legs ever carved by Nature in the brightest mahogany, and they walk like Juno. Their eyes, too, are so lustrous that their long gold ear-rings turn dull beside those brilliant neighbours; and when they are dressed, what with these beauties, and their fine fresh faces, and their many petticoats—striped petticoats, red petticoats, blue petticoats, always clean and smart, and never too long —and their home-made stockings, mulberry-coloured, blue, brown, purple, lilac—which the older women, taking care of the Dutch-looking children, sit in all sorts of places knitting, knitting, knitting from morning to night—and what with their little saucy bright blue jackets, knitted too, and fitting close to their handsome figures; and what with the natural grace with which they wear the commonest cap, or fold the commonest handkerchief round their luxuriant hair—we say, in a word and out of breath, that taking all these premises into our consideration, it has never been a matter of the least surprise to us that we have never once met, in the cornfields, on the dusty roads, by the breezy windmills, on the plots of short sweet grass overhanging the sea—anywhere—a young fisherman and fisherwoman of our French watering-place together, but the arm of that fisherman has invariably been, as a matter of course and without any absurd attempt to disguise so plain a necessity, round the neck or waist of that fisherwoman. And we have had no doubt whatever, standing looking at their uphill streets, house rising above house, and terrace above terrace, and bright garments here and there lying sunning on rough stone parapets, that the pleasant mist on all such objects, caused by their being seen through the brown nets hung across on poles to dry, is, in the eyes of every true young fisherman, a mist of love and beauty, setting off the goddess of his heart.

Moreover it is to be observed that these are an industrious people, and a domestic people, and an honest people. And though we are aware that at the bidding of Bilkins it is our duty to fall down and worship the Neapolitans, we make bold very much to prefer the fishing people of our French watering-place—especially since our last visit to Naples within these twelve months, when we found only four conditions of men remaining in the whole city: to wit, lazzaroni, priests, spies, and soldiers, and all of them beggars ; the paternal government having banished all its subjects except the rascals.

But we can never henceforth separate our French watering-place from our own landlord of two summers, M. Loyal Devasseur, citizen and town-councillor. . Permit us to have the pleasure of presenting M. Loyal Devasseur.

His own family name is simply Loyal; but as he is married, and as in that part of France a husband always adds to his own name the family name of his wife, he writes himself Loyal Devasseur. He owns a compact little estate of some twenty or thirty acres on a lofty hill-side, and on it he has built two country houses, which he lets furnished. They are by many degrees the best houses that are so let near our French watering-place ; we have had the honour of living in both, and can testify. The entrance-hall of the first we inhabited was ornamented with a plan of the estate, representing it as about twice the size of Ireland ; insomuch that when we were yet new to the property (M. Loyal always speaks of it as " La propriété ") we went three miles straight on end in search of the bridge of Austerlitz—which we afterwards found to be immediately outside the window. The Château of the Old Guard, in another part of the grounds, and, according to the plan, about two leagues from the little dining-room, we sought in vain for a week, until, happening one evening to sit upon a bench in the forest (forest in the plan), a few yards from the house-door, we observed at our feet, in the ignominious circumstances of being upside down and greenly rotten, the Old Guard himself: that is to say, the painted effigy of a member of that distinguished corps, seven feet high, and in the act of carrying arms, who had had the misfortune to be blown down in the previous winter. It will be perceived that M. Loyal is a staunch admirer of the great Napoleon. He is an old soldier himself—captain of the National Guard, with a handsome gold vase on his chimney-piece, presented to him by his company—and his respect for the memory of the illustrious general is enthusiastic. Medallions of him, portraits of him, busts of him, pictures of him, are thickly sprinkled all over the property. During the first month of our occupation, it was our affliction to be constantly knocking down Napoleon : if we touched a shelf in a dark corner, he toppled over with a crash ; and every door we opened, shook him to the soul. Yet M. Loyal is not a man of mere castles in the air, or, as he would say, in Spain. He has a specially practical, contriving, clever, skilful eye and hand. His houses are delightful. He unites French elegance and English comfort, in a happy manner quite his own. He has an extraordinary genius for making tasteful little bedrooms in angles of his roofs, which an Englishman would as soon think of turning to any account as he would think of cultivating the Desert. We have ourself reposed deliciously in an elegant chamber of M. Loyal's construction, with our head as nearly in the kitchen chimney-pot as we can conceive it likely for the head of any gentleman, not by profession a Sweep, to be. And into whatsoever strange nook M. Loyal's genius penetrates, it, in that nook, infallibly constructs a cupboard and a row of pegs. In either of our houses, we could have put away the knapsacks and hung up the hats of the whole regiment of Guides.

Aforetime, M. Loyal was a tradesman in the town. You can transact business with no present tradesman in the town, and give your card "chez M. Loyal," but a brighter face shines upon you directly. We doubt if there is, ever was, or ever will be, a man so universally pleasant in the minds of people as M. Loyal is in the minds of the citizens of our French watering-place. They rub their hands and laugh when they speak of him. Ah, but he is such a good child, such a brave boy, such a generous spirit, that Monsieur Loyal ! It is the honest truth. M. Loyal's nature is the nature of a gentleman. He cultivates his ground with his own hands (assisted by one little labourer, who falls into a fit now and then); and he digs and delves from morn to eve in prodigious perspirations—" works always," as he says—but, cover him with dust, mud, weeds, water, any stains you will, you never can cover the gentleman in M. Loyal. A portly, upright, broad-shouldered, brown

faced man, whose soldierly bearing gives him the appearance of being taller than he is, look into the bright eye of
M. Loyal, standing before you in his working-blouse and
cap, not particularly well shaved, and, it may be, very
earthy, and you shall discern in M. Loyal a gentleman
whose true politeness is in grain, and confirmation of whose
word by his bond you would blush to think of. Not without reason is M. Loyal when he tells that story, in his own
vivacious way, of his travelling to Fulham, near London, to
buy all these hundreds and hundreds of trees you now see
upon the Property, then a bare, bleak hill; and of his
sojourning in Fulham three months; and of his jovial
evenings with the market-gardeners; and of the crowning
banquet before his departure, when the market-gardeners rose
as one man, clinked their glasses all together (as the custom
at Fulham is), and cried, "Vive Loyal!"

M. Loyal has an agreeable wife, but no family; and he
loves to drill the children of his tenants, or run races with
them, or do anything with them, or for them, that is good-
natured. He is of a highly convivial temperament, and his
hospitality is unbounded. Billet a soldier on him, and he is
delighted. Five-and-thirty soldiers had M. Loyal billeted on
him this present summer, and they all got fat and red-faced
in two days. It became a legend among the troops that
whosoever got billeted on M. Loyal rolled in clover; and so
it fell out that the fortunate man who drew the billet "M.
Loyal Devasseur" always leaped into the air, though in heavy
marching order. M. Loyal cannot bear to admit anything
that might seem by any implication to disparage the military
profession. We hinted to him once, that we were conscious
of a remote doubt arising in our mind, whether a sou a day
for pocket-money, tobacco, stockings, drink, washing, and
social pleasures in general, left a very large margin for a
soldier's enjoyment. Pardon! said Monsieur Loyal, rather
wincing. It was not a fortune, but—à la bonne heure—it
was better than it used to be! What, we asked him on
another occasion, were all those neighbouring peasants, each
living with his family in one room, and each having a soldier
(perhaps two) billeted on him every other night, required to
provide for those soldiers? "Faith!" said M. Loyal, reluctantly; "a bed, monsieur, and fire to cook with, and a candle.
And they share their supper with those soldiers. It is not
possible that they could eat alone."—"And what allowance

do they get for this?" said we. Monsieur Loyal drew himself up taller, took a step back, laid his hand upon his breast,
and said, with majesty, as speaking for himself and all France,
"Monsieur, it is a contribution to the State!"

It is never going to rain, according to M. Loyal. When
it is impossible to deny that it is now raining in torrents, he
says it will be fine—charming—magnificent—to-morrow. It
is never hot on the Property, he contends. Likewise it is
never cold. The flowers, he says, come out, delighting to
grow there; it is like Paradise this morning; it is like the
Garden of Eden. He is a little fanciful in his language:
smilingly observing of Madame Loyal, when she is absent at
vespers, that she is "gone to her salvation".—allée à son salut.
He has a great enjoyment of tobacco, but nothing would
induce him to continue smoking face to face with a lady.
His short black pipe immediately goes into his breast pocket,
scorches his blouse, and nearly sets him on fire. In the
Town Council and on occasions of ceremony, he appears in
a full suit of black, with a waistcoat of magnificent breadth
across the chest, and a shirt-collar of fabulous proportions.
Good M. Loyal! Under blouse or waistcoat, he carries one
of the gentlest hearts that beat in a nation teeming with
gentle people. He has had losses, and has been at his best
under them. Not only the loss of his way by night in the
Fulham times—when a bad subject of an Englishman, under
pretence of seeing him home, took him into all the night
public-houses, drank "arfanarf" in every one at his expense,
and finally fled, leaving him shipwrecked at Cleefeeway,
which we apprehend to be Ratcliffe Highway—but heavier
losses than that. Long ago a family of children and a mother
were left in one of his houses without money, a whole year.
M. Loyal—anything but as rich as we wish he had been—
had not the heart to say "you must go;" so they stayed on
and stayed on, and paying-tenants who would have come in
couldn't come in, and at last they managed to get helped
home across the water; and M. Loyal kissed the whole group,
and said, "Adieu, my poor infants!" and sat down in their
deserted salon and smoked his pipe of peace.—"The rent,
M. Loyal?" "Eh! well! The rent!" M. Loyal shakes
his head. "Le bon Dieu," says M. Loyal presently, "will
recompense me," and he laughs and smokes his pipe of peace.
May he smoke it on the Property, and not be recompensed,
these fifty years!

There are public amusements in our French watering-place, or it would not be French. They are very popular, and very cheap. The sea-bathing—which may rank as the most favoured daylight entertainment, inasmuch as the French visitors bathe all day long, and seldom appear to think of remaining less than an hour at a time in the water—is astoundingly cheap. Omnibuses convey you, if you please, from a convenient part of the town to the beach and back again ; you have a clean and comfortable bathing-machine, dress, linen, and all appliances ; and the charge for the whole is half-a-franc, or fivepence. On the pier, there is usually a guitar, which seems presumptuously enough to set its tinkling against the deep hoarseness of the sea, and there is always some boy or woman who sings, without any voice, little songs without any tune : the strain we have most frequently heard being an appeal to "the sportsman" not to bag that choicest of game, the swallow. For bathing purposes, we have also a subscription establishment with an esplanade, where people lounge about with telescopes, and seem to get a good deal of weariness for their money ; and we have also an association of individual machine proprietors combined against this formidable rival. M. Féroce, our own particular friend in the bathing line, is one of these. How he ever came by his name we cannot imagine. He is as gentle and ·polite a man as M. Loyal Devasseur himself ; immensely stout withal, and of a beaming aspect. M. Féroce has saved so many people from drowning, and has been decorated with so many medals in consequence, that his stoutness seems a special dispensation of Providence to enable him to wear them ; if his girth were the girth of an ordinary man, he could never hang them on, all at once. It is only on very great occasions that M. Féroce displays his shining honours. At other times they lie by, with rolls of manuscript testifying to the causes of their presentation, in a huge glass case in the red-sofa'd salon of his private residence on the beach, where M. Féroce also keeps his family pictures, his portraits of himself as he appears both in bathing life and in private life, his little boats that rock by clockwork, and his other ornamental possessions.

Then, we have a commodious and gay Theatre—or had, for it is burned down now—where the opera was always preceded by a vaudeville, in which (as usual) everybody, down to the little old man with the large hat and the little cane

and tassel, who always played either my Uncle or my Papa,
suddenly broke out of the dialogue into the mildest vocal
snatches, to the great perplexity of unaccustomed strangers
from Great Britain, who never could make out when they
were singing and when they were talking—and indeed it was
pretty much the same.   But the caterers in the way of
entertainment to whom we are most beholden are the Society
of Welldoing, who are active all the summer, and give the
proceeds of their good works to the poor.   Some of the most
agreeable fêtes they contrive are announced as " Dedicated to
the children ; " and the taste with which they turn a small
public enclosure into an elegant garden beautifully illuminated, and the thorough-going heartiness and energy with
which they personally direct the childish pleasures, are
supremely delightful.   For fivepence a head, we have on these
occasions donkey races with English "Jokeis," and other
rustic sports ; lotteries for toys, roundabouts, dancing on the
grass to the music of an admirable band, fire-balloons and
fireworks.   Further, almost every week all through the
summer—never mind, now, on what day of the week—there
is a fête in some adjoining village (called in that part of the
country a Ducasse), where the people—really *the people*—dance
on the green turf in the open air, round a little orchestra,
that seems itself to dance, there is such an airy motion of
flags and streamers all about it.   And we do not suppose that
between the Torrid Zone and the North Pole there are to be
found male dancers with such astonishingly loose legs,
furnished with so many joints in wrong places, utterly unknown to Professor Owen, as those who here disport themselves.   Sometimes the fête appertains to a particular trade ;
you will see among the cheerful young women at the joint
Ducasse of the milliners and tailors, a wholesome knowledge
of the art of making common and cheap things uncommon
and pretty, by good sense and good taste, that is a practical
lesson to any rank of society in a whole island we could
mention.   The oddest feature of these agreeable scenes is the
everlasting Roundabout (we preserve an English word wherever we can; as we are writing the English language), on the
wooden horses of which machine grown-up people of all ages
are wound round and round with the utmost solemnity, while
the proprietor's wife grinds an organ, capable of only one
tune, in the centre.

As to the boarding-houses of our French watering-place,

they are Legion, and would require a distinct treatise. It is not without a sentiment of national pride that we believe them to contain more bores from the shores of Albion than all the clubs in London.   As you walk timidly in their neighbourhood, the very neckcloths and hats of your elderly compatriots cry to you from the stones of the streets, "We are Bores—avoid us!"   We have never overheard at street corners such lunatic scraps of political and social discussion as among these dear countrymen of ours.   They believe everything that is impossible and nothing that is true.   They carry rumours, and ask questions, and make corrections and improvements on one another, staggering to the human intellect.   And they are for ever rushing into the English library, propounding such incomprehensible paradoxes to the fair mistress of that establishment, that we beg to recommend her to her Majesty's gracious consideration as a fit object for a pension.

The English form a considerable part of the population of our French watering-place, and are deservedly addressed and respected in many ways.   Some of the surface-addresses to them are odd enough, as when a laundress puts a placard outside her house announcing her possession of that curious British instrument, a "Mingle;" or when a tavern-keeper provides accommodation for the celebrated English game of "Nokemdon."   But, to us, it is not the least pleasant feature of our French watering-place that a long and constant fusion of the two great nations there has taught each to like the other, and to learn from the other, and to rise superior to the absurd prejudices that have lingered among the weak and ignorant in both countries equally.

Drumming and trumpeting of course go on for ever in our French watering-place.   Flag-flying is at a premium, too ; but we cheerfully avow that we consider a flag a very pretty object, and that we take such outward signs of innocent liveliness to our heart of hearts.   The people, in the town and in the country, are a busy people who work hard ; they are sober, temperate, good-humoured, light-hearted, and generally remarkable for their engaging manners.   Few just men, not immoderately bilious, could see them in their recreations without very much respecting the character that is so easily, so harmlessly, and so simply, pleased.

BILL-STICKING

IF I had an enemy whom I hated—which Heaven forbid!
—and if I knew of something which sat heavy on his conscience, I think I would introduce that something into
a Posting-Bill, and place a large impression in the hands of
an active sticker. I can scarcely imagine a more terrible
revenge. I should haunt him, by this means, night and
day. I do not mean to say that I would publish his secret,
in red letters two feet high, for all the town to read : I would
darkly refer to it. It should be between him, and me, and
the Posting-Bill. Say, for example, that, at a certain period
of his life, my enemy had surreptitiously possessed himself
of a key. I would then embark my capital in the lock
business, and conduct that business on the advertising principle. In all my placards and advertisements, I would
throw up the line SECRET KEYS. Thus, if my enemy passed
an uninhabited house, he would see his conscience glaring
down on him from the parapets, and peeping up at him
from the cellars. If he took a dead wall in his walk, it
would be alive with reproaches. If he sought refuge in an
omnibus, the panels thereof would become Belshazzar's
palace to him. If he took boat, in a wild endeavour to
escape, he would see the fatal words lurking under the
arches of the bridges over the Thames. If he walked the
streets with downcast eyes, he would recoil from the very
stones of the pavement, made eloquent by lamp-black litho-
graph. If he drove or rode, his way would be blocked up
by enormous vans, each proclaiming the same words over
and over again from its whole extent of surface. Until,
having gradually grown thinner and paler, and having at
last totally rejected food, he would miserably perish, and
I should be revenged. This conclusion I should, no doubt,
celebrate by laughing a hoarse laugh in three syllables, and
folding my arms tight upon my chest agreeably to most of
the examples of glutted animosity that I have had an opportunity of observing in connexion with the Drama—which,

by-the-by, as involving a good deal of noise, appears to me to be occasionally confounded with the Drummer.

The foregoing reflections presented themselves to my mind, the other day, as I contemplated (being newly come to London from the East Riding of Yorkshire, on a house-hunting expedition for next May) an old warehouse which rotting paste and rotting paper had brought down to the condition of an old cheese. It would have been impossible to say, on the most conscientious survey, how much of its front was brick and mortar, and how much decaying and decayed plaster. It was so thickly encrusted with fragments of bills, that no ship's keel after a long voyage could be half so foul. All traces of the broken windows were billed out, the doors were billed across, the water-spout was billed over. The building was shored up to prevent its tumbling into the street ; and the very beams erected against it were less wood than paste and paper, they had been so continually posted and reposted. The forlorn dregs of old posters so encumbered this wreck, that there was no hold for new posters, and the stickers had abandoned the place in despair, except one enterprising man who had hoisted the last masquerade to a clear spot near the level of the stack of chimneys, where it waved and drooped like a shattered flag. Below the rusty cellar-grating, crumpled remnants of old bills torn down rotted away in wasting heaps of fallen leaves. Here and there, some of the thick rind of the house had peeled off in strips, and fluttered heavily down, littering the street ; but still, below these rents and gashes, layers of decomposing posters showed themselves, as if they were interminable. I thought the building could never even be pulled down, but in one adhesive heap of rottenness and poster. As to getting in—I don't believe that if the Sleeping Beauty and her Court had been so billed up, the young Prince could have done it.

Knowing all the posters that were yet legible, intimately, and pondering on their ubiquitous nature, I was led into the reflections with which I began this paper, by considering what an awful thing it would be, ever to have wronged— say M. JULLIEN for example—and to have his avenging name in characters of fire incessantly before my eyes. Or to have injured MADAME TUSSAUD, and undergo a similar retribution. Has any man a self-reproachful thought associated with pills, or ointment ? What an avenging spirit to that man is PROFESSOR HOLLOWAY! Have I sinned in oil? CABBURN pursues me. Have I a dark remembrance associated with any gentlemanly garments, bespoke or ready made? MOSES AND SON are on my track. Did I ever aim a blow at a defenceless fellow-creature's head? That head eternally being measured for a wig, or that worse head which was bald before it used the balsam, and hirsute afterwards—enforcing the benevolent moral, "Better to be bald as a Dutch cheese than come to this,"—undoes me. Have I no sore places in my mind which MECHI touches— which NICOLL probes—which no registered article whatever lacerates? Does no discordant note within me thrill responsive to mysterious watchwords, as "Revalenta Arabica," or "Number One St. Paul's Churchyard"? Then may I enjoy life, and be happy.

Lifting up my eyes, as I was musing to this effect, I beheld advancing towards me (I was then on Cornhill, near to the Royal Exchange) a solemn procession of three advertising vans, of first-class dimensions, each drawn by a very little horse. As the cavalcade approached, I was at a loss to reconcile the careless deportment of the drivers of these vehicles with the terrific announcements they conducted through the city, which being a summary of the contents of a Sunday newspaper, were of the most thrilling kind. Robbery, fire, murder, and the ruin of the United Kingdom —each discharged in a line by itself, like a separate broadside of red-hot shot—were among the least of the warnings addressed to an unthinking people. Yet the Ministers of Fate, who drove the awful cars, leaned forward with their arms upon their knees in a state of extreme lassitude, for want of any subject of interest. The first man, whose hair I might naturally have expected to see standing on end, scratched his head—one of the smoothest I ever beheld— with profound indifference. The second whistled. The third yawned.

Pausing to dwell upon this apathy, it appeared to me, as the fatal cars came by me, that I descried in the second car, through the portal in which the charioteer was seated, a figure stretched upon the floor. At the same time, I thought I smelt tobacco. The latter impression passed quickly from me; the former remained. Curious to know whether this prostrate figure was the one impressible man of the whole capital who had been stricken insensible by the terrors

revealed to him, and whose form had been placed in the car
by the charioteer, from motives of humanity, I followed the
procession. It turned into Leadenhall-market, and halted
at a public-house. Each driver dismounted. I then distinctly heard, proceeding from the second car, where I had
dimly seen the prostrate form, the words :

"And a pipe ! "

The driver entering the public-house with his fellows,
apparently for purposes of refreshment, I could not refrain
from mounting on the shaft of the second vehicle, and
looking in at the portal. I then beheld, reclining on his
back upon the floor, on a kind of mattress or divan, a little
man in a shooting-coat. The exclamation "Dear me,"
which irresistibly escaped my lips, caused him to sit upright
and survey me. I found him to be a good-looking little
man of about fifty, with a shining face, a tight head, a bright
eye, a moist wink, a quick speech, and a ready air. He had
something of a sporting way with him.

He looked at me, and I looked at him, until the driver dis-
placed me by handing in a pint of beer, a pipe, and what
I understand is called "a screw" of tobacco—an object
which has the appearance of a curl-paper taken off the barmaid's head, with the curl in it.

" I beg your pardon," said I, when the removed person of
the driver again admitted of my presenting my face at the
portal. " But—excuse my curiosity, which I inherit from
my mother—do you live here ? "

"That's good, too ! " returned the little man, composedly
laying aside a pipe he had smoked out, and filling the pipe
just brought to him.

"Oh, you *don't* live here then ? " said I.

He shook his head, as he calmly lighted his pipe by means
of a German tinder-box, and replied, " This is my carriage.
When things are flat, I take a ride sometimes, and enjoy
myself. I am the inventor of these wans."

His pipe was now alight. He drank his beer all at once,
and he smoked and he smiled at me.

" It was a great idea ! " said I.

" Not so bad," returned the little man, with the modesty
of merit.

" Might I be permitted to inscribe your name upon the
tablets of my memory ? " I asked.

"There's not much odds in the name," returned the little

man, " —no name particular—I am the King of the Bill-Stickers."

"Good gracious!" said I.

The monarch informed me, with a smile, that he had never been crowned or installed with any public ceremonies, but that he was peaceably acknowledged as King of the Bill-Stickers in right of being the oldest and most respected member of "the old school of bill-sticking." He likewise gave me to understand that there was a Lord Mayor of the Bill-Stickers, whose genius was chiefly exercised within the limits of the city. He made some allusion, also, to an inferior potentate, called "Turkey-legs;" but I did not understand that this gentleman was invested with much power. I rather inferred that he derived his title from some peculiarity of gait, and that it was of an honorary character.

"My father," pursued the King of the Bill-Stickers, "was Engineer, Beadle, and Bill-Sticker to the parish of St. Andrew's, Holborn, in the year one thousand seven hundred and eighty. My father stuck bills at the time of the riots of London."

"You must be acquainted with the whole subject of bill-sticking, from that time to the present!" said I.

"Pretty well so," was the answer.

"Excuse me," said I; "but I am a sort of collector——"

"Not Income-tax?" cried His Majesty, hastily removing his pipe from his lips.

"No, no," said I.

"Water-rate?" said His Majesty.

"No, no," I returned.

"Gas? Assessed? Sewers?" said His Majesty.

"You misunderstand me," I replied, soothingly. "Not that sort of collector at all: a collector of facts."

"Oh, if it's only facts," cried the King of the Bill-Stickers, recovering his good-humour, and banishing the great mistrust that had suddenly fallen upon him, " come in and welcome! If it had been income, or winders, I think I should have pitched you out of the wan, upon my soul!"

Readily complying with the invitation, I squeezed myself in at the small aperture. His Majesty, graciously handing me a little three-legged stool on which I took my seat in a corner, inquired if I smoked.

"I do ;—that is, I can," I answered.

"Pipe and a screw!" said His Majesty to the attendant

P

charioteer. "Do you prefer a dry smoke, or do you moisten it?"

As unmitigated tobacco produces most disturbing effects upon my system (indeed, if I had perfect moral courage, I doubt if I should smoke at all, under any circumstances), I advocated moisture, and begged the Sovereign of the Bill-Stickers to name his usual liquor, and to concede to me the privilege of paying for it. After some delicate reluctance on his part, we were provided, through the instrumentality of the attendant charioteer, with a can of cold rum-and-water, flavoured with sugar and lemon. We were also furnished with a tumbler, and I was provided with a pipe. His Majesty, then observing that we might combine business with conversation, gave the word for the car to proceed; and, to my great delight, we jogged away at a foot pace.

I say to my great delight, because I am very fond of novelty, and it was a new sensation to be jolting through the tumult of the city in that secluded Temple, partly open to the sky, surrounded by the roar without, and seeing nothing but the clouds. Occasionally, blows from whips fell heavily on the Temple's walls, when by stopping up the road longer than usual, we irritated carters and coachmen to madness; but they fell harmless upon us within and disturbed not the serenity of our peaceful retreat. As I looked upward, I felt, I should imagine, like the Astronomer Royal. I was enchanted by the contrast between the freezing nature of our external mission on the blood of the populace, and the perfect composure reigning within those sacred precincts : where His Majesty, reclining easily on his left arm, smoked his pipe and drank his rum-and-water from his own side of the tumbler, which stood impartially between us. As I looked down from the clouds and caught his royal eye, he understood my reflections. "I have an idea," he observed, with an upward glance, "of training scarlet runners across in the season,—making a arbour of it,—and sometimes taking tea in the same, according to the song."

I nodded approval.

"And here you repose and think?" said I.

"And think," said he, "of posters—walls—and hoardings."

We were both silent, contemplating the vastness of the subject. I remembered a surprising fancy of dear THOMAS HOOD's, and wondered whether this monarch ever sighed to repair to the great wall of China, and stick bills all over it.

"And so," said he, rousing himself, "it's facts as you collect?"

"Facts," said I.

"The facts of bill-sticking," pursued His Majesty, in a benignant manner, "as known to myself, air as following. When my father was Engineer, Beadle, and Bill-Sticker to the parish of St. Andrew's, Holborn, he employed women to post bills for him. He employed women to post bills at the time of the riots of London. He died at the age of seventy-five year, and was buried by the murdered Eliza Grimwood, over in the Waterloo Road."

As this was somewhat in the nature of a royal speech, I listened with deference and silently. His Majesty, taking a scroll from his pocket, proceeded, with great distinctness, to pour out the following flood of information:—

"'The bills being at that period mostly proclamations and declarations, and which were only a demy size, the manner of posting the bills (as they did not use brushes) was by means of a piece of wood which they called a 'dabber.' Thus things continued till such time as the State Lottery was passed, and then the printers began to print larger bills, and men were employed instead of women, as the State Lottery Commissioners then began to send men all over England to post bills, and would keep them out for six or eight months at a time, and they were called by the London bill-stickers 'trampers,' their wages at the time being ten shillings per day, besides expenses. They used sometimes to be stationed in large towns for five or six months together, distributing the schemes to all the houses in the town. And then there were more caricature wood-block engravings for posting-bills than there are at the present time, the principal printers, at that time, of posting-bills being Messrs. Evans and Ruffy, of Budge Row; Thoroughgood and Whiting, of the present day; and Messrs. Gye and Balne, Gracechurch Street, City. The largest bills printed at that period were a two-sheet double crown; and when they commenced printing four-sheet bills, two bill-stickers would work together. They had no settled wages per week, but had a fixed price for their work, and the London bill-stickers, during a lottery week, have been known to earn, each, eight or nine pounds per week, till the day of drawing; likewise the men who carried boards in the street used to have one pound per week, and the bill-stickers at that time would not allow any one to wilfully cover or destroy their bills, as they had a society amongst themselves, and very frequently dined together at some public-house where they used to go of an evening to have their work delivered out untoe 'em.'"

All this His Majesty delivered in a gallant manner ; posting it, as it were, before me, in a great proclamation. I took advantage of the pause he now made, to inquire what a "two-sheet double crown" might express ?

"A two-sheet double crown," replied the King, "is a bill thirty-nine inches wide by thirty inches high."

"Is it possible," said I, my mind reverting to the gigantic admonitions we were then displaying to the multitude — which were as infants to some of the posting-bills on the rotten old warehouse—" that some few years ago the largest bill was no larger than that ?"

"The fact," returned the King, "is undoubtedly so." Here he instantly rushed again into the scroll.

"'Since the abolishing of the State Lottery all that good feeling has gone, and nothing but jealousy exists, through the rivalry of each other. Several bill-sticking companies have started, but have failed. The first party that started a company was twelve year ago ; but what was left of the old school and their dependants joined together and opposed them. And for some time we were quiet again, till a printer of Hatton Garden formed a company by hiring the sides of houses ; but he was not supported by the public, and he left his wooden frames fixed up for rent. The last company that started, took advantage of the New Police Act, and hired of Messrs. Grissell and Peto the hoarding of Trafalgar Square, and established a bill-sticking office in Cursitor Street, Chancery Lane, and engaged some of the new bill-stickers to do their work, and for a time got the half of all our work, and with such spirit did they carry on their opposition towards us, that they used to give us in charge before the magistrate, and get us fined ; but they found it so expensive that they could not keep it up, for they were always employing a lot of ruffians from the Seven Dials to come and fight us ; and on one occasion the old bill-stickers went to Trafalgar Square to attempt to post bills, when they were given in custody by the watchman in their employ, and fined at Queen Square five pounds, as they would not allow any of us to speak in the office ; but when they were gone, we had an interview with the magistrate, who mitigated the fine to fifteen shillings. During the time the men were waiting for the fine, this company started off to a public-house that we were in the habit of using, and waited for us coming back, where a fighting scene took place that beggars description. Shortly after this, the principal one day came and shook hands with us, and acknowledged that he had broken up the company, and that he himself had lost five hundred pound in trying to overthrow us. We then took possession of the hoarding in Trafalgar Square; but Messrs. Grissell and Peto would not allow us to post our bills on the said hoarding without paying them—and from first to last we paid upwards of two hundred pounds for that hoarding, and likewise the hoarding of the Reform Club-house, Pall Mall.'"

His Majesty, being now completely out of breath, laid down his scroll (which he appeared to have finished), puffed at his pipe, and took some rum-and-water. I embraced the opportunity of asking how many divisions the art and mystery of bill-sticking comprised? He replied, three—auctioneers' bill-sticking, theatrical bill-sticking, general bill-sticking.

"The auctioneers' porters," said the King, "who do their bill-sticking, are mostly respectable and intelligent, and generally well paid·for their work, whether in town or country. The price paid by the principal auctioneers for country work is nine shillings per day; that is, seven shillings for day's work, one shilling for lodging, and one for paste. Town work is five shillings a day, including paste."

"Town work must be rather hot work," said I, "if there be many of those fighting scenes that beggar description, among the bill-stickers?"

"Well," replied the King, "I an't a stranger, I assure you, to black eyes; a bill-sticker ought to know how to handle his fists a bit. As to that row I have mentioned, that grew out of competition, conducted in an uncompromising spirit. Besides a man in a horse-and-shay continually following us about, the company had a watchman on duty, night and day, to prevent us sticking bills upon the hoarding in Trafalgar Square. We went there, early one morning, to stick bills and to black-wash their bills if we were interfered with. We *were* interfered with, and I gave the word for laying on the wash. It *was* laid on—pretty brisk—and we were all taken to Queen Square: but they couldn't fine *me*. *I* knew that," —with a bright smile—"I'd only give directions—I was only the General."

Charmed with this monarch's affability, I inquired if he had ever hired a hoarding himself.

"Hired a large one," he replied, "opposite the Lyceum Theatre, when the buildings was there. Paid thirty pound for it; let out places on it, and called it 'The External Paper-Hanging Station.' But it didn't answer. Ah!" said His Majesty thoughtfully, as he filled the glass, "Bill-stickers have a deal to contend with. The bill-sticking clause was got into the Police Act by a member of Parliament that employed me at his election. The clause is pretty stiff respecting where bills go; but *he* didn't mind where *his* bills went. It was all right enough, so long as they was *his* bills!"

Fearful that I observed a shadow of misanthropy on the King's cheerful face, I asked whose ingenious invention that was, which I greatly admired, of sticking bills under the arches of the bridges.

"Mine!" said His Majesty. "I was the first that ever stuck a bill under a bridge! Imitators soon rose up, of course.—When don't they? But they stuck 'em at low-water, and the tide came and swept the bills clean away. *I* knew that!" The King laughed.

"What may be the name of that instrument, like an immense fishing-rod," I inquired, "with which bills are posted on high places?"

"The joints," returned His Majesty. "Now, we use the joints where formerly we used ladders—as they do still in country places. Once, when Madame" (Vestris, understood) "was playing in Liverpool, another bill-sticker and me were at it together on the wall outside the Clarence Dock—me with the joints—him on a ladder. Lord! I had my bill up, right over his head, yards above him, ladder and all, while he was crawling to his work. The people going in and out of the docks stood and laughed!—It's about thirty years since the joints come in."

"Are there any bill-stickers who can't read?" I took the liberty of inquiring.

"Some," said the King. "But they know which is the right side up'ards of their work. They keep it as it's given out to 'em. I have seen a bill or so stuck wrong side up'ards. But it's very rare."

Our discourse sustained some interruption at this point, by the procession of cars occasioning a stoppage of about three-quarters of a mile in length, as nearly as I could judge. His Majesty, however, entreating me not to be discomposed by the contingent uproar, smoked with great placidity, and surveyed the firmament.

When we were again in motion, I begged to be informed what was the largest poster His Majesty had ever seen. The King replied, "A thirty-six sheet poster." I gathered, also, that there were about a hundred and fifty bill-stickers in London, and that his Majesty considered an average hand equal to the posting of one hundred bills (single sheets) in a day. The King was of opinion that, although posters had much increased in size, they had not increased in number; as the abolition of the State Lotteries had occasioned a great falling off, especially in the country. Over and above which change, I bethought myself that the custom of advertising in newspapers had greatly increased. The completion of many London improvements, as Trafalgar Square (I particularly observed the singularity of His Majesty's calling *that* an improvement), the Royal Exchange, &c., had of late years reduced the number of advantageous posting-places. Bill-Stickers at present rather confine themselves to districts, than to particular descriptions of work. One man would strike over Whitechapel, another would take round Houndsditch, Shoreditch, and the City Road; one (the King said) would stick to the Surrey side; another would make a beat of the West-end.

His Majesty remarked, with some approach to severity, on the neglect of delicacy and taste, gradually introduced into the trade by the new school: a profligate and inferior race of impostors who took jobs at almost any price, to the detriment of the old school, and the confusion of their own misguided employers. He considered that the trade was overdone with competition, and observed, speaking of his subjects, "There are too many of 'em." He believed, still, that things were a little better than they had been; adducing, as a proof, the fact that particular posting-places were now reserved, by common consent, for particular posters; those places, however, must be regularly occupied by those posters, or, they lapsed and fell into other hands. It was of no use giving a man a Drury Lane bill this week and not next. Where was it to go? He was of opinion that going to the expense of putting up your own board on which your sticker could display your own bills, was the only complete way of posting yourself at the present time; but, even to effect this, on payment of a shilling a week to the keepers of steamboat piers and other such places, you must be able, besides, to give orders for theatres and public exhibitions, or you would be sure to be cut out by somebody. His Majesty regarded the passion for orders, as one of the most unappeasable appetites of human nature. If there were a building, or if there were repairs, going on anywhere, you could generally stand something and make it right with the foreman of the works; but orders would be expected from you, and the man who could give the most orders was the man who would come off best. There was this other objectionable point, in orders, that workmen sold them for drink, and often sold them to persons who were likewise troubled with the weakness of thirst: which led (His Majesty said) to the presentation of your orders at Theatre doors, by individuals who were " too shakery " to derive intellectual profit from the entertainments, and who brought a scandal on you. Finally, His Majesty said that you could hardly put too little in a poster ; what you wanted was, two or three good catch-lines for the eye to rest on—then, leave it alone—and there you were !

These are the minutes of my conversation with His Majesty, as I noted them down shortly afterwards. I am not aware that I have been betrayed into any alteration or suppression. The manner of the King was frank in the extreme ; and he seemed to me to avoid, at once, that slight tendency to repetition which may have been observed in the conversation of His Majesty King George the Third, and that slight under-current of egotism which the curious observer may perhaps detect in the conversation of Napoleon Bonaparte.

I must do the King the justice to say that it was I, and not he, who closed the dialogue. At this juncture, I became the subject of a remarkable optical delusion ; the legs of my stool appeared to me to double up ; the car to spin round and round with great violence ; and a mist to arise between myself and His Majesty. In addition to these sensations, I felt extremely unwell. I refer these unpleasant effects, either to the paste with which the posters were affixed to the van: which may have contained some small portion of arsenic ; or to the printer's ink, which may have contained some equally deleterious ingredient. Of this I cannot be sure. I am only sure that I was not affected, either by the smoke or the rum-and-water. I was assisted out of the vehicle in a state of mind which I have only experienced in two other places—I allude to the Pier at Dover, and to the corresponding portion of the town of Calais—and sat upon a door-step until I recovered. The procession had then disappeared. I have since looked anxiously for the King in several other cars, but I have not yet had the happiness of seeing His Majesty.

"BIRTHS. MRS. MEEK, OF A SON"

My name is Meek. I am, in fact, Mr. Meek. That son is mine and Mrs. Meek's. When I saw the announcement in the *Times*, I dropped the paper. I had put it in, myself, and paid for it, but it looked so noble that it overpowered me.

As soon as I could compose my feelings, I took the paper up to Mrs. Meek's bedside. "Maria Jane," said I (I allude to Mrs. Meek), "you are now a public character." We read the review of our child, several times, with feelings of the strongest emotion; and I sent the boy who cleans the boots and shoes to the office for fifteen copies. No reduction was made on taking that quantity.

It is scarcely necessary for me to say, that our child had been expected. In fact, it had been expected, with comparative confidence, for some months. Mrs. Meek's mother, who resides with us—of the name of Bigby—had made every preparation for its admission to our circle.

I hope and believe I am a quiet man. I will go farther. I *know* I am a quiet man. My constitution is tremulous, my voice was never loud, and, in point of stature, I have been from infancy, small. I have the greatest respect for Maria Jane's Mama. She is a most remarkable woman. I honour Maria Jane's Mama. In my opinion she would storm a town, single-handed, with a hearth-broom, and carry it. I have never known her to yield any point whatever to mortal man. She is calculated to terrify the stoutest heart.

Still—but I will not anticipate.

The first intimation I had of any preparations being in progress, on the part of Maria Jane's Mama, was one afternoon, several months ago. I came home earlier than usual from the office, and, proceeding into the dining-room, found an obstruction behind the door, which prevented it from opening freely. It was an obstruction of a soft nature. On looking in, I found it to be a female.

The female in question stood in the corner behind the door, consuming Sherry Wine. From the nutty smell of that beverage pervading the apartment, I have no doubt she was consuming a second glassful. She wore a black bonnet of large dimensions, and was copious in figure. The expression of her countenance was severe and discontented. The words to which she gave utterance on seeing me, were these, "Oh git along with you, Sir, if *you* please; me and Mrs. Bigby don't want no male parties here!"

That female was Mrs. Prodgit.

I immediately withdrew, of course. I was rather hurt, but I made no remark. Whether it was that I showed a lowness of spirits after dinner, in consequence of feeling that I seemed to intrude, I cannot say. But Maria Jane's Mama said to me on her retiring for the night: in a low distinct voice, and with a look of reproach that completely subdued me: "George Meek, Mrs. Prodgit is your wife's nurse!"

I bear no ill-will towards Mrs. Prodgit. Is it likely that I, writing this with tears in my eyes, should be capable of deliberate animosity towards a female, so essential to the welfare of Maria Jane? I am willing to admit that Fate may have been to blame, and not Mrs. Prodgit; but it is undeniably true, that the latter female brought desolation and devastation into my lowly dwelling.

We were happy after her first appearance; we were sometimes exceedingly so. But whenever the parlour door was opened, and "Mrs. Prodgit!" announced (and she was very often announced), misery ensued. I could not bear Mrs. Prodgit's look. I felt that I was far from wanted, and had no business to exist in Mrs. Prodgit's presence. Between Maria Jane's Mama and Mrs. Prodgit, there was a dreadful, secret, understanding—a dark mystery and conspiracy, pointing me out as a being to be shunned. I appeared to have done something that was evil. Whenever Mrs. Prodgit called after dinner, I retired to my dressing-room—where the temperature is very low, indeed, in the wintry time of the year—and sat looking at my frosty breath as it rose before me, and at my rack of boots; a serviceable article of furniture, but never, in my opinion, an exhilarating object. The length of the councils that were held with Mrs. Prodgit, under these circumstances, I will not attempt to describe. I will merely remark, that Mrs. Prodgit always consumed

Sherry Wine while the deliberations were in progress ; that they always ended in Maria Jane's being in wretched spirits on the sofa ; and that Maria Jane's Mama always received me, when I was recalled, with a look of desolate triumph that too plainly said, " *Now*, George Meek ! You see my child, Maria Jane, a ruin, and I hope you are satisfied ! "

I pass, generally, over the period that intervened between the day when Mrs. Prodgit entered her protest against male parties, and the ever memorable midnight when I brought her to my unobtrusive home in a cab, with an extremely large box on the roof, and a bundle, a bandbox, and a basket, between the driver's legs. I have no objection to Mrs. Prodgit (aided and abetted by Mrs. Bigby, who I never can forget is the parent of Maria Jane) taking entire possession of my unassuming establishment. In the recesses of my own breast, the thought may linger that a man in possession cannot be so dreadful as a woman, and that woman Mrs. Prodgit ; but I ought to bear a good deal, and I hope I can, and do. Huffing and snubbing prey upon my feelings ; but I can bear them without complaint. They may tell in the long run ; I may be hustled about, from post to pillar, beyond my strength ; nevertheless, I wish to avoid giving rise to words in the family.

The voice of Nature, however, cries aloud in behalf of Augustus George, my infant son. It is for him that I wish to utter a few plaintive household words. I am not at all angry ; I am mild—but miserable.

I wish to know why, when my child, Augustus George, was expected in our circle, a provision of pins was made, as if the little stranger were a criminal who was to be put to the torture immediately on his arrival, instead of a holy babe ? I wish to know why haste was made to stick those pins all over his innocent form, in every direction ? I wish to be informed why light and air are excluded from Augustus George, like poisons ? Why, I ask, is my unoffending infant so hedged into a basket-bedstead, with dimity and calico, with miniature sheets and blankets, that I can only hear him snuffle (and no wonder !) deep down under the pink hood of a little bathing-machine, and can never peruse even so much of his lineaments as his nose.

Was I expected to be the father of a French Roll, that the brushes of All Nations were laid in, to rasp Augustus George ? Am I to be told that his sensitive skin was ever

intended by Nature to have rashes brought out upon it, by
the premature and incessant use of those formidable little
instruments?

Is my son a Nutmeg, that he is to be grated on the stiff
edges of sharp frills? Am I the parent of a Muslin boy,
that his yielding surface is to be crimped and small plaited?
Or is my child composed of Paper or of Linen, that impressions of the finer getting-up art, practised by the laundress,
are to be printed off, all over his soft arms and legs, as
I constantly observe them? The starch enters his soul;
who can wonder that he cries?

Was Augustus George intended to have limbs, or to be
born a Torso? I presume that limbs were the intention, as
they are the usual practice. Then, why are my poor child's
limbs fettered and tied up? Am I to be told that there
is any analogy between Augustus George Meek and Jack
Sheppard?

Analyse Castor Oil at any Institution of Chemistry that
may be agreed upon, and inform me what resemblance, in
taste, it bears to that natural provision which it is at once
the pride and duty of Maria Jane to administer to Augustus
George! Yet, I charge Mrs. Prodgit (aided and abetted by
Mrs. Bigby) with systematically forcing Castor Oil on my
innocent son, from the first hour of his birth. When that
medicine, in its efficient action, causes internal disturbance
to Augustus George, I charge Mrs. Prodgit (aided and abetted
by Mrs. Bigby) with insanely and inconsistently administer-
ing opium to allay the storm she has raised! What is the
meaning of this?

If the days of Egyptian Mummies are past, how dare
Mrs. Prodgit require, for the use of my son, an amount of
flannel and linen that would carpet my humble roof? Do
I wonder that she requires it? No! This morning, within
an hour, I beheld this agonising sight. I beheld my son—
Augustus George—in Mrs. Prodgit's hands, and on Mrs.
Prodgit's knee, being dressed. He was at the moment,
comparatively speaking, in a state of nature; having nothing
on but an extremely short shirt, remarkably disproportionate
to the length of his usual outer garments. Trailing from
Mrs. Prodgit's lap, on the floor, was a long narrow roller
or bandage—I should say of several yards in extent. In
this, I saw Mrs. Prodgit tightly roll the body of my unoffending infant, turning him over and over, now presenting

his unconscious face upwards, now the back of his bald
head, until the unnatural feat was accomplished, and the
bandage secured by a pin, which I have every reason
to believe entered the body of my only child. In this
tourniquet, he passes the present phase of his existence.
Can I know it, and smile!

I fear I have been betrayed into expressing myself warmly,
but I feel deeply. Not for myself; for Augustus George.
I dare not interfere. Will any one? Will any publication?
Any doctor? Any parent? Any body? I do not complain that Mrs. Prodgit (aided and abetted by Mrs. Bigby)
entirely alienates Maria Jane's affections from me, and interposes an impassable barrier between us. I do not complain
of being made of no account. I do not want to be of any
account. But Augustus George is a production of Nature
(I cannot think otherwise), and I claim that he should be
treated with some remote reference to Nature. In my
opinion, Mrs. Prodgit is, from first to last, a convention
and a superstition. Are all the faculty afraid of Mrs. Prodgit?
If not, why don't they take her in hand and improve her?

P.S. Maria Jane's Mama boasts of her own knowledge
of the subject, and says she brought up seven children
besides Maria Jane. But how do *I* know that she might
not have brought them up much better? Maria Jane herself is far from strong, and is subject to headaches, and
nervous indigestion. Besides which, I learn from the statistical tables that one child in five dies within the first year
of its life; and one child in three, within the fifth. That
don't look as if we could never improve in these particulars,
I think!

P.P.S. Augustus George is in convulsions.

LYING AWAKE

" MY uncle lay with his eyes half closed, and his nightcap drawn almost down to his nose. His fancy was already wandering, and began to mingle up the present scene with the crater of Vesuvius, the French Opera, the Coliseum at Rome, Dolly's Chop-house in London, and all the farrago of noted places with which the brain of a traveller is crammed ; in a word, he was just falling asleep."

Thus, that delightful writer, WASHINGTON IRVING, in his Tales of a Traveller. But, it happened to me the other night to be lying : not with my eyes half closed, but with my eyes wide open ; not with my nightcap drawn almost down to my nose, for on sanitary principles I never wear a nightcap : but with my hair pitchforked and touzled all over the pillow ; not just falling asleep by any means, but glaringly, persistently, and obstinately, broad awake. Per-haps, with no scientific intention or invention, I was illus-trating the theory of the Duality of the Brain ; perhaps one part of my brain, being wakeful, sat up to watch the other part which was sleepy. Be that as it may, something in me was as desirous to go to sleep as it possibly could be, but something else in me would not go to sleep, and was as obstinate as George the Third.

Thinking of George the Third—for I devote this paper to my train of thoughts as I lay awake : most people lying awake sometimes, and having some interest in the subject— put me in mind of BENJAMIN FRANKLIN, and so Benjamin Franklin's paper on the art of procuring pleasant dreams, which would seem necessarily to include the art of going to sleep, came into my head. Now, as I often used to read that paper when I was a very small boy, and as I recollect everything I read then as perfectly as I forget everything I read now, I quoted " Get out of bed, beat up and turn your pillow, shake the bed-clothes well with at least twenty shakes, then throw the bed open and leave it to cool ; in the meanwhile, continuing undrest, walk about your chamber.

When you begin to feel the cold air unpleasant, then return to your bed, and you will soon fall asleep, and your sleep will be sweet and pleasant." Not a bit of it ! I performed the whole ceremony, and if it were possible for me to be more saucer-eyed than I was before, that was the only result that came of it.

Except Niagara. The two quotations from Washington Irving and Benjamin Franklin may have put it in my head by an American association of ideas ; but there I was, and the Horse-shoe Fall was thundering and tumbling in my eyes and ears, and the very rainbows that I left upon the spray when I really did last look upon it, were beautiful to see. The night-light being quite as plain, however, and sleep seeming to be many thousand miles further off than Niagara, I made up my mind to think a little about Sleep ; which I no sooner did than I whirled off in spite of myself to Drury Lane Theatre, and there saw a great actor and dear friend of mine (whom I had been thinking of in the day) playing Macbeth, and heard him apostrophising " the death of each day's life," as I have heard him many a time, in the days that are gone.

But, Sleep. I *will* think about Sleep. I am determined to think (this is the way I went on) about Sleep. I must hold the word Sleep tight and fast, or I shall be off at a tangent in half a second. I feel myself unaccountably straying, already, into Clare Market. Sleep. It would be curious, as illustrating the equality of sleep, to inquire how many of its phenomena are common to all classes, to all degrees of wealth and poverty, to every grade of education and ignorance. Here, for example, is her Majesty Queen Victoria in her palace, this present blessed night, and here is Winking Charley, a sturdy vagrant, in one of her Majesty's jails. Her Majesty has fallen, many thousands of times, from that same Tower, which *I* claim a right to tumble off now and then. So has Winking Charley. Her Majesty in her sleep has opened or prorogued Parliament, or has held a Drawing Room, attired in some very scanty dress, the deficiencies and improprieties of which have caused her great uneasiness. I, in my degree, have suffered unspeakable agitation of mind from taking the chair at a public dinner at the London Tavern in my night-clothes, which not all the courtesy of my kind friend and host Mr. Bathe could persuade me were quite adapted to the occasion.

Winking Charley has been repeatedly tried in a worse condition. Her Majesty is no stranger to a vault or firmament,
of a sort of floorcloth, with an indistinct pattern distantly
resembling eyes, which occasionally obtrudes itself on her
repose. Neither, am I. Neither is Winking Charley. It is
quite common to all three of us to skim along with airy strides
a little above the ground; also to hold, with the deepest
interest, dialogues with various people, all represented by
ourselves; and to be at our wit's end to know what they are
going to tell us; and to be indescribably astonished by the
secrets they disclose. It is probable that we have all three
committed murders and hidden bodies. It is pretty certain
that we have all desperately wanted to cry out, and have
had no voice; that we have all gone to the play and not
been able to get in; that we have all dreamed much more
of our youth than of our later lives; that—I have lost it!
The thread's broken.

And up I go. I, lying here with the night-light before
me, up I go, for no reason on earth that I can find out, and
drawn by no links that are visible to me, up the Great Saint
Bernard! I have lived in Switzerland, and rambled among
the mountains; but why I should go there now, and why
up the Great Saint Bernard in preference to any other
mountain, I have no idea. As I lie here broad awake, and
with every sense so sharpened that I can distinctly hear
distant noises inaudible to me at another time, I make that
journey, as I really did, on the same summer day, with the
same happy party—ah! two since dead, I grieve to think
—and there is the same track, with the same black wooden
arms to point the way, and there are the same storm-refuges
here and there; and there is the same snow falling at the
top, and there are the same frosty mists, and there is the
same intensely cold convent with its ménagerie smell, and
the same breed of dogs fast dying out, and the same breed
of jolly young monks whom I mourn to know as humbugs,
and the same convent parlour with its piano and the sitting
round the fire, and the same supper, and the same lone
night in a cell, and the same bright fresh morning when
going out into the highly rarefied air was like a plunge into
an icy bath. Now, see here what comes along; and why
does this thing stalk into my mind on the top of a Swiss
mountain!

It is a figure that I once saw, just after dark, chalked

upon a door in a little back lane near a country church—
my first church. How young a child I may have been at
the time I don't know, but it horrified me so intensely—in
connexion with the churchyard, I suppose, for it smokes
a pipe, and has a big hat with each of its ears sticking out
in a horizontal line under the brim, and is not in itself more
oppressive than a mouth from ear to ear, a pair of goggle
eyes, and hands like two bunches of carrots, five in each, can
make it—that it is still vaguely alarming to me to recall (as
I have often done before, lying awake) the running home,
the looking behind, the horror, of its following me ; though
whether disconnected from the door, or door and all, I can't
say, and perhaps never could. It lays a disagreeable train.
I must resolve to think of something on the voluntary
principle.

The balloon ascents of this last season. They will do to
think about, while I lie awake, as well as anything else. I
must hold them tight though, for I feel them sliding away,
and in their stead are the Mannings, husband and wife, hanging on the top of Horsemonger Lane Jail. In connexion
with which dismal spectacle, I recall this curious fantasy of
the mind. That, having beheld that execution, and having
left those two forms dangling on the top of the entrance
gateway—the man's, a limp, loose suit of clothes as if the
man had gone out of them ; the woman's, a fine shape, so
elaborately corseted and artfully dressed, that it was quite
unchanged in its trim appearance as it slowly swung from
side to side—I never could, by my uttermost efforts, for
some weeks, present the outside of that prison to myself
(which the terrible impression I had received continually
obliged me to do) without presenting it with the two figures
still hanging in the morning air. Until, strolling past the
gloomy place one night, when the street was deserted and
quiet, and actually seeing that the bodies were not there,
my fancy was persuaded, as it were, to take them down and
bury them within the precincts of the jail, where they have
lain ever since.

The balloon ascents of last season. Let me reckon them
up. There were the horse, the bull, the parachute, and the
tumbler hanging on—chiefly by his toes, I believe—below
the car. Very wrong, indeed, and decidedly to be stopped.
But, in connexion with these and similar dangerous exhibitions, it strikes me that that portion of the public whom

they entertain, is unjustly reproached. Their pleasure is in the difficulty overcome. They are a public of great faith, and are quite confident that the gentleman will not fall off the horse, or the lady off the bull or out of the parachute, and that the tumbler has a firm hold with his toes. They do not go to see the adventurer vanquished, but triumphant. There is no parallel in public combats between men and beasts, because nobody can answer for the particular beast —unless it were always the same beast, in which case it would be a mere stage-show, which the same public would go in the same state of mind to see, entirely believing in the brute being beforehand safely subdued by the man. That they are not accustomed to calculate hazards and dangers with any nicety, we may know from their rash exposure of themselves in overcrowded steamboats, and unsafe conveyances and places of all kinds. And I cannot help thinking that instead of railing, and attributing savage motives to a people naturally well disposed and humane, it is better to teach them, and lead them argumentatively and reasonably—for they are very reasonable, if you will discuss a matter with them—to more considerate and wise conclusions.

This is a disagreeable intrusion ! Here is a man with his throat cut, dashing towards me as I lie awake ! A recollection of an old story of a kinsman of mine, who, going home one foggy winter night to Hampstead, when London was much smaller and the road lonesome, suddenly encountered such a figure rushing past him, and presently two keepers from a madhouse in pursuit. A very unpleasant creature indeed, to come into my mind unbidden, as I lie awake.

—The balloon ascents of last season. I must return to the balloons. Why did the bleeding man start out of them ? Never mind ; if I inquire, he will be back again. The balloons. This particular public have inherently a great pleasure in the contemplation of physical difficulties overcome ; mainly, as I take it, because the lives of a large majority of them are exceedingly monotonous and real, and further, are a struggle against continual difficulties, and further still, because anything in the form of accidental injury, or any kind of illness or disability is so very serious in their own sphere. I will explain this seeming paradox of mine. Take the case of a Christmas Pantomime. Surely nobody supposes that the young mother in the pit who falls into fits of laughter when the baby is boiled or sat upon, would be at all diverted by such an occurrence off the stage. Nor is the decent workman in the gallery, who is transported beyond the ignorant present by the delight with which he sees a stout gentleman pushed out of a two pair of stairs window, to be slandered by the suspicion that he would be in the least entertained by such a spectacle in any street in London, Paris, or New York. It always appears to me that the secret of this enjoyment lies in the temporary superiority to the common hazards and mischances of life; in seeing casualties, attended when they really occur with bodily and mental suffering, tears, and poverty, happen through a very rough sort of poetry without the least harm being done to any one—the pretence of distress in a pantomime being so broadly humorous as to be no pretence at all. Much as in the comic fiction I can understand the mother with a very vulnerable baby at home, greatly relishing the invulnerable baby on the stage, so in the Cremorne reality I can understand the mason who is always liable to fall off a scaffold in his working jacket and to be carried to the hospital, having an infinite admiration of the radiant personage in spangles who goes into the clouds upon a bull, or upside down, and who, he takes it for granted—not reflecting upon the thing—has, by uncommon skill and dexterity, conquered such mischances as those to which he and his acquaintance are continually exposed.

I wish the Morgue in Paris would not come here as I lie awake, with its ghastly beds, and the swollen saturated clothes hanging up, and the water dripping, dripping all day long, upon that other swollen saturated something in the corner, like a heap of crushed over-ripe figs that I have seen in Italy! And this detestable Morgue comes back again at the head of a procession of forgotten ghost stories. This will never do. I must think of something else as I lie awake; or, like that sagacious animal in the United States who recognised the colonel who was such a dead shot, I am a gone 'Coon. What shall I think of? The late brutal assaults. Very good subject. The late brutal assaults.

(Though whether, supposing I should see, here before me as I lie awake, the awful phantom described in one of those ghost stories, who, with a head-dress of shroud, was always seen looking in through a certain glass door at a certain dead hour—whether, in such a case it would be the least consolation to me to know on philosophical grounds that it was merely my imagination, is a question I can't help asking myself by the way.)

The late brutal assaults. I strongly question the expedi-ency of advocating the revival of whipping for those crimes. It is a natural and generous impulse to be indignant at the perpetration of inconceivable brutality, but I doubt the whipping panacea gravely. Not in the least regard or pity for the criminal, whom I hold in far lower estimation than a mad wolf, but in consideration for the general tone and feeling, which is very much improved since the whipping times. It is bad for a people to be familiarised with such punishments. When the whip went out of Bridewell, and ceased to be flourished at the cart's tail and at the whipping-post, it began to fade out of madhouses, and workhouses, and schools and families, and to give place to a better system everywhere, than cruel driving. It would be hasty, because a few brutes may be inadequately punished, to revive, in any aspect, what, in so many aspects, society is hardly yet happily rid of. The whip is a very contagious kind of thing, and difficult to confine within one set of bounds. Utterly abolish punishment by fine—a barbarous device, quite as much out of date as wager by battle, but particu-larly connected in the vulgar mind with this class of offence —at least quadruple the term of imprisonment for aggra-vated assaults—and above all let us, in such cases, have no Pet Prisoning, vain glorifying, strong soup, and roasted meats, but hard work, and one unchanging and uncom-promising dietary of bread and water, well or ill; and we shall do much better than by going down into the dark to grope for the whip among the rusty fragments of the rack, and the branding iron, and the chains and gibbet from the public roads, and the weights that pressed men to death in the cells of Newgate.

I had proceeded thus far, when I found I had been lying awake so long that the very dead began to wake too, and to crowd into my thoughts most sorrowfully. Therefore, I resolved to lie awake no more, but to get up and go out for a night walk—which resolution was an acceptable relief to me, as I dare say it may prove now to a great many more.

THE GHOST OF ART

I AM a bachelor, residing in rather a dreary set of chambers in the Temple. They are situated in a square court of high houses, which would be a complete well, but for the want of water and the absence of a bucket. I live at the top of the house, among the tiles and sparrows. Like the little man in the nursery-story, I live by myself, and all the bread and cheese I get—which is not much—I put upon a shelf. I need scarcely add, perhaps, that I am in love, and that the father of my charming Julia objects to our union.

I mention these little particulars as I might deliver a letter of introduction. The reader is now acquainted with me, and perhaps will condescend to listen to my narrative.

I am naturally of a dreamy turn of mind; and my abundant leisure—for I am called to the Bar—coupled with much lonely listening to the twittering of sparrows, and the pattering of rain, has encouraged that disposition. In my "top set" I hear the wind howl on a winter night, when the man on the ground floor believes it is perfectly still weather. The dim lamps with which our Honourable Society (supposed to be as yet unconscious of the new discovery called Gas) make the horrors of the staircase visible, deepen the gloom which generally settles on my soul when I go home at night.

I am in the Law, but not of it. I can't exactly make out what it means. I sit in Westminster Hall sometimes (in character) from ten to four; and when I go out of Court, I don't know whether I am standing on my wig or my boots.

It appears to me (I mention this in confidence) as if there were too much talk and too much law—as if some grains of truth were started overboard into a tempestuous sea of chaff.

All this may make me mystical. Still, I am confident that what I am going to describe myself as having seen and heard, I actually did see and hear.

It is necessary that I should observe that I have a great delight in pictures. I am no painter myself, but I have studied pictures and written about them. I have seen all the most famous pictures in the world; my education and reading have been sufficiently general to possess me before-hand with a knowledge of most of the subjects to which a Painter is likely to have recourse; and, although I might be in some doubt as to the rightful fashion of the scabbard of King Lear's sword, for instance, I think I should know King Lear tolerably well, if I happened to meet with him.

I go to all the Modern Exhibitions every season, and of course I revere the Royal Academy. I stand by its forty Academical articles almost as firmly as I stand by the thirty-nine Articles of the Church of England. I am convinced that in neither case could there be, by any rightful possibility, one article more or less.

It is now exactly three years—three years ago, this very month—since I went from Westminster to the Temple, one Thursday afternoon, in a cheap steamboat. The sky was black, when I imprudently walked on board. It began to thunder and lighten immediately afterwards, and the rain poured down in torrents. The deck seeming to smoke with the wet, I went below; but so many passengers were there, smoking too, that I came up again, and buttoning my pea-coat, and standing in the shadow of the paddle-box, stood as upright as I could, and made the best of it.

It was at this moment that I first beheld the terrible Being, who is the subject of my present recollections.

Standing against the funnel, apparently with the intention of drying himself by the heat as fast as he got wet, was a shabby man in threadbare black, and with his hands in his pockets, who fascinated me from the memorable instant when I caught his eye.

Where had I caught that eye before? Who was he? Why did I connect him, all at once, with the Vicar of Wakefield, Alfred the Great, Gil Blas, Charles the Second, Joseph and his Brethren, the Fairy Queen, Tom Jones, the Decameron of Boccaccio, Tam O'Shanter, the Marriage of the Doge of Venice with the Adriatic, and the Great Plague of London? Why, when he bent one leg, and placed one hand upon the back of the seat near him, did my mind associate him wildly with the words, "Number one hundred and forty-two, Portrait of a gentleman?" Could it be that I was going mad?

I looked at him again, and now I could have taken my affidavit that he belonged to the Vicar of Wakefield's family. Whether he was the Vicar, or Moses, or Mr. Burchill, or the Squire, or a conglomeration of all four, I knew not; but I was impelled to seize him by the throat, and charge him with being, in some fell way, connected with the Primrose blood. He looked up at the rain, and then oh Heaven! he became St. John. He folded his arms, resigning himself to the weather, and I was frantically inclined to address him as the Spectator, and firmly demand to know what he had done with Sir Roger de Coverley.

The frightful suspicion that I was becoming deranged, returned on me with redoubled force. Meantime, this awful stranger, inexplicably linked to my distress, stood drying himself at the funnel; and ever, as the steam rose from his clothes, diffusing a mist around him, I saw through the ghostly medium all the people I have mentioned, and a score more, sacred and profane.

I am conscious of a dreadful inclination that stole upon me, as it thundered and lightened, to grapple with this man, or demon, and plunge him over the side. But I constrained myself—I know not how—to speak to him, and in a pause of the storm, I crossed the deck, and said:

"What are you?"

He replied, hoarsely, "A Model."

"A what?" said I.

"A Model," he replied. "I sets to the profession for a bob a-hour." (All through this narrative I give his own words, which are indelibly imprinted on my memory.)

The relief which this disclosure gave me, the exquisite delight of the restoration of my confidence in my own sanity, I cannot describe. I should have fallen on his neck, but for the consciousness of being observed by the man at the wheel.

"You then," said I, shaking him so warmly by the hand, that I wrung the rain out of his coat-cuff, "are the gentleman whom I have so frequently contemplated, in connection with a high-backed chair with a red cushion, and a table with twisted legs."

"I am that Model," he rejoined moodily, "and I wish I was anything else."

"Say not so," I returned. "I have seen you in the society of many beautiful young women ; " as in truth I had, and always (I now remember) in the act of making the most of his legs.

"No doubt," said he. "And you've seen me along with warses of flowers, and any number of table-kivers, and antique cabinets, and warious gammon."

"Sir?" said I.

"And warious gammon," he repeated, in a louder voice. "You might have seen me in armour, too, if you had looked sharp. Blessed if I ha'n't stood in half the suits of armour as ever came out of Pratt's shop : and sat, for weeks together, a-eating nothing, out of half the gold and silver dishes as has ever been lent for the purpose out of Storrses, and Mortimerses, or Garrardses, and Davenportseseses."

Excited, as it appeared, by a sense of injury, I thought he would never have found an end for the last word. But at length it rolled sullenly away with the thunder.

"Pardon me," said I, "you are a well-favoured, well-made man, and yet—forgive me—I find, on examining my mind, that I associate you with—that my recollection indistinctly makes you, in short—excuse me—a kind of powerful monster."

"It would be a wonder if it didn't," he said. "Do you know what my points are?"

"No," said I.

"My throat and my legs," said he. "When I don't set for a head, I mostly sets for a throat and a pair of legs. Now, granted you was a painter, and was to work at my throat for a week together, I suppose you'd see a lot of lumps and bumps there, that would never be there at all, if you looked at me, complete, instead of only my throat. Wouldn't you?"

"Probably," said I, surveying him.

"Why, it stands to reason," said the Model. "Work another week at my legs, and it'll be the same thing. You'll make 'em out as knotty and as knobby, at last, as if they was the trunks of two old trees. Then, take and stick my legs and throat on to another man's body, and you'll make a reg'lar monster. And that's the way the public gets their reg'lar monsters, every first Monday in May, when the Royal Academy Exhibition opens."

"You are a critic," said I, with an air of deference.

"I'm in an uncommon ill humour, if that's it," rejoined the Model, with great indignation. "As if it warn't bad enough for a bob a-hour, for a man to be mixing himself up with that there jolly old furniter that one 'ud think the public know'd the wery nails in by this time—or to be putting on greasy old 'ats and cloaks, and playing tambourines in the Bay o' Naples, with Wesuvius a smokin' according to pattern in the background, and the wines a bearing wonderful in tho middle distance—or to be unpolitely kicking up his legs among a lot o' gals, with no reason whatever in his mind, but to show 'em—as if this warn't bad enough, I'm to go and be thrown out of employment too!"

"Surely no!" said I.

"Surely yes," said the indignant Model. "But I'll grow one."

The gloomy and threatening manner in which he muttered the last words, can never be effaced from my remembrance. My blood ran cold.

I asked of myself, what was it that this desperate Being was resolved to grow. My breast made no response.

I ventured to implore him to explain his meaning. With a scornful laugh, he uttered this dark prophecy:

"I'll grow one. And, mark my words, it shall haunt you!"

We parted in the storm, after I had forced half-a-crown on his acceptance, with a trembling hand. I conclude that something supernatural happened to the steamboat, as it bore his reeking figure down the river; but it never got into the papers.

Two years elapsed, during which I followed my profession without any vicissitudes; never holding so much as a motion, of course. At the expiration of that period, I found myself making my way home to the Temple, one night, in precisely such another storm of thunder and lightning as that by which I had been overtaken on board the steamboat—except that this storm, bursting over the town at midnight, was rendered much more awful by the darkness and the hour.

As I turned into my court, I really thought a thunderbolt would fall, and plough the pavement up. Every brick and stone in the place seemed to have an echo of its own for the thunder. The waterspouts were overcharged, and the rain came tearing down from the house-tops as if they had been mountain-tops.

Mrs. Parkins, my laundress—wife of Parkins the porter, then newly dead of a dropsy—had particular instructions to place a bedroom candle and a match under the staircase lamp on my landing, in order that I might light my candle there, whenever I came home. Mrs. Parkins invariably disregarding all instructions, they were never there. Thus it happened that on this occasion I groped my way into my sitting-room to find the candle, and came out to light it.

What were my emotions when, underneath the staircase lamp, shining with wet as if he had never been dry since our last meeting, stood the mysterious Being whom I had encountered on the steamboat in a thunderstorm, two years before! His prediction rushed upon my mind, and I turned faint.

"I said I'd do it," he observed, in a hollow voice, "and I have done it. May I come in?"

"Misguided creature, what have you done?" I returned.

"I'll let you know," was his reply, "if you'll let me in."

Could it be murder that he had done? And had he been so successful that he wanted to do it again, at my expense?

I hesitated.

"May I come in?" said he.

I inclined my head, with as much presence of mind as I could command, and he followed me into my chambers. There, I saw that the lower part of his face was tied up, in what is commonly called a Belcher handkerchief. He slowly removed this bandage, and exposed to view a long dark beard, curling over his upper lip, twisting about the corners of his mouth, and hanging down upon his breast.

"What is this?" I exclaimed involuntarily, "and what have you become?"

"I am the Ghost of Art!" said he.

The effect of these words, slowly uttered in the thunder-storm at midnight, was appalling in the last degree. More dead than alive, I surveyed him in silence.

"The German taste came up," said he, "and threw me out of bread. I am ready for the taste now."

He made his beard a little jagged with his hands, folded his arms, and said,

"Severity!"

I shuddered. It was so severe.

He made his beard flowing on his breast, and, leaning both hands on the staff of a carpet-broom which Mrs. Parkins had left among my books, said:

"Benevolence."

I stood transfixed. The change of sentiment was entirely in the beard. The man might have left his face alone, or had no face. The beard did everything.

He lay down, on his back, on my table, and with that action of his head threw up his beard at the chin.

"That's death!" said he.

He got off my table and, looking up at the ceiling. cocked his beard a little awry; at the same time making it stick out before him.

"Adoration, or a vow of vengeance," he observed.

He turned his profile to me, making his upper lip very bulky with the upper part of his beard.

"Romantic character," said he.

He looked sideways out of his beard, as if it were an ivy-bush. "Jealousy," said he. He gave it an ingenious twist in the air, and informed me that he was carousing. He made it shaggy with his fingers—and it was Despair; lank—and it was avarice; tossed it all kinds of ways—and it was rage. The beard did everything.

"I am the Ghost of Art," said he. "Two bob a-day now, and more when it's longer! Hair's the true expression. There is no other. I SAID I'D GROW IT, AND I'VE GROWN IT, AND IT SHALL HAUNT YOU!"

He may have tumbled down-stairs in the dark, but he never walked down or ran down. I looked over the banisters, and I was alone with the thunder.

Need I add more of my terrific fate? IT HAS haunted me ever since. It glares upon me from the walls of the Royal Academy, (except when MACLISE subdues it to his genius,) it fills my soul with terror at the British Institution, it lures young artists on to their destruction. Go where I will, the Ghost of Art, eternally working the passions in hair, and expressing everything by beard, pursues me. The prediction is accomplished, and the victim has no rest.

OUT OF TOWN

SITTING, on a bright September morning, among my books and papers at my open window on the cliff overhanging the sea-beach, I have the sky and ocean framed before me like a beautiful picture. A beautiful picture, but with such movement in it, such changes of light upon the sails of ships and wake of steamboats, such dazzling gleams of silver far out at sea, such fresh touches on the crisp wave-tops as they break and roll towards me—a picture with such music in the billowy rush upon the shingle, the blowing of morning wind through the corn-sheaves where the farmers' waggons are busy, the singing of the larks, and the distant voices of children at play—such charms of sight and sound as all the Galleries on earth can but poorly suggest.

So dreamy is the murmur of the sea below my window, that I may have been here, for anything I know, one hundred years. Not that I have grown old, for, daily on the neighbouring downs and grassy hill-sides, I find that I can still in reason walk any distance, jump over anything, and climb up anywhere; but that the sound of the ocean seems to have become so customary to my musings, and other realities seem so to have gone aboard ship and floated away over the horizon, that, for aught I will undertake to the contrary, I am the enchanted son of the King my father, shut up in a tower on the sea-shore, for protection against an old she-goblin who insisted on being my godmother, and who foresaw at the font—wonderful creature!—that I should get into a scrape before I was twenty-one. I remember to have been in a City (my Royal parent's dominions, I suppose), and apparently not long ago either, that was in the dreariest condition. The principal inhabitants had all been changed into old newspapers, and in that form were preserving their window-blinds from dust, and wrapping all their smaller household gods in curl-papers. I walked through gloomy streets where every house was shut up and newspapered, and where my solitary footsteps echoed on the deserted pavements. In the public rides there were no carriages, no horses, no animated existence, but a few sleepy policemen, and a few adventurous boys taking advantage of the devasta- tion to swarm up the lamp-posts. In the Westward streets there was no traffic; in the Westward shops, no business. The water-patterns which the 'Prentices had trickled out on the pavements early in the morning, remained uneffaced by human feet. At the corners of mews, Cochin-China fowls stalked gaunt and savage; nobody being left in the deserted city (as it appeared to me), to feed them. Public Houses, where splendid footmen swinging their legs over gorgeous hammer-cloths beside wigged coachmen were wont to regale, were silent, and the unused pewter pots shone, too bright for business, on the shelves. I beheld a Punch's Show leaning against a wall near Park Lane, as if it had fainted. It was deserted, and there were none to heed its desolation. In Belgrave Square I met the last man—an ostler—sitting on a post in a ragged red waistcoat, eating straw, and mildew- ing away.

If I recollect the name of the little town, on whose shore this sea is murmuring—but I am not just now, as I have premised, to be relied upon for anything—it is Pavilionstone. Within a quarter of a century, it was a little fishing town, and they do say, that the time was, when it was a little smuggling town. I have heard that it was rather famous in the hollands and brandy way, and that coevally with that reputation the lamplighter's was considered a bad life at the Assurance Offices. It was observed that if he were not particular about lighting up, he lived in peace; but that, if he made the best of the oil-lamps in the steep and narrow streets, he usually fell over the cliff at an early age. Now, gas and electricity run to the very water's edge, and the South-Eastern Railway Company screech at us in the dead of night.

But the old little fishing and smuggling town remains, and is so tempting a place for the latter purpose, that I think of going out some night next week, in a fur cap and a pair of petticoat trousers, and running an empty tub, as a kind of archæological pursuit. Let nobody with corns come to Pavilionstone, for there are breakneck flights of ragged steps, connecting the principal streets by back-ways, which will cripple that visitor in half an hour. These are the ways by which, when I run that tub, I shall escape. I shall make a Thermopylæ of the corner of one of them, defend it with my cutlass against the coast-guard until my brave companions have sheered off, then dive into the darkness, and regain my Susan's arms. In connection with these breakneck steps I observe some wooden cottages, with tumble-down out-houses, and back-yards three feet square, adorned with garlands of dried fish, in one of which (though the General Board of Health might object) my Susan dwells.

The South-Eastern Company have brought Pavilionstone into such vogue, with their tidal trains and splendid steam-packets, that a new Pavilionstone is rising up. I am, myself, of New Pavilionstone. We are a little mortary and limey at present, but we are getting on capitally. Indeed, we were getting on so fast, at onè time, that we rather overdid it, and built a street of shops, the business of which may be expected to arrive in about ten years. We are sensibly laid out in general; and with a little care and pains (by no means wanting, so far), shall become a very pretty place. We ought to be, for our situation is delightful, our air is delicious, and our breezy hills and downs, carpeted with wild thyme, and decorated with millions of wild flowers, are, on the faith of a pedestrian, perfect. In New Pavilionstone we are a little too much addicted to small windows with more bricks in them than glass, and we are not over-fanciful in the way of decorative architecture, and we get unexpected sea-views through cracks in the street doors; on the whole, however, we are very snug and comfortable, and well accom-modated. But the Home Secretary (if there be such an officer) cannot too soon shut up the burial-ground of the old parish church. It is in the midst of us, and Pavilionstone will get no good of it, if it be too long left alone.

The lion of Pavilionstone is its Great Hotel. A dozen years ago, going over to Paris by South-Eastern Tidal Steamer, you used to be dropped upon the platform of the main line Pavilionstone Station (not a junction then), at eleven o'clock on a dark winter's night, in a roaring wind; and in the howling wilderness outside the station, was a short omnibus which brought you up by the forehead the instant you got in at the door; and nobody cared about you, and you were alone in the world. You bumped over infinite chalk, until you were turned out at a strange building which had just left off being a barn without having quite begun to be a house, where nobody expected your coming, or knew

what to do with you when you were come, and where you
were usually blown about, until you happened to be blown
against the cold beef, and finally into bed. At five in the
morning you were blown out of bed, and after a dreary
breakfast, with crumpled company, in the midst of confusion,
were hustled on board a steamboat and lay wretched on
deck until you saw France lunging and surging at you with
great vehemence over the bowsprit.

Now, you come down to Pavilionstone in a free and easy
manner, an irresponsible agent, made over in trust to the
South-Eastern Company, until you get out of the railway-
carriage at high-water mark. If you are crossing by the
boat at once, you have nothing to do but walk on board
and be happy there if you can—I can't. If you are going
to our Great Pavilionstone Hotel, the sprightliest porters
under the sun, whose cheerful looks are a pleasant welcome,
shoulder your luggage, drive it off in vans, bowl it away in
trucks, and enjoy themselves in playing athletic games with
it. If you are for public life at our great Pavilionstone
Hotel, you walk into that establishment as if it were your
club; and find ready for you, your news-room, dining-room,
smoking-room, billiard-room, music-room, public breakfast,
public dinner twice a-day (one plain, one gorgeous), hot
baths and cold baths. If you want to be bored, there are
plenty of bores always ready for you, and from Saturday to
Monday in particular, you can be bored (if you like it)
through and through. Should you want to be private at our
Great Pavilionstone Hotel, say but the word, look at the
list of charges, choose your floor, name your figure—there
you are, established in your castle, by the day, week, month,
or year, innocent of all comers or goers, unless you have my
fancy for walking early in the morning down the groves of
boots and shoes, which so regularly flourish at all the
chamber-doors before breakfast, that it seems to me as if
nobody ever got up or took them in. Are you going across
the Alps, and would you like to air your Italian at our Great
Pavilionstone Hotel? Talk to the Manager—always conversational, accomplished, and polite. Do you want to be
aided, abetted, comforted, or advised, at our Great Pavilionstone Hotel? Send for the good landlord, and he is your
friend. Should you, or any one belonging to you, ever be
taken ill at our Great Pavilionstone Hotel, you will not
soon forget him or his kind wife. And when you pay your

bill at our Great Pavilionstone Hotel, you will not be put out of humour by anything you find in it.

A thoroughly good inn, in the days of coaching and post-ing, was a noble place. But no such inn would have been equal to the reception of four or five hundred people, all of them wet through, and half of them dead sick, every day in the year. This is where we shine, in our Pavilionstone Hotel. Again—who, coming and going, pitching and toss-ing, boating and training, hurrying in, and flying out, could ever have calculated the fees to be paid at an old-fashioned house? In our Pavilionstone Hotel vocabulary, there is no such word as fee. Everything is done for you; every service is provided at a fixed and reasonable charge; all the prices are hung up in all the rooms; and you can make out your own bill beforehand, as well as the book-keeper.

In the case of your being a pictorial artist, desirous of studying at small expense the physiognomies and beards of different nations, come, on receipt of this, to Pavilionstone. You shall find all the nations of the earth, and all the styles of shaving and not shaving, hair cutting and hair letting alone, for ever flowing through our hotel. Couriers you shall see by hundreds; fat leathern bags for five-franc pieces, closing with violent snaps, like discharges of fire-arms, by thousands; more luggage in a morning than, fifty years ago, all Europe saw in a week. Looking at trains, steamboats, sick travellers, and luggage, is our great Pavilionstone recrea-tion. We are not strong in other public amusements. We have a Literary and Scientific Institution, and we have a Working Men's Institution—may it hold many gipsy holidays in summer fields, with the kettle boiling, the band of music playing, and the people dancing; and may I be on the hill-side, looking on with pleasure at a wholesome sight too rare in England!—and we have two or three churches, and more chapels than I have yet added up. But public amusements are scarce with us. If a poor theatrical manager comes with his company to give us, in a loft, Mary Bax, or the Murder on the Sand Hills, we don't care much for him—starve him out, in fact. We take more kindly to wax-work, especially if it moves; in which case it keeps much clearer of the second commandment than when it is still. Cooke's Circus (Mr. Cooke is my friend, and always leaves a good name behind him) gives us only a night in passing through. Nor does the travelling menagerie think us worth a longer visit

It gave us a look-in the other day, bringing with it the residentiary van with the stained glass windows, which Her Majesty kept ready-made at Windsor Castle, until she found a suitable opportunity of submitting it for the proprietor's acceptance. I brought away five wonderments from this exhibition. I have wondered ever since, Whether the beasts ever do get used to those small places of confinement; Whether the monkeys have that very horrible flavour in their free state; Whether wild animals have a natural ear for time and tune, and therefore every four-footed creature began to howl in despair when the band began to play; What the giraffe does with his neck when his cart is shut up; and, Whether the elephant feels ashamed of himself when he is brought out of his den to stand on his head in the presence of the whole Collection.

We are a tidal harbour at Pavilionstone, as indeed I have implied already in my mention of tidal trains. At low water, we are a heap of mud, with an empty channel in it where a couple of men in big boots always shovel and scoop: with what exact object, I am unable to say. At that time, all the stranded fishing-boats turn over on their sides, as if they were dead marine monsters; the colliers and other shipping stick disconsolate in the mud; the steamers look as if their white chimneys would never smoke more, and their red paddles never turn again; the green sea-slime and weed upon the rough stones at the entrance, seem records of obsolete high tides never more to flow; the flagstaff-halyards droop; the very little wooden lighthouse shrinks in the idle glare of the sun. And here I may observe of the very little wooden lighthouse, that when it is lighted at night,—red and green,—it looks so like a medical man's, that several distracted husbands have at various times been found, on occasions of premature domestic anxiety, going round and round it, trying to find the Night-bell.

But the moment the tide begins to make, the Pavilion-stone Harbour begins to revive. It feels the breeze of the rising water before the water comes, and begins to flutter and stir. When the little shallow waves creep in, barely overlapping one another, the vanes at the mastheads wake, and become agitated. As the tide rises, the fishing-boats get into good spirits and dance, the flagstaff hoists a bright red flag, the steamboat smokes, cranes creak, horses and carriages dangle in the air, stray passengers and luggage appear. Now, the shipping is afloat, and comes up buoy-antly, to look at the wharf. Now, the carts that have come down for coals, load away as hard as they can load. Now, the steamer smokes immensely, and occasionally blows at the paddle-boxes like a vaporous whale—greatly disturbing nervous loungers. Now, both the tide and the breeze have risen, and you are holding your hat on (if you want to see how the ladies hold *their* hats on, with a stay, passing over the broad brim and down the nose, come to Pavilionstone). Now, everything in the harbour splashes, dashes, and bobs. Now, the Down Tidal Train is telegraphed, and you know (without knowing how you know), that two hundred and eighty-seven people are coming. Now, the fishing-boats that have been out, sail in at the top of the tide. Now, the bell goes, and the locomotive hisses and shrieks, and the train comes gliding in, and the two hundred and eighty-seven come scuffling out. Now, there is not only a tide of water, but a tide of people, and a tide of luggage—all tumbling and flowing and bouncing about together. Now, after infinite bustle, the steamer steams out, and we (on the Pier) are all delighted when she rolls as if she would roll her funnel out, and are all disappointed when she don't. Now, the other steamer is coming in, and the Custom House prepares, and the wharf-labourers assemble, and the hawsers are made ready, and the Hotel Porters come rattling down with van and truck, eager to begin more Olympic games with more luggage. And this is the way in which we go on, down at Pavilionstone, every tide. And if you want to live a life of luggage, or to see it lived, or to breathe sweet air which will send you to sleep at a moment's notice at any period of the day or night, or to disport yourself upon or in the sea, or to scamper about Kent, or to come out of town for the enjoyment of all or any of these pleasures, come to Pavilionstone.

OUT OF THE SEASON

It fell to my lot, this last bleak Spring, to find myself in a watering-place out of the Season. A vicious north-east squall blew me into it from foreign parts, and I tarried in it alone for three days, resolved to be exceedingly busy.

On the first day, I began business by looking for two hours at the sea, and staring the Foreign Militia out of countenance. Having disposed of these important engagements, I sat down at one of the two windows of my room, intent on doing something desperate in the way of literary composition, and writing a chapter of unheard-of excellence —with which the present essay has no connexion.

It is a remarkable quality in a watering-place out of the season, that everything in it will and must be looked at. I had no previous suspicion of this fatal truth; but the moment I sat down to write, I began to perceive it. I had scarcely fallen into my most promising attitude, and dipped my pen in the ink, when I found the clock upon the pier— a red-faced clock with a white rim—importuning me in a highly vexatious manner to consult my watch, and see how I was off for Greenwich time. Having no intention of making a voyage or taking an observation, I had not the least need of Greenwich time, and could have put up with watering-place time as a sufficiently accurate article. The pier-clock, however, persisting, I felt it necessary to lay down my pen, compare my watch with him, and fall into a grave solicitude about half-seconds. I had taken up my pen again, and was about to commence that valuable chapter, when a Custom-house cutter under the window requested that I would hold a naval review of her, immediately.

It was impossible, under the circumstances, for any mental resolution, merely human, to dismiss the Custom-house cutter, because the shadow of her topmast fell upon my paper, and the vane played on the masterly blank chapter. I was therefore under the necessity of going to the other window; sitting astride of the chair there, like

Napoleon bivouacking in the print; and inspecting the cutter as she lay, all, O! that day, in the way of my chapter. She was rigged to carry a quantity of canvas, but her hull was so very small that four giants aboard of her (three men and a boy) who were vigilantly scraping at her, all together, inspired me with a terror lest they should scrape her away. A fifth giant, who appeared to consider himself " below "— as indeed he was, from the waist downwards—meditated, in such close proximity with the little gusty chimney-pipe, that he seemed to be smoking it. Several boys looked on from the wharf, and, when the gigantic attention appeared to be fully occupied, one or other of these would furtively swing himself in mid-air over the Custom-house cutter, by means of a line pendan't from her rigging, like a young spirit of the storm. Presently, a sixth hand brought down two little water-casks; presently afterwards a truck came and delivered a hamper. I was now under an obligation to consider that the cutter was going on a cruise, and to wonder where she was going, and when she was going, and why she was going, and at what date she might be expected back, and who commanded her? With these pressing questions I was fully occupied when the Packet, making ready to go across, and blowing off her spare steam, roared, "Look at me!"

It became a positive duty to look at the Packet preparing to go across; aboard of which, the people newly come down by the railroad were hurrying in a great fluster. The crew had got their tarry overalls on—and one knew what *that* meant—not to mention the white basins, ranged in neat little piles of a dozen each, behind the door of the after-cabin. One lady as I looked, one resigning and far-seeing woman, took her basin from the store of crockery, as she might have taken a refreshment-ticket, laid herself down on deck with that utensil at her ear, muffled her feet in one shawl, solemnly covered her countenance after the antique manner with another, and on the completion of these preparations appeared by the strength of her volition to become insensible. The mail-bags (O that I myself had the sea-legs of a mail-bag!) were tumbled aboard; the Packet left off roaring, warped out, and made at the white line upon the bar. One dip, one roll, one break of the sea over her bows, and Moore's Almanack or the sage Raphael could not have told me more of the state of things aboard, than I knew.

The famous chapter was all but begun now, and would have been quite begun, but for the wind. It was blowing stiffly from the east, and it rumbled in the chimney and shook the house. That was not much; but, looking out into the wind's grey eye for inspiration, I laid down my pen again to make the remark to myself, how emphatically everything by the sea declares that it has a great concern in the state of the wind. The trees blown all one way; the defences of tho harbour reared highest and strongest against the raging point; the shingle flung up on the beach from the same direction; the number of arrows pointed at the common enemy; the sea tumbling in and rushing towards them as if it were inflamed by the sight. This put it in my head that I really ought to go out and take a walk in the wind; so I gave up the magnificent chapter for that day, entirely persuading myself that I was under a moral obligation to have a blow.

I had a good one, and that on the high road—the very high road—on the top of the cliffs, where I met the stage-coach with all the outsides holding their hats on and themselves too, and overtook a flock of sheep with the wool about their necks blown into such great ruffs that they looked like fleecy owls. The wind played upon the light-house as if it were a great whistle, the spray was driven over the sea in a cloud of haze, the ships rolled and pitched heavily, and at intervals long slants and flaws of light mado mountain-steeps of communication between the ocean and the sky. A walk of ten miles brought me to a seaside town without a cliff, which, like the town I had come from, was out of the season too. Half of the houses were shut up; half of the other half were to let; the town might have done as much business as it was doing then, if it had been at the bottom of the sea. Nobody seemed to flourish save the attorney; his clerk's pen was going in the bow-window of his wooden house; his brass door-plate alone was free from salt, and had been polished up that morning. On the beach, among the rough luggers and capstans, groups of storm-beaten boatmen, like a sort of marine monsters, watched under the lee of those objects, or stood leaning forward against the wind, looking out through battered spy-glasses. The parlour bell in the Admiral Benbow had grown so flat with being out of the season, that neither could I hear it ring when I pulled the handle for lunch, nor could the young woman in black stockings and strong shoes, who acted as waiter out of the season, until it had been tinkled three times.

Admiral Benbow's cheese was out of the season, but his home-made bread was good, and his beer was perfect. Deluded by some earlier spring day which had been warm and sunny, the Admiral had cleared the firing out of his parlour stove, and had put some flower-pots in—which was amiable and hopeful in the Admiral, but not judicious: the room being, at that present visiting, transcendantly cold. I therefore took the liberty of peeping out across a little stone passage into the Admiral's kitchen, and, seeing a high settle with its back towards me drawn out in front of the Admiral's kitchen fire, I strolled in, bread and cheese in hand, munching and looking about. One landsman and two boatmen were seated on the settle, smoking pipes and drinking beer out of thick pint crockery mugs—mugs peculiar to such places, with parti-coloured rings round them, and ornaments between the rings like frayed-out roots. The landsman was relating his experience, as yet only three nights old, of a fearful running-down case in the Channel, and therein presented to my imagination a sound of music that it will not soon forget.

"At that identical moment of time," said he (he was a prosy man by nature, who rose with his subject), "the night being light and calm, but with a grey mist upon the water that didn't seem to spread for more than two or three mile, I was walking up and down the wooden causeway next the pier, off where it happened, along with a friend of mine, which his name is Mr. Clocker. Mr. Clocker is a grocer over yonder." (From the direction in which he pointed the bowl of his pipe, I might have judged Mr. Clocker to be a merman, established in the grocery trade in five-and-twenty fathoms of water.) "We were smoking our pipes, and walking up and down the causeway, talking of one thing and talking of another. We were quite alone there, except that a few hovellers" (the Kentish name for 'long-shore boatmen like his companions) "were hanging about their lugs, waiting while the tide made, as hovellers will." (One of the two boatmen, thoughtfully regarding me, shut up one eye; this I understood to mean: first, that he took me into the conversation: secondly, that he confirmed the proposition: thirdly, that he announced himself as a hoveller.)

"All of a sudden Mr. Clocker and me stood rooted to the spot, by hearing a sound come through the stillness, right over the sea, *like a great sorrowful flute or Æolian harp.* We didn't in the least know what it was, and judge of our surprise when we saw the hovellers, to a man, leap into the boats and tear about to hoist sail and get off, as if they had every one of 'em gone, in a moment, raving mad! But *they* knew it was the cry of distress from the sinking emigrant ship."

When I got back to my watering-place out of the season, and had done my twenty miles in good style, I found that the celebrated Black Mesmerist intended favouring the public that evening in the Hall of the Muses, which he had engaged for the purpose. After a good dinner, seated by the fire in an easy chair, I began to waver in a design I had formed of waiting on the Black Mesmerist, and to incline towards the expediency of remaining where I was. Indeed a point of gallantry was involved in my doing so, inasmuch as I had not left France alone, but had come from the prisons of St. Pélagie with my distinguished and unfortunate friend Madame Roland (in two volumes which I bought for two francs each, at the book-stall in the Place de la Concorde, Paris, at the corner of the Rue Royale). Deciding to pass the evening tête-à-tête with Madame Roland, I derived, as I always do, great pleasure from that spiritual woman's society, and the charms of her brave soul and engaging conversation. I must confess that if she had only some more faults, only a few more passionate failings of any kind, I might love her better; but I am content to believe that the deficiency is in me, and not in her. We spent some sadly interesting hours together on this occasion, and she told me again of her cruel discharge from the Abbaye, and of her being re-arrested before her free feet had sprung lightly up half-a-dozen steps of her own staircase, and carried off to the prison which she only left for the guillotine.

Madame Roland and I took leave of one another before midnight, and I went to bed full of vast intentions for next day, in connexion with the unparalleled chapter. To hear the foreign mail-steamers coming in at dawn of day, and to know that I was not aboard or obliged to get up, was very comfortable; so I rose for the chapter in great force.

I had advanced so far as to sit down at my window again

on my second morning, and to write the first half-line of the
chapter and strike it out, not liking it, when my conscience
reproached me with not having surveyed the watering-place
out of the season, after all, yesterday, but with having gone
straight out of it at the rate of four miles and a half an
hour. Obviously the best amends that I could make for
this remissness was to go and look at it without another
moment's delay. So—altogether as a matter of duty—
I gave up the magnificent chapter for another day, and
sauntered out with my hands in my pockets.

All the houses and lodgings ever let to visitors were to
let that morning. It seemed to have snowed bills with To
Let upon them. This put me upon thinking what the
owners of all those apartments did, out of the season; how
they employed their time, and occupied their minds. They
could not be always going to the Methodist chapels, of which
I passed one every other minute. They must have some
other recreation. Whether they pretended to take one
another's lodgings, and opened one another's tea-caddies in
fun? Whether they cut slices off their own beef and
mutton, and made believe that it belonged to somebody
else? Whether they played little dramas of life, as children
do, and said, "I ought to come and look at your apartments,
and you ought to ask two guineas a-week too much, and
then I ought to say I must have the rest of the day to think
of it, and then you ought to say that another lady and
gentleman with no children in family had made an offer
very close to your own terms, and you had passed your
word to give them a positive answer in half an hour, and
indeed were just going to take the bill down when you
heard the knock, and then I ought to take them you
know?" Twenty such speculations engaged my thoughts.
Then, after passing, still clinging to the walls, defaced rags
of the bills of last year's Circus, I came to a back field near
a timber-yard where the Circus itself had been, and where
there was yet a sort of monkish tonsure on the grass, indicating the spot where the young lady had gone round upon
her pet steed Firefly in her daring flight. Turning into the
town again, I came among the shops, and they were emphatically out of the season. The chemist had no boxes of
ginger-beer powders, no beautifying sea-side soaps and
washes, no attractive scents; nothing but his great goggle-
eyed red bottles, looking as if the winds of winter and the

drift of the salt sea had inflamed them. The grocers' hot pickles, Harvey's Sauce, Doctor Kitchener's Zest, Anchovy Paste, Dundee Marmalade, and the whole stock of luxurious helps to appetite, were hybernating somewhere underground. The china-shop had no trifles from anywhere. The Bazaar had given in altogether, and presented a notice on the shutters that this establishment would re-open at Whitsuntide, and that the proprietor in the meantime might be heard of at Wild Lodge, East Cliff. At the Sea-bathing Establishment, a row of neat little wooden houses seven or eight feet high, I *saw* the proprietor in bed in the shower-bath. As to the bathing-machines, they were (how they got there is not for me to say) at the top of a hill at least a mile and a half off. The library, which I had never seen otherwise than wide open, was tight shut; and two peevish bald old gentlemen seemed to be hermetically sealed up inside, eternally reading the paper. That wonderful mystery, the music-shop, carried it off as usual (except that it had more cabinet pianos in stock), as if season or no season were all one to it. It made the same prodigious display of bright brazen wind-instruments, horribly twisted, worth, as I should conceive, some thousands of pounds, and which it is utterly impossible that anybody in any season can ever play or want to play. It had five triangles in the window, six pairs of castanets, and three harps; likewise every polka with a coloured frontispiece that ever was published; from the original one where a smooth male and female Pole of high rank are coming at the observer with their arms a-kimbo, to the Ratcatcher's Daughter. Astonishing establishment, amazing enigma! Three other shops were pretty much out of the season, what they were used to be in it. First, the shop where they sell the sailors' watches, which had still the old collection of enormous timekeepers, apparently designed to break a fall from the masthead: with places to wind them up, like fire-plugs. Secondly, the shop where they sell the sailors' clothing, which displayed the old sou'-westers, and the old oily suits, and the old pea-jackets, and the old one sea-chest, with its handles like a pair of rope ear-rings. Thirdly, the unchangeable shop for the sale of literature that has been left behind. Here, Dr. Faustus was still going down to very red and yellow perdition, under the superintendence of three green personages of a scaly humour, with excrescential serpents growing out of their blade-bones.

Here, the Golden Dreamer and the Norwood Fortune Teller were still on sale at sixpence each, with instructions for making the dumb cake, and reading destinies in tea-cups, and with a picture of a young woman with a high waist lying on a sofa in an attitude so uncomfortable as almost to account for her dreaming at one and the same time of a conflagration, a shipwreck, an earthquake, a skeleton, a church-porch, lightning, funerals performed, and a young man in a bright blue coat and canary pantaloons. Here, were Little Warblers and Fairburn's Comic Songsters. Here, too, were ballads on the old ballad paper and in the old confusion of types; with an old man in a cocked hat, and an arm-chair, for the illustration to Will Watch the bold Smuggler; and the Friar of Orders Grey, represented by a little girl in a hoop, with a ship in the distance. All these as of yore, when they were infinite delights to me!

It took me so long fully to relish these many enjoyments, that I had not more than an hour before bedtime to devote to Madame Roland. We got on admirably together on the subject of her convent education, and I rose next morning with the full conviction that the day for the great chapter was at last arrived.

It had fallen calm, however, in the night, and as I sat at breakfast I blushed to remember that I had not yet been on the Downs. I a walker, and not yet on the Downs! Really, on so quiet and bright a morning this must be set right. As an essential part of the Whole Duty of Man, therefore, I left the chapter to itself—for the present—and went on the Downs. They were wonderfully green and beautiful, and gave me a good deal to do. When I had done with the free air and the view, I had to go down into the valley and look after the hops (which I know nothing about), and to be equally solicitous as to the cherry orchards. Then I took it on myself to cross-examine a tramping family in black (mother alleged, I have no doubt by herself in person, to have died last week), and to accompany eighteenpence, which produced a great effect, with moral admonitions which produced none at all. Finally, it was late in the afternoon before I got back to the unprecedented chapter, and then I determined that it was out of the season, as the place was, and put it away.

I went at night to the benefit of Mrs. B. Wedgington at the Theatre, who had placarded the town with the admonition, "DON'T FORGET IT!" I made the house, according to my calculation, four and ninepence to begin with, and it may have warmed up, in the course of the evening, to half a sovereign. There was nothing to offend any one,—the good Mr. Baines of Leeds excepted. Mrs. B. Wedgington sang to a grand piano. Mr. B. Wedgington did the like, and also took off his coat, tucked up his trousers, and danced in clogs. Master B. Wedgington, aged ten months, was nursed by a shivering young person in the boxes, and the eye of Mrs. B. Wedgington wandered that way more than once. Peace be with all the Wedgingtons from A. to Z. May they find themselves in the Season somewhere!

A POOR MAN'S TALE OF A PATENT

I AM not used to writing for print. What working-man, that never labours less (some Mondays, and Christmas Time and Easter Time excepted) than twelve or fourteen hours a day, is? But I have been asked to put down, plain, what I have got to say; and so I take pen-and-ink, and do it to the best of my power, hoping defects will find excuse.

I was born nigh London, but have worked in a shop at Birmingham (what you would call Manufactories, we call Shops) almost ever since I was out of my time. I served my apprenticeship at Deptford, nigh where I was born, and I am a smith by trade. My name is John. I have been called "Old John" ever since I was nineteen year of age, on account of not having much hair. I am fifty-six year of age at the present time, and I don't find myself with more hair, nor yet with less, to signify, than at nineteen year of age aforesaid.

I have been married five and thirty year, come next April. I was married on All Fools' Day. Let them laugh that win. I won a good wife that day, and it was as sensible a day to me as ever I had.

We have had a matter of ten children, six whereof are living. My eldest son is engineer in the Italian steam-packet "Mezzo Giorno, plying between Marseilles and Naples, and calling at Genoa, Leghorn, and Civita Vecchia." He was a good workman. He invented a many useful little things that brought him in—nothing. I have two sons doing well at Sydney, New South Wales—single, when last heard from. One of my sons (James) went wild and for a soldier, where he was shot in India, living six weeks in hospital with a musket-ball lodged in his shoulder-blade, which he wrote with his own hand. He was the best looking. One of my two daughters (Mary) is comfortable in her circumstances, but water on the chest. The other (Charlotte), her husband run away from her in the basest

manner, and she and her three children live with us. The
youngest, six year old, has a turn for mechanics.

I am not a Chartist, and I never was. I don't mean to
say but what I see a good many public points to complain
of, still I don't think that's the way to set them right. If
I did think so, I should be a Chartist. But I don't think
so, and I am not a Chartist. I read the paper, and hear
discussion, at what we call "a parlour," in Birmingham,
and I know many good men and workmen who are
Chartists. Note. Not Physical force.

It won't be took as boastful in me, if I make the remark
(for I can't put down what I have got to say, without putting
that down before going any further), that I have always been
of an ingenious turn. I once got twenty pound by a screw,
and it's in use now. I have been twenty year, off and on,
completing an. Invention and perfecting it. I perfected of
it, last Christmas Eve at ten o'clock at night. Me and my
wife stood and let some tears fall over the Model, when it
was done and I brought her in to take a look at it.

A friend of mine, by the name of William Butcher, is
a Chartist. Moderate. He is a good speaker. He is very
animated. I have often heard him deliver that what is, at
every turn, in the way of us working-men, is, that too many
places have been made, in the course of time, to provide for
people that never ought to have been provided for; and that
we have to obey forms and to pay fees to support those
places when we shouldn't ought. "True," (delivers William
Butcher), "all the public has to do this, but it falls heaviest
on the working-man, because he has least to spare; and
likewise because impediments shouldn't be put in his way,
when he wants redress of wrong or furtherance of right."
Note. I have wrote down those words from William
Butcher's own mouth. W. B. delivering them fresh for
the aforesaid purpose.

Now, to my Model again. There it was, perfected of, on
Christmas Eve, gone nigh a year, at ten o'clock at night.
All the money I could spare I had laid out upon the
Model; and when times was bad, or my daughter Charlotte's
children sickly, or both, it had stood still, months at a spell.
I had pulled it to pieces, and made it over again with
improvements, I don't know how often. There it stood, at
last, a perfected Model as aforesaid.

William Butcher and me had a long talk, Christmas Day,

A Poor Man's Tale of a Patent

respecting of the Model. William is very sensible. But sometimes cranky. William said, "What will you do with it, John?" I said, "Patent it." William said, "How patent it, John?" I said, "By taking out a Patent." William then delivered that the law of Patent was a cruel wrong. William said, "John, if you make your invention public, before you get a Patent, any one may rob you of the fruits of your hard work. You are put in a cleft stick, John. Either you must drive a bargain very much against yourself, by getting a party to come forward beforehand with the great expenses of the Patent; or, you must be put about, from post to pillar, among so many parties, trying to make a better bargain for yourself, and showing your invention, that your invention will be took from you over your head." I said, "William Butcher, are you cranky? You are sometimes cranky." William said, "No, John, I tell you the truth;" which he then delivered more at length. I said to W. B. I would Patent the invention myself.

My wife's brother, George Bury of West Bromwich (his wife unfortunately took to drinking, made away with everything, and seventeen times committed to Birmingham Jail before happy release in every point of view), left my wife, his sister, when he died, a legacy of one hundred and twenty-eight pound ten, Bank of England Stocks. Me and my wife never broke into that money yet. Note. We might come to be old and past our work. We now agreed to Patent the invention. We said we would make a hole in it—I mean in the aforesaid money—and Patent the invention. William Butcher wrote me a letter to Thomas Joy, in London. T. J. is a carpenter, six foot four in height, and plays quoits well. He lives in Chelsea, London, by the church. I got leave from the shop, to be took on again when I come back. I am a good workman. Not a Teetotaller; but never drunk. When the Christmas holidays were over, I went up to London by the Parliamentary Train, and hired a lodging for a week with Thomas Joy. He is married. He has one son gone to sea.

Thomas Joy delivered (from a book he had) that the first step to be took, in Patenting the invention, was to prepare a petition unto Queen Victoria. William Butcher had delivered similar, and drawn it up. Note. William is a ready writer. A declaration before a Master in Chancery was to be added to it. That, we likewise drew up. After a deal of trouble I found out a Master, in Southampton Buildings, Chancery Lane, nigh Temple Bar, where I made the declaration, and paid eighteen-pence. I was told to take the declaration and petition to the Home Office, in Whitehall, where I left it to be signed by the Home Secretary (after I had found the office out), and where I paid two pound, two, and sixpence. In six days he signed it, and I was told to take it to the Attorney-General's chambers, and leave it there for a report. I did so, and paid four pound, four. Note. Nobody all through, ever thankful for their money, but all uncivil.

My lodging at Thomas Joy's was now hired for another week, whereof five days were gone. The Attorney-General made what they called a Report-of-course (my invention being, as William Butcher had delivered before starting, unopposed), and I was sent back with it to the Home Office. They made a Copy of it, which was called a Warrant. For this warrant, I paid seven pound, thirteen, and six. It was sent to the Queen, to sign. The Queen sent it back, signed. The Home Secretary signed it again. The gentleman throwed it at me when I called, and said, "Now take it to the Patent Office in Lincoln's Inn." I was then in my third week at Thomas Joy's, living very sparing, on account of fees. I found myself losing heart.

At the Patent Office in Lincoln's Inn, they made "a draft of the Queen's bill," of my invention, and a "docket of the bill." I paid five pound, ten, and six, for this. They "engrossed two copies of the bill; one for the Signet Office, and one for the Privy-Seal Office." I paid one pound, seven, and six, for this. Stamp duty over and above, three pound. The Engrossing Clerk of the same office engrossed the Queen's bill for signature. I paid him one pound, one. Stamp duty, again, one pound, ten. I was next to take the Queen's bill to the Attorney-General again, and get it signed again. I took it, and paid five pound more. I fetched it away, and took it to the Home Secretary again. He sent it to the Queen again. She signed it again. I paid seven pound, thirteen, and six, more, for this. I had been over a month at Thomas Joy's. I was quite wore out, patience and pocket.

Thomas Joy delivered all this, as it went on, to William Butcher. William Butcher delivered it again to three Birmingham Parlours, from which it got to all the other

Parlours, and was took, as I have been told since, right
through all the shops in the North of England. · Note.
William Butcher delivered, at his Parlour, in a speech, that
it was a Patent way of making Chartists.

But I hadn't nigh done yet. The Queen's bill was to be
took to the Signet Office in Somerset House, Strand—
where the stamp shop is. The Clerk of the Signet made
"a Signet bill for the Lord Keeper of the Privy Seal."
I paid him four pound, seven. The Clerk of the Lord
Keeper of the Privy Seal made "a Privy-Seal bill for the
Lord Chancellor." I paid him four pound, two. The Privy-
Seal bill was handed over to the Clerk of the Patents, who
engrossed the aforesaid. I paid him five pound, seventeen,
and eight ; at the same time, I paid Stamp-duty for the
Patent, in one lump, thirty pound. I next paid for "boxes
for the Patent," nine and sixpence. Note. Thomas Joy
would have made the same at a profit for eighteen-pence.
I next paid "fees to the Deputy, the Lord Chancellor's
Purse-bearer," two pound, two. I next paid "fees to the
Clerk of the Hanaper," seven pound, thirteen. I next paid
"fees to the Deputy Clerk of the Hanaper," ten shillings.
I next paid, to the Lord Chancellor again, one pound, eleven,
and six. Last of all, I paid "fees to the Deputy Sealer, and
Deputy Chaff-wax," ten shillings and sixpence. I had lodged
at Thomas Joy's over six weeks, and the unopposed Patent
for my invention, for England only, had cost me ninety-six
pound, seven, and eightpence. If I had taken it out for the
United Kingdom, it would have cost me more than three
hundred pound.

Now, teaching had not come up but very limited when
I was young. So much the worse for me, you'll say. I say
the same. William Butcher is twenty year younger than
me. He knows a hundred year more. If William Butcher
had wanted to Patent an invention, he might have been
sharper than myself when hustled backwards and forwards
among all those offices, though I doubt if so patient. Note.
William being sometimes cranky, and consider porters,
messengers, and clerks.

Thereby I say nothing of my being tired of my life, while
I was Patenting my invention. But I put this : Is it
reasonable to make a man feel as if, in inventing an ingenious improvement meant to do good, he had done something wrong ? How else can a man feel, when he is met

by such difficulties at every turn? All inventors taking out a Patent MUST feel so. And look at the expense. How hard on me, and how hard on the country if there's any merit in me (and my invention is took up now, I am thankful to say, and doing well), to put me to all that expense before I can move a finger! Make the addition yourself, and it'll come to ninety-six pound, seven, and eightpence. No more, and no less.

What can I say against William Butcher, about places? Look at the Home Secretary, the Attorney-General, the Patent Office, the Engrossing Clerk, the Lord Chancellor, the Privy Seal, the Clerk of the Patents, the Lord Chancellor's Purse-bearer, the Clerk of the Hanaper, the Deputy Clerk of the Hanaper, the Deputy Sealer, and the Deputy Chaff-wax. No man in England could get a Patent for an Indian-rubber band, or an iron-hoop, without feeing all of them. Some of them, over and over again. I went through thirty-five stages. I began with the Queen upon the Throne. I ended with the Deputy Chaff-wax. Note. I should like to see the Deputy Chaff-wax. Is it a man, or what is it?

What I had to tell, I have told. I have wrote it down. I hope it's plain. Not so much in the handwriting (though nothing to boast of there), as in the sense of it. I will now conclude with Thomas Joy. Thomas said to me, when we parted, "John, if the laws of this country were as honest as they ought to be, you would have come to London— registered an exact description and drawing of your invention—paid half-a-crown or so for doing of it—and therein and thereby have got your Patent."

My opinion is the same as Thomas Joy. Further. In William Butcher's delivering "that the whole gang of Hanapers and Chaff-waxes must be done away with, and that England has been chaffed and waxed sufficient." I agree.

THE NOBLE SAVAGE

To come to the point at once, I beg to say that I have
not the least belief in the Noble Savage. I consider him
a prodigious nuisance, and an enormous superstition. His
calling rum fire-water, and me a pale face, wholly fail to
reconcile me to him. I don't care what he calls me. I call
him a savage, and I call a savage a something highly desirable to be civilised off the face of the earth. I think
a mere gent (which I take to be the lowest form of civilisation) better than a howling, whistling, clucking, stamping,
jumping, tearing savage. It is all one to me, whether he
sticks a fish-bone through his visage, or bits of trees through
the lobes of his ears, or bird's feathers in his head ; whether
he flattens his hair between two boards, or spreads his nose
over the breadth of his face, or drags his lower lip down by
great weights, or blackens his teeth, or knocks them out, or
paints one cheek red and the other blue, or tattoos himself,
or oils himself, or rubs his body with fat, or crimps it with
knives. Yielding to whichsoever of these agreeable eccen-
tricities, he is a savage—cruel, false, thievish, murderous ;
addicted more or less to grease, entrails, and beastly customs ; a wild animal with the questionable gift of boasting ;
a conceited, tiresome, bloodthirsty, monotonous humbug.

Yet it is extraordinary to observe how some people will
talk about him, as they talk about the good old times ; how
they will regret his disappearance, in the course of this
world's development, from such and such lands where his
absence is a blessed relief and an indispensable preparation
for the sowing of the very first seeds of any influence that
can exalt humanity ; how, even with the evidence of himself before them, they will either be determined to believe,
or will suffer themselves to be persuaded into believing,
that he is something which their five senses tell them he
is not.

There was Mr. Catlin, some few years ago, with his

Ojibbeway Indians. Mr. Catlin was an energetic, earnest man, who had lived among more tribes of Indians than I need reckon up here, and who had written a picturesque and glowing book about them. With his party of Indians squatting and spitting on the table before him, or dancing their miserable jigs after their own dreary manner, he called, in all good faith, upon his civilised audience to take notice of their symmetry and grace, their perfect limbs, and the exquisite expression of their pantomime; and his civilised audience, in all good faith, complied and admired. Whereas, as mere animals, they were wretched creatures, very low in the scale and very poorly formed ; and as men and women possessing any power of truthful dramatic expression by means of action, they were no better than the chorus at an Italian Opera in England—and would have been worse if such a thing were possible.

Mine are no new views of the noble savage. The greatest writers on natural history found him out long ago. BUFFON knew what he was, and showed why he is the sulky tyrant that he is to his women, and how it happens (Heaven be praised !) that his race is spare in numbers. For evidence of the quality of his moral nature, pass himself for a moment and refer to his "faithful dog." Has he ever improved a dog, or attached a dog, since his nobility first ran wild in woods, and was brought down (at a very long shot) by POPE? Or does the animal that is the friend of man always degenerate in his low society ?

It is not the miserable nature of the noble savage that is the new thing ; it is the whimpering over him with maudlin admiration, and the affecting to regret him, and the drawing of any comparison of advantage between the blemishes of civilisation and the tenor of his swinish life. There may have been a change now and then in those diseased absurdities, but there is none in him.

Think of the Bushmen. Think of the two men and the two women who have been exhibited about England for some years. Are the majority of persons—who remember the horrid little leader of that party in his festering bundle of hides, with his filth and his antipathy to water, and his straddled legs, and his odious eyes shaded by his brutal hand, and his cry of "Qu-u-u-u-aaa ! " (Bosjesman for something desperately insulting, I have no doubt)—conscious of an affectionate yearning towards that noble savage, or is it idiosyncratic in me to abhor, detest, abominate, and abjure him? I have no reserve on this subject, and will frankly state that, setting aside that stage of the entertainment when he counterfeited the death of some creature he had shot, by laying his head on his hand and shaking his left leg—at which time I think it would have been justifiable homicide to slay him—I have never seen that group sleeping, smoking, and expectorating round their brazier, but I have sincerely desired that something might happen to the charcoal smouldering therein, which would cause the immediate suffocation of the whole of the noble strangers.

There is at present a party of Zulu Kaffirs exhibiting at the St. George's Gallery, Hyde Park Corner, London. These noble savages are represented in a most agreeable manner; they are seen in an elegant theatre, fitted with appropriate scenery of great beauty, and they are described in a very sensible and unpretending lecture, delivered with a modesty which is quite a pattern to all similar exponents. Though extremely ugly, they are much better shaped than such of their predecessors as I have referred to; and they are rather picturesque to the eye, though far from odori- ferous to the nose. What a visitor left to his own inter- pretings and imaginings might suppose these noblemen to be about, when they give vent to that pantomimic expression which is quite settled to be the natural gift of the noble savage, I cannot possibly conceive; for it is so much too luminous for my personal civilisation that it conveys no idea to my mind beyond a general stamping, ramping, and raving, remarkable (as everything in savage life is) for its dire uniformity. But let us—with the interpreter's assist- ance, of which I for one stand so much in need—see what the noble savage does in Zulu Kaffirland.

The noble savage sets a king to reign over him, to whom he submits his life and limbs without a murmur or question, and whose whole life is passed chin deep in a lake of blood; but who, after killing incessantly, is in his turn killed by his relations and friends, the moment a grey hair appears on his head. All the noble savage's wars with his fellow- savages (and he takes no pleasure in anything else) are wars of extermination—which is the best thing I know of him, and the most comfortable to my mind when I look at him. He has no moral feelings of any kind, sort, or description; and his "mission" may be summed up as simply diabolical.

The ceremonies with which he faintly diversifies his life are, of course, of a kindred nature. If he wants a wife he appears before the kennel of the gentleman whom he has selected for his father-in-law, attended by a party of male friends of a very strong flavour, who screech and whistle and stamp an offer of so many cows for the young lady's hand. The chosen father-in-law—also supported by a high-flavoured party of male friends—screeches, whistles, and yells (being seated on the ground, he can't stamp) that there never was such a daughter in the market as his daughter, and that he must have six more cows. The son-in-law and his select circle of backers screech, whistle, stamp, and yell in reply, that they will give three more cows. The father-in-law (an old deluder, overpaid at the beginning) accepts four, and rises to bind the bargain. The whole party, the young lady included, then falling into epileptic convulsions, and screeching, whistling, stamping, and yelling together—and nobody taking any notice of the young lady (whose charms are not to be thought of without a shudder)—the noble savage is considered married, and his friends make demoniacal leaps at him by way of congratulation.

When the noble savage finds himself a little unwell, and mentions the circumstance to his friends, it is immediately perceived that he is under the influence of witchcraft. A learned personage, called an Imyanger or Witch Doctor, is immediately sent for to Nooker the Umtargartie, or smell out the witch. The male inhabitants of the kraal being seated on the ground, the learned doctor, got up like a grizzly bear, appears, and administers a dance of a most terrific nature, during the exhibition of which remedy he incessantly gnashes his teeth, and howls :—"I am the original physician to Nooker the Umtargartie. Yow yow yow! No connexion with any other establishment. Till till till! All other Umtargarties are feigned Umtargarties, Boroo Boroo! but I perceive here a genuine and real Umtargartie, Hoosh Hoosh Hoosh! in whose blood I, the original Imyanger and Nookerer, Blizzerum Boo! will wash these bear's claws of mine. O yow yow yow!" All this time the learned physician is looking out among the attentive faces for some unfortunate man who owes him a cow, or who has given him any small offence, or against whom, without offence, he has conceived a spite. Him he never fails to Nooker as the Umtargartie, and he is instantly killed. In the absence of such an individual, the usual practice is to Nooker the quietest and most gentlemanly person in company. But the nookering is invariably followed on the spot by the butchering.

Some of the noble savages in whom Mr. Catlin was so strongly interested, and the diminution of whose numbers, by rum and small-pox, greatly affected him, had a custom not unlike this, though much more appalling and disgusting in its odious details.

The women being at work in the fields, hoeing the Indian corn, and the noble savage being asleep in the shade, the chief has sometimes the condescension to come forth, and lighten the labour by looking at it. On these occasions, he seats himself in his own savage chair, and is attended by his shield-bearer: who holds over his head a shield of cowhide—in shape like an immense mussel shell—fearfully and wonderfully, after the manner of a theatrical supernumerary. But lest the great man should forget his greatness in the contemplation of the humble works of agriculture, there suddenly rushes in a poet, retained for the purpose, called a Praiser. This literary gentleman wears a leopard's head over his own, and a dress of tigers' tails; he has the appearance of having come express on his hind legs from the Zoological Gardens; and he incontinently strikes up the chief's praises, plunging and tearing all the while. There is a frantic wickedness in this brute's manner of worrying the air, and gnashing out, "O what a delightful chief he is! O what a delicious quantity of blood he sheds! O how majestically he laps it up! O how charmingly cruel he is! O how he tears the flesh of his enemies and crunches the bones! O how like the tiger and the leopard and the wolf and the bear he is! O, row row row row, how fond I am of him!" which might tempt the Society of Friends to charge at a hand-gallop into the Swartz-Kop location and exterminate the whole kraal.

When war is afoot among the noble savages—which is always—the chief holds a council to ascertain whether it is the opinion of his brothers and friends in general that the enemy shall be exterminated. On this occasion, after the performance of an Umsebeuza, or war song,—which is exactly like all the other songs,—the chief makes a speech to his brothers and friends, arranged in single file. No particular order is observed during the delivery of this address, but every gentleman who finds himself excited by the subject, instead of crying " Hear, hear ! " as is the custom with us, darts from the rank and tramples out the life, or crushes the skull, or mashes the face, or scoops out the eyes, or breaks the limbs, or performs a whirlwind of atrocities on the body, of an imaginary enemy. Several gentlemen becoming thus excited at once, and pounding away without the least regard to the orator, that illustrious person is rather in the position of an orator in an Irish House of Commons. But several of these scenes of savage life bear a strong generic resemblance to an Irish election, and I think would be extremely well received and understood at Cork.

In all these ceremonies the noble savage holds forth to the utmost possible extent about himself; from which (to turn him to some civilised account) we may learn, I think, that as egotism is one of the most offensive and contemptible littlenesses a civilised man can exhibit, so it is really incompatible with the interchange of ideas; inasmuch as if we all talked about ourselves we should soon have no listeners, and must be all yelling and screeching at once on our own separate accounts : making society hideous. It is my opinion that if we retained in us anything of the noble savage, we could not get rid of it too soon. But the fact is clearly otherwise. Upon the wife and dowry question, substituting coin for cows, we have assuredly nothing of the Zulu Kaffir left. The endurance of despotism is one great distinguishing mark of a savage always. The improving world has quite got the better of that too. In like manner, Paris is a civilised city, and the Théâtre Français a highly civilised theatre ; and we shall never hear, and never have heard in these later days (of course) of the Praiser there. No, no, civilised poets have better work to do. As to Nookering Umtargarties, there are no pretended Umtargarties in Europe, and no European powers to Nooker them ; that would be mere spydom, subordination, small malice, superstition, and false pretence. And as to private Umtargarties, are we not in the year eighteen hundred and fifty-three, with spirits rapping at our doors ?

To conclude as I began. My position is, that if we have anything to learn from the Noble Savage, it is what to avoid. His virtues are a fable ; his happiness is a delusion ;

his nobility, nonsense. We have no greater justification for being cruel to the miserable object, than for being cruel to a WILLIAM SHAKESPEARE or an ISAAC NEWTON; but he passes away before an immeasurably better and higher power than ever ran wild in any earthly woods, and the world will be all the better when his place knows him no more.

A FLIGHT

WHEN Don Diego de—I forget his name—the inventor of the last new Flying Machines, price so many francs for ladies, so many more for gentlemen—when Don Diego, by permission of Deputy Chaff-wax and his noble band, shall have taken out a Patent for the Queen's dominions, and shall have opened a commodious Warehouse in an airy situation; and when all persons of any gentility will keep at least a pair of wings, and be seen skimming about in every direction; I shall take a flight to Paris (as I soar round the world) in a cheap and independent manner. At present, my reliance is on the South-Eastern Railway Company, in whose Express Train here I sit, at eight of the clock on a very hot morning, under the very hot roof of the Terminus at London Bridge, in danger of being "forced" like a cucumber or a melon, or a pine-apple. And talking of pine-apples, I suppose there never were so many pine-apples in a Train as there appear to be in this Train.

Whew! The hot-house air is faint with pine-apples. Every French citizen or citizeness is carrying pine-apples home. The compact little Enchantress in the corner of my carriage (French actress, to whom I yielded up my heart under the auspices of that brave child, "MEAT-CHELL," at the St. James's Theatre the night before last) has a pine-apple in her lap. Compact Enchantress's friend, confidante, mother, mystery, Heaven knows what, has two pine-apples in her lap, and a bundle of them under the seat. Tobacco-smoky Frenchman in Algerine wrapper, with peaked hood behind, who might be Abd-el-Kader dyed rifle-green, and who seems to be dressed entirely in dirt and braid, carries pine-apples in a covered basket. Tall, grave, melancholy Frenchman, with black Vandyke beard, and hair close-cropped, with expansive chest to waistcoat, and compressive waist to coat: saturnine as to his pantaloons, calm as to his feminine boots, precious as to his jewellery, smooth and white as to his linen: dark-eyed, high-foreheaded, hawk-nosed—got up, one thinks, like Lucifer or Mephistopheles, or Zamiel, transformed into a highly genteel Parisian—has the green end of a pine-apple sticking out of his neat valise.

Whew! If I were to be kept here long, under this forcing-frame, I wonder what would become of me—whether I should be forced into a giant, or should sprout or blow into some other phenomenon! Compact Enchantress is not ruffled by the heat—she is always composed, always compact. O look at her little ribbons, frills, and edges, at her shawl, at her gloves, at her hair, at her bracelets, at her bonnet, at everything about her! How is it accomplished? What does she do to be so neat? How is it that every trifle she wears belongs to her, and cannot choose but be a part of her? And even Mystery, look at *her!* A model. Mystery is not young, not pretty, though still of an average candle-light passability; but she does such miracles in her own behalf, that, one of these days, when she dies, they'll be amazed to find an old woman in her bed, distantly like her. She was an actress once, I shouldn't wonder, and had a Mystery attendant on herself. Perhaps, Compact Enchantress will live to be a Mystery, and to wait with a shawl at the side-scenes, and to sit opposite to Mademoiselle in railway carriages, and smile and talk subserviently, as Mystery does now. That's hard to believe!

Two Englishmen, and now our carriage is full. First Englishman, in the monied interest—flushed, highly respectable—Stock Exchange, perhaps—City, certainly. Faculties of second Englishman entirely absorbed in hurry. Plunges into the carriage, blind. Calls out of window concerning his luggage, deaf. Suffocates himself under pillows of great-coats, for no reason, and in a demented manner. Will receive no assurance from any porter whatsoever. Is stout and hot, and wipes his head, and makes himself hotter by breathing so hard. Is totally incredulous respecting assurance of Collected Guard, that "there's no hurry." No hurry! And a flight to Paris in eleven hours!

It is all one to me in this drowsy corner, hurry or no hurry. Until Don Diego shall send home my wings, my flight is with the South-Eastern Company. I can fly with the South-Eastern, more lazily, at all events, than in the upper air. I have but to sit here thinking as idly as I please, and be whisked away. I am not accountable to anybody for the idleness of my thoughts in such an idle summer flight; my flight is provided for by the South-Eastern and is no business of mine.

The bell! With all my heart. It does not require *me* to do so much as even to flap my wings. Something snorts for me, something shrieks for me, something proclaims to everything else that it had better keep out of my way,—and away I go.

Ah! The fresh air is pleasant after the forcing-frame, though it does blow over these interminable streets, and scatter the smoke of this vast wilderness of chimneys. Here we are—no, I mean there we were, for it has darted far into the rear—in Bermondsey where the tanners live. Flash! The distant shipping in the Thames is gone. Whirr! The little streets of new brick and red tile, with here and there a flagstaff growing like a tall weed out of the scarlet beans, and, everywhere, plenty of open sewer and ditch for the promotion of the public health, have been fired off in a volley. Whizz! Dust-heaps, market-gardens, and waste grounds. Rattle! New Cross Station. Shock! There we were at Croydon. Bur-r-r-r! The tunnel.

I wonder why it is that when I shut my eyes in a tunnel I begin to feel as if I were going at an Express pace the other way. I am clearly going back to London now. Compact Enchantress must have forgotten something, and reversed the engine. No! After long darkness, pale fitful streaks of light appear. I am still flying on for Folkestone. The streaks grow stronger—become continuous—become the ghost of day—become the living day—became I mean—the tunnel is miles and miles away, and here I fly through sunlight, all among the harvest and the Kentish hops.

There is a dreamy pleasure in this flying. I wonder where it was, and when it was, that we exploded, blew into space somehow, a Parliamentary Train, with a crowd of heads and faces looking at us out of cages, and some hats waving. Monied Interest says it was at Reigate Station. Expounds to Mystery how Reigate Station is so many miles from London, which Mystery again develops to Compact Enchantress. There might be neither a Reigate nor a London for me, as I fly away among the Kentish hops and harvest. What do *I* care?

Bang! We have let another Station off, and fly away regardless. Everything is flying. The hop-gardens turn gracefully towards me, presenting regular avenues of hops in rapid flight, then whirl away. So do the pools and rushes, haystacks, sheep, clover in full bloom delicious to the sight and smell, corn-sheaves, cherry-orchards, apple-orchards, reapers, gleaners, hedges, gates, fields that taper off into little angular corners, cottages, gardens, now and then a church. Bang, bang! A double-barrelled Station! Now a wood, now a bridge, now a landscape, now a cutting, now a——Bang! a single-barrelled Station—there was a cricket-match somewhere with two white tents, and then four flying cows, then turnips—now the wires of the electric telegraph are all alive, and spin, and blurr their edges, and go up and down, and make the intervals between each other most irregular: contracting and expanding in the strangest manner. Now we slacken. With a screwing, and a grinding, and a smell of water thrown on ashes, now we stop!

Demented Traveller, who has been for two or three minutes watchful, clutches his great-coats, plunges at the door, rattles it, cries "Hi!" eager to embark on board of impossible packets, far inland. Collected Guard appears. "Are you for Tunbridge, sir?" "Tunbridge? No. Paris." "Plenty of time, sir. No hurry. Five minutes here, sir, for refreshment." I am so blest (anticipating Zamiel, by half a second) as to procure a glass of water for Compact Enchantress.

Who would suppose we had been flying at such a rate, and shall take wing again directly? Refreshment-room full, platform full, porter with watering-pot deliberately cooling a hot wheel, another porter with equal deliberation helping the rest of the wheels bountifully to ice cream. Monied Interest and I re-entering the carriage first, and being there alone, he intimates to me that the French are "no go" as a Nation. I ask why? He says, that Reign of Terror of theirs was quite enough. I ventured to inquire whether he remembers anything that preceded said Reign of Terror? He says not particularly. "Because," I remark, "the harvest that is reaped, has sometimes been sown." Monied Interest repeats, as quite enough for him, that the French are revolutionary,—"and always at it."

Bell. Compact Enchantress, helped in by Zamiel (whom the stars confound!), gives us her charming little side-box look, and smites me to the core. Mystery eating sponge-cake. Pine-apple atmosphere faintly tinged with suspicions of sherry. Demented Traveller flits past the carriage, looking for it. Is blind with agitation, and can't see it. Seems singled out by Destiny to be the only unhappy creature in the flight, who has any cause to hurry himself. Is nearly left behind. Is seized by Collected Guard after the Train is in motion, and bundled in. Still, has lingering suspicions that there must be a boat in the neighbourhood, and *will* look wildly out of window for it.

Flight resumod. Corn-sheaves, hop-gardens, reapers, gleaners, apple-orchards, cherry-orchards, Stations singlo and double-barrelled, Ashford. Compact Enchantress (constantly talking to Mystery, in an exquisite manner) gives a little scream; a sound that seems to come from high up in her precious little head; from behind her bright little eyebrows. "Great Heaven, my pine-apple! My Angel! It is lost!" Mystery is desolated. A search made. It is not lost. Zamiel finds it. I curse him (flying) in the Persian manner. May his face be turned upside down, and jackasses sit upon his uncle's grave!

Now fresher air, now glimpses of unenclosed Down-land with flapping crows flying over it whom we soon outfly, now the Sea, now Folkestone at a quarter after ten. "Tickets ready, gentlemen!" Demented dashes at the door. "For Paris, sir?" No hurry.

Not the least. We are dropped slowly down to the Port, and sidle to and fro (the whole Train) before the insensible Royal George Hotel, for some ten minutes. The Royal George takes no more heed of us than its namesake under water at Spithead, or under earth at Windsor, does. The Royal George's dog lies winking and blinking at us, without taking the trouble to sit up; and the Royal George's "wedding party" at' the open window (who seem, I must say, rather tired of bliss) don't bestow a solitary glance upon us, flying thus to Paris in eleven hours. The first gentleman in Folkestone is evidently used up, on this subject.

Meanwhile, Demented chafes. Conceives that every man's hand is against him, and exerting itself to prevent his getting to Paris. Refuses consolation. Rattles door. Sees smoke on the horizon, and "knows" it's the boat gone without him. Monied Interest resentfully explains that *he* is going to Paris too. Demented signifies that if Monied Interest chooses to be left behind, *he* don't.

"Refreshments in the Waiting-Room, ladies and gentlemen. No hurry, ladies and gentlemen, for Paris. No hurry whatever!"

Twenty minutes' pause, by Folkestone clock, for looking at Enchantress while she eats a sandwich, and at Mystery while she eats of everything there that is eatable, from pork-pie, sausage, jam, and gooseberries, to lumps of sugar. All this time, there is a very waterfall of luggage, with a spray of dust, tumbling slantwise from the pier into the steamboat. All this time, Demented (who has no business with it) watches it with starting eyes, fiercely requiring to be shown *his* luggage. When it at last concludes the cataract, he rushes hotly to refresh—is shouted after, pursued, jostled, brought back, pitched into the departing steamer upside down, and caught by mariners disgracefully.

A lovely harvest-day, a cloudless sky, a tranquil sea. The piston-rods of the engines so regularly coming up from below, to look (as well they may) at the bright weather, and so regularly almost knocking their iron heads against the cross beam of the skylight, and never doing it! Another Parisian actress is on board, attended by another Mystery. Compact Enchantress greets her sister artist—Oh, the Compact One's pretty teeth!—and Mystery greets Mystery. *My* Mystery soon ceases to be conversational—is taken poorly, in a word, having lunched too miscellaneously—and goes below. The remaining Mystery then smiles upon the sister artists (who, I am afraid, wouldn't greatly mind stabbing each other), and is upon the whole ravished.

And now I find that all the French people on board begin to grow, and all the English people to shrink. The French are nearing home, and shaking off a disadvantage, whereas we are shaking it on. Zamiel is the same man, and Abd-el-Kader is the same man, but each seems to come into possession of an indescribable confidence that departs from us—from Monied Interest, for instance, and from me. Just what they gain, we lose. Certain British " Gents " about the steersman, intellectually nurtured at home on parody of everything and truth of nothing, become subdued, and in a manner forlorn; and when the steersman tells them (not exultingly) how he has "been upon this station now eight year, and never see the old town of Bullum yet," one of them, with an imbecile reliance on a reed, asks him what he considers to be the best hotel in Paris?

R

Now, I tread upon French ground, and am greeted by the three charming words, Liberty, Equality, Fraternity, painted up (in letters a little too thin for their height) on the Custom-house wall—also by the sight of large cocked hats, without which demonstrative head-gear nothing of a public nature can be done upon this soil. All the rabid Hotel population of Boulogne howl and shriek outside a distant barrier, frantic to get at us. Demented, by some unlucky means peculiar to himself, is delivered over to their fury, and is presently seen struggling in a whirl-pool of Touters—is somehow understood to be going to Paris—is, with infinite noise, rescued by two cocked hats, and brought into Custom-house bondage with the rest of us.

Here, I resign the active duties of life to an eager being, of preternatural sharpness, with a shelving forehead and a shabby snuff-coloured coat, who (from the wharf) brought me down with his eye before the boat came into port. He darts upon my luggage, on the floor where all the luggage is strewn like a wreck at the bottom of the great deep; gets it proclaimed and weighed as the property of "Monsieur a traveller unknown;" pays certain francs for it, to a certain functionary behind a Pigeon Hole, like a pay-box at a Theatre (the arrangements in general are on a wholesale scale, half military and half theatrical); and I suppose I shall find it when I come to Paris—he says I shall. I know nothing about it, except that I pay him his small fee, and pocket the ticket he gives me, and sit upon a counter, involved in the general distraction.

Railway station. "Lunch or dinner,. ladies and gentlemen. Plenty of time for Paris. Plenty of time!" Large hall, long counter, long strips of dining-table, bottles of wine, plates of meat, roast chickens, little loaves of bread, basins of soup, little caraffes of brandy, cakes, and fruit. Comfortably restored from these resources, I begin to fly again.

I saw Zamiel (before I took wing) presented to Compact Enchantress and Sister Artist, by an officer in uniform, with a waist like a wasp's, and pantaloons like two balloons. They all got into the next carriage together, accompanied by the two Mysteries. They laughed. I am alone in the carriage (for I don't consider Demented anybody) and alone in the world.

Fields, windmills, low grounds, pollard-trees, windmills,

fields, fortifications, Abbeville, soldiering and drumming. I wonder where England is, and when I was there last —about two years ago, I should say. Flying in and out among these trenches and batteries, skimming the clattering drawbridges, looking down into the stagnant ditches, I become a prisoner of state, escaping. I am confined with a comrade in a fortress. Our room is in an upper story. We have tried to get up the chimney, but there's an iron grating across it, imbedded in the masonry. After months of labour, we have worked the grating loose with the poker, and can lift it up. We have also made a hook, and twisted our rugs and blankets into ropes. Our plan is, to go up the chimney, hook our ropes to the top, descend hand over hand upon the roof of the guard-house far below, shake the hook loose, watch the opportunity of the sentinel's pacing away, hook again, drop into the ditch, swim across it, creep into the shelter of the wood. The time is come—a wild and stormy night. We are up the chimney, we are on the guard-house roof, we are swimming in the murky ditch, when lo! "Qui v'là?" a bugle, the alarm, a crash! What is it? Death? No, Amiens.

More fortifications, more soldiering and drumming, more basins of soup, more little loaves of bread, more bottles of wine, more caraffes of brandy, more time for refreshment. Everything good, and everything ready. Bright, unsubstantial-looking, scenic sort of station. People waiting. Houses, uniforms, beards, moustaches, some sabots, plenty of neat women, and a few old-visaged children. Unless it be a delusion born of my giddy flight, the grown-up people and the children seem to change places in France. In general, the boys and girls are little old men and women, and the men and women lively boys and girls.

Bugle, shriek, flight resumed. Monied Interest has come into my carriage. Says the manner of refreshing is "not bad," but considers it French. Admits great dexterity and politeness in the attendants. Thinks a decimal currency may have something to do with their despatch in settling accounts, and don't know but what it's sensible and convenient. Adds, however, as a general protest, that they're a revolutionary people—and always at it.

Ramparts, canals, cathedral, river, soldiering and drumming, open country, river, earthenware manufactures, Creil. Again ten minutes. Not even Demented in a hurry. Station, a drawing-room with a verandah : like a planter's house. Monied Interest considers it a band-box, and not made to last. Little round tables in it, at one of which the Sister Artists and attendant Mysteries are established with Wasp and Zamiel, as if they were going to stay a week.

Anon, with no more trouble than before, I am flying again, and lazily wondering as I fly. What has the South-Eastern done with all the horrible little villages we used to pass through, in the *Diligence?* What have they done with all the summer dust, with all the winter mud, with all the dreary avenues of little trees, with all the ramshackle post-yards, with all the beggars (who used to turn out at night with bits of lighted candle, to look in at the coach windows), with all the long-tailed horses who were always biting one another, with all the big postillions in jack-boots—with all the mouldy cafés that we used to stop at, where a long mildewed table-cloth, set forth with jovial bottles of vinegar and oil, and with a Siamese arrangement of pepper and salt, was never wanting ? Where are the grass-grown little towns, the wonderful little market-places all unconscious of markets, the shops that nobody kept, the streets that nobody trod, the churches that nobody went to, the bells that nobody rang, the tumble-down old buildings plastered with many-coloured bills that nobody read ? Where are the two-and-twenty weary hours of long long day and night journey, sure to be either insupportably hot or insupportably cold ? Where are the pains in my bones, where are the fidgets in my legs, where is the Frenchman with the nightcap who never *would* have the little coupé-window down, and who always fell upon me when he went to sleep, and always slept all night snoring onions ?

A voice breaks in with " Paris ! Here we are ! "

I have overflown myself, perhaps, but I can't believe it. I feel, as if I were enchanted or bewitched. It is barely eight o'clock yet—it is nothing like half-past—when I have had my luggage examined at that briskest of Custom-houses attached to the station, and am rattling over the pavement in a hackney-cabriolet.

Surely, not the pavement of Paris ? Yes, I think it is, too. I don't know any other place where there are all these high houses, all these haggard-looking wine shops, all these billiard tables, all these stocking-makers with flat red or yellow legs of wood for signboard, all these fuel shops with stacks of billets painted outside, and real billets sawing in the gutter, all these dirty corners of streets, all these cabinet pictures over dark doorways representing discreet matrons nursing babies. And yet this morning—I'll think of it in a warm-bath.

Very like a small room that I remember in the Chinese baths upon the Boulevard, certainly; and, though I see it through the steam, I think that I might swear to that peculiar hot-linen basket, like a large wicker hour-glass. When can it have been that I left home? When was it that I paid "through to Paris" at London Bridge, and discharged myself of all responsibility, except the preservation of a voucher ruled into three divisions, of which the first was snipped off at Folkestone, the second aboard the boat, and the third taken at my journey's end? It seems to have been ages ago. Calculation is useless. I will go out for a walk.

The crowds in the streets, the lights in the shops and balconies, the elegance, variety, and beauty of their decorations, the number of the theatres, the brilliant cafés with their windows thrown up high and their vivacious groups at little tables on the pavement, the light and glitter of the houses turned as it were inside out, soon convince me that it is no dream; that I am in Paris, howsoever I got here. I stroll down to the sparkling Palais Royal, up the Rue de Rivoli, to the Place Vendôme. As I glance into a print-shop window, Monied Interest, my late travelling companion, comes upon me, laughing with the highest relish of disdain. "Here's a people!" he says, pointing to Napoleon in the window and Napoleon on the column. "Only one idea all over Paris! A monomania!" Humph! I THINK I have seen Napoleon's match? There WAS a statue, when I came away, at Hyde Park Corner, and another in the City, and a print or two in the shops.

I walk up to the Barrière de l'Etoile, sufficiently dazed by my flight to have a pleasant doubt of the reality of everything about me; of the lively crowd, the overhanging trees, the performing dogs, the hobby-horses, the beautiful perspectives of shining lamps: the hundred and one enclosures, where the singing is, in gleaming orchestras of azure and gold, and where a star-eyed Houri comes round with a box for voluntary offerings. So, I pass to my hotel, enchanted; sup, enchanted; go to bed, enchanted; pushing back this morning (if it really were this morning) into the remoteness of time, blessing the South-Eastern Company for realising the Arabian Nights in these prose days, murmuring, as I wing my idle flight into the land of dreams, "No hurry, ladies and gentlemen, going to Paris in eleven hours. It is so well done, that there really is no hurry!"

THE DETECTIVE POLICE

WE are not by any means devout believers in the old Bow Street Police. To say the truth, we think there was a vast amount of humbug about those worthies. Apart from many of them being men of very indifferent character, and far too much in the habit of consorting with thieves and the like, they never lost a public occasion of jobbing and trading in mystery and making the most of themselves. Continually puffed besides by incompetent magistrates anxious to conceal their own deficiencies, and hand-in-glove with the penny-a-liners of that time, they became a sort of superstition. Although as a Preventive Police they were utterly ineffective, and as a Detective Police were very loose and uncertain in their operations, they remain with some people a superstition to the present day.

On the other hand, the Detective Force organised since the establishment of the existing Police, is so well chosen and trained, proceeds so systematically and quietly, does its business in such a workmanlike manner, and is always so calmly and steadily engaged in the service of the public, that the public really do not know enough of it, to know a tithe of its usefulness. Impressed with this conviction, and interested in the men themselves, we represented to the authorities at Scotland Yard, that we should be glad, if there were no official objection, to have some talk with the Detectives. A most obliging and ready permission being given, a certain evening was appointed with a certain Inspector for a social conference between ourselves and the Detectives, at The Household Words Office in Wellington Street, Strand, London. In consequence of which appointment the party "came off," which we are about to describe. And we beg to repeat that, avoiding such topics as it might for obvious reasons be injurious to the public, or disagreeable to respectable individuals, to touch upon in print, our description is as exact as we can make it.

The reader will have the goodness to imagine the Sanctum

Sanctorum of Household Words.   Anything that best suits
the reader's fancy, will best represent that magnificent
chamber.   We merely stipulate for a round table in the
middle, with some glasses and cigars arranged upon it; and
the editorial sofa elegantly hemmed in between that stately
piece of furniture and the wall.

It is a sultry evening at dusk.   The stones of Wellington
Street are hot and gritty, and the watermen and hackney-
coachmen at the Theatre opposite, are much flushed and
aggravated.   Carriages are constantly setting down the
people who have come to Fairy-Land; and there is a mighty
shouting and bellowing every now and then, deafening us
for the moment, through the open windows.

Just at dusk, Inspectors Wield and Stalker are announced;
but we do not undertake to warrant the orthography of any
of the names here mentioned.   Inspector Wield presents
Inspector Stalker.   Inspector Wield is a middle-aged man of
a portly presence, with a large, moist, knowing eye, a husky
voice, and a habit of emphasising his conversation by the
aid of a corpulent fore-finger, which is constantly in juxta-
position with his eyes or nose.   Inspector Stalker is a
shrewd, hard-headed Scotchman—in appearance not at all
unlike a very acute, thoroughly-trained schoolmaster, from
the Normal Establishment at Glasgow.   Inspector Wield
one might have known, perhaps, for what he is—Inspector
Stalker, never.

The ceremonies of reception over, Inspectors Wield and
Stalker observe that they have brought some sergeants with
them.   The sergeants are presented—five in number, Sergeant Dornton, Sergeant Witchem, Sergeant Mith, Sergeant
Fendall, and Sergeant Straw.   We have the whole Detective
Force from Scotland Yard, with one exception.   They sit
down in a semi-circle (the two Inspectors at the two ends)
at a little distance from the round table, facing the editorial
sofa.   Every man of them, in a glance, immediately takes
an inventory of the furniture and an accurate sketch of the
editorial presence.   The Editor feels that any gentleman in
company could take him up, if need should be, without the
smallest hesitation, twenty years hence.

The whole party are in plain clothes.   Sergeant Dornton
about fifty years of age, with a ruddy face and a high sun-
burnt forehead, has the air of one who has been a Sergeant
in the army—he might have sat to Wilkie for the Soldier

in the Reading of the Will. He is famous for steadily pursuing the inductive process, and, from small beginnings, working on from clue to clue until he bags his man. Sergeant Witchem, shorter and thicker-set, and marked with the small-pox, has something of a reserved and thoughtful air, as if he were engaged in deep arithmetical calculations. He is renowned for his acquaintance with the swell mob. Sergeant Mith, a smooth-faced man with a fresh bright complexion, and a strange air of simplicity, is a dab at housebreakers. Sergeant Fendall, a light-haired, well-spoken, polite person, is a prodigious hand at pursuing private inquiries of a delicate nature. Straw, a little wiry Sergeant of meek demeanour and strong sense, would knock at a door and ask a series of questions in any mild character you choose to prescribe to him, from a charity-boy upwards, and seem as innocent as an infant. They are, one and all, respectable-looking men ; of perfectly good deportment and unusual intelligence ; with nothing lounging or slinking in their manners ; with an air of keen observation and quick perception when addressed ; and generally presenting in their faces, traces more or less marked of habitually leading lives of strong mental excitement. They have all good eyes ; and they all can, and they all do, look full at whomsoever they speak to.

We light the cigars, and hand round the glasses (which are very temperately used indeed), and the conversation begins by a modest amateur reference on the Editorial part to the swell mob. Inspector Wield immediately removes his cigar from his lips, waves his right hand, and says, "Regarding the swell mob, sir, I can't do better than call upon Sergeant Witchem. Because the reason why ? I'll tell you. Sergeant Witchem is better acquainted with the swell mob than any officer in London."

Our heart leaping up when we beheld this rainbow in the sky, we turn to Sergeant Witchem, who very concisely, and in well-chosen language, goes into the subject forthwith. Meantime, the whole of his brother officers are closely interested in attending to what he says, and observing its effect. Presently they begin to strike in, one or two together, when an opportunity offers, and the conversation becomes general. But these brother officers only come in to the assistance of each other—not to the contradiction—and a more amicable brotherhood there could not be. From the swell mob, we diverge to the kindred topics of cracksmen, fences, public-house dancers, area-sneaks, designing young people who go out "gonophing," and other "schools." It is observable throughout these revelations, that Inspector Stalker, the Scotchman, is always exact and statistical, and that when any question of figures arises, everybody as by one consent pauses, and looks to him.

When we have exhausted the various schools of Art—during which discussion the whole body have remained profoundly attentive, except when some unusual noise at the Theatre over the way has induced some gentleman to glance inquiringly towards the window in that direction, behind his next neighbour's back—we burrow for information on such points as the following. Whether there really are any high-way robberies in London, or whether some circumstances not convenient to be mentioned by the aggrieved party, usually precede the robberies complained of, under that head, which quite change their character? Certainly the latter, almost always. Whether in the case of robberies in houses, where servants are necessarily exposed to doubt, innocence under suspicion ever becomes so like guilt in appearance, that a good officer need be cautious how he judges it? Undoubtedly. Nothing is so common or decep-tive as such appearances at first. Whether in a place of public amusement, a thief knows an officer, and an officer knows a thief—supposing them, beforehand, strangers to each other—because each recognises in the other, under all disguise, an inattention to what is going on, and a purpose that is not the purpose of being entertained? Yes. That's the way exactly. Whether it is reasonable or ridiculous to trust to the alleged experiences of thieves as narrated by themselves, in prisons, or penitentiaries, or anywhere? In general, nothing more absurd. Lying is their habit and their trade ; and they would rather lie—even if they hadn't an interest in it, and didn't want to make themselves agree-able—than tell the truth.

From these topics, we glide into a review of the most celebrated and horrible of the great crimes that have been committed within the last fifteen or twenty years. The men engaged in the discovery of almost all of them, and in the pursuit or apprehension of the murderers, are here, down to the very last instance. One of our guests gave chase to and boarded the emigrant ship, in which the murderess last hanged in London was supposed to have embarked. We learn from him that his errand was not announced to the passengers, who may have no idea of it to this hour. That he went below, with the captain, lamp in hand—it being dark, and the whole steerage abed and sea-sick—and engaged the Mrs. Manning who *was* on board, in a conversation about her luggage, until she was, with no small pains, induced to raise her head, and turn her face towards the light. Satisfied that she was not the object of his search, he quietly re-embarked in the Government steamer alongside, and steamed home again with the intelligence.

When we have exhausted these subjects, too, which occupy a considerable time in the discussion, two or three leave their chairs, whisper Sergeant Witchem, and resume their seats. Sergeant Witchem leaning forward a little, and placing a hand on each of his legs, then modestly speaks as follows:

" My brother-officers wish me to relate a little account of my taking Tally-ho Thompson. A man oughtn't to tell what he has done himself; but still, as nobody was with me, and, consequently, as nobody but myself can tell it, I'll do it in the best way I can, if it should meet your approval."

We assure Sergeant Witchem that he will oblige us very much, and we all compose ourselves to listen with great interest and attention.

"Tally-ho Thompson," says Sergeant Witchem, after merely wetting his lips with his brandy-and-water, " Tally-ho Thompson was a famous horse-stealer, couper, and magsman. Thompson, in conjunction with a pal that occasionally worked with him, gammoned a countryman out of a good round sum of money, under pretence of getting him a situation— the regular old dodge—and was afterwards in the 'Hue and Cry' for a horse—a horse that he stole, down in Hertfordshire. I had to look after Thompson, and I applied myself, of course, in the first instance, to discovering where he was. Now, Thompson's wife lived, along with a little daughter, at Chelsea. Knowing that Thompson was somewhere in the country, I watched the house—especially at post-time in the morning—thinking Thompson was pretty likely to write to her. Sure enough, one morning the postman comes up, and delivers a letter at Mrs. Thompson's door. Little girl opens the door, and takes it in. We're not always sure of postmen, though the people at the post-offices are always very obliging. A postman may help us, or he may not,—just as it happens. However, I go across the road, and I say to the postman, after he has left the letter, 'Good morning! how are you?' 'How are *you*?' says he. 'You've just delivered a letter for Mrs. Thompson.' 'Yes, I have.' 'You didn't happen to remark what the post-mark was, perhaps?' 'No,' says he, 'I didn't.' 'Come,' says I, 'I'll be plain with you. I'm in a small way of business, and I have given Thompson credit, and I can't afford to lose what he owes me. I know he's got money, and I know he's in the country, and if you could tell me what the post-mark was, I should be very much obliged to you, and you'd do a service to a tradesman in a small way of business that can't afford a loss.' 'Well,' he said, 'I do assure you that I did not observe what the post-mark was; all I know is, that there was money in the letter—I should say a sovereign.' This was enough for me, because of course I knew that Thompson having sent his wife money, it was probable she'd write to Thompson, by return of post, to acknowledge the receipt. So I said 'Thankee' to the postman, and I kept on the watch. In the afternoon I saw the little girl come out. Of course I followed her. She went into a stationer's shop, and I needn't say to you that I looked in at the window. She bought some writing-paper and envelopes, and a pen. I think to myself, 'That'll do!'—watch her home again—and don't go away, you may be sure, knowing that Mrs. Thompson was writing her letter to Tally-ho, and that the letter would be posted presently. In about an hour or so, out came the little girl again, with the letter in her hand. I went up, and said something to the child, whatever it might have been; but I couldn't see the direction of the letter, because she held it with the seal upwards. However, I observed that on the back of the letter there was what we call a kiss—a drop of wax by the side of the seal—and again, you understand, that was enough for me. I saw her post the letter, waited till she was gone, then went into the shop, and asked to see the Master. When he came out, I told him, 'Now, I'm an Officer in the Detective Force; there's a letter with a kiss been posted here just now, for a man that I'm in search of; and what I have to ask of you, is, that you will let me look at the direction of that letter.' He was very civil—took a lot of letters from

the box in the window—shook 'em out on the counter with
the faces downwards—and there among 'm was the identical
letter with the kiss.   It was directed, Mr. Thomas Pigeon,
Post Office, B——, to be left 'till called for.   Down I went
to B—— (a hundred and twenty miles or so) that night.
Early next morning I went to the Post Office ; saw the
gentleman in charge of that department ; told him who
I was ; and that my object was to see, and track, the party
that should come for the letter for Mr. Thomas Pigeon.
He was very polite, and said, 'You shall have every assistance
we can give you ; you can wait inside the office ; and we'll
take care to let you know when anybody comes for the letter.'
Well, I waited there three days, and began to think that
nobody ever *would* come.   At last the clerk whispered to
me, 'Here !   Detective !   Somebody's come for the letter !'
'Keep him a minute,' said I, and I ran round to the outside
of the office.   There I saw a young chap with the appearance
of an Ostler, holding a horse by the bridle—stretching the
bridle across the pavement, while he waited at the Post
Office window for the letter.   I began to pat the horse, and
that ; and I said to the boy, 'Why, this is Mr. Jones's
Mare !'   'No.   It an't.'   'No ?' said I.   'She's very like
Mr. Jones's Mare !'   'She an't Mr. Jones's Mare, anyhow,'
says he.   'It's Mr. So and So's, of the Warwick Arms.'
And up he jumped, and off he went—letter and all.   I got
a cab, followed on the box, and was so quick after him that
I came into the stable-yard of the Warwick Arms, by one
gate, just as he came in by another.   I went into the bar,
where there was a young woman serving, and called for
a glass of brandy-and-water.   He came in directly, and
handed her the letter.   She casually looked at it, without
saying anything, and stuck it up behind the glass over the
chimney-piece.   What was to be done next ?

"I turned it over in my mind while I drank my brandy-
and-water (looking pretty sharp at the letter the while),
but I couldn't see my way out of it at all.   I tried to get
lodgings in the house, but there had been a horse-fair, or
something of that sort, and it was full.   I was obliged to
put up somewhere else, but I came backwards and forwards
to the bar for a couple of days, and there was the letter
always behind the glass.   At last I thought I'd write a letter
to Mr. Pigeon myself, and see what that would do.   So
I wrote one, and posted it, but I purposely addressed it,

Mr. John Pigeon, instead of Mr. Thomas Pigeon, to see what *that* would do. In the morning (a very wet morning it was) I watched the postman down the street, and cut into the bar, just before he reached the Warwick Arms. In he came presently with my letter. 'Is there a Mr. John Pigeon staying here?' 'No!—stop a bit though,' says the barmaid; and she took down the letter behind the glass. 'No,' says she, 'it's Thomas, and *he* is not staying here. Would you do me a favour, and post this for me, as it is so wet?' The postman said Yes; she folded it in another envelope, directed it, and gave it him. He put it in his hat, and away he went.

"I had no difficulty in finding out the direction of that letter. It was addressed Mr. Thomas Pigeon, Post Office, R——, Northamptonshire, to be left till called for. Off I started directly for R——; I said the same at the Post Office there, as I had said at B——; and again I waited three days before anybody came. At last another chap on horseback came. 'Any letters for Mr. Thomas Pigeon?' 'Where do you come from?' 'New Inn, near R——.' He got the letter, and away *he* went at a canter.

"I made my inquiries about the New Inn, near R——, and hearing it was a solitary sort of house, a little in the horse line, about a couple of miles from the station, I thought I'd go and have a look at it. I found it what it had been described, and sauntered in, to look about me. The landlady was in the bar, and I was trying to get into conversation with her; asked her how business was, and spoke about the wet weather, and so on; when I saw, through an open door, three men sitting by the fire in a sort of parlour, or kitchen; and one of those men, according to the description I had of him, was Tally-ho Thompson!

"I went and sat down among 'em, and tried to make things agreeable; but they were very shy—wouldn't talk at all—looked at me, and at one another, in a way quite the reverse of sociable. I reckoned 'em up, and finding that they were all three bigger men than me, and considering that their looks were ugly—that it was a lonely place—railroad station two miles off—and night coming on—thought I couldn't do better than have a drop of brandy-and-water to keep my courage up. So I called for my brandy-and-water; and as I was sitting drinking it by the fire, Thompson got up and went out.

"Now the difficulty of it was, that I wasn't sure it *was* Thompson, because I had never set eyes on him before ; and what I had wanted was to be quite certain of him. However, there was nothing for it now, but to follow, and put a bold face upon it. I found him talking, outside in the yard, with the landlady. It turned out afterwards that he was wanted by a Northampton officer for something else, and that, knowing that officer to be pock-marked (as I am myself), he mistook me for him. As I have observed, I found him talking to the landlady, outside. I put my hand upon his shoulder—this way—and said, "Tally-ho Thompson, it's no use. I know you. I'm an officer from London, and I take you into custody for felony ! ' 'That be d—d ! ' says Tally-ho Thompson.

"We went back into the house, and the two friends began to cut up rough, and their looks didn't please me at all, I assure you. 'Let the man go. What are you going to do with him?' 'I'll tell you what I'm going to do with him. I'm going to take him to London to-night, as sure as I'm alive. I'm not alone here, whatever you may think. You mind your own business, and keep yourselves to yourselves. It'll be better for you, for I know you both very well.' *I*'d never seen or heard of 'em in all my life, but my bouncing cowed 'em a bit, and they kept off, while Thompson was making ready to go. I thought to myself, however, that they might be coming after me on the dark road, to rescue Thompson ; so I said to the landlady, 'What men have you got in the house, Missis?' 'We haven't got no men here,' she says, sulkily. 'You have got an ostler, I suppose?' 'Yes, we've got an ostler.' 'Let me see him.' Presently he came, and a shaggy-headed young fellow he was. 'Now attend to me, young man,' says I ; 'I'm a Detective Officer from London. This man's name is Thompson. I have taken him into custody for felony. I am going to take him to the railroad station. I call upon you in the Queen's name to assist me ; and mind you, my friend, you'll get yourself into more trouble than you know of, if you don't ! ' You never saw a person open his eyes so wide. ' Now, Thompson, come along ! ' says I. But when I took out the handcuffs, Thompson cries, 'No ! None of that ! I won't stand *them !* I'll go along with you quiet, but I won't bear none of that ! ' 'Tally-ho Thompson,' I said, 'I'm willing to behave as a man to you, if you are willing to behave as a man to me.

Give me your word that you'll come peaceably along, and I don't want to handcuff you.' 'I will,' says Thompson, 'but I'll have a glass of brandy first.' 'I don't care if I've another,' said I. 'We'll have two more, Missis,' said the friends, 'and con-found you, Constable, you'll give your man a drop, won't you?' I was agreeable to that, so we had it all round, and then my man and I took Tally-ho Thompson safe to the railroad, and I carried him to London that night. He was afterwards acquitted, on account of a defect in the evidence; and I understand he always praises me up to the skies, and says I'm one of the best of men."

This story coming to a termination amidst general applause, Inspector Wield, after a little grave smoking, fixes his eye on his host, and thus delivers himself:

"It wasn't a bad plant that of mine, on Fikey, the man accused of forging the Sou'-Western Railway debentures—it was only t'other day—because the reason why? I'll tell you.

"I had information that Fikey and his brother kept a factory over yonder there,"—indicating any region on the Surrey side of the river—"where he bought second-hand carriages; so after I'd tried in vain to get hold of him by other means, I wrote him a letter in an assumed name, saying that I'd got a horse and shay to dispose of, and would drive down next day that he might view the lot, and make an offer—very reasonable it was, I said—a reg'lar bargain. Straw and me then went off to a friend of mine that's in the livery and job business, and hired a turn-out for the day, a precious smart turn-out it was—quite a slap-up thing! Down we drove, accordingly, with a friend (who's not in the Force himself); and leaving my friend in the shay near a public-house, to take care of the horse, we went to the factory, which was some little way off. In the factory, there was a number of strong fellows at work, and after reckoning 'em up, it was clear to me that it wouldn't do to try it on there. They were too many for us. We must get our man out of doors. 'Mr. Fikey at home?' 'No, he ain't.' 'Expected home soon?' 'Why, no, not soon.' 'Ah! Is his brother here?' '*I*'m his brother.' 'Oh! well, this is an ill-convenience, this is. I wrote him a letter yesterday, saying I'd got a little turn-out to dispose of, and I've took the trouble to bring the turn-out down a' purpose, and now he ain't in the way.' 'No, he ain't in the way. You couldn't make it convenient to call again, could you?' 'Why, no, I couldn't. I want to sell; that's the fact; and I can't put it off. Could you find him anywheres?' At first he said No, he couldn't, and then he wasn't sure about it, and then he'd go and try. So at last he went up-stairs, where there was a sort of loft, and presently down comes my man himself in his shirt-sleeves.

"'Well,' he says, 'this seems to be rayther a pressing matter of yours.' 'Yes,' I says, 'it *is* rayther a pressing matter, and you'll find it a bargain—dirt cheap.' 'I ain't in partickler want of a bargain just now,' he says, 'but where is it?' 'Why,' I says, 'the turn-out's just outside. Come and look at it.' He hasn't any suspicions, and away we go. And the first thing that happens is, that the horse runs away with my friend (who knows no more of driving than a child) when he takes a little trot along the road to show his paces. You never saw such a game in your life!

"When the bolt is over, and the turn-out has come to a standstill again, Fikey walks round and round it as grave as a judge—me too. 'There, sir!' I says. 'There's a neat thing!' 'It ain't a bad style of thing,' he says. 'I believe you,' says I. 'And there's a horse!'—for I saw him looking at it. 'Rising eight!' I says, rubbing his fore-legs. (Bless you, there ain't a man in the world knows less of horses than I do, but I'd heard my friend at the Livery Stables say he was eight year old, so I says, as knowing as possible, 'Rising eight.') 'Rising eight, is he?' says he. 'Rising eight,' says I. 'Well,' he says, 'what do you want for it?' 'Why, the first and last figure for the whole concern is five-and-twenty pound!' 'That's very cheap!' he says, looking at me. 'Ain't it?' I says. 'I told you it was a bargain! Now, without any higgling and haggling about it, what I want is to sell, and that's my price. Further, I'll make it easy to you, and take half the money down, and you can do a bit of stiff[1] for the balance.' 'Well,' he says again, 'that's very cheap.' 'I believe you,' says I; 'get in and try it, and you'll buy it. Come! take a trial!'

"Ecod, he gets in, and we get in, and we drive along the road, to show him to one of the railway clerks that was hid in the public-house window to identify him. But the clerk was bothered, and didn't know whether it was him, or wasn't— because the reason why? I'll tell you,—on account of his

[1] Give a bill.

having shaved his whiskers. 'It's a clever little horse,' he says, 'and trots well; and the shay runs light.' 'Not a doubt about it,' I says. 'And now, Mr. Fikey, I may as well make it all right, without wasting any more of your time. The fact is, I'm Inspector Wield, and you're my prisoner.' 'You don't mean that?' he says. 'I do, indeed.' 'Then burn my body,' says Fikey, 'if this ain't *too* bad!'

"Perhaps you never saw a man so knocked over with surprise. 'I hope you'll let me have my coat?' he says. 'By all means.' 'Well, then, let's drive to the factory.' 'Why, not exactly that, I think,' said I; 'I've been there, once before, to-day. Suppose we send for it.' He saw it was no go, so he sent for it, and put it on, and we drove him up to London, comfortable."

This reminiscence is in the height of its success, when a general proposal is made to the fresh-complexioned, smooth-faced officer, with the strange air of simplicity, to tell the "Butcher's Story."

The fresh-complexioned, smooth-faced officer, with the strange air of simplicity, began with a rustic smile, and in a soft, wheedling tone of voice, to relate the Butcher's Story, thus:

"It's just about six years ago, now, since information was given at Scotland Yard of there being extensive robberies of lawns and silks going on, at some wholesale houses in the City. Directions were given for the business being looked into; and Straw, and Fendall, and me, we were all in it."

"When you received your instructions," said we, "you went away, and held a sort of Cabinet Council together!"

The smooth-faced officer coaxingly replied, "Ye-es. Just so. We turned it over among ourselves a good deal. It appeared, when we went into it, that the goods were sold by the receivers extraordinarily cheap—much cheaper than they could have been if they had been honestly come by. The receivers were in the trade, and kept capital shops—establishments of the first respectability—one of 'em at the West End, one down in Westminster. After a lot of watching and inquiry, and this and that among ourselves, we found that the job was managed, and the purchases of the stolen goods made, at a little public-house near Smithfield, down by Saint Bartholomew's; where the Warehouse Porters, who were the thieves, took 'em for that purpose, don't you see? and made appointments to meet the people that went between themselves and the receivers. This public-house was principally used by journeymen butchers from the country, out of place, and in want of situations; so, what did we do, but—ha, ha, ha!—we agreed that I should be dressed up like a butcher myself, and go and live there!"

Never, surely, was a faculty of observation better brought to bear upon a purpose, than that which picked out this officer for the part. Nothing in all creation could have suited him better. Even while he spoke, he became a greasy, sleepy, shy, good-natured, chuckle-headed, unsuspicious, and confiding young butcher. His very hair seemed to have suet in it, as he made it smooth upon his head, and his fresh complexion to be lubricated by large quantities of animal food.

"—So I—ha, ha, ha!" (always with the confiding snigger of the foolish young butcher) "so I dressed myself in the regular way, made up a little bundle of clothes, and went to the public-house, and asked if I could have a lodging there? They says, 'yes, you can have a lodging here,' and I got a bedroom, and settled myself down in the tap. There was a number of people about the place, and coming backwards and forwards to the house; and first one says, and then another says, 'Are you from the country, young man?' 'Yes,' I says, 'I am. I'm come out of Northamptonshire, and I'm quite lonely here, for I don't know London at all, and it's such a mighty big town.' 'It *is* a big town,' they says. 'Oh, it's a *very* big town!' I says. 'Really and truly I never was in such a town. It quite confuses of me!'—and all that, you know.

"When some of the Journeymen Butchers that used the house, found that I wanted a place, they says, 'Oh, we'll get you a place!' And they actually took me to a sight of places, in Newgate Market, Newport Market, Clare, Carnaby—I don't know where all. But the wages was—ha, ha, ha!—was not sufficient, and I never could suit myself, don't you see? Some of the queer frequenters of the house were a little suspicious of me at first, and I was obliged to be very cautious indeed, how I communicated with Straw or Fendall. Sometimes, when I went out, pretending to stop and look into the shop windows, and just casting my eye round, I used to see some of 'em following me; but being perhaps better accustomed than they thought for, to that sort of thing, I used to lead 'em on as far as I thought necessary or convenient—sometimes a long way—and then turn sharp round, and meet 'em, and say, 'Oh, dear, how glad I am to come upon you so fortunate! This London's such a place, I'm blowed if I an't lost again!' And then we'd go back all together, to the public-house, and—ha, ha, ha! and smoke our pipes, don't you see?

"They were very attentive to me, I am sure. It was a common thing, while I was living there, for some of 'em to take me out, and show me London. They showed me the Prisons—showed me Newgate—and when they showed me Newgate, I stops at the place where the Porters pitch their loads, and says, 'Oh dear, is this where they hang the men? Oh Lor!' 'That!' they says, 'what a simple cove he is! *That* ain't it!' And then, they pointed out which *was* it, and I says, 'Lor!' and they says, 'Now you'll know it agen, won't you?' And I said I thought I should if I tried hard—and I assure you I kept a sharp look out for the City Police when we were out in this way, for if any of 'em had happened to know me, and had spoke to me, it would have been all up in a minute. However, by good luck such a thing never happened, and all went on quiet: though the difficulties I had in communicating with my brother officers were quite extraordinary.

"The stolen goods that were brought to the public-house by the Warehouse Porters, were always disposed of in a back parlour. For a long time, I never could get into this parlour, or see what was done there. As I sat smoking my pipe, like an innocent young chap, by the tap-room fire, I'd hear some of the parties to the robbery, as they came in and out, say softly to the landlord, 'Who's that? What does *he* do here?' 'Bless your soul,' says the landlord, 'he's only a'—ha, ha, ha!—'he's only a green young fellow from the country, as is looking for a butcher's sitivation. Don't mind *him!*' So, in course of time, they were so convinced of my being green, and got to be so accustomed to me, that I was as free of the parlour as any of 'em, and I have seen as much as Seventy Pounds' Worth of fine lawn sold there, in one night, that was stolen from a warehouse in Friday Street. After the sale the buyers always stood treat—hot supper, or dinner, or what not—and they'd say on those occasions, 'Come on, Butcher! Put your best leg foremost, young 'un, and walk into it!' Which I used to do—and hear, at table, all manner of

particulars that it was very important for us Detectives
to know.

"This went on for ten weeks. I lived in the public-house
all the time, and never was out of the Butcher's dress—except
in bed. At last, when I had followed seven of the thieves,
and set 'em to rights—that's an expression of ours, don't
you see, by which I mean to say that I traced 'em, and found
out where the robberies were done, and all about 'em—Straw,
and Fendall, and I, gave one another the office, and at a
time agreed upon, a descent was made upon the public-house,
and the apprehensions effected. One of the first things the
officers did, was to collar me—for the parties to the robbery
weren't to suppose yet, that I was anything but a Butcher—
on which the landlord cries out, 'Don't take *him*,' he says,
'whatever you do! He's only a poor young chap from the
country, and butter wouldn't melt in his mouth!' However,
they—ha, ha, ha!—they took me, and pretended to search
my bedroom, where nothing was found but an old fiddle
belonging to the landlord, that had got there somehow or
another. But it entirely changed the landlord's opinion, for
when it was produced, he says, 'My fiddle! The Butcher's
a pur-loiner! I give him into custody for the robbery of
a musical instrument!'

"The man that had stolen the goods in Friday Street was
not taken yet. He had told me, in confidence, that he had
his suspicions there was something wrong (on account of the
City Police having captured one of the party), and that he
was going to make himself scarce. I asked him, 'Where do
you mean to go, Mr. Shepherdson?' 'Why, Butcher,' says
he, 'the Setting Moon, in the Commercial Road, is a snug
house, and I shall hang out there for a time. I shall call
myself Simpson, which appears to me to be a modest sort of
a name. Perhaps you'll give us a look in, Butcher?' 'Well,'
says I, 'I think I *will* give you a call'—which I fully
intended, don't you see, because, of course, he was to be
taken! I went over to the Setting Moon next day, with
a brother officer, and asked at the bar for Simpson. They
pointed out his room, up-stairs. As we were going up,
he looks down over the banisters, and calls out, 'Halloa,
Butcher! is that you?' 'Yes, it's me. How do you find
yourself?' 'Bobbish,' he says; 'but who's that with you?'
'It's only a young man, that's a friend of mine,' I says.
'Come along, then,' says he; 'any friend of the Butcher's

is as welcome as the Butcher!' So I made my friend acquainted with him, and we took him into custody.

"You have no idea, sir, what a sight it was, in Court, when they first knew that I wasn't a Butcher, after all! I wasn't produced at the first examination, when there was a remand; but I was at the second. And when I stepped into the box, in full police uniform, and the whole party saw how they had been done, actually a groan of horror and dismay proceeded from 'em in the dock!

"At the Old Bailey, when their trials came on, Mr. Clark-son was engaged for the defence, and he *couldn't* make out how it was, about the Butcher. He thought, all along, it was a real Butcher. When the counsel for the prosecution said, 'I will now call before you, gentlemen, the Police-officer,' meaning myself, Mr. Clarkson says, 'Why Police-officer? Why more Police-officers? I don't want Police. We have had a great deal too much of the Police. I want the Butcher!' However, sir, he had the Butcher and the Police-officer, both in one. Out of seven prisoners committed for trial, five were found guilty, and some of 'em were trans-ported. The respectable firm at the West End got a term of imprisonment; and that's the Butcher's Story!"

The story done, the chuckle-headed Butcher again resolved himself into the smooth-faced Detective. But he was so extremely tickled by their having taken him about, when he was that Dragon in disguise, to show him London, that he could not help reverting to that point in his narrative; and gently repeating with the Butcher snigger, "'Oh, dear,' I says, 'is that where they hang the men? Oh, Lor!' '*That!*' says they. 'What a simple cove he is!'"

It being now late, and the party very modest in their fear of being too diffuse, there were some tokens of separation; when Sergeant Dornton, the soldierly-looking man, said, looking round him with a smile:

"Before we break up, sir, perhaps you might have some amusement in hearing of the Adventures of a Carpet Bag. They are very short; and, I think, curious."

We welcomed the Carpet Bag, as cordially as Mr. Shep-herdson welcomed the false Butcher at the Setting Moon. Sergeant Dornton proceeded.

"In 1847, I was despatched to Chatham, in search of one Mesheck, a Jew. He had been carrying on, pretty heavily, in the bill-stealing way, getting acceptances from young men of good connexions (in the army chiefly), on pretence of discount, and bolting with the same.

"Mesheck was off, before I got to Chatham. All I could learn about him was, that he had gone, probably to London, and had with him—a Carpet Bag.

"I came back to town, by the last train from Blackwall, and made inquiries concerning a Jew passenger with—a Carpet Bag.

"The office was shut up, it being the last train. There were only two or three porters left. Looking after a Jew with a Carpet Bag, on the Blackwall Railway, which was then the high road to a great Military Depôt, was worse than looking after a needle in a hayrick. But it happened that one of these porters had carried, for a certain Jew, to a certain public-house, a certain—Carpet Bag.

"I went to the public-house, but the Jew had only left his luggage there for a few hours, and had called for it in a cab, and taken it away. I put such questions there, and to the porter, as I thought prudent, and got at this description of—the Carpet Bag.

"It was a bag which had, on one side of it, worked in worsted, a green parrot on a stand. A green parrot on a stand was the means by which to identify that—Carpet Bag.

"I traced Mesheck, by means of this green parrot on a stand, to Cheltenham, to Birmingham, to Liverpool, to the Atlantic Ocean. At Liverpool he was too many for me. He had gone to the United States, and I gave up all thoughts of Mesheck, and likewise of his—Carpet Bag.

"Many months afterwards—near a year afterwards—there was a bank in Ireland robbed of seven thousand pounds, by a person of the name of Doctor Dundey, who escaped to America; from which country some of the stolen notes came home. He was supposed to have bought a farm in New Jersey. Under proper management, that estate could be seized and sold, for the benefit of the parties he had defrauded. I was sent off to America for this purpose.

"I landed at Boston. I went on to New York. I found that he had lately changed New York paper-money for New Jersey paper-money, and had banked cash in New Brunswick. To take this Doctor Dundey, it was necessary to entrap him into the State of New York, which required a deal of artifice and trouble. At one time, he couldn't be drawn into an appointment. At another time, he appointed to come to meet me, and a New York officer, on a pretext I made; and then his children had the measles. At last he came, per steamboat, and I took him, and lodged him in a New York prison called the Tombs; which I dare say you know, sir?"

Editorial acknowledgment to that effect.

"I went to the Tombs, on the morning after his capture, to attend the examination before the magistrate. I was passing through the magistrate's private room, when, happening to look round me to take notice of the place, as we generally have a habit of doing, I clapped my eyes, in one corner, on a—Carpet Bag.

"What did I see upon that Carpet Bag, if you'll believe me, but a green parrot on a stand, as large as life!

"'That Carpet Bag, with the representation of a green parrot on a stand,' said I, 'belongs to an English Jew, name Aaron Mesheck, and to no other man, alive or dead!'

"I give you my word the New York Police Officers were doubled up with surprise.

"'How did you ever come to know that?' said they.

"'I think I ought to know that green parrot by this time,' said I; 'for I have had as pretty a dance after that bird, at home, as ever I had, in all my life!'"

"And was it Mesheck's?" we submissively inquired.

"Was it, sir? Of course it was! He was in custody for another offence, in that very identical Tombs, at that very identical time. And, more than that! Some memoranda, relating to the fraud for which I had vainly endeavoured to take him, were found to be, at that moment, lying in that very same individual—Carpet Bag!"

Such are the curious coincidences and such is the peculiar ability, always sharpening and being improved by practice, and always adapting itself to every variety of circumstances, and opposing itself to every new device that perverted ingenuity can invent, for which this important social branch of the public service is remarkable! For ever on the watch, with their wits stretched to the utmost, these officers have, from day to day and year to year, to set themselves against every novelty of trickery and dexterity that the combined imaginations of all the lawless rascals in England can devise, and to keep pace with every such invention that comes out.

In the Courts of Justice, the materials of thousands of such stories as we have narrated—often elevated into the marvellous and romantic, by the circumstances of the case—are dryly compressed into the set phrase, "in consequence of information I received, I did so and so." Suspicion was to be directed, by careful inference and deduction, upon the right person; the right person was to be taken, wherever he had gone, or whatever he was doing to avoid detection: he is taken; there he is at the bar; that is enough. From information I, the officer, received, I did it; and, according to the custom in these cases, I say no more.

These games of chess, played with live pieces, are played before small audiences, and are chronicled nowhere. The interest of the game supports the player. Its results are enough for Justice. To compare great things with small, suppose LEVERRIER or ADAMS informing the public that from information he had received he had discovered a new planet; or COLUMBUS informing the public of his day that from information he had received he had discovered a new continent; so the Detectives inform it that they have discovered a new fraud or an old offender, and the process is unknown.

Thus, at midnight, closed the proceedings of our curious and interesting party. But one other circumstance finally wound up the evening, after our Detective guests had left us. One of the sharpest among them, and the officer best acquainted with the Swell Mob, had his pocket picked, going home!

THREE "DETECTIVE" ANECDOTES

I. THE PAIR OF GLOVES

"It's a singler story, sir," said Inspector Wield, of the Detective Police, who, in company with Sergeants Dornton and Mith, paid us another twilight visit, one July evening; "and I've been thinking you might like to know it.

"It's concerning the murder of the young woman, Eliza Grimwood, some years ago, over in the Waterloo Road. She was commonly called The Countess, because of her handsome appearance and her proud way of carrying of herself; and when I saw the poor Countess (I had known her well to speak to), lying dead, with her throat cut, on the floor of her bedroom, you'll believe me that a variety of reflections calculated to make a man rather low in his spirits, came into my head.

"That's neither here nor there. I went to the house the morning after the murder, and examined the body, and made a general observation of the bedroom where it was. Turning down the pillow of the bed with my hand, I found, under-neath it, a pair of gloves. A pair of gentleman's dress gloves, very dirty; and inside the lining, the letters TR, and a cross.

"Well, sir, I took them gloves away, and I showed 'em to the magistrate, over at Union Hall, before whom the case was. He says, 'Wield,' he says, 'there's no doubt this is a discovery that may lead to something very important; and what you have got to do, Wield, is to find out the owner of these gloves.'

"I was of the same opinion, of course, and I went at it immediately. I looked at the gloves pretty narrowly, and it was my opinion that they had been cleaned. There was a smell of sulphur and rosin about 'em, you know, which cleaned gloves usually have, more or less. I took 'em over to a friend of mine at Kennington, who was in that line, and I put it to him. 'What do you say now? Have these gloves been cleaned?' 'These gloves have been cleaned,' says he. 'Have you any idea who cleaned them?' says I. 'Not at all,' says he; 'I've a very distinct idea who *didn't* clean 'em, and that's myself. But I'll tell you what, Wield, there ain't above eight or nine reg'lar glove-cleaners in London,'—there were not, at that time, it seems—'and I think I can give you their addresses, and you may find out, by that means, who did clean 'em.' Accordingly, he gave me the directions, and I went here, and I went there, and I looked up this man, and 'I looked- up that man; but, though they all agreed that the gloves had been cleaned, I couldn't find the man, woman, or child, that had cleaned that aforesaid pair of gloves.

"What with this person not being at home, and that person being expected home in the afternoon, and so forth, the inquiry took me three days. On the evening of the third day, coming over Waterloo Bridge from the Surrey side of the river, quite beat, and very much vexed and disappointed, I thought I'd have a shilling's worth of entertainment at the Lyceum Theatre to freshen myself up. So I went into the Pit, at half-price, and I sat myself down next to a very quiet, modest sort of young man. Seeing I was a stranger (which I thought it just as well to appear to be) he told me the names of the actors on the stage, and we got into conversation. When the play was over, we came out together, and I said, 'We've been very companionable and agreeable, and perhaps you wouldn't object to a drain?' 'Well, you're very good,' says he; 'I *shouldn't* object to a drain.' Accordingly, we went to a public-house, near the Theatre, sat ourselves down in a quiet room up-stairs on the first floor, and called for a pint of half-and-half apiece, and a pipe.

"Well, sir, we put our pipes aboard, and we drank our half-and-half, and sat a-talking, very sociably, when the young man says, 'You must excuse me stopping very long,' he says, 'because I'm forced to go home in good time. I must be at work all night.' 'At work all night?' says I. 'You ain't a baker?' 'No,' he says, laughing, 'I ain't a baker.' 'I thought not,' says I, 'you haven't the looks of a baker.' 'No,' says he, 'I'm a glove-cleaner.'

"I never was more astonished in my life, than when I heard them words come out of his lips. 'You're a glove-cleaner, are you?' says I. 'Yes,' he says, 'I am.' 'Then, perhaps,' says I, taking the gloves out of my pocket, 'you

can tell me who cleaned this pair of gloves? It's a rum
story,' I says. 'I was dining over at Lambeth, the other day,
at a free-and-easy—quite promiscuous—with a public company—when some gentleman, he left these gloves behind
him! Another gentleman and me, you see, we laid a wager
of a sovereign, that I wouldn't find out who they belonged to.
I've spent as much as seven shillings already, in trying to
discover; but, if you could help me, I'd stand another seven
and welcome. You see there's TR and a cross, inside.' '*I*
see,' he says. 'Bless you, *I* know these gloves very well!
I've seen dozens of pairs belonging to the same party.'
'No?' says I. 'Yes,' says he. 'Then you know who
cleaned 'em?' says I. 'Rather so,' says he. 'My father
cleaned 'em.'

"'Where does your father live?' says I. 'Just round the
corner,' says the young man, 'near Exeter Street, here. He'll
tell you who they belong to, directly.' 'Would you come
round with me now?' says I. 'Certainly,' says he, 'but you
needn't tell my father that you found me at the play, you
know, because he mightn't like it.' 'All right!' We went
round to the place, and there we found an old man in a white
apron, with two or three daughters, all rubbing and cleaning
away at lots of gloves, in a front parlour. 'Oh, Father!'
says the young man, 'here's a person been and made a bet
about the ownership of a pair of gloves, and I've told him
you can settle it.' 'Good evening, sir,' says I to the old
gentleman. 'Here's the gloves your son speaks of. Letters
TR, you see, and a cross.' 'Oh yes,' he says, 'I know these
gloves very well; I've cleaned dozens of pairs of 'em. They
belong to Mr. Trinkle, the great upholsterer in Cheapside.'
'Did you get 'em from Mr. Trinkle, direct,' says I, 'if you'll
excuse my asking the question?' 'No,' says he; 'Mr. Trinkle
always sends 'em to Mr. Phibbs's, the haberdasher's, opposite
his shop, and the haberdasher sends 'em to me.' 'Perhaps
you wouldn't object to a drain?' says I. 'Not in the least!'
says he. So I took the old gentleman out, and had a little
more talk with him and his son, over a glass, and we parted
ex-cellent friends.

"This was late on a Saturday night. First thing on the
Monday morning, I went to the haberdasher's shop, opposite
Mr. Trinkle's, the great upholsterer's in Cheapside. 'Mr.
Phibbs in the way?' 'My name is Phibbs.' 'Oh! I believe
you sent this pair of gloves to be cleaned?' 'Yes, I did,

for young Mr. Trinkle over the way. There he is in the shop!' 'Oh! that's him in the shop, is it? Him in the green coat?' 'The same individual.' 'Well, Mr. Phibbs, this is an unpleasant affair; but the fact is, I am Inspector Wield of the Detective Police, and I found these gloves under the pillow of the young woman that was murdered the other day, over in the Waterloo Road.' 'Good Heaven!' says he. 'He's a most respectable young man, and if his father was to hear of it, it would be the ruin of him!' 'I'm very sorry for it,' says I, 'but I must take him into custody.' 'Good Heaven!' says Mr. Phibbs, again; 'can nothing be done!' 'Nothing,' says I. 'Will you allow me to call him over here,' says he, 'that his father may not see it done?' 'I don't object to that,' says I; 'but unfortunately, Mr. Phibbs, I can't allow of any communication between you. If any was attempted, I should have to interfere directly. Perhaps you'll beckon him over here?' Mr. Phibbs went to the door and beckoned, and the young fellow came across the street directly; a smart, brisk young fellow.

" 'Good morning, sir,' says I. 'Good morning, sir,' says he. 'Would you allow me to inquire, sir,' says I, 'if you ever had any acquaintance with a party of the name of Grimwood?' 'Grimwood! Grimwood!' says he. 'No! 'You know the Waterloo Road?' 'Oh! of course I know the Waterloo Road!' 'Happen to have heard of a young woman being murdered there?' 'Yes, I read it in the paper, and very sorry I was to read it.' 'Here's a pair of gloves belonging to you, that I found under her pillow the morning afterwards!'

"He was in a dreadful state, sir; a dreadful state! 'Mr. Wield,' he says, 'upon my solemn oath I never was there. I never so much as saw her, to my knowledge, in my life!' 'I am very sorry,' says I. 'To tell you the truth; I don't think you *are* the murderer, but I must take you to Union Hall in a cab. However, I think it's a case of that sort, that, at present, at all events, the magistrate will hear it in private.'

"A private examination took place, and then it came out that this young man was acquainted with a cousin of the unfortunate Eliza Grimwood, and that, calling to see this cousin a day or two before the murder, he left these gloves upon the table. Who should come in, shortly afterwards, but Eliza Grimwood! 'Whose gloves are these?' she says,

taking 'em up. 'Those are Mr. Trinkle's gloves,' says her
cousin. 'Oh!' says she, 'they are very dirty, and of no use
to him, I am sure. I shall take 'em away for my girl to
clean the stoves with.' And she put 'em in her pocket.
The girl had used 'em to clean the stoves, and, I have no
doubt, had left 'em lying on the bedroom mantelpiece, or on
the drawers, or somewhere; and her mistress, looking round
to see that the room was tidy, had caught 'em up and put
'em under the pillow where I found 'em.

"That's the story, sir."

II. THE ARTFUL TOUCH

"One of the most *beautiful* things that ever was done,
perhaps," said Inspector Wield, emphasising the adjective,
as preparing us to expect dexterity or ingenuity rather than
strong interest, "was a move of Sergeant Witchem's. It
was a lovely idea!

"Witchem and me were down at Epsom one Derby Day,
waiting at the station for the Swell Mob. As I mentioned,
when we were talking about these things before, we are
ready at the station when there's races, or an Agricultural
Show, or a Chancellor sworn in for an university, or Jenny
Lind, or anything of that sort; and as the Swell Mob come
down, we send 'em back again by the next train. But some
of the Swell Mob, on the occasion of this Derby that I refer
to, so far kidded us as to hire a horse and shay; start away
from London by Whitechapel, and miles round; come into
Epsom from the opposite direction; and go to work, right
and left, on the course, while we were waiting for 'em at
the Rail. That, however, ain't the point of what I'm going
to tell you.

"While Witchem and me were waiting at the station,
there comes up one Mr. Tatt; a gentleman formerly in the
public line, quite an amateur Detective in his way, and very
much respected. 'Halloa, Charley Wield,' he says. 'What
are you doing here? On the look out for some of your old
friends?' 'Yes, the old move, Mr. Tatt.' 'Come along,' he
says, 'you and Witchem, and have a glass of sherry.' 'We
can't stir from the place,' says I, 'till the next train comes
in; but after that, we will with pleasure.' Mr. Tatt waits,
and the train comes in, and then Witchem and me go off
with him to the Hotel. Mr. Tatt he's got up quite regard-

less of expense, for the occasion ; and in his shirt-front there's
a beautiful diamond prop, cost him fifteen or twenty pound
—a very handsome pin indeed.   We drink our sherry at the
bar, and have had our three or four glasses, when Witchem
cries suddenly, 'Look out, Mr. Wield! stand fast!' and
a dash is made into the place by the Swell Mob—four of 'em
—that have come down as I tell you, and in a moment Mr.
Tatt's prop is gone!   Witchem, he cuts 'em off at the door,
I lay about me as hard as I can, Mr. Tatt shows fight like
a good 'un, and there we are, all down together, heads and
heels, knocking about on the floor of the bar—perhaps you
never see such a scene of confusion!   However, we stick to
our men (Mr. Tatt being as good as any officer), and we take
'em all, and carry 'em off to the station.   The station's full
of people, who have been took on the course; and it's a
precious piece of work to get 'em secured.   However, we do
it at last, and we search 'em ; but nothing's found upon 'em,
and they're locked up ; and a pretty state of heat we are in
by that time, I assure you!

"I was very blank over it, myself, to think that the prop
had been passed away ; and I said to Witchem, when we
had set 'em to rights, and were cooling ourselves along with
Mr. Tatt, 'we don't take much by *this* move, anyway, for
nothing's found upon 'em, and it's only the braggadocia[1],
after all.' 'What do you mean, Mr. Wield?' says Witchem.
'Here's the diamond pin!' and in the palm of his hand
there it was, safe and sound ! 'Why, in the name of wonder,'
says me and Mr. Tatt, in astonishment, 'how did you come
by that?' 'I'll tell you how I come by it,' says he. 'I saw
which of 'em took it ; and when we were all down on the
floor together, knocking about, I just gave him a little touch
on the back of his hand, as I knew his pal would ; and he
thought it was his pal; and gave it me!' It was beautiful,
beau-ti-ful!

"Even that was hardly the best of the case, for that chap
was tried at the Quarter Sessions at Guildford.   You know
what Quarter Sessions are, sir.   Well, if you'll believe me,
while them slow justices were looking over the Acts of
Parliament, to see what they could do to him, I'm blowed if
he didn't cut out of the dock before their faces ! He cut out
of the dock, sir, then and there ; swam across a river ; and

---

[1] Three months' imprisonment as reputed thieves.

got up into a tree to dry himself. In the tree he was took
—an old woman having seen him climb up—and Witchem's
artful touch transported him!"

III. THE SOFA

"What young men will do, sometimes, to ruin themselves
and break their friends' hearts," said Sergeant Dornton, "it's
surprising! I had a case at Saint Blank's Hospital which
was of this sort. A bad case, indeed, with a bad end!"

"The Secretary, and the House-Surgeon, and the Treasurer,
of Saint Blank's Hospital, came to Scotland Yard to give
information of numerous robberies having been committed on
the students. The students could leave nothing in the pockets
of their great-coats, while the great-coats were hanging at
the hospital, but it was almost certain to be stolen. Property
of various descriptions was constantly being lost; and the
gentlemen were naturally uneasy about it, and anxious, for
the credit of the institution, that the thief or thieves should
be discovered. The case was entrusted to me, and I went
to the hospital.

"'Now, gentlemen,' said I, after we had talked it over; 'I
understand this property is usually lost from one room.'

"Yes, they said. It was.

"'I should wish, if you please,' said I, 'to see the room.'

"It was a good-sized bare room down-stairs, with a few
tables and forms in it, and a row of pegs, all round, for hats
and coats.

"'Next, gentlemen,' said I, 'do you suspect anybody?'

"Yes, they said. They did suspect somebody. They were
sorry to say, they suspected one of the porters.

"'I should like,' said I, 'to have that man pointed out to
me, and to have a little time to look after him.'

"He was pointed out, and I looked after him, and then I
went back to the hospital, and said, 'Now, gentlemen, it's
not the porter. He's, unfortunately for himself, a little too
fond of drink, but he's nothing worse. My suspicion is, that
these robberies are committed by one of the students; and
if you'll put me a sofa into that room where the pegs are
—as there's no closet—I think I shall be able to detect the
thief. I wish the sofa, if you please, to be covered with
chintz, or something of that sort, so that I may lie on my
chest, underneath it, without being seen.'

The Sofa

"The sofa was provided, and next day at eleven o'clock, before any of the students came, I went there, with those gentlemen, to get underneath it. It turned out to be one of those old-fashioned sofas with a great cross-beam at the bottom, that would have broken my back in no time if I could ever have got below it. We had quite a job to break all this away in the time; however, I fell to work, and they fell to work, and we broke it out, and made a clear place for me. I got under the sofa, lay down on my chest, took out my knife, and made a convenient hole in the chintz to look through. It was then settled between me and the gentlemen that when the students were all up in the wards, one of the gentlemen should come in, and hang up a great-coat on one of the pegs. And that that great-coat should have, in one of the pockets, a pocket-book containing marked money.

"After I had been there some time, the students began to drop into the room, by ones, and twos, and threes, and to talk about all sorts of things, little thinking there was anybody under the sofa—and then to go up-stairs. At last there came in one who remained until he was alone in the room by himself. A tallish, good-looking young man of one or two and twenty, with a light whisker. He went to a particular hat-peg, took off a good hat that was hanging there, tried it on, hung his own hat in its place, and hung that hat on another peg, nearly opposite to me. I then felt quite certain that he was the thief, and would come back by-and-by.

"When they were all up-stairs, the gentleman came in with the great-coat. I showed him where to hang it, so that I might have a good view of it ; and he went away ; and I lay under the sofa on my chest, for a couple of hours or so, waiting.

"At last, the same young man came down. He walked across the room, whistling—stopped and listened—took another walk and whistled—stopped again, and listened— then began to go regularly round the pegs, feeling in the pockets of all the coats. When he came to THE great-coat, and felt the pocket-book, he was so eager and so hurried that he broke the strap in tearing it open. As he began to put the money in his pocket, I crawled out from under the sofa, and his eyes met mine.

"My face, as you may perceive, is brown now, but it was pale at that time, my health not being good ; and looked as long as a horse's. Besides which, there was a great draught of air from the door, underneath the sofa, and I had tied a handkerchief round my head; so what I looked like, altogether, I don't know. He turned blue—literally blue—when he saw me crawling out, and I couldn't feel surprised at it.

"'I am an officer of the Detective Police,' said I, 'and have been lying here, since you first came in this morning. I regret, for the sake of yourself and your friends, that you should have done what you have; but this case is complete. You have the pocket-book in your hand and the money upon you; and I must take you into custody!'

"It was impossible to make out any case in his behalf, and on his trial he pleaded guilty. How or when he got the means I don't know; but while he was awaiting his sentence, he poisoned himself in Newgate."

We inquired of this officer, on the conclusion of the foregoing anecdote, whether the time appeared long, or short, when he lay in that constrained position under the sofa?

"Why, you see, sir," he replied, "if he hadn't come in, the first time, and I had not been quite sure he was the thief, and would return, the time would have seemed long. But, as it was, I being dead certain of my man, the time seemed pretty short."

ON DUTY WITH INSPECTOR FIELD

How goes the night? Saint Giles's clock is striking nine. The weather is dull and wet, and the long lines of street lamps are blurred, as if we saw them through tears. A damp wind blows and rakes the pieman's fire out, when he opens the door of his little furnace, carrying away an eddy of sparks.

Saint Giles's clock strikes nine. We are punctual. Where is Inspector Field? Assistant Commissioner of Police is already here, enwrapped in oil-skin cloak, and standing in the shadow of Saint Giles's steeple. Detective Sergeant, weary of speaking French all day to foreigners unpacking at the Great Exhibition, is already here. Where is Inspector Field?

Inspector Field is, to-night, the guardian genius of the British Museum. He is bringing his shrewd eye to bear on every corner of its solitary galleries, before he reports "all right." Suspicious of the Elgin marbles, and not to be done by cat-faced Egyptian giants with their hands upon their knees, Inspector Field, sagacious, vigilant, lamp in hand, throwing monstrous shadows on the walls and ceilings, passes through the spacious rooms. If a mummy trembled in an atom of its dusty covering, Inspector Field would say, "Come out of that, Tom Green. I know you!" If the smallest "Gonoph" about town were crouching at the bottom of a classic bath, Inspector Field would nose him with a finer scent than the ogre's, when adventurous Jack lay trembling in his kitchen copper. But all is quiet, and Inspector Field goes warily on, making little outward show of attending to anything in particular, just recognising the Ichthyosaurus as a familiar acquaintance, and wondering, perhaps, how the detectives did it in the days before the Flood.

Will Inspector Field be long about this work? He may be half-an-hour longer. He sends his compliments by Police Constable, and proposes that we meet at St. Giles's Station

House, across the road. Good. It were as well to stand by the fire, there, as in the shadow of Saint Giles's steeple.

Anything doing here to-night? Not much. We are very quiet. A lost boy, extremely calm and small, sitting by the fire, whom we now confide to a constable to take home, for the child says that if you show him Newgate Street, he can show you where he lives—a raving drunken woman in the cells, who has screeched her voice away, and has hardly power enough left to declare, even with the passionate help of her feet and arms, that she is the daughter of a British officer, and, strike her blind and dead, but she'll write a letter to the Queen! but who is soothed with a drink of water—in another cell, a quiet woman, with a child at her breast, for begging—in another, her husband in a smock-frock, with a basket of watercresses—in another, a pickpocket —in another, a meek tremulous old pauper man who has been out for a holiday "and has took but a little drop, but it has overcome him after so many months in the house"—and that's all as yet. Presently, a sensation at the Station House door. Mr. Field, gentlemen!

Inspector Field comes in, wiping his forehead, for he is of a burly figure, and has come fast from the ores and metals of the deep mines of the earth, and from the Parrot Gods of the South Sea Islands, and from the birds and beetles of the tropics, and from the Arts of Greece and Rome, and from the Sculptures of Nineveh, and from the traces of an elder world, when these were not. Is Rogers ready? Rogers is ready, strapped and great-coated, with a flaming eye in the middle of his waist, like a deformed Cyclops. Lead on, Rogers, to Rats' Castle!

How many people may there be in London, who, if we had brought them deviously and blindfold, to this street, fifty paces from the Station House, and within call of Saint Giles's church, would know it for a not remote part of the city in which their lives are passed? How many, who amidst this compound of sickening smells, these heaps of filth, these tumbling houses, with all their vile contents, animate and inanimate, slimily overflowing into the black road, would believe that they breathe *this* air? How much Red Tape may there be, that could look round on the faces which now hem us in—for our appearance here has caused a rush from all points to a common centre—the lowering foreheads, the sallow cheeks, the brutal eyes, the matted hair, the infected, vermin-haunted heaps of rags—and say, "I have thought of this. I have not dismissed the thing. I have neither blustered it away, nor frozen it away, nor tied it up and put it away, nor smoothly said pooh, pooh! to it when it has been shown to me?"

This is not what Rogers wants to know, however. What Rogers wants to know, is, whether you *will* clear the way here, some of you, or whether you won't; because if you don't do it right on end, he'll lock you up! "What! *You* are there, are you, Bob Miles? You haven't had enough of it yet, haven't you? You want three months more, do you? Come away from that gentleman! What are you creeping round there for?"

"What am I a doing, thinn, Mr. Rogers?" says Bob Miles, appearing, villainous, at the end of a lane of light, made by the lantern.

"I'll let you know pretty quick, if you don't hook it. WILL you hook it?"

A sycophantic murmur rises from the crowd. "Hook it, Bob, when Mr. Rogers and Mr. Field tells you! Why don't you hook it, when you are told to?"

The most importunate of the voices strikes familiarly on Mr. Rogers's ear. He suddenly turns his lantern on the owner.

"What! *You* are there, are you, Mister Click? You hook it too—come!"

"What for?" says Mr. Click, discomfited.

"You hook it, will you!" says Mr. Rogers with stern emphasis.

Both Click and Miles *do* "hook it," without another word, or, in plainer English, sneak away.

"Close up there, my men!" says Inspector Field to two constables on duty who have followed. "Keep together, gentlemen; we are going down here. Heads!"

Saint Giles's church strikes half-past ten. We stoop low, and creep down a precipitous flight of steps into a dark close cellar. There is a fire. There is a long deal table. There are benches. The cellar is full of company, chiefly very young men in various conditions of dirt and raggedness. Some are eating supper. There are no girls or women present. Welcome to Rats' Castle, gentlemen, and to this company of noted thieves!

"Well, my lads! How are you, my lads? What have

you been doing to-day ?   Here's some company come to see
you, my lads!   *There's* a plate of beefsteak, sir, for the
supper of a fine young man !   And there's a mouth for
a steak, sir !   Why, I should be too proud of such a mouth
as that, if I had it myself !   Stand up and show it, sir !
Take off your cap.   There's a fine young man for a nice
little party, sir !   An't he ? "

Inspector Field is the bustling speaker.   Inspector Field's
eye is the roving eye that searches every corner of the cellar
as he talks.   Inspector Field's hand is the well-known hand
that has collared half the people here, and motioned their
brothers, sisters, fathers, mothers, male and female friends,
inexorably to New South Wales.   Yet Inspector Field stands
in this den, the Sultan of the place.   Every thief here
cowers before him, like a schoolboy before his schoolmaster.
All watch him, all answer when addressed, all laugh at his
jokes, all seek to propitiate him.   This cellar company alone
—to say nothing of the crowd surrounding the entrance
from the street above, and making the steps shine with
eyes—is strong enough to murder us all, and willing enough
to do it ; but let Inspector Field have a mind to pick out
one thief here, and take him ; let him produce that ghostly
truncheon from his pocket, and say, with his business-air,
"My lad, I want you ! " and all Rats' Castle shall be stricken
with paralysis, and not a finger move against him, as he fits
the handcuffs on !

Where's the Earl of Warwick ?—Here he is, Mr. Field !
Here's the Earl of Warwick, Mr. Field !—O, there you are,
my Lord.   Come for'ard.   There's a chest, sir, not to have
a clean shirt on.   An't it ?   Take your hat off, my Lord.
Why, I should be ashamed if I was you—and an Earl, too—
to show myself to a gentleman with my hat on !—The Earl
of Warwick laughs and uncovers.   All the company laugh.
One pickpocket, especially, laughs with great enthusiasm.
O what a jolly game it is, when Mr. Field comes down—and
don't want nobody !

"So, *you* are here, too, are you, you tall, grey, soldierly-
looking, grave man, standing by the fire ?—Yes, sir.   Good
evening, Mr. Field !—Let us see.   You lived servant to a
nobleman once ?—Yes, Mr. Field.—And what is it you do
now ; I forget ?—Well, Mr. Field, I job about as well as I
can.   I left my employment on account of delicate health.
The family is still kind to me.   Mr. Wix of Piccadilly

is also very kind to me when I am hard up. Likewise
Mr. Nix of Oxford Street. I get a trifle from them occasionally, and rub on as well as I can, Mr. Field. Mr. Field's eye
rolls enjoyingly, for this man is a notorious begging-letter
writer.—Good night, my lads!—Good night, Mr. Field, and
thank'ee, sir!

Clear the street here, half a thousand of you! Cut it,
Mrs. Stalker—none of that—we don't want you! Rogers of
the flaming eye, lead on to the tramps' lodging-house!

A dream of baleful faces attends to the door. Now, stand
back all of you! In the rear Detective Sergeant plants
himself, composedly whistling, with his strong right arm
across the narrow passage. Mrs. Stalker, I am something'd
that need not be written here, if you won't get yourself into
trouble, in about half a minute, if I see that face of yours
again!

Saint Giles's church clock, striking eleven, hums through
our hand from the dilapidated door of a dark outhouse as we
open it, and are stricken back by the pestilent breath that
issues from within. Rogers to the front with the light, and
let us look!

Ten, twenty, thirty—who can count them! Men, women,
children, for the most part naked, heaped upon the floor
like maggots in a cheese! Ho! In that dark corner yonder!
Does anybody lie there? Me sir, Irish me, a widder, with
six children. And yonder? Me sir, Irish me, with me
wife and eight poor babes. And to the left there? Me sir,
Irish me, along with two more Irish boys as is me friends.
And to the right there? Me sir and the Murphy fam'ly,
numbering five blessed souls. And what's this, coiling,
now, about my foot? Another Irish me, pitifully in want
of shaving, whom I have awakened from sleep—and across
my other foot lies his wife—and by the shoes of Inspector
Field lie their three eldest—and their three youngest are at
present squeezed between the open door and the wall. And
why is there no one on that little mat before the sullen fire?
Because O'Donovan, with his wife and daughter, is not come
in from selling Lucifers! Nor on the bit of sacking in the
nearest corner? Bad luck! Because that Irish family is
late to-night, a-cadging in the streets!

They are all awake now, the children excepted, and most
of them sit up, to stare. Wheresoever Mr. Rogers turns
the flaming eye, there is a spectral figure rising, unshrouded,

from a grave of rags. Who is the landlord here?—I am, Mr. Field! says a bundle of ribs and parchment against the wall, scratching itself.—Will you spend this money fairly, in the morning, to buy coffee for 'em all?—Yes, sir, I will! —O he'll do it, sir, he'll do it fair. He's honest! cry the spectres. And with thanks and Good Night sink into their graves again.

Thus, we make our New Oxford Streets, and our other new streets, never heeding, never asking, where the wretches whom we clear out, crowd. With such scenes at our doors, with all the plagues of Egypt tied up with bits of cobweb in kennels so near our homes, we timorously make our Nuisance Bills and Boards of Health, nonentities, and think to keep away the Wolves of Crime and Filth, by our electioneering ducking to little vestrymen and our gentlemanly handling of Red Tape!

Intelligence of the coffee-money has got abroad. The yard is full, and Rogers of the flaming eye is beleaguered with entreaties to show other Lodging Houses. Mine next! Mine! Mine! Rogers, military, obdurate, stiff-necked, im-movable, replies not, but leads away; all falling back before him. Inspector Field follows. Detective Sergeant, with his barrier of arm across the little passage, deliberately waits to close the procession. He sees behind him, without any effort, and exceedingly disturbs one individual far in the rear by coolly calling out, "It won't do, Mr. Michael! Don't try it!"

After council holden in the street, we enter other lodging-houses, public-houses, many lairs and holes; all noisome and offensive; none so filthy and so crowded as where Irish are. In one, The Ethiopian party are expected home presently —were in Oxford Street when last heard of—shall be fetched, for our delight, within ten minutes. In another, one of the two or three Professors who draw Napoleon Buonaparte and a couple of mackerel, on the pavement, and then let the work of art out to a speculator, is refreshing after his labours. In another, the vested interest of the pro-fitable nuisance has been in one family for a hundred years, and the landlord drives in comfortably from the country to his snug little stew in town. In all, Inspector Field is received with warmth. Coiners and smashers droop before him; pickpockets defer to him; the gentle sex (not very gentle here) smile upon him. Half-drunken hags check themselves in the midst of pots of beer, or pints of gin, to drink to Mr. Field, and pressingly to ask the honour of his finishing the draught. One beldame in rusty black has such admiration for him, that she runs a whole street's length to shake him by the hand; tumbling into a heap of mud by the way, and still pressing her attentions when her very form has ceased to be distinguishable through it. Before the power of the law, the power of superior sense— for common thieves are fools beside these men—and the power of a perfect mastery of their character, the garrison of Rats' Castle and the adjacent Fortresses make but a skulking show indeed when reviewed by Inspector Field.

Saint Giles's clock says it will be midnight in half-an-hour, and Inspector Field says we must hurry to the Old Mint in the Borough. The cab-driver is low-spirited, and has a solemn sense of his responsibility. Now, what's your fare, my lad?—O *you* know, Inspector Field, what's the good of asking *me!*

Say, Parker, strapped and great-coated, and waiting in dim Borough doorway by appointment, to replace the trusty Rogers whom we left deep in Saint Giles's, are you ready? Ready, Inspector Field, and at a motion of my wrist behold my flaming eye.

This narrow street, sir, is the chief part of the Old Mint, full of low lodging-houses, as you see by the transparent canvas-lamps and blinds, announcing beds for travellers! But it is greatly changed, friend Field, from my former knowledge of it; it is infinitely quieter and more subdued than when I was here last, some seven years ago? O yes! Inspector Haynes, a first-rate man, is on this station now and plays the Devil with them!

Well, my lads! How are you to-night, my lads? Playing cards here, eh? Who wins?—Why, Mr. Field, I, the sulky gentleman with the damp flat side-curls, rubbing my bleared eye with the end of my neckerchief which is like a dirty eel-skin, am losing just at present, but I suppose I must take my pipe out of my mouth, and be submissive to *you*— I hope I see you well, Mr. Field?—Aye, all right, my lad. Deputy, who have you got up-stairs? Be pleased to show the rooms!

Why Deputy, Inspector Field can't say. He only knows that the man who takes care of the beds and lodgers is always called so. Steady, O Deputy, with the flaring candle in the blacking-bottle, for this is a slushy back-yard, and the wooden staircase outside the house creaks and has holes in it.

Again, in these confined intolerable rooms, burrowed out like the holes of rats or the nests of insect-vermin, but fuller of intolerable smells, are crowds of sleepers, each on his foul truckle-bed coiled up beneath a rug. Halloa here! Come! Let us see you! Show your face! Pilot Parker goes from bed to bed and turns their slumbering heads towards us, as a salesman might turn sheep. Some wake up with an execration and a threat.—What! who spoke? O! If it's the accursed glaring eye that fixes me, go where I will, I am helpless. Here! I sit up to be looked at. Is it me you want? Not you, lie down again! and I lie down, with a woful growl.

Wherever the turning lane of light becomes stationary for a moment, some sleeper appears at the end of it, submits himself to be scrutinised, and fades away into the darkness.

There should be strange dreams here, Deputy. They sleep sound enough, says Deputy, taking the candle out of the blacking-bottle, snuffing it with his fingers, throwing the snuff into the bottle, and corking it up with the candle; that's all *I* know. What is the inscription, Deputy, on all the discoloured sheets? A precaution against loss of linen. Deputy turns down the rug of an unoccupied bed and discloses it. STOP THIEF!

To lie at night, wrapped in the legend of my slinking life; to take the cry that pursues me, waking, to my breast in sleep; to have it staring at me, and clamouring for me, as soon as consciousness returns; to have it for my first-foot on New-Year's day, my Valentine, my Birthday salute, my Christmas greeting, my parting with the old year. STOP THIEF!

And to know that I *must* be stopped, come what will. To know that I am no match for this individual energy and keenness, or this organised and steady system! Come across the street, here, and, entering by a little shop, and yard, examine these intricate passages and doors, contrived for escape, flapping and counter-flapping, like the lids of the conjurer's boxes. But what avail they? Who gets in by a nod, and shows their secret working to us? Inspector Field.

Don't forget the old Farm House, Parker! Parker is not the man to forget it. We are going there, now. It is the old Manor-House of these parts, and stood in the country once. Then, perhaps, there was something, which was not the beastly street, to see from the shattered low fronts of the overhanging wooden houses we are passing under—shut up now, pasted over with bills about the literature and drama of the Mint, and mouldering away. This long paved yard was a paddock or a garden once, or a court in front of the Farm House. Perchance, with a dovecot in the centre, and fowls pecking about—with fair elm trees, then, where discoloured chimney-stacks and gables are now—noisy, then, with rooks which have yielded to a different sort of rookery. It's likelier than not, Inspector Field thinks, as we turn into the common kitchen, which is in the yard, and many paces from the house.

Well, my lads and lasses, how are you all? Where's Blackey, who has stood near London Bridge these five-and-twenty years, with a painted skin to represent disease?—Here he is, Mr. Field!—How are you, Blackey?—Jolly, sa! Not playing the fiddle to-night, Blackey?—Not a night, sa! A sharp, smiling youth, the wit of the kitchen, interposes. He an't musical to-night, sir. I've been giving him a moral lecture; I've been a talking to him about his latter end, you see. A good many of these are my pupils, sir. This here young man (smoothing down the hair of one near him, reading a Sunday paper) is a pupil of mine. I'm a teaching of him to read, sir. He's a promising cove, sir. He's a smith, he is, and gets his living by the sweat of the brow, sir. So do I, myself, sir. This young woman is my sister, Mr. Field. *She's* getting on very well too. I've a deal of trouble with 'em, sir, but I'm richly rewarded, now I see 'em all a doing so well, and growing up so creditable. That's a great comfort, that is, an't it, sir?—In the midst of the kitchen (the whole kitchen is in ecstasies with this impromptu "chaff") 'sits a young, modest, gentle-looking creature, with a beautiful child in her lap. She seems to belong to the company, but is so strangely unlike it. She has such a pretty, quiet face and voice, and is so proud to hear the child admired—thinks you would hardly believe that he is only nine months old! Is she as bad as the rest, I wonder? Inspectorial experience does not engender a belief contrariwise, but prompts the answer, Not a ha'porth of difference!

There is a piano going in the old Farm House as we

approach. It stops. Landlady appears. Has no objections,
Mr. Field, to gentlemen being brought, but wishes it were
at earlier hours, the lodgers complaining of ill-conwenience.
Inspector Field is polite and soothing—knows his woman
and the sex.   Deputy (a girl in this case) shows the way up
a heavy broad old staircase, kept very clean, into clean rooms
where many sleepers are, and where painted panels of an
older time look strangely on the truckle beds.   The sight
of whitewash and the smell of soap—two things we seem by
this time to have parted from in infancy—make the old
Farm House a phenomenon, and connect themselves with
the so curiously misplaced picture of the pretty mother and
child long after we have left it,—long after we have left,
besides, the neighbouring nook with something of a rustic
flavour in it yet, where once, beneath a low wooden colonnade still standing as of yore, the eminent Jack Sheppard
condescended to regale himself, and where, now, two old
bachelor brothers in broad hats (who are whispered in the
Mint to have made a compact long ago that if either should
ever marry, he must forfeit his share of the joint property)
still keep a sequestered tavern, and sit o' nights smoking
pipes in the bar, among ancient bottles and glasses, as our
eyes behold them.

How goes the night now?   Saint George of Southwark
answers with twelve blows upon his bell.   Parker, good
night, for Williams is already waiting over in the region of
Ratcliffe Highway, to show the houses where the sailors
dance.

I should like to know where Inspector Field was born.
In Ratcliffe Highway, I would have answered with confidence, but for his being equally at home wherever we go.
He does not trouble his head as I do, about the river at
night.   *He* does not care for its creeping, black and silent,
on our right there, rushing through sluice-gates, lapping at
piles and posts and iron rings, hiding strange things in its
mud, running away with suicides and accidentally drowned
bodies faster than midnight funeral should, and acquiring
such various experience between its cradle and its grave.   It
has no mystery for *him*.   Is there not the Thames Police?

Accordingly, Williams leads the way.   We are a little
late, for some of the houses are already closing.   No matter.
You show us plenty.   All the landlords know Inspector Field.
All pass him, freely and good-humouredly, wheresoever he

wants to go. So thoroughly are all these houses open to him and our local guide, that, granting that sailors must be entertained in their own way—as I suppose they must, and have a right to be—I hardly know how such places could be better regulated. Not that I call the company very select, or the dancing very graceful—even so graceful as that of the German Sugar Bakers, whose assembly, by the Minories, we stopped to visit—but there is watchful maintenance of order in every house, and swift expulsion where need is. Even in the midst of drunkenness, both of the lethargic kind and the lively, there is sharp landlord supervision, and pockets are in less peril than out of doors. These houses show, singularly, how much of the picturesque and romantic there truly is in the sailor, requiring to be especially addressed. All the songs (sung in a hailstorm of halfpence, which are pitched at the singer without the least tenderness for the time or tune— mostly from great rolls of copper carried for the purpose —and which he occasionally dodges like shot as they fly near his head) are of the sentimental sea sort. All the rooms are decorated with nautical subjects. Wrecks, engagements, ships on fire, ships passing lighthouses on iron-bound coasts, ships blowing up, ships going down, ships running ashore, men lying out upon the main-yard in a gale of wind, sailors and ships in every variety of peril, constitute the illustrations of fact. Nothing can be done in the fanciful way, without a thumping boy upon a scaly dolphin.

How goes the night now? Past one. Black and Green are waiting in Whitechapel to unveil the mysteries of Wentworth Street. Williams, the best of friends must part. Adieu !

Are not Black and Green ready at the appointed place ? O yes ! They glide out of shadow as we stop. Imperturb- able Black opens the cab-door ; Imperturbable Green takes a mental note of the driver. Both Green and Black then open, each his flaming eye, and marshal us the way that we are going.

The lodging-house we want is hidden in a maze of streets and courts. It is fast shut. We knock at the door, and stand hushed looking up for a light at one or other of the begrimed old lattice windows in its ugly front, when another constable comes up—supposes that we want "to see the school." Detective Sergeant meanwhile has got over a rail, opened a gate, dropped down an area, overcome some other little obstacles, and tapped at a window. Now returns. The landlord will send a deputy immediately.

Deputy is heard to stumble out of bed. Deputy lights a candle, draws back a bolt or two, and appears at the door. Deputy is a shivering shirt and trousers by no means clean, a yawning face, a shock head much confused externally and internally. We want to look for some one. You may go up with the light, and take 'em all, if you like, says Deputy, resigning it, and sitting down upon a bench in the kitchen with his ten fingers sleepily twisting in his hair.

Holloa here! Now then! Show yourselves. That'll do. It's not you. Don't disturb yourself any more! So on, through a labyrinth of airless rooms, each man responding, like a wild beast, to the keeper who has tamed him, and who goes into his cage. What, you haven't found him, then? says Deputy, when we came down. A woman mysteriously sitting up all night in the dark by the smouldering ashes of the kitchen fire, says it's only tramps and cadgers here; it's gonophs over the way. A man mysteriously walking about the kitchen all night in the dark, bids her hold her tongue. We come out. Deputy fastens the door and goes to bed again.

Black and Green, you know Bark, lodging-house keeper and receiver of stolen goods?—O yes, Inspector Field.— Go to Bark's next.

Bark sleeps in an inner wooden hutch, near his street door. As we parley on the step with Bark's Deputy, Bark growls in his bed. We enter, and Bark flies out of bed. Bark is a red villain and a wrathful, with a sanguine throat that looks very much as if it were expressly made for hanging, as he stretches it out, in pale defiance, over the half-door of his hutch. Bark's parts of speech are of an awful sort—principally adjectives. I won't, says Bark, have no adjective police and adjective strangers in my adjective premises! I won't, by adjective and substantive! Give me my trousers, and I'll send the whole adjective police to adjective and substantive! Give me, says Bark, my adjective trousers! I'll put an adjective knife in the whole bileing of 'em. I'll punch their adjective heads. I'll rip up their adjective substantives. Give me my adjective trousers! says Bark, and I'll spile the bileing of 'em!

Now, Bark, what's the use of this? Here's Black and Green, Detective Sergeant, and Inspector Field. You know

we will come in.—I know you won't! says Bark. Somebody give me my adjective trousers! Bark's trousers seem
difficult to find. He calls for them as Hercules might for his
club. Give me my adjective trousers! says Bark, and I'll
spile the bileing of 'em.

Inspector Field holds that it's all one whether Bark likes
the visit or don't like it. He, Inspector Field, is an Inspector of the Detective Police, Detective Sergeant *is* Detective Sergeant, Black and Green are constables in uniform.
Don't you be a fool, Bark, or you know it will be the worse
for you.—I don't care, says Bark. Give me my adjective
trousers!

At two o'clock in the morning, we descend into Bark's
low kitchen, leaving Bark to foam at the mouth above, and
Imperturbable Black and Green to look at him. Bark's
kitchen is crammed full of thieves, holding a *conversazione*
there by lamp-light. It is by far the most dangerous assembly we have seen yet. Stimulated by the ravings of
Bark, above, their looks are sullen, but not a man speaks.
We ascend again. Bark has got his trousers, and is in
a state of madness in the passage with his back against a
door that shuts off the upper staircase. We observe, in other
respects, a ferocious individuality in Bark. Instead of "STOP
THIEF!" on his linen, he prints "STOLEN FROM BARK'S!"

Now, Bark, we are going up-stairs!—No, you ain't!—You
refuse admission to the Police, do you, Bark?—Yes, I do!
I refuse it to all the adjective police, and to all the adjective substantives. If the adjective coves in the kitchen was
men, they'd come up now, and do for you! Shut me that
there door! says Bark, and suddenly we are enclosed in
the passage. They'd come up and do for you! cries Bark,
and waits. Not a sound in the kitchen! They'd come up
and do for you! cries Bark again, and waits. Not a sound
in the kitchen! We are shut up, half-a-dozen of us, in
Bark's house in the innermost recesses of the worst part
of London, in the dead of the night—the house is crammed
with notorious robbers and ruffians—and not a man stirs.
No, Bark. They know the weight of the law, and they
know Inspector Field and Co. too well.

We leave bully Bark to subside at leisure out of his passion and his trousers, and, I dare say, to be inconveniently
reminded of this little brush before long. Black and Green
do ordinary duty here, and look serious.

As to White, who waits on Holborn Hill to show the courts that are eaten out of Rotten Gray's Inn Lane, where other lodging-houses are, and where (in one blind alley) the Thieves' Kitchen and Seminary for the teaching of the art to children, is, the night has so worn away, being now

almost at odds with morning, which is which,

that they are quiet, and no light shines through the chinks in the shutters. As undistinctive Death will come here, one day, sleep comes now. The wicked cease from troubling sometimes, even in this life.

DOWN WITH THE TIDE

A VERY dark night it was, and bitter cold; the east wind blowing bleak, and bringing with it stinging particles from marsh, and moor, and fen—from the Great Desert and Old Egypt, may be. Some of the component parts of the sharp-edged vapour that came flying up the Thames at London might be mummy-dust, dry atoms from the Temple at Jerusalem, camels' foot-prints, crocodiles' hatching-places, loosened grains of expression from the visages of blunt-nosed sphynxes, waifs and strays from caravans of turbaned merchants, vegetation from jungles, frozen snow from the Himalayas. O! It was very very dark upon the Thames, and it was bitter bitter cold.

"And yet," said the voice within the great pea-coat at my side, "you'll have seen a good many rivers too, I dare say?"

"Truly," said I, "when I come to think of it, not a few. From the Niagara, downward to the mountain rivers of Italy, which are like the national spirit—very tame, or chafing suddenly and bursting bounds, only to dwindle away again. The Moselle, and the Rhine, and the Rhone; and the Seine, and the Saone; and the St. Lawrence, Mississippi, and Ohio; and the Tiber, the Po, and the Arno; and the——"

Peacoat coughing as if he had had enough of that, I said no more. I could have carried the catalogue on to a teasing length, though, if I had been in the cruel mind.

"And after all," said he, "this looks so dismal?"

"So awful," I returned, "at night. The Seine at Paris is very gloomy too, at such a time, and is probably the scene of far more crime and greater wickedness; but this river looks so broad and vast, so murky and silent, seems such an image of death in the midst of the great city's life, that——"

That Peacoat coughed again. He *could not* stand my holding forth.

We were in a four-oared Thames Police Galley, lying on our oars in the deep shadow of Southwark Bridge—under the corner arch on the Surrey side—having come down with the tide from Vauxhall. We were fain to hold on pretty tight, though close in shore, for the river was swollen and the tide running down very strong. We were watching certain water-rats of human growth, and lay in the deep shade as quiet as mice ; our light hidden and our scraps of conversation carried on in whispers. Above us, the massive iron girders of the arch were faintly visible, and below us its ponderous shadow seemed to sink down to the bottom of the stream.

We had been lying here some half an hour. With our backs to the wind, it is true ; but the wind being in a deter-mined temper blew straight through us, and would not take the trouble to go round. I would have boarded a fireship to get into action, and mildly suggested as much to my friend Pea.

"No doubt," says he as patiently as possible ; "but shore-going tactics wouldn't do with us. River-thieves can always get rid of stolen property in a moment by dropping it overboard. We want to take them *with* the property, so we lurk about and come out upon 'em sharp. If they see us or hear us, over it goes."

Pea's wisdom being indisputable, there was nothing for it but to sit there and be blown through, for another half-hour. The water-rats thinking it wise to abscond at the end of that time without commission of felony, we shot out, disappointed, with the tide.

"Grim they look, don't they ?" said Pea, seeing me glance over my shoulder at the lights upon the bridge, and downward at their long crooked reflections in the river.

"Very," said I, "and make one think with a shudder of Suicides. What a night for a dreadful leap from that parapet ! "

"Aye, but Waterloo's the favourite bridge for making holes in the water from," returned Pea. "By the bye— avast pulling, lads !—would you like to speak to Waterloo on the subject ? "

My face confessing a surprised desire to have some friendly conversation with Waterloo Bridge, and my friend Pea being the most obliging of men, we put about, pulled out of the force of the stream, and in place of going at great speed with the tide, began to strive against it, close in shore again. Every colour but black seemed to have departed from the world. The air was black, the water was black, the barges and hulks were black, the piles were black, the buildings were black, the shadows were only a deeper shade of black upon a black ground. Here and there, a coal fire in an iron cresset blazed upon a wharf; but one knew that it too had been black a little while ago, and would be black again soon. Uncomfortable rushes of water suggestive of gurgling and drowning, ghostly rattlings of iron chains, dismal clankings of discordant engines, formed the music that accompanied the dip of our oars and their rattling in the rullocks. Even the noises had a black sound to me—as the trumpet sounded red to the blind man.

Our dexterous boat's crew made nothing of the tide, and pulled us gallantly up to Waterloo Bridge. Here Pea and I disembarked, passed under the black stone archway, and climbed the steep stone steps. Within a few feet of their summit, Pea presented me to Waterloo (or an eminent toll-taker representing that structure), muffled up to the eyes in a thick shawl, and amply great-coated and fur-capped.

Waterloo received us with cordiality, and observed of the night that it was "a Searcher." He had been originally called the Strand Bridge, he informed us, but had received his present name at the suggestion of the proprietors, when Parliament had resolved to vote three hundred thousand pound for the erection of a monument in honour of the victory. Parliament took the hint (said Waterloo, with the least flavour of misanthropy) and saved the money. Of course the late Duke of Wellington was the first passenger, and of course he paid his penny, and of course a noble lord preserved it evermore. The treadle and index at the toll-house (a most ingenious contrivance for rendering fraud impossible), were invented by Mr. Lethbridge, then property-man at Drury Lane Theatre.

Was it suicide, we wanted to know about? said Waterloo. Ha! Well, he had seen a good deal of that work, he did assure us. He had prevented some. Why, one day a woman, poorish looking, came in between the hatch, slapped down a penny, and wanted to go on without the change! Waterloo suspected this, and says to his mate, "give an eye to the gate," and bolted after her. She had got to the third seat between the piers, and was on the parapet just a going over, when he caught her and gave her in charge. At the police office next morning, she said it was along of trouble and a bad husband.

"Likely enough," observed Waterloo to Pea and myself, as he adjusted his chin in his shawl. "There's a deal of trouble about, you see—and bad husbands too!"

Another time, a young woman at twelve o'clock in the open day, got through, darted along; and, before Waterloo could come near her, jumped upon the parapet, and shot herself over sideways. Alarm given, watermen put off, lucky escape.—Clothes buoyed her up.

"This is where it is," said Waterloo. "If people jump off straight forwards from the middle of the parapet of the bays of the bridge, they are seldom killed by drowning, but are smashed, poor things; that's what *they* are; they dash themselves upon the buttress of the bridge. But you jump off," said Waterloo to me, putting his forefinger in a button-hole of my great-coat; "you jump off from the side of the bay, and you'll tumble, true, into the stream under the arch. What you have got to do, is to mind how you jump in! There was poor Tom Steele from Dublin. Didn't dive! Bless you, didn't dive at all! Fell down so flat into the water, that he broke his breast-bone, and lived two days!"

I asked Waterloo if there were a favourite side of his bridge for this dreadful purpose? He reflected, and thought yes, there was. He should say the Surrey side.

Three decent-looking men went through one day, soberly and quietly, and went on abreast for about a dozen yards: when the middle one, he sung out, all of a sudden, "Here goes, Jack!" and was over in a minute.

Body found? Well. Waterloo didn't rightly recollect about that. They were compositors, *they* were.

He considered it astonishing how quick people were! Why, there was a cab came up one Boxing-night, with a young woman in it, who looked, according to Waterloo's opinion of her, a little the worse for liquor; very handsome she was too—very handsome. She stopped the cab at the gate, and said she'd pay the cabman then, which she did, though there was a little hankering about the fare, because at first she didn't seem quite to know where she wanted to be drove to. However, she paid the man, and the toll too, and looking Waterloo in the face (he thought she knew him, don't you see!) said, "I'll finish it somehow!" Well, the cab went off, leaving Waterloo a little doubtful in his mind, and while it was going on at full speed the young woman jumped out, never fell, hardly staggered, ran along the bridge pavement a little way, passing several people, and jumped over from the second opening. At the inquest it was giv' in evidence that she had been quarrelling at the Hero of Waterloo, and it was brought in jealousy. (One of the results of Waterloo's experience was, that there was a deal of jealousy about.)

"Do we ever get madmen?" said Waterloo, in answer to an inquiry of mine. "Well, we *do* get madmen. Yes, we have had one or two; escaped from 'Sylums, I suppose. One hadn't a halfpenny; and because I wouldn't let him through, he went back a little way, stooped down, took a run, and butted at the hatch like a ram. He smashed his hat rarely, but his head didn't seem no worse—in my opinion on account of his being wrong in it afore. Sometimes people haven't got a halfpenny. If they are really tired and poor we give 'em one and let 'em through. Other people will leave things— pocket-handkerchiefs mostly. I *have* taken cravats and gloves, pocket-knives, tooth-picks, studs, shirt-pins, rings (generally from young gents, early in the morning), but handkerchiefs is the general thing."

"Regular customers?" said Waterloo. "Lord, yes! We have regular customers. One, such a worn-out used-up old file as you can scarcely picter, comes from the Surrey side as regular as ten o'clock at night comes; and goes over, *I* think, to some flash house on the Middlesex side. He comes back, he does, as reg'lar as the clock strikes three in the morning, and then can hardly drag one of his old legs after the other. He always turns down the water-stairs, comes up again, and then goes on down the Waterloo Road. He always does the same thing, and never varies a minute. Does it every night—even Sundays."

I asked Waterloo if he had given his mind to the possibility of this particular customer going down the water-stairs at three o'clock some morning, and never coming up again? He didn't think *that* of him, he replied. In fact, it was Waterloo's opinion, founded on his observation of that file, that he know'd a trick worth two of it.

"There's another queer old customer," said Waterloo, " comes over, as punctual as the almanack, at eleven o'clock on the sixth of January, at eleven o'clock on the fifth of April, at eleven o'clock on the sixth of July, at eleven o'clock on the tenth of October. Drives a shaggy little, rough pony, in a sort of a rattle-trap arm-chair sort of a thing. White hair he has, and white whiskers, and muffles himself up with all manner of shawls. He comes back again the same afternoon, and we never see more of him for three months. He is a captain in the navy—retired—wery old— wery odd—and served with Lord Nelson. He is particular about drawing his pension at Somerset House afore the clock strikes twelve every quarter. I *have* heerd say that he thinks it wouldn't be according to the Act of Parliament, if he didn't draw it afore twelve."

Having related these anecdotes in a natural manner, which was the best warranty in the world for their genuine nature, our friend Waterloo was sinking deep into his shawl again, as having exhausted his communicative powers and taken in enough east wind, when my other friend Pea in a moment brought him to the surface by asking whether he had not been occasionally the subject of assault and battery in the execution of his duty? Waterloo recovering his spirits, instantly dashed into a new branch of his subject. We learnt how "both these teeth "—here he pointed to the places where two front teeth were not—were knocked out by an ugly customer who one night made a dash at him (Waterloo) while his (the ugly customer's) pal and coadjutor made a dash at the toll-taking apron where the money-pockets were ; how Waterloo, letting the teeth go (to Blazes, he observed indefinitely), grappled with the apron-seizer, permitting the ugly one to run away ; and how he saved the bank, and cap- tured his man, and consigned him to fine and imprisonment. Also how, on another night, "a Cove " laid hold of Waterloo, then presiding at the horse-gate of his bridge, and threw him unceremoniously over his knee, having first cut his head open with his whip. How Waterloo "got right," and started after the Cove all down the Waterloo Road, through Stamford Street, and round to the foot of Blackfriars Bridge, where the Cove "cut into" a public-house. How Waterloo cut in too ; but how an aider and abettor of the Cove's, who happened to be taking a promiscuous drain at the bar, stopped Waterloo ; and the Cove cut out again, ran across the road down Holland Street, and where not, and into a beer-shop. How Waterloo breaking away from his detainer was close upon the Cove's heels, attended by no end of people, who, seeing him running with the blood streaming down his face, thought something worse was "up," and roared Fire! and Murder! on the hopeful chance of the matter in hand being one or both. How the Cove was ignominiously taken, in a shed where he had run to hide, and how at the Police Court they at first wanted to make a sessions job of it; but eventually Waterloo was allowed to be "spoke to," and the Cove made it square with Waterloo by paying his doctor's bill (W. was laid up for a week) and giving him "Three, ten." Likewise we learnt what we had faintly suspected before, that your sporting amateur on the Derby day, albeit a captain, can be—"if he be," as Captain Bobadil observes, "so gener-ously minded"—anything but a man of honour and a gentle-man; not sufficiently gratifying his nice sense of humour by the witty scattering of flour and rotten eggs on obtuse civilians, but requiring the further excitement of "bilking the toll," and "pitching into" Waterloo, and "cutting him about the head with his whip;" finally being, when called upon to answer for the assault, what Waterloo described as "Minus," or, as I humbly conceived it, not to be found. Likewise did Waterloo inform us, in reply to my inquiries, admiringly and deferentially preferred through my friend Pea, that the takings at the Bridge had more than doubled in amount, since the reduction of the toll one half. And being asked if the aforesaid takings included much bad money, Waterloo responded, with a look far deeper than the deepest part of the river, *he* should think not!—and so retired into his shawl for the rest of the night.

Then did Pea and I once more embark in our four-oared galley, and glide swiftly down the river with the tide. And while the shrewd East rasped and notched us, as with jagged razors, did my friend Pea impart to me confidences of interest relating to the Thames Police; we between whiles finding "duty boats" hanging in dark corners under banks, like weeds —our own was a "supervision boat"—and they, as they reported "all right!" flashing their hidden light on us, and we flashing ours on them. These duty boats had one sitter in each: an Inspector: and were rowed "Ran-dan," which— for the information of those who never graduated, as I was once proud to do, under a fireman-waterman and winner of Kean's Prize Wherry: who, in the course of his tuition, took hundreds of gallons of rum and egg (at my expense) at the various houses of note above and below bridge; not by any means because he liked it, but to cure a weakness in his

liver, for which the faculty had particularly recommended it
—may be explained as rowed by three men, two pulling an
oar each, and one a pair of sculls.

Thus, floating down our black highway, sullenly frowned
upon by the knitted brows of Blackfriars, Southwark, and
London, each in his lowering turn, I was shown by my friend
Pea that there are, in the Thames Police Force, whose district extends from Battersea to Barking Creek, ninety-eight
men, eight duty boats, and two supervision boats ; and that
these go about so silently, and lie in wait in such dark places,
and so seem to be nowhere, and so may be anywhere, that
they have gradually become a police of prevention, keeping
the river almost clear of any great crimes, even while the
increased vigilance on shore has made it much harder than
of yore to live by "thieving" in the streets. And as to the
various kinds of water-thieves, said my friend Pea, there were
the Tier-rangers, who silently dropped alongside the tiers of
shipping in the Pool, by night, and who, going to the com-
panion-head, listened for two snores—snore number one, the
skipper's ; snore number two, the mate's—mates and skippers
always snoring great guns, and being dead, sure to be hard
at it if they had turned in and were asleep. Hearing the
double fire, down went the Rangers into the skippers' cabins ;
groped for the skippers' inexpressibles, which it was the
custom of those gentlemen to shake off, watch, money, braces,
boots, and all together, on the floor ; and therewith made off
as silently as might be. Then there were the Lumpers, or
labourers employed to unload vessels. They wore loose
canvas jackets with a broad hem in the bottom, turned
inside, so as to form a large circular pocket in which they
could conceal, like clowns in pantomimes, packages of surprising sizes. A great deal of property was stolen in this
manner (Pea confided to me) from steamers ; first, because
steamers carry a larger number of small packages than other
ships ; next, because of the extreme rapidity with which
they are obliged to be unladen for their return voyages.
The Lumpers dispose of their booty easily to marine store
dealers, and the only remedy to be suggested is that marine
store shops should be licensed, and thus brought under the
eye of the police as rigidly as public-houses. Lumpers also
smuggle goods ashore for the crews of vessels. The smuggling
of tobacco is so considerable, that it is well worth the while
of the sellers of smuggled tobacco to use hydraulic presses,

to squeeze a single pound into a package small enough to be contained in an ordinary pocket. Next, said my friend Pea, there were the Truckers—less thieves than smugglers, whose business it was to land more considerable parcels of goods than the Lumpers could manage. They sometimes sold articles of grocery and so forth, to the crews, in order to cloak their real calling, and get aboard without suspicion. Many of them had boats of their own, and made money. Besides these, there were the Dredgermen, who, under pretence of dredging up coals and such like from the bottom of the river, hung about barges and other undecked craft, and when they saw an opportunity, threw any property they could lay their hands on overboard: in order slyly to dredge it up when the vessel was gone. Sometimes, they dexterously used their dredges to whip away anything that might lie within reach. Some of them were mighty neat at this, and the accomplishment was called dry dredging. Then, there was a vast deal of property, such as copper nails, sheathing, hardwood, &c., habitually brought away by shipwrights and other workmen from their employers' yards, and disposed of to marine store dealers, many of whom escaped detection through hard swearing, and their extraordinary artful ways of accounting for the possession of stolen property. Likewise, there were special-pleading practitioners, for whom barges "drifted away of their own selves"—they having no hand in it, except first cutting them loose, and afterwards plundering them—innocents, meaning no harm, who had the misfortune to observe those foundlings wandering about the Thames.

We were now going in and out, with little noise and great nicety, among the tiers of shipping, whose many hulls, lying close together, rose out of the water like black streets. Here and there, a Scotch, an Irish, or a foreign steamer, getting up her steam as the tide made, looked, with her great chimney and high sides, like a quiet factory among the common buildings. Now, the streets opened into clearer spaces, now contracted into alleys; but the tiers were so like houses, in the dark, that I could almost have believed myself in the narrower bye-ways of Venice. Everything was wonderfully still; for it wanted full three hours of flood, and nothing seemed awake but a dog here and there.

So we took no Tier-rangers captive, nor any Lumpers, nor Truckers, nor Dredgermen, nor other evil-disposed person or persons'; but went ashore at Wapping, where the old Thames Police-office is now a station-house, and where the old Court, with its cabin windows looking on the river, is a quaint charge-room: with nothing worse in it usually than a stuffed cat in a glass case, and a portrait, pleasant to behold, of a rare old Thames Police officer, Mr. Superintendent Evans, now succeeded by his son. We looked over the charge books, admirably kept, and found the prevention so good that there were not five hundred entries (including drunken and disorderly) in a whole year. Then, we looked into the store-room; where there was an oakum smell, and a nautical seasoning of dreadnought clothing, rope yarn, boat-hooks, sculls and oars, spare stretchers, rudders, pistols, cutlasses, and the like. Then, into the cell, aired high up in the wooden wall through an opening like a kitchen plate-rack: wherein there was a drunken man, not at all warm, and very wishful to know if it were morning yet. Then, into a better sort of watch and ward room, where there was a squadron of stone bottles drawn up, ready to be filled with hot water and applied to any unfortunate creature who might be brought in apparently drowned. Finally, we shook hands with our worthy friend Pea, and ran all the way to Tower Hill, under strong Police suspicion occasionally, before we got warm.

A WALK IN A WORKHOUSE

On a certain Sunday, I formed one of the congregation assembled in the chapel of a large metropolitan Workhouse. With the exception of the clergyman and clerk, and a very few officials, there were none but paupers present. The children sat in the galleries; the women in the body of the chapel, and in one of the side aisles; the men in the remaining aisle. The service was decorously performed, though the sermon might have been much better adapted to the comprehension and to the circumstances of the hearers. The usual supplications were offered, with more than the usual significancy in such a place, for the fatherless children and widows, for all sick persons and young children, for all that were desolate and oppressed, for the comforting and helping of the weak-hearted, for the raising-up of them that had fallen; for all that were in danger, necessity, and tribulation. The prayers of the congregation were desired "for several persons in the various wards dangerously ill;" and others who were recovering returned their thanks to Heaven.

Among this congregation were some evil-looking young women, and beetle-browed young men; but not many—perhaps that kind of characters kept away. Generally, the faces (those of the children excepted) were depressed and subdued, and wanted colour. Aged people were there, in every variety. Mumbling, blear-eyed, spectacled, stupid, deaf, lame; vacantly winking in the gleams of sun that now and then crept in through the open doors, from the paved yard; shading their listening ears, or blinking eyes, with their withered hands; poring over their books, leering at nothing, going to sleep, crouching and drooping in corners. There were weird old women, all skeleton within, all bonnet and cloak without, continually wiping their eyes with dirty dusters of pocket-handkerchiefs; and there were ugly old crones, both male and female, with a ghastly kind of contentment upon them which was not at all comforting to see.

Upon the whole, it was the dragon, Pauperism, in a very weak and impotent condition; toothless, fangless, drawing his breath heavily enough, and hardly worth chaining up.

When the service was over, I walked with the humane and conscientious gentleman whose duty it was to take that walk, that Sunday morning, through the little world of poverty enclosed within the workhouse walls. It was inhabited by a population of some fifteen hundred or two thousand paupers, ranging from the infant newly born or not yet come into the pauper world, to the old man dying on his bed.

In a room opening from a squalid yard, where a number of listless women were lounging to and fro, trying to get warm in the ineffectual sunshine of the tardy May morning —in the "Itch Ward," not to compromise the truth— a woman such as HOGARTH has often drawn, was hurriedly getting on her gown before a dusty fire. She was the nurse, or wardswoman, of that insalubrious department—herself a pauper—flabby, raw-boned, untidy—unpromising and coarse of aspect as need be. But, on being spoken to about the patients whom she had in charge, she turned round, with her shabby gown half on, half off, and fell a crying with all her might. Not for show, not querulously, not in any mawkish sentiment, but in the deep grief and affliction of her heart; turning away her dishevelled head: sobbing most bitterly, wringing her hands, and letting fall abundance of great tears, that choked her utterance. What was the matter with the nurse of the itch-ward? Oh, "the dropped child" was dead! Oh, the child that was found in the street, and she had brought up ever since, had died an hour ago, and see where the little creature lay, beneath this cloth! The dear, the pretty dear!

The dropped child seemed too small and poor a thing for Death to be in earnest with, but Death had taken it; and already its diminutive form was neatly washed, composed, and stretched as if in sleep upon a box. I thought I heard a voice from Heaven saying, It shall be well for thee, O nurse of the itch-ward, when some less gentle pauper does those offices to thy cold form, that such as the dropped child are the angels who behold my Father's face!

In another room were several ugly old women crouching, witch-like, round a hearth, and chattering and nodding, after the manner of the monkeys. "All well here? And enough to eat?" A general chattering and chuckling; at last an answer from a volunteer. "Oh yes, gentleman! Bless you, gentleman! Lord bless the Parish of St. So-and-So! It feed the hungry, sir, and give drink to the thusty, and it warm them which is cold, so it do, and good luck to the parish of St. So-and-So, and thankee, gentleman!" Elsewhere, a party of pauper nurses were at dinner. "How do *you* get on?" "Oh pretty well, sir! We works hard, and we lives hard—like the sodgers!"

In another room, a kind of purgatory or place of transition, six or eight noisy madwomen were gathered together, under the superintendence of one sane attendant. Among them was a girl of two or three and twenty, very prettily dressed, of most respectable appearance, and good manners, who had been brought in from the house where she had lived as domestic servant (having, I suppose, no friends), on account of being subject to epileptic fits, and requiring to be removed under the influence of a very bad one. She was by no means of the same stuff, or the same breeding, or the same experience, or in the same state of mind, as those by whom she was surrounded; and she pathetically complained that the daily association and the nightly noise made her worse, and was driving her mad—which was perfectly evident. The case was noted for inquiry and redress, but she said she had already been there for some weeks.

If this girl had stolen her mistress's watch, I do not hesitate to say she would have been infinitely better off. We have come to this absurd, this dangerous, this monstrous pass, that the dishonest felon is, in respect of cleanliness, order, diet, and accommodation, better provided for, and taken care of, than the honest pauper.

And this conveys no special imputation on the workhouse of the parish of St. So-and-So, where, on the contrary, I saw many things to commend. It was very agreeable, recollecting that most infamous and atrocious enormity committed at Tooting—an enormity which, a hundred years hence, will still be vividly remembered in the bye-ways of English life, and which has done more to engender a gloomy discontent and suspicion among many thousands of the people than all the Chartist leaders could have done in all their lives—to find the pauper children in this workhouse looking robust and well, and apparently the objects of very great care. In the Infant School—a large, light, airy room at the top of the building—the little creatures, being at dinner, and eating their potatoes heartily, were not cowed by the presence of strange visitors, but stretched out their small hands to be shaken, with a very pleasant confidence. And it was comfortable to see two mangy pauper rocking-horses rampant in a corner. In the girls' school, where the dinner was also in progress, everything bore a cheerful and healthy aspect. The meal was over, in the boys' school, by the time of our arrival there, and the room was not yet quite re-arranged; but the boys were roaming unrestrained about a large and airy yard, as any other schoolboys might have done. Some of them had been drawing large ships upon the schoolroom wall; and if they had a mast with shrouds and stays set up for practice (as they have in the Middlesex House of Correction), it would be so much the better. At present, if a boy should feel a strong impulse upon him to learn the art of going aloft, he could only gratify it, I presume, as the men and women paupers gratify their aspirations after better board and lodging, by smashing as many workhouse windows as possible, and being promoted to prison.

In one place, the Newgate of the Workhouse, a company of boys and youths were locked up in a yard alone; their day-room being a kind of kennel where the casual poor used formerly to be littered down at night. Divers of them had been there some long time. "Are they never going away?" was the natural inquiry. "Most of them are crippled, in some form or other," said the Wardsman, "and not fit for anything." They slunk about, like dispirited wolves or hyænas; and made a pounce at their food when it was served out, much as those animals do. The big-headed idiot shuffling his feet along the pavement, in the sunlight outside, was a more agreeable object everyway.

Groves of babies in arms; groves of mothers and other sick women in bed; groves of lunatics; jungles of men in stone-paved down-stairs day-rooms, waiting for their dinners; longer and longer groves of old people, in up-stairs Infirmary wards, wearing out life, God knows how—this was the scenery through which the walk lay, for two hours. In some of these latter chambers, there were pictures stuck against the wall, and a neat display of crockery and pewter on a kind of side-board; now and then it was a treat to see a plant or two; in almost every ward there was a cat.

In all of these Long Walks of aged and infirm, some old

people were bedridden, and had been for a long time; some were sitting on their beds half-naked; some dying in their beds; some out of bed, and sitting at a table near the fire. A sullen or lethargic indifference to what was asked, a blunted sensibility to everything but warmth and food, a moody absence of complaint as being of no use, a dogged silence and resentful desire to be left alone again, I thought were generally apparent. On our walking into the midst of one of these dreary perspectives of old men, nearly the following little dialogue took place, the nurse not being immediately at hand:

"All well here?"

No answer. An old man in a Scotch cap sitting among others on a form at the table, eating out of a tin porringer, pushes back his cap a little to look at us, claps it down on his forehead again with the palm of his hand, and goes on eating.

"All well here?" (repeated).

No answer. Another old man sitting on his bed, paralytically peeling a boiled potato, lifts his head and stares.

"Enough to eat?"

No answer. Another old man, in bed, turns himself and coughs.

"How are *you* to-day?" To the last old man.

That old man says nothing; but another old man, a tall old man of very good address, speaking with perfect correctness, comes forward from somewhere, and volunteers an answer. The reply almost always proceeds from a volunteer, and not from the person looked at or spoken to.

"We are very old, sir," in a mild, distinct voice. "We can't expect to be well, most of us."

"Are you comfortable?"

"I have no complaint to make, sir." With a half shake of his head, a half shrug of his shoulders, and a kind of apologetic smile.

"Enough to eat?"

"Why, sir, I have but a poor appetite," with the same air as before; "and yet I get through my allowance very easily."

"But," showing a porringer with a Sunday dinner in it; "here is a portion of mutton, and three potatoes. You can't starve on that?"

"Oh dear no, sir," with the same apologetic air. "Not starve."

T

"What do you want?"

"We have very little bread, sir. It's an exceedingly small quantity of bread."

The nurse, who is now rubbing her hands at the questioner's elbow, interferes with, "It ain't much raly, sir. You see they've only six ounces a day, and when they've took their breakfast, there *can* only be a little left for night, sir."

Another old man, hitherto invisible, rises out of his bed-clothes, as out of a grave, and looks on.

"You have tea at night?" The questioner is still addressing the well-spoken old man.

"Yes, sir, we have tea at night."

"And you save what bread you can from the morning, to eat with it?"

"Yes, sir—if we can save any."

"And you want more to eat with it?"

"Yes, sir." With a very anxious face.

The questioner, in the kindness of his heart, appears a little discomposed, and changes the subject.

"What has become of the old man who used to lie in that bed in the corner?"

The nurse don't remember what old man is referred to. There has been such a many old men. The well-spoken old man is doubtful. The spectral old man who has come to life in bed, says, "Billy Stevens." Another old man who has previously had his head in the fireplace, pipes out,

"Charley Walters."

Something like a feeble interest is awakened. I suppose Charley Walters had conversation in him.

"He's dead," says the piping old man.

Another old man, with one eye screwed up, hastily displaces the piping old man, and says:

"Yes! Charley Walters died in that bed, and—and——"

"Billy Stevens," persists the spectral old man.

"No, no! and Johnny Rogers died in that bed, and—and—they're both on 'em dead—and Sam'l Bowyer;" this seems very extraordinary to him; "he went out!"

With this he subsides, and all the old men (having had quite enough of it) subside, and the spectral old man goes into his grave again, and takes the shade of Billy Stevens with him.

As we turn to go out at the door, another previously

invisible old man, a hoarse old man in a flannel gown, is standing there, as if he had just come up through the floor.

"I beg your pardon, sir, could I take the liberty of saying a word?"

"Yes; what is it?"

"I am greatly better in my health, sir; but what I want, to get me quite round," with his hand on his throat, "is a little fresh air, sir. It has always done my complaint so much good, sir. The regular leave for going out comes round so seldom, that if the gentlemen, next Friday, would give me leave to go out walking, now and then—for only an hour or so, sir!——"

Who could wonder, looking through those weary vistas of bed and infirmity, that it should do him good to meet with some other scenes, and assure himself that there was something else on earth? Who could help wondering why the old men lived on as they did; what grasp they had on life; what crumbs of interest or occupation they could pick up from its bare board; whether Charley Walters had ever described to them the days when he kept company with some old pauper woman in the bud, or Billy Stevens ever told them of the time when he was a dweller in the far-off foreign land called Home!

The morsel of burnt child, lying in another room, so patiently, in bed, wrapped in lint, and looking steadfastly at us with his bright quiet eyes when we spoke to him kindly, looked as if the knowledge of these things, and of all the tender things there are to think about, might have been in his mind—as if he thought, with us, that there was a fellow-feeling in the pauper nurses which appeared to make them more kind to their charges than the race of common nurses in the hospitals—as if he mused upon the Future of some older children lying around him in the same place, and thought it best, perhaps, all things considered, that he should die—as if he knew, without fear, of those many coffins, made and unmade, piled up in the store below—and of his unknown friend, "the dropped child," calm upon the box-lid covered with a cloth. But there was something wistful and appealing, too, in his tiny face, as if, in the midst of all the hard necessities and incongruities he pondered on, he pleaded, in behalf of the helpless and the aged poor, for a little more liberty—and a little more bread.

PRINCE BULL. A FAIRY TALE

ONCE upon a time, and of course it was in the Golden Age, and I hope you may know when that was, for I am sure I don't, though I have tried hard to find out, there lived in a rich and fertile country, a powerful Prince whose name was BULL. He had gone through a great deal of fighting, in his time, about all sorts of things, including nothing ; but had gradually settled down to be a steady, peaceable, good-natured, corpulent, rather sleepy Prince.

This Puissant Prince was married to a lovely Princess whose name was Fair Freedom. She had brought him a large fortune, and had borne him an immense number of children, and had set them to spinning, and farming, and engineering, and soldiering, and sailoring, and doctoring, and lawyering, and preaching, and all kinds of trades. The coffers of Prince Bull were full of treasure, his cellars were crammed with delicious wines from all parts of the world, the richest gold and silver plate that ever was seen adorned his sideboards, his sons were strong, his daughters were hand-some, and in short you might have supposed that if there ever lived upon earth a fortunate and happy Prince, the name of that Prince, take him for all in all, was assuredly Prince Bull.

But appearances, as we all know, are not always to be trusted—far from it ; and if they had led you to this conclusion respecting Prince Bull, they would have led you wrong as they often have led me.

For this good Prince had two sharp thorns in his pillow, two hard knobs in his crown, two heavy loads on his mind, two unbridled nightmares in his sleep, two rocks ahead in his course. He could not by any means get servants to suit him, and he had a tyrannical old godmother, whose name was Tape.

She was a Fairy, this Tape, and was a bright red all over. She was disgustingly prim and formal, and could never

bend herself a hair's breadth this way or that way, out of
her naturally crooked shape. But she was very potent in
her wicked art. She could stop the fastest thing in the
world, change the strongest thing into the weakest, and the
most useful into the most useless. To do this she had only
to put her cold hand upon it, and repeat her own name,
Tape. Then it withered away.

At the Court of Prince Bull—at least I don't mean literally at his court, because he was a very genteel Prince, and
readily yielded to his godmother when she always reserved
that for his hereditary Lords and Ladies—in the dominions
of Prince Bull, among the great mass of the community
who were called in the language of that polite country the
Mobs and the Snobs, were a number of very ingenious men,
who were always busy with some invention or other, for
promoting the prosperity of the Prince's subjects, and augmenting the Prince's power. But, whenever they submitted their models for the Prince's approval, his godmother
stepped forward, laid her hand upon them, and said "Tape."
Hence it came to pass, that when any particularly good
discovery was made, the discoverer usually carried it off to
some other Prince, in foreign parts, who had no old god
mother who said Tape. This was not on the whole an
advantageous state of things for Prince Bull, to the best of
my understanding.

The worst of it was, that Prince Bull had in course of
years lapsed into such a state of subjection to this unlucky
godmother, that he never made any serious effort to rid
himself of her tyranny. I have said this was the worst of it,
but there I was wrong, because there is a worse consequence
still, behind. The Prince's numerous family became so down-
right sick and tired of Tape, that when they should have
helped the Prince out of the difficulties into which that evil
creature led him, they fell into a dangerous habit of moodily
keeping away from him in an impassive and indifferent
manner, as though they had quite forgotten that no harm
could happen to the Prince their father, without its inevitably affecting themselves.

Such was the aspect of affairs at the court of Prince Bull,
when this great Prince found it necessary to go to war with
Prince Bear. He had been for some time very doubtful of
his servants, who, besides being indolent and addicted to
enriching their families at his expense, domineered over him

dreadfully; threatening to discharge themselves if they were found the least fault with, pretending that they had done a wonderful amount of work when they had done nothing, making the most unmeaning speeches that ever were heard in the Prince's name, and uniformly showing themselves to be very inefficient indeed. Though, that some of them had excellent characters from previous situations is not to be denied. Well; Prince Bull called his servants together, and said to them one and all, "Send out my army against Prince Bear. Clothe it, arm it, feed it, provide it with all necessaries and contingencies, and I will pay the piper! Do your duty by my brave troops," said the Prince, "and do it well, and I will pour my treasure out like water, to defray the cost. Who ever heard ME complain of money well laid out!" Which indeed he had reason for saying, inasmuch as he was well known to be a truly generous and munificent Prince.

When the servants heard those words, they sent out the army against Prince Bear, and they set the army tailors to work, and the army provision merchants, and the makers of guns both great and small, and the gunpowder makers, and the makers of ball, shell, and shot; and they bought up all manner of stores and ships, without troubling their heads about the price, and appeared to be so busy that the good Prince rubbed his hands, and (using a favourite expression of his), said, "It's all right!" But while they were thus employed, the Prince's godmother, who was a great favourite with those servants, looked in upon them continually all day long, and whenever she popped in her head at the door said, "How do you do, my children? What are you doing here?" "Official business, godmother." "Oho!" says this wicked Fairy. "—Tape!" And then the business all went wrong, whatever it was, and the servants' heads became so addled and muddled that they thought they were doing wonders.

Now, this was very bad conduct on the part of the vicious old nuisance, and she ought to have been strangled, even if she had stopped here; but she didn't stop here, as you shall learn. For a number of the Prince's subjects, being very fond of the Prince's army who were the bravest of men, assembled together and provided all manner of eatables and drinkables, and books to read, and clothes to wear, and tobacco to smoke, and candles to burn, and nailed them up

in great packing-cases, and put them aboard a great many
ships, to be carried out to that brave army in the cold and
inclement country where they were fighting Prince Bear.
Then up comes this wicked Fairy as the ships were weighing
anchor, and says, "How do you do, my children? What are
you doing here?"—"We are going with all these comforts
to the army, godmother."—"Oho!" says she. "A pleasant
voyage, my darlings.—Tape!" And from that time forth,
those enchanted ships went sailing, against wind and tide
and rhyme and reason, round and round the world, and
whenever they touched at any port were ordered off immediately, and could never deliver their cargoes anywhere.

This, again, was very bad conduct on the part of the
vicious old nuisance, and she ought to have been strangled
for it if she had done nothing worse; but she did something
worse still, as you shall learn. For she got astride of an
official broomstick, and muttered as a spell these two
sentences, "On Her Majesty's service," and "I have the
honour to be, sir, your most obedient servant," and presently
alighted in the cold and inclement country where the army
of Prince Bull were encamped to fight the army of Prince
Bear. On the sea-shore of that country, she found piled
together a number of houses for the army to live in, and
a quantity of provisions for the army to live upon, and
a quantity of clothes for the army to wear: while, sitting in
the mud gazing at them, were a group of officers as red to
look at as the wicked old woman herself. So, she said to
one of them, "Who are you, my darling, and how do you
do?"—"I am the Quarter-master General's Department,
godmother, and I am pretty well."—Then she said to
another, "Who are *you*, my darling, and how do *you* do?"
—"I am the Commissariat Department, godmother, and *I*
am pretty well." Then she said to another, "Who are *you*,
my darling, and how do *you* do?"—"I am the Head of the
Medical Department, godmother, and I am pretty well."
Then she said to some gentlemen scented with lavender,
who kept themselves at a great distance from the rest, "And
who are *you*, my pretty pets, and how do *you* do?" And
they answered, "We-aw-are-the-aw-Staff-aw-Department, godmother, and we are very well indeed."—"I am delighted
to see you all, my beauties," says this wicked old Fairy,
"—Tape!" Upon that, the houses, clothes, and provisions,
all mouldered away; and the soldiers who were sound, fell

sick; and the soldiers who were sick, died miserably: and
the noble army of Prince Bull perished.

When the dismal news of his great loss was carried to
the Prince, he suspected his godmother very much indeed;
but he knew that his servants must have kept company
with the malicious beldame, and must have given way to
her, and therefore he resolved to turn those servants out of
their places. So he called to him a Roebuck who had the
gift of speech, and he said, " Good Roebuck, tell them they
must go." So the good Roebuck delivered his message, so
like a man that you might have supposed him to be nothing
but a man, and they were turned out—but not without
warning, for that they had had a long time.

And now comes the most extraordinary part of the history
of this Prince. When he had turned out those servants, of
course he wanted others. What was his astonishment to
find that in all his dominions, which contained no less than
twenty-seven millions of people, there were not above five-
and-twenty servants altogether! They were so lofty about
it, too, that instead of discussing whether they should hire
themselves as servants to Prince Bull, they turned things
topsy-turvy, and considered whether as a favour they
should hire Prince Bull to be their master! While they
were arguing this point among themselves quite at their
leisure, the wicked old red Fairy was incessantly going
up and down, knocking at the doors of twelve of the oldest
of the five-and-twenty, who were the oldest inhabitants in
all that country, and whose united ages amounted to one
thousand, saying, "Will *you* hire Prince Bull for your
master?—Will *you* hire Prince Bull for your master?"
To which one answered, "I will if next door will;" and
another, "I won't if over the way does;" and another, "I
can't if he, she, or they, might, could, would, or should."
And all this time Prince Bull's affairs were going to rack
and ruin.

At last, Prince Bull in the height of his perplexity assumed
a thoughtful face, as if he were struck by an entirely new
idea. The wicked old Fairy, seeing this, was at his elbow
directly, and said, "How do you do, my Prince, and what
are you thinking of?"—"I am thinking, godmother," says
he, "that among all the seven-and-twenty millions of my
subjects who have never been in service, there are men of
intellect and business who have made me very famous both

among my friends and enemies."—"Aye, truly?" says the Fairy.—"Aye, truly," says the Prince.—"And what then?" says the Fairy.—"Why, then," says he, "since the regular old class of servants do so ill, are so hard to get, and carry it with so high a hand, perhaps I might try to make good servants of some of these." The words had no sooner passed his lips than she returned, chuckling, "You think so, do you? Indeed, my Prince?—Tape!" Thereupon he directly forgot what he was thinking of, and cried out lamentably to the old servants, "O, do come and hire your poor old master! Pray do! On any terms!"

And this, for the present, finishes the story of Prince Bull. I wish I could wind it up by saying that he lived happy ever afterwards, but I cannot in my conscience do so; for, with Tape at his elbow, and his estranged children fatally repelled by her from coming near him, I do not, to tell you the plain truth, believe in the possibility of such an end to it.

A PLATED ARTICLE

PUTTING up for the night in one of the chiefest towns of
Staffordshire, I find it to be by no means a lively town. In
fact is as dull and dead a town as any one could desire not
to see. It seems as if its whole population might be imprisoned in its Railway Station. The Refreshment Room
at that Station is a vortex of dissipation compared with the
extinct town-inn, the Dodo, in the dull High Street.

Why High Street? Why not rather Low Street, Flat
Street, Low-Spirited Street, Used-up Street? Where are
the people who belong to the High Street? Can they all
be dispersed over the face of the country, seeking the unfortunate Strolling Manager who decamped from the mouldy
little Theatre last week, in the beginning of his season (as
his play-bills testify), repentantly resolved to bring him back,
and feed him, and be entertained? Or, can they all be
gathered to their fathers in the two old churchyards near
to the High Street—retirement into which churchyards
appears to be a mere ceremony, there is so very little life
outside their confines, and such small discernible difference
between being buried alive in the town, and buried dead in
the town tombs? Over the way, opposite to the staring
blank bow windows of the Dodo, are a little ironmonger's
shop, a little tailor's shop (with a picture of the Fashions in
the small window and a bandy-legged baby on the pavement staring at it)—a watchmaker's shop, where all the
clocks and watches must be stopped, I am sure, for they
could never have the courage to go, with the town in
general, and the Dodo in particular, looking at them. Shade
of Miss Linwood, erst of Leicester Square, London, thou
art welcome here, and thy retreat is fitly chosen! I myself was one of the last visitors to that awful storehouse of
thy life's work, where an anchorite old man and woman
took my shilling with a solemn wonder, and conducting
me to a gloomy sepulchre of needlework dropping to pieces
with dust and age and shrouded in twilight at high noon,

left me there, chilled, frightened, and alone. And now, in ghostly letters on all the dead walls of this dead town, I read thy honoured name, and find that thy Last Supper, worked in Berlin Wool, invites inspection as a powerful excitement!

Where are the people who are bidden with so much cry to this feast of little wool? Where are they? Who are they? They are not the bandy-legged baby studying the fashions in the tailor's window. They are not the two earthy ploughmen lounging outside the saddler's shop, in the stiff square where the Town Hall stands, like a brick and mortar private on parade. They are not the landlady of the Dodo in the empty bar, whose eye had trouble in it and no welcome, when I asked for dinner. They are not the turnkeys of the Town Jail, looking out of the gateway in their uniforms, as if they had locked up all the balance (as my American friends would say) of the inhabitants, and could now rest a little. They are not the two dusty millers in the white mill down by the river, where the great water-wheel goes heavily round and round, like the monotonous days and nights in this forgotten place. Then who are they, for there is no one else? No; this deponent maketh oath and saith that there is no one else, save and except the waiter at the Dodo, now laying the cloth. I have paced the streets, and stared at the houses, and am come back to the blank bow window of the Dodo; and the town clocks strike seven, and the reluctant echoes seem to cry, "Don't wake us!" and the bandy-legged baby has gone home to bed.

If the Dodo were only a gregarious bird—if he had only some confused idea of making a comfortable nest—I could hope to get through the hours between this and bed-time, without being consumed by devouring melancholy. But, the Dodo's habits are all wrong. It provides me with a trackless desert of sitting-room, with a chair for every day in the year, a table for every month, and a waste of side-board where a lonely China vase pines in a corner for its mate long departed, and will never make a match with the candlestick in the opposite corner if it live till Doomsday. The Dodo has nothing in the larder. Even now, I behold the Boots returning with my sole in a piece of paper; and with that portion of my dinner, the Boots, perceiving me at the blank bow window, slaps his leg as he comes across

the road, pretending it is something else. The Dodo ex-
cludes the outer air. When I mount up to my bedroom,
a smell of closeness and flue gets lazily up my nose like
sleepy snuff. The loose little bits of carpet writhe under
my tread, and take wormy shapes. I don't know the ridiculous man in the looking-glass, beyond having met him
once or twice in a dish-cover—and I can never shave *him*
to-morrow morning! The Dodo is narrow-minded as to
towels; expects me to wash on a freemason's apron without
the trimming: when I asked for soap, gives me a stony-
hearted something white, with no more lather in it than
the Elgin marbles. The Dodo has seen better days, and
possesses interminable stables at the back—silent, grass-
grown, broken-windowed, horseless.

This mournful bird can fry a sole, however, which is
much. Can cook a steak, too, which is more. I wonder
where it gets its Sherry? If I were to send my pint of
wine to some famous chemist to be analysed, what would
it turn out to be made of? It tastes of pepper, sugar, bitter-
almonds, vinegar, warm knives, any flat drinks, and a little
brandy. Would it unman a Spanish exile by reminding
him of his native land at all? I think not. If there really
be any townspeople out of the churchyards, and if a caravan
of them ever do dine, with a bottle of wine per man, in
this desert of the Dodo, it must make good for the doctor
next day!

Where was the waiter born? How did he come here?
Has he any hope of getting away from here? Does he ever
receive a letter, or take a ride upon the railway, or see anything but the Dodo? Perhaps he has seen the Berlin Wool.
He appears to have a silent sorrow on him, and it may be
that. He clears the table; draws the dingy curtains of the
great bow window, which so unwillingly consent to meet,
that they must be pinned together; leaves me by the fire
with my pint decanter, and a little thin funnel-shaped wine-
glass, and a plate of pale biscuits—in themselves engendering
desperation.

No book, no newspaper! I left the Arabian Nights in the
railway carriage, and have nothing to read but Bradshaw,
and "that way madness lies." Remembering what prisoners
and shipwrecked mariners have done to exercise their minds
in solitude, I repeat the multiplication table, the pence table,
and the shilling table: which are all the tables I happen to

know. What if I write something? The Dodo keeps no
pens but steel pens; and those I always stick through the
paper, and can turn to no other account.

What am I to do? Even if I could have the bandy-legged
baby knocked up and brought here, I could offer him nothing
but sherry, and that would be the death of him. He would
never hold up his head again if he touched it. I can't go
to bed, because I have conceived a mortal hatred for my
bedroom; and I can't go away, because there is no train
for my place of destination until morning. To burn the
biscuits will be but a fleeting joy; still it is a temporary
relief, and here they go on the fire! Shall I break the
plate? First let me look at the back, and see who made it.
COPELAND.

Copeland! Stop a moment. Was it yesterday I visited
Copeland's works, and saw them making plates? In the
confusion of travelling about, it might be yesterday or it
might be yesterday month; but I think it was yesterday. I appeal to the plate. The plate says, decidedly,
yesterday. I find the plate, as I look at it, growing into
a companion.

Don't you remember (says the plate) how you steamed
away, yesterday morning, in the bright sun and the east
wind, along the valley of the sparkling Trent? Don't you
recollect how many kilns you flew past, looking like the bowls
of gigantic tobacco-pipes, cut short off from the stem and
turned upside down? And the fires—and the smoke—and
the roads made with bits of crockery, as if all the plates
and dishes in the civilised world had been Macadamised
expressly for the laming of all the horses? Of course I do!

And don't you remember (says the plate) how you alighted
at Stoke—a picturesque heap of houses, kilns, smoke, wharfs,
canals, and river, lying (as was most appropriate) in a basin
—and how, after climbing up the sides of the basin to look
at the prospect, you trundled down again at a walking-match
pace, and straight proceeded to my father's, Copeland's, where
the whole of my family, high and low, rich and poor, are
turned out upon the world from our nursery and seminary,
covering some fourteen acres of ground? And don't you
remember what we spring from:—heaps of lumps of clay,
partially prepared and cleaned in Devonshire and Dorset-
shire, whence said clay principally comes—and hills of flint,
without which we should want our ringing sound, and should

never be musical? And as to the flint, don't you recollect that it is first burnt in kilns, and is then laid under the four iron feet of a demon slave, subject to violent stamping fits, who, when they come on, stamps away insanely with his four iron legs, and would crush all the flint in the Isle of Thanet to powder, without leaving off? And as to the clay, don't you recollect how it is put into mills or teazers, and is sliced, and dug, and cut at, by endless knives, clogged and sticky, but persistent—and is pressed out of that machine through a square trough, whose form it takes—and is cut off in square lumps and thrown into a vat, and there mixed with water, and beaten to a pulp by paddle-wheels—and is then run into a rough house, all rugged beams and ladders splashed with white,—superintended by Grindoff the Miller in his working clothes, all splashed with white,—where it passes through no end of machinery-moved sieves all splashed with white, arranged in an ascending scale of fineness (some so fine, that three hundred silk threads cross each other in a single square inch of their surface), and all in a violent state of ague with their teeth for ever chattering, and their bodies for ever shivering! And as to the flint again, isn't it mashed and mollified and troubled and soothed, exactly as rags are in a paper-mill, until it is reduced to a pap so fine that it contains no atom of "grit" perceptible to the nicest taste? And as to the flint and the clay together, are they not, after all this, mixed in the proportion of five of clay to one of flint, and isn't the compound—known as "slip"—run into oblong troughs, where its superfluous moisture may evaporate; and finally, isn't it slapped and banged and beaten and patted and kneaded and wedged and knocked about like butter, until it becomes a beautiful grey dough, ready for the potter's use?

In regard of the potter, popularly so called (says the plate), you don't mean to say you have forgotten that a workman called a Thrower is the man under whose hand this grey dough takes the shapes of the simpler household vessels as quickly as the eye can follow? You don't mean to say you cannot call him up before you, sitting, with his attendant woman, at his potter's wheel—a disc about the size of a dinner-plate, revolving on two drums slowly or quickly as he wills—who made you a complete breakfast-set for a bachelor, as a good-humoured little off-hand joke. You remember how he took up as much dough as he wanted, and, throwing it on his wheel, in a moment fashioned it into a teacup—caught up more clay and made a saucer—a larger dab and whirled it into a teapot—winked at a smaller dab and converted it into the lid of the teapot, accurately fitting by the measurement of his eye alone—coaxed a middle-sized dab for two seconds, broke it, turned it over at the rim, and made a milkpot—laughed, and turned out a slop-basin—coughed, and provided for the sugar?   Neither, I think, are you oblivious of the newer mode of making various articles, but especially basins, according to which improvement a mould revolves instead of a disc?   For you *must* remember (says the plate) how you saw the mould of a little basin spinning round and round, and how the workman smoothed and pressed a handful of dough upon it, and how with an instrument called a profile (a piece of wood, representing the profile of a basin's foot) he cleverly scraped and carved the ring which makes the base of any such basin, and then took the basin off the lathe like a doughy skull-cap to be dried, and afterwards (in what is called a green state) to be put into a second lathe, there to be finished and burnished with a steel burnisher?   And as to moulding in general (says the plate), it can't be necessary for me to remind you that all ornamental articles, and indeed all articles not quite circular, are made in moulds.   For you must remember how you saw the vegetable dishes, for example, being made in moulds; and how the handles of teacups, and the spouts of teapots, and the feet of tureens, and so forth, are all made in little separate moulds, and are each stuck on to the body corporate, of which it is destined to form a part, with a stuff called "slag," as quickly as you can recollect it.   Further, you learnt—you know you did—in the same visit, how the beautiful sculptures in the delicate new material called Parian, are all constructed in moulds ; how, into that material, animal bones are ground up, because the phosphate of lime contained in bones makes it translucent ; how everything is moulded, before going into the fire, one-fourth larger than it is intended to come out of the fire, because it shrinks in that proportion in the intense heat; how, when a figure shrinks unequally, it is spoiled—emerging from the furnace a mis-shapen birth ; a big head and a little body, or a little head and a big body, or a Quasimodo with long arms and short legs, or a Miss Biffin with neither legs nor arms worth mentioning.

And as to the kilns, in which the firing takes place, and in which some of the more precious articles are burnt repeatedly, in various stages of their process towards completion,—as to the kilns (says the plate, warming with the recollection), if you don't remember THEM with a horrible interest, what did you ever go to Copeland's for? When you stood inside of one of those inverted bowls of a pre-Adamite tobacco-pipe, looking up at the blue sky through the open top far off, as you might have looked up from a well, sunk under the centre of the pavement of the Pantheon at Rome, had you the least idea where you were? And when you found yourself surrounded, in that dome-shaped cavern, by innumerable columns of an unearthly order of architecture, supporting nothing, and squeezed close together as if a pre-Adamite Samson had taken a vast Hall in his arms and crushed it into the smallest possible space, had you the least idea what they were? No (says the plate), of course not! And when you found that each of those pillars was a pile of ingeniously made vessels of coarse clay—called Saggers—looking, when separate, like raised-pies for the table of the mighty Giant Blunderbore, and now all full of various articles of pottery ranged in them in baking order, the bottom of each vessel serving for the cover of the one below, and the whole kiln rapidly filling with these, tier upon tier, until the last workman should have barely room to crawl out, before the closing of the jagged aperture in the wall and the kindling of the gradual fire; did you not stand amazed to think that all the year round these dread chambers are heating, white hot—and cooling—and filling—and emptying—and being bricked up —and broken open—humanly speaking, for ever and ever? To be sure you did! And standing in one of those kilns nearly full, and seeing a free crow shoot across the aperture a-top, and learning how the fire would wax hotter and hotter by slow degrees, and would cool similarly through a space of from forty to sixty hours, did no remembrance of the days when human clay was burnt oppress you? Yes, I think so! I suspect that some fancy of a fiery haze and a shortening breath, and a growing heat, and a gasping prayer; and a figure in black interposing between you and the sky (as figures in black are very apt to do), and looking down, before it grew too hot to look and live, upon the Heretic in his edifying agony—I say I suspect (says the plate) that some such fancy was pretty strong upon you when you went out into the air, and blessed God for the bright spring day and the degenerate times!

After that, I needn't remind you what a relief it was to see the simplest process of ornamenting this "biscuit" (as it is called when baked) with brown circles and blue trees—converting it into the common crockery-ware that is exported to Africa, and used in cottages at home. For (says the plate) I am well persuaded that you bear in mind how those particular jugs and mugs were once more set upon a lathe and put in motion; and how a man blew the brown colour (having a strong natural affinity with the material in that condition) on them from a blowpipe as they twirled; and how his daughter, with a common brush, dropped blotches of blue upon them in the right places; and how, tilting the blotches upside down, she made them run into rude images of trees, and there an end.

And didn't you see (says the plate) planted upon my own brother that astounding blue willow, with knobbed and gnarled trunk, and foliage of blue ostrich feathers, which gives our family the title of "willow pattern"? And didn't you observe, transferred upon him at the same time, that blue bridge which spans nothing, growing out from the roots of the willow; and the three blue Chinese going over it into a blue temple, which has a fine crop of blue bushes sprouting out of the roof; and a blue boat sailing above them, the mast of which is burglariously sticking itself into the foundations of a blue villa, suspended sky-high, surmounted by a lump of blue rock, sky-higher, and a couple of billing blue birds, sky-highest—together with the rest of that amusing blue landscape, which has, in deference to our revered ancestors of the Cerulean Empire, and in defiance of every known law of perspective, adorned millions of our family ever since the days of platters? Didn't you inspect the copper-plate on which my pattern was deeply engraved? Didn't you perceive an impression of it taken in cobalt colour at a cylindrical press, upon a leaf of thin paper, streaming from a plunge-bath of soap and water? Wasn't the paper impression daintily spread, by a light-fingered damsel (you *know* you admired her!), over the surface of the plate, and the back of the paper rubbed prodigiously hard—with a long tight roll of flannel, tied up like a round of hung beef—without so much as ruffling the paper, wet as it was? Then (says the plate), was not the paper washed away with a sponge, and didn't there appear, set off upon the plate, *this* identical piece of pre-Raphaelite blue distemper which you now behold? Not to be denied! I had seen all this— and more. I had been shown, at Copeland's, patterns of beautiful design, in faultless perspective, which are causing the ugly old willow to wither out of public favour; and which, being quite as cheap, insinuate good wholesome natural art into the humblest households. When Mr. and Mrs. Sprat have satisfied their material tastes by that equal division of fat and lean which has made their *ménage* immortal; and have, after the elegant tradition, "licked the platter clean," they can—thanks to modern artists in clay— feast their intellectual tastes upon excellent delineations of natural objects.

This reflection prompts me to transfer my attention from the blue plate to the forlorn but cheerfully painted vase on the sideboard. And surely (says the plate) you have not forgotten how the outlines of such groups of flowers as you see there, are printed, just as I was printed, and are after-wards shaded and filled in with metallic colours by women and girls? As to the aristocracy of our order, made of the finer clay—porcelain peers and peeresses;—the slabs, and panels, and table-tops, and tazze; the endless nobility and gentry of dessert, breakfast, and tea services; the gemmed perfume bottles, and scarlet and gold salvers; you saw that they were painted by artists, with metallic colours laid on with camel-hair pencils, and afterwards burnt in.

And talking of burning in (says the plate), didn't you find that every subject, from the willow pattern to the landscape after Turner—having been framed upon clay or porcelain biscuit—has to be glazed? Of course, you saw the glaze— composed of various vitreous materials—laid over every article; and of course you witnessed the close imprisonment of each piece in saggers upon the separate system rigidly enforced by means of fine-pointed earthenware stilts placed between the articles to prevent the slightest communication or contact. We had in my time—and I suppose it is the same now—fourteen hours' firing to fix the glaze and to make it "run" all over us equally, so as to put a good shiny and unscratchable surface upon us. Doubtless, you observed that one sort of glaze—called printing-body—is burnt into the better sort of ware *before* it is printed. Upon this you saw some of the finest steel engravings transferred, to be fixed by an after glazing—didn't you ? Why, of course you did !

Of course I did. I had seen and enjoyed everything that the plate recalled to me, and had beheld with admiration how the rotatory motion which keeps this ball of ours in its place in the great scheme, with all its busy mites upon it, was necessary throughout the process, and could only be dispensed with in the fire. So, listening to the plate's reminders, and musing upon them, I got through the evening after all, and went to bed. I made but one sleep of it— for which I have no doubt I am also indebted to the plate —and left the lonely Dodo in the morning, quite at peace with it, before the bandy-legged baby was up.

OUR HONOURABLE FRIEND

WE are delighted to find that he has got in! Our honourable friend is triumphantly returned to serve in the next Parliament. He is the honourable member for Verbosity— the best represented place in England.

Our honourable friend has issued an address of congratulation to the Electors, which is worthy of that noble constituency, and is a very pretty piece of composition. In electing him, he says, they have covered themselves with glory, and England has been true to herself. (In his preliminary address he had remarked, in a poetical quotation of great rarity, that nought could make us rue, if England to herself did prove but true.)

Our honourable friend delivers a prediction, in the same document, that the feeble minions of a faction will never hold up their heads any more; and that the finger of scorn will point at them in their dejected state, through countless ages of time. Further, that the hireling tools that would destroy the sacred bulwarks of our nationality are unworthy of the name of Englishman; and that so long as the sea shall roll around our ocean-girded isle, so long his motto shall be, No surrender. Certain dogged persons of low principles and no intellect, have disputed whether anybody knows who the minions are, or what the faction is, or which are the hireling tools and which the sacred bulwarks, or what it is that is never to be surrendered, and if not, why not? But, our honourable friend the member for Verbosity knows all about it.

Our honourable friend has sat in several parliaments, and given bushels of votes. He is a man of that profundity in the matter of vote-giving, that you never know what he means. When he seems to be voting pure white, he may be in reality voting jet black. When he says Yes, it is just as likely as not—or rather more so—that he means No. This is the statesmanship of our honourable friend. It is in

this that he differs from mere unparliamentary men. *You*
may not know what he meant then, or what he means now;
but our honourable friend knows, and did from the first
know, both what he meant then, and what he means now;
and when he said he didn't mean it then, he did in fact say
that he means it now. And if you mean to say that you
did not then, and do not now, know what he did mean then,
or does mean now, our honourable friend will be glad to
receive an explicit declaration from you whether you are
prepared to destroy the sacred bulwarks of our nationality.

Our honourable friend, the member for Verbosity, has this
great attribute, that he always means something, and always
means the same thing. When he came down to that House
and mournfully boasted in his place, as an individual member
of the assembled Commons of this great and happy country,
that he could lay his hand upon his heart, and solemnly
declare that no consideration on earth should induce him, at
any time or under any circumstances, to go as far north as
Berwick-upon-Tweed; and when he nevertheless, next year,
did go to Berwick-upon-Tweed, and even beyond it, to
Edinburgh, he had one single meaning, one and indivisible.
And God forbid (our honourable friend says) that he should
waste another argument upon the man who professes that
he cannot understand it ! "I do NOT, gentlemen," said our
honourable friend, with indignant emphasis and amid great
cheering, on one such public occasion. "I do NOT, gentlemen, I am free to confess, envy the feelings of that man whose
mind is so constituted as that he can hold such language to
me, and yet lay his head upon his pillow, claiming to be
a native of that land,

> Whose march is o'er the mountain-wave,
> Whose home is on the deep!"

(Vehement cheering, and man expelled.)

When our honourable friend issued his preliminary address
to the constituent body of Verbosity on the occasion of one
particular glorious triumph, it was supposed by some of his
enemies that even he would be placed in a situation of
difficulty by the following comparatively trifling conjunction
of circumstances. The dozen noblemen and gentlemen whom
our honourable friend supported had "come in" expressly
to do a certain thing. Now, four of the dozen said, at a certain place, that they didn't mean to do that thing, and had

never meant to do it; another four of the dozen said, at another certain place, that they did mean to do that thing, and had always meant to do it; two of the remaining four said, at two other certain places, that they meant to do half of that thing (but differed about which half), and to do a variety of nameless wonders instead of the other half; and one of the remaining two declared that the thing itself was dead and buried, while the other as strenuously protested that it was alive and kicking. It was admitted that the parliamentary genius of our honourable friend would be quite able to reconcile such small discrepancies as these; but there remained the additional difficulty that each of the twelve made entirely different statements at different places, and that all the twelve called everything visible and invisible, sacred and profane, to witness that they were a perfectly impregnable phalanx of unanimity. This, it was apprehended, would be a stumbling-block to our honourable friend.

The difficulty came before our honourable friend in this way. He went down to Verbosity to meet his free and independent constituents, and to render an account (as he informed them in the local papers) of the trust they had confided to his hands—that trust which it was one of the proudest privileges of an Englishman to possess—that trust which it was the proudest privilege of an Englishman to hold. It may be mentioned as a proof of the great general interest attaching to the contest, that a Lunatic whom nobody employed or knew, went down to Verbosity with several thousand pounds in gold, determined to give the whole away —which he actually did; and that all the publicans opened their houses for nothing. Likewise, several fighting men, and a patriotic group of burglars sportively armed with life-preservers, proceeded (in barouches and very drunk) to the scene of action at their own expense; these children of nature having conceived a warm attachment to our honourable friend, and intending, in their artless manner, to testify it by knocking the voters in the opposite interest on the head.

Our honourable friend being come into the presence of his constituents, and having professed with great suavity that he was delighted to see his good friend Tipkisson there, in his working-dress—his good friend Tipkisson being an inveterate saddler, who always opposes him, and for whom he has a mortal hatred—made them a brisk, ginger-beery sort of speech, in which he showed them how the dozen noblemen and gentlemen had (in exactly ten days from their coming in) exercised a surprisingly beneficial effect on the whole financial condition of Europe, had altered the state of the exports and imports for the current half-year, had prevented the drain of gold, had made all that matter right about the glut of the raw material, and had restored all sorts of balances with which the superseded noblemen and gentlemen had played the deuce—and all this, with wheat at so much a quarter, gold at so much an ounce, and the Bank of England discounting good bills at so much per cent. ! He might be asked, he observed in a peroration of great power, what were his principles ? His principles were what they always had been. His principles were written in the countenances of the lion and unicorn; were stamped indelibly upon the royal shield which those grand animals supported, and upon the free words of fire which that shield bore. His principles were, Britannia and her sea-king trident! His principles were, commercial prosperity coexistently with perfect and profound agricultural contentment; but short of this he would never stop. His principles were these,—with the addition of his colours nailed to the mast, every man's heart in the right place, every man's eye open, every man's hand ready, every man's mind on the alert. His principles were these, concurrently with a general revision of something—speaking generally—and a possible readjustment of something else, not to be mentioned more particularly. His principles, to sum up all in a word, were, Hearths and Altars, Labour and Capital, Crown and Sceptre, Elephant and Castle. And now, if his good friend Tipkisson required any further explanation from him, he (our honourable friend) was there, willing and ready to give it.

Tipkisson, who all this time had stood conspicuous in the crowd, with his arms folded and his eyes intently fastened on our honourable friend: Tipkisson, who throughout our honourable friend's address had not relaxed a muscle of his visage, but had stood there, wholly unaffected by the torrent of eloquence, an object of contempt and scorn to mankind (by which we mean, of course, to the supporters of our honourable friend) ; Tipkisson now said that he was a plain man (Cries of " You are indeed ! "), and that what he wanted to know was, what our honourable friend and the dozen noblemen and gentlemen were driving at?

Our honourable friend immediately replied, "At the illimitable perspective."

It was considered by the whole assembly that this happy statement of our honourable friend's political views ought, immediately, to have settled Tipkisson's business and covered him with confusion; but that implacable person, regardless of the exeurations that were heaped upon him from all sides (by which we mean, of course, from our honourable friend's side), persisted in retaining an unmoved countenance, and obstinately retorted that if our honourable friend meant that, he wished to know what *that* meant?

It was in repelling this most objectionable and indecent opposition that our honourable friend displayed his highest qualifications for the representation of Verbosity. His warmest supporters present, and those who were best acquainted with his generalship, supposed that the moment was come when he would fall back upon the sacred bulwarks of our nationality. No such thing. He replied thus: "My good friend Tipkisson, gentlemen, wishes to know what I mean when he asks me what we are driving at, and when I candidly tell him, at the illimitable perspective, he wishes (if I understand him) to know what I mean?" "I do!" says Tipkisson, amid cries of "Shame" and "Down with him." "Gentlemen," says our honourable friend, "I will indulge my good friend Tipkisson by telling him both what I mean and what I don't mean. (Cheers and cries of "Give it him!") Be it known to him then, and to all whom it may concern, that I do mean altars, hearths, and homes, and that I don't mean mosques and Mohammedanism!" The effect of this home-thrust was terrific. Tipkisson (who is a Baptist) was hooted down and hustled out, and has ever since been regarded as a Turkish Renegade who contemplates an early pilgrimage to Mecca. Nor was he the only discomfited man. The charge, while it stuck to him, was magically transferred to our honourable friend's opponent, who was represented in an immense variety of placards as a firm believer in Mahomet; and the men of Verbosity were asked to choose between our honourable friend and the Bible, and our honourable friend's opponent and the Koran. They decided for our honourable friend, and rallied round the illimitable perspective.

It has been claimed for our honourable friend, with much appearance of reason, that he was the first to bend sacred matters to electioneering tactics. However this may be, the fine precedent was undoubtedly set in a Verbosity election : and it is certain that our honourable friend (who was a disciple of Brahma in his youth, and was a Buddhist when we had the honour of travelling with him a few years ago) always professes in public more anxiety than the whole Bench of Bishops, regarding the theological and doxological opinions of every man, woman, and child in the United Kingdom.

As we began by saying that our honourable friend has got in again at this last election, and that we are delighted to find that he has got in, so we will conclude. Our honourable friend cannot come in for Verbosity too often. It is a good sign; it is a great example. It is to men like our honourable friend, and to contests like those from which he comes triumphant, that we are mainly indebted for that ready interest in politics, that fresh enthusiasm in the discharge of the duties of citizenship, that ardent desire to rush to the poll, at present so manifest throughout England. When the contest lies (as it sometimes does) between two such men as our honourable friend, it stimulates the finest emotions of our nature, and awakens the highest admiration of which our heads and hearts are capable.

It is not too much to predict that our honourable friend will be always at his post in the ensuing session. Whatever the question be, or whatever the form of its discussion ; address to the crown, election petition, expenditure of the public money, extension of the public suffrage, education, crime ; in the whole house, in committee of the whole house, in select committee ; in every parliamentary discussion of every subject, everywhere: the Honourable Member for Verbosity will most certainly be found.

OUR SCHOOL

WE went to look at it, only this last Midsummer, and found that the Railway had cut it up·root and branch. A great trunk-line had swallowed the playground, sliced away the schoolroom, and pared off the corner of the house: which, thus curtailed of its proportions, presented itself, in a green stage of stucco, profilewise towards the road, like a forlorn flat-iron without a handle, standing on end.

It seems as if our schools were doomed to be the sport of change. We have faint recollections of a Preparatory Day-School, which we have sought in vain, and which must have been pulled down to make a new street, ages ago. We have dim impressions, scarcely amounting to a belief, that it was over a dyer's shop. We know that you went up steps to it ; that you frequently grazed your knees in doing so ; that you generally got your leg over the scraper, in trying to scrape the mud off a very unsteady little shoe. The mistress of the Establishment holds no place in our memory ; but rampant on one eternal door-mat, in an eternal entry long and narrow, is a puffy pug-dog, with a personal animosity towards us, who triumphs over Time. The bark of that baleful Pug, a certain radiating way he had of snapping at our undefended legs, the ghastly grinning of his moist black muzzle and white teeth, and the insolence of his crisp tail curled like a pastoral crook, all live and flourish. From an otherwise unaccountable association of him with a fiddle, we conclude that he was of French extraction, and his name *Fidèle*. He belonged to some female, chiefly inhabiting a back-parlour, whose life appears to us to have been consumed in sniffing, and in wearing a brown beaver bonnet. For her, he would sit up and balance cake upon his nose, and not eat it until twenty had been counted. To the best of our belief we were once called in to witness this performance; when, unable, even in his milder moments, to endure our presence, he instantly made at us, cake and all.

Why a something in mourning, called "Miss Frost," should still connect itself with our preparatory school, we are unable to say. We retain no impression of the beauty of Miss Frost—if she were beautiful; or of the mental fascinations of Miss Frost—if she were accomplished; yet her name and her black dress hold an enduring place in our remembrance. An equally impersonal boy, whose name has long since shaped itself unalterably into "Master Mawls," is not to be dislodged from our brain. Retaining no vindictive feeling towards Mawls—no feeling whatever, indeed— we infer that neither he nor we can have loved Miss Frost. Our first impression of Death and Burial is associated with this formless pair. We all three nestled awfully in a corner one wintry day, when the wind was blowing shrill, with Miss Frost's pinafore over our heads; and Miss Frost told us in a whisper about somebody being "screwed down." It is the only distinct recollection we preserve of these impalpable creatures, except a suspicion that the manners of Master Mawls were susceptible of much improvement. Generally speaking, we may observe that whenever we see a child intently occupied with its nose, to the exclusion of all other subjects of interest, our mind reverts, in a flash, to Master Mawls.

But the School that was Our School before the Railroad came and overthrew it, was quite another sort of place. We were old enough to be put into Virgil when we went there, and to get Prizes for a variety of polishing on which the rust has long accumulated. It was a School of some celebrity in its neighbourhood—nobody could have said why —and we had the honour to attain and hold the eminent position of first boy. The master was supposed among us to know nothing, and one of the ushers was supposed to know everything. We are still inclined to think the first-named supposition perfectly correct.

We have a general idea that its subject had been in the leather trade, and had bought us—meaning Our School— of another proprietor who was immensely learned. Whether this belief had any real foundation, we are not likely ever to know now. The only branches of education with which he showed the least acquaintance, were, ruling and corporally punishing. He was always ruling ciphering-books with a bloated mahogany ruler, or smiting the palms of offenders with the same diabolical instrument, or viciously drawing a pair of pantaloons tight with one of his large hands, and caning the wearer with the other. We have no doubt whatever that this occupation was the principal solace of his existence.

A profound respect for money pervaded Our School, which was, of course, derived from its Chief. We remember an idiotic goggle-eyed boy, with a big head and half-crowns without end, who suddenly appeared as a parlour-boarder, and was rumoured to have come by sea from some mysterious part of the earth where his parents rolled in gold. He was usually called "Mr." by the Chief, and was said to feed in the parlour on steaks and gravy; likewise to drink currant wine. And he openly stated that if rolls and coffee were ever denied him at breakfast, he would write home to that unknown part of the globe from which he had come, and cause himself to be recalled to the regions of gold. He was put into no form or class, but learnt alone, as little as he liked—and he liked very little—and there was a belief among us that this was because he was too wealthy to be "taken down." His special treatment, and our vague association of him with the sea, and with storms, and sharks, and Coral Reefs occasioned the wildest legends to be circulated as his history. A tragedy in blank verse was written on the subject—if our memory does not deceive us, by the hand that now chronicles these recollections—in which his father figured as Pirate, and was shot for a voluminous catalogue of atrocities: first imparting to his wife the secret of the cave in which his wealth was stored, and from which his only son's half-crowns now issued. Dumbledon (the boy's name) was represented as "yet unborn" when his brave father met his fate; and the despair and grief of Mrs. Dumbledon at that calamity was movingly shadowed forth as having weakened the parlour-boarder's mind. This production was received with great favour, and was twice performed with closed doors in the dining-room. But it got wind, and was seized as libellous, and brought the unlucky poet into severe affliction. Some two years afterwards, all of a sudden one day, Dumbledon vanished. It was whispered that the Chief himself had taken him down to the Docks, and re-shipped him for the Spanish Main; but nothing certain was ever known about his disappearance. At this hour, we cannot thoroughly disconnect him from California.

Our School was rather famous for mysterious pupils. There was another—a heavy young man, with a large double-cased silver watch, and a fat knife the handle of which was a perfect tool-box—who unaccountably appeared one day at a special desk of his own, erected close to that of the Chief, with whom he held familiar converse. He lived in the parlour, and went out for his walks, and never took the least notice of us—even of us, the first boy—unless to give us a deprecatory kick, or grimly to take our hat off and throw it away, when he encountered us out of doors, which unpleasant ceremony he always performed as he passed—not even condescending to stop for the purpose. Some of us believed that the classical attainments of this phenomenon were terrific, but that his penmanship and arithmetic were defective, and he had come there to mend them; others, that he was going to set up a school, and had paid the Chief "twenty-five pound down," for leave to see Our School at work. The gloomier spirits even said that he was going to buy us; against which contingency, conspiracies were set on foot for a general defection and running away. However, he never did that. After staying for a quarter, during which period, though closely observed, he was never seen to do anything but make pens out of quills, write small hand in a secret portfolio, and punch the point of the sharpest blade in his knife into his desk all over it, he too disappeared, and his place knew him no more.

There was another boy, a fair, meek boy, with a delicate complexion and rich curling hair, who, we found out, or thought we found out (we have no idea now, and probably had none then, on what grounds, but it was confidentially revealed from mouth to mouth), was the son of a Viscount who had deserted his lovely mother. It was understood that if he had his rights, he would be worth twenty thousand a year. And that if his mother ever met his father, she would shoot him with a silver pistol, which she carried, always loaded to the muzzle, for that purpose. He was a very suggestive topic. So was a young Mulatto, who was always believed (though very amiable) to have a dagger about him somewhere. But we think they were both outshone, upon the whole, by another boy who claimed to have been born on the twenty-ninth of February, and to have only one birthday in five years. We suspect this

to have been a fiction—but he lived upon it all the time he
was at Our School.

The principal currency of Our School was slate pencil.
It had some inexplicable value, that was never ascertained,
never reduced to a standard.   To have a great hoard of it
was somehow to be rich.   We used to bestow it in charity,
and confer it as a precious boon upon our chosen friends.
When the holidays were coming, contributions were solicited
for certain boys whose relatives were in India, and who
were appealed for under the generic name of "Holiday-
stoppers,"—appropriate marks of remembrance that should
enliven and cheer them in their homeless state.   Personally,
we always contributed these tokens of sympathy in the form
of slate pencil, and always felt that it would be a comfort
and a treasure to them.

Our School was remarkable for white mice.   Red-polls,
linnets, and even canaries, were kept in desks, drawers,
hat-boxes, and other strange refuges for birds ; but white
mice were the favourite stock.   The boys trained the mice
much better than the masters trained the boys.   We recall
one white mouse, who lived in the cover of a Latin
dictionary, who ran up ladders, drew Roman chariots,
shouldered muskets, turned wheels, and even made a very
creditable appearance on the stage as the Dog of Montargis.
He might have achieved greater things, but for having the
misfortune to mistake his way in a triumphal procession to
the Capitol, when he fell into a deep inkstand, and was
dyed black and drowned.   The mice were the occasion of
some most ingenious engineering, in the construction of
their houses and instruments of performance.   The famous
one belonged to a company of proprietors, some of whom
have since made Railroads, Engines, and Telegraphs ; the
chairman has erected mills and bridges in New Zealand.

The usher at Our School, who was considered to know
everything as opposed to the Chief, who was considered to
know nothing, was a bony, gentle-faced, clerical-looking
young man in rusty black.   It was whispered that he was
sweet upon one of Maxby's sisters (Maxby lived close by,
and was a day pupil), and further that he "favoured
Maxby."   As we remember, he taught Italian to Maxby's
sisters on half-holidays.   He once went to the play with
them, and wore a white waistcoat and a rose : which
was considered among us equivalent to a declaration.   We

were of opinion on that occasion, that to the last moment
he expected Maxby's father to ask him to dinner at five
o'clock, and therefore neglected his own dinner at half-past
one, and finally got none. We exaggerated in our imaginations the extent to which he punished Maxby's father's cold
meat at supper; and we agreed to believe that he was
elevated with wine and water when he came home. But
we all liked him; for he had a good knowledge of boys,
and would have made it a much better school if he had had
more power. He was writing master, mathematical master,
English master, made out the bills, mended the pens, and
did all sorts of things. He divided the little boys with the
Latin master (they were smuggled through their rudimentary
books, at odd times when there was nothing else to do),
and he always called at parents' houses to inquire after sick
boys, because he had gentlemanly manners. He was rather
musical, and on some remote quarter-day had bought an old
trombone; but a bit of it was lost, and it made the most
extraordinary sounds when he sometimes tried to play it of
an evening. His holidays never began (on account of the
bills) until long after ours; but in the summer vacations
he used to take pedestrian excursions with a knapsack; and
at Christmas time he went to see his father at Chipping
Norton, who we all said (on no authority) was a dairy-fed
pork-butcher. Poor fellow! He was very low all day on
Maxby's sister's wedding-day, and afterwards was thought
to favour Maxby more than ever, though he had been
expected to spite him. He has been dead these twenty
years. Poor fellow!

Our remembrance of Our Schools presents the Latin
master as a colourless doubled-up near-sighted man with
a crutch, who was always cold, and always putting onions
into his ears for deafness, and always disclosing ends of
flannel under all his garments, and almost always applying
a ball of pocket-handkerchief to some part of his face with
a screwing action round and round. He was a very good
scholar, and took great pains where he saw intelligence and
a desire to learn: otherwise, perhaps not. Our memory
presents him (unless teased into a passion) with as little
energy as colour—as having been worried and tormented
into monotonous feebleness—as having had the best part
of his life ground out of him in a Mill of boys. We remember with terror how he fell asleep one sultry afternoon

with the little smuggled class before him, and awoke not
when the footstep of the Chief fell heavy on the floor; how
the Chief aroused him, in the midst of a dread silence, and
said, "Mr. Blinkins, are you ill, sir?" how he blushingly
replied, "Sir, rather so;" how the Chief retorted with
severity, "Mr. Blinkins, this is no place to be ill in" (which
was very, very true), and walked back solemn as the ghost
in Hamlet, until, catching a wandering eye, he caned that
boy for inattention, and happily expressed his feelings
towards the Latin master through the medium of a
substitute.

There was a fat little dancing-master who used to come in
a gig, and taught the more advanced among us hornpipes
(as an accomplishment in great social demand in after life);
and there was a brisk little French master who used to come
in the sunniest weather, with a handleless umbrella, and to
whom the Chief was always polite, because (as we believed),
if the Chief offended him, he would instantly address the
Chief in French, and for ever confound him before the boys
with his inability to understand or reply.

There was, besides, a serving man whose name was Phil.
Our retrospective glance presents Phil as a shipwrecked
carpenter, cast away upon the desert island of a school, and
carrying into practice an ingenious inkling of many trades.
He mended whatever was broken, and made whatever was
wanted. He was general glazier, among other things, and
mended all the broken windows—at the prime cost (as was
darkly rumoured among us) of ninepence, for every square
charged three-and-six to parents. We had a high opinion
of his mechanical genius, and generally held that the Chief
"knew something bad of him," and on pain of divulgence
enforced Phil to be his bondsman. We particularly remember that Phil had a sovereign contempt for learning:
which engenders in us a respect for his sagacity, as it implies
his accurate observation of the relative positions of the Chief
and the ushers. He was an impenetrable man, who waited
at table between whiles, and throughout "the half" kept
the boxes in severe custody. He was morose, even to the
Chief, and never smiled, except at breaking-up, when, in
acknowledgment of the toast, "Success to Phil! Hooray!"
he would slowly carve a grin out of his wooden face, where
it would remain until we were all gone. Nevertheless, one
time when we had the scarlet fever in the school, Phil

nursed all the sick boys of his own accord, and was like a mother to them.

There was another school not far off, and of course Our School could have nothing to say to that school. It is mostly the way with schools, whether of boys or men. Well! the railway has swallowed up ours, and the locomotives now run smoothly over its ashes.

> So fades and languishes, grows dim and dies,
> All that this world is proud of,

— and is not proud of, too. It had little reason to be proud of Our School, and has done much better since in that way, and will do far better yet.

OUR VESTRY

WE have the glorious privilege of being always in hot water
if we like. We are a shareholder in a Great Parochial
British Joint Stock Bank of Balderdash. We have a Vestry
in our borough, and can vote for a vestryman—might even
be a vestryman, mayhap, if we were inspired by a lofty and
noble ambition. Which we are not.

Our Vestry is a deliberative assembly of the utmost dignity
and importance. Like the Senate of ancient Rome, its awful
gravity overpowers (or ought to overpower) barbarian visitors.
It sits in the Capitol (we mean in the capital building erected
for it), chiefly on Saturdays, and shakes the earth to its centre
with the echoes of its thundering eloquence, in a Sunday
paper.

To get into this Vestry in the eminent capacity of Vestryman, gigantic efforts are made, and Herculean exertions
used. It is made manifest to the dullest capacity at every
election, that if we reject Snozzle we are done for, and that
if we fail to bring in Blunderbooze at the top of the poll, we
are unworthy of the dearest rights of Britons. Flaming
placards are rife on all the dead walls in the borough, public-
houses hang out banners, hackney-cabs burst into full-grown
flowers of type, and everybody is, or should be, in a paroxysm
of anxiety.

At these momentous crises of the national fate, we are
much assisted in our deliberations by two eminent volunteers;
one of whom subscribes himself A Fellow Parishioner, the
other, A Rate-Payer. Who they are, or what they are, or
where they are, nobody knows; but whatever one asserts,
the other contradicts. They are both voluminous writers,
indicting more epistles than Lord Chesterfield in a single
week; and the greater part of their feelings are too big for
utterance in anything less than capital letters. They require
the additional aid of whole rows of notes of admiration, like
balloons, to point their generous indignation; and they

sometimes communicate a crushing severity to stars.   As
thus:

MEN OF MOONEYMOUNT.

Is it, or is it not, a * * * to saddle the parish with a debt
of £2,745 6s. 9d., yet claim to be a RIGID ECONOMIST?

Is it, or is it not, a * * * to state as a fact what is proved
to be *both a moral and a* PHYSICAL IMPOSSIBILITY ?

Is it, or is it not, a * * * to call £2,745 6s. 9d. nothing ;
and nothing, something?

Do you, or do you *not* want a * * * TO REPRESENT YOU IN
THE VESTRY ?

Your consideration of these questions is recommended to
you by

A FELLOW PARISHIONER.

It was to this important public document that one of our
first orators, MR. MAGG (of Little Winkling Street), adverted,
when he opened the great debate of the fourteenth of
November by saying, " Sir, I hold in my hand an anonymous
slander "—and when the interruption, with which he was at
that point assailed by the opposite faction, gave rise to that
memorable discussion on a point of order which will ever be
remembered with interest by constitutional assemblies.   In
the animated debate to which we refer, no fewer than thirty-
seven gentlemen, many of them of great eminence, including
MR. WIGSBY (of Chumbledon Square), were seen upon their
legs at one time ; and it was on the same great occasion that
DOGGINSON—regarded in our Vestry as " a regular John Bull :"
we believe, in consequence of his having always made up his
mind on every subject without knowing anything about it—
informed another gentleman of similar principles on the
opposite side, that if he " cheek'd him," he would resort to
the extreme measure of knocking his blessed head off.

This was a great occasion.   But our Vestry shines habitually.
In asserting its own pre-eminence, for instance, it is very
strong.   On the least provocation, or on none, it will be
clamorous to know whether it is to be " dictated to," or
" trampled on," or " ridden over rough-shod."   Its great
watchword is Self-government.   That is to say, supposing
our Vestry to favour any little harmless disorder like Typhus
Fever, and supposing the Government of the country to be,
by any accident, in such ridiculous hands, as that any of its

authorities should consider it a duty to object to Typhus Fever—obviously an unconstitutional objection—then, our Vestry cuts in with a terrible manifesto about Self-government, and claims its independent right to have as much Typhus Fever as pleases itself. Some absurd and dangerous persons have represented, on the other hand, that though our Vestry may be able to "beat the bounds" of its own parish, it may not be able to beat the bounds of its own diseases; which (say they) spread over the whole land, in an ever-expanding circle of waste, and misery, and death, and widowhood, and orphanage, and desolation. But our Vestry makes short work of any such fellows as these.

It was our Vestry—pink of Vestries as it is—that in support of its favourite principle took the celebrated ground of denying the existence of the last pestilence that raged in England, when the pestilence was raging at the Vestry doors. Dogginson said it was plums; Mr. Wigsby (of Chumbledon Square) said it was oysters; Mr. Magg (of Little Winkling Street) said, amid great cheering, it was the newspapers. The noble indignation of our Vestry with that un-English institution the Board of Health, under those circumstances, yields one of the finest passages in its history. It wouldn't hear of rescue. Like Mr. Joseph Miller's Frenchman, it would be drowned and nobody should save it. Transported beyond grammar by its kindled ire, it spoke in unknown tongues, and vented unintelligible bellowings, more like an ancient oracle than the modern oracle it is admitted on all hands to be. Rare exigencies produce rare things; and even our Vestry, new hatched to the woful time, came forth a greater goose than ever.

But this, again, was a special occasion. Our Vestry, at more ordinary periods, demands its meed of praise.

Our Vestry is eminently parliamentary. Playing at Parliament is its favourite game. It is even regarded by some of its members as a chapel of ease to the House of Commons: a Little Go to be passed first. It has its strangers' gallery, and its reported debates (see the Sunday paper before mentioned), and our Vestrymen are in and out of order, and on and off their legs, and above all are transcendantly quarrelsome, after the pattern of the real original.

Our Vestry being assembled, Mr. Magg never begs to trouble Mr. Wigsby with a simple inquiry. He knows better than that. Seeing the honourable gentleman, associated in

their minds with Chumbledon Square, in his place, he wishes
to ask that honourable gentleman what the intentions of
himself, and those with whom he acts, may be, on the subject
of the paving of the district known as Piggleum Buildings?
Mr. Wigsby replies (with his eye on next Sunday's paper)
that in reference to the question which has been put to him
by the honourable gentleman opposite, he must take leave to
say, that if that honourable gentleman had had the courtesy
to give him notice of that question, he (Mr. Wigsby) would
have consulted with his colleagues in reference to the advisa-
bility, in the present state of the discussions on the new
paving-rate, of answering that question.   But, as the honourable gentleman has NOT had the courtesy to give him
notice of that question (great cheering from the Wigsby
interest), he must decline to give the honourable gentleman
the satisfaction he requires.   Mr. Magg, instantly rising to
retort, is received with loud cries of "Spoke!" from the
Wigsby interest, and with cheers from the Magg side of
the house.   Moreover, five gentlemen rise to order, and one
of them, in revenge for being taken no notice of, petrifies
the assembly by moving that this Vestry do now adjourn;
but is persuaded to withdraw that awful proposal, in consideration of its tremendous consequences if persevered in.
Mr. Magg, for the purpose of being heard, then begs to move,
that you, sir, do now pass to the order of the day; and takes
that opportunity of saying, that if an honourable gentleman
whom he has in his eye, and will not demean himself by
more particularly naming (oh, oh, and cheers), supposes that
he is to be put down by clamour, that honourable gentleman—however supported he may be, through thick and thin,
by a Fellow Parishioner, with whom he is well acquainted
(cheers and counter-cheers, Mr. Magg being invariably backed
by the Rate-Payer)—will find himself mistaken.   Upon this,
twenty members of our Vestry speak in succession concerning
what the two great men have meant, until it appears, after
an hour and twenty minutes, that neither of them meant
anything.   Then our Vestry begins business.

We have said that, after the pattern of the real original,
our Vestry in playing at Parliament is transcendantly quarrelsome.   It enjoys a personal altercation above all things.
Perhaps the most redoubtable case of this kind we have ever
had—though we have had so many that it is difficult to
decide—was that on which the last extreme solemnities

passed between Mr. Tiddypot (of Gumption House) and
Captain Banger (of Wilderness Walk).

In an adjourned debate on the question whether water
could be regarded in the light of a necessary of life;
respecting which there were great differences of opinion,
and many shades of sentiment; Mr. Tiddypot, in a powerful
burst of eloquence against that hypothesis, frequently made
use of the expression that such and such a rumour had
"reached his ears." Captain Banger, following him, and
holding that, for purposes of ablution and refreshment,
a pint of water per diem was necessary for every adult of
the lower classes, and half a pint for every child, cast ridicule
upon his address in a sparkling speech, and concluded by
saying that instead of those rumours having reached the
ears of the honourable gentleman, he rather thought the
honourable gentleman's ears must have reached the rumours,
in consequence of their well-known length. Mr. Tiddypot
immediately rose, looked the honourable and gallant gentleman full in the face, and left the Vestry.

The excitement, at this moment painfully intense, was
heightened to an acute degree when Captain Banger rose,
and also left the Vestry. After a few moments of profound
silence—one of those breathless pauses never to be forgotten—Mr. Chib (of Tucket's Terrace, and the father of the
Vestry) rose. He said that words and looks had passed in
that assembly, replete with consequences which every feeling
mind must deplore. Time pressed. The sword was drawn,
and while he spoke the scabbard might be thrown away.
He moved that those honourable gentlemen who had left
the Vestry be recalled, and required to pledge themselves
upon their honour that this affair should go no farther.
The motion being by a general union of parties unanimously
agreed to (for everybody wanted to have the belligerents
there, instead of out of sight: which was no fun at all),
Mr. Magg was deputed to recover Captain Banger, and
Mr. Chib himself to go in search of Mr. Tiddypot. The
Captain was found in a conspicuous position, surveying the
passing omnibuses from the top step of the front-door
immediately adjoining the beadle's box; Mr. Tiddypot made
a desperate attempt at resistance, but was overpowered by
Mr. Chib (a remarkably hale old gentleman of eighty-two),
and brought back in safety.

Mr. Tiddypot and the Captain being restored to their

places, and glaring on each other, were called upon by the chair to abandon all homicidal intentions, and give the Vestry an assurance that they did so. Mr. Tiddypot remained profoundly silent. The Captain likewise remained profoundly silent, saving that he was observed by those around him to fold his arms like Napoleon Buonaparte, and to snort in his breathing—actions but too expressiv of gunpowder.

The most intense emotion now prevailed. Several members clustered in remonstrance round the Captain, and several round Mr. Tiddypot; but both were obdurate. Mr. Chib then presented himself amid tremendous cheering, and said, that not to shrink from the discharge of his painful duty, he must now move that both honourable gentlemen be taken into custody by the beadle, and conveyed to the nearest police-office, there to be held to bail. The union of parties still continuing, the motion was seconded by Mr. Wigsby— on all usual occasions Mr. Chib's opponent—and rapturously carried with only one dissentient voice. This was Dogginson's, who said from his place "Let 'em fight it out with fistes;" but whose coarse remark was received as it merited.

The beadle now advanced along the floor of the Vestry, and beckoned with his cocked hat to both members. Every breath was suspended. To say that a pin might have been heard to fall, would be feebly to express the all-absorbing interest and silence. Suddenly, enthusiastic cheering broke out from every side of the Vestry. Captain Banger had risen—being, in fact, pulled up by a friend on either side, and poked up by a friend behind.

The Captain said, in a deep determined voice, that he had every respect for that Vestry and every respect for that chair; that he also respected the honourable gentleman of Gumption House; but that he respected his honour more. Hereupon the Captain sat down, leaving the whole Vestry much affected. Mr. Tiddypot instantly rose, and was received with the same encouragement. He likewise said—and the exquisite art of this orator communicated to the observation an air of freshness and novelty—that he too had every respect for that Vestry; that he too had every respect for that chair. That he too respected the honourable and gallant gentleman of Wilderness Walk; but that he too respected his honour more. "Hows'ever," added the distinguished Vestryman, "if the honourable or gallant gentleman's honour is never

more doubted and damaged than it is by me, he's all right."
Captain Banger immediately started up again, and said that
after those observations, involving as they did ample concession to his honour without compromising the honour of
the honourable gentleman, he would be wanting in honour
as well as in generosity, if he did not at once repudiate all
intention of wounding the honour of the honourable gentleman, or saying anything dishonourable to his honourable
feelings. These observations were repeatedly interrupted by
bursts of cheers. Mr. Tiddypot retorted that he well knew
the spirit of honour by which the honourable and gallant
gentleman was so honourably animated, and that he accepted
an honourable explanation, offered in a way that did him
honour; but he trusted that the Vestry would consider that
his (Mr. Tiddypot's) honour had imperatively demanded of
him that painful course which he had felt it due to his
honour to adopt. The Captain and Mr. Tiddypot then
touched their hats to one another across the Vestry, a great
many times, and it is thought that these proceedings
(reported to the extent of several columns in next Sunday's
paper) will bring them in as churchwardens next year.

All this was strictly after the pattern of the real original,
and so are the whole of our Vestry's proceedings. In all
their debates, they are laudably imitative of the windy and
wordy slang of the real original, and of nothing that is better
in it. They have headstrong party animosities, without any
reference to the merits of questions; they tack a surprising
amount of debate to a very little business; they set more
store by forms than they do by substances:—all very like
the real original! It has been doubted in our borough,
whether our Vestry is of any utility; but our own conclusion
is, that it is of the use to the Borough that a diminishing
mirror is to a painter, as enabling it to perceive in a small
focus of absurdity all the surface defects of the real original.

OUR BORE

It is unnecessary to say that we keep a bore. Everybody does. But the bore whom we have the pleasure and honour of enumerating among our particular friends, is such a generic bore, and has so many traits (as it appears to us) in common with the great bore family, that we are tempted to make him the subject of the present notes. May he be generally accepted !

Our bore is admitted on all hands to be a good-hearted man. He may put fifty people out of temper, but he keeps his own. He preserves a sickly solid smile upon his face, when other faces are ruffled by the perfection he has attained in his art, and has an equable voice which never travels out of one key or rises above one pitch. His manner is a manner of tranquil interest. None of his opinions are startling. Among his deepest-rooted convictions, it may be mentioned that he considers the air of England damp, and holds that our lively neighbours—he always calls the French our lively neighbours—have the advantage of us in that particular. Nevertheless he is unable to forget that John Bull is John Bull all the world over, and that England with all her faults is England still.

Our bore has travelled. He could not possibly be a complete bore without having travelled. He rarely speaks of his travels without introducing, sometimes on his own plan of construction, morsels of the language of the country—which he always translates. You cannot name to him any little remote town in France, Italy, Germany, or Switzerland but he knows it well; stayed there a fortnight under peculiar circumstances. And talking of that little place, perhaps you know a statue over an old fountain, up a little court, which is the second—no, the third—stay—yes, the third turning on the right, after you come out of the Post-house, going up the hill towards the market ? You *don't* know that statue ? Nor that fountain ? You surprise him ! They are not usually seen by travellers (most extraordinary, he has never yet met with a single traveller who knew them, except one German, the most intelligent man he ever met in his life!) but he thought that you would have been the man to find them out. And then he describes them, in a circumstantial lecture half an hour long, generally delivered behind a door which is constantly being opened from the other side ; and implores you, if you ever revisit that place, now do go and look at that statue and fountain !

Our bore, in a similar manner, being in Italy, made a dis-covery of a dreadful picture, which has been the terror of a large portion of the civilized world ever since. We have seen the liveliest men paralysed by it, across a broad dining-table. He was lounging among the mountains, sir, basking in the mellow influences of the climate, when he came to *una piccola chiesa*—a little church—or perhaps it would be more correct to say *una piccolissima cappella*—the smallest chapel you can possibly imagine—and walked in. There was nobody inside but a *cieco*—a blind man—saying his prayers, and a *vecchio padre*—old friar—rattling a money-box. But above the head of that friar, and immediately to the right of the altar as you enter—to the right of the altar ? No. To the left of the altar as you enter—or say near the centre—there hung a painting (subject, Virgin and Child) so divine in its expression, so pure and yet so warm and rich in its tone, so fresh in its touch, at once so glowing in its colour and so statuesque in its repose, that our bore cried out in an ecstasy, "That's the finest picture in Italy !" And so it is, sir. There is no doubt of it. It is astonishing that that picture is so little known. Even the painter is un-certain. He afterwards took Blumb, of the Royal Academy (it is to be observed that our bore takes none but eminent people to see sights, and that none but eminent people take our bore), and you never saw a man so affected in your life as Blumb was. He cried like a child ! And then our bore begins his description in detail—for all this is introductory —and strangles his hearers with the folds of the purple drapery.

By an equally fortunate conjunction of accidental circum-stances, it happened that when our bore was in Switzerland, he discovered a Valley, of that superb character, that Cha-mouni is not to be mentioned in the same breath with it. This is how it was, sir. He was travelling on a mule—had been in the saddle some days—when, as he and the guide,

Pierre Blanquo : whom you may know, perhaps ?—our bore is sorry you don't, because he's the only guide deserving of the name—as he and Pierre were descending, towards evening, among those everlasting snows, to the little village of La Croix, our bore, observed a mountain track turning off sharply to the right. At first he was uncertain whether it *was* a track at all, and in fact, he said to Pierre, *" Qu'est que c'est donc, mon ami ?*—What is that, my friend ? "   *" Où, monsieur ? "* said Pierre—" Where, sir ? "   *" Là !*—there ! " said our bore.   *" Monsieur, ce n'est rien de tout*—sir, it's nothing at all," said Pierre.   *"Allons !*—Make haste.   *Il va neiger*—it's going to snow ! "   But our bore was not to be done in that way, and he firmly replied, " I wish to go in that direction—*je veux y aller.*   I am bent upon it—*je suis déterminé.   En avant !*—go ahead ! "   In consequence of which firmness on our bore's part, they proceeded, sir, during two hours of evening, and three of moonlight (they waited in a cavern till the moon was up), along the slenderest track, overhanging perpendicularly the most awful gulfs, until they arrived, by a winding descent, in a valley that possibly, and he may say probably, was never visited by any stranger before. What a valley! Mountains piled on mountains, avalanches stemmed by pine forests ; waterfalls, châlets, mountain-torrents, wooden bridges, every conceivable picture of Swiss scenery ! The whole village turned out to receive our bore. The peasant girls kissed him, the men shook hands with him, one old lady of benevolent appearance wept upon his breast. He was conducted, in a primitive triumph, to the little inn : where he was taken ill next morning, and lay for six weeks, attended by the amiable hostess (the same benevolent old lady who had wept over night) and her charming daughter, Fanchette. It is nothing to say that they were attentive to him ; they doted on him. They called him in their simple way, *l'Ange Anglais*—the English Angel. When our bore left the valley, there was not a dry eye in the place ; some of the people attended him for miles. He begs and entreats of you as a personal favour, that if you ever go to Switzerland again (you have mentioned that your last visit was your twenty-third), you will go to that valley, and see Swiss scenery for the first time. And if you want really to know the pastoral people of Switzerland, and to understand them, mention, in that valley, our bore's name !

Our bore has a crushing brother in the East, who, some-how or other, was admitted to smoke pipes with Mehemet Ali, and instantly became an authority on the whole range of Eastern matters, from Haroun Alraschid to the present Sultan. He is in the habit of expressing mysterious opinions on this wide range of subjects, but on questions of foreign policy more particularly, to our bore, in letters; and our bore is continually sending bits of these letters to the newspapers (which they never insert), and carrying other bits about in his pocket-book. It is even whispered that he has been seen at the Foreign Office, receiving great consideration from the messengers, and having his card promptly borne into the sanctuary of the temple. The havoc committed in society by this Eastern brother is beyond belief. Our bore is always ready with him. We have known our bore to fall upon an intelligent young sojourner in the wilderness, in the first sentence of a narrative, and beat all confidence out of him with one blow of his brother. He became omniscient, as to foreign policy, in the smoking of those pipes with Mehemet Ali. The balance of power in Europe, the machinations of the Jesuits, the gentle and humanising influence of Austria, the position and prospects of that hero of the noble soul who is worshipped by happy France, are all easy reading to our bore's brother. And our bore is so provokingly self-denying about him! "I don't pretend to more than a very general knowledge of these subjects myself," says he, after enervating the intellects of several strong men, "but these are my brother's opinions, and I believe he is known to be well-informed."

The commonest incidents and places would appear to have been made special, expressly for our bore. Ask him whether he ever chanced to walk, between seven and eight in the morning, down St. James's Street, London, and he will tell you, never in his life but once. But it's curious that that once was in eighteen thirty; and that as our bore was walking down the street you have just mentioned, at the hour you have just mentioned—half-past seven—or twenty minutes to eight. No! Let him be correct!—exactly a quarter before eight by the palace clock—he met a fresh-coloured, grey-haired, good-humoured looking gentleman, with a brown umbrella, who, as he passed him, touched his hat and said, "Fine morning, sir, fine morning!"—William the Fourth!

Ask our bore whether he has seen Mr. Barry's new Houses of Parliament, and he will reply that he has not yet inspected them minutely, but that you remind him that it was his singular fortune to be the last man to see the old Houses of Parliament before the fire broke out. It happened in this way. Poor John Spine, the celebrated novelist, had taken him over to South Lambeth to read to him the last few chapters of what was certainly his best book—as our bore told him at the time, adding, "Now, my dear John, touch it, and you'll spoil it!"—and our bore was going back to the club by way of Millbank and Parliament Street, when he stopped to think of Canning, and look at the Houses of Parliament. Now, you know far more of the philosophy of Mind than our bore does, and are much better able to explain to him than he is to explain to you why or wherefore, at that particular time, the thought of fire should come into his head. But it did. It did. He thought, What a national calamity if an edifice connected with so many associations should be consumed by fire! At that time there was not a single soul in the street but himself. All was quiet, dark, and solitary. After contemplating the building for a minute—or, say a minute and a half, not more—our bore proceeded on his way, mechanically repeating, What a national calamity if such an edifice, connected with such associations, should be destroyed by—— A man coming towards him in a violent state of agitation completed the sentence, with the exclamation, Fire! Our bore looked round, and the whole structure was in a blaze.

In harmony and union with these experiences, our bore never went anywhere in a steamboat but he made either the best or the worst voyage ever known on that station. Either he overheard the captain say to himself, with his hands clasped, "We are all lost!" or the captain openly declared to him that he had never made such a run before, and never should be able to do it again. Our bore was in that express train on that railway, when they made (unknown to the passengers) the experiment of going at the rate of a hundred miles an hour. Our bore remarked on that occasion to the other people in the carriage, "This is too fast, but sit still!" He was at the Norwich musical festival when the extraordinary echo for which science has been wholly unable to account, was heard for the first and last time. He and the bishop heard it at the same moment, and caught each other's eye. He was present at that illumination of St. Peter's, of which the Pope is known to have remarked, as he looked at it out of his window in the Vatican, " *O Cielo! Questa cosa non sara fatta, mai ancora, come questa*—O Heaven! this thing will never be done again, like this!" He has seen every lion he ever saw, under some remarkably propitious circumstances. He knows there is no fancy in it, because in every case the showman mentioned the fact at the time, and congratulated him upon it.

At one period of his life, our bore had an illness. It was an illness of a dangerous character for society at large. Innocently remark that you are very well, or that somebody else is very well; and our bore, with a preface that one never knows what a blessing health is until one has lost it, is reminded of that illness, and drags you through the whole of its symptoms, progress, and treatment. Innocently remark that you are not well, or that somebody else is not well, and the same inevitable result ensues. You will learn how our bore felt a tightness about here, sir, for which he couldn't account, accompanied with a constant sensation as if he were being stabbed—or, rather, jobbed—that expresses it more correctly—jobbed—with a blunt knife. Well, sir! This went on, until sparks began to flit before his eyes, water-wheels to turn round in his head, and hammers to beat incessantly thump, thump, thump, all down his back—along the whole of the spinal vertebræ. Our bore, when his sensations had come to this, thought it a duty he owed to himself to take advice, and he said, Now, whom shall I consult? He naturally thought of Callow, at that time one of the most eminent physicians in London, and he went to Callow. Callow said, " Liver!" and prescribed rhubarb and calomel, low diet, and moderate exercise. Our bore went on with this treatment, getting worse every day, until he lost confidence in Callow, and went to Moon, whom half the town was then mad about. Moon was interested in the case; to do him justice he was very much interested in the case; and he said, " Kidneys!" He altered the whole treatment, sir—gave strong acids, cupped, and blistered. This went on, our bore still getting worse every day, until he openly told Moon it would be a satisfaction to him if he would have a consultation with Clatter. The moment Clatter saw our bore, he said, " Accumulation of fat about the heart!" Snugglewood, who was called in with him,

differed, and said, "Brain!" But what they all agreed
upon was, to lay our bore upon his back, to shave his head,
to leech him, to administer enormous quantities of medicine,
and to keep him low; so that he was reduced to a mere
shadow, you wouldn't have known him, and nobody considered it possible that he could ever recover. This was his
condition, sir, when he heard of Jilkins—at that period in
a very small practice, and living in the upper part of a house
in Great Portland Street; but still, you understand, with
a rising reputation among the few people to whom he was
known. Being in that condition in which a drowning man
catches at a straw, our bore sent for Jilkins. Jilkins came.
Our bore liked his eye, and said, "Mr. Jilkins, I have a pre-
sentiment that you will do me good." Jilkins's reply was
characteristic of the man. It was, "Sir, I mean to do you
good." This confirmed our bore's opinion of his eye, and
they went into the case together—went completely into it.
Jilkins then got up, walked across the room, came back, and
sat down. His words were these. "You have been hum-
bugged. This is a case of indigestion, occasioned by deficiency of power in the Stomach. Take a mutton chop in
half-an-hour, with a glass of the finest old sherry that can
be got for money. Take two mutton chops to-morrow, and
two glasses of the finest old sherry. Next day, I'll come
again." In a week our bore was on his legs, and Jilkins's
success dates from that period!

Our bore is great in secret information. He happens
to know many things that nobody else knows. He can
generally tell you where the split is in the Ministry; he
knows a deal about the Queen; and has little anecdotes to
relate of the royal nursery. He gives you the judge's
private opinion of Sludge the murderer, and his thoughts
when he tried him. He happens to know what such a man
got by such a transaction, and it was fifteen thousand five
hundred pounds, and his income is twelve thousand a year.
Our bore is also great in mystery. He believes, with an
exasperating appearance of profound meaning, that you saw
Parkins last Sunday?—Yes, you did.—Did he say anything
particular?—No, nothing particular.—Our bore is surprised
at that.—Why?—Nothing. Only he understood that Parkins had come to tell you something.—What about?—
Well! our bore is not at liberty to mention what about.
But he believes you will hear that from Parkins himself,

soon, and he hopes it may not surprise you as it did him.
Perhaps, however, you never heard about Parkins's wife's
sister?—No.—Ah! says our bore, that explains it!

Our bore is also great in argument. He infinitely enjoys
a long humdrum, drowsy interchange of words of dispute
about nothing. He considers that it strengthens the mind,
consequently, he "don't see that," very often. Or, he would
be glad to know what you mean by that. Or, he doubts
that. Or, he has always understood exactly the reverse of
that. Or, he can't admit that. Or, he begs to deny that.
Or, surely you don't mean that. And so on. He once
advised us; offered us a piece of advice, after the fact,
totally impracticable and wholly impossible of acceptance,
because it supposed the fact, then eternally disposed of, to
be yet in abeyance. It was a dozen years ago, and to this
hour our bore benevolently wishes, in a mild voice, on
certain regular occasions, that we had thought better of his
opinion.

The instinct with which our bore finds out another bore,
and closes with him, is amazing. We have seen him pick
his man out of fifty men, in a couple of minutes. They
love to go (which they do naturally) into a slow argument
on a previously exhausted subject, and to contradict each
other, and to wear the hearers out, without impairing their
own perennial freshness as bores. It improves the good
understanding between them, and they get together afterwards, and bore each other amicably. Whenever we see
our bore behind a door with another bore, we know that
when he comes forth, he will praise the other bore as one
of the most intelligent men he ever met. And this bringing us to the close of what we had to say about our bore,
we are anxious to have it understood that he never bestowed this praise on us.

A MONUMENT OF FRENCH FOLLY

It was profoundly observed by a witty member of the Court of Common Council, in Council assembled in the City of London, in the year of our Lord one thousand eight hundred and fifty, that the French are a frog-eating people, who wear wooden shoes.

We are credibly informed, in reference to the nation whom this choice spirit so happily disposed of, that the caricatures and stage representations which were current in England some half a century ago, exactly depict their present condition. For example, we understand that every Frenchman, without exception, wears a pigtail and curl-papers. That he is extremely sallow, thin, long-faced, and lantern-jawed. That the calves of his legs are invariably undeveloped; that his legs fail at the knees, and that his shoulders are always higher than his ears. We are likewise assured that he rarely tastes any food but soup maigre, and an onion; that he always says, "By Gar! Aha! Vat you tell me, sare?" at the end of every sentence he utters; and that the true generic name of his race is the Mounseers, or the Parly-voos. If he be not a dancing-master, or a barber, he must be a cook; since no other trades but those three are congenial to the tastes of the people, or permitted by the Institutions of the country. He is a slave, of course. The ladies of France (who are also slaves) invariably have their heads tied up in Belcher handkerchiefs, wear long earrings, carry tambourines, and beguile the weariness of their yoke by singing in head voices through their noses—principally to barrel-organs.

It may be generally summed up, of this inferior people, that they have no idea of anything.

Of a great Institution like Smithfield, they are unable to form the least conception. A Beast Market in the heart of Paris would be regarded an impossible nuisance. Nor have they any notion of slaughter-houses in the midst of a city.

One of these benighted frog-eaters would scarcely understand your meaning, if you told him of the existence of
such a British bulwark.

It is agreeable, and perhaps pardonable, to indulge in
a little self-complacency when our right to it is thoroughly
established. At the present time, to be rendered memorable
by a final attack on that good old market which is the
(rotten) apple of the Corporation's eye, let us compare ourselves, to our national delight and pride as to these two
subjects of slaughter-house and beast-market, with the
outlandish foreigner.

The blessings of Smithfield are too well understood to
need recapitulation ; all who run (away from mad bulls and
pursuing oxen) may read. Any market-day they may be
beheld in glorious action. Possibly the merits of our
slaughter-houses are not yet quite so generally appreciated.

Slaughter-houses, in the large towns of England, are
always (with the exception of one or two enterprising towns)
most numerous in the most densely crowded places, where
there is the least circulation of air. They are often underground, in cellars ; they are sometimes in close back yards ;
sometimes (as in Spitalfields) in the very shops where the
meat is sold. Occasionally, under good private management,
they are ventilated and clean. For the most part, they are
unventilated and dirty ; and, to the reeking walls, putrid
fat and other offensive animal matter clings with a tenacious
hold. The busiest slaughter-houses in London are in the
neighbourhood of Smithfield, in Newgate Market, in Whitechapel, in Newport Market, in Leadenhall Market, in Clare
Market. All these places are surrounded by houses of a
poor description, swarming with inhabitants. Some of them
are close to the worst burial-grounds in London. When the
slaughter-house is below the ground, it is a common practice to throw the sheep down areas, neck and crop—which
is exciting, but not at all cruel. When it is on the level
surface, it is often extremely difficult of approach. Then,
the beasts have to be worried, and goaded, and pronged,
and tail-twisted, for a long time before they can be got in—
which is entirely owing to their natural obstinacy. When
it is not difficult of approach, but is in a foul condition,
what they see and scent makes them still more reluctant to
enter—which is their natural obstinacy again. When they
do get in at last, after no trouble and suffering to speak of

(for there is nothing in the previous journey into the heart of London, the night's endurance in Smithfield, the struggle out again, among the crowded multitude, the coaches, carts, waggons, omnibuses, gigs, chaises, phaetons, cabs, trucks, dogs, boys, whoopings, roarings, and ten. thousand other distractions), they are represented to be in a most unfit state to be killed, according to microscopic examinations made of their fevered blood by one of the most distinguished physiologists in the world, PROFESSOR OWEN—but that's humbug. When they *are* killed, at last, their reeking carcases are hung in impure air, to become, as the same Professor will explain to you, less nutritious and more unwholesome—but he is only an *un*common counsellor, so don't mind *him*. In half a quarter of a mile's length of Whitechapel, at one time, there shall be six hundred newly slaughtered oxen hanging up, and seven hundred sheep—but the more the merrier—proof of prosperity. Hard by Snow Hill and Warwick Lane, you shall see the little children, inured to sights of brutality from their birth, trotting along the alleys, mingled with troops of horribly busy pigs, up to their ankles in blood—but it makes the young rascals hardy. Into the imperfect sewers of this overgrown city, you shall have the immense mass of corruption, engendered by these practices, lazily thrown out of sight, to rise, in poisonous. gases, into your house at night, when your sleeping children will most readily absorb them, and to find its languid way, at last, into the river that you drink—but the French are a frog-eating people who wear wooden shoes, and it's O the roast beef of England, my boy, the jolly old English roast beef.

It is quite a mistake—a new-fangled notion altogether—to suppose that there is any natural antagonism between putrefaction and health. They know better than that, in the Common Council. You may talk about Nature, in her wisdom, always warning man through his sense of smell, when he draws near to something dangerous; but that won't go down in the City. Nature very often don't mean anything. Mrs. .Quickly says that prunes are ill for a green wound; but whosoever says that putrid animal substances are ill for a green wound, or for robust vigour, or for anything or for anybody, is a humanity-monger and a humbug. Britons never, never, never, &c., therefore. And prosperity to cattle-driving, cattle-slaughtering, bone-crushing,' blood-boiling, trotter-scraping, tripe-dressing, paunch-cleaning, gut-spinning, hide-preparing, tallow-melting, and other salubrious proceedings, in the midst of hospitals, church-yards, workhouses, schools, infirmaries, refuges, dwellings, provision-shops, nurseries, sick-beds, every stage and baiting-place in the journey from birth to death!

These *un*common counsellors, your Professor Owens and fellows, will contend that to tolerate these things in a civilised city, is to reduce it to a worse condition than BRUCE found to prevail in ABYSSINIA. For there (say they) the jackals and wild dogs came at night to devour the offal; whereas, here there are no such natural scavengers, and quite as savage customs. Further, they will demonstrate that nothing in Nature is intended to be wasted, and that besides the waste which such abuses occasion in the articles of health and life—main sources of the riches of any com-munity—they lead to a prodigious waste of changing matters, which might, with proper preparation, and under scientific direction, be safely applied to the increase of the fertility of the land. Thus (they argue) does Nature ever avenge infractions of her beneficent laws, and so surely as Man is determined to warp any of her blessings into curses, shall they become curses, and shall he suffer heavily. But this is cant. Just as it is cant of the worst description to say to the London Corporation, "How can you exhibit to the people so plain a spectacle of dishonest equivocation, as to claim the right of holding a market in the midst of the great city, for one of your vested privileges, when you know that when your last market holding charter was granted to you by King Charles the First, Smithfield stood IN THE SUBURBS OF LONDON, and is in that very charter so de-scribed in those five words?"—which is certainly true, but has nothing to do with the question.

Now to the comparison, in these particulars of civilisa-tion, between the capital of England, and the capital of that frog-eating and wooden-shoe wearing country, which the illustrious Common Councilman so sarcastically settled.

In Paris, there is no Cattle Market. Cows and calves are sold within the city, but the Cattle Markets are at Poissy, about thirteen miles off, on a line of railway; and at Sceaux, about five miles off. The Poissy market is held every Thursday; the Sceaux market, every Monday. In Paris, there are no slaughter-houses, in our acceptation of the term. There are five public Abattoirs—within the walls, though in the suburbs—and in these all the slaughtering for the city must be performed. They are managed by a Syndicat or Guild of Butchers, who confer with the Minister of the Interior on all matters affecting the trade, and who are consulted when any new regulations are contemplated for its government. They are, likewise, under the vigilant superintendence of the police. Every butcher must be licensed: which proves him at once to be a slave, for we don't license butchers in England—we only license apothecaries, attorneys, post-masters, publicans, hawkers, retailers of tobacco, snuff, pepper, and vinegar—and one or two other little trades, not worth mentioning. Every arrangement in connexion with the slaughtering and sale of meat, is matter of strict police regulation. (Slavery again, though we certainly have a general sort of Police Act here.)

But, in order that the reader may understand what a monument of folly these frog-eaters have raised in their abattoirs and cattle-markets, and may compare it with what common counselling has done for us all these years, and would still do but for the innovating spirit of the times, here follows a short account of a recent visit to these places:

It was as sharp a February morning as you would desire to feel at your fingers' ends when I turned out—tumbling over a chiffonier with his little basket and rake, who was picking up the bits of coloured paper that had been swept out, over-night, from a Bon-Bon shop—to take the Butchers' Train to Poissy. A cold, dim light just touched the high roofs of the Tuileries which have seen such changes, such distracted crowds, such riot and bloodshed ; and they looked as calm, and as old, all covered with white frost, as the very Pyramids. There was not light enough, yet, to strike upon the towers of Notre Dame across the water ; but I thought of the dark pavement of the old Cathedral as just beginning to be streaked with grey ; and of the lamps in the "House of God," the Hospital close to it, burning low and being quenched ; and of the keeper of the Morgue going about with a fading lantern, busy in the arrangement of his terrible waxwork for another sunny day.

The sun was up, and shining merrily when the butchers and I, announcing our departure with an engine shriek to sleepy Paris, rattled away for the Cattle Market. Across

the country, over the Seine, among a forest of scrubby trees
—the hoar frost lying cold in shady places, and glittering
in the light—and here we are at Poissy! Out leap the
butchers, who have been chattering all the way like madmen,
and off they straggle for the Cattle Market (still chattering,
of course, incessantly), in hats and caps of all shapes, in
coats and blouses, in calf-skins, cow-skins, horse-skins, furs,
shaggy mantles, hairy coats, sacking, baize, oil-skin, anything
you please that will keep a man and a butcher warm, upon
a frosty morning.

Many a French town have I seen, between this spot of
ground and Strasburgh or Marseilles, that might sit for your
picture, little Poissy! Barring the details of your old
church, I know you well, albeit we make acquaintance,
now, for the first time. I know your narrow, straggling,
winding streets, with a kennel in the midst, and lamps
slung across. I know your picturesque street-corners,
winding up-hill Heaven knows why or where! I know
your tradesmen's inscriptions, in letters not quite fat enough;
your barbers' brazen basins dangling over little shops; your
Cafés and Estaminets, with cloudy bottles of stale syrup in
the windows, and pictures of crossed billiard cues outside.
I know this identical grey horse with his tail rolled up in
a knot like the "back hair" of an untidy woman, who
won't be shod, and who makes himself heraldic by clattering
across the street on his hind-legs, while twenty voices shriek
and growl at him as a Brigand, an accursed Robber, and
an everlastingly-doomed Pig. I know your sparkling town-
fountain, too, my Poissy, and am glad to see it near a cattle-
market, gushing so freshly, under the auspices of a gallant
little sublimated Frenchman wrought in metal, perched
upon the top. Through all the land of France I know this
unswept room at The Glory, with its peculiar smell of
beans and coffee, where the butchers crowd about the stove,
drinking the thinnest of wine from the smallest of tumblers;
where the thickest of coffee-cups mingle with the longest of
loaves, and the weakest of lump sugar; where Madame at
the counter easily acknowledges the homage of all entering
and departing butchers; where the billiard-table is covered
up in the midst like a great bird-cage—but the bird may
sing by-and-by!

A bell! The Calf Market! Polite departure of butchers.
Hasty payment and departure on the part of amateur-Visitor.

Madame reproaches Ma'amselle for too fine a susceptibility
in reference to the devotion of a Butcher in a bear-skin.
Monsieur, the landlord of The Glory, counts a double handful
of sous, without an unobliterated inscription, or an undamaged
crowned head, among them.

There is little noise without, abundant space, and no confusion. The open area devoted to the market is divided
into three portions: the Calf Market, the Cattle Market,
the Sheep Market. Calves at eight, cattle at ten, sheep at
mid-day. All is very clean.

The Calf Market is a raised platform of stone, some three
or four feet high, open on all sides, with a lofty over-
spreading roof, supported on stone columns, which give it
the appearance of a sort of vineyard from Northern Italy.
Here, on the raised pavement, lie innumerable calves, all
bound hind-legs and fore-legs together, and all trembling
violently—perhaps with cold, perhaps with fear, perhaps
with pain; for this mode of tying, which seems to be an
absolute superstition with the peasantry, can hardly fail to
cause great suffering. Here they lie patiently in rows,
among the straw, with their stolid faces and inexpressive
eyes, superintended by men and women, boys and girls; here
they are inspected by our friends, the butchers, bargained
for, and bought. Plenty of time; plenty of room; plenty
of good humour. "Monsieur François in the bear-skin, how
do you do, my friend? You come from Paris by the train?
The fresh air does you good. If you are in want of three or
four fine calves this market morning, my angel, I, Madame
Doche, shall be happy to deal with you. Behold these
calves, Monsieur François! Great Heaven, you are doubtful!
Well, sir, walk round and look about you. If you find better
for the money, buy them. If not, come to me!" Monsieur
François goes his way leisurely, and keeps a wary eye upon
the stock. No other butcher jostles Monsieur François; Monsieur François jostles no other butcher. Nobody is flustered
and aggravated. Nobody is savage. In the midst of the
country blue frocks and red handkerchiefs, and the butchers'
coats, shaggy, furry, and hairy: of calf-skin, cow-skin, horse-
skin, and bear-skin: towers a cocked hat and a blue cloak.
Slavery! For *our* Police wear great-coats and glazed hats.

But now the bartering is over, and the calves are sold.
"Ho! Gregoire, Antoine, Jean, Louis! Bring up the carts,
my children! Quick, brave infants! Hola! Hi!"

The carts, well littered with straw, are backed up to the edge of the raised pavement, and various hot infants carry calves upon their heads, and dexterously pitch them in, while other hot infants, standing in the carts, arrange the calves, and pack them carefully in straw. Here is a promising young calf, not sold, whom Madame Doche unbinds. Pardon me, Madame Doche, but I fear this mode of tying the four legs of a quadruped together, though strictly à la mode, is not quite right. You observe, Madame Doche, that the cord leaves deep indentations in the skin, and that the animal is so cramped at first as not to know, or even remotely suspect that he *is* unbound, until you are so obliging as to kick him, in your delicate little way, and pull his tail like a bell-rope. Then, he staggers to his knees, not being able to stand, and stumbles about like a drunken calf, or the horse at Franconi's, whom you may have seen, Madame Doche, who is supposed to have been mortally wounded in battle. But what is this rubbing against me, as I apostrophise Madame Doche? It is another heated infant with a calf upon his head. "Pardon, Monsieur, but will you have the politeness to allow me to pass?" "Ah, sir, willingly. I am vexed to obstruct the way." On he staggers, calf and all, and makes no allusion whatever either to my eyes or limbs.

Now, the carts are all full. More straw, my Antoine, to shake over these top rows; then, off we will clatter, rumble, jolt, and rattle, a long row of us, out of the first town-gate, and out at the second town-gate, and past the empty sentry-box, and the little thin square bandbox of a guardhouse, where nobody seems to live: and away for Paris, by the paved road, lying, a straight straight line, in the long long avenue of trees. We can neither choose our road, nor our pace, for that is all prescribed to us. The public convenience demands that our carts should get to Paris by such a route, and no other (Napoleon had leisure to find that out, while he had a little war with the world upon his hands), and woe betide us if we infringe orders.

Droves of oxen stand in the Cattle Market, tied to iron bars fixed into posts of granite. Other droves advance slowly down the long avenue, past the second town-gate, and the first town-gate, and the sentry-box, and the bandbox, thawing the morning with their smoky breath as they come along. Plenty of room; plenty of time. Neither man nor beast is driven out of his wits by coaches, carts, waggons, omnibuses, gigs, chaises, phaetons, cabs, trucks, boys, whoopings, roarings, and multitudes. No tail-twisting is necessary —no iron pronging is necessary. There are no iron prongs here. The market for cattle is held as quietly as the market for calves. In due time, off the cattle go to Paris; the drovers can no more choose their road, nor their time, nor the numbers they shall drive, than they can choose their hour for dying in the course of nature.

Sheep next. The sheep-pens are up here, past the Branch Bank of Paris established for the convenience of the butchers, and behind the two pretty fountains they are making in the Market. My name is Bull: yet I think I should like to see as good twin fountains—not to say in Smithfield, but in England anywhere. Plenty of room; plenty of time. And here are sheep-dogs, sensible as ever, but with a certain French air about them—not without a suspicion of dominoes —with a kind of flavour of moustache and beard—demonstrative dogs, shaggy and loose where an English dog would be tight and close—not so troubled with business calculations as our English drovers' dogs, who have always got their sheep upon their minds, and think about their work, even resting, as you may see by their faces; but dashing, showy, rather unreliable dogs: who might worry me instead of their legitimate charges if they saw occasion—and might see it somewhat suddenly.

The market for sheep passes off like the other two; and away they go, by *their* allotted road to Paris. My way being the Railway, I make the best of it at twenty miles an hour; whirling through the now high-lighted landscape; thinking that the inexperienced green buds will be wishing, before long, they had not been tempted to come out so soon; and wondering who lives in this or that château, all window and lattice, and what the family may have for breakfast this sharp morning.

After the Market comes the Abattoir. What abattoir shall I visit first? Montmartre is the largest. So I will go there.

The abattoirs are all within the walls of Paris, with an eye to the receipt of the octroi duty; but they stand in open places in the suburbs, removed from the press and bustle of the city. They are managed by the Syndicat or Guild of Butchers, under the inspection of the Police. Certain smaller items of the revenue derived from them are in part retained by the Guild for the payment of their expenses, and in part devoted by it to charitable purposes in connexion with the trade. They cost six hundred and eighty thousand pounds; and they return to the city of Paris an interest on that outlay, amounting to nearly six and a-half per cent.

Here, in a sufficiently dismantled space is the Abattoir of Montmartre, covering nearly nine acres of ground, surrounded by a high wall, and looking from the outside like a cavalry barrack. At the iron gates is a small functionary in a large cocked hat. "Monsieur desires to see the abattoir? Most certainly." State being inconvenient in private transactions, and Monsieur being already aware of the cocked hat, the functionary puts it into a little official bureau which it almost fills, and accompanies me in the modest attire—as to his head—of ordinary life.

Many of the animals from Poissy have come here. On the arrival of each drove, it was turned into yonder ample space, where each butcher who had bought, selected his own purchases. Some, we see now, in these long perspectives of stalls with a high overhanging roof of wood and open tiles rising above the walls. While they rest here, before being slaughtered, they are required to be fed and watered, and the stalls must be kept clean. A stated amount of fodder must always be ready in the loft above; and the supervision is of the strictest kind. The same regulations apply to sheep and calves; for which, portions of these perspectives are strongly railed off. All the buildings are of the strongest and most solid description.

After traversing these lairs, through which, besides the upper provision for ventilation just mentioned, there may be a thorough current of air from opposite windows in the side walls, and from doors at either end, we traverse the broad, paved, court-yard until we come to the slaughter-houses. They are all exactly alike, and adjoin each other, to the number of eight or nine together, in blocks of solid building. Let us walk into the first.

It is firmly built and paved with stone. It is well lighted, thoroughly aired, and lavishly provided with fresh water. It has two doors opposite each other; the first, the door by which I entered from the main yard; the second, which is opposite, opening on another smaller yard, where the sheep and calves are killed on benches. The pavement

of that yard, I see, slopes downward to a gutter, for its
being more easily cleansed. The slaughter-house is fifteen
feet high, sixteen feet and a-half wide, and thirty-three feet
long. It is fitted with a powerful windlass, by which one
man at the handle can bring the head of an ox down to the
ground to receive the blow from the pole-axe that is to fell
him—with the means of raising the carcass and keeping it
suspended during the after-operation of dressing—and with
hooks on which carcasses can hang, when completely prepared, without touching the walls. Upon the pavement
of this first stone chamber, lies an ox scarcely dead. If
I except the blood draining from him, into a little stone
well in a corner of the pavement, the place is free from
offence as the Place de la Concorde. It is infinitely purer
and cleaner, I know, my friend the functionary, than the
Cathedral of Notre Dame. Ha, ha! Monsieur is pleasant,
but, truly, there is reason, too, in what he says.

I look into another of these slaughter-houses. "Pray
enter," says a gentleman in bloody boots. "This is a calf
I have killed this morning. Having a little time upon my
hands, I have cut and punctured this lace pattern in the
coats of his stomach. It is pretty enough. I did it to divert
myself."—"It is beautiful, Monsieur, the slaughterer!" He
tells me I have the gentility to say so.

I look into rows of slaughter-houses. In many, retail
dealers, who have come here for the purpose, are making
bargains for meat. There is killing enough, certainly, to
satiate an unused eye; and there are steaming carcasses
enough, to suggest the expediency of a fowl and salad for
dinner; but everywhere, there is an orderly, clean, well-
systematised routine of work in progress—horrible work at
the best, if you please; but so much the greater reason
why it should be made the best of. I don't know (I think
I have observed, my name is Bull) that a Parisian of the
lowest order is particularly delicate, or that his nature is
remarkable for an infinitesimal infusion of ferocity; but
I do know, my potent, grave, and common counselling
Signors, that he is forced, when at this work, to submit
himself to a thoroughly good system, and to make an
Englishman very heartily ashamed of you.

Here, within the walls of the same abattoir, in other
roomy and commodious buildings, are a place for converting
the fat into tallow and packing it for market—a place for

cleansing and scalding calves' heads and sheep's feet —
a place for preparing tripe—stables and coach-houses for
the butchers — innumerable conveniences, aiding in the
diminution of offensiveness to its lowest possible point, and
the raising of cleanliness and supervision to their highest.
Hence, all the meat that goes out of the gate is sent away
in clean covered carts. And if every trade connected with
the slaughtering of animals were obliged by law to be
carried on in the same place, I doubt, my friend, now
reinstated in the cocked hat (whose civility these two francs
imperfectly acknowledge, but appear munificently to repay),
whether there could be better regulations than those which
are carried out at the Abattoir of Montmartre. Adieu, my
friend, for I am away to the other side of Paris, to the
Abattoir of Grenelle! And there I find exactly the same
thing on a smaller scale, with the addition of a magnificent
Artesian well, and a different sort of conductor, in the
person of a neat little woman with neat little eyes, and
a neat little voice, who picks her neat little way among the
bullocks in a very neat little pair of shoes and stockings.

Such is the Monument of French Folly which a foreigneer-
ing people have erected, in a national hatred and antipathy
for common counselling wisdom. That wisdom, assembled
in the City of London, having distinctly refused, after
a debate of three days long, and by a majority of nearly
seven to one, to associate itself with any Metropolitan
Cattle-Market unless it be held in the midst of the City,
it follows that we shall lose the inestimable advantages of
common counselling protection, and be thrown, for a market,
on our own wretched resources. In all human probability
we shall thus come, at last, to erect a monument of folly
very like this French monument. If that be done, the
consequences are obvious. The leather trade will be ruined,
by the introduction of American timber, to be manufactured
into shoes for the fallen English; the Lord Mayor will be
required, by the popular voice, to live entirely on frogs;
and both these changes will (how, is not at present quite
clear, but certainly somehow or other) fall on that unhappy
landed interest which is always being killed, yet is always
found to be alive—and kicking.

THE LAMPLIGHTER

CHARACTERS

The Astrologer, a crazy old man, who has spent fifteen years in fruitless experiments in attempting to discover the philosopher's stone.

Miss Fanny Barker, niece to the astrologer.

Emma, daughter of the astrologer.

Galileo Isaac Newton Flamstead, Christian names of the son of the astrologer.

Tom Grig, a lamplighter.

Mr. Mooney ("The Gifted"), a learned but very absent-minded philosopher.

THE LAMPLIGHTER

"If you talk of Murphy and Francis Moore, gentlemen," said the lamplighter who was in the chair, "I mean to say that neither of 'em ever had any more to do with the stars than Tom Grig had."

"And what had *he* to do with 'em?" asked the lamplighter who officiated as vice.

"Nothing at all," replied the other; "just exactly nothing at all."

"Do you mean to say you don't believe in Murphy, then?" demanded the lamplighter who had opened the discussion.

"I mean to say I believe in Tom Grig," replied the chairman. "Whether I believe in Murphy, or not, is a matter between me and my conscience; and whether Murphy believes in himself, or not, is a matter between him and his conscience. Gentlemen, I drink your healths."

The lamplighter who did the company this honour, was seated in the chimney-corner of a certain tavern, which has been, time out of mind, the Lamplighters' House of Call. He sat in the midst of a circle of lamplighters, and was the cacique, or chief of the tribe.

If any of our readers have had the good fortune to behold a lamplighter's funeral, they will not be surprised to learn that lamplighters are a strange and primitive people; that they rigidly adhere to old ceremonies and customs which have been handed down among them from father to son since the first public lamp was lighted out of doors; that they intermarry, and betroth their children in infancy; that they enter into no plots or conspiracies (for who ever heard of a traitorous lamplighter?); that they commit no crimes against the laws of their country (there being no instance of a murderous or burglarious lamplighter) ; that they are, in short, notwithstanding their apparently volatile and restless character, a highly moral and reflective people: having among themselves as many traditional observances as the Jews, and being, as a body, if not as old as the hills, at least as old as the streets. It is an article of their creed that the first faint glimmering of true civilization shone in the first street-light maintained at the public expense. They trace their existence and high position in the public esteem, in a direct line to the heathen mythology ; and hold that the history of Prometheus himself is but a pleasant fable, whereof the true hero is a lamplighter.

"Gentlemen," said the lamplighter in the chair, "I drink your healths."

"And, perhaps, Sir," said the vice, holding up his glass, and rising a little way off his seat and sitting down again, in token that he recognised and returned the compliment, "perhaps you will add to that condescension by telling us who Tom Grig was, and how he came to be connected in your mind with Francis Moore, Physician."

"Hear, hear, hear !" cried the lamplighters generally.

"Tom Grig, gentlemen," said the chairman, "was one of us ; and it happened to him, as it don't often happen to a public character in our line, that he had his what-you-may-call-it cast."

"His head ? " said the vice.

"No," replied the chairman, "not his head."

"His face, perhaps ? " said the vice. "No, not his face." "His legs ? " "No, not his legs." Nor yet his arms, nor his hands, nor his feet, nor his chest, all of which were severally suggested.

"His nativity, perhaps ? "

"That's it," said the chairman, awakening from his thoughtful attitude at the suggestion. "His nativity. That's what Tom had cast, gentlemen."

"In plaister ? " asked the vice.

"I don't rightly know how it's done," returned the chairman. "But I suppose it was."

And there he stopped as if that were all he had to say ; whereupon there arose a murmur among the company, which at length resolved itself into a request, conveyed through the vice, that he would go on. This being exactly what the chairman wanted, he mused for a little time, performed that agreeable ceremony which is popularly termed wetting one's whistle, and went on thus:

"Tom Grig, gentlemen, was, as I have said, one of us; and I may go further, and say he was an ornament to us, and such a one as only the good old times of oil and cotton could have produced. Tom's family, gentlemen, were all lamplighters."

"Not the ladies, I hope?" asked the vice.

"They had talent enough for it, Sir," rejoined the chairman, "and would have been, but for the prejudices of society. Let women have their rights, Sir, and the females of Tom's family would have been every one of 'em in office. But that emancipation hasn't come yet, and hadn't then, and consequently they confined themselves to the bosoms of their families, cooked the dinners, mended the clothes, minded the children, comforted their husbands, and attended to the house-keeping generally. It's a hard thing upon the women, gentlemen, that they are limited to such a sphere of action as this; very hard."

"I happen to know all about Tom, gentlemen, from the circumstance of his uncle by his mother's side having been my particular friend. His (that's Tom's uncle's) fate was a melancholy one. Gas was the death of him. When it was first talked of, he laughed. He wasn't angry; he laughed at the credulity of human nature. 'They might as well talk,' he says, 'of laying on an everlasting succession of glow-worms;' and then he laughed again, partly at his joke, and partly at poor humanity.

"In course of time, however, the thing got ground, the experiment was made, and they lighted up Pall Mall. Tom's uncle went to see it. I've heard that he fell off his ladder fourteen times that night, from weakness, and that he would certainly have gone on falling till he killed himself, if his last tumble hadn't been into a wheelbarrow which was going his way, and humanely took him home. 'I foresee in this,' says Tom's uncle faintly, and taking to his bed as he spoke —'I foresee in this,' he says, 'the breaking up of our profession. There's no more going the rounds to trim by daylight, no more dribbling down of the oil on the hats and bonnets of ladies and gentlemen when one feels in spirits. Any low fellow can light a gas-lamp. And it's all up.' In this state of mind, he petitioned the government for—I want a word again, gentlemen—what do you

x

call that which they give to people when it's found out, at last, that they've never been of any use, and have been paid too much for doing nothing ? "

"Compensation ? " suggested the vice.

"That's it," said the chairman. "Compensation. They didn't give it him, though, and then he got very fond of his country all at once, and went about saying that gas was a death-blow to his native land, and that it was a plot of the radicals to ruin the country and destroy the oil and cotton trade for ever, and that the whales would go and kill themselves privately, out of sheer spite and vexation at not being caught. At last he got right-down cracked ; called his tobacco-pipe a gas-pipe ; thought his tears were lamp-oil ; and went on with all manner of nonsense of that sort, till one night he hung himself on a lamp-iron in Saint Martin's Lane, and there was an end of *him*.

"Tom loved him, gentlemen, but he survived it. He shed a tear over his grave, got very drunk, spoke a funeral oration that night in the watch-house, and was fined five shillings for it, in the morning. Some men are none the worse for this sort of thing. Tom was one of 'em. He went that very afternoon on a new beat : as clear in his head, and as free from fever as Father Mathew himself.

"Tom's new beat, gentlemen, was—I can't exactly say where, for that he'd never tell ; but I know it was in a quiet part of town, where there were some queer old houses. I have always had it in my head that it must have been somewhere near Canonbury Tower in Islington, but that's a matter of opinion. Wherever it was, he went upon it, with a bran-new ladder, a white hat, a brown holland jacket and trousers, a blue neckerchief, and a sprig of full-blown double wall-flower in his button-hole. Tom was always genteel in his appearance, and I have heard from the best judges, that if he had left his ladder at home that afternoon, you might have took him for a lord.

"He was always merry, was Tom, and such a singer, that if there was any encouragement for native talent, he'd have been at the opera. He was on his ladder, lighting his first lamp, and singing to himself in a manner more easily to be conceived than described, when he hears the clock strike five, and suddenly sees an old gentleman with a telescope in his hand, throw up a window and look at him very hard.

"Tom didn't know what could be passing in this old gentleman's mind. He thought it likely enough that he might be saying within himself, 'Here's a new lamplighter—a good-looking young fellow—shall I stand something to drink?' Thinking this possible, he keeps quite still, pretending to be very particular about the wick, and looks at the old gentleman sideways, seeming to take no notice of him.

"Gentlemen, he was one of the strangest and most mysterious-looking files that ever Tom clapped his eyes on. He was dressed all slovenly and untidy, in a great gown of a kind of bed-furniture pattern, with a cap of the same on his head; and a long old flapped waistcoat; with no braces, no strings, very few buttons—in short, with hardly any of those artificial contrivances that hold society together. Tom knew by these signs, and by his not being shaved, and by his not being over-clean, and by a sort of wisdom not quite awake, in his face, that he was a scientific old gentleman. He often told me that if he could have conceived the possibility of the whole Royal Society being boiled down into one man, he should have said the old gentleman's body was that Body."

"The old gentleman claps the telescope to his eye, looks all round, sees nobody else in sight, stares at Tom again, and cries out very loud:

"'Hal-loa!'

"'Halloa, Sir,' says Tom from the ladder; 'and halloa again, if you come to that.'

"'Here's an extraordinary fulfilment,' says the old gentleman, 'of a prediction of the planets.'

"'Is there?' says Tom. 'I'm very glad to hear it.'

"'Young man,' says the old gentleman, 'you don't know me.'

"'Sir,' says Tom, 'I have not that honour; but I shall be happy to drink your health, notwithstanding.'

"'I read,' cries the old gentleman, without taking any notice of this politeness on Tom's part—'I read what's going to happen, in the stars.'

"Tom thanked him for the information, and begged to know if anything particular was going to happen in the stars, in the course of a week or so; but the old gentleman, correcting him, explained that he read in the stars what was going to happen on dry land, and that he was acquainted with all the celestial bodies.

"'I hope they're all well, Sir,' says Tom,—'everybody.'

"'Hush!' cries the old gentleman. 'I have consulted the book of Fate with rare and wonderful success. I am versed in the great sciences of astrology and astronomy. In my house here, I have every description of apparatus for observing the course and motion of the planets. Six months ago, I derived from this source, the knowledge that precisely as the clock struck five this afternoon a stranger would present himself—the destined husband of my young and lovely niece—in reality of illustrious and high descent, but whose birth would be enveloped in uncertainty and mystery. Don't tell me yours isn't,' says the old gentleman, who was in such a hurry to speak that he couldn't get the words out fast enough, 'for I know better.'

"Gentlemen, Tom was so astonished when he heard him say this, that he could hardly keep his footing on the ladder, and found it necessary to hold on by the lamp-post. There *was* a mystery about his birth. His mother had always admitted it. Tom had never known who was his father, and some people had gone so far as to say that even *she* was in doubt.

"While he was in this state of amazement, the old gentleman leaves the window, bursts out of the house-door, shakes the ladder, and Tom, like a ripe pumpkin, comes sliding down into his arms.

"'Let me embrace you,' he says, folding his arms about him, and nearly lighting up his old bed-furniture gown at Tom's link. 'You're a man of noble aspect. Everything combines to prove the accuracy of my observations. You have had mysterious promptings within you,' he says; 'I know you have had whisperings of greatness, eh?' he says.

"'I think I have,' says Tom—Tom was one of those who can persuade themselves to anything they like—'I've often thought I wasn't the small beer I was taken for.'

"'You were right,' cries the old gentleman, hugging him again. 'Come in. My niece awaits us.'

"'Is the young lady tolerable good-looking, Sir?' says Tom, hanging fire rather, as he thought of her playing the piano, and knowing French, and being up to all manner of accomplishments.

"'She's beautiful!' cries the old gentleman, who was in such a terrible bustle that he was all in a perspiration. 'She has a graceful carriage, an exquisite shape, a sweet voice, a countenance beaming with animation and expression ; and the eye,' he says, rubbing his hands, ' of a startled fawn.'

"Tom supposed this might mean, what was called among his circle of acquaintance, 'a game eye ;' and, with a view to this defect, inquired whether the young lady had any cash.

" ' She has five thousand pounds,' cries the old gentleman. ' But what of that ? what of that ? A word in your ear. I'm in search of the philosopher's stone. I have very nearly found it—not quite. It turns everything to gold ; that's its property.'

"Tom naturally thought it must have a deal of property ; and said that when the old gentleman did get it, he hoped he'd be careful to keep it in the family.

" ' Certainly,' he says, ' of course. Five thousand pounds! What's five thousand pounds to us ? What's five million ? ' he says. ' What's five thousand million ? Money will be nothing to us. We shall never be able to spend it fast enough.'

" ' We'll try what we can do, Sir,' says Tom.

" ' We will,' says the old gentleman. ' Your name ? '

" ' Grig,' says Tom.

The old gentleman embraced him again, very tight ; and without speaking another word, dragged him into the house in such an excited manner, that it was as much as Tom could do to take his link and ladder with him, and put them down in the passage.

"Gentlemen, if Tom hadn't been always remarkable for his love of truth, I think you would still have believed him when he said that all this was like a dream. There is no better way for a man to find out whether he is really asleep or awake, than calling for something to eat. If he's in a dream, gentlemen, he'll find something wanting in the flavour, depend upon it.

"Tom explained his doubts to the old gentleman, and said that if there was any cold meat in the house, it would ease his mind very much to test himself at once. The old gentleman ordered up a venison pie, a small ham, and a bottle of very old Madeira. At the first mouthful of pie and the first glass of wine, Tom smacks his lips and cries out, ' I'm awake—wide awake ;' and to prove that he was so, gentlemen, he made an end of 'em both.

" When Tom had finished his meal (which he never spoke of afterwards without tears in his eyes), the old gentleman hugs him again, and says, 'Noble stranger! let us visit my young and lovely niece.' Tom, who was a little elevated with the wine, replies, 'The noble stranger is agreeable!' At which words the old gentleman took him by the hand, and led him to the parlour; crying as he opened the door, 'Here is Mr. Grig, the favourite of the planets!'

"I will not attempt a description of female beauty, gentlemen, for every one of us has a model of his own that suits his own taste best. In this parlour that I'm speaking of, there were two young ladies; and if every gentleman present, will imagine two models of his own in their places, and will be kind enough to polish 'em up to the very highest pitch of perfection, he will then have a faint conception of their uncommon radiance.

"Besides these two young ladies, there was their waiting-woman, that under any other circumstances Tom would have looked upon as a Venus; and besides her, there was a tall, thin, dismal-faced young gentleman, half man and half boy, dressed in a childish suit of clothes very much too short in the legs and arms; and looking, according to Tom's comparison, like one of the wax juveniles from a tailor's door, grown up and run to seed. Now, this youngster stamped his foot upon the ground and looked very fierce at Tom, and Tom looked fierce at him—for to tell the truth, gentlemen, Tom more than half suspected that when they entered the room he was kissing one of the young ladies; and for anything Tom knew, you observe, it might be *his* young lady—which was not pleasant.

" 'Sir,' says Tom, 'before we proceed any further, will you have the goodness to inform me who this young Salamander' —Tom called him that for aggravation, you perceive, gentlemen—'who this young Salamander may be?'

" 'That, Mr. Grig,' says the old gentleman, 'is my little boy. He was christened Galileo Isaac Newton Flamstead. Don't mind him. He's a mere child.'

" 'And a very fine child too,' says Tom—still aggravating, you'll observe—'of his age, and as good as fine, I have no doubt. How do you do, my man?' with which kind and patronising expressions, Tom reached up to pat him on the head, and quoted two lines about little boys, from Doctor Watts's Hymns, which he had learnt at a Sunday School.

"It was very easy to see, gentlemen, by this youngster's frowning and by the waiting-maid's tossing her head and turning up her nose, and by the young ladies turning their backs and talking together at the other end of the room, that nobody but the old gentleman took very kindly to the noble stranger. Indeed, Tom plainly heard the waiting-woman say of her master, that so far from being able to read the stars as he pretended, she didn't believe he knew his letters in 'em, or at best that he had got further than words in one syllable; but Tom, not minding this (for he was in spirits after the Madeira), looks with an agreeable air towards the young ladies, and, kissing his hand to both, says to the old gentleman, 'Which is which?'

"'This,' says the old gentleman, leading out the hand-somest, if one of 'em could possibly be said to be handsomer than the other—'this is my niece, Miss Fanny Barker.'

"'If you'll permit me, Miss,' says Tom, 'being a noble stranger and a favourite of the planets, I will conduct myself as such.' With these words, he kisses the young lady in a very affable way, turns to the old gentleman, slaps him on the back, and says, 'When's it to come off, my buck?'

"The young lady coloured so deep, and her lip trembled so much, gentlemen, that Tom really thought she was going to cry. But she kept her feelings down, and turning to the old gentleman, says, 'Dear uncle, though you have the abso-lute disposal of my hand and fortune, and though you mean well in disposing of 'em thus, I ask you whether you don't think this is a mistake? Don't you think, dear uncle,' she says, 'that the stars must be in error? Is it not possible that the comet may have put 'em out?'

"'The stars,' says the old gentleman, 'couldn't make a mistake if they tried. Emma,' he says to the other young lady.

"'Yes, papa,' says she.

"'The same day that makes your cousin Mrs. Grig will unite you to the gifted Mooney. No remonstrance—no tears. Now, Mr. Grig, let me conduct you to that hallowed ground, that philosophical retreat, where my friend and partner, the gifted Mooney of whom I have just now spoken, is even now pursuing those discoveries which shall enrich us with the precious metal, and make us masters of the world. Come, Mr. Grig,' he says.

"'With all my heart, Sir,' replies Tom; 'and luck to the gifted Mooney, say I—not so much on his account as for our worthy selves!' With this sentiment, Tom kissed his hand to the ladies again, and followed him out; having the gratification to perceive, as he looked back, that they were all hanging on by the arms and legs of Galileo Isaac Newton Flamstead, to prevent him from following the noble stranger, and tearing him to pieces.

"Gentlemen, Tom's father-in-law that was to be, took him by the hand, and having lighted a little lamp, led him across a paved court-yard at the back of the house, into a very large, dark, gloomy room: filled with all manner of bottles, globes, books, telescopes, crocodiles, alligators, and other scientific instruments of every kind. In the centre of this room was a stove or furnace, with what Tom called a pot, but which in my opinion was a crucible, in full boil. In one corner was a sort of ladder leading through the roof; and up this ladder the old gentleman pointed, as he said in a whisper:

"'The observatory. Mr. Mooney is even now watching for the precise time at which we are to come into all the riches of the earth. It will be necessary for he and I, alone in that silent place, to cast your nativity before the hour arrives. Put the day and minute of your birth on this piece of paper, and leave the rest to me.'

"'You don't mean to say,' says Tom, doing as he was told and giving him back the paper, 'that I'm to wait here long, do you? It's a precious dismal place.'

"'Hush!' says the old gentleman. 'It's hallowed ground. Farewell!'

"'Stop a minute,' says Tom. 'What a hurry you're in! What's in that large bottle yonder?'

"'It's a child with three heads,' says the old gentleman; 'and everything else in proportion.'

"'Why don't you throw him away?' says Tom. 'What do you keep such unpleasant things here for?'

"'Throw him away!' cries the old gentleman. 'We use him constantly in astrology. He's a charm.'

"'I shouldn't have thought it,' says Tom, 'from his appearance. *Must* you go, I say?'

"The old gentleman makes him no answer, but climbs up the ladder in a greater bustle than ever. Tom looked after his legs till there was nothing of him left, and then sat down to wait; feeling (so he used to say) as comfortable as if he was going to be made a freemason, and they were heating the pokers.

"Tom waited so long, gentlemen, that he began to think it must be getting on for midnight at least, and felt more dismal and lonely than ever he had done in all his life. He tried every means of whiling away the time, but it never had seemed to move so slow. First, he took a nearer view of the child with three heads, and thought what a comfort it must have been to his parents. Then he looked up a long telescope which was pointed out of the window, but saw nothing particular, in consequence of the stopper being on at the other end. Then he came to a skeleton in a glass case, labelled, 'Skeleton of a Gentleman—prepared by Mr. Mooney,'—which made him hope that Mr. Mooney might not be in the habit of preparing gentlemen that way without their own consent. A hundred times, at least, he looked into the pot where they were boiling the philosopher's stone down to the proper consistency, and wondered whether it was nearly done. 'When it is,' thinks Tom, 'I'll send out for sixpenn'orth of sprats, and turn 'em into gold fish for a first experiment.' Besides which, he made up his mind, gentlemen, to have a country-house and a park; and to plant a bit of it with a double row of gas-lamps a mile long, and go out every night with a French-polished mahogany ladder, and two servants in livery behind him, to light 'em for his own pleasure.

"At length and at last, the old gentleman's legs appeared upon the steps leading through the roof, and he came slowly down: bringing along with him, the gifted Mooney. This Mooney, gentlemen, was even more scientific in appearance than his friend; and had, as Tom often declared upon his word and honour, the dirtiest face we can possibly know of, in this imperfect state of existence.

"Gentlemen, you are all aware that if a scientific man isn't absent in his mind, he's of no good at all. Mr. Mooney was so absent, that when the old gentleman said to him, 'Shake hands with Mr. Grig,' he put out his leg. 'Here's a mind, Mr. Grig!' cries the old gentleman in a rapture. 'Here's philosophy! Here's rumination! Don't disturb him,' he says, 'for this is amazing!'

"Tom had no wish to disturb him, having nothing particular to say; but he was so uncommonly amazing, that the old gentleman got impatient, and determined to give him an electric shock to bring him to—'for you must know, Mr. Grig,' he says, 'that we always keep a strongly charged battery, ready for that purpose.' These means being resorted to, gentlemen, the gifted Mooney revived with a loud roar, and he no sooner came to himself than both he and the old gentleman looked at Tom with compassion, and shed tears abundantly.

"'My dear friend,' says the old gentleman to the Gifted, 'prepare him.'

"'I say,' cries Tom, falling back, 'none of that, you know. No preparing by Mr. Mooney if you please.'

"'Alas!' replies the old gentleman, 'you don't understand us. My friend, inform him of his fate.—I can't.'

"The Gifted mustered up his voice, after many efforts, and informed Tom that his nativity had been carefully cast, and he would expire at exactly thirty-five minutes, twenty-seven seconds, and five-sixths of a second past nine o'clock, a.m., on that day two months.

"Gentlemen, I leave you to judge what were Tom's feelings at this announcement, on the eve of matrimony and endless riches. 'I think,' he says in a trembling voice, 'there must be a mistake in the working of that sum. Will you do me the favour to cast it up again?'—'There is no mistake,' replies the old gentleman, 'it is confirmed by Francis Moore, Physician. Here is the prediction for to-morrow two months.' And he showed him the page, where sure enough were these words—'The decease of a great person may be looked for, about this time.'

"'Which,' says the old gentleman, 'is clearly you, Mr. Grig.'

"'Too clearly,' cries Tom, sinking into a chair, and giving one hand to the old gentleman, and one to the Gifted. 'The orb of day has set on Thomas Grig for ever!'

"At this affecting remark, the Gifted shed tears again, and the other two mingled their tears with his, in a kind—if I may use the expression—of Mooney and Co.'s entire. But the old gentleman recovering first, observed that this was only a reason for hastening the marriage, in order that Tom's distinguished race might be transmitted to posterity; and requesting the Gifted to console Mr. Grig during his temporary absence, he withdrew to settle the preliminaries with his niece immediately.

"And now, gentlemen, a very extraordinary and remark-able occurrence took place ; for as Tom sat in a melancholy way in one chair, and the Gifted sat in a melancholy way in another, a couple of doors were thrown violently open, the two young ladies rushed in, and one knelt down in a loving attitude at Tom's feet, and the other at the Gifted's. So far, perhaps, as Tom was concerned—as he used to say—you will say there was nothing strange in this : but you will be of a different opinion when you understand that Tom's young lady was kneeling to the Gifted, and the Gifted's young lady was kneeling to Tom.

" 'Halloa ! stop a minute !' cries Tom ; 'here's a mistake. I need condoling with by sympathising woman, under my afflicting circumstances ; but we're out in the figure. Change partners, Mooney.'

" 'Monster !' cries Tom's young lady, clinging to the Gifted.

" 'Miss !' says Tom.   ' Is *that* your manners ?'

" 'I abjure thee !' cries Tom's young lady.   'I renounce thee. I never will be thine. Thou,' she says to the Gifted, 'art the object of my first and all-engrossing passion. Wrapt in thy sublime visions, thou hast not perceived my love ; but, driven to despair, I now shake off the woman and avow it. Oh, cruel, cruel man !' With which reproach she laid her head upon the Gifted's breast, and put her arms about him in the tenderest manner possible, gentlemen.

" 'And I,' says the other young lady, in a sort of ecstasy, that made Tom start—'I hereby abjure my chosen husband too. Hear me, Goblin !'—this was to the Gifted—'Hear me ! I hold thee in the deepest detestation. The maddening interview of this one night has filled my soul with love—but not for thee. It is for thee, for thee, young man,' she cries to Tom. 'As Monk Lewis finely observes, Thomas, Thomas, I am thine, Thomas, Thomas, thou art mine : thine for ever, mine for ever !' with which words, she became very tender likewise.

"Tom and the Gifted, gentlemen, as you may believe, looked at each other in a very awkward manner, and with thoughts not at all complimentary to the two young ladies. As to the Gifted, I have heard Tom say often, that he was certain he was in a fit, and had it inwardly.

" 'Speak to me ! Oh, speak to me !' cries Tom's young lady to the Gifted.

"'I don't want to speak to anybody,' he says, finding his voice at last, and trying to push her away. 'I think I had better go. I'm—I'm frightened,' he says, looking about as if he had lost something.

"'Not one look of love!' she cries. 'Hear me while I declare——'

"'I don't know how to look a look of love,' he says, all in a maze. 'Don't declare anything. I don't want to hear anybody.'

"'That's right!' cries the old gentleman (who it seems had been listening). 'That's right! Don't hear her. Emma shall marry you to-morrow, my friend, whether she likes it or not, and *she* shall marry Mr. Grig.'

"Gentlemen, these words were no sooner out of his mouth than Galileo Isaac Newton Flamstead (who it seems had been listening too) darts in, and spinning round and round, like a young giant's top, cries, 'Let her. Let her. I'm fierce; I'm furious. I give her leave. I'll never marry anybody after this—never. It isn't safe. She is the falsest of the false,' he cries, tearing his hair and gnashing his teeth.; 'and I'll live and die a bachelor!'

"'The little boy,' observed the Gifted gravely, 'albeit of tender years, has spoken wisdom. I have been led to the contemplation of woman-kind, and will not adventure on the troubled waters of matrimony.'

"'What!' says the old gentleman, 'not marry my daughter! Won't you, Mooney? Not if I make her? Won't you? Won't you?'

"'No,' says Mooney, 'I won't. And if anybody asks me any more, I'll run away, and never come back again.'

"'Mr. Grig,' says the old gentleman, 'the stars must be obeyed. You have not changed your mind because of a little girlish folly—eh, Mr. Grig?'

"Tom, gentlemen, had had his eyes about him, and was pretty sure that all this was a device and trick of the waiting-maid, to put him off his inclination. He had seen her hiding and skipping about the two doors, and had observed that a very little whispering from her pacified the Salamander directly. 'So,' thinks Tom, 'this is a plot—but it won't fit.'

"'Eh, Mr. Grig?' says the old gentleman.

"'Why, Sir,' says Tom, pointing to the crucible, 'if the soup's nearly ready——'

"'Another hour beholds the consummation of our labours,' returned the old gentleman.

"'Very good,' says Tom, with a mournful air. 'It's only for two months, but I may as well be the richest man in the world even for that time. I'm not particular, I'll take her, Sir. I'll take her.'

"The old gentleman was in a rapture to find Tom still in the same mind, and drawing the young lady towards him by little and little, was joining their hands by main force, when all of a sudden, gentlemen, the crucible blows up, with a great crash; everybody screams; the room is filled with smoke; and Tom, not knowing what may happen next, throws himself into a Fancy attitude, and says, 'Come on, if you're a man!' without addressing himself to anybody in particular.

"'The labours of fifteen years,' says the old gentleman, clasping his hands and looking down upon the Gifted, who was saving the pieces, 'are destroyed in an instant!'—And I am told, gentlemen, by-the-bye, that this same philosopher's stone would have been discovered a hundred times at least, to speak within bounds, if it wasn't for the one unfortunate circumstance that the apparatus always blows up, when it's on the very point of succeeding.

"Tom turns pale when he hears the old gentleman expressing himself to this unpleasant effect, and stammers out that if it's quite agreeable to all parties, he would like to know exactly what has happened, and what change has really taken place in the prospects of that company.

"'We have failed for the present, Mr. Grig,' says the old gentleman, wiping his forehead. 'And I regret it the more, because I have in fact invested my niece's five thousand pounds in this glorious speculation. But don't be cast down,' he says, anxiously—'in another fifteen years, Mr. Grig——'

"'Oh!' cries Tom, letting the young lady's hand fall. 'Were the stars very positive about this union, Sir?'

"'They were,' says the old gentleman.

"'I'm sorry to hear it,' Tom makes answer, 'for it's no go, Sir.'

"'No what!' cries the old gentleman.

"'Go, Sir,' says Tom, fiercely. 'I forbid the banns.' And with these words—which are the very words he used—he sat himself down in a chair, and, laying his head upon the table, thought with a secret grief of what was to come to pass on that day two months.

"Tom always said, gentlemen, that that waiting-maid was the artfullest minx he had ever seen; and he left it in writing in this country when he went to colonize abroad, that he was certain in his own mind she and the Salamander had blown up the philosopher's stone on purpose, and to cut him out of his property. I believe Tom was in the right, gentlemen; but whether or no, she comes forward at this point, and says, 'May I speak, Sir?' and the old gentleman answering, 'Yes, you may,' she goes on to say that 'the stars are no doubt quite right in every respect, but Tom is not the man.' And she says, 'Don't you remember, Sir, that when the clock struck five this afternoon, you gave Master Galileo a rap on the head with your telescope, and told him to get out of the way?' 'Yes, I do,' says the old gentleman. 'Then,' says the waiting-maid, 'I say he's the man, and the prophecy is fulfilled.' The old gentleman staggers at this, as if somebody had hit him a blow on the chest, and cries, 'He! why he's a boy!' Upon that, gentlemen, the Salamander cries out that he'll be twenty-one next Lady-day; and complains that his father has always been so busy with the sun round which the earth revolves, that he has never taken any notice of the son that revolves round him; and that he hasn't had a new suit of clothes since he was fourteen; and that he wasn't even taken out of nankeen frocks and trousers till he was quite unpleasant in 'em; and touches on a good many more family matters to the same purpose. To make short of a long story, gentlemen, they all talk together, and cry together, and remind the old gentleman that as to the noble family, his own grandfather would have been lord mayor if he hadn't died at a dinner the year before; and they show him by all kinds of arguments that if the cousins are married, the prediction comes true every way. At last, the old gentleman being quite convinced, gives in; and joins their hands; and leaves his daughter to marry anybody she likes; and they are all well pleased; and the Gifted as well as any of them.

"In the middle of this little family party, gentlemen, sits Tom all the while, as miserable as you like. But, when everything else is arranged, the old gentleman's daughter says, that their strange conduct was a little device of the waiting-maid's to disgust the lovers he had chosen for 'em, and will he forgive her? and if he will, perhaps he might even find her a husband—and when she says that, she looks uncommon hard at Tom. Then the waiting-maid says that, oh dear! she couldn't abear Mr. Grig should think she wanted him to marry her; and that she had even gone so far as to refuse the last lamplighter, who was now a literary character (having set up as a bill-sticker); and that she hoped Mr. Grig would not suppose she was on her last legs by any means, for the baker was very strong in his attentions at that moment, and as to the butcher, he was frantic. And I don't know how much more she might have said, gentlemen (for, as you know, this kind of young women are rare ones to talk), if the old gentleman hadn't cut in suddenly, and asked Tom if he'd have her, with ten pounds to recompense him for his loss of time and disappointment, and as a kind of bribe to keep the story secret.

"'It don't much matter, Sir,' says Tom, 'I ain't long for this world. Eight weeks of marriage, especially with this young woman, might reconcile me to my fate. I think,' he says, 'I could go off easy after that.' With which he embraces her with a very dismal face, and groans in a way that might move a heart of stone—even of philosopher's stone.

"'Egad,' says the old gentleman, 'that reminds me—this bustle put it out of my head—there was a figure wrong. He'll live to a green old age—eighty-seven at least!'

"'How much, Sir?' cries Tom.

"'Eighty-seven!' says the old gentleman.

"Without another word, Tom flings himself on the old gentleman's neck; throws up his hat; cuts a caper; defies the waiting-maid; and refers her to the butcher.

"'You won't marry her!' says the old gentleman, angrily.

"'And live after it!' says Tom. 'I'd sooner marry a mermaid with a small-tooth comb and looking-glass.'

"'Then take the consequences,' says the other.

"With those words—I beg your kind attention here, gentlemen, for it's worth your notice—the old gentleman wetted the forefinger of his right hand in some of the liquor from the crucible that was spilt on the floor, and drew a small triangle on Tom's forehead. The room swam before his eyes, and he found himself in the watch-house."

"Found himself *where?*" cried the vice, on behalf of the company generally.

"In the watch-house," said the chairman. "It was late at night, and he found himself in the very watch-house from which he had been let out that morning."

"Did he go home?" asked the vice.

"The watch-house people rather objected to that," said the chairman; "so he stopped there that night, and went before the magistrate in the morning. 'Why, you're here again, are you?' says the magistrate, adding insult to injury; 'we'll trouble you for five shillings more, if you can conveniently spare the money.' Tom told him he had been enchanted, but it was of no use. He told the contractors the same, but they wouldn't believe him. It was very hard upon him, gentlemen, as he often said, for was it likely he'd go and invent such a tale? They shook their heads and told him he'd say anything but his prayers—as indeed he would; there's no doubt about that. It was the only imputation on his moral character that ever *I* heard of."

TO BE READ AT DUSK

CHARACTERS

Carolina, maid to the young bride.

Clara, a young bride, on her wedding-trip.

Signor Dellombra, a dark, remarkable-looking, accomplished man, of a secret and reserved air.

An English Gentleman, Clara's husband.

Giovanni Baptista, a Genoese courier.

James, a bachelor in business with his brother.

John, twin-brother to James.

A Neapolitan Courier.

A Swiss Courier

Wilhelm, a German courier.

TO BE READ AT DUSK

ONE, two, three, four, five. There were five of them.

Five couriers, sitting on a bench outside the convent on the summit of the Great St. Bernard in Switzerland, looking at the remote heights, stained by the setting sun, as if a mighty quantity of red wine had been broached upon the mountain top, and had not yet had time to sink into the snow.

This is not my simile. It was made for the occasion by the stoutest courier, who was a German. None of the others took any more notice of it than they took of me, sitting on another bench on the other side of the convent door, smoking my cigar, like them, and—also like them—looking at the reddened snow, and at the lonely shed hard by, where the bodies of belated travellers, dug out of it, slowly wither away, knowing no corruption in that cold region.

The wine upon the mountain top soaked in as we looked; the mountain became white; the sky, a very dark blue; the wind rose; and the air turned piercing cold. The five couriers buttoned their rough coats. There being no safer man to imitate in all such proceedings than a courier, I buttoned mine.

The mountain in the sunset had stopped the five couriers in a conversation. It is a sublime sight, likely to stop conversation. The mountain being now out of the sunset, they resumed. Not that I had heard any part of their previous discourse; for indeed, I had not then broken away from the American gentleman, in the travellers' parlour of the convent, who, sitting with his face to the fire, had undertaken to realise to me the whole progress of events which had led to the accumulation by the Honourable

Ananias Dodger of one of the largest acquisitions of dollars ever made in our country.

"My God!" said the Swiss courier, speaking in French, which I do not hold (as some authors appear to do) to be such an all-sufficient excuse for a naughty word, that I have only to write it in that language to make it innocent; "if you talk of ghosts——"

"But I *don't* talk of ghosts," said the German.

"Of what then?" asked the Swiss.

"If I knew of what then," said the German, "I should probably know a great deal more."

It was a good answer, I thought, and it made me curious. So I moved my position to that corner of my bench which was nearest to them, and leaning my back against the convent wall, heard perfectly, without appearing to attend.

"Thunder and lightning!" said the German, warming, "when a certain man is coming to see you, unexpectedly; and, without his own knowledge, sends some invisible messenger, to put the idea of him into your head all day, what do you call that? When you walk along a crowded street—at Frankfort, Milan, London, Paris—and think that a passing stranger is like your friend Heinrich, and then that another passing stranger is like your friend Heinrich, and so begin to have a strange foreknowledge that presently you'll meet your friend Heinrich—which you do, though you believed him at Trieste—what do you call *that?*"

"It's not uncommon, either," murmured the Swiss and the other three.

"Uncommon!" said the German. "It's as common as cherries in the Black Forest. It's as common as maccaroni at Naples. And Naples reminds me! When the old Marchesa Senzanima shrieks at a card-party on the Chiaja—as I heard and saw her, for it happened in a Bavarian family of mine, and I was overlooking the service that evening—I say, when the old Marchesa starts up at the card-table, white through her rouge, and cries, 'My sister in Spain is dead! I felt her cold touch on my back!'—and when that sister *is* dead at the moment—what do you call that?"

"Or when the blood of San Gennaro liquefies at the request of the clergy—as all the world knows that it does regularly once a year, in my native city," said the Neapolitan courier after a pause, with a comical look, "what do you call that?"

"*That!*" cried the German. "Well, I think I know a name for that."

"Miracle?" said the Neapolitan, with the same sly face.

The German merely smoked and laughed; and they all smoked and laughed.

"Bah!" said the German, presently. "I speak of things that really do happen. When I want to see the conjurer, I pay to see a professed one, and have my money's worth. Very strange things do happen without ghosts. Ghosts! Giovanni Baptista, tell your story of the English bride. There's no ghost in that, but something full as strange. Will any man tell me what?"

As there was a silence among them, I glanced around. He whom I took to be Baptista was lighting a fresh cigar. He presently went on to speak. He was a Genoese, as I judged.

"The story of the English bride?" said he. "Basta! one ought not to call so slight a thing a story. Well, it's all one. But it's true. Observe me well, gentlemen, it's true. That which glitters is not always gold: but what I am going to tell, is true."

He repeated this more than once.

Ten years ago, I took my credentials to an English gentleman at Long's Hotel, in Bond Street, London, who was about to travel—it might be for one year, it might be for two. He approved of them; likewise of me. He was pleased to make inquiry. The testimony that he received was favourable. He engaged me by the six months, and my entertainment was generous.

He was young, handsome, very happy. He was enamoured of a fair young English lady, with a sufficient fortune, and they were going to be married. It was the wedding-trip, in short, that we were going to take. For three months' rest in the hot weather (it was early summer then) he had hired an old place on the Riviera, at an easy distance from my city, Genoa, on the road to Nice. Did I know that place? Yes; I told him I knew it well. It was an old palace with great gardens. It was a little bare, and it was a little dark and gloomy, being close surrounded by trees; but it was spacious, ancient, grand, and on the seashore. He said it had been so described to him exactly, and he was well pleased that I knew it. For its being a little bare of furniture, all such places were. For its being a little gloomy, he had hired it principally for the gardens, and he and my mistress would pass the summer weather in their shade.

"So all goes well, Baptista?" said he.

"Indubitably, signore; very well."

We had a travelling chariot for our journey, newly built for us, and in all respects complete. All we had was complete; we wanted for nothing. The marriage took place. They were happy. I was happy, seeing all so bright, being so well situated, going to my own city, teaching my language in the rumble to the maid, la bella Carolina, whose heart was gay with laughter: who was young and rosy.

The time flew. But I observed—listen to this, I pray! (and here the courier dropped his voice)—I observed my mistress sometimes brooding in a manner very strange; in a frightened manner; in an unhappy manner; with a cloudy, uncertain alarm upon her. I think that I began to notice this when I was walking up hills by the carriage side, and master had gone on in front. At any rate, I remember that it impressed itself upon my mind one evening in the South of France, when she called to me to call master back; and when he came back, and walked for a long way, talking encouragingly and affectionately to her, with his hand upon the open window, and hers in it. Now and then, he laughed in a merry way, as if he were bantering her out of something. By-and-by, she laughed, and then all went well again.

It was curious. I asked la bella Carolina, the pretty little one, Was mistress unwell?—No.—Out of spirits?—No.—Fearful of bad roads, or brigands?—No. And what made it more mysterious was, the pretty little one would not look at me in giving answer, but *would* look at the view.

But one day she told me the secret.

"If you must know," said Carolina, "I find, from what I have overheard, that mistress is haunted."

"How haunted?"

"By a dream."

"What dream?"

"By a dream of a face. For three nights before her marriage, she saw a face in a dream—always the same face, and only One."

"A terrible face?"

"No. The face of a dark, remarkable-looking man, in black, with black hair and a grey moustache—a handsome man except for a reserved and secret air. Not a face she ever saw, or at all like a face she ever saw. Doing nothing in the dream but looking at her fixedly, out of darkness."

"Does the dream come back?"

"Never. The recollection of it, is all her trouble."

"And why does it trouble her?"

Carolina shook her head.

"That's master's question," said la bella. "She don't know. She wonders why, herself. But I heard her tell him, only last night, that if she was to find a picture of that face in our Italian house (which she is afraid she will) she did not know how she could ever bear it."

Upon my word, I was fearful after this (said the Genoese courier) of our coming to the old palazzo, lest some such ill-starred picture should happen to be there. I knew there were many there; and, as we got nearer and nearer to the place, I wished the whole gallery in the crater of Vesuvius. To mend the matter, it was a stormy dismal evening when we, at last, approached that part of the Riviera. It thundered; and the thunder of my city and its environs, rolling among the high hills, is very loud. The lizards ran in and out of the chinks in the broken stone wall of the garden, as if they were frightened; the frogs bubbled and croaked their loudest; the sea-wind moaned, and the wet trees dripped; and the lightning—body of San. Lorenzo, how it lightened!

We all know what an old palace in or near Genoa is—how time and the sea air have blotted it—how the drapery painted on the outer walls has peeled off in great flakes of plaster—how the lower windows are darkened with rusty bars of iron—how the courtyard is overgrown with grass—how the outer buildings are dilapidated—how the whole pile seems devoted to ruin. Our palazzo was one of the true kind. It had been shut up close for months. Months?—years!—it had an earthy smell, like a tomb. The scent of the orange trees on the broad back terrace, and of the lemons ripening on the wall, and of some shrubs that grew around a broken fountain, had got into the house somehow, and had never been able to get out again. There was, in every room, an aged smell, grown faint with confinement. It pined in all the cupboards and drawers. In the little rooms of communication between great rooms, it was stifling. If you turned a picture

—to come back to the pictures—there it still was, clinging to the wall behind the frame, like a sort of bat.

The lattice-blinds were close shut, all over the house. There were two ugly grey old women in the house, to take care of it; one of them with a spindle, who stood winding and mumbling in the doorway, and who would as soon have let in the devil as the air. Master, mistress, la bella Carolina, and I, went all through the palazzo. I went first, though I have named myself last, opening the windows and the lattice-blinds, and shaking down on myself splashes of rain, and scraps of mortar, and now and then a dozing mosquito, or a monstrous, fat, blotchy, Genoese spider.

When I had let the evening light into a room, master, mistress, and la bella Carolina, entered. Then we looked round at all the pictures, and I went forward again into another room. Mistress secretly had great fear of meeting with the likeness of that face—we all had; but there was no such thing. The Madonna and Bambino, San Francisco, San Sebastiano, Venus, Santa Caterina, Angels, Brigands, Friars, Temples at Sunset, Battles, White Horses, Forests, Apostles, Doges, all my old acquaintances many times repeated?—yes Dark handsome man in black, reserved and secret, with black hair and grey moustache, looking fixedly at mistress out of darkness?—no.

At last we got through all the rooms and all the pictures, and came out into the gardens. They were pretty well kept, being rented by a gardener, and were large and shady. In one place there was a rustic theatre, open to the sky; the stage a green slope; the coulisses, three entrances upon a side, sweet-smelling leafy screens. Mistress moved her bright eyes, even there, as if she looked to see the face come in upon the scene; but all was well.

"Now, Clara," master said, in a low voice, "you see that it is nothing? You are happy."

Mistress was much encouraged. She soon accustomed herself to that grim palazzo, and would sing, and play the harp, and copy the old pictures, and stroll with master under the green trees and vines all day. She was beautiful. He was happy. He would laugh and say to me, mounting his horse for his morning ride before the heat:

"All goes well, Baptista!"

"Yes, signore, thank God, very well."

We kept no company. I took la bella to the Duomo and

Annunciata, to the Café, to the Opera, to the village Festa, to the Public Garden, to the Day Theatre, to the Marionetti. The pretty little one was charmed with all she saw. She learnt Italian—heavens! miraculously! Was mistress quite forgetful of that dream? I asked Carolina sometimes. Nearly, said la bella—almost. It was wearing out.

One day master received a letter, and called me.

" Baptista ! "

" Signore ! "

" A gentleman who is presented to me will dine here to-day. He is called the Signor Dellombra. Let me dine like a prince."

It was an odd name. I did not know that name. But there had been many noblemen and gentlemen pursued by Austria on political suspicions, lately, and some names had changed. Perhaps this was one. Altro! Dellombra was as good a name to me as another.

When the Signor Dellombra came to dinner (said the Genoese courier in the low voice, into which he had subsided once before), I showed him into the reception-room, the great sala of the old palazzo. Master received him with cordiality, and presented him to mistress. As she rose, her face changed, she gave a cry, and fell upon the marble floor.

Then I turned my head to the Signor Dellombra, and saw that he was dressed in black, and had a reserved and secret air, and was a dark remarkable-looking man, with black hair and a grey moustache.

Master raised mistress in his arms, and carried her to her own room, where I sent la bella Carolina straight. La bella told me afterwards that mistress was nearly terrified to death, and that she wandered in her mind about her dream, all night.

Master was vexed and anxious—almost angry, and yet full of solicitude. The Signor Dellombra was a courtly gentleman, and spoke with great respect and sympathy of mistress's being so ill. The African wind had been blowing for some days (they had told him at his hotel of the Maltese Cross), and he knew that it was often hurtful. He hoped the beautiful lady would recover soon. He begged permission to retire, and to renew his visit when he should have the happiness of hearing that she was better. Master would not allow of this, and they dined alone.

He withdrew early. Next day he called at the gate, on

horseback, to inquire for mistress. He did so two or three times in that week.

What I observed myself, and what la bella Carolina told me, united to explain to me that master had now set his mind on curing mistress of her fanciful terror. He was all kindness, but he was sensible and firm. He reasoned with her, that to encourage such fancies was to invite melancholy, if not madness. That it rested with herself to be herself. That if she once resisted her strange weakness, so successfully as to receive the Signor Dellombra as an English lady would receive any other guest, it was for ever conquered. To make an end, the signore came again, and mistress received him without marked distress (though with constraint and apprehension still), and the evening passed serenely. Master was so delighted with this change, and so anxious to confirm it, that the Signor Dellombra became a constant guest. He was accomplished in pictures, books, and music; and his society, in any grim palazzo, would have been welcome.

I used to notice, many times, that mistress was not quite recovered. She would cast down her eyes and droop her head, before the Signor Dellombra, or would look at him with a terrified and fascinated glance, as if his presence had some evil influence or power upon her. Turning from her to him, I used to see him in the shaded gardens, or the large half-lighted sala, looking, as I might say, "fixedly upon her out of darkness." But, truly, I had not forgotten la bella Carolina's words describing the face in the dream.

After his second visit I heard master say:

"Now, see, my dear Clara, it's over! Dellombra has come and gone, and your apprehension is broken like glass."

"Will he—will he ever come again?" asked mistress.

"Again? Why, surely, over and over again! Are you cold?" (she shivered).

"No, dear—but—he terrifies me: are you sure that he need come again?"

"The surer for the question, Clara!" replied master, cheerfully.

But he was very hopeful of her complete recovery now, and grew more and more so every day. She was beautiful. He was happy.

"All goes well, Baptista?" he would say to me again.

"Yes, signore, thank God; very well."

We were all (said the Genoese courier, constraining himself to speak a little louder), we were all at Rome for the Carnival. I had been out, all day, with a Sicilian, a friend of mine, and a courier, who was there with an English family. As I returned at night to our hotel, I met the little Carolina, who never stirred from home alone, running distractedly along the Corso.

"Carolina! What's the matter?"

"O Baptista! O, for the Lord's sake! where is my mistress?"

"Mistress, Carolina?"

"Gone since morning—told me, when master went out on his day's journey, not to call her, for she was tired with not resting in the night (having been in pain), and would lie in bed until the evening; then get up refreshed. She is gone!—she is gone! Master has come back, broken down the door, and she is gone! My beautiful, my good, my innocent mistress!"

The pretty little one so cried, and raved, and tore herself that I could not have held her, but for her swooning on my arm as if she had been shot. Master came up—in manner, face, or voice, no more the master that I knew, than I was he. He took me (I laid the little one upon her bed in the hotel, and left her with the chamber-women), in a carriage, furiously through the darkness, across the desolate Campagna. When it was day, and we stopped at a miserable post-house, all the horses had been hired twelve hours ago, and sent away in different directions. Mark me! by the Signor Dellombra, who had passed there in a carriage, with a frightened English lady crouching in one corner.

I never heard (said the Genoese courier, drawing a long breath) that she was ever traced beyond that spot. All I know is, that she vanished into infamous oblivion, with the dreaded face beside her that she had seen in her dream.

"What do you call *that*?" said the German courier, triumphantly. "Ghosts! There are no ghosts *there!* What do you call this, that I am going to tell you? Ghosts! There are no ghosts *here!*"

I took an engagement once (pursued the German courier) with an English gentleman, elderly and a bachelor, to travel through my country, my Fatherland. He was a merchant who traded with my country and knew the language, but who had never been there since he was a boy—as I judge, some sixty years before.

His name was James, and he had a twin-brother John, also a bachelor. Between these brothers there was a great affection. They were in business together, at Goodman's Fields, but they did not live together. Mr. James dwelt in Poland Street, turning out of Oxford Street, London; Mr. John resided by Epping Forest.

Mr. James and I were to start for Germany in about a week. The exact day depended on business. Mr. John came to Poland Street (where I was staying in the house), to pass that week with Mr. James. But he said to his brother on the second day, "I don't feel very well, James. There's not much the matter with me; but I think I am a little gouty. I'll go home and put myself under the care of my old house-keeper, who understands my ways. If I get quite better, I'll come back and see you before you go. If I don't feel well enough to resume my visit where I leave it off, why *you* will come and see *me* before you go." Mr. James, of course, said he would, and they shook hands—both hands, as they always did—and Mr. John ordered out his old-fashioned chariot and rumbled home.

It was on the second night after that—that is to say, the fourth in the week—when I was awoke out of my sound sleep by Mr. James coming into my bedroom in his flannel-gown, with a lighted candle. He sat upon the side of my bed, and looking at me, said:

"Wilhelm, I have reason to think I have got some strange illness upon me."

I then perceived that there was a very unusual expression in his face.

"Wilhelm," said he, "I am not afraid or ashamed to tell you what I might be afraid or ashamed to tell another man. You come from a sensible country, where mysterious things are inquired into and are not settled to have been weighed and measured—or to have been unweighable and unmeasur-able—or in either case to have been completely disposed of, for all time—ever so many years ago. I have just now seen the phantom of my brother."

I confess (said the German courier) that it gave me a little tingling of the blood to hear it.

"I have just now seen," Mr. James repeated, looking full at me, that I might see how collected he was, " the phantom of my brother John. I was sitting up in bed, unable to sleep, when it came into my room, in a white dress, and regarding me earnestly, passed up to the end of the room, glanced at some papers on my writing-desk, turned, and, still looking earnestly àt me as it passed the bed, went out at the door. Now, I am not in the least mad, and am not in the least disposed to invest that phantom with any external existence out of myself. I think it is a warning to me that I am ill; and I think I had better be bled."

I got out of bed directly (said the German courier) and began to get on my clothes, begging him not to be alarmed, and telling him that I would go myself to the doctor. I was just ready, when we heard a loud knocking and ringing at the street door. My room being an attic at the back, and Mr. James's being the second-floor room in the front, we went down to his room, and put up the window, to see what was the matter.

"Is that Mr. James?" said a man below, falling back to the opposite side of the way to look up.

"It is," said Mr. James, "and you are my brother's man, Robert."

"Yes, Sir. I am sorry to say, Sir, that Mr. John is ill. He is very bad, Sir. It is even feared that he may be lying at the point of death. He wants to see you, Sir. I have a chaise here. Pray come to him. Pray lose no time."

Mr. James and I looked at one another. "Wilhelm," said he, "this is strange. I wish you to come with me!" I helped him to dress, partly there and partly in the chaise; and no grass grew under the horses' iron shoes between Poland Street and the Forest.

Now, mind! (said the German courier) I went with Mr. James into his brother's room, and I saw and heard myself what follows.

His brother lay upon his bed, at the upper end of a long bed-chamber. His old housekeeper was there, and others were there: I think three others were there, if not four, and they had been with him since early in the afternoon. He was in white, like the figure—necessarily so, because he had his night-dress on. He looked like the figure—necessarily so, because he looked earnestly at his brother when he saw him come into the room.

But, when his brother reached the bed-side, he slowly

raised himself in bed, and looking full upon him, said these words :

"JAMES, YOU HAVE SEEN ME BEFORE, TO-NIGHT—AND YOU KNOW IT !"

And so died !

I waited, when the German courier ceased, to hear something said of this strange story. The silence was unbroken. I looked round, and the five couriers were gone : so noiselessly that the ghostly mountain might have absorbed them into its eternal snows. By this time, I was by no means in a mood to sit alone in that awful scene, with the chill air coming solemnly upon me—or, if I may tell the truth, to sit alone anywhere. So I went back into the convent-parlour, and, finding the American gentleman still disposed to relate the biography of the Honourable Ananias Dodger, heard it all out.

SUNDAY UNDER
THREE HEADS

DEDICATION

TO THE RIGHT REVEREND THE BISHOP OF LONDON

My Lord,

You were among the first, some years ago, to expatiate on the vicious addiction of the lower classes of society, to Sunday excursions; and were thus instrumental in calling forth occasional demonstrations of those extreme opinions on the subject, which are very generally received with derision, if not with contempt.

Your elevated station, my Lord, affords you countless opportunities of increasing the comforts and pleasures of the humbler classes of society—not by the expenditure of the smallest portion of your princely income, but by merely sanctioning with the influence of your example, their harmless pastimes and innocent recreations.

That your Lordship would ever have contemplated Sunday recreations with so much horror, if you had been at all acquainted with the wants and necessities of the people who indulged in them, I cannot imagine possible. That a Prelate of your elevated rank has the faintest conception of the extent of those wants, and the nature of those necessities, I do not believe.

For these reasons, I venture to address this little Pamphlet to your Lordship's consideration. I am quite conscious that the outlines I have drawn, afford but a very imperfect description of the feelings they are intended to illustrate; but I claim for them one merit—their truth and freedom from exaggeration. I may have fallen short of the mark, but I have never overshot it: and while I have pointed out what appears to me to be injustice on the part of others, I hope I have carefully abstained from committing it myself.

I am, My Lord,

Your Lordship's most obedient, humble Servant,

TIMOTHY SPARKS.

June, 1836.

SUNDAY UNDER
THREE HEADS

I

AS IT IS

THERE are few things from which I derive greater pleasure, than walking through some of the principal streets of London on a fine Sunday, in summer, and watching the cheerful faces of the lively groups with which they are thronged. There is something, to my eyes at least, exceedingly pleasing in the general desire evinced by the humbler classes of society to appear neat and clean on this their only holiday. There are many grave old persons, I know, who shake their heads with an air of profound wisdom, and tell you that poor people dress too well now-a-days; that when they were children, folks knew their stations in life better; that you may depend upon it, no good will come of this sort of thing in the end,—and so forth: but I fancy I can discern in the fine bonnet of the working-man's wife, or the feather-bedizened hat of his child, no inconsiderable evidence of good feeling on the part of the man himself, and an affectionate desire to expend the few shillings he can spare from his week's wages, in improving the appearance and adding to the happiness of those who are nearest and dearest to him. This may be a very heinous and unbecoming degree of vanity, perhaps, and the money might possibly be applied to better uses; it must not be forgotten, however, that it might very easily be devoted to worse: and if two or three faces can be rendered happy and contented, by a trifling improvement of outward appearance, I cannot help thinking that the object is very cheaply purchased, even at the expense of a smart gown, or a gaudy riband. There is a great deal of very unnecessary cant about the over-dressing of the common people. There is not a manufacturer or tradesman in existence, who would not employ a man who takes a reasonable degree of pride in the appearance of himself and those about him, in preference to a sullen slovenly fellow, who works doggedly on, regardless of his own clothing and that of his wife and children, and seeming to take pleasure or pride in nothing.

The pampered aristocrat, whose life is one continued round of licentious pleasures and sensual gratifications; or the gloomy enthusiast, who detests the cheerful amusements he can never enjoy, and envies the healthy feelings he can never know, and who would put down the one and suppress the other, until he made the minds of his fellow-beings as be-sotted and distorted as his own;—neither of these men can by possibility form an adequate notion of what Sunday really is, to those whose lives are spent in sedentary or laborious occupations, and who are accustomed to look forward to it through their whole existence, as their only day of rest from toil, and innocent enjoyment.

The sun that rises over the quiet streets of London on a bright Sunday morning, shines till his setting, on gay and happy faces. Here and there, so early as six o'clock, a young man and woman in their best attire may be seen hurrying along on their way to the house of some acquaintance, who is included in their scheme of pleasure for the day; from whence, after stopping to take "a bit of breakfast," they sally forth, accompanied by several old people, and a whole crowd of young ones, bearing large hand-baskets full of provisions, and Belcher handkerchiefs done up in bundles, with the neck of a bottle sticking out at the top, and closely-packed apples bulging out at the sides,—and away they hurry along the streets leading to the steam-packet wharfs, which are already plentifully sprinkled with parties bound for the same destination. Their good humour and delight know no bounds—for it is a delightful morning, all blue over head, and nothing like a cloud in the whole sky; and even the air of the river at London Bridge is something to them, shut up as they have been, all the week, in close streets and heated rooms. There are dozens of steamers to all sorts of places—Gravesend, Greenwich, and Richmond; and such numbers of people, that when you have once sat down on the deck, it is all but a moral impossibility to get up again—to say nothing of walking about, which is entirely out of the question. Away they go, joking and laughing, and eating and drinking, and admiring everything they see, and pleased with everything they hear, to climb Windmill Hill, and catch a glimpse of the rich corn-fields and beautiful orchards of Kent; or to stroll among the fine old trees of Greenwich Park, and survey the wonders of Shooter's Hill and Lady James's Folly; or to glide past the beautiful meadows of Twickenham and Richmond, and to gaze with a delight which only people like them can know, on every lovely object in the fair prospect around. Boat follows boat, and coach succeeds coach, for the next three hours; but all are filled, and all with the same kind of people—neat and clean, cheerful and contented.

They reach their places of destination, and the taverns are crowded; but there is no drunkenness or brawling, for the class of men who commit the enormity of making Sunday excursions, take their families with them: and this in itself would be a check upon them, even if they were inclined to dissipation, which they really are not. Boisterous their mirth may be, for they have all the excitement of feeling that fresh air and green fields can impart to the dwellers in crowded cities, but it is innocent and harmless. The glass is circulated, and the joke goes round; but the one is free from excess, and the other from offence; and nothing but good humour and hilarity prevail.

In streets like Holborn and Tottenham Court Road, which form the central market of a large neighbourhood, inhabited by a vast number of mechanics and poor people, a few shops are open at an early hour of the morning; and a very poor man, with a thin and sickly woman by his side, may be seen with their little basket in hand, purchasing the scanty quantity of necessaries they can afford, which the time at which the man receives his wages, or his having a good deal of work to do, or the woman's having been out charing till a late hour, prevented their procuring over-night. The coffee-shops too, at which clerks and young men employed in counting-houses can procure their breakfasts, are also open. This class comprises, in a place like London, an enormous number of people, whose limited means prevent their engaging for their lodgings any other apartment than a bedroom, and who have consequently no alternative but to take their breakfasts at a coffee-shop, or go without it altogether. All these places, however, are quickly closed; and by the time the church bells begin to ring, all appearance of traffic has ceased. And then, what are the signs of immorality that meet the eye? Churches are well filled, and Dissenters' chapels are crowded to suffocation. There is no preaching to empty benches, while the drunken and dissolute populace run riot in the streets.

Here is a fashionable church, where the service commences at a late hour, for the accommodation of such members of the congregation—and they are not a few—as may happen to have lingered at the Opera far into the morning of the Sabbath ; an excellent contrivance for poising the balance between God and Mammon, and illustrating the ease with which a man's duties to both may be accommodated and adjusted. How the carriages rattle up, and deposit their richly-dressed burdens beneath the lofty portico ! The powdered footmen glide along the aisle, place the richly-bound prayer-books on the pew desks, slam the doors, and hurry away, leaving the fashionable members of the congregation to inspect each other through their glasses, and to dazzle and glitter in the eyes of the few shabby people in the free seats. The organ peals forth, the hired singers commence a short hymn, and the congregation condescendingly rise, stare about them, and converse in whispers. The clergyman enters the reading-desk,—a young man of noble family and elegant demeanour, notorious at Cambridge for his knowledge of horse-flesh and dancers, and celebrated at Eton for his hopeless stupidity. The service commences. Mark the soft voice in which he reads, and the impressive manner in which he applies his white hand, studded with brilliants, to his perfumed hair. Observe the graceful emphasis with which he offers up the prayers for the King, the Royal Family, and all the Nobility ; and the nonchalance with which he hurries over the more uncomfortable portions of the service, the seventh commandment for instance, with a studied regard for the taste and feeling of his auditors, only to be equalled by that displayed by the sleek divine who succeeds him, who murmurs, in a voice kept down by rich feeding, most comfortable doctrines for exactly twelve minutes, and then arrives at the anxiously expected " Now to God," which is the signal for the dismissal of the congregation. The organ is again heard ; those who have been asleep wake up, and those who have kept awake, smile and seem greatly relieved ; bows and congratulations are exchanged, the livery servants are all bustle and commotion, bang go the steps, up jump the footmen, and off rattle the carriages : the inmates discoursing on the dresses of the congregation, and congratulating themselves on having set so excellent an example to the community in general, and Sunday-pleasurers in particular.

Enter a less orthodox place of religious worship, and observe the contrast. A small close chapel with a white-washed wall, and plain deal pews and pulpit, contains a closely-packed congregation, as different in dress as they are opposed in manner, to that we have just quitted. The hymn is sung—not by paid singers, but by the whole assembly at the loudest pitch of their voices, unaccompanied by any musical instrument, the words being given out, two lines at a time, by the clerk. There is something in the sonorous quavering of the harsh voices, in the lank and hollow faces of the men, and the sour solemnity of the women, which bespeaks this a stronghold of intolerant zeal and ignorant enthusiasm. The preacher enters the pulpit. He is a coarse, hard-faced man of forbidding aspect, clad in rusty black, and bearing in his hand a small plain Bible from which he selects some passage for his text, while the hymn is concluding. The congregation fall upon their knees, and are hushed into profound stillness as he delivers an extempore prayer, in which he calls upon the Sacred Founder of the Christian faith to bless his ministry, in terms of disgusting and impious familiarity not to be described. He begins his oration in a drawling tone, and his hearers listen with silent attention. He grows warmer as he proceeds with his subject, and his gesticulation becomes proportionately violent. He clenches his fists, beats the book upon the desk before him, and swings his arms wildly about his head. The congregation murmur their acquiescence in his doctrines : and a short groan occasionally bears testimony to the moving nature of his eloquence. Encouraged by these symptoms of approval, and working himself up to a pitch of enthusiasm amounting almost to frenzy, he denounces sabbath-breakers with the direst vengeance of offended Heaven. He stretches his body half out of the pulpit, thrusts forth his arms with frantic gestures, and blasphemously calls upon the Deity to visit with eternal torments those who turn aside from the word, as interpreted and preached by—himself. A low moaning is heard, the women rock their bodies to and fro, and wring their hands; the preacher's fervour increases, the perspiration starts upon his brow, his face is flushed, and he clenches his hands convulsively, as he draws a hideous and appalling picture of the horrors preparing for the wicked in a future state. A great excitement is visible among his hearers, a scream is heard, and some young girl falls senseless on the floor. There is a momentary rustle, but it is only for a moment—all eyes are turned towards the preacher. He pauses, passes his handkerchief across his face, and looks complacently round. His voice resumes its natural tone, as with mock humility he offers up a thanksgiving for having been successful in his efforts, and having been permitted to rescue one sinner from the path of evil. He sinks back into his seat, exhausted with the violence of his ravings; the girl is removed, a hymn is sung, a petition for some measure for securing the better observance of the Sabbath, which has been prepared by the good man, is read; and his worshipping admirers struggle who shall be the first to sign it.

But the morning service has concluded, and the streets are again crowded with people. Long rows of cleanly-dressed charity children, preceded by a portly beadle and a withered schoolmaster, are returning to their welcome dinner; and it is evident, from the number of men with beer-trays who are running from house to house, that no inconsiderable portion of the population are about to take theirs at this early hour. The bakers' shops, in the humbler suburbs especially, are filled with men, women, and children, each anxiously waiting for the Sunday dinner. Look at the group of children who surround that working man who has just emerged from the baker's shop at the corner of the street, with the reeking dish, in which a diminutive joint of mutton simmers above a vast heap of half-browned potatoes. How the young rogues clap their hands, and dance round their father, for very joy at the prospect of the feast: and how anxiously the youngest and chubbiest of the lot lingers on tiptoe by his side, trying to get a peep into the interior of the dish. They turn up the street, and the chubby-faced boy trots on as fast as his little legs will carry him, to herald the approach of the dinner to "Mother" who is standing with a baby in her arms on the doorstep, and who seems almost as pleased with the whole scene as the children themselves; whereupon "baby" not precisely understanding the importance of the business in hand, but clearly perceiving that it is something unusually lively, kicks and crows most lustily, to the unspeakable delight of all the children and both the parents: and the dinner is borne into the house amidst a shouting of small voices, and jumping of fat legs, which would fill Sir Andrew Agnew with astonishment; as well it might, seeing that Baronets, generally speaking, eat pretty comfortable dinners all the week through, and cannot be expected to understand what people feel, who only have a meat dinner on one day out of every seven.

The bakings being all duly consigned to their respective owners, and the beer-man having gone his rounds, the church bells ring for afternoon service, the shops are again closed, and the streets are more than ever thronged with people; some who have not been to church in the morning, going to it now; others who have been to church, going out for a walk; and others—let us admit the full measure of their guilt—going for a walk, who have not been to church at all. I am afraid the smart servant of all work, who has been loitering at the corner of the square for the last ten minutes, is one of the latter class. She is evidently waiting for somebody, and though she may have made up her mind to go to church with him one of these mornings, I don't think they have any such intention on this particular afternoon. Here he is, at last. The white trousers, blue coat, and yellow waistcoat—and more especially that cock of the hat—indicate, as surely as inanimate objects can, that Chalk Farm and not the parish church is their destination. The girl colours up, and puts out her hand with a very awkward affectation of indifference. He gives it a gallant squeeze, and away they walk, arm in arm, the girl just looking back towards her "place" with an air of conscious self-importance, and nodding to her fellow-servant who has gone up to the two-pair-of-stairs window, to take a full view of "Mary's young man," which being communicated to William, he takes off his hat to the fellow-servant: a proceeding which affords unmitigated satisfaction to all parties, and impels the fellow-servant to inform Miss Emily confidentially, in the course of the evening, "that the young man as Mary keeps company with, is one of the most genteelest young men as ever she see."

The two young people who have just crossed the road, and

are following this happy couple down the street, are a fair specimen of another class of Sunday-pleasurers. There is a dapper smartness, struggling through very limited means, about the young man, which induces one to set him down at once as a junior clerk to a tradesman or attorney. The girl no one could possibly mistake. You may tell a young woman in the employment of a large dress-maker, at any time, by a certain neatness of cheap finery and humble following of fashion which pervade her whole attire; but unfortunately there are other tokens not to be misunderstood —the pale face with its hectic bloom, the slight distortion of form which no artifice of dress can wholly conceal, the unhealthy stoop, and the short cough—the effects of hard work and close application to a sedentary employment, upon a tender frame. They turn towards the fields. The girl's countenance brightens, and an unwonted glow rises in her face. They are going to Hampstead or Highgate, to spend their holiday afternoon in some place where they can see the sky, the fields, and trees, and breathe for an hour or two the pure air, which so seldom plays upon that poor girl's form, or exhilarates her spirits.

I would to God, that the iron-hearted man who would deprive such people as these of their only pleasures, could feel the sinking of heart and soul, the wasting exhaustion of mind and body, the utter prostration of present strength and future hope, attendant upon that incessant toil which lasts from day to day, and from month to month; that toil which is too often protracted until the silence of midnight, and resumed with the first stir of morning. How marvellously would his ardent zeal for other men's souls diminish after a short probation, and how enlightened and comprehensive would his views of the real object and meaning of the institution of the Sabbath become!

The afternoon is far advanced—the parks and public drives are crowded. Carriages, gigs, phaetons, stanhopes, and vehicles of every description, glide smoothly on. The promenades are filled with loungers on foot, and the road is thronged with loungers on horseback. Persons of every class are crowded together, here, in one dense mass. The plebeian, who takes his pleasure on no day but Sunday, jostles the patrician, who takes his from year's end to year's end. You look in vain for any outward signs of profligacy or debauchery. You see nothing before you but a vast number of people, the denizens of a large and crowded city, in the needful and rational enjoyment of air and exercise.

It grows dusk. The roads leading from the different places of suburban resort, are crowded with people on their return home, and the sound of merry voices rings through the gradually darkening fields. The evening is hot and sultry. The rich man throws open the sashes of his spacious dining-room, and quaffs his iced wine in splendid luxury. The poor man, who has no room to take his meals in, but the close apartment to which he and his family have been confined throughout the week, sits in the tea-garden of some famous tavern, and drinks his beer in content and comfort. The fields and roads are gradually deserted, the crowd once more pour into the streets, and disperse to their several homes; and by midnight all is silent and quiet, save where a few stragglers linger beneath the window of some great man's house, to listen to the strains of music from within, or stop to gaze upon the splendid carriages which are waiting to convey the guests from the dinner-party of an Earl.

There is a darker side to this picture, on which, so far from its being any part of my purpose to conceal it, I wish to lay particular stress. In some parts of London, and in many of the manufacturing towns of England, drunkenness and profligacy in their most disgusting forms, exhibit in the open streets on Sunday a sad and a degrading spectacle. We need go no farther than St. Giles's, or Drury Lane, for sights and scenes of a most repulsive nature. Women with scarcely the articles of apparel which common decency requires, with forms bloated by disease, and faces rendered hideous by habitual drunkenness—men reeling and staggering along—children in rags and filth—whole streets of squalid and miserable appearance, whose inhabitants are lounging in the public road, fighting, screaming, and swearing—these are the common objects which present themselves in, these are the well-known characteristics of, that portion of London to which I have just referred.

And why is it that all well-disposed persons are shocked, and public decency scandalised, by such exhibitions?

These people are poor—that is notorious. It may be said that they spend in liquor, money with which they might purchase necessaries, and there is no denying the fact; but let it be remembered that even if they applied every farthing of their earnings in the best possible way, they

would still be very, very poor. Their dwellings are necessarily uncomfortable, and to a certain degree unhealthy.
Cleanliness might do much, but they are too crowded
together, the streets are too narrow, and the rooms too
small, to admit of their ever being rendered desirable
habitations. They work very hard all the week. We know
that the effect of prolonged and arduous labour is to
produce, when a period of rest does arrive, a sensation of
lassitude which it requires the application of some stimulus
to overcome. What stimulus have they? Sunday comes,
and with it a cessation of labour. How are they to employ
the day, or what inducement have they to employ it in
recruiting their stock of health? They see little parties, on
pleasure excursions, passing through the streets; but they
cannot imitate their example, for they have not the means.
They may walk, to be sure, but it is exactly the inducement
to walk that they require. If every one of these men knew
that by taking the trouble to walk two or three miles he
would be enabled to share in a good game of cricket, or
some athletic sport, I very much question whether any of
them would remain at home.

But you hold out no inducement, you offer no relief from
listlessness, you provide nothing to amuse his mind, you
afford him no means of exercising his body. Unwashed and
unshaven, he saunters moodily about, weary and dejected.
In lieu of the wholesome stimulus he might derive from
nature, you drive him to the pernicious excitement to be
gained from art. He flies to the gin-shop as his only resource; and when, reduced to a worse level than the lowest
brute in the scale of creation, he lies wallowing in the
kennel, your saintly lawgivers lift up their hands to heaven,
and exclaim for a law which shall convert the day intended
for rest and cheerfulness, into one of universal gloom,
bigotry, and persecution.

AS SABBATH BILLS WOULD MAKE IT

THE provisions of the bill introduced into the House of
Commons by Sir Andrew Agnew, and thrown out by that
House on the motion for the second reading, on the 18th of
May in the present year, by a majority of 32, may very
fairly be taken as a test of the length to which the fanatics,
of which the honourable Baronet is the distinguished leader,
are prepared to go. No test can be fairer; because while on
the one hand this measure may be supposed to exhibit all
that improvement which mature reflection and long deliberation may have suggested, so on the other it may very
reasonably be inferred, that if it be quite as severe in its
provisions, and to the full as partial in its operation, as
those which have preceded it, and experienced a similar
fate, the disease under which the honourable Baronet and
his friends labour, is perfectly hopeless, and beyond the
reach of cure.

The proposed enactments of the bill are briefly these:—
All work is prohibited on the Lord's day, under heavy
penalties, increasing with every repetition of the offence.
There are penalties for keeping shops open—penalties for
drunkenness—penalties for keeping open houses of entertainment—penalties for being present at any public meeting
or assembly—penalties for letting carriages, and penalties
for hiring them—penalties for travelling in steam-boats, and
penalties for taking passengers—penalties on vessels commencing their voyage on Sunday—penalties on the owners
of cattle who suffer them to be driven on the Lord's day—
penalties on constables who refuse to act, and penalties for
resisting them when they do. In addition to these trifles,
the constables are invested with arbitrary, vexatious, and
most extensive powers; and all this in a bill which sets
out with a hypocritical and canting declaration that

"nothing is more acceptable to God than the *true and sincere* worship of Him according to His holy will, and that it is the bounden duty of Parliament to promote the observance of the Lord's day, by protecting every class of society against being required to sacrifice their comfort, health, religious privileges, and conscience, for the convenience, enjoyment, or supposed advantage of any other class on the Lord's day"! The idea of making a man truly moral through the ministry of constables, and sincerely religious under the influence of penalties, is worthy of the mind which could form such a mass of monstrous absurdity as this bill is composed of.

The House of Commons threw the measure out certainly, and by so doing retrieved the disgrace—so far as it could be retrieved—of placing among the printed papers of Parliament, such an egregious specimen of legislative folly; but there was a degree of delicacy and forbearance about the debate that took place, which I cannot help thinking as unnecessary and uncalled for, as it is unusual in Parliamentary discussions. If it had been the first time of Sir Andrew Agnew's attempting to palm such a measure upon the country, we might well understand, and duly appreciate, the delicate and compassionate feeling due to the supposed weakness and imbecility of the man, which prevented his proposition being exposed in its true colours, and induced this Hon. Member to bear testimony to his excellent motives, and that Noble Lord to regret that he could not—although he had tried to do so—adopt any portion of the bill. But when these attempts have been repeated again and again; when Sir Andrew Agnew has renewed them session after session, and when it has become palpably evident to the whole House that

> His impudence of proof in every trial,
> Kens no polite, and heeds no plain denial—

it really becomes high time to speak of him and his legislation, as they appear to deserve, without that gloss of politeness, which is all very well in an ordinary case, but rather out of place when the liberties and comforts of a whole people are at stake.

In the first place, it is by no means the worst characteristic of this bill, that it is a bill of blunders: it is, from beginning to end, a piece of deliberate cruelty, and crafty injustice. If the rich composed the whole population of this country, not a single comfort of one single man would be affected by it. It is directed exclusively, and without the exception of a solitary instance, against the amusements and recreations of the poor. This was the bait held out by the Hon. Baronet to a body of men, who cannot be supposed to have any very strong sympathies in common with the poor, because they cannot understand their sufferings or their struggles. This is the bait, which will in time prevail, unless public attention is awakened, and public feeling exerted, to prevent it.

Take the very first clause, the provision that no man shall be allowed to work on Sunday—"That no person, upon the Lord's day, shall do, or hire, or employ any person to do any manner of labour, or any work of his or her ordinary calling." What class of persons does this affect? The rich man? No. Menial servants, both male and female, are specially exempted from the operation of the bill. "Menial servants" are among the poor people. The bill has no regard for them. The Baronet's dinner must be cooked on Sunday, the Bishop's horses must be groomed, and the Peer's carriage must be driven. So the menial servants are put utterly beyond the pale of grace;—unless indeed, they are to go to heaven through the sanctity of their masters, and possibly they might think even that rather an uncertain passport.

There is a penalty for keeping open houses of entertainment. Now, suppose the bill had passed, and that half-a-dozen adventurous licensed victuallers, relying upon the excitement of public feeling on the subject, and the consequent difficulty of conviction (this is by no means an improbable supposition), had determined to keep their houses and gardens open, through the whole Sunday afternoon, in defiance of the law. Every act of hiring or working, every act of buying or selling, or delivering, or causing anything to be bought or sold, is specifically made a separate offence—mark the effect. A party, a man and his wife and children, enter a tea-garden, and the informer stations himself in the next box, from whence he can see and hear everything that passes. "Waiter!" says the father. "Yes, Sir." "Pint of the best ale!" "Yes, Sir." Away runs the waiter to the bar, and gets the ale from the landlord. Out comes the informer's note-book—penalty on the father for hiring, on the waiter for delivering, and on the landlord for selling, on the Lord's day. But it does not stop here. The waiter delivers the ale, and darts off, little suspecting the penalties in store for him. "Hollo," cries the father, "waiter!" "Yes, Sir." "Just get this little boy a biscuit, will you?" "Yes, Sir." Off runs the waiter again, and down goes another case of hiring, another case of delivering, and another case of selling; and so it would go on *ad infinitum*, the sum and substance of the matter being, that every time a man or woman cried "Waiter!" on Sunday, he or she would be fined not less than forty shillings, nor more than a hundred; and every time a waiter replied, "Yes, Sir," he and his master would be fined in the same amount: with the addition of a new sort of window duty on the landlord, to wit, a tax of twenty shillings an hour for every hour beyond the first one, during which he should have his shutters down on the Sabbath.

With one exception, there are perhaps no clauses in the whole bill, so strongly illustrative of its partial operation, and the intention of its framer, as those which relate to travelling on Sunday. Penalties of ten, twenty, and thirty pounds, are mercilessly imposed upon coach proprietors who shall run their coaches on the Sabbath; one, two, and ten pounds upon those who hire, or let to hire, horses and carriages upon the Lord's day, but not one syllable about those who have no necessity to hire, because they have carriages and horses of their own; not one word of a penalty on liveried coachmen and footmen. The whole of the saintly venom is directed against the hired cabriolet, the humble fly, or the rumbling hackney-coach, which enables a man of the poorer class to escape for a few hours from the smoke and dirt, in the midst of which he has been confined throughout the week: while the escutcheoned carriage and the dashing cab may whirl their wealthy owners to Sunday feasts and private oratorios, setting constables, informers, and penalties, at defiance. Again, in the description of the places of public resort which it is rendered criminal to attend on Sunday, there are no words comprising a very fashionable promenade. Public discussions, public debates, public lectures and speeches, are cautiously guarded against; for it is by their means that the people become enlightened enough to deride the last efforts of bigotry and superstition. There is a stringent provision for punishing the poor man who spends an hour in a news-room, but there is nothing to prevent the rich one from lounging away the day in the Zoological Gardens.

There is, in four words, a mock proviso, which affects to forbid travelling "with any animal" on the Lord's day. This, however, is revoked, as relates to the rich man, by a subsequent provision. We have then a penalty of not less than fifty, nor more than one hundred pounds, upon any person participating in the control, or having the command of any vessel which shall commence her voyage on the Lord's day, should the wind prove favourable. The next time this bill is brought forward (which will no doubt be at an early period of the next session of Parliament) perhaps it will be better to amend this clause by declaring, that from and after the passing of the act, it shall be deemed unlawful for the wind to blow at all upon the Sabbath. It would remove a great deal of temptation from the owners and captains of vessels.

The reader is now in possession of the principal enacting clauses of Sir Andrew Agnew's bill, with the exception of one, for preventing the killing or taking of "*fish, or other wild animals,*" and the ordinary provisions which are inserted for form's sake in all acts of Parliament. I now beg his attention to the clauses of exemption.

They are two in number. The first exempts menial servants from any rest, and all poor men from any recreation: outlaws a milkman after nine o'clock in the morning, and makes eating-houses lawful for only two hours in the afternoon; permits a medical man to use his carriage on Sunday, and declares that a clergyman may either use his own, or hire one.

The second is artful, cunning, and designing; shielding the rich man from the possibility of being entrapped, and affecting at the same time, to have a tender and scrupulous regard for the interests of the whole community. It declares, "that nothing in this act contained, shall extend to works of piety, charity, or necessity."

What is meant by the word "necessity" in this clause? Simply this—that the rich man shall be at liberty to make use of all the splendid luxuries he has collected around him, on any day in the week, because habit and custom have rendered them "necessary" to his easy existence; but that

the poor man who saves his money to provide some little
pleasure for himself and family at lengthened intervals, shall
not be permitted to enjoy it. It is not "necessary" to him:
—Heaven knows, he very often goes long enough without it.
This is the plain English of the clause. The carriage and
pair of horses, the coachman, the footman, the helper, and
the groom, are "necessary" on Sundays, as on other days, to
the bishop and the nobleman; but the hackney-coach, the
hired gig, or the taxed cart, cannot possibly be "necessary"
to the working-man on Sunday, for he has it not at other
times. The sumptuous dinner and the rich wines are
"necessaries" to a great man in his own mansion: but the
pint of beer and the plate of meat degrade the national
character in an eating-house.

Such is the bill for promoting the true and sincere worship
of God according to his Holy Will, and for protecting every
class of society against being required to sacrifice their
health and comfort on the Sabbath. Instances in which its
operation would be as unjust as it would be absurd, might
be multiplied to an endless amount; but it is sufficient to
place its leading provisions before the reader. In doing so,
I have purposely abstained from drawing upon the imagination for possible cases; the provisions to which I have
referred, stand in so many words upon the bill as printed
by order of the House of Commons; and they can neither
be disowned nor explained away.

Let us suppose such a bill as this to have actually passed
both branches of the legislature; to have received the royal
assent; and to have come into operation. Imagine its effect
in a great city like London.

Sunday comes, and brings with it a day of general gloom
and austerity. The man who has been toiling hard all the
week, has been looking towards the Sabbath, not as to a day
of rest from labour, and healthy recreation, but as one of
grievous tyranny and grinding oppression. The day which
his Maker intended as a blessing, man has converted into
a curse. Instead of being hailed by him as his period of
relaxation, he finds it remarkable only as depriving him
of every comfort and enjoyment. He has many children
about him, all sent into the world at an early age to struggle
for a livelihood; one is kept in a warehouse all day, with an
interval of rest too short to enable him to reach home,
another walks four or five miles to his employment at the

docks, a third earns a few shillings weekly as an errand boy, or office messenger; and the employment of the man himself, detains him at some distance from his home from morning till night. Sunday is the only day on which they could all meet together, and enjoy a homely meal in social comfort; and now they sit down to a cold and cheerless dinner: the pious guardians of the man's salvation having, in their regard for the welfare of his precious soul, shut up the bakers' shops. The fire blazes high in the kitchen chimney of these well-fed hypocrites, and the rich steams of the savoury dinner scent the air. What care they to be told that this class of men have neither a place to cook in—nor means to bear the expense, if they had?

Look into your churches—diminished congregations, and scanty attendance. People have grown sullen and obstinate, and are becoming disgusted with, the faith which condemns them to such a day as this, once in every seven. And as you cannot make people religious by Act of Parliament, or force them to church by constables, they display their feeling by staying away.

Turn into the streets, and mark the rigid gloom that reigns over everything around. The roads are empty, the fields are deserted, the houses of entertainment are closed. Groups of filthy and discontented-looking men are idling about at the street corners, or sleeping in the sun; but there are no decently-dressed people of the poorer class passing to and fro. Where should they walk to? It would take them an hour, at least, to get into the fields, and when they reached them they could procure neither bite nor sup without the informer and the penalty. Now and then a carriage rolls smoothly on, or a well-mounted horseman, followed by a liveried attendant, canters by; but with these exceptions, all is as melancholy and quiet as if a pestilence had fallen on the city.

Bend your steps through the narrow and thickly-inhabited streets, and observe the sallow faces of the men and women who are lounging at the doors, or lolling from the windows. Regard well the closeness of these crowded rooms, and the noisome exhalations that rise from the drains and kennels; and then laud the triumph of religion and morality, which condemns people to drag their lives out in such stews as these, and makes it criminal for them to eat or drink in the fresh air, or under the clear sky. Here and there, from some half-opened window, the loud shout of drunken revelry strikes upon the ear, and the noise of oaths and quarrelling— the effect of the close and heated atmosphere—is heard on all sides. See how the men all rush to join the crowd that are making their way down the street, and how loud the execra- tions of the mob become as they draw nearer. They have assembled round a little knot of constables, who have seized the stock-in-trade, heinously exposed on Sunday, of some miserable walking-stick seller, who follows clamouring for his property. The dispute grows warmer and fiercer, until at last some of the more furious among the crowd rush forward to restore the goods to their owner. A general conflict takes place; the sticks of the constables are exercised in all directions; fresh assistance is procured; and half a dozen of the assailants are conveyed to the station-house, struggling, bleeding, and cursing. The case is taken to the police-office on the following morning; and after a frightful amount of perjury on both sides, the men are sent to prison for resisting the officers, their families to the workhouse to keep them from starving : and there they both remain for a month afterwards, glorious trophies of the sanctified enforcement of the Christian Sabbath. Add to such scenes as these the profligacy, idleness, drunkenness, and vice, that will be committed to an extent which no man can foresee, on Monday, as an atonement for the restraint of the preceding day; and you have a very faint and imperfect picture of the religious effects of this Sunday legislation, supposing it could ever be forced upon the people.

But let those who advocate the cause of fanaticism reflect well upon the probable issue of their endeavours. They may by perseverance, succeed with Parliament. Let them ponder on the probability of succeeding with the people. You may deny the concession of a political question for a time, and a nation will bear it patiently. Strike home to the comforts of every man's fireside—tamper with every man's freedom and liberty—and one month, one week, may rouse a feeling abroad which a king would gladly yield his crown to quell, and a peer would resign his coronet to allay.

It is the custom to affect a deference for the motives of those who advocate these measures, and a respect for the feelings by which they are actuated. They do not deserve it. If they legislate in ignorance, they are criminal and dishonest; if they do so with their eyes open, they commit wilful injustice; in either case, they bring religion into contempt. But they do NOT legislate in ignorance. Public prints, and public men, have pointed out to them again and again the consequences of their proceedings. If they persist in thrusting themselves forward, let those consequences rest upon their own heads, and let them be content to stand upon their own merits.

It may be asked, what motives can actuate a man who has so little regard for the comfort of his fellow-beings, so little respect for their wants and necessities, and so distorted a notion of the beneficence of his Creator. I reply, an envious, heartless, ill-conditioned dislike to seeing those whom fortune has placed below him, cheerful and happy— an intolerant confidence in his own high worthiness before God, and a lofty impression of the demerits of others— pride, selfish pride, as inconsistent with the spirit of Christianity itself, as opposed to the example of its Founder upon earth.

To these may be added another class of men—the stern and gloomy enthusiasts, who would make earth a hell, and religion a torment: men who, having wasted the earlier part of their lives in dissipation and depravity, find themselves when scarcely past its meridian, steeped to the neck in vice, and shunned like a loathsome disease. Abandoned by the world, having nothing to fall back upon, nothing to remember but time mis-spent, and energies misdirected, they turn their eyes and not their thoughts to Heaven, and delude themselves into the impious belief, that in denouncing the lightness of heart of which they cannot partake, and the rational pleasures from which they never derived enjoyment, they are more than remedying the sins of their old career, and—like the founders of monasteries and builders of churches, in ruder days—establishing a good set claim upon their Maker.

III

THE supporters of Sabbath Bills, and more especially the extreme class of Dissenters, lay great stress upon the declarations occasionally made by criminals from the condemned cell or the scaffold, that to Sabbath-breaking they attribute their first deviation from the path of rectitude; and they point to these statements, as an incontestable proof of the evil consequences which await a departure from that strict and rigid observance of the Sabbath, which they uphold. I cannot help thinking that in this, as in almost every other respect connected with the subject, there is a considerable degree of cant, and a very great deal of wilful blindness. If a man be viciously disposed—and with very few exceptions, not a man dies by the executioner's hands, who has not been in one way or other a most abandoned and profligate character for many years—if a man be viciously disposed, there is no doubt that he will turn his Sunday to bad account, that he will take advantage of it to dissipate with other bad characters as vile as himself; and that in this way he may trace his first yielding to temptation, possibly his first commission of crime, to an infringement of the Sabbath. But this would be an argument against any holiday at all. If his holiday had been Wednesday instead of Sunday, and he had devoted it to the same improper uses, it would have been productive of the same results. It is too much to judge of the character of a whole people by the confessions of the very worst members of society. It is not fair to cry down things which are harmless in themselves, because evil-disposed men may turn them to bad account. Who ever thought of deprecating the teaching poor people to write because some porter in a warehouse had committed forgery? Or into what man's head did it ever enter, to prevent the crowding of churches because it afforded a temptation for the picking of pockets?

When the Book of Sports, for allowing the peasantry of England to divert themselves with certain games in the open air, on Sundays, after evening service, was published by Charles the First, it is needless to say the English people were comparatively rude and uncivilised. And yet it is extraordinary to how few excesses it gave rise, even in that day, when men's minds were not enlightened, or their passions moderated, by the influence of education and refinement. That some excesses were committed through its means, in the remoter parts of the country, and that it was discontinued in those places in consequence, cannot be denied: but generally speaking, there is no proof whatever on record, of its having had any tendency to increase crime, or to lower the character of the people.

The Puritans of that time were as much opposed to harmless recreations and healthful amusements as those of the present day, and it is amusing to observe that each in their generation advance precisely the same description of arguments. In the British Museum there is a curious pamphlet got up by the Agnews of Charles's time, entitled " A Divine Tragedie lately acted, or a Collection of sundry memorable examples of God's Judgements upon Sabbath Breakers, and other like Libertines in their unlawful Sports, happening within the realme of England, in the compass only of two yeares last past, since the Booke (of Sports) was published, worthy to be knowne and considered of all men, especially such who are guilty of the sinne, or archpatrons thereof." This amusing document contains some fifty or sixty veritable accounts of balls of fire that fell into church-yards and upset the sporters, and sporters that quarrelled and upset one another, and so forth: and among them is one anecdote containing an example of a rather different kind, which I cannot resist the temptation of quoting, as strongly illustrative of the fact, that this blinking of the question has not even the recommendation of novelty.

"A woman about Northampton, the same day that she heard the booke for sports read, went immediately, and having 3. pence in her purse, hired a fellow to goe to the next towne to fetch a Minstrell, who coming, she with others fell a dauncing, which continued within night ; at which time shee was got with child, which at the birth shee mur-thering, was detected and apprehended, and being convented before the justice, shee confessed it, and withal told the occasion of it, saying it was her falling to sport on the Sabbath, upon the reading of the Booke, so as for this treble sinfull act, her presumptuous profaning of the Sabbath, w$^{h.}$ brought her adultory and that murther. Shee was according to the Law both of God and man, put to death. Much sinne and misery followeth upon Sabbath-breaking."

It is needless to say that if the young lady near Northampton had "fallen to sport" of such a dangerous description, on any other day but Sunday, the first result would probably have been the same: it never having been distinctly shown that Sunday is more favourable to the propagation of the human race than any other day in the week. The second result—the murder of the child—does not speak very highly for the amiability of her natural disposition; and the whole story, supposing it to have had any foundation at all, is about as much chargeable upon the Book of Sports, as upon the Book of Kings. Such "sports" have taken place in Dissenting Chapels before now; but religion has never been blamed in consequence; nor has it been proposed to shut up the chapels on that account.

The question, then, very fairly arises, whether we have any reason to suppose that allowing games in the open air on Sundays, or even providing the means of amusement for the humbler classes of society on that day, would be hurtful and injurious to the character and morals of the people.

I was travelling in the west of England a summer or two back, and was induced by the beauty of the scenery, and the seclusion of the spot, to remain for the night in a small village, distant about seventy miles from London. The next morning was Sunday; and I walked out towards the church. Groups of people—the whole population of the little hamlet apparently—were hastening in the same direction. Cheerful and good-humoured congratulations were heard on all sides, as neighbours overtook each other, and walked on in company. Occasionally I passed an aged couple, whose married daughter and her husband were loitering by the side of the old people, accommodating their rate of walking to their feeble pace, while a little knot of children hurried on before; stout young labourers in clean round frocks; and buxom girls with healthy, laughing faces, were plentifully sprinkled about in couples, and the whole scene was one of quiet and tranquil contentment, irresistibly captivating. The morning was bright and pleasant, the hedges were green and blooming, and a thousand delicious scents were wafted on the air, from the wild flowers which blossomed on either side of the footpath. The little church was one of those venerable simple buildings which abound in the English counties ; half overgrown with moss and ivy, and standing in the centre of a little plot of ground, which, but for the green mounds with which it was studded, might have passed for a lovely meadow. I fancied that the old clanking bell which was now summoning the congregation together, would seem less terrible when it rung out the knell of a departed soul, than I had ever deemed possible before—that the sound would tell only of a welcome to calmness and rest, amidst the most peaceful and tranquil scene in nature.

I followed into the church—a low-roofed building with small arched windows, through which the sun's rays streamed upon a plain tablet on the opposite wall, which had once recorded names, now as undistinguishable on its worn surface, as were the bones beneath, from the dust into which they had resolved. The impressive service of the Church of England was spoken—not merely *read*—by a grey-headed minister, and the responses delivered by his auditors, with an air of sincere devotion as far removed from affectation or display, as from coldness or indifference. The psalms were accompanied by a few instrumental performers, who were stationed in a small gallery extending across the church at the lower end, over the door : and the voices were led by the clerk, who it was evident derived no slight pride and gratification from this portion of the service. The discourse was plain, unpretending, and well adapted to the comprehension of the hearers. At the conclusion of the service, the villagers waited in the churchyard to salute the clergyman as he passed ; and two or three, I observed, stepped aside, as if communicating some little difficulty, and asking his advice. This, to guess from the homely bows, and other rustic expressions of gratitude, the old gentleman readily conceded. He seemed intimately acquainted with the circumstances of all his parishioners ; for I heard him inquire after one man's youngest child, another man's wife, and so forth ; and that he was fond of his joke, I discovered from overhearing him ask a stout, fresh-coloured young fellow, with a very pretty bashful-looking girl on his arm, "when those banns were to be put up?"—an inquiry which made the young fellow more fresh-coloured, and the girl more bashful, and which, strange to say, caused a great many other girls who were standing round, to colour up also, and look anywhere but in the faces of their male companions.

As I approached this spot in the evening about half an hour before sunset, I was surprised to hear the hum of voices, and occasionally a shout of merriment from the meadow beyond the churchyard; which I found, when I reached the stile, to be occasioned by a very animated game of cricket, in which the boys and young men of the place were engaged, while the females and old people were scattered about: some seated on the grass watching the progress of the game, and others sauntering about in groups of two or three, gathering little nosegays of wild roses and hedge flowers. I could not but take notice of one old man in particular, with a bright-eyed grand-daughter by his side, who was giving a sunburnt young fellow some instructions in the game, which he received with an air of profound deference, but with an occasional glance at the girl, which induced me to think that his attention was rather distracted from the old gentleman's narration of the fruits of his experience. When it was his turn at the wicket, too, there was a glance towards the pair every now and then, which the old grandfather very complacently considered as an appeal to his judgment of a particular hit, but which a certain blush in the girl's face, and a downcast look of the bright eye, led me to believe was intended for somebody else than the old man,—and understood by somebody else, too, or I am much mistaken.

I was in the very height of the pleasure which the contemplation of this scene afforded me, when I saw the old clergyman making his way towards us. I trembled for an angry interruption to the sport, and was almost on the point of crying out, to warn the cricketers of his approach; he was so close upon me, however, that I could do nothing but remain still, and anticipate the reproof that was preparing. What was my agreeable surprise to see the old gentleman standing at the stile, with his hands in his pockets, surveying the whole scene with evident satisfaction! And how dull I must have been, not to have known till my friend the grandfather (who, by-the-bye, said he had been a wonderful cricketer in his time) told me, that it was the clergyman himself who had established the whole thing: that it was his field they played in; and that it was he who had purchased stumps, bats, ball, and all!

It is such scenes as this I would see near London on a Sunday evening. It is such men as this who would do more in one year to make people properly religious, cheerful, and contented, than all the legislation of a century could ever accomplish.

It will be said—it has been very often—that it would be matter of perfect impossibility to make amusements and exercises succeed in large towns, which may be very well adapted to a country population. Here, again, we are called upon to yield to bare assertions on matters of belief and opinion, as if they were established and undoubted facts. That there is a wide difference between the two cases, no one will be prepared to dispute; that the difference is such as to prevent the application of the same principle to both, no reasonable man, I think, will be disposed to maintain. The great majority of the people who make holiday on Sunday now, are industrious, orderly, and well-behaved persons. It is not unreasonable to suppose that they would be no more inclined to an abuse of pleasures provided for them, than they are to an abuse of the pleasures they provide for themselves; and if any people, for want of something better to do, resort to criminal practices on the Sabbath as at present observed, no better remedy for the evil can be imagined, than giving them the opportunity of doing something which will amuse them, and hurt nobody else.

The propriety of opening the British Museum to respectable people on Sunday, has lately been the subject of some discussion. I think it would puzzle the most austere of the Sunday legislators to assign any valid reason for opposing so sensible a proposition. The Museum contains rich specimens from all the vast museums and repositories of Nature, and rare and curious fragments of the mighty works of art, in bygone ages: all calculated to awaken contemplation and inquiry, and to tend to the enlightenment and improvement of the people. But attendants would be necessary, and a few men would be employed upon the Sabbath. They certainly would; but how many? Why, if the British Museum, and the National Gallery, and the Gallery of

Practical Science, and every other exhibition in London, from which knowledge is to be derived and information gained, were to be thrown open on a Sunday afternoon, not fifty people would be required to preside over the whole: and it would take treble the number to enforce a Sabbath bill in any three populous parishes.

I should like to see some large field, or open piece of ground, in every outskirt of London, exhibiting each Sunday evening on a larger scale, the scene of the little country meadow. I should like to see the time arrive, when a man's attendance to his religious duties might be left to that religious feeling which most men possess in a greater or less degree, but which was never forced into the breast of any man by menace or restraint. I should like to see the time when Sunday might be looked forward to, as a recognised day of relaxation and enjoyment, and when every man might feel, what few men do now, that religion is not incompatible with rational pleasure and needful recreation.

How different a picture would the streets and public places then present! The museums, and repositories of scientific and useful inventions, would be crowded with ingenious mechanics and industrious artisans, all anxious for information, and all unable to procure it at any other time. The spacious saloons would be swarming with practical men: humble in appearance, but destined, perhaps, to become the greatest inventors and philosophers of their age. The labourers who now lounge away the day in idleness and intoxication, would be seen hurrying along, with cheerful faces and clean attire, not to the close and smoky atmosphere of the public-house, but to the fresh and airy fields. Fancy the pleasant scene. Throngs of people, pouring out from the lanes and alleys of the metropolis, to various places of common resort at some short distance from the town, to join in the refreshing sports and exercises of the day—the children gambolling in crowds upon the grass, the mothers looking on, and enjoying themselves the little game they seem only to direct; other parties strolling along some pleasant walks, or reposing in the shade of the stately trees; others again intent upon their different amusements. Nothing should be heard on all sides, but the sharp stroke of the bat as it sent the ball skimming along the ground, the clear ring of the quoit, as it struck upon the iron peg: the noisy murmur of many voices, and the loud shout of mirth and delight, which would awaken the echoes far and wide, till the fields rung with it. The day would pass away in a series of enjoyments which would awaken no painful reflections when night arrived ; for they would be calculated to bring with them only health and contentment. The young would lose that dread of religion, which the sour austerity of its professors too often inculcates in youthful bosoms; and the old would find less difficulty in persuading them to respect its observances. The drunken and dissipated, deprived of any excuse for their misconduct, would no longer excite pity but disgust. Above all, the more ignorant and humble class of men, who now partake of many of the bitters of life, and taste but few of its sweets, would naturally feel attachment and respect for that code of morality, which, regarding the many hardships of their station, strove to alleviate its rigours, and endeavoured to soften its asperity.

This is what Sunday might be made, and what it might be made without impiety or profanation. The wise and beneficent Creator who places men upon earth, requires that they shall perform the duties of that station of life to which they are called, and He can never intend that the more a man strives to discharge those duties, the more he shall be debarred from happiness and enjoyment. Let those who have six days in the week for all the world's pleasures, appropriate the seventh to fasting and gloom, either for their own sins or those of other people, if they like to bewail them ; but let those who employ their six days in a worthier manner, devote their seventh to a different purpose. Let divines set the example of true morality : preach it to their flocks in the morning, and dismiss them to enjoy true rest in the afternoon ; and let them select for their text, and let Sunday legislators take for their motto, the words which fell from the lips of that Master, whose precepts they misconstrue, and whose lessons they pervert —" The Sabbath was made for man, and not man to serve the Sabbath."

HUNTED DOWN

CHARACTERS

MR. ADAMS, clerk in a life-assurance office.

MR. MELTHAM (also called by the assumed names of MAJOR BANKS and MR. ALFRED BECKWITH), actuary of the Inestimable Life Assurance Company.

MISS MARGARET NINER, Mr. Slinkton's niece.

MR. SAMPSON, chief manager of a life-assurance company, and the narrator of the story.

MR. JULIUS SLINKTON, a well-educated and agreeable gentleman, but a hypocritical villain.

HUNTED DOWN

CHAPTER I

Most of us see some romances in life. In my capacity as Chief Manager of a Life Assurance Office, I think I have within the last thirty years seen more romances than the generality of men, however unpromising the opportunity may, at first sight, seem.

As I have retired, and live at my ease, I possess the means that I used to want, of considering what I have seen, at leisure. My experiences have a more remarkable aspect, so reviewed, than they had when they were in progress. I have come home from the Play now, and can recall the scenes of the Drama upon which the curtain has fallen, free from the glare, bewilderment, and bustle of the Theatre.

Let me recall one of these Romances of the real world.

There is nothing truer than physiognomy, taken in connexion with manner. The art of reading that book of which Eternal Wisdom obliges every human creature to present his or her own page with the individual character written on it, is a difficult one, perhaps, and is little studied. It may require some natural aptitude, and it must require (for everything does) some patience and some pains. That these are not usually given to it,—that numbers of people accept a few stock commonplace expressions of the face as the whole list of characteristics, and neither seek nor know the refinements that are truest,—that You, for instance, give a great deal of time and attention to the reading of music, Greek, Latin, French, Italian, Hebrew, if you please, and do not qualify yourself to read the face of the master or mistress looking over your shoulder teaching it to you,—I assume to be five hundred times more probable than improbable. Perhaps a little self-sufficiency may be at the bottom of this; facial expression requires no study from you, you think; it comes by nature to you to know enough about it, and you are not to be taken in.

I confess, for my part, that I *have* been taken in, over and over again. I have been taken in by acquaintances, and I have been taken in (of course) by friends; far oftener by friends than by any other class of persons. How came I to be so deceived? Had I quite misread their faces?

No. Believe me, my first impression of those people, founded on face and manner alone, was invariably true. My mistake was in suffering them to come nearer to me and explain themselves away.

CHAPTER II

The partition which separated my own office from our general outer office in the City was of thick plate-glass. I could see through it what passed in the outer office, without hearing a word. I had it put up in place of a wall that had been there for years,—ever since the house was built. It is no matter whether I did or did not make the change in order that I might derive my first impression of strangers, who came to us on business, from their faces alone, without being influenced by anything they said. Enough to mention that I turned my glass partition to that account, and that a Life-Assurance Office is at all times exposed to be practised upon by the most crafty and cruel of the human race.

It was through my glass partition that I first saw the gentleman whose story I am going to tell.

He had come in without my observing it, and had put his hat and umbrella on the broad counter, and was bending over it to take some papers from one of the clerks. He was about forty or so, dark, exceedingly well dressed in black,—being in mourning,—and the hand he extended with a polite air, had a particularly well-fitting black kid glove upon it. His hair, which was elaborately brushed and oiled, was parted straight up the middle; and he presented this parting to the clerk, exactly (to my thinking) as if he had said, in so many words: "You must take me, if you please, my friend, just as I show myself. Come straight up here, follow the gravel path, keep off the grass, I allow no trespassing."

I conceived a very great aversion to that man the moment I thus saw him.

He had asked for some of our printed forms, and the clerk was giving them to him and explaining them. An obliged and agreeable smile was on his face, and his eyes met those of the clerk with a sprightly look. (I have known a vast quantity of nonsense talked about bad men not looking you in the face. Don't trust that conventional idea. Dishonesty will stare honesty out of countenance, any day in the week, if there is anything to be got by it.)

I saw, in the corner of his eyelash, that he became aware of my looking at him. Immediately he turned the parting in his hair toward the glass partition, as if he said to me with a sweet smile, "Straight up here, if you please. Off the grass!"

In a few moments he had put on his hat and taken up his umbrella, and was gone.

I beckoned the clerk into my room, and asked, "Who was that?"

He had the gentleman's card in his hand. "Mr. Julius Slinkton, Middle Temple."

"A barrister, Mr. Adams?"

"I think not, Sir."

"I should have thought him a clergyman, but for his having no Reverend here," said I.

"Probably, from his appearance," Mr. Adams replied, "he is reading for orders."

I should mention that he wore a dainty white cravat, and dainty linen altogether.

"What did he want, Mr. Adams?"

"Merely a form of proposal. Sir, and form of reference."

"Recommended here? Did he say?"

"Yes, he said he was recommended here by a friend of yours. He noticed you, but said that as he had not the pleasure of your personal acquaintance he would not trouble you."

"Did he know my name?"

"O yes, Sir! He said, 'There *is* Mr. Sampson, I see!'"

"A well-spoken gentleman, apparently?"

"Remarkably so, Sir."

"Insinuating manners, apparently?"

"Very much so, indeed, Sir."

"Hah!" said I. "I want nothing at present, Mr. Adams."

Within a fortnight of that day I went to dine with a friend of mine, a merchant, a man of taste, who buys pictures and books, and the first man I saw among the company was Mr. Julius Slinkton. There he was, standing before the fire, with good large eyes and an open expression of face; but still (I thought) requiring everybody to come at him by the prepared way he offered, and by no other.

I noticed him ask my friend to introduce him to Mr. Sampson, and my friend did so. Mr. Slinkton was very happy to see me. Not too happy; there was no over-doing of the matter; happy in a thoroughly well-bred, perfectly unmeaning way.

"I thought you had met," our host observed.

"No," said Mr. Slinkton. "I did look in at Mr. Sampson's office, on your recommendation; but I really did not feel justified in troubling Mr. Sampson himself, on a point in the everyday routine of an ordinary clerk."

I said I should have been glad to show him any attention on our friend's introduction.

"I am sure of that," said he, "and am much obliged. At another time, perhaps, I may be less delicate. Only, however, if I have real business; for I know, Mr. Sampson, how precious business time is, and what a vast number of impertinent people there are in the world."

I acknowledged his consideration with a slight bow. "You were thinking," said I, "of effecting a policy on your life."

"O dear no! . I am afraid I am not so prudent as you pay me the compliment of supposing me to be, Mr. Sampson. I merely inquired for a friend. But you know what friends are in such matters. Nothing may ever come of it. I have the greatest reluctance to trouble men of business with inquiries for friends, knowing the probabilities to be a thousand to one that the friends will never follow them up. People are so fickle, so selfish, so inconsiderate. Don't you, in your business, find them so every day, Mr. Sampson?"

I was going to give a qualified answer; but he turned his smooth, white parting on me with its "Straight up here, if you please!" and I answered "Yes."

"I hear, Mr. Sampson," he resumed presently, for our friend had a new cook, and dinner was not so punctual as usual, "that your profession has recently suffered a great loss."

"In money?" said I.

He laughed at my ready association of loss with money, and replied, "No, in talent and vigour."

Not at once following out his allusion, I considered for a moment. "*Has* it sustained a loss of that kind?" said I. "I was not aware of it."

"Understand me, Mr. Sampson. I don't imagine that you have retired. It is not so bad as that. But Mr. Meltham——"

"O, to be sure!" said I. "Yes! Mr. Meltham, the young actuary of the 'Inestimable.'"

"Just so," he returned in a consoling way.

"He is a great loss. He was at once the most profound, the most original, and the most energetic man I have ever known connected with Life Assurance."

I spoke strongly ;' for I had a high esteem and admiration for Meltham ; and my gentleman had indefinitely conveyed to me some suspicion that he wanted to sneer at him. He recalled me to my guard by presenting that trim pathway up his head, with its infernal "Not on the grass, if you please— the gravel."

"You knew him, Mr. Slinkton."

"Only by reputation. To have known him as an acquaint-ance or as a friend, is an honour I should have sought if he had remained in society, though I might never have had the good fortune to attain it, being a man of far inferior mark. He was scarcely above thirty, I suppose?"

"About thirty."

"Ah!" he sighed in his former consoling way. "What creatures we are! To break up, Mr. Sampson, and become incapable of business at that time of life!—Any reason assigned for the melancholy fact?"

("Humph!" thought I, as I looked at him. "But I won't go up the track, and I will go on the grass.")

"What reason have you heard assigned, Mr. Slinkton?" I asked, point-blank.

"Most likely a false one. You know what Rumour is, Mr. Sampson. I never repeat what I hear ; it is the only way of paring the nails and shaving the head of Rumour. But when *you* ask me what reason I have heard assigned for Mr. Meltham's passing away from among men, it is another thing. I am not gratifying idle gossip then. I was told, Mr. Sampson, that Mr. Meltham had relinquished all his avocations and all his prospects, because he was, in fact, broken-hearted. A disappointed attachment I heard,—though it hardly seems probable, in the case of a man so distinguished and so attractive."

"Attractions and distinctions are no armour against death," said I.

"O, she died? Pray pardon me. I did not hear that. That, indeed, makes it very, very sad. Poor Mr. Meltham! She died? Ah, dear me! Lamentable, lamentable!"

I still thought his pity was not quite genuine, and I still suspected an unaccountable sneer under all this, until he said, as we were parted, like the other knots of talkers, by the announcement of dinner:

"Mr. Sampson, you are surprised to see me so moved on behalf of a man whom I have never known. I am not so disinterested as you may suppose. I have suffered, and recently too, from death myself. I have lost one of two charming nieces, who were my constant companions. She died young—barely three-and-twenty; and even her remaining sister is far from strong. The world is a grave!"

He said this with deep feeling, and I felt reproached for the coldness of my manner. Coldness and distrust had been engendered in me, I knew, by my bad experiences; they were not natural to me; and I often thought how much I had lost in life, losing trustfulness, and how little I had gained, gaining hard caution. This state of mind being habitual to me, I troubled myself more about this conversation than I might have troubled myself about a greater matter. I listened to his talk at dinner, and observed how readily other men responded to it, and with what a graceful instinct he adapted his subjects to the knowledge and habits of those he talked with. As, in talking with me, he had easily started the subject I might be supposed to understand best, and to be the most interested in, so, in talking with others, he guided himself by the same rule. The company was of a varied character; but he was not at fault, that I could discover, with any member of it. He knew just as much of each man's pursuit as made him agreeable to that man in reference to it, and just as little as made it natural in him to seek modestly for information when the theme was broached.

As he talked and talked—but really not too much, for the rest of us seemed to force it upon him—I became quite angry with myself. I took his face to pieces in my mind, like a watch, and examined it in detail. I could not say much against any of his features separately; I could say even less against them when they were put together. "Then is it not monstrous," I asked myself, "that because a man happens to part his hair straight up the middle of his head, I should permit myself to suspect, and even to detest him?"

(I may stop to remark that this was no proof of my sense. An observer of men who finds himself steadily repelled by some apparently trifling thing in a stranger is right to give it great weight. It may be the clue to the whole mystery. A hair or two will show where a lion is hidden. A very little key will open a very heavy door.)

I took my part in the conversation with him after a time, and we got on remarkably well. In the drawing-room I asked the host how long he had known Mr. Slinkton. He answered, not many months; he had met him at the house of a celebrated painter then present, who had known him well when he was travelling with his nieces in Italy for their health. His plans in life being broken by the death of one of them, he was reading with the intention of going back to college as a matter of form, taking his degree, and going into orders. I could not but argue with myself that here was the true explanation of his interest in poor Meltham, and that I had been almost brutal in my distrust on that simple head.

CHAPTER III

On the very next day but one I was sitting behind my glass partition, as before, when he came into the outer office, as before. The moment I saw him again without hearing him, I hated him worse than ever.

It was only for a moment that I had this opportunity; for he waved his tight-fitting black glove the instant I looked at him, and came straight in.

"Mr. Sampson, good-day! I presume, you see, upon your kind permission to intrude upon you. I don't keep my word in being justified by business, for my business here—if I may so abuse the word—is of the slightest nature."

I asked, was it anything I could assist him in?

"'I thank you, no. I merely called to inquire outside whether my dilatory friend had been so false to himself as to be practical and sensible. But, of course, he has done nothing. I gave him your papers with my own hand, and he was hot upon the intention, but of course he has done nothing. Apart from the general human disinclination to do anything that ought to be done, I dare say there is a specialty about assuring one's life. You find it like will-making. People are so superstitious, and take it for granted they will die soon afterwards."

"Up here, if you please; straight up here, Mr. Sampson. Neither to the right nor to the left." I almost fancied I could hear him breathe the words as he sat smiling at me, with that intolerable parting exactly opposite the bridge of my nose.

"There is such a feeling sometimes, no doubt," I replied; "but I don't think it obtains to any great extent."

"Well," said he, with a shrug and a smile, "I wish some good angel would influence my friend in the right direction. I rashly promised his mother and sister in Norfolk to see it done, and he promised them that he would do it. But I suppose he never will."

He spoke for a minute or two on indifferent topics, and went away.

I had scarcely unlocked the drawers of my writing-table next morning, when he reappeared. I noticed that he came straight to the door in the glass partition, and did not pause a single moment outside.

"Can you spare me two minutes, my dear Mr. Sampson?"

"By all means."

"Much obliged," laying his hat and umbrella on the table; "I came early, not to interrupt you. The fact is, I am taken by surprise in reference to this proposal my friend has made."

"Has he made one?" said I.

"Ye-es," he answered, deliberately looking at me; and then a bright idea seemed to strike him—"or he only tells me he has. Perhaps that may be a new way of evading the matter. By Jupiter, I never thought of that!"

Mr. Adams was opening the morning's letters in the outer office. "What is the name, Mr. Slinkton?" I asked.

"Beckwith."

I looked out at the door and requested Mr. Adams, if there

were a proposal in that name, to bring it in. He had already laid it out of his hand on the counter. It was easily selected from the rest, and he gave it me. Alfred Beckwith. Proposal to effect a policy with us for two thousand pounds. Dated yesterday.

"From the Middle Temple, I see, Mr. Slinkton."

"Yes. He lives on the same staircase with me; his door is opposite. I never thought he would make me his reference though."

"It seems natural enough that he should."

"Quite so, Mr. Sampson; but I never thought of it. Let me see." He took the printed paper from his pocket. "How am I to answer all these questions?"

"According to the truth, of course," said I.

"O, of course!" he answered, looking up from the paper with a smile; "I meant they were so many. But you do right to be particular. It stands to reason that you must be particular. Will you allow me to use your pen and ink?"

"Certainly."

"And your desk?"

"Certainly."

He had been hovering about between his hat and his umbrella for a place to write on. He now sat down in my chair, at my blotting-paper and inkstand, with the long walk up his head in accurate perspective before me, as I stood with my back to the fire.

Before answering each question he ran over it aloud, and discussed it. How long had he known Mr. Alfred Beckwith? That he had to calculate by years upon his fingers. What were his habits? No difficulty about them; temperate in the last degree, and took a little too much exercise, if anything. All the answers were satisfactory. When he had written them all, he looked them over, and finally signed them in a very pretty hand. He supposed he had now done with the business. I told him he was not likely to be troubled any farther. Should he leave the papers there? If he pleased. Much obliged. Good morning.

I had had one other visitor before him; not at the office, but at my own house. That visitor had come to my bedside when it was not yet daylight, and had been seen by no one else but by my faithful confidential servant.

A second reference paper (for we required always two) was

sent down into Norfolk, and was duly received back by post. This, likewise, was satisfactorily answered in every respect. Our forms were all complied with ; we accepted the proposal, and the premium for one year was paid.

CHAPTER IV

FOR six or seven months I saw no more of Mr. Slinkton. He called once at my house, but I was not at home ; and he once asked me to dine with him in the Temple, but I was engaged. His friend's assurance was effected in March. Late in September or early in October I was down at Scarborough for a breath of sea-air, where I met him on the beach. It was a hot evening ; he came toward me with his hat in his hand ; and there was the walk I had felt so strongly disinclined to take in perfect order again, exactly in front of the bridge of my nose.

He was not alone, but had a young lady on his arm.

She was dressed in mourning, and I looked at her with great interest. She had the appearance of being extremely delicate, and her face was remarkably pale and melancholy; but she was very pretty. He introduced her as his niece, Miss Niner.

"Are you strolling, Mr. Sampson ? Is it possible you can be idle ? "

It *was* possible, and I *was* strolling.

"Shall we stroll together ? "

"With pleasure."

The young lady walked between us, and we walked on the cool sea sand, in the direction of Filey.

"There have been wheels here," said Mr. Slinkton. "And now I look again, the wheels of a hand-carriage ! Margaret, my love, your shadow without doubt ! "

"Miss Niner's shadow ? " I repeated, looking down at it on the sand.

"Not that one," Mr. Slinkton returned, laughing. " Margaret, my dear, tell Mr. Sampson."

"Indeed," said the young lady, turning to me, "there is nothing to tell—except that I constantly see the same invalid old gentleman at all times, wherever I go. I have mentioned it to my uncle, and he calls the gentleman my shadow."

"Does he live in Scarborough?" I asked.

"He is staying here."

"Do you live in Scarborough?"

"No, I am staying here. My uncle has placed me with a family here, for my health."

"And your shadow?" said I, smiling.

"My shadow," she answered, smiling too, "is—like myself —not very robust, I fear; for I lose my shadow sometimes, as my shadow loses me at other times. We both seem liable to confinement to the house. I have not seen my shadow for days and days; but it does oddly happen, occasionally, that wherever I go, for many days together, this gentleman goes. We have come together in the most unfrequented nooks on this shore."

"Is this he?" said I, pointing before us.

The wheels had swept down to the water's edge, and described a great loop on the sand in turning. Bringing the loop back towards us, and spinning it out as it came, was a hand-carriage, drawn by a man.

"Yes," said Miss Niner, "this really is my shadow, uncle."

As the carriage approached us and we approached the carriage, I saw within it an old man, whose head was sunk on his breast, and who was enveloped in a variety of wrappers. He was drawn by a very quiet but very keen-looking man, with iron-grey hair, who was slightly lame. They had passed us, when the carriage stopped, and the old gentleman within, putting out his arm, called to me by my name. I went back, and was absent from Mr. Slinkton and his niece for about five minutes.

When I rejoined them, Mr. Slinkton was the first to speak. Indeed, he said to me in a raised voice before I came up with him:

"It is well you have not been longer, or my niece might have died of curiosity to know who her shadow is, Mr. Sampson."

"An old East India Director," said I. "An intimate friend of our friend's, at whose house I first had the pleasure of meeting you. A certain Major Banks. You have heard of him?"

"Never."

"Very rich, Miss Niner; but very old, and very crippled.

An amiable man, sensible—much interested in you. He has just been expatiating on the affection that he has observed to exist between you and your uncle."

Mr. Slinkton was holding his hat again, and he passed his hand up the straight walk, as if he himself went up it serenely, after me.

"Mr. Sampson," he said, tenderly pressing his niece's arm in his, "our affection was always a strong one, for we have had but few near ties. We have still fewer now. We have associations to bring us together, that are not of this world, Margaret."

"Dear uncle!" murmured the young lady, and turned her face aside to hide her tears.

"My niece and I have such remembrances and regrets in common, Mr. Sampson," he feelingly pursued, "that it would be strange indeed if the relations between us were cold or indifferent. If I remember a conversation we once had together, you will understand the reference I make. Cheer up, dear Margaret. Don't droop, don't droop. My Margaret! I cannot bear to see you droop!"

The poor young lady was very much affected, but controlled herself. His feelings, too, were very acute. In a word, he found himself under such great need of a restorative, that he presently went away, to take a bath of sea-water, leaving the young lady and me sitting by a point of rock, and probably presuming—but that you will say was a pardonable indulgence in a luxury—that she would praise him with all her heart.

She did, poor thing! With all her confiding heart, she praised him to me, for his care of her dead sister, and for his untiring devotion in her last illness. The sister had wasted away very slowly, and wild and terrible fantasies had come over her toward the end, but he had never been impatient with her, or at a loss; had always been gentle, watchful, and self-possessed. The sister had known him, as she had known him, to be the best of men, the kindest of men, and yet a man of such admirable strength of character, as to be a very tower for the support of their weak natures while their poor lives endured.

"I shall leave him, Mr. Sampson, very soon," said the young lady; "I know my life is drawing to an end; and when I am gone, I hope he will marry and be happy. I am sure he has lived single so long, only for my sake, and for my poor, poor sister's."

The little hand-carriage had made another great loop on the damp sand, and was coming back again, gradually spinning out a slim figure of eight, half a mile long.

"Young lady," said I, looking around, laying my hand upon her arm, and speaking in a low voice, "time presses. You hear the gentle murmur of that sea?"

She looked at me with the utmost wonder and alarm, saying,

"Yes!"

"And you know what a voice is in it when the storm comes?"

"Yes!"

"You see how quiet and peaceful it lies before us, and you know what an awful sight of power without pity it might be, this very night!"

"Yes!"

"But if you had never heard or seen it, or heard of it in its cruelty, could you believe that it beats every inanimate thing in its way to pieces, without mercy, and destroys life without remorse?"

"You terrify me, Sir, by these questions!"

"To save you, young lady, to save you! For God's sake, collect your strength and collect your firmness! If you were here alone, and hemmed in by the rising tide on the flow to fifty feet above your head, you could not be in greater danger than the danger you are now to be saved from."

The figure on the sand was spun out, and straggled off into a crooked little jerk that ended at the cliff very near us.

"As I am, before Heaven and the Judge of all mankind, your friend, and your dead sister's friend, I solemnly entreat you, Miss Niner, without one moment's loss of time, to come to this gentleman with me!"

If the little carriage had been less near to us, I doubt if I could have got her away; but it was so near that we were there before she had recovered the hurry of being urged from the rock. I did not remain there with her two minutes. Certainly within five, I had the inexpressible satisfaction of seeing her—from the point we had sat on, and to which I had returned—half supported and half carried up some rude steps notched in the cliff, by the figure of an active man. With that figure beside her, I knew she was safe anywhere.

I sat alone on the rock, awaiting Mr. Slinkton's return. The twilight was deepening and the shadows were heavy, when he came round the point, with his hat hanging at his button-hole, smoothing his wet hair with one of his hands, and picking out the old path with the other and a pocket-comb.

"My niece not here, Mr. Sampson?" he said, looking about.

"Miss Niner seemed to feel a chill in the air after the sun was down, and has gone home."

He looked surprised, as though she were not accustomed to do anything without him ; even to originate so slight a proceeding.

"I persuaded Miss Niner," I explained.

"Ah!" said he. "She is easily persuaded—for her good. Thank you, Mr. Sampson ; she is better within doors. The bathing-place was farther than I thought, to say the truth."

"Miss Niner is very delicate," I observed.

He shook his head and drew a deep sigh. "Very, very, very. You may recollect my saying so. The time that has since intervened has not strengthened her. The gloomy shadow that fell upon her sister so early in life seems, in my anxious eyes, to gather over her, ever darker, ever darker. Dear Margaret, dear Margaret! But we must hope."

The hand-carriage was spinning away before us at a most indecorous pace for an invalid vehicle, and was making most irregular curves upon the sand. Mr. Slinkton, noticing it after he had put his handkerchief to his eyes, said:

"If I may judge from appearances, your friend will be upset, Mr. Sampson."

"It looks probable, certainly," said I.

"The servant must be drunk."

"The servants of old gentlemen will get drunk sometimes," said I.

"The major draws very light, Mr. Sampson."

"The major does draw light," said I.

By this time the carriage, much to my relief, was lost in the darkness. We walked on for a little, side by side over the sand, in silence. After a short while he said, in a voice still affected by the emotion that his niece's state of health had awakened in him,

"Do you stay here long, Mr. Sampson?"

"Why, no. I am going away to-night."

"So soon? But business always holds you in request. Men like Mr. Sampson are too important to others, to be spared to their own need of relaxation and enjoyment."

"I don't know about that," said I. "However, I am going back."

"To London?"

"To London."

"I shall be there too, soon after you."

I knew that as well as he did. But I did not tell him so. Any more than I told him what defensive weapon my right hand rested on in my pocket, as I walked by his side. Any more than I told him why I did not walk on the sea side of him with the night closing in.

We left the beach, and our ways diverged. We exchanged good night, and had parted indeed, when he said, returning,

"Mr. Sampson, *may* I ask? Poor Meltham, whom we spoke of,—dead yet?"

"Not when I last heard of him ; but too broken a man to live long, and hopelessly lost to his old calling."

"Dear, dear, dear !" said he, with great feeling. "Sad, sad, sad ! The world is a grave !" And so went his way.

It was not his fault if the world were not a grave ; but I did not call that observation after him, any more than I had mentioned those other things just now enumerated. He went his way, and I went mine with all expedition. This happened, as I have said, either at the end of September or beginning of October. The next time I saw him, and the last time, was late in November.

CHAPTER V

I HAD a very particular engagement to breakfast in the Temple. It was a bitter north-easterly morning, and the sleet and slush lay inches deep in the streets. I could get no conveyance, and was soon wet to the knees ; but I should have been true to that appointment, though I had to wade to it up to my neck in the same impediments.

The appointment took me to some chambers in the Temple. They were at the top of a lonely corner house overlooking the river. The name, MR. ALFRED BECKWITH, was painted on the outer door. On the door opposite, on the same landing, the name MR. JULIUS SLINKTON. The doors of both sets of chambers stood open, so that anything said aloud in one set could be heard in the other.

I had never been in those chambers before. They were dismal, close, unwholesome, and oppressive; the furniture, originally good, and not yet old, was faded and dirty,—the rooms were in great disorder; there was a strong prevailing smell of opium, brandy, and tobacco; the grate and fire-irons were splashed all over with unsightly blotches of rust; and on a sofa by the fire, in the room where breakfast had been prepared, lay the host, Mr. Beckwith, a man with all the appearances of the worst kind of drunkard, very far advanced upon his shameful way to death.

"Slinkton is not come yet," said this creature, staggering up when I went in; "I'll call him.—Halloa! Julius Cæsar! Come and drink!" As he hoarsely roared this out, he beat the poker and tongs together in a mad way, as if that were his usual manner of summoning his associate.

The voice of Mr. Slinkton was heard through the clatter from the opposite side of the staircase, and he came in. He had not expected the pleasure of meeting me. I have seen several artful men brought to a stand, but I never saw a man so aghast as he was when his eyes rested on mine.

"Julius Cæsar," cried Beckwith, staggering between us, "Mist' Sampson! Mist' Sampson, Julius Cæsar! Julius, Mist' Sampson, is the friend of my soul. Julius keeps me plied with liquor, morning, noon, and night. Julius is a real benefactor. Julius threw the tea and coffee out of window when I used to have any. Julius empties all the water-jugs of their contents, and fills 'em with spirits. Julius winds me up and keeps me going.—Boil the brandy, Julius!"

There was a rusty and furred saucepan in the ashes,—the ashes looked like the accumulation of weeks,—and Beckwith, rolling and staggering between us as if he were going to plunge headlong into the fire, got the saucepan out, and tried to force it into Slinkton's hand.

"Boil the brandy, Julius Cæsar! Come! Do your usual office. Boil the brandy!"

He became so fierce in his gesticulations with the saucepan, that I expected to see him lay open Slinkton's head with it. I therefore put out my hand to check him. He reeled back to the sofa, and sat there panting, shaking, and red-eyed, in his rags of dressing-gown, looking at us both. I noticed then that there was nothing to drink on the table but brandy, and nothing to eat but salted herrings, and a hot, sickly, highly-peppered stew.

"At all events, Mr. Sampson," said Slinkton, offering me the smooth gravel path for the last time, "I thank you for interfering between me and this unfortunate man's violence. However you came here, Mr. Sampson, or with whatever motive you came here, at least I thank you for that."

"Boil the brandy," muttered Beckwith.

Without gratifying his desire to know how I came there, I said, quietly, "How is your niece, Mr. Slinkton?"

He looked hard at me, and I looked hard at him.

"I am sorry to say, Mr. Sampson, that my niece has proved treacherous and ungrateful to her best friend. She left me without a word of notice or explanation. She was misled, no doubt, by some designing rascal. Perhaps you may have heard of it."

"I did hear that she was misled by a designing rascal. In fact, I have proof of it."

"Are you sure of that?" said he.

"Quite."

"Boil the brandy," muttered Beckwith. "Company to breakfast, Julius Cæsar. Do your usual office,—provide the usual breakfast, dinner, tea, and supper. Boil the brandy!"

The eyes of Slinkton looked from him to me, and he said, after a moment's consideration,

"Mr. Sampson, you are a man of the world, and so am I. I will be plain with you."

"O no, you won't," said I, shaking my head.

"I tell you, Sir, I will be plain with you."

"And I tell you you will not," said I. "I know all about you. *You* plain with any one? Nonsense, nonsense!"

"I plainly tell you, Mr. Sampson, he went on, with a manner almost composed, "that I understand your object. You want to save your funds, and escape from your liabilities; these are old tricks of trade with you Office-gentlemen. But you will not do it, Sir; you will not succeed. You have not an easy adversary to play against, when you play against me. We shall have to inquire, in due time, when and how Mr. Beckwith fell into his present habits. With that remark, Sir, I put this poor creature, and his incoherent wanderings of speech, aside, and wish you a good morning and a better case next time."

While he was saying this, Beckwith had filled a half-pint glass with brandy. At this moment, he threw the brandy at his face, and threw the glass after it. Slinkton put his hands up, half blinded with the spirit, and cut with the glass across the forehead. At the sound of the breakage, a fourth person came into the room, closed the door, and stood at it; he was a very quiet but very keen-looking man, with iron-grey hair, and slightly lame.

Slinkton pulled out his handkerchief, assuaged the pain in his smarting eyes, and dabbled the blood on his forehead. He was a long time about it, and I saw that in the doing of it, a tremendous change came over him, occasioned by the change in Beckwith,—who ceased to pant and tremble, sat upright, and never took his eyes off him. I never in my life saw a face in which abhorrence and determination were so forcibly painted as in Beckwith's then.

"Look at me, you villain," said Beckwith, "and see me as I really am. I took these rooms, to make them a trap for you. I came into them as a drunkard, to bait the trap for you. You fell into the trap, and you will never leave it alive. On the morning when you last went to Mr. Sampson's office, I had seen him first. Your plot has been known to both of us, all along, and you have been counter-plotted all along. What? Having been cajoled into putting that prize of two thousand pounds in your power, I was to be done to death with brandy, and, brandy not proving quick enough, with something quicker? Have I never seen you, when you thought my senses gone, pouring from your little bottle into my glass? Why, you Murderer and Forger, alone here with you in the dead of night, as I have so often been, I have had my hand upon the trigger of a pistol, twenty times, to blow your brains out!"

This sudden starting up of the thing that he had supposed to be his imbecile victim into a determined man, with a settled resolution to hunt him down and be the death of him, mercilessly expressed from head to foot, was, in the first shock, too much for him. Without any figure of speech, he staggered under it. But there is no greater mistake than to suppose that a man who is a calculating criminal, is, in any phase of his guilt, otherwise than true to himself, and perfectly consistent with his whole character. Such a man commits murder, and murder is the natural culmination of his course; such a man has to outface murder, and will do it with hardihood and effrontery. It is a sort of fashion to express surprise that any notorious criminal, having such crime upon his conscience, can so brave it out. Do you think that if he had it on his conscience at all, or had a conscience to have it upon, he would ever have committed the crime?

Perfectly consistent with himself, as I believe all such monsters to be, this Slinkton recovered himself. and showed a defiance that was sufficiently cold and quiet. He was white, he was haggard, he was changed : but only as a sharper who had played for a great stake and had been outwitted and had lost the game.

" Listen to me, you villain," said Beckwith, " and let every word you hear me say be a stab in your wicked heart. When I took these rooms, to throw myself in your way and lead you on to the scheme that I knew my appearance and supposed character and habits would suggest to such a devil, how did I know that? Because you were no stranger to me. I knew you well. And I knew you to be the cruel wretch who, for so much money, had killed one innocent girl while she trusted him implicitly, and who was by inches killing another."

Slinkton took out a snuff-box, took a pinch of snuff, and laughed.

" But see here," said Beckwith, never looking away, never raising his voice, never relaxing his face, never unclenching his hand. " See what a dull wolf you have been, after all ! The infatuated drunkard who never drank a fiftieth part of the liquor you plied him with, but poured it away, here, there, everywhere—almost before your eyes ; who bought over the fellow you set to watch him and to ply him, by out-bidding you in his bribe, before he had been at his work three days—with whom you have observed no caution, yet who was so bent on ridding the earth of you as a wild beast, that he would have defeated you if you had been ever so prudent—that drunkard whom you have, many a time, left on the floor of this room, and who has even let you go out of it, alive and undeceived, when you have turned him over with your foot—has, almost as often, on the same night, within an hour, within a few minutes, watched you awake, had his hand at your pillow when you were asleep, turned over your papers, taken samples from your bottles and packets of powder, changed their contents, rifled every secret of your life ! "

He had had another pinch of snuff in his hand, but had

gradually let it drop from between his fingers to the floor; where he now smoothed it out with his foot, looking down at it the while.

"That drunkard," said Beckwith, "who had free access to your rooms at all times, that he might drink the strong drinks that you left in his way and be the sooner ended, holding no more terms with you than he would hold with a tiger, has had his master-key for all your locks, his test for all your poisons, his clue to your cipher-writing. He can tell you, as well as you can tell him, how long it took to complete that deed, what doses there were, what intervals, what signs of gradual decay upon mind and body; what distempered fancies were produced, what observable changes, what physical pain. He can tell you, as well as you can tell him, that all this was recorded day by day, as a lesson of experience for future service. He can tell you, better than you can tell him, where that journal is at this moment."

Slinkton stopped the action of his foot, and looked at Beckwith.

"No," said the latter, as if answering a question from him. "Not in the drawer of the writing-desk that opens with a spring; it is not there, and it never will be there again.

"Then you are a thief!" said Slinkton.

Without any change whatever in the inflexible purpose, which it was quite terrific even to me to contemplate, and from the power of which I had always felt convinced it was impossible for this wretch to escape, Beckwith returned,

"And I am your niece's shadow, too."

With an imprecation Slinkton put his hand to his head, tore out some hair, and flung it to the ground. It was the end of the smooth walk; he destroyed it in the action, and it will soon be seen that his use for it was past.

Beckwith went on: "Whenever you left here, I left here. Although I understood that you found it necessary to pause in the completion of that purpose, to avert suspicion, still I watched you close, with the poor confiding girl. When I had the diary, and could read it word by word,—it was only about the night before your last visit to Scarborough,—you remember the night? you slept with a small flat vial tied to your wrist,—I sent to Mr. Sampson, who was kept out of view. This is Mr. Sampson's trusty servant standing by the door. We three saved your niece among us."

Slinkton looked at us all, took an uncertain step or two from the place where he had stood, returned to it, and glanced about him in a very curious way,—as one of the meaner reptiles might, looking for a hole to hide in. I noticed at the same time, that a singular change took place in the figure of the man,—as if it collapsed within his clothes, and they consequently became ill-shapen and ill-fitting.

"You shall know," said Beckwith, "for I hope the knowledge will be bitter and terrible to you, why you have been pursued by one man, and why, when the whole interest that Mr. Sampson represents would have expended any money in hunting you down, you have been tracked to death at a single individual's charge. I hear you have had the name of Meltham on your lips sometimes?"

I saw, in addition to those other changes, a sudden stoppage come upon his breathing.

"When you sent the sweet girl whom you murdered (you know with what artfully made-out surroundings and probabilities you sent her) to Meltham's office, before taking her abroad to originate the transaction that doomed her to the grave, it fell to Meltham's lot to see her and to speak with her. It did not fall to his lot to save her, though I know he would freely give his own life to have done it. He admired her;—I would say he loved her deeply, if I thought it possible that you could understand the word. When she was sacrificed, he was thoroughly assured of your guilt. Having lost her, he had but one object left in life, and that was to avenge her and destroy you."

I saw the villain's nostrils rise and fall convulsively; but I saw no moving at his mouth.

"That man Meltham," Beckwith steadily pursued, "was as absolutely certain that you could never elude him in this world, if he devoted himself to your destruction with his utmost fidelity and earnestness, and if he divided the sacred duty with no other duty in life, as he was certain that in achieving it he would be a poor instrument in the hands of Providence, and would do well before Heaven in striking you out from among living men. I am that man, and I thank God that I have done my work!"

If Slinkton had been running for his life from swift-footed savages, a dozen miles, he could not have shown more emphatic signs of being oppressed at heart and labouring for breath, than he showed now, when he looked at the pursuer who had so relentlessly hunted him down. .

"You never saw me under my right name before; you see me under my right name now. You shall see me once again in the body, when you are tried for your life. You shall see me once again in the spirit, when the cord is round your neck, and the crowd are crying against you!"

When Meltham had spoken these last words, the miscreant suddenly turned away his face, and seemed to strike his mouth with his open hand. At the same instant, the room was filled with a new and powerful odour, and, almost at the same instant, he broke into a crooked run, leap, start, —I have no name for the spasm,—and fell, with a dull weight that shook the heavy old doors and windows in their frames.

That was the fitting end of him.

When we saw that he was dead, we drew away from the room, and Meltham, giving me his hand, said, with a weary air,

"I have no more work on earth, my friend. But I shall see her again elsewhere."

It was in vain that I tried to rally him. He might have saved her, he said; he had not saved her, and he reproached himself; he had lost her, and he was broken-hearted.

"The purpose that sustained me is over, Sampson, and there is nothing now to hold me to life. I am not fit for life; I am weak and spiritless; I have no hope and no object; my day is done."

In truth, I could hardly have believed that the broken man who then spoke to me was the man who had so strongly and so differently impressed me when his purpose was before him. I used such entreaties with him, as I could; but he still said, and always said, in a patient, undemonstrative way,—nothing could avail him,—he was broken-hearted.

He died early in the next spring. He was buried by the side of the poor young lady for whom he had cherished those tender and unhappy regrets; and he left all he had to her sister. She lived to be a happy wife and mother; she married my sister's son, who succeeded poor Meltham; she is living now, and her children ride about the garden on my walking-stick when I go to see her.

HOLIDAY ROMANCE

CHARACTERS

CAPTAIN BOLDHEART, master of the schooner *Beauty;* hero of Master Robin Redforth's romance.

WILLIAM BOOZEY, one of the crew of the *Beauty.*

BROWN, a vicious, greedy (grown-up) boy, in Miss Nettie Ashford's romance.

PRINCE CERTAINPERSONIO, a young gentleman who "marries" Princess Alicia.

THE MASTER LATIN-GRAMMAR, an old teacher and enemy of Captain Boldheart.

MR. JAMES ORANGE, the husband of Mrs. Orange.

PICKLES, a fishmonger in Miss Alice Rainbird's romance.

LIEUTENANT-COLONEL ROBIN REDFORTH, a young gentleman aged nine, assuming the part of a bloodthirsty pirate.

WILLIAM TINKLING, Esq., a young gentleman eight years old, to whom Miss Nettie Ashford is "married."

TOM, an impudent boy ; cousin to Captain Boldheart.

PRINCESS ALICIA, the heroine of Miss Alice Rainbird's romance.

MRS. ALICUMPAINE, a character in Miss Nettie Ashford's romance.

MRS. BLACK, one of Mrs. Lemon's pupils.

MISS DROWVEY, a schoolmistress in partnership with Miss Grimmer.

FAIRY GRANDMARINA, godmother of the Princess Alicia.

MISS GRIMMER, a schoolmistress.

MRS. LEMON, the proprietress of a preparatory school for grown-up pupils.

ALICE RAINBIRD, the "bride" of Robin Redforth.

HOLIDAY ROMANCE

IN FOUR PARTS

PART I

INTRODUCTORY ROMANCE FROM THE PEN OF WILLIAM TINKLING, ESQ.[1]

THIS beginning-part is not made out of anybody's head, you know. It's real. You must believe this beginning-part more than what comes after, else you won't understand how what comes after came to be written. You must believe it all; but you must believe this most, please. I am the editor of it. Bob Redforth (he's my cousin, and shaking the table on purpose) wanted to be the editor of it; but I said he shouldn't because he couldn't. *He* has no idea of being an editor.

Nettie Ashford is my bride. We were married in the right-hand closet in the corner of the dancing-school, where first we met, with a ring (a green one) from Wilkingwater's toy-shop. *I* owed for it out of my pocket-money. When the rapturous ceremony was over, we all four went up the lane and let off a cannon (brought loaded in Bob Redforth's waistcoat-pocket) to announce our nuptials. It flew right up when it went off, and turned over. Next day, Lieut.-Col. Robin Redforth was united, with similar ceremonies, to Alice Rainbird. This time the cannon burst with a most terrific explosion, and made a puppy bark.

My peerless bride was, at the period of which we now treat, in captivity at Miss Grimmer's. Drowvey and Grim-

[1] Aged eight,

mer is the partnership, and opinion is divided which is the greatest beast. The lovely bride of the colonel was also immured in the dungeons of the same establishment. A vow was entered into, between the colonel and myself, that we would cut them out on the following Wednesday when walking two and two.

Under the desperate circumstances of the case, the active brain of the colonel, combining with his lawless pursuit (he is a pirate), suggested an attack with fireworks. This, however, from motives of humanity, was abandoned as too expensive.

Lightly armed with a paper-knife buttoned up under his jacket, and waving the dreaded black flag at the end of a cane, the colonel took command of me at two P.M. on the eventful and appointed day. He had drawn out the plan of attack on a piece of paper, which was rolled up round a hoop-stick. He showed it to me. My position and my full-length portrait (but my real ears don't stick out horizontal) was behind a corner lamp-post, with written orders to remain there till I should see Miss Drowvey fall. The Drowvey who was to fall was the one in spectacles, not the one with the large lavender bonnet. At that signal I was to rush forth, seize my bride, and fight my way to the lane. There a junction would be effected between myself and the colonel; and putting our brides behind us, between ourselves and the palings, we were to conquer or die.

The enemy appeared,—approached. Waving his black flag, the colonel attacked. Confusion ensued. Anxiously I awaited my signal; but my signal came not. So far from falling, the hated Drowvey in spectacles appeared to me to have muffled the colonel's head in his outlawed banner, and to be pitching into him with a parasol. The one in the lavender bonnet also performed prodigies of valour with her fists on his back. Seeing that all was for the moment lost, I fought my desperate way hand to hand to the lane. Through taking the back road, I was so fortunate as to meet nobody, and arrived there uninterrupted.

It seemed an age ere the colonel joined me. He had been to the jobbing tailor's to be sewn up in several places, and attributed our defeat to the refusal of the detested Drowvey to fall. Finding her so obstinate, he had said to her "Die, recreant!" but had found her no more open to reason on that point than the other.

My blooming bride appeared, accompanied by the colonel's

bride, at the dancing-school next day. What? Was her face averted from me? Hah? Even so. With a look of scorn, she put into my hand a bit of paper, and took another partner. On the paper was pencilled, "Heavens! Can I write the word? Is my husband a cow?"

In the first bewilderment of my heated brain, I tried to think what slanderer could have traced my family to the ignoble animal mentioned above. Vain were my endeavours. At the end of that dance I whispered the colonel to come into the cloak-room, and I showed him the note.

"There is a syllable wanting," said he, with a gloomy brow.

"Hah! What syllable?" was my inquiry.

"She asks, can she write the word? And no; you see she couldn't," said the colonel, pointing out the passage.

"And the word was?" said I.

"Cow—cow—coward," hissed the pirate-colonel in my ear, and gave me back the note.

Feeling that I must for ever tread the earth a branded boy,—person I mean,—or that I must clear up my honour, I demanded to be tried by a court-martial. The colonel admitted my right to be tried. Some difficulty was found in composing the court, on account of the Emperor of France's aunt refusing to let him come out. He was to be the president. Ere yet we had appointed a substitute, he made his escape over the back-wall, and stood among us, a free monarch.

The court was held on the grass by the pond. I recognised, in a certain admiral among my judges, my deadliest foe. A cocoa-nut had given rise to language that I could not brook; but confiding in my innocence, and also in the knowledge that the President of the United States (who sat next him) owed me a knife, I braced myself for the ordeal.

It was a solemn spectacle, that court. Two executioners with pinafores reversed led me in. Under the shade of an umbrella I perceived my bride, supported by the bride of the pirate-colonel. The president, having reproved a little female ensign for tittering, on a matter of life or death, called upon me to plead, "Coward or no coward, guilty or not guilty?" I pleaded in a firm tone, "No coward and not guilty." (The little female ensign being again reproved by the president for misconduct, mutinied, left the court, and threw stones.)

My implacable enemy, the admiral, conducted the case against me. The colonel's bride was called to prove that I had remained behind the corner lamp-post during the engagement. I might have been spared the anguish of my own bride's being also made a witness to the same point, but the admiral knew where to wound me. Be still, my soul, no matter. The colonel was then brought forward with his evidence.

It was for this point that I had saved myself up, as the turning-point of my case. Shaking myself free of my guards, —who had no business to hold me, the stupids, unless I was found guilty,—I asked the colonel what he considered the first duty of a soldier? Ere he could reply, the President of the United States rose and informed the court, that my foe, the admiral, had suggested "Bravery," and that prompting a witness wasn't fair. The president of the court immediately ordered the admiral's mouth to be filled with leaves, and tied up with string. I had the satisfaction of seeing the sentence carried into effect before the proceedings went further.

I then took a paper from my trousers-pocket, and asked, "What do you consider, Col. Redford, the first duty of a soldier? Is it obedience?"

"It is," said the colonel.

"Is that paper—please to look at it—in your hand?"

"It is," said the colonel.

"Is it a military sketch?"

"It is," said the colonel.

"Of an engagement?"

"Quite so," said the colonel.

"Of the late engagement?"

"Of the late engagement."

"Please to describe it, and then hand it to the president of the court."

From that triumphant moment my sufferings and my dangers were at an end. The court rose up and jumped, on discovering that I had strictly obeyed orders. My foe, the admiral, who though muzzled was malignant yet, contrived to suggest that I was dishonoured by having quitted the field. But the colonel himself had done as much, and gave his opinion, upon his word and honour as a pirate, that when all was lost the field might be quitted without disgrace. I was going to be found "No coward and not guilty," and my blooming bride was going to be publicly restored to my arms in a procession, when an unlooked-for event disturbed the general rejoicing. This was no other than the Emperor of

France's aunt catching hold of his hair. The proceedings abruptly terminated, and the court tumultuously dissolved.

It was when the shades of the next evening but one were beginning to fall, ere yet the silver beams of Luna touched the earth, that four forms might have been descried slowly advancing towards the weeping willow on the borders of the pond, the now deserted scene of the day before yesterday's agonies and triumphs. On a nearer approach, and by a practised eye, these might have been identified as the forms of the pirate-colonel with his bride, and of the day before yesterday's gallant prisoner with his bride.

On the beauteous faces of the Nymphs dejection sat enthroned. All four reclined under the willow for some minutes without speaking, till at length the bride of the colonel poutingly observed, "It's of no use pretending any more, and we had better give it up."

"Hah!" exclaimed the pirate.   "Pretending?"

"Don't go on like that; you worry me," returned his bride.

The lovely bride of Tinkling echoed the incredible declaration.   The two warriors exchanged stony glances.

"If," said the bride of the pirate-colonel, "grown up people won't do what they ought to do, and will put us out, what comes of our pretending?"

"We only get into scrapes," said the bride of Tinkling.

"You know very well," pursued the colonel's bride, "that Miss Drowvey wouldn't fall. You complained of it yourself. And you know how disgracefully the court-martial ended. As to our marriage; would my people acknowledge it at home?"

"Or would my people acknowledge ours?" said the bride of Tinkling.

Again the two warriors exchanged stony glances.

"If you knocked at the door and claimed me, after you were told to go away," said the colonel's bride, "you would only have your hair pulled, or your ears, or your nose."

"If you persisted in ringing at the bell and claiming me," said the bride of Tinkling to that gentleman, "you would have things dropped on your head from the window over the handle, or you would be played upon by the garden-engine."

"And at your own homes," resumed the bride of the colonel, "it would be just as bad. You would be sent to bed, or something equally undignified. Again, how would you support us?"

The pirate-colonel replied in a courageous voice, "By rapine!" But his bride retorted, "Suppose the grown-up people wouldn't be rapined?" "Then," said the colonel, "they should pay the penalty in blood."—"But suppose they should object," retorted his bride, "and wouldn't pay the penalty in blood or anything else?"

A mournful silence ensued.

"Then do you no longer love me, Alice?" asked the colonel.

"Redforth! I am ever thine," returned his bride.

"Then do you no longer love me, Nettie?" asked the present writer.

"Tinkling! I am ever thine," returned my bride.

We all four embraced. Let me not be misunderstood by the giddy. The colonel embraced his own bride, and I embraced mine. But two times two make four.

"Nettie and I," said Alice mournfully, "have been considering our position. The grown-up people are too strong for us. They make us ridiculous. Besides, they have changed the times. William Tinkling's baby brother was christened yesterday. What took place? Was any king present? Answer, William."

I said No, unless disguised as Great-uncle Chopper.

"Any queen?"

There had been no queen that I knew of at our house. There might have been one in the kitchen: but I didn't think so, or the servants would have mentioned it.

"Any fairies?"

None that were visible.

"We had an idea among us, I think," said Alice, with a melancholy smile, "we four, that Miss Grimmer would prove to be the wicked fairy, and would come in at the christening with her crutch-stick, and give the child a bad gift. Was there anything of that sort? Answer, William."

I said that ma had said afterwards (and so she had), that Great-uncle Chopper's gift was a shabby one; but she hadn't said a bad one. She had called it shabby, electrotyped, second-hand, and below his income.

"It must be the grown-up people who have changed all this," said Alice. "*We* couldn't have changed it, if we had been so inclined, and we never should have been. Or perhaps Miss Grimmer *is* a wicked fairy after all, and won't act up to it because the grown-up people have persuaded her not to. Either way, they would make us ridiculous if we told them what we expected."

"Tyrants!" muttered the pirate-colonel.

"Nay, my Redforth," said Alice, "say not so. Call not names, my Redforth, or they will apply to pa."

"Let 'em," said the colonel. "I do not care. Who's he?"

Tinkling here undertook the perilous task of remonstrating with his lawless friend, who consented to withdraw the moody expressions above quoted.

"What remains for us to do?" Alice went on in her mild, wise way. "We must educate, we must pretend in a new manner, we must wait."

The colonel clenched his teeth,—four out in front, and a piece of another, and he had been twice dragged to the door of a dentist-despot, but had escaped from his guards. "How educate? How pretend in a new manner? How wait?"

"Educate the grown-up people," replied Alice. "We part to-night. Yes, Redforth,"—for the colonel tucked up his cuffs,—"part to-night! Let us in these next holidays, now going to begin, throw our thoughts into something educational for the grown-up people, hinting to them how things ought to be. Let us veil our meaning under a mask of romance; you, I, and Nettie. William Tinkling being the plainest and quickest writer, shall copy out. Is it agreed?"

The colonel answered sulkily, "I don't mind." He then asked, "How about pretending?"

"We will pretend," said Alice, "that we are children; not that we are those grown-up people who won't help us out as they ought, and who understand us so badly."

The colonel, still much dissatisfied, growled, "How about waiting?"

"We will wait," answered little Alice, taking Nettie's hand in hers, and looking up to the sky, "we will wait—ever constant and true—till the times have got so changed as that everything helps us out, and nothing makes us ridiculous, and the fairies have come back. We will wait—ever constant and true—till we are eighty, ninety, or one hundred. And then the fairies will send *us* children, and we will help them out, poor pretty little creatures, if they pretend ever so much."

"So we will, dear," said Nettie Ashford, taking her round the waist with both arms and kissing her. "And now if my husband will go and buy some cherries for us, I have got some money."

In the friendliest manner I invited the colonel to go with me; but he so far forgot himself as to acknowledge the invitation by kicking out behind, and then lying down on his stomach on the grass, pulling it up and chewing it. When I came back, however, Alice had nearly brought him out of his vexation, and was soothing him by telling him how soon we should all be ninety.

As we sat under the willow-tree and ate the cherries (fair, for Alice shared them out), we played at being ninety. Nettie complained that she had a bone in her old back, and it made her hobble; and Alice sang a song in an old woman's way, but it was very pretty, and we were all merry. At least, I don't know about merry exactly, but all comfortable.

There was a most tremendous lot of cherries; and Alice always had with her some neat little bag or box or case, to hold things. In it that night was a tiny wine-glass. So Alice and Nettie said they would make some cherry-wine to drink our love at parting.

Each of us had a glassful, and it was delicious; and each of us drank the toast, "Our love at parting." The colonel drank his wine last; and it got into my head directly that it got into his directly. Anyhow, his eyes rolled immediately after he had turned the glass upside down; and he took me on one side and proposed in a hoarse whisper, that we should "Cut 'em out still."

"How did he mean?" I asked my lawless friend.

"Cut our brides out," said the colonel, "and then cut our way, without going down a single turning, bang to the Spanish main!"

We might have tried it, though I didn't think it would answer; only we looked round and saw that there was nothing but moonlight under the willow-tree, and that our pretty, pretty wives were gone. We burst out crying. The colonel gave in second, and came to first; but he gave in strong.

We were ashamed of our red eyes, and hung about for half-an-hour to whiten them. Likewise a piece of chalk round the rims, I doing the colonel's, and he mine, but afterwards found in the bedroom looking-glass not natural, besides inflammation. Our conversation turned on being ninety. The colonel told me he had a pair of boots that wanted soling and heeling; but he thought it hardly worth while to mention it to his father, as he himself should so soon be ninety, when he thought shoes would be more convenient.

The colonel also told me, with his hand upon his hip, that he felt himself already getting on in life, and turning rheumatic. And I told him the same. And when they said at our house at supper (they are always bothering about something) that I stooped, I felt so glad !

This is the end of the beginning-part that you were to believe most.

PART II

ROMANCE. FROM THE PEN OF MISS ALICE RAINBIRD [1]

THERE was once a king, and he had a queen; and he was the manliest of his sex, and she was the loveliest of hers. The king was, in his private profession, under government. The queen's father had been a medical man out of town.

They had nineteen children, and were always having more. Seventeen of these children took care of the baby; and Alicia, the eldest, took care of them all.   Their ages varied from seven years to seven months.

Let us now resume our story.

One day the king was going to the office, when he stopped at the fishmonger's to buy a pound and a half of salmon not too near the tail, which the queen (who was a careful house-keeper) had requested him to send home.   Mr. Pickles, the fishmonger, said, "Certainly, Sir ; is there any other article ? Good morning."

The king went on towards the office in a melancholy mood ; for quarter-day was such a long way off, and several of the dear children were growing out of their clothes.   He had not proceeded far, when Mr. Pickles's errand-boy came running after him, and said, "Sir, you didn't notice the old lady in our shop."

"What old lady ?" inquired the king.   "I saw none."

Now the king had not seen any old lady, because this old lady had been invisible to him, though visible to Mr. Pickles's boy.   Probably because he messed and splashed the water about to that degree, and flopped the pairs of soles down in that violent manner, that, if she had not been visible to him, he would have spoilt her clothes.

[1] Aged seven.

Just then the old lady came trotting up. She was dressed in shot-silk of the richest quality, smelling of dried lavender.

"King Watkins the First, I believe?" said the old lady.

"Watkins," replied the king, "is my name."

"Papa, if I am not mistaken, of the beautiful Princess Alicia?" said the old lady.

"And of eighteen other darlings," replied the king.

"Listen. You are going to the office," said the old lady.

It instantly flashed upon the king that she must be a fairy, or how could she know that?

"You are right," said the old lady, answering his thoughts. "I am the good Fairy Grandmarina. Attend! When you return home to dinner, politely invite the Princess Alicia to have some of the salmon you bought just now."

"It may disagree with her," said the king.

The old lady became so very angry at this absurd idea, that the king was quite alarmed, and humbly begged her pardon.

"We hear a great deal too much about this thing disagreeing, and that thing disagreeing," said the old lady, with the greatest contempt it was possible to express. "Don't be greedy. I think you want it all yourself."

The king hung his head under this reproof, and said he wouldn't talk about things disagreeing any more.

"Be good, then," said the Fairy Grandmarina, "and don't. When the beautiful Princess Alicia consents to partake of the salmon,—as I think she will,—you will find she will leave a fish-bone on her plate. Tell her to dry it, and to rub it, and to polish it till it shines like mother-of-pearl, and to take care of it as a present from me."

"Is that all?" asked the king.

"Don't be impatient, Sir," returned the fairy Grandmarina, scolding him severely. "Don't catch people short, before they have done speaking. Just the way with you grown-up persons. You are always doing it."

The king again hung his head, and said he wouldn't do so any more.

"Be good, then," said the Fairy Grandmarina, "and don't! Tell the Princess Alicia, with my love, that the fish-bone is a magic present which can only be used once; but that it will bring her, that once, whatever she wishes for, PROVIDED SHE WISHES FOR IT AT THE RIGHT TIME. That is the message. Take care of it."

The king was beginning, "Might I ask the reason?" when the fairy became absolutely furious.

"*Will* you be good, Sir?" she exclaimed, stamping her foot on the ground. "The reason for this, and the reason for that, indeed! You are always wanting the reason. No reason. There! Hoity toity me! I am sick of your grown-up reasons."

The king was extremely frightened by the old lady's flying into such a passion, and said he was very sorry to have offended her, and he wouldn't ask for reasons any more.

"Be good, then," said the old lady, "and don't!"

With those words, Grandmarina vanished, and the king went on and on and on, till he came to the office. There he wrote and wrote and wrote, till it was time to go home again. Then he politely invited the Princess Alicia, as the fairy had directed him, to partake of the salmon. And when she had enjoyed it very much, he saw the fish-bone on her plate, as the fairy had told him he would, and he delivered the fairy's message, and the Princess Alicia took care to dry the bone, and to rub it, and to polish it, till it shone like mother-of-pearl.

And so, when the queen was going to get up in the morning, she said, "O, dear me, dear me; my head, my head!" and then she fainted away.

The Princess Alicia, who happened to be looking in at the chamber-door, asking about breakfast, was very much alarmed when she saw her royal mamma in this state, and she rang the bell for Peggy, which was the name of the lord chamberlain. But remembering where the smelling-bottle was, she climbed on a chair and got it; and after that she climbed on another chair by the bedside, and held the smelling-bottle to the queen's nose; and after that she jumped down and got some water; and after that she jumped up again and wetted the queen's forehead; and, in short, when the lord chamberlain came in, that dear old woman said to the little princess, "What a trot you are! I couldn't have done it better myself!"

But that was not the worst of the good queen's illness. O, no! She was very ill indeed, for a long time. The Princess Alicia kept the seventeen young princes and princesses quiet, and dressed and undressed and danced the baby, and made the kettle boil, and heated the soup, and swept the hearth, and poured out the medicine, and nursed the queen, and did all that ever she could, and was as busy, busy, busy as busy could be ; for there were not many servants at that palace for three reasons : because the king was short of money, because a rise in his office never seemed to come, and because quarter-day was so far off that it looked almost as far off and as little as one of the stars.

But on the morning when the queen fainted away, where was the magic fish-bone ? Why, there it was in the Princess Alicia's pocket ! She had almost taken it out to bring the queen to life again, when she put it back, and looked for the smelling-bottle.

After the queen had come out of her swoon that morning, and was dozing, the Princess Alicia hurried upstairs to tell a most particular secret to a most particularly confidential friend of hers, who was a duchess. People did suppose her to be a doll ; but she was really a duchess, though nobody knew it except the princess.

This most particular secret was the secret about the magic fish-bone, the history of which was well known to the duchess, because the princess told her everything. The princess kneeled down by the bed on which the duchess was lying, full-dressed and wide awake, and whispered the secret to her. The duchess smiled and nodded. People might have supposed that she never smiled and nodded ; but she often did, though nobody knew it except the princess.

Then the Princess Alicia hurried downstairs again, to keep watch in the queen's room. She often kept watch by herself in the queen's room ; but every evening, while the illness lasted, she sat there watching with the king. And every evening the king sat looking at her with a cross look, wondering why she never brought out the magic fish-bone. As often as she noticed this, she ran upstairs, whispered the secret to the duchess over again, and said to the duchess besides, "They think we children never have a reason or a meaning ! " And the duchess, though the most fashionable duchess that ever was heard of, winked her eye.

" Alicia," said the king, one evening, when she wished him good night.

" Yes, papa."

" What is become of the magic fish-bone ? "

" In my pocket, papa ! "

" I thought you had lost it ? "

" O, no, papa ! "

" Or forgotten it ? "

"No, indeed, papa."

And so another time the dreadful little snapping pug-dog, next door, made a rush at one of the young princes as he stood on the steps coming home from school, and terrified him out of his wits; and he put his hand through a pane of glass, and bled, bled, bled. When the seventeen other young princes and princesses saw him bleed, bleed, bleed, they were terrified out of their wits too, and screamed themselves black in their seventeen faces all at once. But the Princess Alicia put her hands over all their seventeen mouths, one after another, and persuaded them to be quiet because of the sick queen. And then she put the wounded prince's hand in a basin of fresh cold water, while they stared with their twice seventeen are thirty-four, put down four and carry three, eyes. and then she looked in the hand for bits of glass, and there were fortunately no bits of glass there. And then she said to two chubby-legged princes, who were sturdy though small, "Bring me in the royal rag-bag: I must snip and stitch and cut and contrive." So these two young princes tugged at the royal rag-bag, and lugged it in; and the Princess Alicia sat down on the floor, with a large pair of scissors and a needle and thread, and snipped and stitched and cut and contrived, and made a bandage, and put it on, and it fitted beautifully; and so when it was all done, she saw the king her papa looking on by the door.

"Alicia."

"Yes, papa."

"What have you been doing?"

"Snipping, stitching, cutting, and contriving, papa."

"Where is the magic fish-bone?"

"In my pocket, papa."

"I thought you had lost it?"

"O, no, papa."

"Or forgotten it?"

"No, indeed, papa."

After that, she ran upstairs to the duchess, and told her what had passed, and told her the secret over again; and the duchess shook her flaxen curls, and laughed with her rosy lips.

Well! and so another time the baby fell under the grate. The seventeen young princes and princesses were used to it; for they were almost always falling under the grate or down the stairs; but the baby was not used to it yet. and it gave him a swelled face and a black eye. The way the poor little darling came to tumble was, that he was out of the Princess Alicia's lap just as she was sitting, in a great coarse apron that quite smothered her, in front of the kitchen-fire, beginning to peel the turnips for the broth for dinner; and the way she came to be doing that was, that the king's cook had run away that morning with her own true love, who was a very tall but very tipsy soldier. Then the seventeen young princes and princesses, who cried at everything that happened, cried and roared. But the Princess Alicia (who couldn't help crying a little herself) quietly called to them to be still, on account of not throwing back the queen upstairs, who was fast getting well, and said, "Hold your tongues, you wicked little monkeys, every one of you, while I examine baby!" Then she examined baby, and found that he hadn't broken anything; and she held cold iron to his poor dear eye, and smoothed his poor dear face, and he presently fell asleep in her arms. Then she said to the seventeen princes and princesses, "I am afraid to let him down yet, lest he should wake and feel pain; be good, and you shall all be cooks." They jumped for joy when they heard that, and began making themselves cooks' caps out of old newspapers. So to one she gave the salt-box, and to one she gave the barley, and to one she gave the herbs, and to one she gave the turnips, and to one she gave the carrots, and to one she gave the onions, and to one she gave the spice-box, till they were all cooks, and all running about at work, she sitting in the middle, smothered in the great coarse apron, nursing baby. By-and-by the broth was done; and the baby woke up, smiling like an angel, and was trusted to the sedatest princess to hold, while the other princes and princesses were squeezed into a far-off corner to look at the Princess Alicia turning out the saucepanful of broth, for fear (as they were always getting into trouble) they should get splashed and scalded. When the broth came tumbling out, steaming beautifully, and smelling like a nosegay good to eat, they clapped their hands. That made the baby clap his hands; and that, and his looking as if he had a comic toothache, made all the princes and princesses laugh. So the Princess Alicia said, "Laugh and be good; and after dinner we will make him a nest on the floor in a corner, and he shall sit in his nest and see a dance of eighteen cooks." That delighted the young princes and princesses, and they ate up all the broth, and washed up all the plates and dishes, and cleared away, and pushed the table into a corner; and then they in their cooks' caps, and the Princess Alicia in the smothering coarse apron that belonged to the cook that had run away with her own true love that was the very tall but very tipsy soldier, danced a dance of eighteen cooks before the angelic baby, who forgot his swelled face and his black eye, and crowed with joy.

And so then, once more the Princess Alicia saw King Watkins the First, her father, standing in the doorway look-ing on, and he said, "What have you been doing, Alicia?"

"Cooking and contriving, papa."

"What else have you been doing, Alicia?"

"Keeping the children light-hearted, papa."

"Where is the magic fish-bone, Alicia?"

"In my pocket, papa."

"I thought you had lost it?"

"O, no, papa!"

"Or forgotten it?"

"No, indeed, papa."

The king then sighed so heavily, and seemed so low-spirited, and sat down so miserably, leaning his head upon his hand, and his elbow upon the kitchen-table pushed away in the corner, that the seventeen princes and princesses crept softly out of the kitchen, and left him alone with the Princess Alicia and the angelic baby.

"What is the matter, papa?"

"I am dreadfully poor, my child."

"Have you no money at all, papa?"

"None, my child."

"Is there no way of getting any, papa?"

"No way," said the king. "I have tried very hard, and I have tried all ways."

When she heard those last words, the Princess Alicia began to put her hand into the pocket where she kept the magic fish-bone.

"Papa," said she, "when we have tried very hard, and tried all ways, we must have done our very, very best?"

"No doubt, Alicia."

"When we have done our very, very best, papa, and that is not enough, then I think the right time must have come for asking help of others." This was the very secret con-nected with the magic fish-bone, which she had found out for herself from the good Fairy Grandmarina's words, and which she had so often whispered to her beautiful and fashionable friend, the duchess.

So she took out of her pocket the magic fish-bone, that had been dried and rubbed and polished till it shone like mother-of-pearl; and she gave it one little kiss, and wished it was quarter-day. And immediately it *was* quarter-day; and the king's quarter's salary came rattling down the chimney, and bounced into the middle of the floor.

But this was not half of what happened,—no, not a quarter; for immediately afterwards the good Fairy Grandmarina came riding in, in a carriage and four (peacocks), with Mr. Pickles's boy up behind, dressed in silver and gold, with a cocked-hat, powdered-hair, pink silk stockings, a jewelled cane, and a nosegay. Down jumped Mr. Pickles's boy, with his cocked-hat in his hand, and wonderfully polite (being entirely changed by enchantment), and handed Grandmarina out; and there she stood, in her rich shot-silk smelling of dried lavender, fanning herself with a sparkling fan.

"Alicia, my dear," said this charming old fairy, "how do you do? I hope I see you pretty well? Give me a kiss."

The Princess Alicia embraced her; and then Grandmarina turned to the king, and said rather sharply, "Are you good?"

The king said he hoped so.

"I suppose you know the reason *now*, why my god-daughter here," kissing the princess again, "did not apply to the fish-bone sooner?" said the fairy.

The king made a shy bow.

"Ah! but you didn't *then*?" said the fairy.

The king made a shyer bow.

"Any more reasons to ask for?" said the fairy.

The king said, No, and he was very sorry.

"Be good, then," said the fairy, "and live happy ever afterwards."

Then Grandmarina waved her fan, and the queen came in most splendidly dressed; and the seventeen young princes and princesses, no longer grown out of their clothes, came in, newly fitted out from top to toe, with tucks in everything to admit of its being let out. After that, the fairy tapped the Princess Alicia with her fan; and the smothering coarse apron flew away, and she appeared exquisitely dressed, like a little bride, with a wreath of orange-flowers and a silver veil. After that, the kitchen dresser changed of itself into a wardrobe, made of beautiful woods and gold and looking-glass, which was full of dresses of all sorts, all for her and all exactly fitting her. After that, the angelic baby came in, running alone, with his face and eye not a bit the worse, but much the better. Then Grandmarina begged to be introduced to the duchess; and, when the duchess was brought down, many compliments passed between them.

A little whispering took place between the fairy and the duchess; and then the fairy said out loud, "Yes, I thought she would have told you." Grandmarina then turned to the king and queen, and said, "We are going in search of Prince Certainpersonio. The pleasure of your company is requested at church in half an hour precisely. So she and the Princess Alicia got into the carriage; and Mr. Pickles's boy handed in the duchess, who sat by herself on the opposite seat; and then Mr. Pickles's boy put up the steps and got up behind, and the peacocks flew away with their tails behind.

Prince Certainpersonio was sitting by himself, eating barley-sugar, and waiting to be ninety. When he saw the peacocks, followed by the carriage, coming in at the window, it immediately occurred to him that something uncommon was going to happen.

"Prince," said Grandmarina, "I bring you your bride."

The moment the fairy said those words, Prince Certainpersonio's face left off being sticky, and his jacket and corduroys changed to peach-bloom velvet, and his hair curled, and a cap and feather flew in like a bird and settled on his head. He got into the carriage by the fairy's invitation; and there he renewed his acquaintance with the duchess, whom he had seen before.

In the church were the prince's relations and friends, and the Princess Alicia's relations and friends, and the seventeen princes and princesses, and the baby, and a crowd of the neighbours. The marriage was beautiful beyond expression. The duchess was bridesmaid, and beheld the ceremony from the pulpit, where she was supported by the cushion of the desk.

Grandmarina gave a magnificent wedding-feast afterwards, in which there was everything and more to eat, and everything and more to drink. The wedding-cake was delicately ornamented with white satin ribbons, frosted silver, and white lilies, and was forty-two yards round.

When Grandmarina had drunk her love to the young couple, and Prince Certainpersonio had made a speech, and everybody had cried, Hip, hip, hip, hurrah! Grandmarina announced to the king and queen that in future there would be eight quarter-days in every year, except in leap-year, when there would be ten. She then turned to Certainpersonio and Alicia, and said, "My dears, you will have thirty-five children, and they will all be good and beautiful. Seventeen of your children will be boys, and eighteen will be girls. The hair of the whole of your children will curl naturally. They will never have the measles, and will have recovered from the whooping-cough before being born."

On hearing such good news, everybody cried out "Hip, hip, hip, hurrah!" again.

"It only remains," said Grandmarina in conclusion, "to make an end of the fish-bone."

So she took it from the hand of the Princess Alicia, and it instantly flew down the throat of the dreadful little snapping pug-dog, next door, and choked him, and he expired in convulsions.

PART III

ROMANCE. FROM THE PEN OF LIEUT.-COL ROBIN REDFORTH [1]

THE subject of our present narrative would appear to have devoted himself to the pirate profession at a comparatively early age. We find him in command of a splendid schooner of one hundred guns loaded to the muzzle, ere yet he had had a party in honour of his tenth birthday.

It seems that our hero, considering himself spited by a Latin-grammar master, demanded the satisfaction due from one man of honour to another. Not getting it, he privately withdrew his haughty spirit from such low company, bought a second-hand pocket-pistol, folded up some sandwiches in a paper bag, made a bottle of Spanish liquorice-water, and entered on a career of valour.

It were tedious to follow Boldheart (for such was his name) through the commencing stages of his story. Suffice it, that we find him bearing the rank of Capt. Boldheart, reclining in full uniform on a crimson hearth-rug spread out

[1] Aged nine.

upon the quarter-deck of his schooner "The Beauty," in the China seas. It was a lovely evening; and, as his crew lay grouped about him, he favoured them with the following melody:

O landsmen are folly!
O pirates are jolly!
O diddleum Dolly,
Di.
Chorus.—Heave yo.

The soothing effect of these animated sounds floating over the waters, as the common sailors united their rough voices to take up the rich tones of Boldheart, may be more easily conceived than described.

It was under these circumstances that the look-out at the masthead gave the word, "Whales!"

All was now activity.

"Where away?" cried Capt. Boldheart, starting up.

"On the larboard bow, Sir," replied the fellow at the masthead, touching his hat. For such was the height of discipline on board of "The Beauty," that, even at that height, he was obliged to mind it, or be shot through the head.

"This adventure belongs to me," said Boldheart. "Boy, my harpoon. Let no man follow;" and leaping alone into his boat, the captain rowed with admirable dexterity in the direction of the monster.

All was now excitement.

"He nears him!" said an elderly seaman, following the captain through his spy-glass.

"He strikes him!" said another seaman, a mere stripling, but also with a spy-glass.

"He tows him towards us!" said another seaman, a man in the full vigour of life, but also with a spy-glass.

In fact, the captain was seen approaching, with the huge bulk following. We will not dwell on the deafening cries of "Boldheart! Boldheart!" with which he was received, when, carelessly leaping on the quarter-deck, he presented his prize to his men. They afterwards made two thousand four hundred and seventeen pound ten and sixpence by it.

Ordering the sail to be braced up, the captain now stood W.N.W. "The Beauty" flew rather than floated over the dark blue waters. Nothing particular occurred for a fortnight, except taking, with considerable slaughter, four

Spanish galleons, and a snow from South America, all richly
laden. Inaction began to tell upon the spirits of the men.
Capt. Boldheart called all hands aft, and said, "My lads, I
hear there are discontented ones among ye. Let any such
stand forth."

After some murmuring, in which the expressions. "Ay,
ay, Sir!" "Union Jack," "Avast," "Starboard," "Port,"
"Bowsprit," and similar indications of a mutinous under-
current, though subdued, were audible, Bill Boozey, captain
of the foretop, came out from the rest. His form was that
of a giant, but he quailed under the captain's eye.

"What are your wrongs?" said the captain.

"Why, d'ye see, Capt. Boldheart," replied the towering
mariner, "I've sailed, man and boy, for many a year, but I
never yet know'd the milk served out for the ship's company's teas to be so sour as 'tis aboard this craft."

At this moment the thrilling cry, "Man overboard!"
announced to the astonished crew that Boozey, in stepping
back, as the captain (in mere thoughtfulness) laid his hand
upon the faithful pocket-pistol which he wore in his belt,
had lost his balance, and was struggling with the foaming
tide.

All was now stupefaction.

But with Captain Boldheart, to throw off his uniform coat,
regardless of the various rich orders with which it was
decorated, and to plunge into the sea after the drowning giant,
was the work of a moment. Maddening was the excitement
when boats were lowered; intense the joy when the captain
was seen holding up the drowning man with his teeth; deafening the cheering when both were restored to the main deck of
"The Beauty." And, from the instant of his changing his
wet clothes for dry ones, Capt. Boldheart had no such
devoted though humble friend as William Boozey.

Boldheart now pointed to the horizon, and called the
attention of his crew to the taper spars of a ship lying snug
in harbour under the guns of a fort.

"She shall be ours at sunrise," said he. "Serve out a
double allowance of grog, and prepare for action."

All was now preparation.

When morning dawned, after a sleepless night, it was
seen that the stranger was crowding on all sail to come out
of the harbour and offer battle. As the two ships came
nearer to each other, the stranger fired a gun and hoisted

Roman colours. Boldheart then perceived her to be the Latin-grammar master's bark. Such indeed she was, and had been tacking about the world in unavailing pursuit, from the time of his first taking to a roving life.

Boldheart now addressed his men, promising to blow them up if he should feel convinced that their reputation required it, and giving orders that the Latin-grammar master should be taken alive. He then dismissed them to their quarters, and the fight began with a broadside from "The Beauty." She then veered around, and poured in another. "The Scorpion" (so was the bark of the Latin-grammar master appropriately called) was not slow to return her fire; and a terrific cannonading ensued, in which the guns of "The Beauty" did tremendous execution.

The Latin-grammar master was seen upon the poop, in the midst of the smoke and fire, encouraging his men. To do him justice, he was no craven, though his white hat, his short grey trousers, and his long snuff-coloured surtout reaching to his heels (the self-same coat in which he had spited Boldheart), contrasted most unfavourably with the brilliant uniform of the latter. At this moment, Boldheart, seizing a pike and putting himself at the head of his men, gave the word to board.

A desperate conflict ensued in the hammock-nettings,—or somewhere in about that direction,—until the Latin-grammar master, having all his masts gone, his hull and rigging shot through, and seeing Boldheart slashing a path towards him, hauled down his flag himself, gave up his sword to Boldheart, and asked for quarter. Scarce had he been put into the captain's boat, ere "The Scorpion" went down with all on board.

On Capt. Boldheart's now assembling his men, a circumstance occurred. He found it necessary with one blow of his cutlass to kill the cook, who, having lost his brother in the late action, was making at the Latin-grammar master in an infuriated state, intent on his destruction with a carving-knife.

Capt. Boldheart then turned to the Latin-grammar master, severely reproaching him with his perfidy, and put it to his crew what they considered that a master who spited a boy deserved.

They answered with one voice, "Death."

"It may be so," said the captain; "but it shall never be

said that Boldheart stained his hour of triumph with the blood of his enemy. Prepare the cutter."

The cutter was immediately prepared.

"Without taking your life," said the captain, "I must yet for ever deprive you of the power of spiting other boys. I shall turn you adrift in this boat. You will find in her two oars, a compass, a bottle of rum, a small cask of water, a piece of pork, a bag of biscuits, and my Latin grammar. Go! and spite the natives, if you can find any."

Deeply conscious of this bitter sarcasm, the unhappy wretch was put into the cutter, and was soon left far behind. He made no effort to row, but was seen lying on his back with his legs up, when last made out by the ship's telescopes.

A stiff breeze now beginning to blow, Capt. Boldheart gave orders to keep her S.S.W., easing her a little during the night by falling off a point or two W. by W., or even by W.S., if she complained much. He then retired for the night, having in truth much need of repose. In addition to the fatigues he had undergone, this brave officer had received sixteen wounds in the engagement, but had not mentioned it.

In the morning a white squall came on, and was succeeded by other squalls of various colours. It thundered and lightened heavily for six weeks. Hurricanes then set in for two months. Waterspouts and tornadoes followed. The oldest sailor on board—and he was a very old one—had never seen such weather. "The Beauty" lost all idea where she was, and the carpenter reported six feet two of water in the hold. Everybody fell senseless at the pumps every day.

Provisions now ran very low. Our hero put the crew on short allowance, and put himself on shorter allowance than any man in the ship. But his spirit kept him fat. In this extremity, the gratitude of Boozey, the captain of the foretop, whom our readers may remember, was truly affecting. The loving though lowly William repeatedly requested to be killed, and preserved for the captain's table.

We now approach a change of affairs.

One day during a gleam of sunshine, and when the weather had moderated, the man at the masthead—too weak now to touch his hat, besides its having been blown away—called out,

"Savages !"

All was now expectation.

Presently fifteen hundred canoes, each paddled by twenty savages, were seen advancing in excellent order. They were of a light green colour (the savages were), and sang, with great energy, the following strain:

> Choo a choo a choo tooth.
> Muntch, muntch. Nycey!
> Choo a choo a choo tooth.
> Muntch, muntch. Nycey!

As the shades of night were by this time closing in, these expressions were supposed to embody this simple people's views of the evening hymn. But it too soon appeared that the song was a translation of "For what we are going to receive," &c.

The chief, imposingly decorated with feathers of lively colours, and having the majestic appearance of a fighting parrot, no sooner understood (he understood English perfectly) that the ship was "The Beauty," Capt. Boldheart, than he fell upon his face on the deck, and could not be persuaded to rise until the captain had lifted him up, and told him he wouldn't hurt him. All the rest of the savages also fell on their faces with marks of terror, and had also to be lifted up one by one. Thus the fame of the great Boldheart had gone before him, even among these children of Nature.

Turtles and oysters were now produced in astonishing numbers; and on these and yams the people made a hearty meal. After dinner the chief told Capt. Boldheart that there was better feeding up at the village, and that he would be glad to take him and his officers there. Apprehensive of treachery, Boldheart ordered his boat's crew to attend him completely armed. And well were it for other commanders if their precautions—but let us not anticipate.

When the canoes arrived at the beach, the darkness of the night was illumined by the light of an immense fire. Ordering his boat's crew (with the intrepid though illiterate William at their head) to keep close and be upon their guard, Boldheart bravely went on, arm in arm with the chief.

But how to depict the captain's surprise when he found a ring of savages singing in chorus that barbarous translation of "For what we are going to receive," &c., which has been given above, and dancing hand in hand round the Latin-grammar master, in a hamper with his head shaved, while two savages floured him, before putting him to the fire to be cooked!

Boldheart now took counsel with his officers cn the course to be adopted. In the meantime, the miserable captive never ceased begging pardon and imploring to be delivered. On the generous Boldheart's proposal, it was at length resolved that he should not be cooked, but should be allowed to remain raw, on two conditions, namely :

1. That he should never, under any circumstances, presume to teach any boy anything any more.

2. That, if taken back to England, he should pass his life in travelling to find out boys who wanted their exercises done, and should do their exercises for those boys for nothing, and never say a word about it.

Drawing the sword from its sheath, Boldheart swore him to these conditions on its shining blade. The prisoner wept bitterly, and appeared acutely to feel the errors of his past career.

The captain then ordered his boat's crew to make ready for a volley, and after firing to re-load quickly. " And expect a score or two on ye to go head over heels," murmured William Boozey ; " for I'm a-looking at ye." With those words, the derisive though deadly William took a good aim. " Fire ! "

The ringing voice of Boldheart was lost in the report of the guns and the screeching of the savages. Volley after volley awakened the numerous echoes. Hundreds of savages were killed, hundreds wounded, and thousands ran howling into the woods. The Latin-grammar master had a spare night-cap lent him, and a long-tail coat, which he wore hind side before. He presented a ludicrous though pitiable appearance, and serve him right.

We now find Capt. Boldheart, with this rescued wretch on board, standing off for other islands. At one of these, not a cannibal island, but a pork and vegetable one, he married (only in fun on his part) the king's daughter. Here he rested some time, receiving from the natives great quantities of precious stones, gold dust, elephants' teeth, and sandal wood, and getting very rich. This, too, though he almost every day made presents of enormous value to his men.

The ship being at length as full as she could hold of all sorts of valuable things, Boldheart gave orders to weigh the anchor, and turn " The Beauty's" head towards England. These orders were obeyed with three cheers ; and ere the sun went down full many a hornpipe had been danced on deck by the uncouth though agile William.

We next find Capt. Boldheart about three leagues off Madeira, surveying through his spy-glass a stranger of suspicious appearance making sail towards him. On his firing a gun ahead of her to bring her to, she ran up a flag, which he instantly recognised as the flag from the mast in the back-garden at home.

Inferring from this, that his father had put to sea to seek his long-lost son, the captain sent his own boat on board the stranger to inquire if this was so, and, if so, whether his father's intentions were strictly honourable. The boat came back with a present of greens and fresh meat, and reported that the stranger was "The Family," of twelve hundred tons, and had not only the captain's father on board, but also his mother, with the majority of his aunts and uncles, and all his cousins. It was further reported to Boldheart that the whole of these relations had expressed themselves in a becoming manner, and were anxious to embrace him and thank him for the glorious credit he had done them. Boldheart at once invited them to breakfast next morning on board "The Beauty," and gave orders for a brilliant ball that should last all day.

It was in the course of the night that the captain discovered the hopelessness of reclaiming the Latin-grammar master. That thankless traitor was found out, as the two ships lay near each other, communicating with "The Family" by signals, and offering to give up Boldheart. He was hanged at the yard-arm the first thing in the morning, after having it impressively pointed out to him by Boldheart that this was what spiters came to.

The meeting between the captain and his parents was attended with tears. His uncles and aunts would have attended their meeting with tears too, but he wasn't going to stand that. His cousins were very much astonished by the size of his ship and the discipline of his men, and were greatly overcome by the splendour of his uniform. He kindly conducted them round the vessel, and pointed out everything worthy of notice. He also fired his hundred guns, and found it amusing to witness their alarm.

The entertainment surpassed everything ever seen on board ship, and lasted from ten in the morning until seven the next morning. Only one disagreeable incident occurred. Capt.

Boldheart found himself obliged to put his cousin Tom in irons, for being disrespectful. On the boy's promising amendment, however, he was humanely released after a few hours' close confinement.

Boldheart now took his mother down into the great cabin, and asked after the young lady with whom, it was well known to the world, he was in love. His mother replied that the object of his affections was then at school at Margate, for the benefit of sea-bathing (it was the month of September,) but that she feared the young lady's friends were still opposed to the union. Boldheart at once resolved, if necessary, to bombard the town.

Taking the command of his ship with this intention, and putting all but fighting men on board "The Family," with orders to that vessel to keep in company, Boldheart soon anchored in Margate Roads. Here he went ashore well-armed, and attended by his boat's crew (at their head the faithful though ferocious William), and demanded to see the mayor, who came out of his office.

"Dost know the name of yon ship, mayor?" asked Bold heart fiercely.

"No," said the mayor, rubbing his eyes, which he could scarce believe, when he saw the goodly vessel riding at anchor.

"She is named 'The Beauty,'" said the captain.

"Hah!" exclaimed the mayor, with a start. "And you, then, are Capt. Boldheart?"

"The same."

A pause ensued. The mayor trembled.

"Now, mayor," said the captain, "choose! Help me to my bride, or be bombarded."

The mayor begged for two hours' grace, in which to make inquiries respecting the young lady. Boldheart accorded him but one; and during that one placed William Boozey sentry over him, with a drawn sword, and instructions to accompany him wherever he went, and to run him through the body if he showed a sign of playing false.

At the end of the hour the mayor re-appeared more dead than alive, closely waited on by Boozey more alive than dead.

"Captain," said the mayor, "I have ascertained that the young lady is going to bathe. Even now she waits her turn for a machine. The tide is low, though rising. I, in one of our town-boats, shall not be suspected. When she comes forth in her bathing-dress into the shallow water from behind the hood of the machine, my boat shall intercept her and prevent her return. Do you the rest."

"Mayor," returned Capt. Boldheart, "thou hast saved thy town."

The captain then signalled his boat to take him off, and, steering her himself, ordered her crew to row towards the bathing-ground, and there to rest upon their oars. All happened as had been arranged. His lovely bride came forth, the mayor glided in behind her, she became confused, and had floated out of her depth, when, with one skilful touch of the rudder and one quivering stroke from the boat's crew, her adoring Boldheart held her in his strong arms. There her shrieks of terror were changed to cries of joy.

Before "The Beauty" could get under way, the hoisting of all the flags in the town and harbour, and the ringing of all the bells, announced to the brave Boldheart that he had nothing to fear. He therefore determined to be married on the spot, and signalled for a clergyman and clerk, who came off promptly in a sailing-boat named "The Skylark." Another great entertainment was then given on board "The Beauty," in the midst of which the mayor was called out by a messenger. He returned with the news that government had sent down to know whether Capt. Boldheart, in acknowledgment of the great services he had done his country by being a pirate, would consent to be made a lieutenant-colonel. For himself he would have spurned the worthless boon ; but his bride wished it, and he consented.

Only one thing further happened before the good ship "Family" was dismissed, with rich presents to all on board. It is painful to record (but such is human nature in some cousins) that Capt. Boldheart's unmannerly Cousin Tom was actually tied up to receive three dozen with a rope's end "for cheekiness and making game," when Capt. Boldheart's lady begged for him, and he was spared. "The Beauty" then refitted, and the captain and his bride departed for the Indian Ocean to enjoy themselves for evermore.

PART IV

ROMANCE.　FROM THE PEN OF MISS NETTIE ASHFORD [1]

THERE is a country, which I will show you when I get into
maps, where the children have everything their own way. It
is a most delightful country to live in.　The grown-up people
are obliged to obey the children, and are never allowed to sit
up to supper, except on their birthdays.　The children order
them to make jam and jelly and marmalade, and tarts and
pies and puddings, and all manner of pastry.　If they say
they won't, they are put in the corner till they do.　They are
sometimes allowed to have some; but when they have some,
they generally have powders given them afterwards.

One of the inhabitants of this country, a truly sweet young
creature of the name of Mrs. Orange, had the misfortune
to be sadly plagued by her numerous family.　Her parents
required a great deal of looking after, and they had connexions and companions who were scarcely ever out of
mischief.　So Mrs. Orange said to herself, "I really cannot
be troubled with these torments any longer: I must put
them all to school."

Mrs. Orange took off her pinafore, and dressed herself very
nicely and took up her baby, and went out to call upon
another lady of the name of Mrs. Lemon, who kept a preparatory establishment.　Mrs. Orange stood upon the scraper
to pull at the bell, and give a ring-ting-ting.

Mrs. Lemon's neat little housemaid, pulling up her socks
as she came along the passage, answered the ring-ting-ting.

"Good morning," said Mrs. Orange.　"Fine day.　How do
you do?　Mrs. Lemon at home!"

"Yes, ma'am."

"Will you say Mrs. Orange and baby?"

"Yes, ma'am.　Walk in."

Mrs. Orange's baby was a very fine one, and real wax all
over.　Mrs. Lemon's baby was leather and bran.　However,

[1] Aged half-past six.

when Mrs. Lemon came into the drawing-room with her baby in her arms, Mrs. Orange said politely. "Good morning. Fine day. How do you do? And how is little Tootleum-boots?"

"Well, she is but poorly. Cutting her teeth, ma'am," said Mrs. Lemon.

"O, indeed, ma'am!" said Mrs. Orange. "No fits, I hope?"

"No, ma'am."

"How many teeth has she, ma'am?"

"Five, ma'am."

"My Emilia, ma'am, has eight," said Mrs. Orange. "Shall we lay them on the mantelpiece side by side, while we converse?"

"By all means, ma'am," said Mrs. Lemon. "Hem!"

"The first question is, ma'am," said Mrs. Orange, "I don't bore you?"

"Not in the least, ma'am," said Mrs. Lemon. "Far from it, I assure you."

"Then pray *have* you," said Mrs. Orange,—"*have* you any vacancies?"

"Yes, ma'am. How many might you require?"

"Why, the truth is, ma'am," said Mrs. Orange, "I have come to the conclusion that my children,"—O, I forgot to say that they call the grown-up people children in that country!—"that my children are getting positively too much for me. Let me see. Two parents, two intimate friends of theirs, one godfather, two godmothers, and an aunt. *Have* you as many as eight vacancies?"

"I have just eight, ma'am," said Mrs. Lemon.

"Most fortunate! Terms moderate, I think?"

"Very moderate, ma'am."

"Diet good, I believe?"

"Excellent, ma'am."

"Unlimited?"

"Unlimited."

"Most satisfactory! Corporal punishment dispensed with?"

"Why, we do occasionally shake," said Mrs. Lemon, "and we have slapped. But only in extreme cases."

"*Could* I, ma'am," said Mrs. Orange,—"*could* I see the establishment?"

"With the greatest of pleasure, ma'am," said Mrs. Lemon.

Mrs. Lemon took Mrs. Orange into the schoolroom, where

there were a number of pupils. "Stand up, children," said Mrs. Lemon ; and they all stood up.

Mrs. Orange whispered to Mrs. Lemon, "There is a pale, bald child, with red whiskers, in disgrace. Might I ask what he has done ? "

"Come here, White," said Mrs. Lemon, "and tell this lady what you have been doing."

"Betting on horses," said White sulkily.

"Are you sorry for it, you naughty child?" said Mrs. Lemon.

"No," said White. "Sorry to lose, but shouldn't be sorry to win."

"There's a vicious boy for you, ma'am," said Mrs. Lemon. "Go along with you, Sir. This is Brown, Mrs. Orange. O, a sad case, Brown's ! Never knows when he has had enough. Greedy. How is your gout, Sir ? "

"Bad," said Brown.

"What else can you expect ? " said Mrs. Lemon. "Your stomach is the size of two. Go and take exercise directly. Mrs. Black, come here to me. Now, here is a child, Mrs. Orange, ma'am, who is always at play. She can't be kept at home a single day together; always gadding about and spoiling her clothes. Play, play, play, play, from morning to night, and to morning again. How can she expect to improve ? "

"Don't expect to improve," sulked Mrs. Black. "Don't want to."

"There is a specimen of her temper, ma'am," said Mrs. Lemon. "To see her when she is tearing about, neglecting everything else, you would suppose her to be at least good-humoured. But bless you! ma'am, she is as pert and flouncing a minx as ever you met with in all your days ! "

"You must have a great deal of trouble with them, ma'am," said Mrs. Orange.

"Ah, I have, indeed, ma'am ! " said Mrs. Lemon. "What with their tempers, what with their quarrels, what with their never knowing what's good for them, and what with their always wanting to domineer, deliver me from these unreasonable children ! "

"Well, I wish you good morning, ma'am," said Mrs. Orange.

"Well, I wish you good morning, ma'am," said Mrs. Lemon.

So Mrs. Orange took up her baby and went home, and told the family that plagued her so that they were all going to be sent to school. They said they didn't want to go to school; but she packed up their boxes, and packed them off.

"O dear me, dear me! Rest and be thankful!" said Mrs. Orange, throwing herself back in her little armchair. "Those troublesome troubles are got rid of, please the pigs!"

Just then another lady, named Mrs. Alicumpaine, came calling at the street-door with a ring-ting-ting.

"My dear Mrs. Alicumpaine," said Mrs. Orange, "how do you do? Pray stay to dinner. We have but a simple joint of sweet-stuff, followed by a plain dish of bread and treacle; but, if you will take us as you find us, it will be *so* kind!"

"Don't mention it," said Mrs. Alicumpaine. "I shall be too glad. But what do you think I have come for, ma'am? Guess, ma'am."

"I really cannot guess, ma'am," said Mrs. Orange.

"Why, I am going to have a small juvenile party to-night," said Mrs. Alicumpaine; "and if you and Mr. Orange and baby would but join us, we should be complete."

"More than charmed, I am sure!" said Mrs. Orange.

"So kind of you!" said Mrs. Alicumpaine. "But I hope the children won't bore you!"

"Dear things! Not at all," said Mrs. Orange. "I dote upon them."

Mr. Orange here came home from the city; and he came, too, with a ring-ting-ting.

"James love," said Mrs. Orange, "you look tired. What has been doing in the city to-day?"

"Trap, bat, and ball, my dear," said Mr. Orange; "and it knocks a man up."

"That dreadfully anxious city, ma'am," said Mrs. Orange to Mrs. Alicumpaine; "so wearing, is it not?"

"O, so trying!" said Mrs. Alicumpaine. "John has lately been speculating in the peg-top ring; and I often say to him at night, 'John, *is* the result worth the wear and tear?'"

Dinner was ready by this time: so they sat down to dinner; and while Mr. Orange carved the joint of sweet-stuff, he said, "It's a poor heart that never rejoices. Jane, go down to the cellar, and fetch a bottle of the Upest ginger-beer."

At tea-time, Mr. and Mrs. Orange, and baby, and Mrs. Alicumpaine went off to Mrs. Alicumpaine's house. The children had not come yet; but the ball-room was ready for them, decorated with paper flowers.

"How very sweet!" said Mrs. Orange. "The dear things! How pleased they will be!"

"I don't care for children myself," said Mr. Orange, gaping.

"Not for girls?" said Mrs. Alicumpaine. "Come! you care for girls?"

Mr. Orange shook his head, and gaped again. "Frivolous and vain, ma'am."

"My dear James," cried Mrs. Orange, who had been peeping about. "do look here. Here's the supper for the darlings, ready laid in the room behind the folding-doors. Here's their little pickled salmon, I do declare! And here's their little salad, and their little roast beef and fowls, and their little pastry, and their wee, wee, wee champagne!"

"Yes, I thought it best, ma'am," said Mrs. Alicumpaine, "that they should have their supper by themselves. Our table is in the corner here, where the gentlemen can have their wineglass of negus, and their egg-sandwich, and their quiet game at beggar-my-neighbour, and look on. As for us, ma'am, we shall have quite enough to do to manage the company."

"O, indeed, you may say so! Quite enough, ma'am," said Mrs. Orange.

The company began to come. The first of them was a stout boy, with a white top-knot and spectacles. The housemaid brought him in and said, "Compliments, and at what time was he to be fetched?" Mrs. Alicumpaine said, "Not a moment later than ten. How do you do, Sir? Go and sit down." Then a number of other children came; boys by themselves, and girls by themselves, and boys and girls together. They didn't behave at all well. Some of them looked through quizzing-glasses at others, and said, "Who are those? Don't know them." Some of them looked through quizzing-glasses at others, and said, "How do?" Some of them had cups of tea or coffee handed to them by others, and said, "Thanks; much!" A good many boys stood about, and felt their shirt-collars. Four tiresome fat boys *would* stand in the doorway, and talk about the newspapers, till Mrs. Alicumpaine went to them and said, "My dears, I really cannot allow you to prevent people from coming in. I shall be truly sorry to do it; but, if you put yourself in everybody's way, I must positively send you home." One boy, with a beard and a large white waistcoat, who stood straddling on the hearth-rug warming his coat-tails, *was* sent home. "Highly incorrect, my dear," said Mrs. Alicumpaine, handing him out of the room, "and I cannot permit it."

There was a children's band,—harp, cornet, and piano.— and Mrs. Alicumpaine and Mrs. Orange bustled among the children to persuade them to take partners and dance. But they were so obstinate! For quite a long time they would not be persuaded to take partners and dance. Most of the boys said, "Thanks; much! But not at present." And most of the rest of the boys said, "Thanks; much! But never do."

"O, these children are very wearing!" said Mrs. Alicumpaine to Mrs. Orange.

"Dear things! I dote upon them; but they ARE wearing," said Mrs. Orange to Mrs. Alicumpaine.

At last they did begin in a slow and melancholy way to slide about to the music; though even then they wouldn't mind what they were told, but would have this partner, and wouldn't have that partner, and showed temper about it. And they wouldn't smile,—no, not on any account they wouldn't; but, when the music stopped, went round and round the room in dismal twos, as if everybody else was dead.

"O, it's very hard indeed to get these vexing children to be entertained!" said Mrs. Alicumpaine to Mrs. Orange.

"I dote upon the darlings; but it is hard," said Mrs. Orange to Mrs. Alicumpaine.

They were trying children, that's the truth. First, they wouldn't sing when they were asked; and then, when everybody fully believed they wouldn't, they would. "If you serve us so any more, my love," said Mrs. Alicumpaine to a tall child, with a good deal of white back, in mauve silk trimmed with lace, "it will be my painful privilege to offer you a bed, and to send you to it immediately."

The girls were so ridiculously dressed, too, that they were in rags before supper. How could the boys help treading on their trains? And yet when their trains were trodden on, they often showed temper again, and looked as black, they did! However, they all seemed to be pleased when Mrs. Alicumpaine said, "Supper is ready, children!" And they went crowding and pushing in, as if they had had dry bread for dinner.

"How are the children getting on?" said Mr. Orange to Mrs. Orange, when Mrs. Orange came to look after baby. Mrs. Orange had left baby on a shelf near Mr. Orange while he played at beggar-my-neighbour, and had asked him to keep his eye upon her now and then.

"Most charmingly, my dear!" said Mrs. Orange. "So droll to see their little flirtations and jealousies! Do come and look!"

"Much obliged to you, my dear," said Mr. Orange; "but I don't care about children myself."

So Mrs. Orange, having seen that baby was safe, went back without Mr. Orange to the room where the children were having supper.

"What are they doing now?" said Mrs. Orange to Mrs. Alicumpaine.

"They are making speeches, and playing at parliament," said Mrs. Alicumpaine to Mrs. Orange.

On hearing this, Mrs. Orange set off once more back again to Mr. Orange, and said, "James dear, do come. The children are playing at parliament."

"Thank you, my dear," said Mr. Orange, "but I don't care about parliament myself."

So Mrs. Orange went once again without Mr. Orange to the room where the children were having supper, to see them playing at parliament. And she found some of the boys crying, "Hear, hear, hear!" while other boys cried "No, no!" and others, "Question!" "Spoke!" and all sorts of nonsense that ever you heard. Then one of those tiresome fat boys who had stopped the doorway told them he was on his legs (as if they couldn't see that he wasn't on his head, or on his anything else) to explain, and that, with the permission of his honourable friend, if he would allow him to call him so (another tiresome boy bowed), he would proceed to explain. Then he went on for a long time in a sing-song (whatever he meant), did this troublesome fat boy, about that he held in his hand a glass; and about that he had come down to that house that night to discharge what he would call a public duty; and about that, on the present occasion, he would lay his hand (his other hand) upon his heart, and would tell honourable gentlemen that he was about to open the door to general approval. Then he opened the door by saying, "To our hostess!" and everybody else said "To our hostess!" and then there were cheers. Then another tiresome boy started up in sing-song, and then half-a-dozen noisy and nonsensical boys at once. But at last Mrs. Alicumpaine said, "I cannot have this din. Now, children, you have played at parliament very nicely; but parliament gets tiresome after a little while, and it's time you left off, for you will soon be fetched."

After another dance (with more tearing to rags than before supper), they began to be fetched; and you will be very glad to be told that the tiresome fat boy who had been on his legs was walked off first without any ceremony. When they were all gone, poor Mrs. Alicumpaine dropped upon a sofa, and said to Mrs. Orange, "These children will be the death of me at last, ma'am,—they will indeed!"

"I quite adore them, ma'am," said Mrs. Orange; "but they DO want variety."

Mr. Orange got his hat, and Mrs. Orange got her bonnet and her baby, and they set out to walk home. They had to pass Mrs. Lemon's preparatory establishment on their way.

"I wonder, James dear," said Mrs. Orange, looking up at the window, "whether the precious children are asleep!"

"I don't care much whether they are or not, myself," said Mr. Orange.

"James dear!"

"You dote upon them, you know," said Mr. Orange. "That's another thing."

"I do," said Mrs. Orange rapturously. "O, I DO!"

"I don't," said Mr. Orange.

"But I was thinking, James love," said Mrs. Orange, pressing his arm, "whether our dear, good, kind Mrs. Lemon would like them to stay the holidays with her."

"If she was paid for it, I daresay she would," said Mr. Orange.

"I adore them, James," said Mrs. Orange, "but SUPPOSE we pay her, then!"

This was what brought that country to such perfection, and made it such a delightful place to live in. The grown-up people (that would be in other countries) soon left off being allowed any holidays after Mr. and Mrs Orange tried the experiment; and the children (that would be in other countries) kept them at school as long as ever they lived, and made them do whatever they were told.

GEORGE SILVERMAN'S
EXPLANATION

CHARACTERS

LADY FAREWAY, widow of Sir Gaston Fareway, Bart.; a penurious and managing woman.

ADELINA FAREWAY, her daughter; pupil of George Silverman.

MR. FAREWAY, the second son of Lady Fareway; a young man of more than average abilities, but idle and luxurious.

BROTHER GIMBLET, an elderly drysalter; an expounder in Brother Hawkyard's congregation.

MR. VERITY HAWKYARD ("Brother Hawkyard"), an exhorter in a congregation of an obscure denomination; George Silverman's guardian or patron.

GEORGE SILVERMAN, the narrator of the story; an orphan brought up under the guardianship of Brother Hawkyard, eventually becoming a clergyman.

SYLVIA, a girl at a farm-house.

MR. GRANVILLE WHARTON, a pupil of George Silverman's.

GEORGE SILVERMAN'S
EXPLANATION

FIRST CHAPTER

I⊤ happened in this wise—

But, sitting with my pen in my hand looking at those words again, without descrying any hint in them of the words that should follow, it comes into my mind that they have an abrupt appearance. They may serve, however, if I let them remain, to suggest how very difficult I find it to begin to explain my explanation. An uncouth phrase: and yet I do not see my way to a better.

SECOND CHAPTER

I⊤ happened in *this* wise—

But, looking at those words, and comparing them with my former opening, I find they are the self-same words repeated. This is the more surprising to me, because I employ them in quite a new connexion. For indeed I declare that my intention was to discard the commencement I first had in my thoughts, and to give the preference to another of an entirely different nature, dating my explanation from an anterior period of my life. I will make a third trial, without erasing this second failure, protesting that it is not my design to conceal any of my infirmities, whether they be of head or heart.

THIRD CHAPTER

Not as yet directly aiming at how it came to pass, I will come upon it by degrees. The natural manner, after all, for God knows that is how it came upon me.

My parents were in a miserable condition of life, and my infant home was a cellar in Preston. I recollect the sound of father's Lancashire clogs on the street pavement above, as being different in my young hearing from the sound of all other clogs; and I recollect, that, when mother came down the cellar-steps, I used tremblingly to speculate on her feet having a good or an ill-tempered look,—on her knees,—on her waist,—until finally her face came into view, and settled the question. From this it will be seen that I was timid, and that the cellar-steps were steep, and that the doorway was very low.

Mother had the gripe and clutch of poverty upon her face, upon her figure, and not least of all upon her voice. Her sharp and high-pitched words were squeezed out of her, as by the compression of bony fingers on a leathern bag; and she had a way of rolling her eyes about and about the cellar, as she scolded, that was gaunt and hungry. Father, with his shoulders rounded, would sit quiet on a three-legged stool, looking at the empty grate, until she would pluck the stool from under him, and bid him go bring some money home. Then he would dismally ascend the steps; and I, holding my ragged shirt and trousers together with a hand (my only braces), would feint and dodge from mother's pursuing grasp at my hair.

A worldly little devil was mother's usual name for me. Whether I cried for that I was in the dark, or for that it was cold, or for that I was hungry, or whether I squeezed myself into a warm corner when there was a fire, or ate voraciously when there was food, she would still say, "O you worldly little devil!" And the sting of it was, that I quite well knew myself to be a worldly little devil. Worldly as to wanting to be housed and warmed, worldly as to wanting to be fed, worldly as to the greed with which I inwardly compared how much I got of those good things with how much father and mother got, when, rarely, those good things were going.

Sometimes they both went away seeking work ; and then I would be locked up in the cellar for a day or two at a time. I was at my worldliest then. Left alone, I yielded myself up to a worldly yearning for enough of anything (except misery), and for the death of mother's father, who was a machine-maker at Birmingham, and on whose decease, I had heard mother say, she would come into a whole courtful of houses "if she had her rights." Worldly little devil, I would stand about, musingly fitting my cold bare feet into cracked bricks and crevices of the damp cellar-floor, —walking over my grandfather's body, so to speak, into the courtful of houses, and selling them for meat and drink, and clothes to wear.

At last a change came down into our cellar. The universal change came down even as low as that,—so will it mount to any height on which a human creature can perch,—and brought other changes with it.

We had a heap of I don't know what foul litter in the darkest corner, which we called "the bed." For three days mother lay upon it without getting up, and then began at times to laugh. If I had ever heard her laugh before, it had been so seldom that the strange sound frightened me. It frightened father too ; and we took it by turns to give her water. Then she began to move her head from side to side, and sing. After that, she getting no better, father fell a-laughing and a-singing ; and then there was only I to give them both water, and they both died.

FOURTH CHAPTER

WHEN I was lifted out of the cellar by two men, of whom one came peeping down alone first, and ran away and brought the other, I could hardly bear the light of the street. I was sitting in the road-way, blinking at it, and at a ring of people collected around me, but not close to me, when, true to my character of worldly little devil, I broke silence by saying, " I am hungry and thirsty ! "

"Does he know they are dead ? " asked one of another

"Do you know your father and mother are both dead of fever?" asked a third of me severely.

"I don't know what it is to be dead. I supposed it meant that, when the cup rattled against their teeth, and the water spilt over them. I am hungry and thirsty." That was all I had to say about it.

The ring of people widened outward from the inner side as I looked around me; and I smelt vinegar, and what I know to be camphor, thrown in towards where I sat. Presently some one put a great vessel of smoking vinegar on the ground near me; and then they all looked at me in silent horror as I ate and drank of what was brought for me. I knew at the time they had a horror of me, but I couldn't help it.

I was still eating and drinking, and a murmur of discussion had begun to arise respecting what was to be done with me next, when I heard a cracked voice somewhere in the ring say, "My name is Hawkyard, Mr. Verity Hawkyard, of West Bromwich." Then the ring split in one place; and a yellow-faced, peak-nosed gentleman, clad all in iron-grey to his gaiters, pressed forward with a policeman and another official of some sort. He came forward close to the vessel of smoking vinegar; from which he sprinkled himself carefully, and me copiously.

"He had a grandfather at Birmingham, this young boy, who is just dead too," said Mr. Hawkyard.

I turned my eyes upon the speaker, and said in a ravening manner, "Where's his houses?"

"Hah! Horrible wordliness on the edge of the grave," said Mr. Hawkyard, casting more of the vinegar over me, as if to get my devil out of me. "I have undertaken a slight —a ve-ry slight—trust in behalf of this boy; quite a voluntary trust: a matter of mere honour, if not of mere sentiment: still I have taken it upon myself, and it shall be (O, yes, it shall be!) discharged."

The bystanders seemed to form an opinion of this gentleman much more favourable than their opinion of me.

"He shall be taught," said Mr. Hawkyard, "(O, yes, he shall be taught!) but what is to be done with him for the present? He may be infected. He may disseminate infection." The ring widened considerably. "What is to be done with him?"

He held some talk with the two officials. I could distin-

guish no word save "Farm-house." There was another
sound several times repeated, which was wholly meaningless
in my ears then, but which I knew afterwards to be
"Hoghton Towers."

"Yes," said Mr. Hawkyard. "I think that sounds
promising; I think that sounds hopeful. And he can be
put by himself in a ward, for a night or two, you say?"

It seemed to be the police-officer who had said so; for it
was he who replied, Yes! It was he, too, who finally took
me by the arm, and walked me before him through the streets,
into a whitewashed room in a bare building, where I had
a chair to sit in, a table to sit at, an iron bedstead and good
mattress to lie upon, and a rug and blanket to cover me.
Where I had enough to eat too, and was shown how to
clean the tin porringer in which it was conveyed to me,
until it was as good as a looking-glass. Here, likewise,
I was put in a bath, and had new clothes brought to me;
and my old rags were burnt, and I was camphored and
vinegared and disinfected in a variety of ways.

When all this was done,—I don't know in how many days
or how few, but it matters not,—Mr. Hawkyard stepped in
at the door, remaining close to it, and said, "Go and stand
against the opposite wall, George Silverman. As far off as
you can. That'll do. How do you feel?"

I told him that I didn't feel cold, and didn't feel hungry,
and didn't feel thirsty. That was the whole round of
human feelings, as far as I knew, except the pain of being
beaten.

"Well," said he, "you are going, George, to a healthy
farm-house to be purified. Keep in the air there as much as
you can. Live an out-of-door life there, until you are fetched
away. You had better not say much—in fact, you had
better be very careful not to say anything—about what your
parents died of, or they might not like to take you in.
Behave well, and I'll put you to school; O, yes! I'll put you
to school, though I'm not obligated to do it. I am a servant
of the Lord, George; and I have been a good servant to
him, I have, these five-and-thirty years. The Lord has had
a good servant in me, and he knows it."

What I then supposed him to mean by this, I cannot
imagine. As little do I know when I began to comprehend
that he was a prominent member of some obscure denomination or congregation, every member of which held forth to

the rest when so inclined, and among whom he was called Brother Hawkyard. It was enough for me to know, on that day in the ward, that the farmer's cart was waiting for me at the street corner. I was not slow to get into it; for it was the first ride I ever had in my life.

It made me sleepy, and I slept. First, I stared at Preston streets as long as they lasted; and, meanwhile, I may have had some small dumb wondering within me whereabouts our cellar was; but I doubt it. Such a worldly little devil was I, that I took no thought who would bury father and mother, or where they would be buried, or when. The question whether the eating and drinking by day, and the covering by night, would be as good at the farm-house as at the ward superseded those questions.

The jolting of the cart on a loose stony road awoke me; and I found that we were mounting a steep hill, where the road was a rutty by-road through a field. And so, by frag-ments of an ancient terrace, and by some rugged outbuildings that had once been fortified, and passing under a ruined gateway we came to the old farm-house in the thick stone wall outside the old quadrangle of Hoghton Towers: which I looked at like a stupid savage, seeing no specialty in, seeing no antiquity in; assuming all farm-houses to resemble it; assigning the decay I noticed to the one potent cause of all ruin that I knew,—poverty; eyeing the pigeons in their flights, the cattle in their stalls, the ducks in the pond, and the fowls pecking about the yard, with a hungry hope that plenty of them might be killed for dinner while I stayed there; wondering whether the scrubbed dairy vessels, drying in the sunlight, could be goodly porringers out of which the master ate his belly-filling food, and which he polished when he had done, according to my ward experience; shrinkingly doubtful whether the shadows, passing over that airy height on the bright spring day, were not something in the nature of frowns,—sordid, afraid, unadmiring,—a small brute to shudder at.

To that time I had never had the faintest impression of duty. I had had no knowledge whatever that there was anything lovely in this life. When I had occasionally slunk up the cellar-steps into the street, and glared in at shop-windows, I had done so with no higher feelings than we may suppose to animate a mangy young dog or wolf-cub. It is equally the fact that I had never been alone, in the sense of holding unselfish converse with myself. I had been solitary often enough, but nothing better.

Such was my condition when I sat down to my dinner that day, in the kitchen of the old farm-house. Such was my condition when I lay on my bed in the old farm-house that night, stretched out opposite the narrow mullioned window, in the cold light of the moon, like a young vampire.

FIFTH CHAPTER

What do I know now of Hoghton Towers? Very little; for I have been gratefully unwilling to disturb my first impressions. A house, centuries old, on high ground a mile or so removed from the road between Preston and Blackburn, where the first James of England, in his hurry to make money by making baronets, perhaps made some of those remunerative dignitaries. A house, centuries old, deserted and falling to pieces, its woods and gardens long since grass-land or ploughed up, the Rivers Ribble and Darwen glancing below it, and a vague haze of smoke, against which not even the supernatural prescience of the first Stuart could foresee a counterblast, hinting at steam-power, powerful in two distances.

What did I know then of Hoghton Towers? When I first peeped in at the gate of the lifeless quadrangle, and started from the mouldering statue becoming visible to me like its guardian ghost; when I stole round by the back of the farm-house, and got in among the ancient rooms, many of them with their floors and ceilings falling, the beams and rafters hanging dangerously down, the plaster dropping as I trod, the oaken panels stripped away, the windows half walled up, half broken; when I discovered a gallery commanding the old kitchen, and looked down between balustrades upon a massive old table and benches, fearing to see I know not what dead-alive creatures come in and seat themselves, and look up with I know not what dreadful eyes, or lack of eyes, at me; when all over the house I was awed by gaps and chinks where the sky stared sorrowfully at me, where the birds passed, and the ivy rustled, and the stains of winter weather blotched the rotten floors; when down at the bottom of dark pits of staircase, into which the stairs had sunk, green leaves trembled, butterflies fluttered, and bees hummed in and out through the broken doorways; when encircling the whole ruin were sweet scents, and sights of fresh green growth, and ever-renewing life, that I had never dreamed of, —I say, when I passed into such clouded perception of these things as my dark soul could compass, what did I know then of Hoghton Towers?

I have written that the sky stared sorrowfully at me. Therein have I anticipated the answer. I knew that all these things looked sorrowfully at me; that they seemed to sigh or whisper, not without pity for me, "Alas! poor worldly little devil!"

There were two or three rats at the bottom of one of the smaller pits of broken staircase when I craned over and looked in. They were scuffling for some prey that was there; and, when they started and hid themselves close together in the dark, I thought of the old life (it had grown old already) in the cellar.

How not to be this worldly little devil? how not to have a repugnance towards myself as I had towards the rats? I hid in a corner of one of the smaller chambers, frightened at myself, and crying (it was the first time I had ever cried for any cause not purely physical), and I tried to think about it. One of the farm-ploughs came into my range of view just then; and it seemed to help me as it went on with its two horses up and down the field so peacefully and quietly.

There was a girl of about my own age in the farm-house family, and she sat opposite to me at the narrow table at meal-times. It had come into my mind, at our first dinner, that she might take the fever from me. The thought had not disquieted me then. I had only speculated how she would look under the altered circumstances, and whether she would die. But it came into my mind now, that I might try to prevent her taking the fever by keeping away from her. I knew I should have but scrambling board if I did; so much the less worldly and less devilish the deed would be, I thought.

From that hour, I withdrew myself at early morning into secret corners of the ruined house, and remained hidden there until she went to bed. At first, when meals were ready, I used to hear them calling me; and then my resolution weakened. But I strengthened it again by going farther off into the ruin, and getting out of hearing. I often watched for her at the dim windows; and, when I saw that she was fresh and rosy, felt much happier.

Out of this holding her in my thoughts, to the humanising of myself, I suppose some childish love arose within me. I felt, in some sort, dignified by the pride of protecting her,— by the pride of making the sacrifice for her. As my heart swelled with that new feeling, it insensibly softened about mother and father. It seemed to have been frozen before, and now to be thawed. The old ruin and all the lovely things that haunted it were not sorrowful for me only, but sorrowful for mother and father as well. Therefore did I cry again, and often too.

The farm-house family conceived me to be of a morose temper, and were very short with me; though they never stinted me in such broken fare as was to be got out of regular hours. One night when I lifted the kitchen latch at my usual time, Sylvia (that was her pretty name) had but just gone out of the room. Seeing her ascending the opposite stairs, I stood still at the door. She had heard the clink of the latch, and looked round.

"George," she called to me in a pleased voice, "to-morrow is my birthday; and we are to have a fiddler, and there's a party of boys and girls coming in a cart, and we shall dance. I invite you. Be sociable for once, George."

"I am very sorry miss," I answered; "but I—but, no; I can't come."

"You are a disagreeable, ill-humoured lad," she returned disdainfully; "and I ought not to have asked you. I shall never speak to you again."

As I stood with my eyes fixed on the fire, after she was gone, I felt that the farmer bent his brows upon me.

"Eh, lad!" said he; "Sylvy's right. You're as moody and broody a lad as never I set eyes on yet."

I tried to assure him that I meant no harm; but he only said coldly, "Maybe not, maybe not! There, get thy supper, get thy supper; and then thou canst sulk to thy heart's content again."

Ah! if they could have seen me next day, in the ruin, watching for the arrival of the cart full of merry young guests; if they could have seen me at night, gliding out from behind the ghostly statue, listening to the music and the fall of dancing feet, and watching the lighted farm-house windows from the quadrangle when all the ruin was dark;

if they could have read my heart, as I crept up to bed by the
back way, comforting myself with the reflection, "They will
take no hurt from me,"—they would not have thought mine
a morose or an unsocial nature.

It was in these ways that I began to form a shy disposition ; to be of a timidly silent character under misconstruc-
tion ; to have an inexpressible, perhaps a morbid, dread of
ever being sordid or worldly.   It was in these ways that my
nature came to shape itself to such a mould, even before it
was affected by the influences of the studious and retired life
of a poor scholar.

SIXTH CHAPTER

Brother Hawkyard (as he insisted on my calling him) put
me to school, and told me to work my way.   "You are all
right, George," he said.   "I have been the best servant the
Lord has had in his service for this five-and-thirty year (O, I
have !) ; and he knows the value of such a servant as I have
been to him (O, yes, he does !) ; and he'll prosper your
schooling as a part of my reward.   That's what *he*'ll do,
George.   He'll do it for me."

From the first I could not like this familiar knowledge of
the ways of the sublime, inscrutable Almighty, on Brother
Hawkyard's part.   As I grew a little wiser, and still a little
wiser, I liked it less and less.   His manner, too, of confirming
himself in a parenthesis,—as if, knowing himself, he doubted
his own word,—I found distasteful.   I cannot tell how much
these dislikes cost me ; for I had a dread that they were
worldly.

As time went on, I became a Foundation-boy on a good
foundation, and I cost Brother Hawkyard nothing.   When I
had worked my way so far, I worked yet harder, in the hope
of ultimately getting a presentation to college and a fellowship.   My health has never been strong (some vapour from
the Preston cellar cleaves to me, I think) ; and what with
much work and some weakness, I came again to be regarded
—that is, by my fellow-students—as unsocial.

All through my time as a foundation-boy, I was within a
few miles of Brother Hawkyard's congregation; and whenever

I was what we called a leave-boy on a Sunday, I went over there at his desire. Before the knowledge became forced upon me that outside their place of meeting these brothers and sisters were no better than the rest of the human family, but on the whole were, to put the case mildly, as bad as most, in respect of giving short weight in their shops, and not speaking the truth,—I say, before this knowledge became forced upon me, their prolix addresses, their inordinate conceit, their daring ignorance, their investment of the Supreme Ruler of heaven and earth with their own miserable meannesses and littlenesses, greatly shocked me. Still, as their term for the frame of mind that could not perceive them to be in an exalted state of grace was the "worldly" state, I did for a time suffer tortures under my inquiries of myself whether that young worldly-devilish spirit of mine could secretly be lingering at the bottom of my non-appreciation.

Brother Hawkyard was the popular expounder in this assembly, and generally occupied the platform (there was a little platform with a table on it, in lieu of a pulpit) first, on a Sunday afternoon. He was by trade a drysalter. Brother Gimblet, an elderly man with a crabbed face, a large dog's-eared shirt-collar, and a spotted blue neckerchief reaching up behind to the crown of his head, was also a drysalter and an expounder. Brother Gimblet professed the greatest admiration for Brother Hawkyard but (I had thought more than once) bore him a jealous grudge.

Let whosoever may peruse these lines kindly take the pains here to read twice my solemn pledge, that what I write of the language and customs of the congregation in question I write scrupulously, literally, exactly, from the life and the truth.

On the first Sunday after I had won what I had so long tried for, and when it was certain that I was going up to college, Brother Hawkyard concluded a long exhortation thus:

"Well, my friends and fellow-sinners, now I told you when I began, that I didn't know a word of what I was going to say to you (and no, I did not!), but that it was all one to me, because I knew the Lord would put into my mouth the words I wanted."

("That's it!" from Brother Gimblet.)

"And he did put into my mouth the words I wanted"

("So he did!" from Brother Gimblet.)

"And why?"

("Ah, let's have that!" from Brother Gimblet.)

"Because I have been his faithful servant for five-and-thirty years, and because he knows it. For five-and-thirty years! And he knows it, mind you! I got those words that I wanted on account of my wages. I got 'em from the Lord, my fellow-sinners. Down! I said, 'Here's a heap of wages due; let us have something down, on account.' And I got it down, and I paid it over to you; and you won't wrap it up in a napkin, nor yet in a towel, nor yet pocketankercher, but you'll put it out at good interest. Very well. Now, my brothers and sisters and fellow-sinners, I am going to conclude with a question, and I'll make it so plain (with the help of the Lord, after five-and-thirty years, I should, rather hope!) as that the Devil shall not be able to confuse it in your heads,—which he would be overjoyed to do."

("Just his way. Crafty old blackguard!" from Brother Gimblet.)

"And the question is this, Are the angels learned?"

("Not they. Not a bit on it!" from Brother Gimblet, with the greatest confidence.)

"Not they. And where's the proof? sent ready-made by the hand of the Lord. Why, there's one among us here now, that has got all the learning that can be crammed into him. *I* got him all the learning that could be crammed into him. His grandfather" (this I had never heard before) "was a brother of ours. He was Brother Parksop. That's what he was. Parksop; Brother Parksop. His worldly name was Parksop, and he was a brother of this brotherhood. Then wasn't he Brother Parksop?"

("Must be. Couldn't help hisself!" from Brother Gimblet.)

"Well, he left that one now here present among us to the care of a brother-sinner of his (and that brother-sinner, mind you, was a sinner of a bigger size in his time than any of you; praise the Lord!), Brother Hawkyard. Me. *I* got him without fee or reward,—without a morsel of myrrh, or frankincense, nor yet amber, letting alone the honeycomb,—all the learning that could be crammed into him. Has it brought him into our temple, in the spirit? No. Have we had any ignorant brothers and sisters that didn't know round O from crooked S, come in among us meanwhile? Many. Then the angels are *not* learned; then they don't so much as know their alphabet. And now, my friends and fellow-sinners, having brought it to that, perhaps some brother present—perhaps you, Brother Gimblet—will pray a bit for us?"

Brother Gimblet undertook the sacred function, after having drawn his sleeve across his mouth, and muttered, "Well! I don't know as I see my way to hitting any of you quite in the right place neither." He said this with a dark smile, and then began to bellow. What we were specially to be preserved from, according to his solicitations, was, despoilment of the orphan, suppression of testamentary intentions on the part of a father or (say) grandfather, appropriation of the orphan's house-property, feigning to give in charity to the wronged one from whom we withheld his due; and that class of sins. He ended with the petition, "Give us peace!" which, speaking for myself, was very much needed after twenty minutes of his bellowing.

Even though I had not seen him when he rose from his knees, steaming with perspiration, glance at Brother Hawkyard, and even though I had not heard Brother Hawkyard's tone of congratulating him on the vigour with which he had roared, I should have detected a malicious application in this prayer. Unformed suspicions to a similar effect had sometimes passed through my mind in my earlier school-days, and had always caused me great distress; for they were worldly in their nature, and wide, very wide, of the spirit that had drawn me from Sylvia. They were sordid suspicions, without a shadow of proof. They were worthy to have originated in the unwholesome cellar. They were not only without proof, but against proof; for was I not myself a living proof of what Brother Hawkyard had done? and without him, how should I ever have seen the sky look sorrowfully down upon that wretched boy at Hoghton Towers?

Although the dread of a relapse into a stage of savage selfishness was less strong upon me as I approached manhood, and could act in an increased degree for myself, yet I was always on my guard against any tendency to such relapse. After getting these suspicions under my feet, I had been troubled by not being able to like Brother Hawkyard's manner, or his professed religion. So it came about, that, as I walked back that Sunday evening, I thought it would be an act of reparation for any such injury my struggling thoughts had unwillingly done him, if I wrote, and placed in his hands, before going to college, a full acknowledgment of his goodness to me, and an ample tribute of thanks. It might serve as an implied vindication of him against any dark scandal from a rival brother and expounder, or from any other quarter.

Accordingly, I wrote the document with much care. I may add with much feeling too ; for it affected me as I went on. Having no set studies to pursue, in the brief interval between leaving the Foundation and going to Cambridge, I determined to walk out to his place of business, and give it into his own hands.

It was a winter afternoon, when I tapped at the door of his little counting-house, which was at the farther end of his long, low shop. As I did so (having entered by the back yard, where casks and boxes were taken in, and where there was the inscription, " Private way to the counting-house "), a shopman called to me from the counter that he was engaged.

"Brother Gimblet" (said the shopman, who was one of the brotherhood) "is with him."

I thought this all the better for my purpose, and made bold to tap again. They were talking in a low tone, and money was passing; for I heard it being counted out.

"Who is it?" asked Brother Hawkyard, sharply.

"George Silverman," I answered, holding the door open. "May I come in?"

Both brothers seemed so astounded to see me that I felt shyer than usual. But they looked quite cadaverous in the early gaslight, and perhaps that accidental circumstance exaggerated the expression of their faces.

"What is the matter?" asked Brother Hawkyard.

" Ay! what is the matter?" asked Brother Gimblet.

"Nothing at all," I said, diffidently producing my docu-ment: "I am only the bearer of a letter from myself."

"From yourself, George?" cried Brother Hawkyard.

" And to you," said I.

"And to me, George?"

He turned paler, and opened it hurriedly; but looking over it, and seeing generally what it was, became less hurried, recovered his colour, and said, "Praise the Lord!"

" That's it!" cried Brother Gimblet. "Well put! Amen."

Brother Hawkyard then said, in a livelier strain, "You must know, George, that Brother Gimblet and I are going to make our two businesses one. We are going into partnership. We are settling it now. Brother Gimblet is to take one clear half of the profits (O, yes! he shall have it; he shall have it to the last farthing)."

"D.V. !" said Brother Gimblet, with his right fist firmly clinched on his right leg.

"There is no objection," pursued Brother Hawkyard, "to my reading this aloud, George?"

As it was what I expressly desired should be done, after yesterday's prayer, I more than readily begged him to read it aloud. He did so; and Brother Gimblet listened with a crabbed smile.

"It was in a good hour that I came here," he said, wrinkling up his eyes. "It was in a good hour, likewise, that I was moved yesterday to depict for the terror of evil-doers a character the direct opposite of Brother Hawkyard's. But it was the Lord that done it: I felt him at it while I was perspiring."

After that it was proposed by both of them that I should attend the congregation once more before my final departure. What my shy reserve would undergo, from being expressly preached at and prayed at, I knew beforehand. But I reflected that it would be for the last time, and that it might add to the weight of my letter. It was well known to the brothers and sisters that there was no place taken for me in *their* paradise; and if I showed this last token of deference to Brother Hawkyard, notoriously in despite of my own sinful inclinations, it might go some little way in aid of my statement that he had been good to me, and that I was grateful to him. Merely stipulating, therefore, that no express endeavour should be made for my conversion,—which would involve the rolling of several brothers and sisters on the floor, declaring that they felt all their sins in a heap on their left side, weighing so many pounds avoirdupois, as I knew from what I had seen of those repulsive mysteries,—I promised.

Since the reading of my letter, Brother Gimblet had been at intervals wiping one eye with an end of his spotted blue neckerchief, and grinning to himself. It was, however, a habit that brother had, to grin in an ugly manner even when expounding. I call to mind a delighted snarl with which he used to detail from the platform the torments reserved for the wicked (meaning all human creation except the brotherhood), as being remarkably hideous.

I left the two to settle their articles of partnership, and count money ; and I never saw them again but on the following Sunday. Brother Hawkyard died within two or three years, leaving all he possessed to Brother Gimblet, in virtue of a will dated (as I have been told) that very day.

Now I was so far at rest with myself, when Sunday came, knowing that I had conquered my own mistrust, and righted Brother Hawkyard in the jaundiced vision of a rival, that I went, even to that coarse chapel, in a less sensitive state than usual. How could I foresee that the delicate, perhaps the diseased, corner of my mind, where I winced and shrunk when it was touched, or was even approached, would be handled as the theme of the whole proceedings?

On this occasion it was assigned to Brother Hawkyard to pray, and to Brother Gimblet to preach. The prayer was to open the ceremonies ; the discourse was to come next. Brothers Hawkyard and Gimblet were both on the platform ; Brother Hawkyard on his knees at the table, unmusically ready to pray ; Brother Gimblet sitting against the wall, grinningly ready to preach.

" Let us offer up the sacrifice of prayer, my brothers and sisters and fellow-sinners." Yes ; but it was I who was the sacrifice. It was our poor, sinful, worldly-minded brother here present who was wrestled for. The now-opening career of this our unawakened brother might lead to his becoming a minister of what was called "the church." That was what *he* looked to. The church. Not the chapel, Lord. The church. No rectors, no vicars, no archdeacons, no bishops, no archbishops, in the chapel, but, O Lord ! many such in the church. Protect our sinful brother from his love of lucre. Cleanse from our unawakened brother's breast his sin of worldly-mindedness. The prayer said infinitely more in words, but nothing more to any intelligible effect.

Then Brother Gimblet came forward, and took (as I knew he would) the text, " My kingdom is not of this world." Ah ! but whose was, my fellow-sinners ? Whose ? Why, our brother's here present was. The only kingdom he had an idea of was of this world. ("That's it !" from several of the congregation.) What did the woman do when she lost the piece of money? Went and looked for it. What should our brother do when he lost his way ? ("Go and look for it," from a sister.) Go and look for it, true. But must he look for it in the right direction, or in the wrong? ("In the right," from a brother.) There spake the prophets! He must look for it in the right direction, or he couldn't find it. But he had turned his back upon the right direction, and he wouldn't find it. Now, my fellow-sinners, to show you the difference betwixt worldly-mindedness and unworldly-mindedness, betwixt kingdoms not of this world and kingdoms *of* this world, here was a letter wrote by even our worldly-minded brother unto Brother Hawkyard. Judge, from hearing of it read, whether Brother Hawkyard was the faithful steward that the Lord had in his mind only t'other day, when, in this very place, he drew you the picter of the unfaithful one; for it was him that done it, not me. Don't doubt that!

Brother Gimblet then groaned and bellowed his way through my composition, and subsequently through an hour. The service closed with a hymn, in which the brothers unanimously roared, and the sisters unanimously shrieked at me, That I by wiles of worldly gain was mocked, and they on waters of sweet love were rocked; that I with mammon struggled in the dark, while they were floating in a second ark.

I went out from all this with an aching heart and a weary spirit: not because I was quite so weak as to consider these narrow creatures interpreters of the Divine Majesty and Wisdom, but because I was weak enough to feel as though it were my hard fortune to be misrepresented and misunderstood, when I most tried to subdue any risings of mere worldliness within me, and when I most hoped that, by dint of trying earnestly, I had succeeded.

SEVENTH CHAPTER

My timidity and my obscurity occasioned me to live a secluded life at college, and to be little known. No relative ever came to visit me, for I had no relative. No intimate friends broke in upon my studies, for I made no intimate friends. I supported myself on my scholarship, and read much. My college time was otherwise not so very different from my time at Hoghton Towers.

Knowing myself to be unfit for the noisier stir of social

existence, but believing myself qualified to do my duty in a
moderate, though earnest way, if I could obtain some small
preferment in the Church, I applied my mind to the clerical
profession. In due sequence I took orders, was ordained, and
began to look about me for employment. I must observe
that I had taken a good degree, that I had succeeded in
winning a good fellowship, and that my means were ample
for my retired way of life. By this time I had read with
several young men ; and the occupation increased my income,
while it was highly interesting to me. I once accidentally
overheard our greatest don say, to my boundless joy, "That
he heard it reported of Silverman that his gift of quiet
explanation, his patience, his amiable temper, and his con-
scientiousness made him the best of coaches." May my
"gift of quiet explanation" come more seasonably and
powerfully to my aid in this present explanation than I
think it will !

It may be in a certain degree owing to the situation of my
college-rooms (in a corner where the daylight was sobered),
but it is in a much larger degree referable to the state of my
own mind, that I seem to myself, on looking back to this
time of my life, to have been always in the peaceful shade.
I can see others in the sunlight ; I can see our boats' crews
and our athletic young men on the glistening water, or
speckled with the moving lights of sunlit leaves ; but I
myself am always in the shadow looking on. Not unsym-
pathetically,—God forbid !—but looking on alone, much as
I looked at Sylvia from the shadows of the ruined house,
or looked at the red gleam shining through the farmer's
windows, and listened to the fall of dancing feet, when all
the ruin was dark that night in the quadrangle.

I now come to the reason of my quoting that laudation
of myself above given. Without such reason, to repeat it
would have been mere boastfulness.

Among those who had read with me was Mr. Fareway,
second son of Lady Fareway, widow of Sir Gaston Fareway,
baronet. This young gentleman's abilities were much above
the average ; but he came of a rich family, and was idle and
luxurious. He presented himself to me too late, and afterwards came to me too irregularly, to admit of my being of
much service to him. In the end, I considered it my duty
to dissuade him from going up for an examination which he
could never pass ; and he left college without a degree.

After his departure, Lady Fareway wrote to me, representing the justice of my returning half my fee, as I had been of so little use to her son. Within my knowledge a similar demand had not been made in any other case; and I most freely admit that the justice of it had not occurred to me until it was pointed out. But I at once perceived it, yielded to it, and returned the money.

Mr. Fareway had been gone two years or more, and I had forgotten him, when he one day walked into my rooms as I was sitting at my books.

Said he, after the usual salutations had passed, "Mr. Silverman, my mother is in town here, at the hotel, and wishes me to present you to her."

I was not comfortable with strangers, and I dare say I betrayed that I was a little nervous or unwilling. "For," said he, without my having spoken, "I think the interview may tend to the advancement of your prospects."

It put me to the blush to think that I should be tempted by a worldly reason, and I rose immediately.

Said Mr. Fareway, as we went along, "Are you a good hand at business?"

"I think not," said I.

Said Mr. Fareway then, "My mother is."

"Truly?" said I.

"Yes: my mother is what is usually called a managing woman. Doesn't make a bad thing, for instance, even out of the spendthrift habits of my eldest brother abroad. In short, a managing woman. This is in confidence."

He had never spoken to me in confidence, and I was surprised by his doing so. I said I should respect his confidence, of course, and said no more on the delicate subject. We had but a little way to walk, and I was soon in his mother's company. He presented me, shook hands with me, and left us two (as he said) to business.

I saw in my Lady Fareway a handsome, well-preserved lady of somewhat large stature, with a steady glare in her great round dark eyes that embarrassed me.

Said my lady, "I have heard from my son, Mr. Silverman, that you would be glad of some preferment in the church."

I gave my lady to understand that was so.

"I don't know whether you are aware," my lady proceeded, "that we have a presentation to a living? I say *we* have; but, in point of fact, *I* have."

I gave my lady to understand that I had not been aware of this.

Said my lady, "So it is : indeed I have two presentations, —one to two hundred a year, one to six. Both livings are in our county,—North Devonshire,—as you probably know. The first is vacant. Would you like it ?"

What with my lady's eyes, and what with the suddenness of this proposed gift, I was much confused.

"I am sorry it is not the larger presentation," said my lady, rather coldly ; "though I will not, Mr. Silverman, pay you the bad compliment of supposing that *you* are, because that would be mercenary,—and mercenary I am persuaded you are not."

Said I, with my utmost earnestness, "Thank you, Lady Fareway, thank you, thank you ! I should be deeply hurt if I thought I bore the character."

"Naturally," said my lady. "Always detestable, but par-ticularly in a clergyman. You have not said whether you will like the living ?"

With apologies for my remissness or indistinctness, I as-sured my lady that I accepted it most readily and gratefully. I added that I hoped she would not estimate my appreciation of the generosity of her choice by any flow of words; for I was not a ready man in that respect when taken by surprise or touched at heart.

"The affair is concluded," said my lady; "concluded. You will find the duties very light, Mr. Silverman. Charm-ing house ; charming little garden, orchard, and all that. You will be able to take pupils. By-the-bye ! No : I will return to the word afterwards. What was I going to men-tion, when it put me out ?"

My lady stared at me, as if I knew. And I didn't know. And that perplexed me afresh.

Said my lady, after some consideration, "O, of course, how very dull of me ! The last incumbent,—least mercenary man I ever saw,—in consideration of the duties being so light and the house so delicious, couldn't rest, he said, un-less I permitted him to help me with my correspondence, accounts, and various little things of that kind ; nothing in themselves, but which it worries a lady to cope with. Would Mr. Silverman also like to—— ? Or shall I—— ?"

I hastened to say that my poor help would be always at her ladyship's service.

" I am absolutely blessed," said my lady, casting up her eyes (and so taking them off me for one moment), "in having to do with gentlemen who cannot endure an approach to the idea of being mercenary!" She shivered at the word. "And now as to the pupil."

"The——?" I was quite at a loss.

"Mr. Silverman, you have no idea what she is. She is," said my lady, laying her touch upon my coat-sleeve, "I do verily believe, the most extraordinary girl in this world. Already knows more Greek and Latin than Lady Jane Grey. And taught herself! Has not yet, remember, derived a moment's advantage from Mr. Silverman's classical acquirements. To say nothing of mathematics, which she is bent upon becoming versed in, and in which (as I hear from my son and others) Mr. Silverman's reputation is so deservedly high!"

Under my lady's eyes I must have lost the clue, I felt persuaded; and yet I did not know where I could have dropped it.

"Adelina," said my lady, "is my only daughter. If I did not feel quite convinced that I am not blinded by a mother's partiality; unless I was absolutely sure that when you know her, Mr. Silverman, you will esteem it a high and unusual privilege to direct her studies,—I should introduce a mercenary element into this conversation, and ask you on what terms——"

I entreated my lady to go no further. My lady saw that I was troubled, and did me the honour to comply with my request.

EIGHTH CHAPTER

EVERYTHING in mental acquisition that her brother might have been, if he would, and everything in all gracious charms and admirable qualities that no one but herself could be,—this was Adelina.

I will not expatiate upon her beauty; I will not expatiate upon her intelligence, her quickness of perception, her powers of memory, her sweet consideration, from the first moment, for the slow-paced tutor who ministered to her wonderful gifts. I was thirty then; I am over sixty now: she is ever present to me in these hours as she was in those, bright and beautiful and young, wise and fanciful and good.

When I discovered that I loved her, how can I say? In the first day? in the first week? in the first month? Impossible to trace. If I be (as I am) unable to represent to myself any previous period of my life as quite separable from her attracting power, how can I answer for this one detail?

Whensoever I made the discovery, it laid a heavy burden on me. And yet, comparing it with the far heavier burden that I afterwards took up, it does not seem to me now to have been very hard to bear. In the knowledge that I did love her, and that I should love her while my life lasted, and that I was ever to hide my secret deep in my own breast, and she was never to find it, there was a kind of sustaining joy or pride, or comfort, mingled with my pain.

But later on,—say, a year later on,—when I made another discovery, then indeed my suffering and my struggle were strong. That other discovery was—

These words will never see the light, if ever, until my heart is dust; until her bright spirit has returned to the regions of which, when imprisoned here, it surely retained some unusual glimpse of remembrance; until all the pulses that ever beat around us shall have long been quiet; until all the fruits of all the tiny victories and defeats achieved in our little breasts shall have withered away. That discovery was that she loved me.

She may have enhanced my knowledge, and loved me for that; she may have over-valued my discharge of duty to her, and loved me for that; she may have refined upon a playful compassion which she would sometimes show for what she. called my want of wisdom, according to the light of the world's dark lanterns, and loved me for that; she may —she must—have confused the borrowed light of what I had only learned, with its brightness in its pure, original rays; but she loved me at that time, and she made me know it.

Pride of family and pride of wealth put me as far off from her in my lady's eyes as if I had been some domesticated creature of another kind. But they could not put me farther from her than I put myself when I set my merits against hers. More than that. They could not put me, by millions of fathoms, half so low beneath her as I put myself when in imagination I took advantage of her noble trustfulness, took the fortune that I knew she must possess in her own right, and left her to find herself, in the zenith of her beauty and genius, bound to poor rusty, plodding me.

No! Worldliness should not enter here at any cost. If I had tried to keep it out of other ground, how much harder was I bound to try to keep it out from this sacred place!

But there was something daring in her broad, generous character, that demanded at so delicate a crisis to be delicately and patiently addressed. After many and many a bitter night (O, I found I could cry for reasons not purely physical, at this pass of my life!) I took my course.

My lady had, in our first interview, unconsciously over-stated the accommodation of my pretty house. There was room in it for only one pupil. He was a young gentleman near coming of age, very well connected, but what is called a poor relation. His parents were dead. The charges of his living and reading with me were defrayed by an uncle; and he and I were to do our utmost together for three years towards qualifying him to make his way. At this time he had entered into his second year with me. He was well-looking, clever, energetic, enthusiastic, bold; in the best sense of the term, a thorough young Anglo-Saxon.

I resolved to bring these two together.

NINTH CHAPTER

SAID I, one night, when I had conquered myself, "Mr. Granville,"—Mr. Granville Wharton his name was,—"I doubt if you have ever yet so much as seen Miss Fareway."

"Well, Sir," returned he, laughing, "you see her so much yourself, that you hardly leave another fellow a chance of seeing her."

"I am her tutor, you know," said I.

And there the subject dropped for that time. But I so contrived as that they should come together shortly afterwards. I had previously so contrived as to keep them asunder; for while I loved her,—I mean before I had determined on my sacrifice,—a lurking jealousy of Mr. Granville lay within my unworthy breast.

It was quite an ordinary interview in the Fareway Park·
but they talked easily together for some time: like takes to
like, and they had many points of resemblance. Said Mr.
Granville to me, when he and I sat at our supper that night,
"Miss Fareway is remarkably beautiful, Sir, remarkably engaging. Don't you think so?" "I think so," said I. And
I stole a glance at him, and saw that he had reddened and
was thoughtful. I remember it most vividly, because the
mixed feeling of grave pleasure and acute pain that the
slight circumstance caused me was the first of a long, long
series of such mixed impressions under which my hair
turned slowly grey.

I had not much need to feign to be subdued; but I
counterfeited to be older than I was in all respects (Heaven
knows! my heart being all too young the while), and feigned
to be more of a recluse and bookworm than I had really
become, and gradually set up more and more of a fatherly
manner towards Adelina. Likewise I made my tuition less
imaginative than before; separated myself from my poets
and philosophers; was careful to present them in their own
light, and me, their lowly servant, in my own shade. Moreover, in the matter of apparel I was equally mindful; not
that I had ever been dapper that way; but that I was
slovenly now.

As I depressed myself with one hand, so did I labour to
raise Mr. Granville with the other; directing his attention
to such subjects as I too well knew most interested her, and
fashioning him (do not deride or misconstrue the expression,
unknown reader of this writing; for I have suffered!) into
a greater resemblance to myself in my solitary one strong
aspect. And gradually, gradually, as I saw him take more
and more to these thrown-out lures of mine, then did I come
to know better and better that love was drawing him on, and
was drawing her from me.

So passed more than another year; every day a year in its
number of my mixed impressions of grave pleasure and acute
pain; and then these two, being of age and free to act legally
for themselves, came before me hand in hand (my hair being
now quite white), and entreated me that I would unite them
together. "And indeed, dear tutor," said Adelina, "it is but
consistent in you that you should do this thing for us, seeing
that we should never have spoken together that first time
but for you, and that but for you we could never have met

so often afterwards." The whole of which was literally true; for I had availed myself of my many business attendances on, and conferences with, my lady, to take Mr. Granville to the house, and leave him in the outer room with Adelina.

I knew that my lady would object to such a marriage for her daughter, or to any marriage that was other than an exchange of her for stipulated lands, goods, and moneys. But looking on the two, and seeing with full eyes that they were both young and beautiful; and knowing that they were alike in the tastes and acquirements that will outlive youth and beauty; and considering that Adelina had a fortune now, in her own keeping; and considering further that Mr. Granville, though for the present poor, was of a good family that had never lived in a cellar in Preston; and believing that their love would endure, neither having any great discrepancy to find out in the other,—I told them of my readiness to do this thing which Adelina asked of her dear tutor, and to send them forth, husband and wife, into the shining world with golden gates that awaited them.

It was on a summer morning that I rose before the sun to compose myself for the crowning of my work with this end; and my dwelling being near to the sea, I walked down to the rocks on the shore, in order that I might behold the sun in his majesty.

The tranquillity upon the deep, and on the firmament, the orderly withdrawal of the stars, the calm promise of coming day, the rosy suffusion of the sky and waters, the ineffable splendour that then burst forth, attuned my mind afresh after the discords of the night. Methought that all I looked on said to me, and that all I heard in the sea and in the air said to me, "Be comforted, mortal, that thy life is so short. Our preparation for what is to follow has endured, and shall endure, for unimaginable ages."

I married them. I knew that my hand was cold when I placed it on their hands clasped together; but the words with which I had to accompany the action I could say without faltering, and I was at peace.

They being well away from my house and from the place after our simple breakfast, the time was come when I must do what I had pledged myself to them that I would do,—break the intelligence to my lady.

I went up to the house, and found my lady in her ordinary business-room. She happened to have an unusual amount of commissions to intrust to me that day; and she had filled my hands with papers before I could originate a word.

"My lady," I then began, as I stood beside her table.

"Why, what's the matter?" she said quickly, looking up.

"Not much, I would fain hope, after you shall have prepared yourself, and considered a little."

"Prepared myself; and considered a little! You appear to have prepared *your*self but indifferently, anyhow, Mr. Silverman." This mighty scornfully, as I experienced my usual embarrassment under her stare.

Said I, in self-extenuation once for all, "Lady Fareway, I have but to say for myself that I have tried to do my duty."

"For yourself?" repeated my lady. "Then there are others concerned, I see. Who are they?"

I was about to answer, when she made towards the bell with a dart that stopped me, and said, "Why, where is Adelina?"

"Forbear! be calm, my lady. I married her this morning to Mr. Granville Wharton."

She set her lips, looked more intently at me than ever, raised her right hand, and smote me hard upon the cheek.

"Give me back those papers! give me back those papers!" She tore them out of my hands, and tossed them on her table. Then seating herself defiantly in her great chair, and folding her arms, she stabbed me to the heart with the unlooked-for reproach, "You worldly wretch!"

"Worldly?" I cried. "Worldly?"

"This, if you please,"—she went on with supreme scorn, pointing me out as if there were some one there to see,— "this, if you please, is the disinterested scholar, with not a design beyond his books! This, if you please, is the simple creature whom any one could overreach in a bargain! This, if you please, is Mr. Silverman! Not of this world; not he! He has too much simplicity for this world's cunning. He has too much singleness of purpose to be a match for this world's double-dealing. What did he give you for it?"

"For what? And who?"

"How much," she asked, bending forward in her great chair, and insultingly tapping the fingers of her right hand on the palm of her left,—"how much does Mr. Granville Wharton pay you for getting him Adelina's money? What is the amount of your percentage upon Adelina's fortune? What were the terms of the agreement that you proposed to this boy when you, the Rev. George Silverman, licensed to marry, engaged to put him in possession of this girl? You made good terms for yourself, whatever they were. He would stand a poor chance against your keenness."

Bewildered, horrified, stunned by this cruel perversion, I could not speak. But I trust that I looked innocent, being so.

"Listen to me, shrewd hypocrite," said my lady, whose anger increased as she gave it utterance; "attend to my words, you cunning schemer, who have carried this plot through with such a practised double face that I have never suspected you. I had my projects for my daughter; projects for family connexion; projects for fortune. You have thwarted them, and overreached me; but I am not one to be thwarted and overreached without retaliation. Do you mean to hold this living another month?"

"Do you deem it possible, Lady Fareway, that I can hold it another hour, under your injurious words?"

"Is it resigned, then?"

"It was mentally resigned, my lady, some minutes ago."

"Don't equivocate, Sir. *Is* it resigned?"

"Unconditionally and entirely; and I would that I had never, never come near it!"

"A cordial response from me to *that* wish, Mr. Silverman! But take this with you, Sir. If you had not resigned it, I would have had you deprived of it. And though you have resigned it, you will not get quit of me as easily as you think for. I will pursue you with this story. I will make this nefarious conspiracy of yours, for money, known. You have made money by it, but you have at the same time made an enemy by it. *You* will take good care that the money sticks to you; I will take good care that the enemy sticks to you."

Then said I finally, "Lady Fareway, I think my heart is broken. Until I came into this room just now, the possibility of such mean wickedness as you have imputed to me never dawned upon my thoughts. Your suspicions——"

"Suspicions! Pah!" said she indignantly. "Certainties."

"Your certainties, my lady, as you call them, your suspicions as I call them, are cruel, unjust, wholly devoid of foundation in fact. I can declare no more; except that I have not acted for my own profit or my own pleasure. I have not in this proceeding considered myself. Once again,

I think my heart is broken.. If I have unwittingly done any wrong with a righteous motive, that is some penalty to pay."

She received this with another and more indignant "Pah!" and I made my way out of her room (I think I felt my way out with my hands, although my eyes were open), almost suspecting that my voice had a repulsive sound, and that I was a repulsive object.

There was a great stir made, the bishop was appealed to, I received a severe reprimand, and narrowly escaped suspension. For years a cloud hung over me, and my name was tarnished. But my heart did not break, if a broken heart involves death; for I lived through it.

They stood by me, Adelina and her husband, through it all. Those who had known me at college, and even most of those who had only known me there by reputation, stood by me too. Little by little, the belief widened that I was not capable of what was laid to my charge. At length I was presented to a college-living in a sequestered place, and there I now pen my explanation. I pen it at my open window in the summer-time, before me, lying in the churchyard, equal resting-place for sound hearts, wounded hearts, and broken hearts. I pen it for the relief of my own mind, not foreseeing whether or no it will ever have a reader.